PRINCIPLES AND METHODS OF

Adapted Physical Education and Recreation

Adapted Physical Education and Recreation

David Auxter, Ed.D.

Senior Scientist
Research Institute for Independent Living
Edgewater, Maryland

Jean Pyfer, P.E.D.

Chair of Kinesiology
Texas Woman's University
Denton, Texas

Carol Huettig, Ph.D.

Adapted Physical Education Specialist
Dallas Independent School District
Dallas, Texas

SEVENTH EDITION

with *278* illustrations

M Mosby

St. Louis   Baltimore   Boston   Chicago   London   Philadelphia   Sydney   Toronto

Editor: Vicki Malinee
Developmental Editor: Cathy Waller
Project Manager: Gayle May Morris
Production Editor: Deborah L. Vogel
Book Designer: Susan Lane

SEVENTH EDITION

Copyright © 1993 by Mosby–Year Book, Inc.

A Mosby imprint of Mosby–Year Book, Inc.

Previous editions copyrighted 1969, 1973, 1977, 1981, 1985, 1989

Printed in the United States of America

Mosby–Year Book, Inc.
11830 Westline Industrial Drive
St. Louis, Missouri 63146

Library of Congress Cataloging-in-Publication Data

Auxter, David.
    Principles and methods of adapted physical education and
recreation/David Auxter, Jean Pyfer, Carol Huettig : with 278
illustrations.—7th ed.
      p. cm.
    Includes bibliographical references and index.
    ISBN 0-8016-6749-6 :
    1. Physical education for handicapped children—Study and
teaching—United States. 2. Handicapped children—United States–
Recreation. I. Pyfer, Jean. II. Huettig, Carol. III. Title.
IV. Title: Adapted physical education and recreation.
GV445.A94 1992   92-30699
371.9′04486—dc20   CIP

93 94 95 96 97 CL/DC 9 8 7 6 5 4 3 2 1

Preface

There has been recent legislation that will require new initiatives by those who administer and conduct physical education and recreation programs for children with disabilities. The sixth edition stressed procedures for conducting physical education and recreation programs that, if employed, would yield benefits in physical and motor skill development. These methods for conducting scientific physical education instruction now need to be applied to the transition of skills learned in the public schools to independent physically active lifestyles in community, leisure, recreation, and sports programs.

Transitional Services: Infant, Toddler, and Preschool Physical Education

Since the publication of the sixth edition, the U.S. Congress has passed the Individuals with Disabilities Education Act (IDEA) and the Americans with Disabilities Act (ADA). Common to both of these pieces of legislation is the notion that physically active healthful lifestyles of the disabled acquired in school should be transferred to meaningful real life behavior in the community. Thus there is a need for the physical education resources of the public schools to be coordinated with community recreation resources to enable attainment of the physical skills in meaningful settings outside of school. The seventh edition of *Principles and Methods of Adapted Physical Education and Rec-*reation assists with providing knowledge to achieve this end.

Content Features

The goal of physical education programs for the disabled is the use of motor skill to enable adaption to social life, community living, and recreational environments. The seventh edition provides a comprehensive practical approach for the adapted physical education teacher. It provides insights into the full spectrum of sports and physical activity that enable the development of community-based recreational sport activity and healthful lifestyles of physical activity through the physical education program. In addition, it is descriptive of procedures that enable physical benefits for the disabled. New legislation requires that many aspects of the human service system need to be coordinated in the conduction of an adapted physical education program. Some of these aspects are the regular physical education program, the special education program, school administrative functions in both special and regular education, parental activity, and related services (e.g., physicians, nurses, occupational therapists, physical therapists, psychologists, and others).

However, it is now necessary to coordinate school activities with those of the community in the "transition process." The seventh edition assists with this process.

New to this Edition

A variety of sources contributed to the seventh edition. There is a considerable body of literature related to physical education for disabled individuals that has emerged since the last edition. This was examined, and decisions were made in selection of the information that was most applicable for conduction of physical education programs for the disabled. New methods, particularly for infant, toddler, and preschool-aged disabled children, have developed since the sixth edition and have been included in this text. Thus the physical education curricula, which previously were extended to reach more severely disabled children need now be designed to reach younger disabled children.

The seventh edition has undergone thorough external review as well as an extensive study of recent professional literature since the last edition. Furthermore, Dr. Carol Huettig has been added as a new author of the seventh edition. Dr. Huettig has had extensive experience in both academic and applied settings. She currently works in the public schools and brings live practical experience to the authorship of the book. Consequently, there have been several modifications to the previous edition. Some of these modifications are as follows:

1. Throughout the book, greater focus has been placed on practical considerations for conducting physical education programs for the disabled individuals of all ages.
2. Chapter 1 presents an update on the legal entitlements in physical education for the disabled. It addresses new relevant procedures that are necessary to conform with new legislation of the Individuals with Disabilities Education Act (IDEA) and the Americans with Disabilities Act (ADA).
3. New procedures and techniques for integrating disabled children with nondisabled children in lesser restricted physical education environments are discussed with respect to supplemental aids and services.
4. The chapters on Assessment, Programming, and Facilitating Learning have been reorganized to improve understanding for conduction of individualized instruction for the disabled.
5. New federal initiatives of transitional living (movement of children from school with skills for productive independent adult community life) is thoroughly discussed throughout this edition in light of recent federal regulations.
6. A thorough discussion of the impact of drugs on children's development is included in the chapters on emotional disturbances and specific learning disabilities.
7. A new chapter on autism (Chapter 8) has been added to the seventh edition.
8. The medical conditions included in the chapter on "Other Conditions" have been expanded.
9. Procedures for conducting physical fitness programs have been updated with state-of-the-art techniques.
10. The newly adapted (1992) definition of mental retardation is presented and discussed.

Pedagogical Aids

The learning aids of the previous edition have been updated in the seventh edition. Almost all of the photographs have been replaced to better portray the content that is expressed in the narrative of the text. New objectives, chapter summaries, student learning activities, and suggested readings strengthen this edition. In addition, there has been a thorough update to the *Instrutor's Manual* for this textbook.

Acknowledgments

Many persons contributed their efforts in the preparation of the seventh edition. We wish to acknowledge Barbara Brandis for her invaluable assistance on the use of drug treatments for the disabled.

We would like to express our thanks to Art Reinhardt, Adapted Physical Education Specialist, Stevens Point (Wisconsin) Area Public Schools, a professional always on the "cutting edge" of the field.

We would also like to express our thanks to the following professionals in the Dallas Independent School District: Dr. Herman Saettler, Director of Special Education; Alberta Pingel, "second in command;" Judy Achilles, Supervisor of Speech and Language Programs; Carmen Anderson, Director of Occupational and Physical Therapy; Fran Hammer, Supervisor of Vision and Adapted Physical Education; Jeri Hodges, Director of Computer Technology; Virginia Nelson, Supervisor of the Autism Program; Cathy Orr, Occupational Therapist; and Dr. Rebecca Yates, Speech and Language Therapist.

We would like to thank the following individuals for providing photographs for use within the text: Jennifer Wright, Director of Adapted Physical Education, Jefferson Parish Schools; Betsy Latsch, Director of Recreation and Rehabilitation, Northern Wisconsin Center for the Developmentally Disabled; and Jeri Hodges, Director of Computer Technology, Dallas Independent School District.

We would also like to express our thanks to the following individuals and programs for providing us with the opportunities to photograph: Tony Omernik, Director, Wisconsin Lions Camp, Rosholt, Wisconsin; Texas Special Olympics and Wisconsin Special Olympics; Callier Center for Communicative Disorders, Dallas, Texas; and the Department of Special Education of the Dallas Independent School District.

Comments and criticisms from users of the sixth edition were carefully considered for this edition. A panel of reviewers currently teaching adapted physical education courses in colleges and universities were selected to assist with the revised manuscript to meet the needs of the instructors and their students. There was close scrutiny of the book to verify that content was appropriate for training modern physical educators and that it applied to physical education settings in the real world. To these colleagues, we would like to express our sincere appreciation.

Peter Aufsesser
San Diego State University
Paul Bishop
Kearney State College
Michael Churton
University of Central Florida
Claire Foret
University of Southwest Louisiana
Lynne Heilbuth
Oklahoma State University
Reba Sims
Southwest Missouri State University

Finally, we wish to extend our appreciation to Cathy Waller of Mosby-Year Book for her outstanding editorial work on this book.

David Auxter
Jean Pyfer
Carol Huettig

Contents

12 *Hearing Impairments, 268*

13 *Visual Impairments, 284*

14 *Posture and Body Mechanics, 304*

15 *Physical and Motor Development, 344*

16 *Other Conditions, 365*

PART FOUR

ORGANIZATION AND ADMINISTRATION

17 *The Individual Education Program Process, 390*

PRINCIPLES AND METHODS OF

Adapted Physical Education and Recreation

PART ONE

THE SCOPE

IN THIS SECTION we provide a historical overview of societal

attitudes toward individuals with disabilities. In the 1990s the

United States is still attempting to implement the commitment

to protecting individual and civil rights of persons with

disabilities mandated by legislation of the 1970s. The mandates

and detailed procedures to follow for compliance with the laws

are presented in this section. Effective teaching methods and

types of assessment to meet specific needs are discussed.

Courtesy Wilderness Inquiry

OBJECTIVES

Describe the nature and prevalence of disabling conditions.

Explain the history of services to persons with disabilities.

Cite the impact of legislation for provision of physical education services to individuals with disabilities.

Describe the effects of disabling conditions as they relate to social forces during school and postschool years.

Explain the role of the physical education teacher within the context of a generic human delivery system.

Cite the significance of labeling on physical education programming for individuals with disabling conditions.

Trace the status of implementing physical education programs for individuals with disabling conditions with respect to conformance to federal legislation.

Educating People with Disabilities

*A*ssumptions about how persons with disabilities are to be physically educated are changing. To meet the needs of students with disabling conditions, physical educators must be prepared for the changing service patterns. When the Education of the Handicapped Act of 1975 (P.L. 94-142)[54] (originally known as the Education for All Handicapped Children Act) was enacted, physical education was the only educational curriculum specifically named. This singular identification has placed unique opportunities and responsibilities on the physical education profession to serve persons with disabilities. During the past years a great transition in the professional fields that deliver assistance to individuals who have motor disabilities has taken place. In our affluent society no longer must a person be relegated to living in isolation due to lack of physical and motor abilities prerequisite to independent domestic and recreational physical activity.

Physical education teachers instruct children with a variety of disabling conditions in many different instructional settings. The mission of the physical educa-

tion teacher is to promote the development of motor skills and abilities so that children can live healthful and productive lives and engage in independent recreational and sport activities of their choosing. This chapter is concerned with the nature of disabling conditions, the benefits of the physical education program, and the service delivery system in physical education to serve these populations.

PREVALENCE

The number of children with disabling conditions is fundamental to knowledge of personnel demands and other resources needed to serve this population. Prevalence refers to the number of people in a given cate-

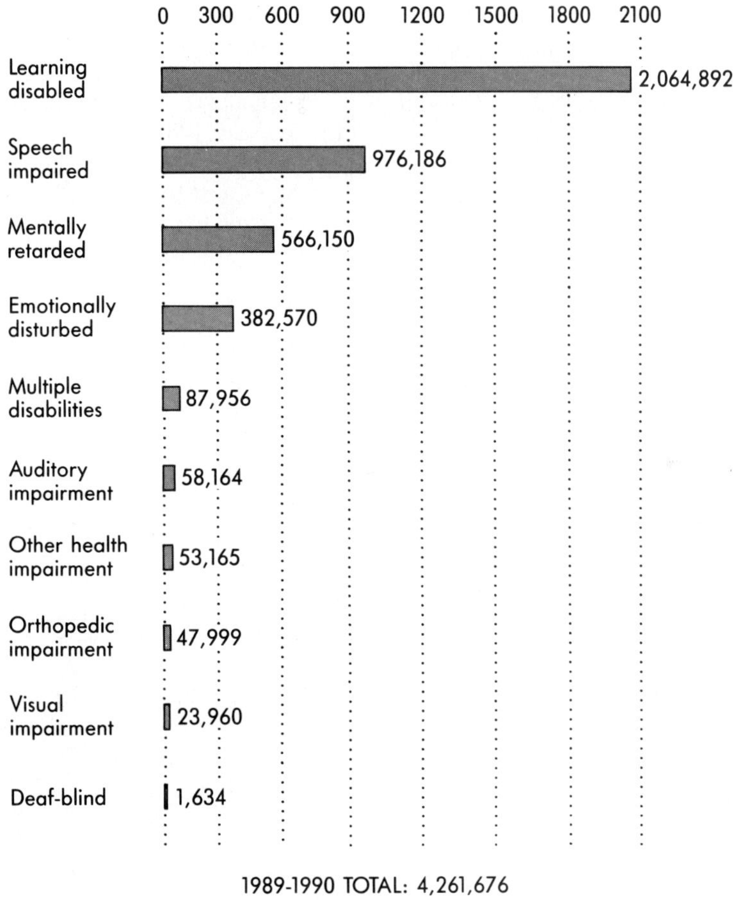

FIGURE 1-1. Number of children aged 6 to 21 years, identified by handicapping condition, who received special education in the United States during the 1989-90 school year. (Source: From Thirteenth Annual Report to Congress on the Implementation of the Individuals with Disabilities Education Act US Department of Education, p 13, 1991.)

gory in a population group during a specific time interval (i.e., the number of mentally retarded children who are of school age this year). Figure 1-1 shows the prevalence of school enrollment of children by disabling conditions during the 1989-1990 school year. Each year the U.S. Department of Education, Office of Special Education and Rehabilitation Services (OSERS) reports to Congress pertinent facts about disabled populations. Some of the most recent facts are: (1) there are over 4.2 million children with disabilities aged 6 to 21 years who receive special education services; (2) children with disabilities in special education represent approximately 11% of the entire school-age population; (3) about twice as many males as females receive special education; (4) approximately 90% of school-aged children who receive special education are mildly handicapped;[24] and (5) the three largest categories of children with disabilities are learning disabilities, speech and language impairment, and mental retardation.

The incidence of children with disabilities in the public schools does not represent the magnitude of the need of persons who can benefit from special physical activity designed to accommodate the needs of individuals. In addition to those conditions outlined in the Education of the Handicapped Act, other special needs may qualify a child for special physical education considerations.

In a given year nearly 467 million acute (short-term) illnesses and injuries occur in our population. Approximately 68 million persons are injured annually, and more than three times as many have colds, sinus infections, influenza, and other respiratory tract diseases. Furthermore, accidents are responsible for an estimated 10.2 million disabling injuries per year. Of this number, 380,000 prove to be permanent impairments.[13] Paralysis, orthopedic disorders, hearing defects, speech defects, and heart disease also represent a considerable number of those conditions reported.

The number of individuals with multiple disabilities also is increasing. The reasons are many, but the primary ones seem to be the higher rate of survival among infants born prematurely and advanced techniques of medical science that are keeping children with one or more disabilities alive.

HISTORICAL IMPLICATIONS
Early History

In highly developed countries the current level of concern for the well-being of the individual has evolved gradually over thousands of years. One characteristic of the typical early primitive cultures was their preoccupation with survival. Historians speculate that members of many early primitive societies who were unable to contribute to their own care were either put to death, allowed to succumb in a hostile environment, or forced to suffer a low social status. In some societies, persons displaying obvious behavioral deviations were considered from converse points of view—either filled with evil or touched by divine powers.

Humanitarianism

Great social and cultural progress occurred during the Renaissance. The seed of social consciousness had been planted. From this time on a genuine concern for the individual developed, giving each person dignity. With a desire for social reform came a multitude of movements to improve life. Reforms dealing with peace, prison conditions, poverty, and insanity were organized, and many social and moral problems were attacked in the first decade of the nineteenth century.

During the latter part of the nineteenth century and the early part of the twentieth century, emphasis was placed on development of instructional methodology to educate intellectually disabled persons. This work had a significant impact on modern pedagogy. The Montessori approach was developed for work with the

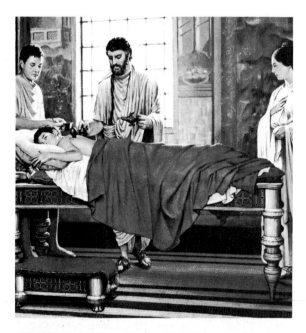

FIGURE 1-2. Galen treating an ill child by cupping. (Courtesy Parke, Davis, & Co, Detroit.)

mentally retarded during the early part of the twentieth century. This was a didactic system in which learners used sequential materials that could accommodate the ability levels of each child. The Montessori approach was a forerunner of individualized instructional programming, which is widely used at present.

World War I was a period that greatly advanced medical and surgical techniques designed to ameliorate many physically disabling conditions. In addition, individuals were restored to usefulness by vocational and workshop programs. During the interim between World War I and World War II, state and federal legislation was enacted to promote vocational rehabilitation for both civilians and the military disabled. The Smith-Sears Act of 1918 and the National Civilian Vocational Rehabilitation Act of 1920 were the forerunners of the Social Security Act of 1935 and the Vocational Rehabilitation Act of 1943, which provided disabled individuals with both physical and vocational rehabilitation.

With World War II came thousands of ill and incapacitated service personnel. Means were employed to restore them to function as useful and productive members of society. Physical medicine became a new medical specialty. Many services heretofore considered hospital services became autonomous ancillary medical fields. The paramedical specialties of physical therapy, occupational therapy, and corrective therapy considerably decreased the recovery time of many patients.

However, the main impetus for aiding the disabled did not occur until early in the twentieth century and as late as the early 1960s for the mentally retarded and the emotionally disturbed. The contributions of figures such as President Franklin D. Roosevelt, supporting the fight against crippling diseases such as poliomyelitis, and the Kennedy family, working to help the mentally retarded, can hardly be overlooked when discussing the humanitarian concerns in the United States.

Physical Activity

The relationship of physical activity to functional development and well-being has long been valued. In 460 BC Hippocrates used exercise to strengthen muscles and aid rehabilitation. Galen (30 BC) recommended specific exercises for muscle tonus, and Erasistratus advocated walking for dropsy. The fundamental value of the exercise was the physical well-being of the individual achieved through specific exercise regimens.

After World War II an emerging philosophy was social participation in sports and games. Such activity provided an opportunity to meet social-recreational needs as well as promote physical and organic develop-

FIGURE 1-3. Pinel unchains the insane. (Courtesy Parke, Davis, & Co, Detroit.)

ment. In 1952 the Committee on Adapted Physical Education adopted the following resolution to accommodate children with disabilities in physical education programs[1]:

> It consisted of a diversified program of developmental activities, games, sports, and rhythms suited to the interests, capacities, and limitations of students with disabilities who may not safely or successfully engage in unrestricted participation in the vigorous activities of the general education program.

The evolution of instructional and behavioral technologies enabled maximization of the motor skill potential of persons with disabilities. Consider the work of Gold,[22] who trained another teacher to teach a person who was legally blind and deaf, physically handicapped, and mentally retarded (IQ of 28) to assemble a complex 16-part Bendix bicycle coaster brake in 20 trials.

The technology Gold used in the motor task of the bicycle brake assembly is equally effective in the development of other physical and motor tasks. Recent advancements in applied behavioral analysis and research and demonstration for developing motor skills for indi-

...ities promise exciting work in the

...OF DISABLING CONDITIONS

...abilities are grouped according to ...teristics. A name is then ascribed to each ... : term *developmental disabilities* represents all disabilities collectively. Although each state or authority may have differing definitions of developmental disability or specific handicaps, this text is concerned with current federal definitions.

Section 504 of the Rehabilitation Act of 1973 (P.L. 93-112) defines a disabled school-aged person as anyone who has a physical or mental impairment that substantially limits one or more major life activities such as:

□ Caring for one's self
□ Performing manual tasks
□ Walking
□ Seeing
□ Hearing
□ Speaking
□ Breathing
□ Learning
□ Working

Students who don't qualify for special education services under the Individuals with Disabilities Education Act (IDEA) of 1990 (see p. 9) but who might be eligible under Section 504 (if their impairments substantially limit one or more of their major life activities) include those with the following conditions:

□ Drug or alcohol dependency
□ Attention deficit disorder or attention deficit hyperactive disorder
□ Other health needs such as insulin-dependent diabetes, severe allergies, arthritis, epilepsy, or temporary disabilities
□ Communicable diseases, such as the human immunodeficiency virus (HIV)
□ Social maladjustment
□ Learning disabilities without a severe discrepancy between ability and achievement
□ Removal from special education because s/he no longer meets eligibility criteria under IDEA[35]

The scope of special education for the exceptional child is broad. Programs of instruction can be offered in a number of places, depending on the needs of the child. Special education is available in hospitals, special residential and day schools, and special classes for children with disabilities within the regular schools, as well as in-home instruction. However, the majority of students with disabilities attend regular schools.

The concern of all persons is that every individual with disabilities should have the opportunity to reach full potential through an individualized education program.

PHYSICAL EDUCATION FOR PERSONS WITH DISABILITIES

Persons with disabilities engage in physical activity that is administered by many different types of personnel and carried out in a variety of settings. Following are some of the terms associated with physical activity for persons with disabilities:

FIGURE 1-4. An obstacle course facilitates the development of wheelchair mobility. (Courtesy Adapted Physical Education Department, Jefferson Parish Public School System, Louisiana.)

adapted physical education Modification of traditional physical activities to enable the child with disabilities to participate safely, successfully, and with satisfaction

corrective physical education Activity designed to habilitate or rehabilitate deficiencies in posture or mechanical alignment of the body

special physical education Another term used to describe adapted pysical education

remedial physical education Activity designed to habilitate or rehabilitate functional motor movements and develop physical and motor prerequisites for functional skills[26]

disorder General mental, physical, or psychological malfunction of the processes[26]

disabled Describes an individual who has lost physical, social, or psychological functioning that significantly interferes with normal growth and development[26]

disability A limitation that is imposed on the individual by environmental demands and that is related to the individual's ability to adapt to environmental demands[26]

habilitation An educational term that indicates the handicapped person is to be taught basic skills needed for independence[26]

New Definition of Physical Education

There is and has been a traditional curriculum common to most physical education programs. For the most part physical education activities include participation in sports and development of sufficient physical fitness to accomplish the activities of daily living and maintenance of health.

Traditionally, good teaching implies accommodation of the individual needs of the learner to enable successful participation. Special accommodations are made in the teaching of skills, and adaptations are made to include children in sport activity and group games. Physical education for individuals with disabilities was specifically defined in P.L. 94-142. It included all of the previous definitions mentioned but was simply stated. We have accepted the following P.L. 94-142 definition for use in this textbook[54]:

1. The term means the development of:
    a. Physical and motor fitness
    b. Fundamental motor skills and patterns
    c. Skills in aquatics, dance, and individual and group games and sports (including intramural and lifetime sports)
2. The term includes special physical education, adapted physical education, movement education, and motor development

The two essential components of physical education for people with disabilities are teaching the defined curricula of physical education and conducting an individualized program for the child.

Benefits of Physical Education for Students with Disabilities

When a child is identified as having a disability, it serves notice to educators and parents that the child risks becoming dependent on others for social living skills. The physical educator can make a major contribution to reduce this risk and facilitate independent living through physical activity in the following ways:

☐ Develop recreational motor skills for independent functioning in the community.

☐ Develop physical fitness for maintenance of health.

☐ Develop ambulatory skills to master mobility in domestic and community environments.

☐ Develop physical and motor prerequisites to self-help skills required for independent living.

☐ Develop physical and motor prerequisites to vocational skills required for independent living.

☐ Develop prerequisite motor skills necessary for participation in self-fulfilling social activity.

The physical education program is a vital part of the total education program, which is designed to maximize the potential for self-sufficient living in the community.

It has long been argued that participation in sports develops the social characteristics of participants. Participation alone may not, however, benefit individuals with disabilities. Early studies on the social benefits of mainstreaming students with disabilities indicated that under certain conditions the person with a disability could be adversely affected.[38] There is some recent evidence that when the conditions of participation are well controlled (e.g., appropriate activities are offered at the ability level of the learner) and environments are designed that include a carefully structured modeling process, social development can be fostered through physical activity and sport.[11] To ensure that social benefits occur to all persons, the social environment should be constructed so that there is a match between the environmental demands of the sport/physical activity and the social capabilities of the participants. Furthermore, the participants without disabilities must be supportive of the socialization process.

Scope of Physical Education for Students with Disabilities

Public policy requires that children with disabilities be provided with physical education. The scope of physical education has been defined by federal regulations (development of physical and motor fitness, fundamental motor patterns and skills, and team and lifetime sport skills). The incorporation of physical education into the Education of the Handicapped Act has led to

FIGURE 1-5. The only limits are those imposed by others. (Courtesy Wisconsin Lions Camp, Rosholt, Wisconsin.)

many opportunities for services to children with disabilities, such as the following:

□ Teaching motor skills to all children with disabilities, who will use these skills in recreational environments in the community
□ Teaching the person with disabilities to generalize skills obtained in instructional settings into the community[7]
□ Helping develop the fundamental motor skills, such as walking for persons with impaired ambulation
□ Developing prerequisite physical and motor fitness

for the severely involved so they may develop self-help skills, such as feeding and dressing
□ Being involved directly and meaningfully with severely and profoundly disabled persons, for whom the primary education program is motor

Clearly, the physical education program is vital to every person with a disability. Often the need for physical education bears a direct relationship to the severity of the disabling condition. Profoundly mentally retarded persons often have an educational program of development of ambulation skills, self-care skills, and communication. The physical education profession is needed to develop the fundamental skills of ambulation and the physical and motor prerequisites for the self-help skills. The mentally impaired often rely on recreational motor skills for their leisure.

Physical Education: an Integral Part of Special Education

The content and purposes of physical education were well known long before the evolution of the instructional procedures that have been identified with effective intervention systems for children with disabilities. However, individualized formats of instruction have added new meaning to the physical education profession. The focus of physical education for persons with disabilities has had the following benefits for the physical education profession:

1. It has enabled an identifiable body of content that is the physical education curriculum (defined by federal law), developed out of a substantial history and tradition.
2. It now has unique integrity with the recognized procedure and products associated with special education (specially designed instruction to meet unique needs as set forth in the individualized education program).
3. The integrated disciplines of special and physical education rely on accurate language to meet public policy demands.

As a matter of public policy, including physical education as an integral part of special education has made adapted physical education a unique discipline.

Coordination of Services

The mission of physical education for persons with disabilities is to improve their quality of life. However, for physical education programs to be of greatest benefit, they must be carried over into daily leisure activities in the community after school. This requires coordination of services and resources in the home, school, and other community agencies.

Parents often mediate for children with school and community. For them to maximize opportunities for their children they need to know specifically the benefits and the skills that are developed in school physical education programs and opportunities in the community where these acquired skills can be expressed. Therefore physical education teachers and parents of children with disabilities should meet frequently to ensure that the school programs meet the child's needs for participation in the community.

LEGISLATION FOR INDIVIDUALS WITH DISABILITIES

There has been a steady history of government and social policy supporting the development of individuals with disabilities so they may have greater opportunities to participate in independent life in the community. The most recent legislation is the Individuals with Disabilities Education Act (IDEA)[56] of 1990. This act expands on the Education of the Handicapped Act of 1975 (P.L. 94-142) and the 1983 (P.L. 98-199) and 1986 (P.L. 99-457) amendments to the act. These federal laws mandate more extensive services to a broader range of individuals.

□ P.L. 98-199 provided incentives to states to identify and provide services to handicapped infants and preschool children ages 3 to 5 years.

□ P.L. 99-457 expanded the definition of handicapped to include children from birth through 2 years of age who are diagnosed with a physical or mental condition and/or who are highly likely to experience developmental delays.

Highly likely factors that may contribute to developmental delays include environmental conditions such as poor housing, poor parental care, and/or limited parenting skills. The law provides funding to assist states with planning, developing, and implementing a statewide comprehensive multidisciplinary program for children who qualify for services.

Services to be included in the state plan are family training, counseling, and home visits; special instruction; speech pathology and audiology; occupational therapy; physical therapy; psychological services; medical services; early identification, screening and assessment services; and health services.[32]

The Individuals with Disabilities Education Act of 1990 (P.L. 101-476)[56] replaced the term *handicapped* with *disability* and expanded on the types of services that must be offered and conditions that qualify children for services. Additional services that must be made available are transition, assistive technology, recreation therapy, and social work. Transition services that will promote movement from school to postschool activities must be included in the individual education plan of all students with disabilities at least by age 16 years. Assistive technology services that are now required include evaluating students' needs for equipment that will maintain, improve, or increase their functional capabilities; purchasing the equipment; customizing it; and training the student, their families, and school personnel in the use of the equipment. The law also requires schools to include the related services of recreation therapy and social work in the student's individual education program.[35]

IDEA expands eligibility for all services to children with autism and children with traumatic brain injury. These conditions and physical education programming concerns are discussed in later chapters of this book. Table 1-1 depicts legislation ensuring the rights of individuals with disabilities.

Accommodation of Individual Difference

Each child with a disability should have an individualized physical education program (IEP). The activities of the program should promote the acquisition of a skill, and each activity should begin at the child's present level of ability and progress in a sequence of small steps. It also is expected that aids will be introduced and the environment modified to enable successful participation. Tasks that meet the needs of the specific learner should be selected, and the length of participation on the tasks should be commensurate with the amount of self-sufficiency the child needs to develop.

For example, consider a young severely involved child who has difficulty sitting erect because of insufficient abdominal strength. Sit-ups might be selected as an activity to strengthen the muscles. The angle of inclination of a board on which the child does the sit-ups can make the task more or less difficult. (The angle of the board reflects the angle of the child's body, with his back against the board.) If the board is flat on the floor (180°), the task is of considerable difficulty. If the board is perpendicular to the floor (90°), the degree of difficulty is diminished to zero. Alteration of the position of the board between 180° and 90° enables a sequence of difficulty. The variance of the distance of the movement and the length of the lever arm on which gravity acts provide a sequence that can accommodate a wide range of abilities. The student might participate in this activity for 5 minutes out of each physical education period to develop this specific muscle group.

TABLE 1-1

Federal legislation impacting individuals with disabilities

1961   *P.L. 87-276 Special Education Act*

Designed to train professionals to prepare teachers of deaf children.

1965   *P.L. 89-10 Elementary and Secondary Education Act*

Enabled the states and local school districts through provision of monies from the federal government to develop programs for economically disadvantaged children.

1966   *P.L. 89-750 Amendments to the Elementary and Secondary Act*

Created the Bureau of Education for the Handicapped.

1973   *P.L. 93-112, Section 504 of the Rehabilitation Act*

Actually adopted and declared that handicapped people cannot be excluded from any program or activity receiving federal funds on the basis of being handicapped alone.

1974   *P.L. 93-247 Child Abuse and Prevention Act*

Created systems to protect children from abuse. Mandated that a person who suspects child abuse must report it.

1975   *P.L. 94-142 Education for All Handicapped Children Act*

Created a free appropriate public education for all handicapped children between the ages of 3 and 21 years. Required that an individual education program (IEP) be developed for each handicapped child and that students with disabilities pursue their programs in the least restrictive environment. Physical education was identified as a direct service to be provided to these students with disabilities. Intramural and interscholastic competition is to be provided to the same extent as for nonhandicapped students.

1983   *P.L. 98-199 Amendments to the Education for All Handicapped Children Act*

States were required to collect data to determine the anticipated service needs for children with disabilities. It provided incentives to the states to provide services to handicapped infants and preschool children.

1986   *P.L. 99-372 Handicapped Children's Protection Act*

Attorney's fees were reimbursed to parents who were forced to go to court to secure an appropriate education for their child. Parents who prevailed in a hearing or a court case could recover the cost incurred for lawyers to represent them.

1986   *P.L. 99-457 Education for All Handicapped Children Amendments of 1986*

States were to develop comprehensive interdisciplinary services for handicapped infants and toddlers, birth through age 2 years, and to expand services for preschool children aged 3 through 5 years.

1987   *Reauthorization of the Child Abuse Prevention and Treatment Act*

The National Center on Child Abuse and Neglect was directed to study the incidence of abuse of children with disabilities and the incidence of disabilities that result from abuse.

1990   *P.L. 101-476 Individuals with Disabilities Education Act*

Replaced the term "handicapped" with "disability" and expanded on the types of services offered and conditions covered.

1990   *P.L. 101-336 Americans with Disabilities Act*

Widened civil rights protections for the disabled to all public accommodations and addressed private discrimination.

Concepts from Legislation

Three primary concepts that have emerged from legislation have implications for the conduction of physical education for students with disabilities: (1) school personnel must spell out achievable objectives in detail and be held accountable for subsequent evaluation; (2) parents must be fully informed of the nature of the programs in which their children participate; and (3) the education should take place in the most integrated setting, with children without disabilities in regular class, if possible. Each of these components of the educational delivery system requires the focus to be on the individual needs and learning of children with specific disabilities.

FIGURE 1-6. Competitive tennis provides opportunities for challenge and personal growth. (Courtesy National Foundation of Wheelchair Tennis.)

Intramurals and Interscholastic Sports

Children with disabilities need the same opportunities as all other children for participation in intramural and interscholastic sports activities. Furthermore, these opportunities ideally should be provided in the most integrated setting. However, provisions should be made to separate students with disabilities from other children during participation "when it is necessary to ensure the health and safety of the students, or to take into account their interest," and only if no qualified student with a disability is denied the opportunity to compete for teams that are not separate or different.[52] The central theme of the provision of equal opportunity in intramural and interscholastic participation for persons with disabilities is that of "reasonable accommodation" for these learners (Section 84:37).[52]

Recreational Sports Opportunities

Recreational sports opportunities for persons with disabilities vary at differing stages of life. In preschool and infant programs for children with disabilities, the focus is on motor development that is prerequisite to a wide variety of physical activities. When the individual enters the public school there are three opportunities for participation in recreational sports activity. One is the physical education instructional program, which teaches the student the physical skills and knowledge necessary to play games and then actually generalizes the skills into play. A second environment that may be available in some schools is an intramural program. Here the student with disabilities has opportunity to express the skills learned in physical education class in recreational play activity within the schools. A third source of opportunity for the child with a disability is community-based recreational programs that may take the form of integrated activity with other children in the community (YMCAs/YWCAs and Little Leagues). In addition, organizations that advocate for specific disabling conditions may organize physical activity to enable participation for specific groups (e.g., Special Olympics for mentally retarded individuals and wheelchair sports for orthopedically impaired persons).

When the individuals with disabilities are postschool aged, there are basically two options for recreational sports participation. One is the generic community recreation services that are available to other citizens. The second is a disabled-only program that has been developed for a specific categorical disabled group (e.g., blind, orthopedically impaired, mentally retarded). However, a third avenue of sports participation entitled Unified Sports League has been developed through Special Olympics International. In this program equal numbers of disabled and nondisabled individuals form teams in a league and engage in meaningful sports activity in the community. The eventual objective is the transition of the individual with disabilities from mixed play to independent recreational sports activity in the community.

Three barriers that prevent individuals with disabilities from participation in community recreation programs are lack of information on the existence of such services, physical barriers that prevent access, and inadequate transporation.

Due Process

When a person's civil rights are violated, that person is entitled to due process (the right to be heard in a formal hearing). Due process complaints under the Education of the Handicapped Act are usually filed to resolve the content or procedures employed in conduction of the IEP or placement in an appropriate setting. A hearing also may be possible through an Office of Civil Rights (OCR) complaint under Section 504 of the Rehabilitation Act of 1973. Lack of opportunity for participation in intramural and interscholastic activities would most likely be addressed through the OCR forum. Due process is a safeguard for achieving the goal of quality and equal educational opportunity for all children with disabling conditions.

Least Restrictive Environment
Legal precedents

Traditionally, persons with disabilities have been segregated in isolated settings. These segregated settings have hospital-like characteristics and are removed from the daily activities of the normal community. At one time it was believed that if sufficient numbers of persons who had special problems were in one place, they could be better served because management would be easier. However, beginning in the early part of the twentieth century, legal precedents were set for what is known as the doctrine of the *least restrictive environment*. Confinement to an institution massively curtails one's liberty, which also occurs when decisions about one's welfare are made by others. Such infringements exist when others decide when one will arise in the morning, when one goes to bed in the evening, when and what one will eat, where one will live, where one will toilet and wash, if and where one can work, when one can work, and what one will do. It is decided what health services will be provided and

when and where, and the extent of those provisions. There often is little recreation; when there is, the restrictions surrounding it are extensive. Clearly, institutionalized living is, in many instances, incarceration with no crime committed by the incarcerated.

Legal background

Equal educational opportunity to children with disabilities in the public schools did not come about by chance. Rather, many laws and court cases important to the education of children who had special needs made their education a fluid and dynamic process. The concept of educating children with disabilities in regular public schools had its roots in the *Brown v. Board of Education of Topeka* decision that established the right of all children to an equal education opportunity. The court wrote:

> [Education] is required in the performance of our most basic responsibilities. . . . It is the very foundation of good citizenship. Today it is a principle in preparing him [sic] for later . . . training, and in helping him adjust normally to his environment. In these days, it is doubtful that any child may reasonably be expected to succeed in life if he is denied the opportunity of an education. Such an opportunity, where the state has undertaken to provide it, is a right which must be made available *to all on equal terms.*[10] *(Italics added.)*

Brown v. Board of Education of Topeka set the precedent for the legal influences of education for individuals with disabilities. Additional court decisions that had an impact on education of individuals with disabilities are delineated in Table 1-2.

Courts have conducted an extensive investigation of denial of unconditional inclusion of a child with disabilities in regular classes and concluded the following[25]:

> There are a great number of other spina bifida children throughout the State of West Virginia who are attending public schools in the regular classroom situation, the great majority of which have more severe disabilities than the plaintiff child Trina Hairston, including children having body braces, shunts, Cunningham clips, and ostomies, and requiring the use of walkers and confinement to wheelchairs. The needless exclusion of these children and other children who are able to function adequately from the regular classroom situation would be a great disservice to these children. . . . A major goal of the educational process is the socialization process that takes place in the regular classroom, with the resulting capability to interact in a social way with one's peers. It is therefore imperative that every child receive an education with his or her peers insofar as it is at all possible. This conclusion is further enforced by the critical importance of education in this society.

TABLE 1-2

Court decisions that impacted education of handicapped persons

1954 **Brown V. Board of Education (Kansas)**

Segregated education in public schools was ruled unconstitutional.

1967 **Hobson V. Hanson (Washington, D.C.)**

The use of standardized tests to track students for special education placement that discriminated against the black and poor children was declared unconstitutional.

1970 **Diana V. State Board of Education (California)**

Children cannot be placed in special education on the basis of culturally biased tests.

1972 **Mills V. Board of Education of the District of Columbia**

Every child has a right to equal opportunity for education.
Emotionally disturbed children cannot be excluded from school, and lack of funds is not an acceptable excuse for lack of educational opportunity.

1972 **Larry B. V. Riles (California)**

IQ tests cannot be used as a sole basis for placing children in special classes.

1979 **Armstrong V. Kline (Pennsylvania)**

Children with disabilities who regress and cannot recoup their gains over extended layoffs from school are entitled to an extended school year through the summer.

1982 **Rowley V. Hendrik (Hudson, New York School District)**

Declared a handicapped child's right to a personalized program of instruction and necessary supportive services and required that the individual education program be reasonably calculated so the child may benefit from it.

1984 **Irving Independent School District V. Tatro (Texas)**

Ruled that services needed to enable a child to reach, enter, exit, or remain in school were required.

1986 **Doe V. Maher (California)**

Children with disabilities cannot be excluded from school for misbehavior that is handicap-related. Educational services can be stopped if the misbehavior is not related to the handicapping condition.

1988 **Polk V. Central Susquehanna Intermediate Unit (Ohio)**

A school district cannot have a blanket policy that no child will get one-to-one physical therapy by a licensed physical therapist if that is what is needed.

1990 **Chester County Intermediate Unit V. Pennsylvania Blue Shield**

If a doctor states that a service (in this case, physical therapy) is necessary to enable the child to benefit from education, the school district, not the insurance company, should pay for the service.

1990 **Cordrey V. Euckert (Ohio)**

A child is entitled to an extended school year if it would be not merely beneficial but a necessary component of an appropriate education for the child. Empirical regression data are not the only permissable evidence of need.

Legislation

The rights of the developmentally disabled have been enhanced through three major pieces of federal legislation. This legislation includes the Rehabilitation Act of 1973, the Education of the Handicapped Act of 1975, and the Americans with Disabilities Act (ADA) of 1990. These three pieces of legislation have similarities as well as differences.

The purpose of all three acts was to provide equal opportunity for individuals with developmental disabilities. The similarities are: (1) equity of services for individuals with disabilities when compared to those without disabilities; (2) accessibility to environments so there is equal opportunity to derive benefits from services; (3) accommodation for the disabling condition for the provision of equal opportunity; and (4) encouragement of integration of individuals with and without disabilities. All of the acts apply these basic principles but focus on different contexts.

The Education of the Handicapped Act of 1975 (P.L. 94-142) focuses on educational settings and is designed to provide equal education opportunity for individuals with disabilities. The primary accommodation is the individual education program (IEP). This act has been amended and retitled the Individuals with Disabilities Education Act.

Rehabilitation Act of 1973 is general civil rights legislation that applies to social services within the community as well as within the public schools. Its enforcement is restricted to those agencies that receive federal assistance. The Americans with Disabilities Act of 1990,[55] however, widens civil rights protections for the disabled to *all* public accommodations and addresses private discrimination.

Each of the three major pieces of legislation focuses on the integration, or inclusion, of individuals with disabilities. Testimony by social scientists, which indicated that segregation and restriction of children from culturally relevant social learning experiences was undesirable, convinced Congress of such worth. Senator Stafford of Vermont made the following points before Congress[42]:

> For far too long children with disabilities have been denied access to the regular school system because of an inability to climb the steps to the schoolhouse door, and not for any other reason. This has led to segregated classes for those children with physical handicaps. This is an isolation that is in many cases unnecessary. It is an isolation for the handicapped child and for the "normal" child as well. The sooner we are able to bring the two together, the more likely that the attitudes of each toward one another will change for the better. . . . I firmly believe that if we are to teach all of our children to love and understand each other, we must give them every opportunity to see what "different" children are like. . . . If we allow and, indeed, encourage children with disabilities and children without disabilities to be educated together as early as possible, their attitudes toward each other in later life will not be such obstacles to overcome. A child who goes to school every day with another child who is confined to a wheelchair will understand far better in later life the limitations and abilities of such an individual when he or she is asked to work with, or is in a position to hire, such an individual.

Social integration of individuals with disabilities is a matter of public policy. Procedures should be taken to ensure that to the maximum extent appropriate children with disabilities are educated with children who are not[42] and that they be moved to special classes and programs only when a regular class cannot meet their needs. The fundamental premise of integration, or inclusion, in the schools is that it prepares all individuals for life in a world in which they must live and work with one another.

Brown and co-workers[9] addressed the reasons surrounding improved learning that schooling severely disabled children with nondisabled children provides. For the most part these benefits reflect those of the integration concept proposed by Congress. They maintain the following position[8]:

Long-term heterogeneous interactions between severely disabled and nondisabled students facilitate the development of the skills, attitudes, and values that will prepare both groups to be sharing, participating, contributing members of complex, postschool communities. Stated another way, separate education is not equal education. . . . Segregated service delivery models have at least the following disadvantages:

1. Exposure to student models without disabilities is absent or minimal.
2. Students with severe disabilities tend to learn "handicapped" skills, attitudes, and values.
3. Teachers tend to strive for the resolution of problems related to the child's disability at the expense of developing functional community-referenced skills.
4. Most comparisons between students are made in relation to degrees of disability rather than to standards of performance for individuals without disabilities.
5. Lack of exposure to severely involved students with disabilities limits the probability that the skills, attitudes, and values of students without disabilities will become more constructive, tolerant, and appropriate.

Certainly, it is possible that interaction may not take place even if students with severe disabilities are in the physical presence of students without disabilities. However, unless these students occupy the same space, interaction is impossible. . . . In the future, students with severe disabilities, upon the completion of formal schooling, will live in public, minimally segregated, heterogeneous communities, where they will constantly interact with other citizens. Thus, the educational experience should be representative and help prepare both students with severe disabilities and students without disabilities to function adaptively in integrated communities.

THE AMERICANS WITH DISABILITIES ACT: IMPLICATIONS FOR PHYSICAL EDUCATION AND RECREATION

The Americans with Disabilities Act (ADA) went into effect in January 1992. As President George Bush said at the signing ceremony, "This historic Act is the world's first comprehensive declaration of equality for people with disability. . . . Legally, it will provide our disabled community with a powerful expansion of protections and basic civil rights." The Act was recommended to Congress in a report called, "Toward Independence" produced by the National Council on Disability. The Act builds on and expands on rights created by the Rehabilitation Act of 1973.

Basically, the law prohibits discrimination by places of public accommodation against those with disabilities. More important, the Act declares that our society will provide equal opportunity to citizens with disabilities in all aspects of American life, including recreation. This philosophy, reflected in a public law, should heighten social awareness of the recreational rights and needs of individuals with disabilities.[57]

Public Accommodation

Prior to the ADA there was a lack of federal legislation to prevent private enterprise from discriminating against disabled individuals. However, the ADA mandated that operators of establishments offering services to the public cannot discriminate because of a person's disability and, subsequently, prevent "full and equal" enjoyment of services or accomodations offered by the establishment. Community recreational facilities, as well as most health and physical fitness facilities, are included under this law.

Reasonable Accommodation

To assure the inclusion of persons with disabilities to the maximum extent possible, the ADA requires that services of public accommodations be provided to permit use of facilities by all individuals, regardless of capability. The main instrument for greater inclusion of the disabled in society is application of principles of "reasonable accommodation" in applied settings. This may require modification of policies, practices, and/or procedures, including provision of auxiliary aids or services, or both. However, when accommodations for inclusion alter the nature of the service or result in an undue hardship to the operators, such accommodations are exempt from implementation.[27]

Implications for Physical Education and Recreation

The ADA vastly enlarges the rights of people with disabilities, freeing them from discrimination in community recreation environments and enabling them to use nearly every recreational facility and service common to life in the United States. These rights will create many new opportunities for disabled persons to achieve recreational independence in the community. In this respect, the ADA will greatly enhance the educational and rehabilitation process by creating real opportunities for recreational freedom. Not only does the ADA facilitate recreational independence for the disabled, it also makes a major contribution to the fundamental outcomes of physical education for children and youth with disabilities. The "transition" clause of IDEA should ensure that skills attained in physical education will be generalized from school to independent community recreation settings. Thus physical educa-

tion programs that incorporate community based assessment of physical education needs of the disabled will have increased opportunities to conduct effective programs that link skills learned in school with meaningful recreational experiences within the community.

Continuum of Lesser Restrictive Environments

There are continua of lesser restrictive environments in educational settings and in the community. The lesser restrictive environment in the community where the individual will live life as an adult is very important, but frequently not very well defined. In the school setting the lesser restrictive environments are fairly well defined with respect to matching the severity of a problem of an individual with the setting in which the individual with a disability will be placed.

One purpose of the Education of the Handicapped Act was to provide education in the least restrictive environment. Thus implementation procedures require first an IEP and then placement in the least restrictive environment. There has recently been considerable discussion in the literature of different models of least restrictive environment in physical education.[2,21,30] Options range from full-time regular physical education to full-time adapted physical education in a special school or facility with various placement options in between. Some special education professionals advocate placing all students with disabilities in regular education.[44,45]

Although least restrictive environment is an essential component of the Education of the Handicapped Act, there have been misconceptions regarding how it should be implemented.[2,48] Concepts that are related to, but different from, least restrictive environment are mainstreaming, integration, normalization or inclusion, and the regular education initiative.[23,40] Mainstreaming is placing a child with a disability into a "regular" class, even if this may not be the child's least restrictive environment. Integration, on the other hand, is descriptive of educational placement of students with disabilities in environments with nondisabled students; in these environments the individual with a disability is considered a full member of the social group and is an active participant in all activities of the group.

The principle of normalization, or inclusion, refers to routines of life that are typical for individuals without disabilities.[46] Normalization should apply to all aspects of the least restrictive environment. The U.S. Department of Education, Office of Special Education and Rehabilitation Services is required to report least restrictive environment placements. The continuum of

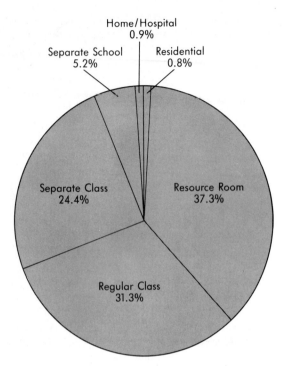

FIGURE 1-7. Percentage of all students with disabilities aged 3 to 21 years served in six educational placements. (Source: From Thirteenth Annual Report to Congress on the Implementation of the Individuals with Disabilities Education Act US Department of Education, p 22, 1991.)

least restrictive environment placement, as reported by this agency, with the percent of total disabled population appears in Figure 1-7. The continua of placements from the least to most restrictive is as follows: (1) regular class—31.3%; (2) resource room (child receives special instruction services outside the "regular" class)—37.3%; (3) separate or segregated class—24.4%; (4) separate school—5.2%; (5) home/hospital—0.9%; and residential—0.8%.

The regular education initiative is a "trend" toward wholesale inclusion of children with disabilities into regular education. The regular education initiative will be discussed further throughout the text.

If we expect students with disabilities to live and work in society, we must prepare them by first integrating them in school. The school, in a sense, becomes a microcosm of the society.[5] Thus the least restrictive environment is considered to be the setting that most closely resembles regular class; the most restrictive is a setting that is removed from the local school that nondisabled students attend.

Effects of labeling on placement

The wisdom of placing individuals with disabilities into specific categories such as "mentally retarded" or "specific learning disability" has been argued for many years. Stainback and Stainback[43] believe that the classification of exceptional children by category of disabling condition may actually interfere with assessment and instructional planning that is directed toward the real learning needs of each student. They state[43]:

> [T]hese categories often do not reflect the specific educational needs and interests of students in relation to such services. For example, some students categorized as behavioral disordered may need self-control training, while some students not so labeled may need self-control training as part of their educational experience. Such categories . . . actually interfere with providing some students with the services they require to progress toward their individual educational goals. Eligibility for educational and related services . . . should be based on the abilities, interests, and needs of each student as they relate to instructional options, rather than on the student's inclusion in a categorical group.

With the recent advances in instructional technology for individualization of instruction, tailoring instruction to the needs of each student irrespective of disabling condition is possible.[37,58] Whenever possible, this instruction should be provided in the regular class, since the regular class has been found to be effective at age levels ranging from preschool[20,29] to high school[59] with exceptional children whose disability ranged from mild[50] to severe.[7,17] However, these successes were primarily in academic areas.

The research describing benefits of integration of students with disabilities with nondisabled students in physical education settings is less clear. Watkinson and Titus[60] report that the value of integration in physical activities cannot realistically be determined because little research has been done in this area. Review of research on the effects of integration in physical education reported by Sherrill[39] indicates that the effects of integration on social and physical development of individuals with disabilities may be negative. On the other hand, the findings from Special Olympics mixed teams indicate that planned interventions with appropriately trained and committed personnel can yield great benefits to all players in community-based sport activity.[11] While the benefits of inclusion in physical education at present are at best mixed, Heward and Orlansky[28] identify six variables that need to be considered and controlled before mainstreaming may be successful. These are (1) knowledge of the student, (2) knowledge of the regular class teacher, (3) knowledge of the nondisabled peer, (4) knowledge of the parents of students with disabilities, (5) knowledge of the parents of children without disabilities and (6) knowledge of the school administrator. As Taylor, Viklen, and Searl[49] observed, decisions concerning the educational program of students with disabilities are based on that child's needs and the environment. Not all children with the same disability should be placed in the same setting. The goal, instead, is to find an appropriate least restrictive environment for each child. Reynolds, Wang, and Walberg[37] call for the joining of demonstrably effective practices from special education to establish a general education system that better serves all students, particularly those who require greater than usual educational support. Implementing such programs would require many changes in our present school systems. Change in most school systems does not occur very rapidly; however, if we are able to serve all students to the best of our ability, changes are needed and necessary.

Community-based lesser restrictive environments

Special Olympics International has designed a model of lesser restrictive environments to promote integration of mentally retarded individuals into independent recreational activity in the community.[41] The continuum of services is as follows: (1) Special Olympics training with mentally retarded individuals only; (2) mixed participation with a one-to-one ratio of nondisabled peers and mentally retarded players; and (3) individualized participation in generic recreational sport services in the community. This continuum applies to specific sport activities because while an individual may be capable of participating in unrestricted recreation in some sport skills (e.g., bowling and distance running or weight-lifting), this may not be the case for that individual in games such as softball, basketball, or volleyball.

Fundamental concepts of least restrictive environment

Despite legal support for the principle of least restrictive environment, school placement of children with specific disabilities will be argued in informal discussions and formal hearings. The following points are critical to the concepts of least restrictive environment:

□ The placement of children with disabilities must be flexible and reevaluated. Appropriate action should be taken on the reevaluation.

□ The desirable placement goal is movement of the child to less restrictive environments where it is pos-

FIGURE 1-8. A parent is a child's first teacher.

sible to participate in normal community and school activities with nondisabled children.

□ The placement of children with disabilities occurs after development of the IEP.

□ Eventual placement of students with disabilities into less restrictive, more normalizing environments requires individual programs so that they can develop motor and social skills necessary for participation with nondisabled children in a variety of settings.

ACCOMMODATING THE STUDENT WITH DISABILITIES IN INTEGRATED SETTINGS

Many argue that teaching children with heterogeneous learning characteristics is impractical; however, growing numbers of educators take exception to that position. Initiatives were taken by the U.S. Office of Education in the 1960s and 1970s to encourage innovative ways to accommodate individual differences. Programmed instruction had proved to be extremely productive in the development of knowledge and skills for all persons, individuals with disabilities included. With considerable federal investment, learning research laboratories developed systems for individualization of *all* children. Materials are now available that enable all children to participate at their current level of educa-

for specific types of tasks are included in subsequent chapters.

Successful teaching of individuals with disabilities in regular classes requires teaching skills that enable the accommodation of heterogeneous groups through individualization of instruction. It also requires teachers who can modify rules, environments, and tasks to promote meaningful play among students with and without disabilities.

Progress of children advancing on a continuum of least restrictive environments requires (1) periodic review of educational progress, (2) frequent assessment of what least restrictive environment means for a particular child at a particular time, and (3) possible modifications in the type of delivery of services that may produce optimum progress in the future.[18]

MOST APPROPRIATE PLACEMENT

Children with disabilities should be placed in settings that most appropriately meet their physical education needs. Clearly, these children should not be placed in regular classes if it is not in their best interest. Appropriate placement requires consideration of several variables, such as the characteristics of the regular class teacher, the nature of the activity the child is to perform, and available support services.

Needs of the Child

Children with disabilities have physical, social, and emotional needs that are to be met in physical education class. To accomplish this, the following four conditions should be met:

1. The instructional level of activity should be commensurate with the ability level of the child. Some form of individualized instruction should be provided.
2. Activities should be modified to accommodate individual differences in group games.
3. The social environment should be such that it can promote interaction (see Chapter 6).
4. Activities should enable participation rather than spectatorship.

Teacher Qualities

The characteristics of classes that restrict individual liberties for free association with peers vary. Teachers may possess different skills for accommodation of individual differences when teaching specific content. Teacher attitudes toward acceptance of all children in their class and their ability to accommodate children with disabilities are considerations for appropriate placement.

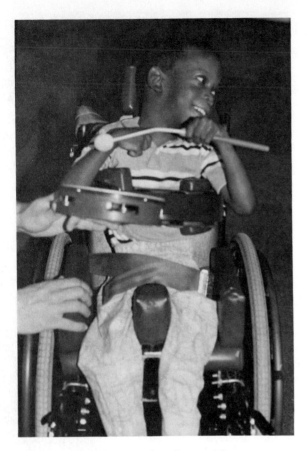

FIGURE 1-9. Make a joyous noise.

tional performance.[61,62] Certain training programs for physical education teachers, as a matter of course, prepare their teachers to conduct the IEP for all children, disabled or not, in the regular class.[3]

Prerequisite to the conduction of physical education skills with individualized formats are (1) prearranged written physical education skills with written objectives and (2) a training system that enables learners to direct and evaluate their own learning. Learners with disbilities at mental age 6 are usually able to convert stick figures into objective performance.[62] We want to emphasize that such individualized instruction for accommodation of individual differences applies only to the development of skills for each individual. Play in group games requires procedures for modification of tasks, rules, and the environment to enable accommodation in group play. Descriptions of procedures for modification of specific disabling conditions

FIGURE 1-10. Recreation and leisure activities provide opportunities for joy throughout the lifespan. (Courtesy Recreation Services, Division Care and Treatment Facilities, Department of Health and Social Services, Northern Wisconsin Center for the Developmentally Delayed.)

Nature of the Activity

Some activities enable accommodation of differences more so than others. Individual sport skills such as tumbling and gymnastics do not depend on the performance or ability of others. Skill development in sports is not particularly difficult to individualize in a regular physical education class. The application of these sport skills in competition is much more difficult. The nature of the activity and ability of the teacher to implement participation in the activity are relevant to the placement of the child with disabilities in a regular class.

All children should be placed in an environment where they may participate successfully and safely.

THE ROLE OF THE ADAPTED PHYSICAL EDUCATOR

The function of the adapted physical education teacher is clear in the Education of the Handicapped Act. The physical educator is to develop physical and motor fitness, fundamental motor skills and patterns, team sports skills, and knowledge of rules and strategies that go with participation in physical activity. However,

over the past decade the actual duties of physical education teachers who serve students with disabilities have become clouded. Factors contributing to this confusion include: (1) lack of certification standards for adapted physical educators in most states, (2) failure by the states to enforce the physical education requirement, and (3) willingness on the part of states and individual school districts to permit inadequately prepared individuals and professionals to deliver physical education to students with disabilities.

Since the enactment of the Education of the Handicapped Act only nine states have developed certification, endorsement, or approval in adapted physical education.[17] Further, in a review of state plans conducted by Bundschuh,[12] 30 states indicated a need for adapted physical education teachers, whereas 18 states did not indicate adapted physical education as a needed area. Of the 18 who reported no need, only two states had either endorsements or approval in adapted physical education. State departments of education apparently have not enforced or provided the necessary information of needs assessment in federal surveys to clarify

...the adapted physical education teacher. As a ... many other professionals have become involved ... the motor planning for students with disabilities. Most of these are adjunctive services of the medical profession (e.g., occupational therapy, corrective therapy, physical therapy).

Preparation and subsequent employment of adapted physical educators is perhaps the key factor in assuring that children with disabilities receive appropriate physical education services.[15] There is evidence that few universities have comprehensively addressed the issue of quality assurance in adapted physical education.[19] There is also evidence that there has been a significant reduction of adapted physical education teachers being trained and placed in the school systems of this country. As a result, the needs of children with disabilities relative to adapted physical education continue to go unfulfilled.[6] There is a need for teachers to be trained so that they can provide quality assurances in physical education to individuals with disabilities.

COMMUNITY-BASED PROGRAMMING

A relationship should be established between skills learned by students in instructional environments and the application of those skills to natural environments in the community. Such programming in physical education starts with the needs of the student for successful participation in physical activity in neighborhood and recreational centers and opportunities in the community. This requires mutual relationships between students with disabilities and the total community environment, both physical and social.

Community-Based Physical Education Programs

The major goal of the Education of the Handicapped Act was to provide an education so that individuals with disabilities could become independent adults in the community. Prerequisite to independent living is the acquisition of the physical and motor skills that will enable these individuals to participate in domestic, recreational, and vocational life in the community. The physical and motor skills attained in instructional settings in the schools should be generalized into physical activity in the community. For the most part, disabled individuals can make the adaptation to community recreational life. However, many such individuals, particularly those with severe involvement, may find it difficult to generalize what was taught in the public schools to community sport and physical activity. To overcome this problem one of the recent initiatives in education for persons with disabilities is community-based assessment and programming, which is a system

that provides specific curriculum content for an individual. The school curriculum focuses on behaviors and skills that an adult will be able to use in the community environment.[29] This system requires that there be a relationship between the curricula for children with and without disabilities in the local school district and that the relationship between the school's curriculum and the physical, sport, and recreational skills learned permits participation in independent recreation in that community. Thus to maximize opportunity for independent recreational programming for persons with disabilities, matches must be made on two levels. Community-based assessment and programming assures the linkage between community, school curricula, and the needs of the child. The key to the curriculum process is generalization. For the instructional content to have value, the student must learn skills that can be generalized from the instructional setting to independent recreational, physical, and sport activity in the community.

NORMALIZATION

Normalization "means making available to the handicapped patterns and conditions of everyday life which are as close as possible to the norms and patterns of the mainstream of society."[33] For this to occur, society's view of persons with disabilities must be consistent with the following conditions:

□ They must be perceived by society as human beings, not as subhuman (vegetables, animals, etc.).

□ They must be perceived by society as possessing a legal and constitutional identity (due process of law for involuntary institutionalization as well as equal opportunity in education, housing, and employment).

□ They must be viewed as persons who can adapt to their environment and acquire skills for as long as they live.

□ They must be provided opportunity by society to take full advantage of their culture.

□ Services must be provided by trained personnel with technical competence in education and habilitation.

□ The human services that care for the disabled provide opportunity for skill development must be valued and well understood by society.

□ Persons with disabilities must be provided opportunities to play valued roles and lead valued lives in our culture.

In the past, many persons with disabilities were considered social deviants. Wolfensberger[63] indicates that a person may be regarded as deviant if some characteristic or attribute is judged different by others who

FIGURE 1-11. The joy of success. (Photo by Jo Arms, Courtesy Texas Special Olympics.)

EDUCATIONAL ACCOUNTABILITY

When applied to the teaching process, the concept of accountability means that a particular program, method, or intervention can be demonstrated to cause a significant positive change in one or more behaviors.[48] It is accepted policy that written records be maintained on each student with a disability to document specific progress toward preestablished goals and objectives. Technical procedures for the appropriate selection of objectives for specific learners have been developed.[4,22] Once these specific meaningful behaviors have been defined, it is then possible to apply accepted behavioral principles to develop them with this sophisticated technology.

Coordination of Delivery of Services

There has been considerable emphasis on the belief that programs for persons with disabilities should be of an interdisciplinary nature. However, according to Stone,[47] problems have existed in the delivery of services within the system. Professionals within the system have taken on the roles, functions, and goals of each other. This has happened because of inadequate planning or coordination and without consideration of the effectiveness of the various professionals in their new roles. As a result we have homogenized professionals who no longer have defined expertise and programs that are less than desirable. Although Stone was not addressing physical education specifically, his view may well relate to the coordination of physical education and the related services (therapies). Role confusion can lead to duplication of services in some programs and voids in others, which results in a lack of comprehensive programming for children with disabilities.

Public policymakers have assigned educational functions to those who are to provide direct services and those who provide indirect services. Direct services are those such as physical education that teach curricula sanctioned by school boards. Related services help children with disabilities gain benefits from the intended outcomes of the direct services (e.g., physical therapy, occupational therapy, and recreational therapy).

The Concept of Related Services

Before a related service such as physical therapy, occupational therapy, or recreational therapy can be implemented in the curriculum, it should be determined whether the limitations of that particular child are such that direct services (physical education) cannot effectively deal with the child's educational problem. A re-

consider the characteristic or attribute important and who value this difference negatively. An overt and negatively valued characteristic that is associated with a deviance is a *stigma.* For instance, members of ethnic minorities, persons with cosmetic disfigurements, dwarfs, and children with disabling conditions have, unfortunately, been considered deviant.

Deviance is a social perception. It is not characteristic of a person but rather of an observer's values as they pertain to social norms.[63] When a person is perceived as deviant or is stereotyped, as is the case with many children with disabilities, he or she is prescribed to a role that carries great expectancies by the person without disabilities. Furthermore, most of these social perceptions clearly reflect prejudices that have little relationship to reality. As Wolfensberger indicates, the lack of objective verification is not a crucial element in the shaping of a social judgment or social policy.

FIGURE 1-12. Motorized wheelchair slalom race. (Courtesy Texas Special Olympics.)

lated service should be provided when a child cannot make the expected progress in skill development in physical education. For instance, if it is decided that a child with a disability does not have the prerequisite strength of a specific muscle group to acquire a sport skill and that the physical educator cannot rectify the problem, a physical therapist may be called on to provide a related service. The physical therapist designs a program for the specific muscle group to establish prerequisite strength; then the child can acquire the skills to be taught by the physical educator. The physical therapist's plan should include measurement of developmental progress in terms of the strength of the specific muscle group. In addition, the physical therapist and those who plan for the related service should indicate the dates of initiation of services, the dates of termination of services, and the duration of the training. However, the development of the skill to be taught in the physical education class is the responsibility of the physical educator. The development of the physical prerequisites (of a pathological nature) to a skill is the responsibility of the related service provider. Such a procedure streamlines services, with greater emphasis on the education of the child, and upgrades the quality of instruction.

CURRENT STATUS OF ADAPTED PHYSICAL EDUCATION

Physical education for individuals with disabilities has been mandated for over 15 years. As a result of the mandated physical education programs, there are undoubtedly several model programs in operation. However, from a national perspective, even with financial assistance from the federal government to develop adapted physical education teachers and programs, physical education for students with disabilities is still inadequate.[15] Loovis[34] indicates it is painfully clear that physical education for students with disabilities remains a woefully neglected and underdeveloped area of public school programming. One reason students with disabilities are not receiving adequate instuction in physical education is because they are inappropriately placed. By law, children with disabilities should be placed in the most appropriate, least restrictive setting that meets their needs. The least restrictive environment is the desirable setting; yet, not all individuals with disabilities belong in regular class. Data revealed that 68% of children with disabilities were provided services in a regular education program.[51] However, the incidence of individuals with disabilities receiving physical education in regular class may be considerably more than in academic subjects. The North Carolina State Department of Public Instruction[36] reports that 87% of their children with disabilities are receiving physical education in the regular physical education program. Thus it may well be that many children with disabilities are inappropriately placed in the lesser restrictive environment. Defacto integration of students with disabilities into regular education is almost exclusively by administrative decree. Efforts must be made to ensure these students are provided an appropriate physical education that will promote their eventual ability to perform as independently as is humanly possible. Parents and educators must insist that students with disabilities are appropriately placed in physical education on the basis of individual test results and that qualified adapted physical educators provide appropriate programming to ensure educational gains.

SUMMARY

Concern for the needs of disabled individuals surfaced during the Renaissance; however, social reforms directed toward improving the quality of life for the disabled did not begin until the nineteenth century. World Wars I and II provided the impetus to develop rehabilitation programs to improve the function of disabled persons. Focus on upgrading the opportunities for mentally retarded individuals became a reality in the 1960s. A national effort to provide school and community services for all persons with disabilities began with the Rehabilitation Act of 1973 and the Education of the Handicapped Act of 1975. These two pieces of legislation mandated appropriate physical education programs and opportunities to participate in intramurals and interscholastic sports for school-age citizens with disabilities. The Individuals with Disabilities Education Act of 1990 and the Americans with Disabilities Act of 1990 extended the provisions of earlier legislation.

Physical education for students with disabilities is a comprehensive service delivery system designed to identify problems of children in physical and motor fitness, fundamental motor patterns and skills, and sport skills and games. Services include assessment, individualized education programming, and coordination of activities with related resources and services. These services may be delivered by specialists who possess skills to conduct instruction for students with disabilities in regular or segregated classes. Special physical education may serve both children with and without disabilities. Specially designed physical education also may occur in any setting on the least restrictive alternative continuum.

An estimated 10% to 20% of the total school-age population at sometime during their education will perform inadequately on physical education tasks. Many of these children have disabilities and need an individualized education program in physical education. The physical education program should develop physical and motor fitness, fundamental motor patterns and skills, and skill development that enables participation in team and lifetime sports. The physical education curriculum and teachers must be able to service children with sensory, physical, mental, and social-emotional handicaps. The services should be provided for children with disabilities in environments where they have an opportunity to engage in culturally relevant learning experiences with their peers. This would be the regular class if possible. However, each child with a disability must be placed in the school environment that is most appropriate for the specific child. The physical educator must coordinate the services with the special education teacher, related services, school administrators, and parents. All parties are cooperatively involved with the physical education program for the special child.

REVIEW QUESTIONS

1. What are the three most prevalent disabling conditions?
2. What is a historical theme in services for the disabled?
3. What is a legal definition of physical education?
4. What are some benefits of a quality physical education program for children with disabilities?
5. Describe the purposes of the Rehabilitation Act of 1973, the Education of the Handicapped Act, the Individuals with Disabilities Education Act, and the Americans with Disabilities Act.
6. What are the entitlements of students with disabilities for intramural and interscholastic sports under federal legislation?
7. What is the difference between least restrictive environment and least restrictive alternative?
8. What is community-based physical education programming?
9. Describe some principles of normalization.
10. What is a related service? What is the relationship of a related service to a direct service?
11. Why is physical education an integral part of special education?
12. What are some of the roles and tasks of physical education teachers of students with disabilities?
13. What are some opportunities for individuals with disabilities to participate in sports and physical activities?
14. What is the present status of physical education for individuals with disabilities as compared to the legislative entitlements of these children?

STUDENT ACTIVITIES

1. Interview a person with a disability or the teacher or parent of a child with disabilities to determine enjoyable physical activities.
2. Provide physical activity for a child with a specific disabling condition. Indicate your feelings before and after the teaching experience.
3. Select two environments where services for persons with disabilities are delivered. One environment should be more restrictive than the other. Describe the differences between the two environments.
4. Identify two or three skills of a child with disabilities that would assist self-sufficient living in the community where the child lives.
5. Visit and interview a physical education teacher of the students with disabilities. Survey the tasks that are performed while the teacher conducts the class.
6. Interview some students with disabilities of different ages to determine their interests.
7. Discuss the view of another professional on the impact that labeling has on subsequent conduction of physical education programs for individuals with disabilities.
8. Interview an adapted physical education teacher, the parents of a child with a disability, or a student with disabilities to determine what types of programs have benefitted the social and physical development of the disabled individual.

REFERENCES

1. American Association of Health, Physical Education, and Recreation: Guiding principles for adapted physical education, *J Health Phys Educ Rec,* p 15, April 1952.
2. Aufsesser PM: Mainstreaming and the least restrictive environment: how do they differ? *Palaestra* 7:31-34, 1991.
3. Auxter DM: Integration of the mentally retarded training programs, *J Health Phys Educ Rec,* pp 61-62, Sept, 1970.
4. Bellamy T, Peterson L, Close D: Habilitation of the severely and profoundly retarded: illustrations of competence, *Educ Train Ment Retard* 10:174-186, 1975.
5. Bliton G, Schroeder HJ: *The new future for children with substantial handicaps: the second wave of LRE,* Bloomington, 1986, Indiana University Developmental Training Center.
6. Bokee M: *Adapted physical education, therapeutic recreation, and arts for the handicapped,* Washington, DC, 1986, US Department of Education.
7. Brinker RP: Interactions between severely mentally retarded students and other students in integrated and segregated public school settings, *Am J Ment Defic* 11:587-594, 1985.
8. Brown L et al: A strategy for developing chronological age appropriate and functional curricular content for severely handicapped adolescents and young adults, *J Spec Educ* 13:81-90, 1979.
9. Brown L et al: Toward the realization of the least restrictive educational environments for handicapped students, *Position paper,* University of Wisconsin-Madison, Grant no. OEG 0-73-6137, 1977, US Department of Education, Office of Special Education.
10. *Brown v The Board of Education,* 347 U.S., 483, 1954.
11. Budoff M: *Massachusetts mixed softball: a final report,* Washington, DC, 1987, Special Olympics International.
12. Bundschuh E: *Needs assessment in special education,* CSPD-PE project, Athens, Ga, 1985, University of Georgia.
13. Carroll C, Miller D: Health: the science of human adaptation, Dubuque, Iowa, 1982, Wm C Brown Group.
14. Churton MW: Impact of the Education of the Handicapped Act on adapted physical education: a ten-year overview, *Adapt Phys Act Q* 1:81, 1987.
15. Churton MW: Addressing personnel preparation needs to meet the challenges of the future, *Adapt Phys Act Q* 3:118-123, 1986.
16. Condon ME et al: Acceptance of handicapped students by nonhandicapped peers, *J Assoc Persons Severe Handicaps* 11:216-219, 1986.
17. Cowden J, Tymeson G: *Certification in adapted/special physical education: national status update,* Dekalb, Ill, 1984, Northern Illinois University.
18. Cratty BJ: *Adapted physical education for handicapped children and youth,* Denver, 1980, Love Publishing Co.
19. DePauw K: Nationwide survey of professional preparation in adapted physical education, *Calif Assoc Health Phys Educ Rec J* 42:28, 1979.
20. Esposito BG, Reed TM: The effects of contact with handicapped persons on young children's attitudes, *Except Child* 54:224-229, 1986.
21. French R: *Serving the handicapped: least restrictive environment (LRE). Usage in physical education.* Presentation at the Preconvention Symposium at the National Convention of the American Alliance for Health, Physical Education, Recreation and Dance, New Orleans, April 1990.
22. Gold M: *Task analysis: a statement and example using acquisition and production of complex assembly task by the retarded blind,* Urbana-Champaign, Ill, 1975, Institute for Child Behavior and Development, University of Illinois.
23. Grosse S: Is the mainstream always a better place to be? *Palaestra* 7:40-49, 1991.
24. Hagerty GJ, Abramson M: Impediments for implementing national policy change for mildly handicapped students, *Except Child* 53:315-323, 1987.
25. *Hairston v Drosick,* 423 F Suppl 180 (SD W Va, 1976).
26. Hardman ML, Drew CJ, Egan MW: *Human exceptionality, society, school and family,* Boston, 1987, Allyn & Bacon.
27. Herbert HL: The Americans with Disabilities Act, *Fitness Management,* March 1991.
28. Heward WL, Orlansky MD: *Exceptional children,* Columbus, Ohio, 1988, Merrill Publishing Co.

29. Howell K, Moorehead MK: Curriculum based evaluation in special and remedial education, Columbus, Ohio, 1987, Merrill Publishing Co.

30. Jansma P, Decker J: *Project LRE/PE: least restrictive environment usage in physical education.* Washington, DC, 1990, United States Department of Education, Office of Special Education.

31. Jenkins JR, Speltz ML, Odom SL: Integrating normal and handicapped preschoolers: effects on child development and social interaction, *Except Child* 52:7-17, 1985.

32. Kelly L: Problematic issues for adapted physical education- implementation of PL 99-457, *J Health Phys Educ Rec,* pp 44-48, 1991.

33. Kennedy MM, Danielson LC: Where are unserved children with disabilities? *Educ Train Ment Retard* 13:408-413, 1978.

34. Loovis ME: Placement of students with disabilities: the perpetual dilemma, *Adapt Phys Act Q* 3:193-198, 1986.

35. Martin R: *Special education law: changes for the nineties.* Urbana, Ill, 1991, Carle Center for Health Law and Ethics.

36. North Carolina State Department of Public Instruction, CSPD report, Raleigh, NC, 1986, Division of Exceptional Children.

37. Reynolds MC, Wang MC, Walberg HJ: The necessary restructuring of special and regular education, *Except Child* 53:391-398, 1987.

38. Sherrill C: *Adapted physical education and recreation, ed 3,* Dubuque, Iowa, 1986, Wm C Brown Group.

39. Sherrill C: *Sports and disabled athletes, the 1984 scientific congress, vol 9,* Champaign, Ill, 1986, Human Kinetics Publishers.

40. Snell ME, Eichner SJ: *Integration for students with profound disablities.* In Brown F, Lehr DH, editors: *Persons with profound disabilities: issues and practices,* Baltimore, 1989, Paul H Brookes.

41. Songster T: *Integration technology in recreational sports for the mentally retarded, a proposal for the office of special education and rehabilitation services,* Washington, DC, 1987, Special Olympics International.

42. Stafford J: *Congress Rec* 121:10961, 1975.

43. Stainback W, Stainback S: A rationale for the merger of special and regular education, *Except Child* 51:102-111, 1984.

44. Stainback W, Stainback S: *Support networks for inclusive schooling: interdependent integrated education,* Baltimore, 1990, Paul H. Brookes.

45. Stainback S, Stainback W, Forest M: *Educating all students in the mainstream of regular education,* Baltimore, 1989, Paul H. Brookes.

46. Stein JU: An international perspective of normalization and least restrictive environments, *Palaestra* 7:50-53, 1991.

47. Stone A: *Mental health and law: a system in transition,* Washington, DC, 1976, US Department of Health, Education, and Welfare.

48. Taylor SJ: Caught in the continuum: a critical analysis of the principle of the least restrictive environment, *J Assoc Persons Severe Handicaps,* 13:41-53, 1988.

49. Taylor SJ, Viklen D, Searl SJ: Preparing for life: a manual for parents on least restrictive environment, Boston, 1986, Federation for Children with Special Needs.

50. Thomas G, Jackson G: The whole school approach to integration, Br J Spec Educ 13:27-29, 1986.

51. US Department of Education: *Eighth annual report to Congress,* Washington, DC, 1986.

52. US Department of Education: *Thirteenth annual report to Congress,* Washington, DC, 1991.

53. US Department of Health, Education, and Welfare: 504 Regulations for the Rehabilitation Act of 1973, Rehabilitation Act Amendments of 1974, and Education of the Handicapped Act, *Fed Reg* 45:339-395, 1990.

54. US 94th Congress: Public Law 94-142, Nov 29, 1975.

55. US 101st Congress: Public Law 101-336, Aug 9, 1990.

56. US 101st Congress: Public Law 101-476, Oct 30, 1990.

57. Verville RE: The Americans with Disabilities Act, *Arch Phys Med Rehabil* 71:1010-1013, 1990.

58. Wang MC, Reynolds MC: Avoiding the "Catch 22" in special education reform, *Except Child* 51:497-502, 1985.

59. Warger CL, Aldinger LE, Okun KA: *Mainstreaming in the secondary school: the role of the regular teacher,* Bloomington, Ind, 1983, Phi Delta Kappa Educational Foundation.

60. Watkinson EJ, Titus JA: Integrating the mentally handicapped in physical activity: a review and discussion, *Can J Except Child* 2:48-53, 1985.

61. Wessel J: *Fundamental skills,* Northbrook, Ill, 1976, Hubbard Press.

62. White C: Acquisition of lateral balance between trainable mentally retarded children and kindergarten children in an individually prescribed instructional program, Unpublished master's thesis, 1972, Slippery Rock State College, Pa.

63. Wolfensberger W: *Principles of normalization,* Toronto, 1972, National Institute on Mental Retardation.

SUGGESTED READINGS

Eichstaedt CB, Kalakian LH: *Developmental/adapted physical education,* New York, 1987, Macmillan Publishing.

Hardman ML, Drew CJ, Egan MW: *Human exceptionality, society, school and family,* Boston, 1987, Allyn & Bacon.

Heward WL, Orlansky MD: *Exceptional children,* Columbus, Ohio, 1988, Merrill Publishing.

Explain the difference between a general ability and a specific motor skill.

Describe the purpose of making a functional adaptation to a specific skill.

State the purpose of developing general abilities that are prerequisites to motor skills.

Delineate the difference in purpose between task analysis of functional skills for independence and development of general abilities.

Explain the appropriate application of developmental and task-specific approaches and their differences.

Describe a classification system of sensory inputs and general and motor-specific abilities.

Courtesy Alabama's Special Camp for Children and Adults—Easter Seals

Approaches to Teaching People with Disabilities

Physical educators who teach individuals with disabilities agree that their primary goal is to facilitate development of purposeful skills for each student. There are, however, a variety of different approaches to programming from which physical educators can select. They range from general physical education activities believed to benefit all children, regardless of degree of function, to developmentally sequenced activities that serve as building blocks of motor development, to activities that enhance very specific skills.

Which approach a physical educator selects depends on the age of the students, the teacher's knowledge of motor development and ability to accurately assess and interpret motor performance levels, and the goals the teacher is attempting to achieve in the physical education program.

LEVELS OF FUNCTION

The ultimate goal of physical education for children with disabilities is to equip them with motor skills that contribute to independent living. To plan these programs systematically, it is desirable to distinguish clearly the levels of function that contribute to acquisition of the many specific sport skills.

Each of three levels makes a unique contribution to independent functioning: (1) basic input functions, (2) general abilities, and (3) specific skills (Fig. 2-2). The physical educator who understands the interrelatedness of these levels and can select intervention activities to facilitate functioning at any given level, depending on a student's needs, will realize success. Those who do not understand the interrelatedness of each level or who ignore the prerequisites will not be successful in helping students reach their full capabilities.

Basic input functions depend on the integrity and operation of the sensory input systems. These systems include primitive and equilibrium reflexes, the vestibular system, refractive and orthoptic vision, audition, and the tactile and kinesthetic systems. Before information can reach the central nervous system for processing, these systems must be intact and operational. The physical educator who automatically assumes these systems are functioning and that adequate stimulation is reaching the central nervous system disregards an important component of purposeful movement.

The second level of functioning is made up of abilities. Like basic input functions, these prerequisites enhance the acquisition of skill. If the sensory input systems are functioning, abilities develop concurrently with movement experiences. Abilities prerequisite to skills include the perceptual-motor, physical, and motor fitness categories. They are not as readily forgotten and are maintained longer than are skills. Examples of perceptual-motor abilities are balance, cross-lateral integration, laterality, directionality, body image, and spatial awareness. Physical fitness prerequisites are strength, flexibility, muscular endurance, and cardiovascular endurance. Motor fitness requires agility and motor coordination.

FIGURE 2-1. An outdoor ropes course is a stimulating learning environment. (Courtesy Wisconsin Lions Camp, Rosholt, Wisconsin.)

The uppermost level of functioning is skill. Skills are motor behaviors that are either specific to a sport or specific to functional living. Examples of skills are shooting a basketball, serving a tennis ball, climbing stairs, and sitting down in a chair. Proficiency at skills is usually developed through repetitious practice of the skill itself. Many activities associated with individual and team sports that require practice are skills. However, skills also can be nonspecific general tasks, such

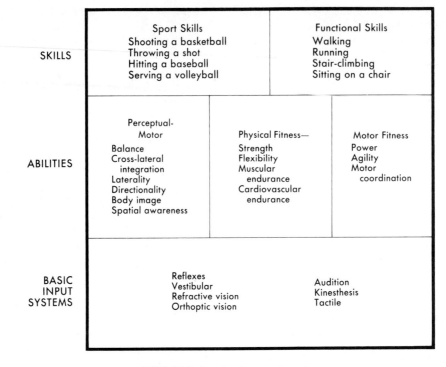

FIGURE 2-2. Levels of motor learning.

as walking or running, that are practiced through repetition to the point that proficiency is achieved.

FACILITATING SKILL DEVELOPMENT

Children with disabilities often have difficulty learning chronologically age-appropriate skills for sports and games. When deficits in skills become apparent, curriculum decisions and instructional strategies must be made. Both single and combination strategies can be employed:

☐ Provide no specific intervention to alleviate the problem and hope that children will "grow out" of the deficit.
☐ Provide a general physical education program that is believed to benefit all children and hope the handicapped students will benefit from it.
☐ Make functional adaptations that enable immediate participation.
☐ Teach the prerequisites specific to the skill and make functional adaptations while the student is learning the specific skill.
☐ Determine which prerequisites are deficient; then select activities to facilitate function in deficient areas.

No Intervention

Fortunately, the number of people who believe children, if left alone, will grow out of motor deficits is decreasing. However, that position is still voiced by some. Observation of the number of adults, both with and without disabilities, who demonstrate lack of motor skills should be enough to silence the advocates of "no intervention needed." Longitudinal studies of children with delayed motor development are on the increase. In a 1982 study Vinzant[5] followed up on children who had been tested in the University of Kansas Perceptual-Motor Clinic and were found to have sensory input and general ability deficits. However, because of uncontrollable circumstances (e.g., living too far from the clinic to bring children for intervention, no available transportation, lack of interest), the children did not receive an intervention program specific to their needs. Eight children who had been tested 1 to 2 years earlier were located and retested using the original battery of tests. In every case the children demonstrated the same deficits (except in the reflex area) that had been identified during the original testing sessions. Other studies have shown that children who were identified at ages 6 and 7 years as being clumsy and/or having poor motor control who were not provided with an intervention program demonstrated motor and behavior, as well as academic difficulties into their teen years.[2,3] It can be concluded that waiting for a child to grow out of motor delays may indeed be a very long wait.

General Physical Education Program Intervention

There are physical educators who believe that the only stimulus children need to develop motor skills is a variety of interesting activities to keep them moving. The failure of these programs to promote motor development is documented in the studies that report improvement in self-concept but no motor ability gain. Self-concept is important, but if the goal of the program is improved motor skill, it would appear that a different intervention strategy is needed in these cases.

Functional Adaptations

Functional adaptations are modifications such as using an assistive device, changing the demands of the task, or changing the rules to permit students with disabilities to participate. Making functional adaptations in accord with a child's needs may enable immediate participation in age-appropriate activities selected to enhance specific skills. Following is a list of functional adaptations for children with deficits:

☐ Blind children can receive auditory or tactual clues to help them locate objects or position their bodies in the activity area.

☐ The blind read through touch and can be instructed in appropriate movement patterns through manual kinesthetic guidance (i.e., the instructor manually moves the student through the correct pattern) or verbal instructions.

☐ Deaf children can learn to read lips or learn signing so that they understand the instructions for an activity.

☐ Children with physical disabilities may have to use crutches or other devices to enable them to move.

☐ An asthmatic child may be permitted to play goalie in a soccer game, which requires smaller cardiovascular demands than the running positions.

☐ Rules may be simplified to accommodate the retarded child's limited comprehension level but still permit participation in a vigorous activity.

In these examples functional adaptations are necessary for the student with a disability to participate in chronologically age-appropriate physical education activities. The approach is useful when the only motor prerequisites lacking are those that are a result of the student's disabling condition or when mainstreaming the student to promote social interaction is being done in addition to the adapted physical education program.

Teach specific skills: top, down

Teaching the skill directly is known as the task-specific approach. Advocates of this approach stress what skills an individual will need for productive independence as an adult in the community where he or she lives. In the case of the physical educator, the targeted behaviors focus on recreational sports skills that an individual would have an opportunity to participate in as an adult in the community. Prerequisites that are not the specific skill itself must relate to functional skills that can be used in the community for recreational purposes or provide a health benefit. The top, down approach places emphasis on the end of the skill sequence, the final motor countdown as an adult, rather than what is to be taught next. When using the top, down approach it is necessary to carefully monitor the progress of learners with disabilities as they move from elementary to middle schools to high schools and then into adult life. To ensure that functional skills are being taught it is necessary to gather information about the lesser restrictive environments the individual will function in as an adult. The focus of this approach emphasizes teaching skills and behaviors that are absolutely necessary for a person to function in a community environment.

To determine which skills an individual has in relation to skills that will be needed for ultimate functioning in the community requires the completion of an ecological inventory (community-based assessment). The ecological inventory provides critical information about current and future school and community environments. It requires intense study of those persons who are successful in the environments where individuals with disabilities may live and participate in activity. From these component repertoires of nondisabled populations, specific behaviors for learners with disabilities can be selected. It is through ecological assessment that age-appropriate skills are identified for instruction of populations with disabilities. Selecting age-appropriate skills tends to maximize the normalization process during the life of a person with a disability. When using ecological assessment data, a major departure from traditional procedures is the need to take students to the natural environment to do part of the instruction. Thus the skills needed to interact effectively with the environment are practiced in the natural setting.

The task-specific approach is a top, down strategy. When using this approach to assess the students' repertoires, the educator can determine which motor skills are present and which are yet to be taught. Once the skills to be taught are determined, they are prioritized, task analyses of the specific skills to be taught are completed, each skill is evaluated to determine which component parts are missing, and the specific missing components are taught using the direct teaching method. If inefficient movements are found, the teacher investigates the ability components for deficits. If problems are found at the ability level, specific sensory input systems believed to contribute to the deficits at the ability level are tested. When deficiencies are found, activities are selected to promote development at the lowest level first.

The task-specific approach may be the most realistic and expedient type to use with individuals with severe

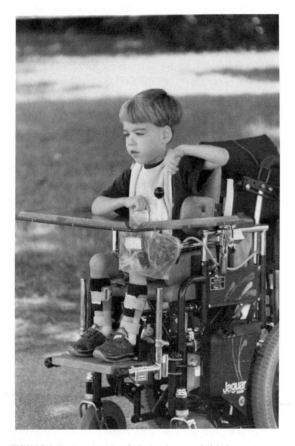

FIGURE 2-3. A motorized chair gives a child the opportunity to control his destiny. (Courtesy Dallas Independent School District.)

disabilities, but it may be inappropriate for higher functioning children with disabilities. The essential question to ask when trying to decide whether to use this approach is: "How much time is available?" Facilitating basic input systems and abilities prior to teaching specific skills takes time, perhaps years. Also, there is evidence that children under the age of 12 years respond more readily than do older individuals. When the individual with a disability is older and severely involved and there is a limited amount of time available to develop functional skills needed to live in a natural environment, the task-specific approach may be the best intervention strategy.

Eliminate deficiencies: bottom, up

Motor development is a progressive process. For each of us to learn to move efficiently, we must first be able to take environmental information into the central nervous system. Then it must be processed or integrated so that it can be used to direct movement patterns and skills. Only after the information is received and processed can the brain direct the muscles to work. If anything goes wrong before the information reaches the muscles, movement is inefficient or nonexistent. Advocates of the developmental approach agree that the ultimate goal of education is to produce productive adults who can function independently in their communities. To achieve this goal the developmentalist would intervene in a child's life as early as possible to determine whether age-appropriate basic input systems, abilities, and skills were functional. If any age-appropriate skills, abilities, and/or basic input systems were found to be deficient when the child was tested, then the developmentalist would select activities to promote development of the deficient areas. Thus if a child was found to have a severe orthoptic (eye alignment) problem that would interfere with eye-hand coordination development, the child would be referred to a visual behavioral specialist for correction of the problem. If a child demonstrated failure to develop equilibrium reactions and/or adequate vestibular (inner ear) function, which are critical for balance development, activities to promote development in those areas would be prescribed.

The developmental approach can be considered a bottom, up strategy (see Fig. 2-2). That is, the developmentalist first evaluates each of the sensory input systems and then tests the ability components to determine which deficits are in evidence. Once the deficits are identified, activities that promote functioning of each sensory input system found to be lacking are selected. The rationale is to progress to activities that fa-

TABLE 2-1

Teaching approaches and their relation to growth and development principals

Principle	Implication	Bottom, up teaching approach	Top, down teaching approach
Each individual is unique.	Every child has a different motor profile.	Test for sensory input deficits and intervene to eliminate those before testing and programming for higher level abilities and skills.	Test for specific functional motor skill deficits. If some are found, probe down into specific abilities that contribute to those skills. If deficits are found, probe down into sensory input areas.
	Every child learns at his or her own rate.	Select activities that appeal to the child and use those until the deficits are eliminated	Program activities at the highest level of dysfunction. If the child does not learn quickly, probe down into contributing components for deficits.
Children advance from one stage of development to a higher, more complex stage of development.	Activities are selected appropriate to level of development.	Select activities that are appropriate for the stage of development the child demonstrates.	Select activities specific to the skill deficits the child demonstrates. Begin an intervention program at the developmental level the child demonstrates.
	Progression to the next stage of development depends on physiological maturation and learning.	When a child appears to have mastered one stage of development, select activities appropriate for the next level of development.	When a child masters lower levels of a specific skill, select activities to promote learning of a more complex aspect of that skill.
Children learn when they are ready.	As neurological maturation takes place, we are capable of learning more.	Test from the bottom up and begin instruction with the lowest neurological deficit found.	Analyze a specific task from the top down until present level of educational performance is found.
	There are critical periods of learning.	It is assumed the child will learn fastest if instruction is begun at the developmental stage at which the child is functioning.	Level of instruction determined by empirical testing verifies that the child is ready to learn.
Development proceeds from simple to complex.	Development begins with simple movements that eventually combine with other movements to form patterns.	Eliminate reflex and sensory input delays before teaching higher level abilities and skills.	Functional skill deficits are identified. The pattern of the skill is analyzed to determine contributing components. Behavioral programs are constructed and implemented to develop pattern deficits.
	Development progresses from large to small movements (from gross to fine patterns).	Promote reflex and vestibular development to stabilize balance. Once balance becomes automatic, control of the limbs will follow.	Program to synthesize patterns that contribute to a specific skill.

cilitate development of the ability components. Only after each of these building blocks is in place will the developmentalist attempt to teach the specific sport or functional skills.

McLaughlin[4] documented the value of the approach when she followed up on learning disabled children who had received this type of evaluation and intervention at the University of Kansas Perceptual-Motor Clinic. Before intervention the children demonstrated varied sensory input and ability deficits. One to two years after the deficits had been eliminated and the children released from the clinic program, every child was demonstrating age-appropriate motor skills.

It should be apparent that the developmental approach is not only time-consuming, it also requires extensive knowledge of sensory input system function and ability level developmental trends. Fortunately for individuals lacking the knowledge base, some available models suggest both testing techniques and intervention strategies for the teacher. These models are discussed in detail in Chapter 4.

When attempting to determine whether to use a bottom, up approach in the adapted physical education program, the teacher must again ask: "How much time is available?" The younger the child and the more time available to the teacher, the more appropriate it is to use this strategy. Examples of how each of these two teaching methods are applied to achieve the same principles are given in Tables 2-1 through 2-7.

Combining Approaches

Note that when using either top, down task-specific or bottom, up developmental approaches, considerable individual attention to each child is necessary. Therefore, in order for these approaches to be effective, the teacher must work with small groups of children with similar problems or with each child on a one-to-one basis. Children involved in such intensive learning environments often do not have an opportunity to interact with their peers in regular physical education classes. Separating the children with disabilities from their normal peers fosters the labeling of children as

---

TABLE 2-2

Teaching approaches and their relation to the generalization process*

Principle	Implication	Bottom, up teaching approach	Top, down teaching approach
Generalization procedures	Activities to promote generalization are selected in particular ways.	Activity is selected to develop sensory input systems, reflexes, and abilities that are believed to be prerequisite to many skills that could be used in a variety of environments.	Functional age-appropriate activities are selected to promote appropriate skills in a variety of natural environments.
Generalization process	There is a degree to which the learning environment matches the natural environment.	At the basic levels (reflexes, sensory inputs, and abilities) the environment is controlled only to ensure that the basics are learned. No attention is paid to the type of environment the eventual skills will be used in.	Skills are practiced in environments that correspond closely to the environment in which the skill will be used (e.g., practice shooting baskets in the gym).
Retention	The more meaningful the skill, the longer it is remembered.	It is believed that once basic reflexes, sensory input systems, and abilities emerge, they remain stable (unless the child is traumatized in some way).	Activities are reviewed immediately after a lesson and then periodically to ensure retention.
Overlearning	Overlearning occurs when a skill or activity is practiced after it has been learned.	Overlearning occurs as the basic levels are interwoven into higher skill levels.	Ability levels prerequisite to skills should be substantially greater than minimum entry requirements needed to fulfill the needs of the task.

*A task is not considered learned until it can be demonstrated in a variety of environments.

TABLE 2-3

The relation of teaching approaches to attention of the learner

Principle	Implication	Bottom, up teaching approach	Top, down teaching approach
Get the attention of the learner.	Help the child attend to relevant rather than irrelevant cues.	Permit the child to participate in a free activity of his or her choice each day if the child enters the room and immediately focuses on the beginning task.	Bats, balls, and other play equipment should be kept out of sight until time of use.
	Give a signal (sometimes called a "ready signal") that indicates a task is to begin.	Structure each day's lesson the same way so the child knows that when a given activity ends, the next activity will begin.	Teach the child precise signals that indicate a task should begin.
Provide the appropriate stimulation.	Stimulate the child to focus on the desired learning task.	Make the activities enjoyable so that the child will want to continue the task.	Use precise, detailed instruction that is designed around eliciting attention through the use of the following hierarchy: 1. Visual or verbal input only 2. Combine visual and verbal input 3. Combine visual, verbal, and kinesthetic instruction.

TABLE 2-4

Managing the intructional environment through teaching approaches

Principle	Implication	Bottom, up teaching approach	Top, down teaching approach
Impose limits for use of equipment, facilities, and student conduct.	Children should learn to adhere to rules that are necessary in social context.	Students are not permitted access to equipment and areas unless they have been given permission by the teacher.	The equipment and facilities a student has access to are specified in the behavioral program.
Control the social interaction among children.	Inappropriate social behavior among children may disrupt class instruction.	The teacher must consider the performance level and emotional stability of each child when grouping children for activites.	Tasks and environments are structured to reduce adverse interaction with peers.
Do not strive for control in all situations.	Children with disabilities must develop social skills that will promote social interaction in the natural environment. For this to occur, students must have an opportunity to adjust to situations independent from supervision or with minimum supervision.	Select activities that will meet the long-range goals of the students and promote social interaction. Pair children so that their interaction contributes to both students' objectives. Example: A child who needs kinesthetic stimulation might be given the task of pulling a child who needs to ride a scooter for tonic labyrinthine prone inhibition.	Permit the students to interact with others as long as progress toward short-term objectives is occurring.

"different" and inhibits social interactions necessary for sound development. One way to overcome the perils of separation is to permit the child with disabilities to engage in physical activity with peers in addition to receiving individual attention in an adapted physical education class.

This approach is workable if functional adaptations are made while the child is engaging in the regular physical education class. This combination of interventions will work if either an indirect method of teaching is used with a movement education or problem-solving program or when direct teaching methods are employed. During direct teaching the standard functional adaptations such as those enumerated earlier can be used. Regardless of whether the teacher selects an indirect or direct teaching method, it is important to remember that all children must experience success when interacting with their peers. Successful interaction with others is necessary for the development of a healthy, positive self-concept. As teachers we must be sensitive to promoting the overall growth of our students.

INCIDENTAL VERSUS PLANNED LEARNING

Most individuals learn from everyday interaction with the environment. This is particularly true if the environment is varied and the learner possesses all the prerequisites needed to convert environmental stimulation (i.e., fully functioning sensory input systems, certain ability traits, and possibly some skills). This is known as *incidental learning.* The more ready an individual is (i.e., the more developed cognitive and motor functions are), the more that can be gained from interaction with the environment. Conversely, the fewer the number of developed prerequisites, the less a person gains from environmental exchanges.

The individual with a disability is often denied opportunities to interact with varied environments. This is a hindrance because for the central nervous system to develop normally, a wide variety of stimulation is

TABLE 2-5

Nature of activity and quality of experience as they relate to two teaching approaches

Principle	Implication	Bottom, up teaching approach	Top, down teaching approach
Learning occurs best when goals and objectives are clear.	Clear goals provide incentives for children to learn.	The desired outcome is clear to the teacher (e.g., 5 seconds of postrotatory nystagmus). The child may be advised of another goal (e.g., stay on the spinning scooter until it stops).	The goal and ongoing measurement of the attainment of the objectives that lead to the goal are shared by the teacher and the child.
The student should be actively involved in the learning process.	The greater the amount of learning time and the lesser the amount of dead time, the more learning that will occur.	The child stays active because activities that are enjoyable to the child are selected.	When and if the child learns to self-instruct and self-evaluate or do so with the help of peer tutors, the student will be active throughout the period. The well-managed class will have children work on nonspecific activities when not participating in behavioral programs.
Discourage stereotyped play activities that develop rigid behaviors.	Permitting children to participate in the same activity day after day deters learning.	The teacher must initiate new activites as soon as lack of progress is evidenced.	The ongoing collection of data makes lack of progress immediately apparent to the teacher and the child and serves notice that the activity should be changed.
Program more for success than failure.	Every satisfying experience decreases anxiety and increases confidence.	The teacher selects activities the child enjoys and gains a feeling of accomplishment from.	The increment of the step sizes in the behavioral program is constantly modified to match the ability of the learner.

TABLE 2-6

Training regimens as they relate to teaching approaches

Principle	Implication	Bottom, up teaching approach	Top, down teaching approach
Rate of learning is affected by initial skill level and length of time practicing the skill.	Beginning students who are learning a new skill learn at a faster rate than intermediate and advanced learners; however, plateaus in learning do occur after initial learning.	At reflex and sensory input levels plateaus may not be seen because learning is not cognitive. At ability levels (perceptual-motor, coordination, etc.) plateaus are apparent. Observe progress with care and change activities if plateaus are observed.	Plateaus will be identified immediately because of the precise data being collected. Provide rest between training trials and terminate activity before failure sets in.
The nature of the learner, the task, and the stage of the learner in learning the task must be considered.	Some research indicates that in the initial stages of motor learning distributed practice is more effective than mass practice.	Use specific time frames (e.g., 5 minutes) each day for each objective.	Highly organized lessons during which accurate data on progress are gathered provide immediate feedback about the effectiveness of the practice trials. When lack of progress becomes apparent, change the activity or the learning strategy.
	Short practices are better than long practices Frequent practices are more effective than infrequent practices.	Divide the lesson plan into several activities. Provide activities for each objective daily or several times weekly.	
Stop instruction at or before the point of satiation on the task.	Plateauing occurs when a person is satiated wtih learning a task.	Selecting tasks that are novel may prevent satiation.	Monitor the increment of the step size carefully because as long as the learner can be reinforced with success on challenging tasks, the child may withstand satiation.
		Use a variety of activities to reach the same objective.	Use a variety of different types of programs for the child to move to so that satiation is countered.
Use the method of teaching that is best for the learner (whole, part, part-whole).	When the whole method is used, the entire task is taught at one time. The task is demonstrated (using visual and verbal cues); child is challenged to learn the skill.	When working toward reflex normality or when stimulating sensory input systems, the entire task is presented.	Use this method when teaching complex tasks. If a child has difficulty with any part of the task, shape the response through programming.
	When the part method is used, break the task down into component parts and teach the parts using backward or forward chaining.	When teaching toward perceptual-motor abilities (e.g., size discrimination), teach the child to recognize differences between sizes.	Break the skill into parts and teach each specific part.
	The part-whole method involves teaching the component parts of the skill and then synthesizing the parts into the whole skill.	When teaching perceptual-motor abilities such as size discrimination, after teaching the learner to discriminate between two or three different sets of sizes, combine the sets gradually until the child can discriminate between a large set of different sizes.	Because it is difficult to establish behaviors in which one is built on the other, divide the skill into natural divisions, teach each section, and then combine them.

TABLE 2-7

Relation of teaching approaches to motivation techniques

Principle	Implication	Bottom, up teaching approach	Top, down teaching approach
Children will learn better if the activity is pleasurable.	As a rule, children enjoy tasks at which they can be successful and dislike tasks where the failure risk is high.	Tasks that are enjoyable to children are selected to reach the specific objective.	Learning steps are sequenced close enough to ensure success.
Provide knowledge of results on task success.	Knowledge of results provides information to the learner as to the correctness of performance. Learners tend to persist at tasks they are successful with.	The students may or may not be advised about the specific objective the teacher is trying to reach; however, the child is advised about the objective to accomplish. Example: In trying to inhibit a positive support reflex, the teacher's objective may be to have the child demonstrate ability to flex the hips, knees, and ankles when there is pressure on the bottom of the feet. The child may be told that the objective is to stop bouncing on the trampoline 3 out of 5 times on command by doing a partial squat when the feet hit the bed of the trampoline.	Precise objectives should be built into the behavioral program to provide immediate feedback as to whether the task was mastered.
Apply a system of reinforcement for attainment of objectives.	Reinforcement strengthens the recurrence of behavior.	The teacher tells the child when he or she has done a good job.	Specific behaviors in a structured hierarchy are reinforced when the behavior occurs because the learner then progresses to the next step in the hierarchy.
The social context of learning should be considered.	Learning is influenced by the presence or absence of others. Each student is influenced in some way by competition/cooperation with peers and the presence of absence of spectators or the teacher.	The child is made to feel as comfortable as possible so that the activity is enjoyable. It is believed that when the child feels successful, he or she will want to engage in play/competition with peers.	Social conditions will be directed toward the generalization of social behavior that exists in natural environments.

necessary. Thus attempts to protect these children from interaction with the environment often delay their development. Because of these delays, learners with disabilities do not always gain as much from incidental learning as do other learners.

Teachers of children with disabilities must be particularly sensitive to the needs of their students. Until a teacher determines the needs of students, appropriate intervention strategies cannot be planned. The adapted physical education teacher must ensure that each stu-

dent's motor learning improves. The general approach of providing a wide variety of activities to all students gives no assurance that motor learning will result. It is true that the children may have fun and could possibly gain some physical fitness from their activities; however, the students will not make the same gains as would be possible if carefully planned intervention strategies were used.

Although the debate will continue as to the relative effectiveness of a developmental model (e.g., bottom, up) as compared with a task-specific (top, down) approach, there are certain tenets upon which both positions can agree. These are as follows:

1. The goals of instruction should not be isolated target behaviors but natural clusters of skills that lead to independent functioning in the community.
2. A critical component of instruction is the specific functional response that has cultural relevance.
3. Motor behavior as a result of instruction should be more durable over time for generalization.
4. After targeting critical behaviors (i.e., locomotion), generalization of the skill is important.
5. There are many ways of achieving the end results of acquisition of motor behaviors that directly relate to independent functioning in the community.[1]

SUMMARY

The goal of a physical education program for students with disabilities is development of motor behaviors that assist ultimate functional responses in community environments. Maximizing performance of the many specific skills of the physical education curriculum is the unique role of the adapted physical educator. Individuals with disabilities often possess limited motor skills. Thus the physical educator must determine which skills are needed and select appropriate intervention strategies to ensure that learning occurs. Teaching specific skills, fostering developmental sequences, and employing functional adaptations are three acceptable intervention strategies. The amount of time available, the age and readiness level of the learner, and the capabilities of the adapted physical education teacher dictate which intervention strategy to use.

REVIEW QUESTIONS

1. What is the relationship between specific functional motor skills and general ability prerequisites to these skills?
2. What are some examples of making functional adaptations for age-appropriate motor skills, and what are arguments for and against such functional adaptations?
3. What are some of the general abilities of a physical-motor and perceptual-motor structure?
4. Describe functional levels of prerequisites to specific skills.
5. What are some strategies and options for teaching chronologically age-appropriate motor skills to children with disabilities?
6. What are the differences between bottom, up (developmental) and top, down (task-specific) approaches?
7. What value is there to combining a bottom, up approach with a top, down approach?

8. Name two sensory input systems, two general abilities, and two specific skills.
9. What is meant by *incidental learning?* Why are some children with disabilities unable to learn as much through incidental learning as children with disabilities?

STUDENT ACTIVITIES

1. Talk with adapted physical education teachers about how they determine what objectives and activities to use with their students with disabilities. Try to decide whether the teachers are using a "top, down," "bottom, up," or combination of these two approaches.
2. Observe a mainstreamed physical education class. Make a list of the functional adaptations used during the class. Select the two adaptations you believe aided the children most and tell why those adaptations were so helpful.
3. List the ways in which a top, down testing and teaching approach would differ from a bottom, up testing and teaching approach.

REFERENCES

1. Evans IM, Meyer LH: *An educative approach to behavior problems,* Baltimore, 1985, Paul H Brookes.
2. Gillberg I, Gillberg C, Groth J: Children with pre-school minor neurodevelopmental disorders vs neurodevelopmental profiles at age 13, *Dev Med Child Neurol* 31:14-24, 1989.
3. Losse A et al: Clumsiness in children—do they grow out of it? A 10-year follow-up study, *Dev Med Child Neurol* 33:55-68, 1991.
4. McLaughlin E: Follow-up study on children remediated for perceptual-motor dysfunction at the University of Kansas perceptual motor clinic, Unpublished master's thesis, 1980, University of Kansas.
5. Vinzant D: Follow-up study on children tested but not remediated for perceptual-motor dysfunction, Unpublished master's thesis, 1982, University of Kansas.

SUGGESTED READINGS

Falvey MA: *Community based curriculum: instructional strategies for students with severe handicaps,* Baltimore, 1986, Paul H Brookes.
Guess D, Noonan MJ: Curricula and instructional procedures for severely handicapped students, *Focus on Except Child* 14:1-12, 1982.
Kohen-Raz R: *Learning disabilities and postural control,* London, 1986, Freund Publishing House.
Seaman JA, DePauw K: *The new adapted physical education,* Palo Alto, Calif, 1989, Mayfield Publishing.
Wheman P, Renzaglia A, Bates P: *Functional living skills for moderately and severely handicapped individuals,* Austin, Tex, 1985, PRO-ED.
Wilcox B, Bellamy T: An alternative curriculum for youth and adults with severe disabilities, Baltimore, 1987, Paul H Brookes.

PART TWO

KEY TECHNIQUES

TYPES OF PHYSICAL AND MOTOR PROBLEMS learners demonstrate are

common to many children; however, each child has a unique

profile that must be identified before appropriate programming

can be determined. In this section specific clues for determining

each individual's present level of functioning, regardless of

disability, and precise programming techniques are described.

3

OBJECTIVES

List the different types of assessment.

Explain the different purposes of assessment.

Provide examples of each of the different types of assessment.

Describe how to use the different types of assessment to achieve a specific outcome.

Explain adverse physical education performance.

Courtesy Dallas Independent School District

Types and Purposes of Assessment

*T*here has been a distinct shift during the 1980s and 1990s from using tests to classify, accept, or reject students to assessment tailored to meet the instructional needs of children. Traditionally, normative-referenced standardized tests have been used to determine how a child was performing in relation to other children of the same age and sex. Often such test results were used to predict the success a child might achieve in school. When test results were used in this manner, above average normative-referenced test performance levels tended to be perceived by teachers as desirable objectives in and of themselves. Unfortunately, this usage often distorted the true purpose of education, particularly the education of students with disabilities.

The court decision in *Armstrong v. Kline* in 1979[1] emphasized that the educational aim for individuals with disabilities is to provide instruction that helps them develop physical and motor skills that will contribute to self-sufficient and independent living. Thus adequate physical education assessment for the child with disabilities requires use of test items that will assist in the design of appropriate educational environments and instructional procedures for the child. This latter perspective of assessment requires us to challenge traditional uses of testing and seek new and different ways of determining performance levels. As Haring[10] said, we must begin to think of assessment as measurement of individual performance at any time to determine status in cumulative skill or knowledge.

PURPOSES OF ASSESSMENT

Motor assessment instruments provide different types of information. It is important to match the selection of the instrument with the purpose of the assessment. Just as a teacher should select an educational intervention to match the particular target physical skills of instruction, so must an assessment instrument match the purpose. Assessments are used to gain information for the purposes of screening, placement, curriculum development, and student evaluation.[23] In addition, assessing individuals with disabilities may also be for the purpose of diagnosis, instructional planning (i.e., use of the diagnostic information to design an individual education plan [IEP] based on the student's needs), and program evaluation (i.e., determining the effectiveness of the special physical education intervention). As Heward and Orlansky[11] indicate, assessment is coming to be seen not as an isolated exercise, but as an inseparable part of the student's ongoing educational program. Today, assessment often is accomplished in natural settings such as the disabled child's regular physical education class, the home, and the community.

SCREENING AND ASSESSMENT OF TODDLERS

Prior to passage of P.L. 99-457, The Education of the Handicapped Amendments of 1986, assessment and intervention efforts directed toward children under 5 years of age focused on those children with obvious disabilities such as Down syndrome, cerebral palsy, or visual impairments. P.L. 99-457 represents a major step toward meeting the needs of individuals with disabilities because in addition to serving children with recognized disabilities, infants and toddlers with less-well defined problems, who are highly likely to experience developmental delays, now qualify for services. This inclusion has far-reaching implications for screening, assessment, and intervention activities.

Tasks and opportunities relevant to screening and assessment outlined in P.L. 99-457 include:

1. Use of a multidisciplinary approach to screen and assess children from birth through 5 years of age
2. Identifying infants and young children with known disabilities and developmental delays; and at states' discretion, identifying children birth through 2 years of age who are at risk for developmental delays (including physical delays)
3. Planning comprehensive services for young children with special needs, including a model of periodic rescreening and reassessment
4. Involving the family in all levels of assessment, identification, and intervention

Levels of services included in the law are:

1. Child Find activities
2. Developmental and health screening, including administration of screening instruments, questioning of parents, and administration of medical, vision, and hearing examinations
3. Diagnostic testing including formal testing, parent interviews, and home observation
4. Individual program planning[17]

Traditionally, many adapted physical educators serving young children with disabilities have been involved with Child Find searches and developmental screening. However, the expansion of services mandated by P.L. 99-457 has enabled the physical educator to become more fully involved in identifying and remediating delays evidenced by a wider range of young children. This is a distinct opportunity to have a positive impact on the lives of growing numbers of at-risk children in those critical early periods of life prior to school age.

GUIDELINES FOR SCREENING AND ASSESSMENT OF PRESCHOOLERS

The following guidelines for screening and assessing young children are recommended by Meisels and Provence[18]:

1. Screening and assessment are services—as part of the intervention process—and not only as means of identification and measurement.
2. Processes, procedures, and instruments in-

tended for screening and assessment should be used only for their specified purposes.

3. Multiple sources of information should be included in screening and assessment.

4. Developmental screening should take place on a recurrent or periodic basis. It is inappropriate to screen young children only once during their early years. Reassessment should continue after services have been initiated.

5. Developmental screening should be viewed as only one path to more in-depth assessment. Failure to qualify for services based on a single source of screening information should not become a barrier to further evaluation for inter-

---

TABLE 3-1

Selected motor assessment instruments for preschool children

Test	Source	Age	Components	Reference
Bayley Scales of Infant Development (1969)	The Psychological Corp. 757 3rd Avenue New York, NY 10017	2-30 mo	Posture, locomotor, fine motor	Normative
Brigance Diagnostic Inventory (1978)	Curiculum Assoc., Inc. 5 Esquire Road North Biller, MA 10862	Birth-7 yr	Preambulatory, motor skills, fine motor, gross motor, self-help skills	Criterion
Denver Developmental Screening (1967)	LODOCA Project & Publishing Foundation E. 51st Avenue & Lincoln Street Denver, CO 80216	Birth-6 yr	Fine motor, gross motor	Domain
Callier-Azusa Scale (1978)	The University of Texas at Dallas The Callier Center for Communication Disorders 1966 Inwood Road Dallas, TX 75235	Birth-7 yr	Postural control, locomotion, fine motor, visual motor, visual development, auditory development, tactile development, daily living skills	Criterion
Early Screening Profiles (1990)	American Guidance Service Circle Pines, MI 55014	2.0-6.11 yr	Gross motor, fine motor	Normative
Hawaii Early Learning Profile (HELP) (1988)	VORT Corp. P.O. Box 601321 Palo Alto, CA 94306	0-36 mo	Gross motor, fine motor, self-help	Criterion
Learning Accomplishment Profile (LAP) (1974)	Kaplan Press P.O. Box 5128 Winston-Salem, NC 27113	1 mo-6 yr	Fine motor, gross motor, self-help	Criterion
Milani-Comparetti Motor Development Screening (1987 Rev.)	Meyer Children's Rehabilitation Institute U. of Nebraska Medical Center Omaha, NE 68131	Birth-24 mo	Primitive reflexes, equilibrium reflexes, gross motor	Criterion
Miller Assessment for Preschoolers (1988 Rev)	The Psychological Corp. 555 Academic Court San Antonio, TX 78204-2498	2.9-5.9 yr	Sense of position & movement, touch, basic movement patterns, gross motor, fine motor	Normative
Movement Assessment of Infants (1980)	Movement Assessment of Infants P.O. Box 4631 Rolling Bay, WA 98061	Birth-12 mo	Muscle tone, primitive reflexes, equilibrium reflexes, volitional movement	Criterion
Peabody Developmental Motor Scales (1983)	DLM Teaching Resources Corp. One DLM Park Allen, TX 75002	Birth-83 mo	Fine motor, gross motor	Criterion

vention services if other risk factors (e.g. environmental, medical, familial) are present.

6. Screening and assessment procedures should be reliable and valid.
7. Family members should be an integral part of the screening and assessment process. Information provided by family members is critically important for determining whether to initiate more in-depth assessment and for designing appropriate intervention strategies. Parents should be accorded complete informed consent at all stages of the screening process.
8. During screening or assessment of developmental strengths and problems, the more relevant and familiar the tasks and setting are to the child and the child's family, the more likely it is that the results will be valid.
9. All tests, procedures, and processes intended for screening and assessment must be culturally sensitive.
10. Extensive and comprehensive training is needed by those who screen and assess very young children.

Selected motor assessment instruments that are appropriate for use with preschool children are included in Table 3-1.

ADVERSE PHYSICAL EDUCATION PERFORMANCE

Once a child reaches school age there are two criteria for determining whether the child has a disability: (1) psychological or medical verification that a handicap exists, and (2) adverse performance in the physical education class. Unless a child has been identified in the preschool years or has an obvious sensory, physical, motor, mental, or emotional impairment, that child is not judged as having adverse performance in a physical education class unless he or she demonstrates below-average standards in the regular class. When a child's performance level is below the performance standard of the majority of children in the regular class, the child is said to demonstrate *adverse physical education performance.* Regardless of the type of disability, a child does not qualify for an IEP in physical education unless adverse performance is identified.

Children who are classified as educable mentally retarded, learning disabled, partially sighted, hearing impaired, health impaired, or emotionally disturbed may demonstrate adverse physical education performance early in the formal schooling years. They are identified through observation or measurement standards set for normal children of the same age. Acceptable standards

for passing are set by each school district. More severely handicapped individuals usually have been identified before entering school.

Regardless of when the adverse performance is identified, it is necessary to determine what skills the individual must acquire to eliminate adverse performance. The type of physical education class the child is placed in depends on the severity of the problem.

Adverse educational performance is determined by assessing the student's performance against the curriculum standards of a local school district. When deficits are found, the logical remedy is curriculum-based assessment and programming. However, in some cases essential prerequisites (e.g., basic abilities) for the physical education curriculum tasks may be so insufficiently developed that it is unlikely that the student will be able to attain the motor skill standards of the regular physical education class. When this is the case, then it may be desirable for the physical education teacher to determine which developmental delays need to be programmed for before entering the regular physical education class (see Chapter 4).

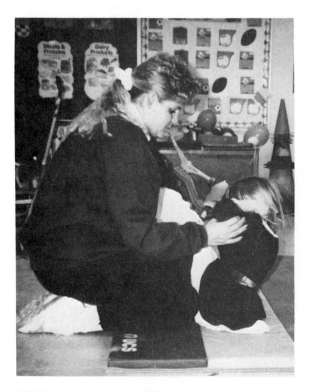

FIGURE 3-1. Assessing a child's abdominal strength. (Photo by Jo Arms, Courtesy Albuquerque, New Mexico Public Schools.)

TABLE 3-2

Selected motor tests for school-aged children

Test	Source	Population	Components	Norms
AAHPERD Health-Related Fitness Test (1976)	AAHPERD 1900 Association Dr. Reston, VA 22091	Normal; ages 5-18 yr	Body composition, cardiorespiratory endurance, flexibility, strength	Domain-referenced
AAHPERD Special Fitness Test for Mildly Mentally Retarded (1976)	AAHPERD 1900 Association Dr. Reston, VA 22091	Mildly mentally retarded; ages 8-18 yr	Strength, power, agility, coordination, and cardiovascular endurance	Domain-referenced
AAHPERD Fitness Test for Moderately Retarded (1975)	AAHPERD 1900 Association Dr. Reston, VA 22091	Moderately mentally retarded; ages 6-20 yr	Hopping, skipping, tumbling, target throw, flexibility	Domain-referenced
Bruininks-Oseretsky Test of Motor Proficiency (1978)	American Guidance Services Publishers' Building Circle Pines, MN 55014	Normal, mentally retarded, learning disabled; ages 4½-14½ yr	Speed and agility, balance, bilateral coordination, strength, fine motor, response speed, hand-eye coordination, upper limb speed and dexterity	Domain-referenced
I CAN (1978)	Hubbard Scientific Co. P.O. Box 104 Northbrook, IL 60062	Ambulatory individuals of any age	Preprimary motor and play skills; primary skills; sport, leisure, and recreation skills	Criterion-referenced
Ohio State University Scale of Intra Gross Motor Assessment (OSU-SIGMA) (1979)	Mohican Publishing Co. P.O.Box 295 Loundonville, OH 44842	Normal; ages 2½-14 yr	Basic locomotor skills, ladder climbing, stair climbing, throwing and catching	Criterion-referenced
Oregon Data-Based Physical Education Program (1985)	PRO-ED Publishing Co. 5341 Industrial Oaks Dr Blvd. Austin, TX 78735	Severely disabled, any age	Movement concepts, elementary games, physical fitness, lifetime leisure skills	Criterion-referenced
PROJECT ACTIVE Basic Motor Ability Test (1976)	Dr. T. Vodola Township of Ocean School District 163 Monmouth Rd. Oakhurst, MJ 07755	Normal, mentally retarded, learning disabled, emotionally disturbed; ages preschool thru adult	Balance/posture, gross body coordination, hand-eye coordination and accuracy, foot-eye accuracy	Criterion-referenced
Physical and Motor Skill Levels of Individuals with Mental Retardation: Mild, Moderate and Down Syndrome Ages 6-21 (1991)	Illinois State University Dept. of Health, Physical Education, Recreation & Dance McCormick Hall, Rm 101 Normal, IL 61761-6901	Mild and moderate mental retardation and Down syndrome; ages 6-21 yr	Balance, body composition, muscular strength and endurance, power, flexibility, cardiorespiratory endurance, hand-eye coordination	Norm-referenced
Project UNIQUE (1985)	Human Kinetics Publishers, Inc. Box 5076 Champaign, IL 61820	Visually impaired, auditory impaired, orthopedically impaired; ages 10 to 17 yr	Body composition, muscular strength and endurance, speed, power, flexibility, coordination, cardiorespiratory endurance	Domain-referenced for each disability
Purdue Perceptual Motor Survey (1966)	Charles E. Merrill 936 Eastwind Dr. Westerville, OH 43081	Normal, learning disabled, mildly retarded, emotionally disturbed; ages 6 to 10 yr	Balance and posture, body image and differentiation, perceptual-motor match, ocular control, form perception	Criterion-referenced
Test of Gross Motor Development (TGMD) (1965)	PRO-ED Publishing Co. 5341 Industrial Oaks Blvd. Austin TX 78735	Normal, ages 3-10 yr	Run, gallop, hop, leap, horizontal jump, skip, slide, two-handed strike, bounce, catch, kick, throw	Domain-referenced and criterion-referenced

All children with disabilities must take their physical education in the least restrictive environment. If it is determined that the goals specified on the IEP can be reached in the regular physical education class, that is where the child is placed. If it is determined that a more personalized setting is necessary for the child to develop the motor skills needed to eventually function effectively in a regular physical education class, that child could be placed in a self-contained adapted physical education class until those goals are reached. Moderately to severely disabled persons whose goals are to develop self-help skills that will contribute to self-sufficiency in a restricted number of community and domestic environments may be permanently placed in the self-contained adapted physical education class. The important point is that placement is to be based on the individual student's needs. Wholesale placement of students with disabilities into regular physical education classes *does not* satisfy the least restrictive environment requirement. What environment is least restrictive depends on the individual's needs and hence the goals set for that person. *Least restrictive* implies that progress toward goals can be realized. If a student is not making progress toward specific goals, the environment may be too restrictive. Progress should be carefully monitored to ensure that the educational environment is permitting progress to occur.

To design appropriate physical education programs for students with disabilities, behaviors that contribute to adverse educational performance must be identified and plans formulated to improve the motor functioning of each student.

ASSESSMENT TOOLS

There are several forms of assessment. Each can contribute in some way to enhancing our selection of appropriate educational environments and instructional procedures for the individual with a disability. These include standardized normative-referenced tests, criterion-referenced tests, domain-referenced tests, content-referenced tests, community-based assessments, surveys and inventories, and treatment-referenced assessments (see Table 3-2 for specific examples).

Standardized Normative-Referenced Tests
Definition

Normative-referenced tests are administered under similar conditions (standardized) to a large number of people (sampling population). Most often the sampling population includes both sexes, who vary in age and performance levels but do not demonstrate any disabling conditions. The scores (norms) achieved by the sampling population are placed on a continuum from high to low and are classified according to percentiles, age equivalencies, and/or stanines. Scores of individuals who later use the test are compared with the norms to determine which percentile, age, or stanine level the scores match (see Tables 3-3 and 3-4).

Purpose

The purpose of the normative-referenced test is to permit comparison of an individual's performance level with the performance of the sampling population. Federal law requires that one criterion for determining whether an individual has a disability is the administration of clinical tests by medical or psychological personnel. Most often a clinical disability is interpreted to mean that the child performs below average on a standardized normative-referenced test; that is, his or her scores are found to fall significantly below the mean.

Comments

There is considerable discussion in the literature concerning the value and use of normative-referenced assessment. The controversy focuses on the use made of the test results. When the test results are used to limit the educational opportunities available to students, protests appear justified; however, when the results are used to facilitate appropriate placement and enhance program planning, information from normative-referenced tests is perceived more favorably.

Hively, Hofmeister, and Reichle are three educators who voice alarm at the misuse of normative-referenced testing. Hively accurately claims that "to a large extent, our contemporary educational culture has been dominated by the image of norm-referenced testing. Many of us are wearing norm-referenced blinders."[12] Hofmeister[13] feels that many teachers have identified the ethical and curriculum support problems of normative-referenced testing. According to him, potential problems of normative-referenced testing consist of the following:

☐ Evaluation procedures are often administered, controlled, and developed by personnel outside the school and classroom.

☐ When results of such evaluations are sent directly to superiors, there is some uneasiness about how the results will be used.

☐ The curriculum may be controlled by the test rather than by the needs of the children.

Reichle et al.[22] expressed other concerns and limitations of standardized normative-referenced tests. Some of these follow:

TABLE 3-3

Norms for the standing long jump in the AAHPERD physical fitness test

Percentile rank	Test scores (meters)*			Percentile rank
	11 years	12 years	13 years	
100th	2.56	2.26	2.59	100th
95th	1.87	1.98	2.15	95th
90th	1.82	1.90	2.08	90th
85th	1.77	1.85	2.03	85th
80th	1.75	1.82	1.95	80th
75th	1.70	1.80	1.90	75th
70th	1.67	1.75	1.87	70th
65th	1.67	1.72	1.82	65th
60th	1.65	1.70	1.82	60th
55th	1.62	1.67	1.77	55th
50th	1.57	1.65	1.75	50th
45th	1.57	1.62	1.70	45th
40th	1.52	1.60	1.67	40th
35th	1.49	1.57	1.65	35th
30th	1.47	1.54	1.60	30th
25th	1.42	1.52	1.57	25th
20th	1.39	1.47	1.52	20th
15th	1.34	1.44	1.47	15th
10th	1.29	1.37	1.39	10th
5th	1.21	1.26	1.32	5th
0	0.91	0.96	0.99	0

From the American Alliance for Health, Physical Education, Recreation and Dance, Reston, Va.
*To convert to centimeters, move the decimal point two places to the right (1.95 m = 195 cm).

□ They do not address or directly examine behaviors in the instructional program.

□ They do not recommend or reflect a scope and sequence of behaviors to be trained.

□ There are limits in the translation of the results of the tests into instructional objectives.

□ They limit options in formats for application of results to heterogeneous groups such as individuals with disabilities.

□ As a rule they do not relate to the critical skills in the learner's environment.

When normative-referenced test results are used to label students as competent (within average performance) or incompetent (below average performance), or are not tied to the curriculum taught, concerns about their use are justified. However, when these test results are used to enhance the quality of education planning for a student, their usefulness becomes more apparent.

Pyfer[20] proposed two benefits that can be derived from normative-referenced test results: (1) if a child's test results show the learner to be below average, the child must be provided with appropriate intervention; and (2) normative-referenced test results used in con-

junction with criterion- and domain-referenced test results can provide an overall profile of a child's developmental level, which enables more accurate selection of an appropriate intervention strategy.

A common complaint voiced by physical educators working in the schools is that school administrators interpret the Education of the Handicapped Act of 1975 (originally known as the Education for All Handicapped Children Act) as a mainstreaming law for the subjects' physical education, art, and music. That is to say, often an administrative decision is made that the least restrictive environment for students with handicapping conditions is placement into regular physical education, art, and music classes. In fact, the physical education class may be a very "restrictive" environment due to large class size, noise level, and expected activity level.

In reality, the need for special education (classroom and physical education) must be determined on the basis of standardized test results. Hence it can be justifiably argued that the child with an assessed clinical disability who performs significantly below average on a standardized normative-referenced test does indeed qualify for some type of special physical education intervention. The type and extent of the intervention cannot be determined by the standardized normative-referenced test results. Additional testing would be required to pinpoint the extent of the learner's limitation and determine which type of intervention is appropriate.

The type of additional testing necessary depends primarily on the age and types of performance problems evidenced by the child. Young children who demonstrate balance problems need to be tested further to determine whether underlying deficiencies such as abnormal reflex development or delayed vestibular functioning are causing the balance problem. Children with poor catching and kicking skills need to be screened for depth perception function. Older children with cardiovascular endurance deficits need to be examined for cardiovascular abnormalities before an intervention program is developed. The standardized normative test results provide clues about what type of motor behavior the child is having difficulty with. Additional types of testing are useful in pinpointing more precisely the reason the child is performing poorly on the standardized normative-referenced test (see box, pp. 72-73).

Again, the use of normative-referenced standardized test results solely to label a child incompetent and not to improve the instructional program for the child has little or no value in education. Such test results do have value when they are used to determine whether a child has an assessed clinical disability. Once it has been determined that a child qualifies for special physical education, tests that can be related to the curriculum taught in the physical education program should be selected. Federal regulations require that adverse physical education performance must be present before a child qualifies for special intervention strategies to be used on his or her behalf. The adverse performance can be eliminated if appropriate educational programming is implemented. The more severe the performance deficits, the greater the need for in-depth probing for the cause of the deficiencies (see also Chapter 4).

Process-oriented analysis assessment. Traditionally normative-referenced tests are used to measure an intrinsic ability. Scores at or above the fiftieth percentile are interpreted as the only acceptable standard of performance. As a result, individuals with disabilities who score below the fiftieth percentile are judged to be defective. However, true performance actually depends on a myriad of factors that the student brings to the test situation,[25] including motivational, emotional, physical, and motor characteristics. In their test, Stott, Henderson, and Moyes[25] attempt to determine the behavioral sources of poor performance by assessing the types of demonstrated motor faults that can be treated through professional intervention. The intent of this type of process-oriented analysis is to bridge the gap between assessment and programming by systematically measuring performance outcomes of intervention strategies. Using assessment data to monitor a student's progress is considerably different from using assessment data to produce a composite score that places an individual on a normative scale. Stott, Henderson, and Moyes[25] believe that there is no present method of assisting the nervous system in a way that will directly correspond to motor functions. Thus their format for assessing gains is to analyze each test task by observing

---

TABLE 3-4

Normative data expressed in percentiles on perceptual items of a basic motor ability test for 7-year-old boys

Percentiles	Bead stringing	Target throwing			Marble transfer		
		Right hand	Left hand	Total	Right hand	Left hand	Total
100	15	12	10	22	20	21	41
90	14	12	8	20	19	20	39
80	12	11	7	18	18	16	34
70	11	10	7	17	16	16	32
60	10	9	6	15	14	13	27
50	9	9	5	14	13	12	25
40	7	8	5	13	11	10	21
30	6	7	5	12	10	10	20
20	5	6	5	11	9	8	17
10	3	6	5	11	8	7	15

From Arnheim DD, Sinclair WA: *The clumsy child,* ed 2, St Louis, 1979. Mosby—Year Book.

control of the body during varying environmental demands.

Criterion-Referenced Tests

Definition

Donlon[4] defines criterion-referenced testing in two ways. One is the classic concept derived from use in learning research. The criterion is an arbitrarily established level of mastery that represents an educational goal. The score simply indicates whether an individual has demonstrated performance above, at, or below the criterion level. How far away from the goal a person performed is not considered. Criterion-referenced tests also demonstrate the level of consistency of performance. Measure of consistency is often used when constructing instructional objectives; for example, to hit a target of specific size *three times in a row* or make *seven out of ten foul shots*. When criterion testing is designed in this manner, it usually is tied to established levels of mastery in curriculum content.

Criterion-referenced assessment is useful for instructional purposes when it meets other conditions. Glaser[9] indicates that a criterion-referenced test is deliberately constructed to give scores that tell what kinds of behaviors individuals can demonstrate. This definition implies classes of behaviors that define different achievement levels and their important nuances. Nitko[19] says that the obtained score must be capable of expressing objectively and meaningfully the individual's performance characteristics in these classes of behavior.

The demands of a criterion-referenced test must be achievable in the context of an instructional program and the behaviors assessed must be teachable.[22] Following are examples of criterion-referenced statements:

1. Throw a 4-inch ball a distance of 20 feet so that it hits a 2 × 2 foot target 5 out of 5 times.
2. Perform a military press with a 70-pound weight for 10 repetitions.
3. Run a mile in 6 minutes and 15 seconds.
4. Swim a distance of 25 yards in 30 seconds.
5. Play 30 minutes of volleyball without a rule violation.

Purpose

Criterion-referenced tests are used to determine whether instructional content in the physical education class has been mastered. These tests are derived for the most part from arbitrary judgments concerning what each instructor or school district wants to teach or what students are to learn. Logic must be applied to match assessments with behavior that children are expected to display in natural environments. For instance, if one is teaching throwing so that a child can play softball, a logical criterion-referenced test might be to accurately throw a ball a distance equal to that between third and first base after fielding the ball.

Criterion-referenced assessment involves instructional items and the prerequisite skills contained within a curriculum. Well-structured criterion-referenced assessment should make it possible to generate individual prescriptions for each child that include prerequisite behaviors and subtasks stated in behavioral terms.

Comments

As mentioned before, criterion-referenced assessment should be constructed so that meeting the performance standard prepares individuals to perform in natural environments (i.e., daily life settings in the community). With this type of assessment it is possible, and often desirable, for testing itself to take place in natural environments. For instance, if an instructor wants to determine whether a student knows how to bowl, the subtasks required to accomplish an effective bowling ball delivery are written out in proper sequence, and the student's performance is observed while executing a ball delivery on a bowling lane.

Criterion test items may be selected through the process of logical thought or derived from normative-referenced tests. As was mentioned earlier, when normative-referenced tests are used for this purpose, there must be a cutoff standard below which the student is declared disabled or said to demonstrate adverse performance. This cutoff point could become one of the criterion-referenced test items. When criterion test items are used in this way, they become the performance level a child must achieve to be moved out of the "disabled" category.

However, criterion-referenced assessment reaches its full potential only when integrated into the day-by-day functioning so that it is not perceived by the student as an artificial testing activity.[9] It is valuable for individualizing instruction and monitoring instructional goals.

Domain-Referenced Tests

Definition

Domain-referenced testing involves the measure of a general ability. To do this, one usually tests a specific behavior and then makes inferences about a student's general capability. For instance, if a student cannot walk a balance beam heel-to-toe for its entire length, it might be said that the child lacks dynamic balance. Usually several domains are sampled in one test. The outcome of domain-referenced assessment is a student profile of general abilities believed to be important for success in a physical education program.

There is disagreement among professionals about what is included in specific domains as well as about terminology associated with each domain. Some of the physical fitness domains are muscular strength, cardiovascular endurance, muscular endurance, and flexibility. Hypothesized domains for motor fitness are power, motor speed, speed of limb movement, static and dynamic balance, fundamental locomotor skill, and gross body agility. Perceptual-motor domains are spatial orientation, body image and differentiation, ocular control, form perception, perception of position in space, perceptual constancy, tactile discrimination, visual closure, memory, and others (see also Chapter 4). Table 3-5 represents a domain-referenced physical fitness test.

Purpose

Domain-referenced tests provide information about abilities that are prerequisites to specific skills. If children have learning problems that adversely affect mastery of specific skills, it is helpful to identify the specific abilities that might alleviate the learning problems. Once deficient domains have been identified, activities are selected and administered to strengthen the domains of weakness. For instance, if a child lacks enough arm strength to support body weight, it is not possible for him or her to perform a handstand. It is also unlikely that this child would have sufficient strength to perform many other gymnastic activities. Programming specific activities to strengthen the arms may general-

ize into facilitating the learning of all skills for which arm strength is prerequisite.

Or, consider a child who cannot walk up a staircase effectively because of a lack of balance. Among other prerequisites to walking up stairs is standing on one foot, raising the other foot at least 9 inches, and placing it on the stair tread. Failure to maintain balance at this level of proficiency impedes normal stair climbing. Thus domain-referenced testing provides a general overview of the abilities and aptitudes that constitute many skills found in physical education curricula.

Transfer and *generalization* are the underlying assumptions in domain-referenced testing. The central thrust of domain-referenced testing is to define concrete domains of competence and to demonstrate transfer from immediate goals in domains to specific skill activities. As competencies in the domains are acquired, one should see corresponding increases in actual physical education skills.

Comments

Normative-referenced and non–criterion-referenced test batteries are often constructed to measure domains. However, the generalization of performance on a domain-referenced test to performance on skills is a subject of debate. This is particularly the case in perceptual-motor training. There could be several reasons why identifying weaknesses in perceptual-motor domains and then attempting to ameliorate those weaknesses through training would not result in generalization to physical skills. One obvious problem is the assumption that each perceptual-motor domain measures a discrete entity. That is to say, there is evidence to suggest that each of the several domains in the perceptual-motor classification is constructed from other

---

TABLE 3-5

Domain-referenced physical fitness test*

Domain	Name of test	Performance measure
Extent of flexibility	Sit and reach test	Inches (plus or minus) from the toes
Dynamic flexibility	Bend, straighten, and twist test	Repetitions over time
Static strength	Grip strength hand dynamometer	Pounds of force applied to the dynamometer
Dynamic strength	Chin-ups	Repetitions
Explosive strength	Two-footed standing broad jump	Distance in feet and inches
Trunk strength	Bent-leg sit-ups	Repetitions over time
Stamina	12-minute run	Distance traveled in 12 minutes
Gross body coordination	Rope jump (24-inch rope)	Number of successful jumps in a specified number of trials
Gross body equilibrium	Balance stick test	Number of seconds balance is held on a stick of a specified width

*This domain-referenced test is based on the factor analysis found in Fleishman EA: *Structure and measurement of physical fitness,* Englewood Cliffs, NJ, 1965, Prentice-Hall, Inc.

pieces of information. For instance, a study reported by Werbel[27] demonstrated that children who evidence body image and differentiation problems also evidence balance and posture delays. It could be that if a student tests low in body image and differentiation, the true source of the problem could actually be poor balance or other basic abilities.

A second problem with perceptual-motor domains is their failure to be validated by factor analytic studies. In 1983 Pyfer[21] reported on an analysis of a battery of tests administered to 126 children referred for testing because of suspected perceptual-motor problems. The analysis yielded the following factors: (1) hand control and static balance, (2) visual-motor control, (3) social classification, (4) age of parents, (5) hand speed, and (6) reflex development. In the future, through careful research, the commonly accepted perceptual-motor domains may prove to be more theoretical than real constructs.

It also is important to realize that the ability or lack of ability of a learner to generalize may also affect the success of using this form of diagnostic remedial approach to facilitate specific skills. Arguments have been made that only by teaching specific skills through programmed instruction will perceptual, physical, and motor domains represented in the skill develop. For instance, in the example of the child who was unable to walk up stairs because of the inability to balance on one foot, the criterion needed to climb the stairs might be to raise the foot 9 inches from the floor (an additional inch is needed to clear an 8-inch stair tread). This behavior could be shaped by having the child practice placing the foot on objects that were ½ inch to 9 inches high. Increments of step sizes could be matched to the learner's ability. It must, however, be remembered that before using the shaping method, the teacher must ascertain that the learner has reached the prerequisite stages of development (i.e., has adequate vestibular and depth perception development) to permit the shaping to be effective.

If the learner demonstrates prerequisite stages of development, the application of the shaping procedure would do two things. It would guarantee the attainment of prerequisites for a functional skill of stair climbing and at the same time develop the balancing domain, which could be generalized to other skills that require balance. Under these circumstances domain-referenced testing and criterion-referenced testing would co-exist. There would be measurement over the domain of balance without setting a criterion for it, but a criterion would be set for attainment of a specific functional skill (stair climbing).

Domains can be validated only by showing that training in them facilitates learning of other valued skills. Hofmeister[13] says that professionals should represent themselves fairly to practitioners in education. He points out that virtually no existing data support the use of predicting performance in specific skills from domain-referenced tests and that criterion-referenced instruments developed along this approach must still be considered unvalidated. Until the time that such validation occurs, perhaps the task-analysis approach specifying specific domains and criterion performance within the context of the skill is the plausible approach.

Content-Referenced Tests

To this point we have discussed normative-referenced, criterion-referenced, and domain-referenced testing. Each has a different purpose. Normative-referenced assessment determines deficiencies according to normal groups. Domain-referenced assessment specifies strengths and weaknesses of general abilities related to motor skills to be acquired. Criterion-referenced assessments, for the most part, determine what pupils can and cannot do in the instructional content of the curriculum. Baker[2] stated that most objectives do not present sufficient information regarding how a teacher should alter instruction to improve learning. Content-referenced assessment attempts to remedy this.

Definition

Content-referenced assessment is the process of determining which activities or components of a task have and have not been mastered. There are two types of content analyses. One is the traditional behavioral analysis of a skill to determine which steps in skill acquisition have and have not been mastered. The unmastered components of the skill then become objectives for instruction. When all objectives are acquired the task most likely will be mastered. The other type of content-referenced assessment is the process of determining where on a continuum or a hierarchy a person is performing. Elley's[5] descriptions indicate that to determine an individual's status a behavioral hierarchy is needed. More simply, content-referenced assessment entails developing a series of small learning steps (or pieces of information), placing them in a hierarchy, and then determining where in this sequence a person is performing.

Purpose

Content-referenced testing is used to determine which short-range objectives leading to a behavioral goal a student can perform. It does not compare children with others, but rather ascertains how close a student is to realizing a behavioral goal. As French and Jansma[7] indicate, this process enables the physical educator to provide an individual pupil with instructional activity based on the first short-range objective (in a sequence) the pupil was not able to demonstrate. A pupil's progress from one developmentally sequenced short-term objective to the next in the sequence eventually leads to the acquisition of a major or terminal motor skill. It is easy to understand how this process fits into the IEP process: content-referenced assessment focuses on narrow and specific elements of behavior that lead to goals. In content-referenced testing the teacher always knows the next objective because the objectives are arranged in a hierarchy of easier to more difficult (complex) tasks before any testing or teaching takes place.

Following is a hierarchy of balance objectives. The action of each objective is to stand on one foot, and the criterion for each objective is 5 seconds. A standard condition for all objectives is for the heel of the free leg to be as high as the supporting knee. The tasks are made more difficult by altering the conditions of the sequence of objectives. Conditions of objectives are altered so hierarchies are expressed for each set of conditions. The conditions that are altered are variations of eye position, arm position, and placement of the foot.

Action: Balance on one foot.

Standard condition: Raise the heel of the free leg as high as the supporting knee.

Conditions	Criterion
1. Eyes anywhere, arms at sides, foot flat	For 5 seconds
2. Eyes anywhere, arms in front, foot flat	For 5 seconds
3. Eyes up, arms at sides, foot flat	For 5 seconds
4. Eyes up, arms in front, foot flat	For 5 seconds
5. Eyes anywhere, arms at sides, heel raised 2 inches	For 5 seconds
6. Eyes anywhere, arms in front, heel raised 2 inches	For 5 seconds
7. Eyes closed, arms at sides, foot flat	For 5 seconds
8. Eyes up, arms at sides, heel raised 2 inches	For 5 seconds
9. Eyes up, arms in front, heel raised 2 inches	For 5 seconds
10. Eyes closed, arms in front, foot flat	For 5 seconds
11. Eyes closed, arms at sides, heel raised 2 inches	For 5 seconds
12. Eyes closed, arms in front, heel raised 2 inches	For 5 seconds

The balance sequence begins with an objective in which the teacher can specify the positions of the eyes, arms, and free heel. The criterion (5 seconds) for each objective remains the same; however, the difficulty of the task is increased from easy to difficult as the positions of the eyes, arms, and heel of the supporting foot are changed. Each objective in the hierarchy becomes the balance content that is to be taught. Placement of the learner within the hierarchy could represent content-referenced testing. The placement would indicate what the learner could and could not do in that sequence of activities.

Although the series of tasks may not be a true hierarchy, altering the conditions forms a hierarchy from simple to more difficult. The tasks are graded in difficulty because (1) standing on the ball of the foot is more difficult than standing with the foot flat, (2) balancing with the eyes closed is more difficult than balancing with the eyes open, and (3) arm placement in front of the body demands greater balance than if they are placed at the sides. The conditions are simply altered to make the task more or less difficult. Criteria for exit from the program can be made by the teacher, depending on how much balance the learner needs to perform sports (or functional) skills satisfactorily.

To content-reference assess an individual in this sequence, one might have the student attempt to perform the odd-numbered objectives in the sequence until he or she is unable to perform an objective. When a step in the hierarchy is missed, one should digress one step back and test. The last mastered task would be the present level of educational performance. Once it is determined where in the continuum the learner is functioning, the learner begins at that point and progresses through the sequence at his or her own rate until the educational goal is reached.[7]

I CAN

Up to this point our discussion of content-referenced testing has concerned analyzing the components of a task that must be mastered to perform the main task and determining what an individual can and cannot do on a hierarchical continuum of activities. There are other ways to incorporate criterion levels of achievement into content-referenced testing. The I CAN[28] series is an example of this combination. In that series of activities the task analysis of the sit-up (and other activities) addresses not only the proper form, but also higher levels of proficiency. For example, skill levels 3 and 4 require sequentially more repetitions with appropriate age and sex criteria. Thus for this specific skill I CAN has embodied content-referenced test-

I CAN

PERFORMANCE OBJECTIVE:
TO DEMONSTRATE A FUNCTIONAL LEVEL OF
ABDOMINAL STRENGTH AND ENDURANCE

SKILL LEVELS	FOCAL POINTS FOR ACTIVITY
1. To perform a bent leg sit-up with assistance.	Given a verbal request, a demonstration, and physical assistance (complete assistance through entire movement), the student can perform a bent leg sit-up 2 out of 3 times, without resistance, in this manner: a. Starting position on back with knees flexed 90 degrees, feet flat on floor, arms clasped behind neck, partner holding ankles b. Curl up by tucking chin and lifting trunk, touching elbows to knees c. Return to starting position by uncurling trunk and lowering head in a controlled movement.
2. To perform a bent leg sit-up with partial assistance. 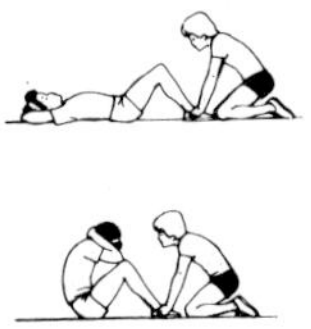	Given a verbal request, a demonstration, and partial assistance (support student's trunk as he sits up), the student can perform a bent leg sit-up 2 out of 3 times in this manner: a. Independently assume starting position on back with knees flexed 90 degrees, feet flat on floor, arms clasped behind neck, partner holding ankles b. Initiate curl-up by tucking chin and lifting trunk; complete curl-up by touching elbows to knees c. Independently return to starting position by uncurling trunk and lowering head in a controlled movement.

I CAN

PERFORMANCE OBJECTIVE:
TO DEMONSTRATE A FUNCTIONAL LEVEL OF
ABDOMINAL STRENGTH AND ENDURANCE

SKILL LEVELS	FOCAL POINTS FOR ACTIVITY
3. To perform a bent leg sit-up without assistance. 	Given a verbal request and a demonstration, the student can perform two consecutive bent leg sit-ups without assistance by curling up and lifting the trunk, touching the elbows to the knees, and returning in a controlled fashion to the starting position.
4. To demonstrate an appropriate level of abdominal endurance and strength.	Given a verbal request, a demonstration, and a command to "start" and "stop," the student can demonstrate consecutive bent leg sit-ups in this manner: a. Start and stop on command b. Meet the minimal performance criteria for individual's age and sex. (See table 1.)
5. To maintain an appropriate level of abdominal endurance and strength through activity participation.	Given the ability to perform the bent leg sit-up at the appropriate age and sex criteria (see Table 1), the student can maintain that criteria over a 12-week period.

FIGURE 3-2. The I CAN program provides a task analysis (focal points for activity) and tests performance at the appropriate age and sex criteria. (From I CAN Primary Skills, Janet A Wessel, Director. Reprinted with permission of the publisher, Hubbard.)

ing through task analysis of the behavior and criterion-referenced testing by increasing the number of repetitions while meeting age- and sex-appropriate criteria (Fig. 3-2).

The arrangement of any given step in the hierarchical sequence can be controlled by the teacher. Ensuring that each step in the sequence is appropriate for the specific learner is the teacher's responsibility as well. Entering criterion levels of performance in the sequence is an additional check on the student's progress.

The sit-up and balance tasks focus on a sequence that is inherent in the task being assessed. That is, the balancing task focuses on different aspects of balancing on one foot, and the sit-up task includes graduated sit-ups. In each of these examples it is assumed that the learner possesses all of the prerequisite components necessary to achieve at least the simplest step in the sequence. It should be pointed out that this is not always true when dealing with learners who have disabilities. In some cases underlying prerequisites, such as vestibular development or depth perception, may be deficient. If a student is having difficulty realizing success with sequential steps in a hierarchy, the teacher may have to determine whether lower level components are functioning satisfactorily. This type of probing is another form of content-referenced testing. For example, if the task is to balance on one foot with eyes open, hands on hips, and the free leg bent 90 degrees for 5 seconds, and if the learner cannot execute the task according to the criteria, the teacher can either (1) administer a balance test to determine whether the learner demonstrates a vestibular delay, or (2) administer a cover test to determine whether orthoptic visual problems (depth perception difficulties) could be interfering with the learner's ability to use the eyes to help maintain balance (see Chapter 4).

This can be considered a deep probing content-referenced assessment. If a vestibular development delay or an orthoptic problem is found, these prerequisite components should be corrected by knowledgeable professionals before the learner can be expected to perform the task to standard. Table 3-6 includes tests that can be used to probe for suspected underlying deficiencies.

Comments

The advantages of activity sequences that are prerequisite to content-referenced assessment consist of the following:

1. Sequences identify what skills learners do and do not perform and what skills are to be taught next.
2. Sequences eliminate the need for the concept of readiness.
3. The teacher never waits for a learner to be ready to learn a given skill, but begins to teach the prerequisite skills specified in the skill sequence.
4. Skill sequences make individualization of instruction easier.

With content-referenced assessment, testing becomes an integral part of the educational process.[9] To accommodate the learner with disabilities, the increments in the learning continuum must be small. When this sequence of steps is used, it provides information to the students and teachers about how a student is

TABLE 3-6

Components tested by fine domain-referenced tests

	Purdue PMS	Bayley	Stott	Bruininks-Oseretsky	Basic motor ability test
Strength	X	X		X	
Flexibility	X				X
Endurance					
Agility				X	
Power					
Balance	X	X	X	X	X
Speed			X	X	
Vision	X	X			
Eye-hand coordination				X	X
Kinesthetic awareness	X				
Tactile discrimination	X		X	X	
Rhythm	X				
Gross motor	X	X	X	X	X
Fine motor		X	X	X	X

progressing toward a goal and can provide clues to selection of appropriate teaching strategies.

Programmed instruction or task analysis (see Chapter 4) is an essential prerequisite of content assessment because it permits each task to be treated as a test of competence. Achieving each step in the sequence reinforces the learner's belief in personal competence and provides incentive to continue to try. Programmed instruction becomes programmed testing, and the outcome of each test is used to make an instructional decision. If the learner reaches the next step in the sequence, the teaching strategy is continued. If the learner fails to achieve the next step, the teaching strategy is modified to better facilitate the learner's success. It should be kept in mind that using this procedure to test and teach will prove successful only if the programmed instruction or task analysis contains every step necessary to accomplish the goal. Inadequate or poorly sequenced steps will lead to learner and teacher frustration.

When programmed instruction or task analysis is in use, each behavior becomes an objective and learning principles can be applied to teaching because there is precise definition of what is to be learned. When content-referenced testing is a part of the education process, there is provision for open measures that are public. They are precisely repeatable and mutually understandable so that all concerned parties know where students are in their educational development and how far they must go to achieve measurable educational goals.[8] Content-referenced tests may be more practical and appropriate than other tests because they reflect what is actually being taught on a daily basis and focus on raw data that reflect a pupil's precise performance.

Assessing Specific Sports Skills

Two basic forms associated with content-referenced testing are task analysis of specific instructional content that has not yet been mastered and improvement of skill proficiency after it is performed in some manner.

Content Task Analysis of a Softball Throw

1. Demonstrate the correct grip 100% of the time.
   a. Select a softball.
   b. Hold the ball with the first and second fingers spread on top, thumb under the ball and the third and fourth fingers on the side.
   c. Grasp the ball with the fingertips.
2. Demonstrate the proper step pattern for throwing the softball 3 out of 5 times.
   a. Identify the restraining line.
   b. Take a side step with the left foot.
   c. Follow with a shorter side step with the right foot.
3. Demonstrate the proper throwing technique and form 3 out of 5 times.
   a. Grip ball correctly.
   b. Bend rear knee.
   c. Rotate hips and pivot left foot, turning body to the right.
   d. Bring right arm back with the ball behind the right ear and bent right elbow leading (in front of) hand.
   e. Bend left elbow and point it at a 45-degree angle.
   f. Step straight ahead with the left foot.
   g. Keep the right hip back and low and the right arm bent with the ball behind the ear and the elbow leading.

h. Start the throwing motion by pushing down hard with the right foot.
i. Straighten the right knee and rotate the hips, shifting the weight to the left foot.
j. Keep the upper body in line with the direction of throw and the eyes focused on the target.
k. Whip the left arm to the rear, increasing the speed of the right arm.
l. Extend the right arm fully forward, completing the release by snapping the wrist and releasing the ball at a 45 degree angle.
m. Follow through by bringing the hand completely down and the right foot forward to the front restraining line.
4. Throw a softball on command 3 out of 5 times.
   a. Assume READY position between the front and back restraining lines with feet apart.
   b. Point the shoulder of the nonthrowing arm towards the restraining line.
   c. Focus eyes in the direction of the throw.
   d. Remain behind the front restraining line.
   e. Throw the softball on command.
   f. Execute smooth integration of skill sequence.

Permission for the Special Olympics Sports Skills Instructional Program provided by Special Olympics, created by The Joseph P. Kennedy, Jr. Foundation. Authorized and accredited by Special Olympics, Inc., for the Benefit of Mentally Retarded Citizens.

In motor skills the development of form and increased levels of proficiency usually occur at the same time. Both forms of assessment make instructional decisions for a specific learner easier.

The task analyses for the Special Olympics sports curriculum are examples of breaking a skill into teachable components. While the specific skill is taught, assessments can be made to determine which specific components can and cannot be done by a learner. In the softball throw 19 observable components are listed. Using the task analysis of the throw to teach from involves content-referenced assessment because there is a direct relationship between assessment and the end result of the instruction. This also might be considered criterion-referenced testing because a standard of mastery could be set for all 19 components of the task (see box on p. 54).

Community-Based Assessment

A community-based assessment strategy is a top, down approach that focuses on the natural environment both as the source of curriculum content and as a location for training the individual to meet the identified needs.[24] This strategy examines current community environments where the individual with a disability is expected to utilize the physical, motor, and sport skills in a domestic and/or recreational context. These environments are then divided into subenvironments, and physical and motor activities needed to participate in each subenvironment are identified. Students' motor skills are then assessed to determine whether discrepancies exist between present levels of performance and those identified as being needed to function in the community environments.

Persons with disabilities are often perceived as being dependent on others, including government, for the duration of their lives. The purpose of special education and physical education is to alleviate continued dependence on others. If, through testing, it is determined that a student is on the borderline between normal and below-normal functioning, special education can help the individual move into the range of normal functioning. Educational remedies should be directed toward raising the student's ability to perform curriculum tasks adequately. If, on the other hand, the student is judged to be so deficient in ability that he or she is unable to compete on an equal basis in a normal adult society, then the education of that student should focus on more practical things. Probably the most practical approach is to develop the student's ability to function in specific community living environments. Toward this end, community-based assessments should be provided for students with moderate to severe disabili-

ties. Following is a list of community-based behaviors from which assessments can be made to determine which needs are to be developed that lead toward independent participation. Behaviors that are deficient can be content referenced through task analysis and programmed instructional procedures.

1. Participates in recreational swimming at the Ford City YMCA.
2. Bowls once a week at the Ford City Bowlodrome.
3. Participates at Smith's Miniature Golf complex at least five times during the summer.
4. Jogs 10 miles per week.
5. Participates in a church summer league softball program.
6. Participates in the Ford City volleyball recreation program during December through February.

Definition

Community-based assessments are strategies for defining what skills and knowledge an individual will need to function adequately in a community environment. The process for conducting a community-based assessment is aptly described by Brown et al.[3] The steps suggested follow:

1. Delineate the most relevant and functional least restrictive current and subsequent school and nonschool environments.
2. Analyze these environments and divide them into subenvironments (school, home, neighborhood, playground, etc.).
3. Designate the most relevant and functional activities that occur in these environments.
4. Determine the skills needed to participate in the activities and describe possible adaptations that allow participation.
5. Design and implement instructional programs to teach students the skills necessary for participation in chronologically age-appropriate activities in the natural environments.

Purpose

The community-based assessment and the IEP should define which skills are mastered and which are not. When environments are changed, new skills are needed for adaptation. There should be a match between skill functionality and instructional tasks. This lowers the risk of requiring unnecessary steps in the generalization process.

Comments

Brown et al.[3] use the term *ecological inventory* to describe a checklist of the behaviors that the student should learn to become self-sufficient in the natural environment. Learner performance is studied across a variety of tasks that occur throughout the day.[22] The community-based assessment provides detailed information on how the behaviors are to be performed by the individual. Once these behaviors are defined to the extent that they can be subjected to either task analysis or programmed instruction, either content- or criterion-referenced testing and programming can be applied to facilitate development. The analysis of the functional skills will identify missing prerequisites. Objectives of the IEP should be related to those functional activities.

Community-based assessment and programming are based on the principle of partial participation. Whatever the learners *can* do, they do. Only the amount of assistance needed to function successfully in a natural environment is provided. Adaptations to help persons accommodate to the environment are (1) personal assistance, (2) adapted materials and devices, (3) adapted social environments, and (4) skill sequences.

Curriculum-Based Assessment

A curriculum-based assessment determines whether the student with disabilities is learning specific physical education content. (For a more in-depth description see Howell and Moorehead[14] and Tucker.[26]) Curriculum-based assessment may be developed in two ways. One is from the ecological inventory, which was described earlier. The second is through examining the local physical education curriculum that exists for students without disabilities in the public schools. Usually, it is assumed that children with less severe disabilities will make progress toward being successful in the regular physical education curricula. However, the more severely disabled student may need an ecological assessment to determine the specific functional motor skills that will directly contribute to self-sufficient motor behavior in communities where they are likely to live.

Other Types of Assessment Instruments
Inventories

Inventory assessments are composed of checklists of tasks to be accomplished. Usually they are not in sequential order, and there is little or no functional relationship between the tasks. Even though the activities are not behaviorally stated, they are nevertheless useful.

One of the most prevalent checklists used is the one to determine acquired swimming skill (see box above). Two problems arise from the use of such checklists.

Swimming Checklist

1. Splash water.
2. Wash face with water.
3. Move down steps into water.
4. Wade in water.
5. Move backward in water.
6. Place nose in water.
7. Submerge head in water.
8. Blow ping-pong ball across pool.
9. With mouth in water, blow bubbles.
10. Jump while in water.
11. Squat underwater.
12. With hands on steps, bring legs up to floating position.
13. With hands on steps, kick fast.
14. While held in prone position, recover.
15. Retrieve objects from 2 feet of water.
16. Roll over from a prone float position.
17. Prone glide and recover.

First, it is possible that the student could master all of the tasks and still not be able to swim. Second, one may be able to swim but not be proficient in many of the subtasks. Checklists are inventories of characteristics and provide a guide for selection of activities, but they are not objectives. Thus programmed instruction or task analysis as it relates to the task to be learned must still be done. One cannot determine specific behavioral performance in natural environments from checklists.

Formative assessment

Many physical education sport skills are taught in a specified form. Once the desirable form is decided on, the sport skill is divided into observable portions. These portions or elements are often called *coaching points*. The formative assessment is similar to, but different from, classic task analysis. For instance, in classic task analysis of tying a shoe, all of the many steps in the task must be mastered before the shoe can be tied. However, in throwing a ball, the ball may be propelled by a novice even though the form of the task is not exactly the way the instructor wants it. Usually, there are two ways of assessing a physical skill performance. One is the formative assessment, which is used to determine if a student replicated a desired form. The other is content-referenced assessment, which generally measures skill proficiency on a continuum of speed, distance, number of repetitions, and so on. In throwing a ball, accuracy and distance of the throw would be measured if one were using content-referenced assessment.

Treatment-referenced testing

According to Donlon,[4] treatment-referenced tests are designed to determine which teaching strategy would be most successful with a given student. When using treatment-referenced tests, careful study is made of antecedents and consequences that bring about desired changes. This assessment form results from recognition that learners are different, and thus different intervention strategies may have to be used. If one strategy does not work, more information is gathered and another treatment form is tried. This approach is often used to control disruptive behavior or bring about positive cognitive change in people with learning disabilities.

ABC analysis

Another type of assessment that is directly related to determining the intervention procedure for the teacher to administer is ABC analysis.[24] *A* is for antecedent; *B* is for behavior; and *C* is for consequence. In this assessment procedure, there is a functional analysis of behavior in a systematic way. Events that occur before and after the target physical or motor skill are observed and recorded. When using this approach, the physical education teacher attempts to identify aspects of the physical and social environment that appear to lead to attainment of the objectives of instruction and to identify events that reinforce or maintain the desired objectives. Using this approach presumes that behavior is a direct result of environmental conditions.[6]

Tests with multiple characteristics

Assessment instruments do not always fit neatly into the specific classification system that has been described so far. Rather, instruments may possess characteristics of several different types of tests. Furthermore, a specific test may be used for more than one purpose.

There are several assessment instruments available in the physical education literature. Many of these tests are commercial domain-referenced tests with norms (see Table 3-2). Table 3-6 indicates the names of several tests, domains covered by each test, and whether the tests can be used for placement, programming, or both.

Milani-Comparetti development chart. This chart is a normative-referenced assessment instrument for determining achievement of motor milestones. It is domain-referenced in that it classifies the maturation of reflexes (evoked responses) and postural control as

A Developmental Checklist of Walking Behaviors

WALKING BEHAVIORS	NORMATIVE DEVELOPMENT
Stands alone	13 months
Walks alone	14 months
Walks sideways	16.5 months
Walks backward	16.9 months
Runs flat footed (no support phase)	18 months
Transfers weight from heel to toe	24 months
Walks with one foot on beam 2½ inches wide and 4 inches high	27.6 months
Walks on tiptoes	31 months
Walks a 1 inch line for 10 feet	37 months
Walks a circular path 21½ feet without stepping off	45 months
Walks on a 4-inch × 8-foot balance beam	56 months

they lead to active locomotion. The comprehensiveness of definitive domains found in the Milani-Comparetti chart is limited (see Fig. 3-3).

Developmental checklists. Whereas the items in the Milani-Comparetti chart are for the most part arranged in prerequisite order (e.g., lying down precedes sitting, sitting precedes standing), not all developmental checklists are placed in that order. The developmental checklist of walking behavior in the box below[27] for example, can be used primarily for assessing normative-referenced attainment of specific skills. When these checklists are used as criterion assessments, specific programs can be designed from them. Once a specific behavior on the checklist is achieved to criterion, that specific program is discontinued.

A diagnostic normative-referenced checklist is shown above.

Assessing developmental stages of a specific skill. Two types of normative-referenced, developmental checklists of motor behaviors have been described. The first included chronologically sequenced behaviors in which one behavior is prerequisite to the other. The second encompassed specific skills that mature at specific chronological ages. Some specific skills progress through stages of development. Each development stage is descriptive in nature and represents a step to-

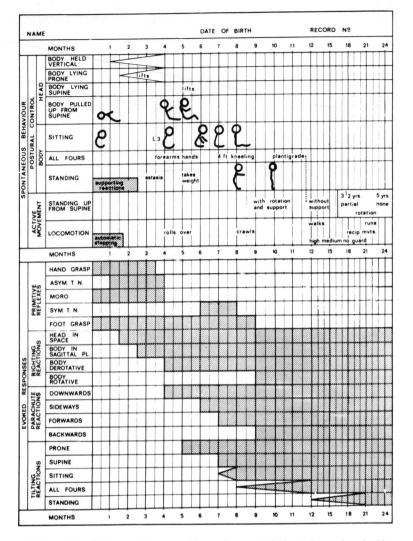

FIGURE 3-3. The Milani-Comparetti Developmental Chart. (Reproduced with permission of The Association for the Severely Handicapped.)

ward a mature locomotor behavior. Assessments can be made by comparing the performance of the learner against the known stages of development of the pattern. Developmental lag on that specific pattern can be determined. Descriptions of the stages in acquiring the ability to throw appear in Fig. 3-4.

Checklists. Content-referenced assessments for a top, down approach may be designed to test deficiencies in both performance and abilities related to a skill. Specific motor skills are task analyzed into observable components, and both desirable and undesirable be-

haviors are included. Content assessment can be made by observing performance of the skill. This type of assessment is unique because the teacher checks off not only what efficient components of the skill the performer demonstrates, but also the errors demonstrated (see box on pp. 60-61).

Hyde[15] developed a similar instrument for screening kindergarten children for developmental delays (see box on p. 62).

Such checklists are useful for screening one student or a whole class of students before beginning a unit of

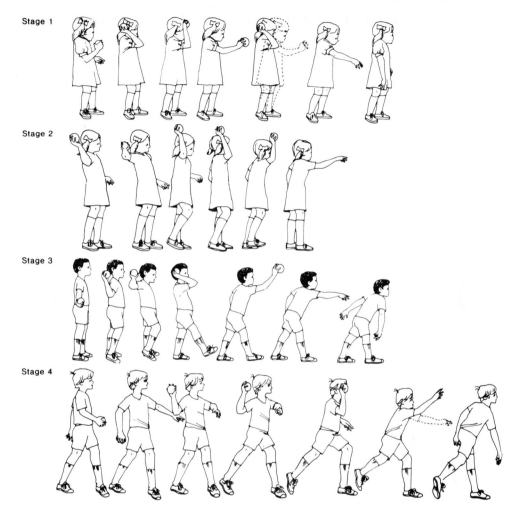

FIGURE 3-4. Developmental stages of throwing. (Redrawn from Sherrill C: Adapted physical education and recreation, ed 2, Dubuque, Iowa; © 1981 by William C Brown Publishers.)

instruction. Through the use of the checklist the teacher can determine which tasks a student can already execute and which tasks need to be taught.

Behavioral checklists that indicate abnormal behavior are also widely used (see box on p. 61).

The Special Olympics Sport Skill Guides require extensive application of different forms of assessment. These include content (task analysis and performance) and criterion (mastery of all parts of the content task analysis) assessments. The guides also have a checklist of performance of skills. Worthy of note is that the checklists require assessment of the skills as they are performed in competition. The items included in the checklists are behavioral outcomes of either the component parts of the task or the measure of performance.

In their assessment of water orientation, Killian, Arena-Ronda, and Bruno[16] have added another dimension to checklist analysis. In addition to assessing the general observed behavior, they apply a five-point scale that reveals the type of interaction that occurs between the tester and the student. The five-point rating scale is listed on p. 63.[16]

Anatomical Functional Content-Referenced Checklist for Walking

Directions: (1) Study the four phases of the walk (heel strike, midstance, push-off, and midswing). Study the child to see if the walking pattern fits in column I (normal and mature). (2) Determine behaviorally the deficit related to a specific phase at a specific anatomical location. (3) When a behavioral deficit has been determined anatomically and in a specific phase of the pattern, pair it with column III to determine potential weak muscles, which may contribute to deficient walking. The initial survey to determine specific muscles that need programmed instructional objectives is complete. Integrated programming would involve (a) matching activity with muscles to be developed, (b) constructing a sequence of objectives that develop the activity, and (c) matching task differently to ability level of the learner. This assessment system assesses *only* strength deficits related to walking.

I: Mature, normal walking pattern	II: Immature, pathological walking pattern	III: Weak muscles that may contribute to deficit
Phase 1: heel strike 1. Pelvis has slight anterior rotation	Pelvis has posterior rotation.	Back extensors and flexors
2. Heel strike knee is extended	Knee is locked in hyperextension.	Knee extensors and flexors
3. Heel strike foot at right angle to leg.	Heel strike foot placed flat on floor with slapping.	Ankle dorsiflexors
4. Heel strike leg is in vertical alignment with pelvis.	Heel strike leg is in abduction at the hip	Hip abductors
5. Plantar surface of forefoot of heel strike leg is visible.	Plantar surface of heel strike leg is not visible.	Ankle dorsiflexors
6. Head and trunk vertical.	Head and trunk tip to support leg, pelvis tilts upward on the swing leg side.	Hip abductors of the support leg side
Phase 2: midstance 7. Pelvis is tilted slightly downward on the side of the swing leg.	Exaggerated downward tilt of the pelvis on the swing leg side.	Hip abductors of the support side
8. Support leg is in slight lateral rotation.	Exaggerated outward rotation of the hip on the support leg side.	Hip abductors, medial rotators, knee extensors, and foot evertors of the support side leg
9. Toes of support foot are in direction of travel.	Toes of the support foot turn out; toes of the support foot turn in.	Foot invertors and evertors
Phase 3: push-off 10. Support leg is slightly rotated laterally.	Support leg is in exaggerated lateral rotation.	Hip and knee extensors of the support leg
11. Slight anterior rotation of the pelvis.	Exaggerated anterior rotation of the pelvis.	Abdominals and hip extensors
12. Push-off ankle is plantar-flexed.	Push-off ankle has limited plantar flexion.	Ankle plantar flexors
13. Toes of the push-off ankle are hyperextended.	Toes are straight.	Ankle plantar flexors

Anatomical Functional Content-Referenced Checklist for Walking—cont'd

I: Mature, normal walking pattern	II: Immature, pathological walking pattern	III: Weak muscles that may contribute to deficit
14. Plantar surface of foot	Plantar surface of foot at mid-push-off is not visible.	Ankle plantar flexors, hip and knee extensors
Phase 4: midswing		
15. Swing foot is at right angle to the leg.	Toes of swing foot drag on the floor.	Hip and knee flexors and ankle dorsiflexors
16. Hip and knees of the swing foot are flexed (toes clear floor).	Exaggerated hip and knee flexion of the forefoot of swing leg is dropped.	Ankle dorsiflexors
17. Pelvis has very slight anterior rotation.	Pelvis has posterior rotation.	Back extensors and hip flexors
18. Head and trunk are vertical.	Trunk is displaced to support leg; pelvis is lifted on swing leg side.	Hip and knee flexors and ankle dorsiflexors
19. Swing leg is in vertical alignment with the pelvis and has slight medial rotation at the hip.	Swing leg is laterally rotated at the hip.	Hip medial rotators
20. Swing foot is at right angle to the leg with slight eversion.	Forefoot of the swing leg is dropped (eversion is not available).	Ankle dorsiflexors and foot evertors

Checklist of Abnormal Behavior

1. Talks out
2. Does not follow directions
3. Limited range of interests
4. Self-stimulating behavior
5. Self-abusive
6. Hyperactive
7. Inattentive

Checklist of Gymnastic Skills

1. Stork stand
2. Cartwheel
3. Roundoff
4. Forward roll
5. Backward roll
6. Tip-up
7. Headstand
8. Inchworm
9. Log roll
10. Front scale

Motor Development Checklist

Name _____   Examiner _____
Birthdate _____ Sex _____   Date

Category	Special Notes and Remarks		
Static balance	___ does not attempt tasks	___ heel-toe stand, 5 secs ___ balance on preferred foot, arms hung relaxed at sides ___ ___ ___ ___ ___ 5 secs	___ heel-toe stand, eyes closed, 5 secs ___ balance on preferred foot, arms hung relaxed at sides, eyes closed ___ ___ ___ ___ ___ 10 secs ___ 5 secs ___ ___ ___ ___ ___ 10 secs

Hopping reflex	___ no response
	___ no righting of head.
	___ trunk
	no step in direction of push
	   ___ right ___ left
	   ___ forward ___ backward
		___ head and body right themselves
		___ step or hop in direction of push
		___ right ___ left
		___ forward ___ backward	

Running pattern	___ loses balance ___ almost ___ twists trunk ___ leans excessively ___ jerky, uneven rhythm	___ elbows away from body in arm swing ___ limited arm swing ___ short strides	___ full arm swing in opposition with legs ___ elbows near body in swing ___ even flow and rhythm
Jumping pattern	___ loses balance on landing ___ no use of arms ___ twists or bends sideways	___ arms at side for balance ___ legs bent throughout jump	___ arms back as legs bend ___ arms swing up as legs extend ___ lands softly with control
Throwing pattern	___ pushing or shoving object ___ loss of balance ___ almost	___ body shifts weight from back to front without stepping	___ steps forward with same foot as throwing arm. ___ steps forward with foot opposite throwing arm
Catching pattern	___ loses balance ___ almost ___ shies away ___ traps or scoops	___ arms stiff in front of body	___ arms bent at sides of body ___ arms "give" as catch ___ uses hands
Kicking pattern	___ misses ___ off center	___ arms at sides or out to sides ___ uses from knee down to kick	___ kicks "through" ball ___ arm opposition ___ uses full leg to kick ___ can kick with either foot

Courtesy Beverly Hyde.

Spontaneous (SP): a behavior in which a subject performs one of the 13 tasks prior to an instructor's verbal directions.

Verbal (VB): the subject performs the specified task after the instructor's verbal directions.

Verbal with demonstration (DMO): the subject performs the specified task after the instructor's verbal directions and with visual cues.

Physical guidance (PG): the instructor manipulates the subject's body through the specified task; verbal cues and visual cues accompany the manipulation.

Objection (OBJ): the subject is unwilling to attempt the task; this response involves both passive and active objection.

As a rule, behavioral checklists assess a series of behaviors that may be found in a physical education curriculum. Once it has been determined whether a student can perform the tasks on the checklist, items that cannot be performed can be broken down and organized for content-referenced testing (see column II in box on pp. 60-61).

Surveys. Postural screening is an example of a survey assessment. The objective of the postural survey is to identify postural misalignments. A widely used postural survey chart is presented in Fig. 3-5.

Once the postural screening is completed, further procedures are required before appropriate intervention activities can be initiated. Steps in the follow-up procedure include:

1. Identify the muscles that are too tight and those which are weak and causing the postural misalignment.
2. Select activities that will strengthen the weakened muscles and stretch the tight muscles.
3. Construct a behavioral intervention program for the specific task.
4. Grade the exercises (content reference the task) so that you begin the intervention program at a reasonable level for that specific learner (see Chapter 4 for more detailed procedures).

This specific survey is also a form of normative-referenced assessment. In Fig. 3-5 the figures in the left column represent the norm, or the desired posture. The figures in the middle and right columns represent deviations from the norm.

USING ASSESSMENT FOR PLACEMENT

Assessment is sometimes used to classify performers so that competition between individuals is as equal as possible. To classify competitors, performance in the skill is observed to determine what the athlete is capable of doing. Once the abilities of the performers are determined, those with similar capabilities compete against one another. A running classification for physically disabled performers follows:

1. Move a wheelchair forward continuously a distance of 10 yards.
2. Move a wheelchair forward continuously a distance of 30 yards.
3. Move a wheelchair continuously up a 10-degree incline that is a length of 10 yards.
4. Move a walker continuously a distance of 10 yards.
5. Move a walker continuously a distance of 30 yards.
6. Move with crutches a distance of 10 yards.
7. Move with crutches a distance of 25 yards.
8. Move with a cane continuously a distance of 15 yards.
9. Move with a cane continuously a distance of 30 yards.
10. Move independently over a distance of 10 yards.
11. Move independently a distance of 30 yards.
12. Run a distance of 30 yards (flight phase).

Considerations when Assessing Individuals with Severe Disabilities

When the purpose of assessment is for instructional purposes of individuals with severe disabilities, Wilcox and Bellamy[29] suggest the following guidelines:

1. Focus the assessment on important sport tasks and physical activities that are community-based rather than on presumed prerequisites.
2. Assess the capabilites of the individual with disabilities to determine what activities the individual can participate in today rather than emphasizing skill development for later use.
3. Assess functional motor, physical, sport, and play activities rather than non-functional assumed prerequisite activity.
4. Assess in a manner in which there is continuity between the assessment and the programming (individual assessment must relate directly in content and focus to program planning and intervention decisions).
5. Assess in relation to local performance needs which reflect the demands and opportunities in the local community.

Wilcox and Bellamy[29] argue that standardized assessments are frequently irrelevant to specific program planning decisions that must be made for individuals with severe disabilities.

POSTURE RATING CHART

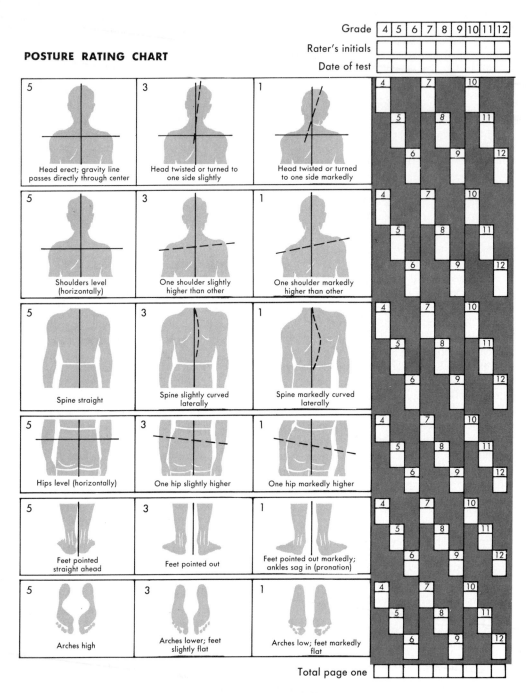

Grade | 4 | 5 | 6 | 7 | 8 | 9 | 10 | 11 | 12

Rater's initials

Date of test

5 — Head erect; gravity line passes directly through center
3 — Head twisted or turned to one side slightly
1 — Head twisted or turned to one side markedly

5 — Shoulders level (horizontally)
3 — One shoulder slightly higher than other
1 — One shoulder markedly higher than other

5 — Spine straight
3 — Spine slightly curved laterally
1 — Spine markedly curved laterally

5 — Hips level (horizontally)
3 — One hip slightly higher
1 — One hip markedly higher

5 — Feet pointed straight ahead
3 — Feet pointed out
1 — Feet pointed out markedly; ankles sag in (pronation)

5 — Arches high
3 — Arches lower; feet slightly flat
1 — Arches low; feet markedly flat

Total page one

FIGURE 3-5. New York State Postural Survey. (Courtesy New York State Education Department.)

SUMMARY

Federal laws mandate that individuals with disabling conditions and those who are highly likely (at-risk) to experience developmental delays be provided with assessment and intervention services. Three fundamental purposes of testing are (1) comparing performance of an individual to a normal population, (2) determining appropriate intervention strategies, and (3) adapting instruction to the ability level of the individual learner. Standardized normative-referenced assessment is used for determining status of an individual in a normal group; that is, it can help determine developmental lag on a specific test item. In some cases this type of test is used for instructional grouping. Recent developments in assessment enable the tester to look at reasons why a child is demonstrating a specific deficit on a specific test item. This type of assessment is called process assessment. Domain-referenced and criterion-referenced assessments indicate what needs to be taught. Domain-referenced assessment identifies deficient physical, motor, or perceptual characteristics, and criterion-referenced tests indicate what skills in the curriculum need to be taught to encourage mastery. Checklists usually do not have criterion measures but provide a rough guide for skills and subskills that are to be taught to master large areas of the curriculum. Surveys are useful in determining areas of intended emphasis in the physical education curriculum. Community-based assessment refers to behaviors identified from ecological study that relate to self-sufficiency for more severely disabled children. Curriculum-based assessment determines the amount of learning the student with disabilities is gaining from a specific physical education curriculum.

The two types of assessment used in daily instruction of curriculum tasks to children with disabilities are content-referenced and treatment-referenced assessment. Content-referenced assessment involves ongoing study of the learning in the instructional content so that it is adapted to the ability level of the learner. Treatment-referenced assessment enables formation of a hypothesis of instructional strategies to facilitate learning. The ABC analysis is an assessment technique that may assist the teacher in selecting beneficial intervention strategies. All types of assessment do not fall into these neat categories. Most of the assessment techniques need to be employed to conduct efficient individualized physical education programs for individuals with disabilities.

REVIEW QUESTIONS

1. What is the difference between a content- and normative-referenced test?
2. When would one use a normative-referenced test? A content-referenced test?
3. What are some potential problems of normative-referenced tests?
4. What is the purpose of a domain-referenced test?
5. What are professional concerns with the use of domain-referenced tests?
6. Activity sequences are prerequisite to content-referenced tests. What advantages do content-referenced tests have for direct instruction?
7. What is a community-based test and when should it be used?
8. What are the purposes of treatment-referenced tests?
9. How does a developmental checklist differ from a content-referenced checklist?
10. What are the purposes of surveys?
11. What are the purposes of assessment?
12. Give two examples of each of the following types of tests: (a) standardized normative-referenced, (b) criterion-referenced, (c) domain-referenced, and (d) content-referenced.
13. When is it appropriate to use each of the following types of tests: (a) standardized normative-referenced, (b) criterion-referenced, (c) domain-referenced, and (d) content-referenced.
14. What is an ABC analysis?
15. What is a curriculum-based assessment?
16. How does a process-oriented assessment differ from traditional normative-referenced assessments?
17. How does a curriculum-based assessment differ from an ecological inventory?
18. What tasks and opportunities relevant to screening and assessment are outlined in P.L. 99-457

STUDENT ACTIVITIES

1. Identify ten assessment tools. Analyze each one and try to classify the assessment instrument.
2. Set up a physical fitness program. Explain how you would incorporate standardized normative-referenced tests, criterion-referenced assessment, domain-referenced assessment, and content-referenced assessment.
3. Study some data bases of children with disabilities (hypothetical if need be) and indicate the types of assessments that were used to gather the data.
4. Observe teachers assessing learners. Indicate the types of assessment used.
5. Make an assessment of a child or another student using a test item from a normative-referenced test, a criterion-referenced test, a domain-referenced test, a community-based assessment, an inventory, and a survey.
6. Interview a teacher of adapted physical education. Find out what types of tests the person uses to evaluate students with disabilities and why these tests are used. Ask to see a copy of these tests. Determine what type of test (normative-referenced, criterion-referenced, domain-referenced, and/or content-referenced) each is.
7. Compare and contrast normative- and criterion-referenced tests. How are they similar? How do they differ?

8. Make a list of behaviors a person with disabilities would need to master to bowl successfully in your community.

9. Conduct an ABC analysis on a severely disabled child for two physical education tasks.

10. Conduct a curriculum-based assessment for a student with a disability in a limited number of curriculum tasks.

REFERENCES

1. *Armstrong v Kline.* United States District Court for the Eastern District of Pennsylvania Civil Action, 1979.

2. Baker E: Beyond objectives: domain-referenced tests for evaluation and instructional improvement, *Educ Tech* 14:1016, 1974.

3. Brown L et al: A strategy for developing chronological-age-appropriate and functional curricular content for severely handicapped adolescents and young adults, *J Spec Educ* 13:81-90, 1979.

4. Donlon T: *Referencing test scores: introductory concepts.* In Hively W, Reynolds M, editors: *Domain-referenced testing in special education,* Reston, Va, 1975, The Council for Exceptional Children.

5. Elley W: *The development of a set for content-referenced tests of reading,* 1971, New Zealand Council of Educational Research.

6. Evans IM, Meyer L: *An educative approach to behavior problems,* Baltimore, 1985, Paul H Brookes Publishing.

7. French R, Jansma P: *Special physical education,* Columbus, Ohio, 1982, Charles E Merrill Publishing.

8. Gay L: *Educational evaluation and measurement,* Columbus, Ohio, 1980, Charles E Merrill Publishing.

9. Glaser R: Educational psychology and education, *Am Psychol* 28:7, 1973.

10. Haring NG: *Developing effective individualized educational programs for severely handicapped children and youth,* Columbus, Ohio, 1977, Special Press.

11. Heward WL, Orlansky MD: *Exceptional children, ed 3,* Columbus, Ohio, 1988, Merrill Publishing.

12. Hively W, Reynolds M: *Domain-refereced testing in special education,* Reston, Va, 1975, The Council for Exceptional Children.

13. Hofmeister A: *Integrating criterion-referenced testing and instruction.* In Hively W, Reynolds M, editors: *Domain-referenced testing in special education,* Reston, Va, 1975, The Council for Exceptional Children.

14. Howell K, Moorehead MK: *Curriculum based evaluation in special and remedial education,* Columbus, Ohio, 1987, Merrill Publishing.

15. Hyde BJ: A motor development checklist of selected categories for kindergarten children, *Unpublished thesis,* University of Kansas, 1980.

16. Killian KJ, Arena-Ronda S, Bruno L: Refinement of two instruments that assess water orientation in atypical swimmers, *Adapt Phys Act Q* 4:25-37, 1987.

17. Meisels SJ: *Developmental screening in early childhood: the interaction of research and social policy.* In Breslow L, Fielding JE, Love LB, editors: *Annual review of public health,* vol 9, Palo Alto, Cal, 1988, Annual Reviews.

18Meisels S, Provence S: *Screening and assessment: guidelines for identifying young disabled and developmentally vulnerable children and their families,* Washington, DC, 1989, National Center for Clinical Infant Programs.

18. Nitko AJ: Problems in the development of criterion-referenced tests: the IPI experience, *Unpublished working paper,* University of Pittsburgh, 1975.

19. Pyfer JL: Criteria for placement in physical education experiences, *Except Educ Q* 3:10-16, 1982.

20. Pyfer JL: Sensory-perceptual-motor characteristics of learning disabled children: a validation study, *Unpublished paper,* Denton, Tex, 1983, Texas Woman's University.

21. Reichle J et al: *Curricula for the severely handicapped: components and evaluation criteria.* In Wilcox B, York R, editors: *Quality education for the severely handicapped,* Washington, DC, 1980, US Department of Education, Office of Special Education.

22. Salvia J, Yesseldyke JE: *Assessment in special and remedial education, ed 3,* Boston, 1984, Houghton Mifflin.

23. Snell M: *Systematic instruction of persons with moderate and severe handicaps,* Columbus, Ohio, 1987, Charles E Merrill Publishing.

24. Stott D, Henderson SE, Moyes FA: The Henderson revision of the test of motor impairment: a comprehensive approach to assessment, *Adapt Phys Educ Q* 3:204-216, 1986.

25. Tucker JA: Curriculum based assessment: an introduction, *Except Child* 52:199-204, 1985.

26. Werbel VJ: Reflex dysfunction, *Unpublished thesis,* University of Kansas, 1975.

27. Wessel J: *I CAN Skills,* Glenview, Ill, 1979, Hubbard Press.

28. Wilcox B, Bellamy T: *A comprehensive guide to the activities catalog: an alternative curriculum for youth and adults with severe disabilities,* Baltimore, 1987, Paul H Brookes Publishing.

SUGGESTED READINGS

Meisels S, Provence S: *Screening and assessment: guidelines for identifying young disabled and developmentally vulnerable children and their families,* Washington, DC, 1989, National Center for Clinical Infant Programs.

Snell M: *Systematic instruction of persons with severe handicaps,* Columbus, Ohio, 1987, Charles E Merrill Publishing.

Werder JK, Kalakian LH: Assessment in adapted physical education, Minneapolis, 1985, Burgess Publishers.

4

OBJECTIVES

Determine the unique physical education needs through domain- and criterion-referenced assessment procedures.

Determine present levels of physical education performance from task analyses.

Cite specific examples of clues to devlopmental delays.

Explain the difference between sensory input system and general ability delays.

Write an instructional objective and alter conditions and criteria to accommodate the present level of ability and plot progress of acquisition of higher ordered objectives.

Describe educational validity of physical education outcomes.

Prioritize and evaluate physical education goals.

The Camden, New Jersey, Post Courier, Courtesy National Amputee Golf Association

Programming to Meet Individual Needs

A statement often voiced by educators is that educational settings must be structured to meet the unique needs of the student. In the past such a phrase has represented a desire more than a reality; however, current diagnostic and instructional procedures have been so refined that unique educational needs can be met through precise measures. As a result of these improved techniques both school personnel and parents are able to determine whether a child is truly progressing through the specific tasks included in the individual education program (IEP).

A unique physical education need can be identified through evaluation of a student's performance. If there is a discrepancy between a child's performance level and a standard on a test, and if that discrepancy represents a delay in development, then it can be said that the child has a unique need. Needs may be expressed through skill requirements (shooting a basketball, serving a tennis ball, climbing stairs), through domains of abilities (strength, flexibility, hand-eye coordination), or by sensory input functions (vestibular, kinesthetic, visual). Progress on skills, abilities, and sensory input functions is evidence that unique needs are being met.

It should be pointed out that a need does not necessarily have to represent a deficit. Rather, it may be a skill that a child is interested in developing further. Very often when a skill is identified, continued participation in that skill enhances the individual's satisfaction. Physical skills can be developed further through participation in intramural and interscholastic competition and can provide opportunity for participation in the community.

In this chapter techniques for determining present levels of students' performances and ways to improve performance are discussed. Specific suggestions for programming to meet students' basic input systems, domains of abilities, and skill needs are presented.

DETERMINING UNIQUE NEEDS

The first step in determining a unique need is to identify the present level of educational performance. We identify present level of educational performance by testing. This crucial step requires skill in selecting the appropriate instrument and then understanding what the test measures.

Very often in physical education teachers select domain- or criterion-referenced tests because they are designed to differentiate between system inputs, abilities, and the skills measured by those instruments. That is, the test is designed to measure reflexes, physical fitness, perceptual-motor performance, coordination, or perhaps locomotor skills. These types of tests also describe how the student being tested compares with other children or a standard of performance; but that information might not be useful in preparing a program for the child. We are not implying that these tests are never helpful; but it is important to keep in mind that the information gained from such tests simply provides a profile of the student, which is limited to the input

systems, abilities, and skills measured by the test. What is needed in addition is information about the status of the components that make up or contribute to each task being tested. Until the functional level of the components that contribute to the ability or skill is known, we cannot determine what is causing the performance deficiency.

The entire process can be compared with that of starting a car's engine. We know that when we turn the ignition key, the criterion for success is that the engine start. If the engine does not start, we must determine what is preventing the performance of the engine and correct the condition before the car can be driven. Someone has to evaluate the components or parts that contribute to starting the engine (battery, spark plugs, wiring, starter, etc.). Once the faulty part is found and replaced or corrected, the engine should start. In the same way, when our students do not perform to expected standards, we must analyze the various components to determine which ones are faulty and then correct those components before the child is able to function at normal levels.

The procedures a teacher should follow to determine and meet unique needs of students are as follows:

1. Select a test that measures the skills and abilities you are interested in evaluating.
2. Administer the test.
3. Study the results to determine which skills and abilities are deficient.
4. Analyze each area found to be deficient to determine the components that contribute to the performance.
5. Once the underdeveloped components are identified, establish goals and objectives that are specific to these components.
6. Select activities that contribute to progress toward these goals and objectives.
7. Develop a teaching sequence that permits objective monitoring of progress.

Selecting an Evaluation Instrument

Several tests and what is measured by each are presented in Chapter 3. Review these tests before deciding which one to use. Keep in mind the age and comprehension level of your students as well as what areas you believe are important to evaluate. The greater the number of input systems, abilities, and skills measured by a test, the broader the student profile you are able to develop from the results. Teachers who select six- to ten-item tests because little time is required to administer such a test gain limited information about the capabilities of their students. At the other extreme, educators who spend much of their time administering a great number of tests may end up with a great overall profile of each child but have little time left for programming activities that will help the child develop. A balance between developing a useful profile and spending time administering the test must be found.

Administering the Test

Specific procedures for administering tests are discussed in Chapter 3. Some practical considerations to keep in mind include the following:

1. How a child performs a task often can be more informative than whether the child is successful with the movement. Watch for extraneous arm, trunk, or leg movements and unusual head positioning as the child performs.
2. Keep the testing conditions as comfortable as possible. Children perform better when the surroundings are free from distractions, the evaluator is relaxed and reinforcing, and the lighting and temperature are comfortable.
3. Test when a child is fresh. Midmorning and midafternoon are better times to test than early morning, just before lunch, or late in the day.
4. Keep the number of observers to a minimum. Children with disabilities are often hesitant about performing in front of peers or parents. When they are insecure about their ability to perform, they will try too hard or fail to give their best effort if people are watching them.
5. Repeat trials when you think the child might be able to perform adequately if given more time or is less tense. If a child is having difficulty with a given task, go on to easier tasks until he or she regains some confidence. Then go back to a task that was failed earlier.
6. Observe the child on different days if possible. Children are just like adults—they have their good days and their bad days. If the testing can be spread over 2 or 3 days, the child will have the opportunity to show different performance levels.
7. Gather information about what is going on in the child's life. Children who have just suffered a trauma, are excited about an upcoming event, or have been removed from their favorite activity for the testing session will not perform to their best levels.
8. Limit testing time to reasonable periods. Children will perform best for a period of 30 to 60 minutes. If the time is too brief, the child does not have time to get warmed up and into the procedure. If you go beyond 1 hour of testing time, fatigue and distractibility often interfere with performance.

A sensitive evaluator keeps the child's best interests in mind at all times. Focusing on the test rather than the child distorts test results and gives an inaccurate picture of the child's true capabilities.

Studying the Results for Deficit Areas

Once you have the test results in hand, it is important to analyze them as soon as possible. The shorter the time lapse between administering and interpreting the results, the easier it is to remember how the student performed individual tasks in the test. When interpreting the test results, usually any total or subtest score that falls beyond one standard deviation below the mean or below the 25th percentile or 1 year below the performance expected for the age of the child is considered a deficit area. But do not rely on those scores alone. Poor performance on individual tasks is a clue to deficit areas. If a child does well on push-ups but poorly on sit-ups, we cannot conclude that strength is adequate. Rather, we note that sit-up ability is a very definite unique need. Make a list of the test items performed below expectations for that age group.

Analyzing Deficit Areas

After determining areas or tasks that appear to be deficient, it is necessary to ascertain how far below the desired level of performance the child is functioning on each task. That is, it is necessary to determine what the present level of educational performance is on each task. Until it is known at what level the child is functioning, progress on activity programming cannot proceed. For a program to be effective, intervention must begin at the level at which the child is functioning and build up from there. Two distinct techniques for pinpointing students' present levels of educational performance are the "top, down" and "bottom, up" approaches. Task analysis is a top, down probing technique for determining the components that contribute to a task and whether they are present. The developmental approach is a bottom, up technique that attempts to determine whether basic sensory input systems and abilities that contribute to broad areas of performance are adequately functioning.

"Top, down" approach

There are several types of task analyses from which present levels of educational performance can be determined. Three types and their descriptions are listed in Table 4-1.

Content analysis of discrete tasks involves breaking the task down into the variety of parts that make up the task. For instance, to be able to execute a lay-up shot in basketball, the individual must be able to perform each of the following parts: (1) bounce a basketball with one hand, (2) bounce a basketball at waist height with one hand, (3) run while bouncing a basketball at waist height, (4) take a short step and jump ver-

---

TABLE 4-1

Task analyses and educational performance

Type of task analysis	Type of task	Examples
Content analysis of discrete tasks	Discrete tasks broken down into the many parts that make up the entire task	Feeding, dressing, lay-up shot in basketball, square dancing
Content analysis of continuous skills	Identifying errors in continuous patterns	Running, jumping, walking, throwing
Prerequisite task analysis	Prerequisite components that contribute to a motor behavior are identified	Any skill

---

tically off the foot opposite the shooting hand, (5) time the jump to occur just before the body reaches the area under the basket, (6) release the ball at the top of the jump, (7) direct the ball to a point on the backboard that will permit the ball to rebound from the backboard into the basket, and (8) control the body when coming down from the jump.

To determine which part of the task is contributing to the student's inability to perform the lay-up, the student should be observed executing the entire movement. When the deficient parts are found, the educator knows those parts must be corrected to improve the student's performance on the task.

Content analysis of continuous skills requires the ability to observe one pattern to determine if any mechanically inefficient movements are occurring. To be

---

Content Analysis of a Continuous Skill
Standing long jump

IMMATURE PATTERN	MATURE PATTERN

Preliminary crouch

IMMATURE PATTERN	MATURE PATTERN
1. Little crouch	1. Crouch with at least 90 degrees (hips and knees)
2. Trunk upright	2. Trunk parallel to ground
3. Arms: no backward swing prior to takeoff	3. Arms swing up as weight is shifted forward

Takeoff

IMMATURE PATTERN	MATURE PATTERN
4. Simultaneous extension of hips and knees	4. Successive extension of hips, knees, and ankles
5. Takeoff more than 45 degrees	5. Takeoff at 45 degrees
6. Uncoordinated swing of arms and legs	6. Arms in straight line with body at takeoff
7. Incomplete knee and hip extension	7. Flexion at hip and knees

Flight

IMMATURE PATTERN	MATURE PATTERN
8. Incomplete knee extension at end of flight	8. Knees extended at end of flight

Landing

IMMATURE PATTERN	MATURE PATTERN
9. Toes or balls of feet contact the ground before heel	9. Heels hit first
10 Incomplete spinal and hip flexion at moment of contact	10 Immediate giving in to gravity
11. Center of gravity too far back at moment of impact	11. Center of gravity enables recovery of body over base
12. Hands touch the ground	12. Arms reach forward and up to assist in maintaining balance

From Sherrill C: *Adapted physical education and recreation,* ed 3, Dubuque, Iowa. Copyright 1985 by William C. Brown Publishers.

able to analyze patterns, the teacher must be familiar with the ideal, or the mechanically efficient pattern. Once the mature pattern is firmly in mind, the teacher can observe the student executing the pattern and identify which components are being executed incorrectly. The box on p. 70 is an example of how content analysis can be used to determine mechanical insufficiencies.

Prerequisite task analysis is a process of probing into each of the underlying components that contribute to ability to perform a task and attempting to determine which of the prerequisites are lacking. An example of using prerequisite task analysis to determine which components contribute to stair climbing appears in the box below.

When probing for prerequisite deficiencies, whole tests, parts of tests, or single test items can be administered to determine which components are deficient. The box below includes specific suggestions of test observations that can be used to probe for prerequisite deficiencies.

Persons with severe disabilities are often nonambulatory, and locomotor skills such as running, hopping, galloping, leaping, and skipping are beyond their capabilities. For these individuals to gain greater independence, they must develop a means of locomotion that is within their capabilities. Since one cannot observe their locomotor pattern to determine their present level of performance, an alternative method of assessing their performance is required. An anatomical task analysis that evaluates prerequisities to the locomotor pattern is an appropriate alternative method of assessing their performance level.

An anatomical task analysis involves evaluating the function level of the joints and muscles that contribute to the pattern. If a person cannot walk, an anatomical analysis might include evaluation of the range of motion at the hip, knee, and ankle as well as strength and endurance of the muscles used to hold the body erect and move the legs. It is common for a child to have a deficient gait as a result of loss of range of motion in the ankle, knee, or hip.

If a child cannot perform any part of a movement pattern or skill with direct instruction, an attempt should be made to identify prerequisite deficiencies. If any such deficiencies are determined, activities should be selected to facilitate development in that specific area.

The continuous and task analyses procedures described thus far are "top, down" approaches for determining present levels of performance. Some educators, however, prefer a "bottom, up" or developmental approach for determining present levels of performance.

"Bottom, Up" approach

The bottom, up or developmental approach is a technique used to determine whether any basic deficiencies exist. The developmentalist will begin by examining sensory input systems (reflexes, vestibular function, ocular alignment and control, visual tracking, and kinesthetic functioning) and domains of abilities to determine level of functioning. If deficits are apparent at those levels, intervention strategies will be selected to facilitate development in those areas. Parts of tests can be used to construct a comprehensive bottom, up evaluation. The box on pp. 72-73 is an example of such an approach.

It is also possible to use a simple sensory input systems screening test to determine the presence of basic deficits. The test presented in Table 4-2 is an easy-to-administer bottom, up evaluation instrument.

It should be evident that using both a comprehensive evaluation and programming from the basic level up is time consuming. There is, however, evidence that this approach is effective in eventually eliminating skill deficiencies.

Regardless of whether a top, down task analysis or a bottom, up development evaluation is conducted, once specific deficits have been identified the teacher is ready to select goals and objectives and begin appropriate intervention.

ESTABLISHING GOALS AND OBJECTIVES
Long-range Goals

Once the physical educator has determined what the present level of educational performance is, long-range

---

Prerequisite Task Analysis
Stair climbing

Task components	Contributing prerequisites
Raise foot the height of the step (9 inches)	Balance, flexor strength in knee and hip
Place the foot on at least half the tread	Depth perception, kinesthetic perception, and spatial relations
Straighten the leg placed on the tread	Extensor strength in hip and knee
Raise the trailing leg so that advancing two steps is possible	Dynamic balance and bilateral coordination.

Comprehensive Test for Prerequisite Components

I. Basic level
  A. Reflex abnormalities: administer some or an entire battery of reflex tests (Fiorintino's Reflex Testing Methods for Evaluating CNS Development, Milani-Comparetti Developmental Chart; Barnes, Crutchfield, and Heriza's Reflex Evaluation; Bobath's Reflex Evaluation)
  B. Tactile deficiencies
    1. Localization of single points of stimulation to hands and cheeks compared with localization of double points of stimulation to hands, to cheeks, to hand and cheek on same side of the body and opposite sides of the body (Southern California Sensory Integration Tests)
    2. Aversion to being touched that is expressed verbally or physically
    3. Response to tactile praise
    4. Excessive signs of fidgeting or discomfort when seated
  C. Vestibular delays
    1. Postrotatory nystagmus test: nystagmus should be approximately half as long as the spinning time (Southern California Postrotatory Nystagmus Test)
    2. Compare ability to balance on one foot with eyes open and eyes closed (ability to balance with eyes open but not with eyes closed may indicate vestibular delay). (Bruininks-Oseretsky Test of Motor Proficiency and Southern California Sensory Integration Tests)
    3. Changing constancy board performance (deQuiros and Schrager)
    4. Caloric tests given by physicians
  D. Visual problems
    1. Refractive: Snellen chart
    2. Orthoptic (depth perception)
      a. Cover test: single and alternating
      b. Stereo Fly Test
      c. Convergence/divergence (Purdue Perceptual-Motor Survey)
      d. Biopter
      e. Figure-ground subtest score (Frostig Developmental Test of Visual Perception)
  E. Kinesthetic deficiencies
    1. Finger-to-nose test (Bruininks-Oseretsky Test of Motor Proficiency)
    2. Overflow while performing "angels in the snow" (Purdue Perceptual-Motor Survey)
    3. Imitation of movement (Purdue Perceptual-Motor Survey)
  F. Auditory deficiencies
    1. Directions need to be repeated
    2. Auditory distractibility
    3. Difficulty remembering directions or performing verbal commands in proper sequence
II. Domains of abilities
  A. Static balance delays
    1. Marked discrepancy between ability to balance on either foot
    2. Marked decrease in ability to balance as the base of support is narrowed (Bruininks-Oseretsky Test of Motor Proficiency)
  B. Dynamic balance problems
    1. Trouble with directional movements (forward, backward, sideways) on the low balance beam (Purdue Perceptual-Motor Survey)
    2. Inability to walk heel-to-toe (Bruininks-Oseretsky Test of Motor Proficiency)
  C. Body image delays
    1. Identification of body parts: note errors and/or hesitancy when locating body parts (Purdue Perceptual-Motor Survey)
    2. Self-drawing: note maturity of drawing for age, inclusion of detail for age, and any body parts omitted from the drawing (Goodenough-Harris)

D. Cross-lateral integration delays
   1. Any indication of midline jump when visually tracking (Purdue Perceptual-Motor Survey)
   2. Lack of arm/leg opposition when throwing (Bruininks-Oseretsky Test of Motor Proficiency)
   3. Difficulty coordinating tapping on opposite sides of the body (Bruininks-Oseretsky Test of Motor Proficiency)
   4. Difficulty isolating movements on opposite sides of the body while performing "angels in the snow" (Purdue Perceptual-Motor Survey)
   5. Avoidance of midline crossing during desk activities
E. Spatial awareness delays
   1. Difficulty walking backward (Bruininks-Oseretsky Test of Motor Proficiency and Purdue Perceptual-Motor Survey)
   2. Crowding letters together when printing words
   3. Drawing forms by connecting dots (Frostig Development Test of Visual Perception, Southern California Sensory Intergration Tests)
   4. Obstacle course: difficulty moving over, under, or through objects (Purdue Perceptual-Motor Survey)
   5. Position in space subtest score (Frostig Developmental Test of Visual Perception)
   6. Organization of drawn geometric forms (Purdue Perceptual-Motor Survey)
   7. Space visualization subtest (Southern California Sensory Integration Tests)
F. Form perception and constancy delays
   1. Accuracy when reproducing geometric forms (Purdue Perceptual-Motor Survey and Bruininks-Oseretsky Test of Motor Proficiency)
   2. Manual form perception (Southern California Sensory Integration Tests)
G. Strength insufficiencies
   1. Static (absolute) strength: a brief maximum contraction measured by a dynamometer or tensiometer
   2. Explosive: muscular contraction through range of motion measured by machines such as Cybex, Orthotron, long jump, or jump and reach
   3. Dynamic: repeated isotonic contractions usually measured by functional tests such as sit-ups or push-ups (total number possible with no time limit)
H. Endurance insufficiencies
   1. Muscular: ability to engage in repeated muscular contractions in a given period of time; usually any dynamic strength test (sit-ups or push-ups) that measures number of repetitions within a given period of time (Bruininks-Oseretsky Test of Motor Proficiency)
   2. Cardiovascular: an individual's capacity to use oxygen during physical activity, tested one of several ways
      a. Vital capacity (Vo_2 test)
      b. Compare resting and working heart rate (Harvard Step Test or bicycle ergometer)
      c. Distance covered in a set amount of time (9-minute run)
      d. Time needed to cover a set distance (300-yard, 600-yard, or mile run)
I. Flexibility: range of motion limitations
   1. Functional tests such as the sit and reach
   2. Goniometer
   3. Flexometer
J. Agility: inability to change direction in space, measured with functional tests such as obstacle run or shuttle run
K. Excessive body fat: caliper measurements
L. Speed: 30- or 50-yard dash

TABLE 4-2

Sensory input systems screening test

	Pass	Fail

Reflex test items—check pass or fail

1. Tonic labyrinthine supine—(TLS)
   While lying on back can bend knees to chest, wrap arms around knees, and touch head to knees. Child should be able to hold position for 10 seconds.
2. Tonic labrinthine prone—(TLP)
   While lying face down on mat with arms at side, child can lift head and upper body and hold off mat for 5 seconds.
3. Positive support reaction—(PSR)
   Child is able to jump into air and, upon landing, flex ankles, knees, and hips while maintaining balance for 5 seconds.
4. Equilibrium reactions
   When placed on a tilt board, child will move hands out to side and maintain balance for 3 seconds when the board is suddenly tipped 15 degrees to one side and then to other side (check each side independently).
   Check child in each of these positions:
   1. Seated, start with hands in lap—move right
   2. Seated, start with hands in lap—move left
   3. On two knees, start with hands on hips—move right
   4. On two knees, start with hands on hips—move left
   Place child on all fours on tilt board and tip board 15 degrees to one side and then to the other. Child can maintain "all fours" position while holding head in a neutral position.
   5. When tipped to right
   6. When tipped to left

Vestibular test items—check pass or fail

1. Seat child in a desk chair that can be rotated 360 degrees. Have child rest hands in lap or on arms of chair. Child should tip head down slightly (30 degrees). Turn chair 10 complete turns in 20 seconds (1 complete rotation every 2 seconds). Stop chair and watch child's eyes. Child's eye should flick back and forth for 7 to 13 seconds. After a 2-minute rest, repeat turning procedure in opposite direction. Check eye movement again.
   1. Turn to right
   2. Turn to left

Fixation (ocular control)—check pass or fail

1. Child should sit in a chair facing a seated evaluator. Child can fixate with both eyes on an object held 18 inches in front of the nose at eye level for 10 seconds.
2. Child should sit in a chair facing a seated evaluator. Cover child's left eye with your hand or a card. Child can fixate with right eye on an object held 18 inches in front of the nose at eye level for 10 seconds.
3. Child should sit in a chair facing a seated evaluator. Cover child's right eye with your hand or a card. Child can fixate with left eye on an object held 18 inches in front of the nose at eye level for 10 seconds.
   Note: Any tendency to turn the head to one side, blink excessively, or for the eyes to water could be an indication that the child needs to be referred to a visual developmental specialist for a refractive and orthoptic visual exam.

Ocular alignment (depth perception)—check pass or fail

Note: On all of the following items start with the child looking at the object with both eyes. Then cover one eye and begin your observation.
1. Child is seated in a chair facing a seated evaluator. Child can fixate on an object held 18 inches in front of the nose at eye level without moving right eye as left eye is covered for 3 seconds. (Note whether the right eye moves and in what direction.)
2. Child is seated in a chair facing a seated evaluator. Child can fixate on an object held 18 inches in front of the nose at eye level without moving left eye as right eye is covered for 3 seconds. (Note whether the left eye moves and in what direction.)

TABLE 4-2

Sensory input systems screening test

	Pass	Fail
Convergence-divergence ocular control—check pass or fail		
1. Child is seated in a chair facing a seated evaluator. Child can visually follow with both eyes an object moved slowly from 18 inches directly in front of the nose (eye level) to 4 inches from the eyes (midpoint) and back to 18 inches. (Note whether the eyes move equally without jerking.)		
Visual tracking—check pass or fail		
1. Child is seated in a chair facing a seated evaluator. Child can visually pursue with both eyes without moving the head an object held 18 inches from the eyes as the object is moved in the following patterns:		
a. A square (12-inch sides)		
b. A circle (8- to 10-inch diameter)		
c. An X (10-inch lines)		
d. A horizontal line (12 inches)		
2. Child is seated in a chair with left eye covered facing a seated evaluator. Child can visually pursue with the right eye without moving the head an object held 18 inches from the eyes as the object is moved in the following patterns:		
a. A square (12-inch sides)		
b. A circle (8- to 10-inch diameter)		
c. An X (10-inch lines)		
d. A horizontal line (12 inches)		
3. Child is seated in a chair with right eye covered facing a seated evaluator. Child can visually pursue with the left eye without moving the head an object held 18 inches from the eyes as the object is moved in the following patterns:		
a. A square (12-inch sides)		
b. A circle (8- to 10-inch diameter)		
c. An X (10-inch lines)		
d. A horizontal line (12 inches)		
Note: During all tracking tasks note any tendency for the eyes to (1) jump when the object moves across the midline of the body, (2) jump ahead of the object, (3) jerk while pursuing the object, (4) water, or (5) blink excessively. The watering and/or excessive blinking could be an indicator of visual stress, and such cases should be referred to a visual developmental specialist for a refractive and orthoptic visual exam.		
Kinesthesis—check pass or fail		
1. Can touch finger to nose three times in alternating succession with index fingers while eyes are closed. (Failure if the child misses the tip of the nose by more than 1 inch.)		

Courtesy of Jean L Pyfer, Texas Woman's University Denton, Texas, and Robert Strauss, Trinity University, San Antonio, Texas.

goals can be developed. Goals are specific target behaviors that the child should be able to demonstrate after instruction has been given. Goals are usually written annually because in most school systems the life of an IEP is 1 year.

Goals should be written in behavioral terms that are measurable and reflect an improvement over the present level of educational performance. For instance, if through testing it is determined that a 10-year-old child functions at the 7-year, 6-month level in relation to hand-eye coordination (as measured by a specific test), a reasonable annual goal could be: "Johnny will demonstrate hand-eye coordination (on the Jones test)

at the 9-year, 6-month level by May 15." If Mary scores at the 5th percentile in physical fitness as measured by the AAHPERD Health-Related Physical Fitness Test, an appropriate annual goal could read: "By May 15 Mary will score at the 15th percentile in all areas measured by the AAHPERD Health-Related Physical Fitness Test." This directs attention toward improvement on a test that may not directly relate to functional skills for self-sufficiency.

School personnel, parents, and (when appropriate) the student with a disability should agree on annual goals based on the evaluation at the beginning of the school year. Everyone is then clear about the behaviors of concern to the physical education teacher. It is not mandatory that the student reach each annual goal; however, goals are necessary before the steps leading to the goals (the short-term objectives) can be selected. That is, before we can decide how to get where we are going, we must know what our destination is.

Prioritizing Physical Education Instructional Goals

The mission of the physical education program for students with disabilities is to provide opportunities and experiences that develop skills that can be used to participate in independent recreational physical activity in community settings. However, there simply is not enough time to teach students with disabilities all of the functional skills they will need in the natural community recreational environment. Therefore goals need to be prioritized. Top priority should be given to motor behaviors that are particularly crucial to maximiz-

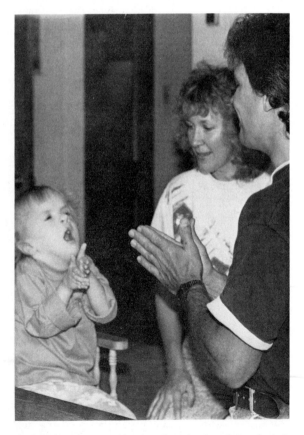

FIGURE 4-1. Parents stimulate learning in a home-based program.

ing participation in everyday physical activity as well as recreational environments.[10]

Short-term Objectives

The annual goal is a specific, predetermined learning experience that, if mastered, extends a child's present level of performance. There is an intricate balance between present level of performance, goals, and objectives. Because goals are specific to the needs of each handicapped student, any given individual can have a series of goals that represent different levels of performance in each of the curriculum areas.

Before selecting goals for a learner the teacher must determine at what level the student is performing. When a student demonstrates an inability to perform a specific behavior, the teacher must determine what prerequisites are needed for the individual to achieve mastery of the task. Until this question is fully answered, it is restated until the student's present level of performance is discovered. Then a reasonable long-range goal is stated. The short-term objectives follow; they represent increasingly difficult steps leading from present level of performance to each annual goal. It is necessary to keep detailed records on each learner to monitor where the child is performing in the learning sequence. The mastery of one objective is prerequisite to the next complex or more difficult objective.

In addition to the hierarchical linkage between the present level of performance, the annual goals, and each of the short-term objectives, the annual goals and short-term objectives must incorporate four concepts: (1) possess an action (what?), (2) establish conditions under which the action should occur (how?), (3) establish a criterion for mastery of a specific task (at what level?), and (4) lie outside the child's present level of educational performance.

The action concept

The action portion of the instructional objective indicates *what* the learner will do when performing the task. It is important that the action be stated in verb form, such as throw, strike, kick, sit up, or serve a volleyball.

Conditions

The conditions under which the action should occur describe *how* the learner is to perform at the task. It is important to be explicit. Changing the conditions makes a task easy or more difficult, inefficient or efficient, simple or more complex. Examples of conditions are: "With eyes closed and nonsupporting leg bent to 90 degrees, the student will . . ." "From a prone posi-

---

General Objective: Develop the Elbow Extensors and Arm Flexors With Push-up Activity

Specification of conditions	Rationale
1. Straighten back and hips to 180 degrees.	Bending either part of body reduces length of resistance arm and decreases degree of difficulty of task.
2. Place hands shoulder width apart on floor.	Spreading hands wider than shoulder width increases difficulty of task.
3. Tuck chin against sternum.	Raising head while performing tends to bend the back and shorten resistance arm.
4. Touch forehead to floor.	Touching forehead indicates starting and ending position of push-up.
5. Straighten arms to 180 degrees.	Straightening arms indicates degree of movement of arms (will count as one repetition).
6. Support weight on hyperextended toes, which rest on floor.	Supporting weight indicates the point of the fulcrum to control length of resistance arm.

---

tion the learner will . . ." "Keeping the back straight and arms at the side of the body the student will . . ."

Statements of conditions are particularly necessary to ensure appropriate *levels* of difficulty in developmental sequences that lead to long-range goals. If the conditions are not specified, it is impossible to determine what the true capability of a student is and what activities are needed to advance the developmental level. If the conditions are not precise, it is unclear how the student is to perform the task, and once again the *value* of the objective is lost. The conditions for performing a push-up and the rationales for specifying these conditions are presented in the box above.

Acceptable and Unacceptable Instructional Objectives

There are three essential features to sound instructional objectives: (1) there must be justification that the objectives are relevant to the learner; (2) objectives must possess the capability of being reproduced when implemented by independent instructors; and (3) there must be agreement on what is to be taught and when it has been mastered by the student. When behaviors are stated in the form of objectives, behavioral principles for facilitating learning can be applied (see Chapter 6). Examples of acceptable and unacceptable objectives are presented in Table 4-3.

The acceptable objectives include what, how, and at what level the behaviors are to be performed. The unacceptable objectives fail for several reasons, as discussed below:

1. Run as fast as you can. *Conditions:* The condi-

tion, distance, or environmental arrangements such as hurdles or nature of the course are not specified. *Criterion:* Neither an objective, measurable distance nor a specified time has been included in the objective. "As fast as you can" is subjective. The students may believe they are running as fast as they can, but the teacher may have a different opinion.

2. Walk on a balance beam without falling off. *Conditions:* The width of the balance beam, the position of the arms, and where the eyes are positioned make the task more or less difficult. None

---

TABLE 4-3

Acceptable and unacceptable objectives

Action	Condition	Criterion
Acceptable objectives		
Run	1 mile	In 5 minutes 30 seconds
Walk	On a balance beam 4 inches wide, heel to toe, eyes closed, and hands on hips	For 8 feet
Swim	Using the American crawl in a 25-yard pool for 50 yards	In 35 seconds
Unacceptable objectives		
Run		As fast as you can
Walk	On a balance beam	Without falling off
Swim		To the end of the pool

of these is specified. *Criterion:* The distance to be traveled or distance over time is not specified.

3. Swim to the end of the pool. *Conditions:* The type of stroke is not specified. *Criterion:* Swimming pools are different lengths. It is unclear what exact distance the student is to swim.

MEASURING TASK PERFORMANCE

Measurement is an integral part of instruction for children with disabilities. It enables adapted physical education teachers to secure information needed to make precise instructional decisions for skill development.

The criterion for mastery of a task is the standard at which the task should be performed. Being able to perform the task to criterion level indicates mastery of the task and hence pupil progress. Reaching a criterion serves notice that one prerequisite in a series has been mastered and that the student is ready to begin working toward the next step. Measures for task mastery can take several forms:

□ Number of repetitions (10 repetitions)
□ Number of repetitions over time (20 repetitions in 15 seconds)
□ Distance traveled (8 feet on a balance beam without stepping off)
□ Distance traveled over time (200 yards in 25 seconds)
□ Number of successive trials without a miss (4 times in a row)
□ Specified number of successful responses in a block of trials (3 out of 5)
□ Number of degrees of movement (flexibility in degrees of movement from starting to ending positions)
□ Mastery of all the stated conditions of the task

The intent of the instructional process is to add new behaviors to present levels of performance. Therefore instructional objectives are not valid unless they are directed toward the acquisition of behaviors beyond what a learner is capable of doing. That is why teachers assess each learner on a continuum of activities to determine present level of performance *before* instructional objectives are selected.

Measurement and Instruction

One of the best ways to determine whether an individual physical education program is effective is to gather progress data on a regular basis. It is relatively easy to determine whether instructional objectives are being met when records are kept of the number of trials required to learn each step as well as whether the learner passed or failed each trial. The Data Based

Gymnasium[5] is one program that includes numerous motor skill activities and tasks that are sequenced in such a way as to facilitate record keeping. Systematic data gathering is necessary to ensure the development of physical motor skills and sport activities as well as the development of cognitive aspects of rules and applications of strategies of games. A number of useful texts exist that explain how to observe, record, chart, and graph behavior.[8,18]

Wessel and Kelly[18] also support the data-based physical education process. These two authors have proposed an achievement-based curriculum (ABC) model for designing an entire physical education program that systematizes the concepts and steps necessary to implement individualized programs. They stress the importance of evaluation and the need for the individualized approach toward teaching physical education that meets the needs of *all* students including those with disabilities. This approach greatly facilitates the mainstreaming process. If instruction is individualized for all persons, then students with disabilities are easily included in the regular class. The model utilizes criterion-referenced testing for measuring present educational performance levels as well as individual progress. This system, like the Data Based Gymnasium program, enables physical educators to be accountable for what happens in the day-to-day class experiences of each person with a disability in their class.

SELECTING ACTIVITIES AND INSTRUCTIONAL STRATEGIES

Once a child's present level of performance has been determined and objectives have been selected and sequenced, the teacher can determine which instructional strategies to use. Physical educators have traditionally included exercises, individual stunts and tumbling, games, sports, rhythmic activities, and gymnastics in their curricula. Often these activities are selected according to teacher bias. More recently, particularly since the mandates of the Education of the Handicapped Act of 1975 (P.L. 94-142) became effective, greater care is being exercised by teachers in selecting activities to include in their programs. Activities should be selected on the basis of what they can contribute to the instructional objectives of the students.

Activities

Once the evaluation of the learner's needs has been carefully completed and the behavioral objectives clearly stated, the physical educator is ready to select activities that will enable the student to progress. The

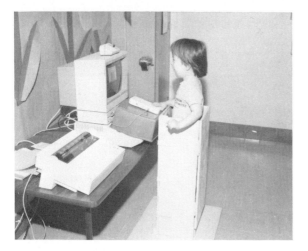

FIGURE 4-2. Assistive devices help a child use computer technology. (Courtesy of Dallas Independent School District.)

three most important factors to keep in mind when selecting activities are (1) appropriateness for the specific objectives, (2) adequate practice time to ensure that learning will occur, and (3) modification of the activity to make it increasingly more difficult.

The physical education activities selected depend on whether the teacher is using a bottom, up or top, down instructional strategy. When using the bottom, up approach, initial attention is focused on the basic input systems followed by domains of abilities.

The vestibular, visual, kinesthetic, tactile, reflex, and auditory systems are considered basic input systems because sensations arising from these systems' receptors provide the basic "stuff" from which perceptual-motor abilities and motor skills are built. These systems normally develop during the first 5 years of life. After they are functioning, perceptual-motor and motor skill development occurs. Should any one or a combination of these systems fail to fully develop, all motor development is delayed and/or interfered with in some way. For this reason, it is imperative to identify and remediate basic input system delays as early in life as possible. When it becomes too late to attempt to facilitate development of any of these systems is not really known; however, some writers suggest that if such delays are still present at age 12 years, the educators' time might better be spent teaching the child to accommodate to the delay.

Reflexes

Reflexes are innate responses that all normal children develop (Table 4-4). Reflexes that affect movement are

of interest to the physical educator because students whose reflex maturation is delayed have inefficient movement patterns. In general, there is a series of reflexes that should appear and disappear during the first year of life. These early (primitive) reflexes are layered over by (integrated into) voluntary movement patterns. As a child begins to experience movement, a different set of reflexes appears. These later automatic patterns are equilibrium reflexes. They help maintain upright posture.

A child would be considered developmentally delayed in reflex development if any of the following conditions existed:

1. The primitive reflexes do not appear during the first year of life.
2. The primitive reflexes appear at the normal time but do not disappear by the end of the first year.
3. The equilibrium reflexes do not appear by the end of the first year of life.
4. Equilibrium reflexes do not persist throughout life.

Primitive Reflexes

Tonic labyrinthine reflexes (supine and prone) help maintain trunk extension when the child is supine and help maintain trunk flexion when prone. If either of these reflexes does not become integrated, the following movement problems will be exhibited:

1. Supine
   a. Difficulty doing sit-ups
   b. A tendency to extend the trunk during the backward roll
   c. Rolling over on side when trying to rise from a back-lying position
2. Prone
   a. Difficulty doing a full push-up
   b. Inability to extend body fully when lying belly down on a scooter

These two reflexes are under control of the labyrinthine portion of the inner ear. To facilitate integration of these reflexes the physical educator should have the child perform activities that require lifting the head against the pull of gravity.

To promote integration of the tonic labyrinthine supine reflex the child should do activities such as the following, which require flexing the head and body from a back-lying position:

1. Hold knees to chest and rock back-and-forth several times
2. Egg rolls
3. V-sits
4. Partial sit-ups

TABLE 4-4

Primitive and equilibrium reflex development

Reflex	Age	Age inhibited	Effect on movement patterns
Primitive reflexes			
Flexor withdrawal	Birth	2 months	Uncontrolled flexion of leg when pressure is applied to sole of foot
Extensor thrust	Birth	2 months	Uncontrolled extension of leg when pressure is applied to sole of foot
Crossed extension 1	Birth	2 months	Uncontrolled extension of flexed leg when opposite leg is suddenly flexed
Crossed extension 2	Birth	2 months	Leg adducts and internally rotates, and foot plantar flexes when opposite leg is tapped medially at level of knee (scissor gait)
Asymmetrical tonic neck	Birth	4-6 months	Extension of arm and leg on face side or increase in extension tone; flexion of arm and leg on skull side or increase in flexor tone when head is turned
Symmetrical tonic neck 1	Birth	4-6 months	Arms flex or flexor tone dominates; legs extend or extensor tone dominates when head is ventroflexed while child is in quadruped position
Symmetrical tonic neck 2	Birth	4-6 months	Arms extend or extensor tone dominates; legs flex or flexor tone dominates when head is dorsiflexed while child is in quadruped position
Tonic labyrinthine, supine position	Birth	4 months	Extensor tone dominates when child is in supine position
Tonic labyrinthine, prone position	Birth	4 months	Flexor tone dominates in arms, hips, and legs when child is in prone position
Positive supporting reaction	Birth	4 months	Increase in extensor tone in legs when sudden pressure is applied to both feet simultaneously
Negative supporting reaction	Birth	4 months	Marked increased in flexor tone in legs when sudden pressure is applied to both feet simulataneously
Neck righting	Birth	6 months	Body rotated as a whole in the same direction the head is turned
Landau reflex	6 months	3 years	Spine, arms, and legs extend when head is dorsiflexed while child is held in supine position; spine, arms, and legs flex when head is ventroflexed while child is held in supine position

TABLE 4-4—cont'd

Primitive and equilibrium reflex development—cont'd

Reflex	Age	Age inhibited	Effect on movement patterns
Equilibrium reflexes			
Body righting	6 months	Throughout life	When child is in supine position and initiates full body roll, there is segmented rotation of the body (i.e., head turns, then shoulders, then pelvis)
Labyrinthine righting 1	2 months	Throughout life	When child is blindfolded and held in prone position, head raises to a point where child's face is vertical
Labyrinthine righting 2	6 months	Throughout life	When child is blindfolded and held in supine position, head raises to a point where face is vertical
Labyrinthine righting 3	6-8 months	Throughout life	When child is blindfolded and held in an upright position and is suddenly tilted right, head does not right itself to an upright position.
Labyrinthine righting 4	6-8 months	Throughout life	Same as labyrinthine righting 3, but child is tilted to left
Optical righting 1	2 months	Throughout life	Same as labyrinthine righting 1, but child is not blindfolded.
Optical righting 2	6 months	Throughout life	Same as labyrinthine righting 2, but child is not blindfolded
Optical righting 3	6-9 months	Throughout life	Same as labyrinthine righting 3, but child is not blindfolded
Optical righting 4	6-8 months	Throughout life	Same as labyrinthine righting 4, but child is not blindfolded
Amphibian reaction	6 months	Throughout life	While child is in prone position with legs extended and arms extended overhead, flexion of arm, hip, and knee on same side can be elicited when pelvis on that side is lifted
Protective extensor	6 months	Throughout life	While child is held by pelvis and is extended in air, arms extend when the child's head is moved suddenly toward the floor
Equilibrium-supine position	6 months	Throughout life	While child is supine on a tiltboard with arms and legs suspended, if the board is suddenly tilted to one side, there is righting of the head and thorax and abduction and extension of the arm and leg on the raised side

Continued.

TABLE 4-4

Primitive and equilibrium reflex development—cont'd

Reflex	Age	Age inhibited	Effect on movement patterns
Equilibrium reflexes—cont'd			
Equilibrium-prone position	6 months	Throughout life	Same as equilibrium-supine, except child is prone on tiltboard
Equilibrium-quadruped position	8 months	Throughout life	While child balances on all fours, if suddenly tilted to one side, righting of head and thorax and abduction extension of arm and leg occur on raised side
Equilibrium-sitting position	10-12 months	Throughout life	While child is seated on chair, if pulled or tilted to one side, righting of head and thorax and abduction-extension of arm and leg occur on raised side (side opposite pull)
Equilibrium-kneeling position	15 months	Throughout life	While child kneels on both knees, if suddenly pulled to one side, righting of the head and thorax and abduction-extension of the arm and leg occur on the raised side
Hopping 1	15-18 months	Throughout life	While child is standing upright, if moved to the left or right, head and thorax move right and child hops sideways to maintain balance
Hopping 2	15-18 months	Throughout life	While child is standing upright, if moved forward, head and thorax move right and child hops forward to maintain balance
Hopping 3	15-18 months	Throughout life	While child is standing upright, if moved backward, head and thorax move right and child hops backward to maintain balance
Dorsiflexion	15-18 months	Throughout life	While child is standing upright, if tilted backward, head and thorax move right and feet dorsiflex
See-saw	15 months	Throughout life	While child stands on one foot, another person holds arm and free foot on same side; when arm is pulled forward and laterally, head and thorax move right and held leg abducts and extends
Simian position	15-18 months	Throughout life	While child squats down, if tilted to one side, head and thorax move right and arm and leg on raised side abduct and extend

Data from Fiorentino MR: Reflex testing methods for evaluating CNS development, Springfield, Ill, 1970, Charles C Thomas Publishers.

To promote integration of the tonic labyrinthine prone reflex the physical educator should have the child do activities such as the following, which require extension of the head and body starting in a front-lying position:

1. Wing lifts
2. While lying prone on a scooter, roll down a ramp and toss a bean bag through a hula hoop extended overhead
3. Seal walk while looking at the ceiling
4. Rock back and forth on tummy while holding ankles with hands

The *positive support* reflex causes the legs to extend and the feet to plantar flex when the child is standing. Clues to its presence are apparent if there is an inability to bend the knees when attempting to jump or no "give" at the knees and hips on landing.

When the *negative support* reflex is present, there is flexion of the knees, hips, and ankles when pressure is removed from the feet. Inability to inhibit the expression of the reflex causes the following problems:

1. During vertical jumps, the legs will bend as soon as the weight is taken off the feet; hence, explosive power is lost
2. Inability to maintain extension of the legs while bouncing on a trampoline

Both of these reflexes are caused from pressure to the soles of the feet. A child may have either the positive or negative support reflex, but not both at the same time. To facilitate integration of these reflexes the physical educator should use activities that increase pressure on the soles of the feet, while the child controls the position of the legs.

To eliminate the positive support reaction the child should flex the lower limbs while applying pressure to the soles of the feet. The following activities are suggested:

1. Bounce on an air mat and suddenly stop by bending the knees
2. Play stoop tag
3. Bunny hop
4. Bounce on inner tubes and/or small trampolines (with the child's hands being held to reduce the chance of falling)

To eliminate the negative support reaction the child should extend the lower limbs while applying pressure to the soles of the feet. The following activities are suggested:

1. While lying prone on a gym scooter, use the feet to push off from the wall; keep legs extended as long as the scooter is moving across the floor
2. Bounce while sitting on a "hippity-hop" ball

3. Practice jumping up vertically and putting a mark on the wall
4. Bounce on an air mat and try to keep legs straight

Presence of the *asymmetrical tonic neck* reflex enables extension of the arm on the face side and flexion of the arm on the skull side when the head is turned. Positioning the arms in this fashion when the head is turned is often referred to as the *classic fencer's position.* Early in life it serves to direct the child's visual attention toward the extended hand. If it persists beyond the tenth month of life, it interferes with bringing the hands to the midline when the head is turned and thus prevents turning the head while creeping and throwing and catching a ball.

Activities that facilitate integration of this reflex include movements that require the child to turn the head toward his or her flexed limbs, such as:

1. Practice touching the chin to various parts of the body (e.g., shoulder, wrist, knee).
2. Balance on hands and knees while holding a bean bag between the chin and one shoulder. Then place the hand on the face side of the body on the hip.
3. Hold a bean bag between the chin and one shoulder. Crawl down the mat while keeping the object between the chin and shoulder.
4. Do a no-hands ball relay where the students have to hold a tennis ball between their chin and chest, and pass it to one another without using their hands or feet.

By means of the *symmetrical tonic neck* reflex, the upper limbs tend to flex and the lower limbs extend during ventroflexion of the head. If the head is dorsiflexed, the upper limbs extend and the lower limbs flex. If this reflex does not become fully integrated within the first year of life, the child will demonstrate the following:

1. Instead of using a cross pattern creep, the child will bunny hop both knees up to the hands.
2. If, while creeping, the child lowers the head, the arms will tend to collapse.
3. If, while creeping, the child lifts the head to look around, movement of the limbs ceases.

Activities that require the child to keep the arms extended while the head is flexed, and the arms flexed while the head is extended will promote integration of this reflex. Examples of such activities include the following:

1. While balancing on hands and knees, look down between the legs, then look up at the ceiling. Keep the arms extended and the legs flexed.

2. With extended arms push against a cage ball while looking down at the floor.
3. Practice doing standing push-ups against a wall while looking at the ceiling.
4. Do pull-ups (look up when pulling up, and look down when letting one's self down).

Equilibrium Reflexes

The *protective extensor thrust* causes immediate extension of the arms when the head and upper body are tipped suddenly forward. The purpose of the reflex is to protect the head and body during a fall. The reflex is used during handsprings and vaulting. If the reflex does not emerge, the child will tend to hit the head when falling.

To develop this reflex the child needs to practice extending the arms and taking the weight on the hands when the head and upper body are tipped toward the floor. The following activities represent ways to accomplish this:

1. While the child is lying prone on a cage ball, roll the ball slowly so that the head, shoulders, and arms are lowered toward the floor. Roll the ball far enough so that the child's weight gradually comes to rest on his or her hands.
2. Practice handstands while someone holds the child's feet in the air.
3. Practice mule kicks.
4. Wheelbarrow with a partner holding the child's knees.

Presence of the *body righting* reflex enables segmental rotation of the trunk and hips when the head is turned. As a result of this segmental turning children can maintain good postural alignment and maintenance of body positions. Without it, for example, when doing a log roll, the child will tend to turn the knees, then the hips, and then the shoulders.

To promote development of the body righting reflex, the child should practice turning the head first, then the shoulders, followed by the hips. The child should start slowly and then increase the speed both from a standing position and back-lying position.

Labyrinthine and *optical righting reactions* cause the head to move to an upright position when the body is suddenly tipped. Once the head rights itself, the body follows. Thus these reflexes help us maintain an upright posture during a quick change of position. Without these reflexes the child will fall down often during running and dodging games and even tends to avoid vigorous running games.

The labyrinthine reflexes are under control of the inner ear, whereas the optical righting reactions are

FIGURE 4-3. A child with multiple disabilities learns to move on a scooter. (Courtesy of Dallas Independent School District.)

primarily controlled by the eyes. Labyrinthine reflexes are facilitated when the head is moved in opposition to gravity. Any activity requiring the child to move the head in opposition to the pull of gravity will promote development of this reflex (see tonic labyrinthine prone and supine activities). Clinical observation indicates poorly developed optical righting reactions most frequently accompany orthoptic visual problems (poor depth perception). Once the depth perception problem is corrected, the optical righting reactions begin to appear.

Like the labyrinthine and righting reactions, the other equilibrium reactions help us maintain an upright position when the center of gravity is suddenly moved beyond the base of support. If the equilibrium reactions are not fully developed, children fall down often, fall off chairs, and avoid vigorous running games.

Almost all of these types of equilibrium reactions are the result of stimulation of muscle spindles and/or the golgi tendon apparatus. Both muscle spindle and golgi tendon apparatus reactions result from sudden stretch (or contraction) of the muscles and tendons. To promote these equilibrium reactions, the child should participate in activities such as the following, which place sudden stretch (or contracture) on the muscles and tendons.

1. Bouncing on an air mat while lying down, balancing on all fours, or balancing on the knees
2. Tug of war
3. Crack the whip
4. Wrestling
5. Scooter activities with a partner pulling or pushing the child who is seated on the scooter

Vestibular System

The vestibular receiving mechanism is located in the inner ear. As the body moves, sensory impulses from the vestibular system are sent to the cerebellum and to the brainstem. From these two areas, information about the position of the head is sent to the extraocular muscles of the eye, to the somatosensory strip in the cerebral cortex, to the stomach, to the cerebellum, and down the spinal cord. Accurate information from this mechanism is needed to help position the eyes and to maintain static and dynamic balance. When maturation of the system is delayed, students may demonstrate the following problems:

1. Inability to balance on one foot (particularly with the eyes closed)
2. Inability to walk a balance beam without watching the feet
3. Inability to walk heel to toe
4. Inefficient walking and running patterns
5. Delays in ability to hop and to skip

Children who demonstrate the clues listed above and who fail to demonstrate nystagmus after spinning are believed to have vestibular development delays and are in need of activities to facilitate development. *Concentrated activities to remediate balance problems that result from poor vestibular function should be administered by someone trained in observing the responses of such a child.* However, some activities can be done in fun, nonthreatening ways in a physical education class or on a playground with the supervision of parents or teachers.

Caution: Anyone who uses vestibular stimulation activities with children should observe closely for signs of sweating, paleness, flushing of the face, nausea, and loss of consciousness. These are all indications that the activities should be stopped immediately. Also, spinning activities should not be used with seizure-prone children. Avoid rapid spinning activities.

The following vestibular stimulation activities should be nonthreatening to most children:

1. Log roll on a mat.
2. Spin self while prone on a gym scooter by crossing hand-over-hand, stop and change direction.
3. Lie on a blanket and roll self up and then unroll.
4. Let the child spin himself or herself on a scooter, play on spinning playground equipment, go down a ramp prone on a gym scooter, or other such nonthreatening activities that give the child an opportunity to respond to changes of his or her position in space (movement or spinning should not be so fast as to be disorienting or disorganizing).

Visual System

Both refractive and orthoptic vision are important for efficient motor performance. Refractive vision is the process by which the light rays are bent as they enter the eyes. When light rays are bent precisely, vision is sharpest and clearest. Individuals who have poor refractive vision are said to be nearsighted (myopic) or farsighted (hyperopic) or have astigmatism. The following problems are demonstrated by children with refractive visual problems:

1. Tendency to squint
2. Tendency to rub the eyes frequently
3. Redness of the eyes

Orthoptic vision refers to the ability to use the extraocular muscles of the eyes in unison. When the extraocular muscles are balanced, images entering each eye strike each retina at precisely the same point so that the images transmitted to the visual center of the brain match. The closer the match of the images from the eye, the better the depth perception. The greater the discrepancy between the two images that reach the visual center, the poorer the depth perception. Clues to orthoptic problems (poor depth perception) follow:

1. Turning the head when catching a ball
2. Inability to catch a ball or a tendency to scoop the ball into the arms
3. Tendency to kick a ball off center or miss it entirely
4. Persisting to ascend and descend stairs one at a time
5. Avoidance of climbing apparatus

The physical educator is not trained to test for or correct refractive and orthoptic visual problems. However, a simple screening test that can be used to determine whether the possibility of a serious orthoptic (depth perception) problem exists is described in the screening test for developmental delays (see Table 4-2). Individuals who fail the ocular alignment portion of the screening test should be professionally evaluated by a behavioral visual specialist (optometrist or ophthalmologist who has specialized training in orthoptics). Students suspected of having refractive vision problems should be evaluated by either an optometrist or ophthalmologist.

Kinesthetic System

The kinesthetic receptors are specialized proprioceptors located in the joints, muscles, and tendons throughout the body. Information from the kinesthetic receptors informs the central nervous system about the position of the limbs in space. As these joint receptors fire, sensory impulses are sent to the brain and are recorded as spatial maps. As the kinesthetic system becomes more developed, judgment about the rate, amount, and amplitude of motion needed to perform a task improves. Refined movement is not possible without kinesthetic awareness. Possible signs of developmental delays of the kinesthetic system are

1. Inability to move a body part on command without assistance
2. No awareness of the position of body parts in space
3. Messy handwriting
4. Poor skill in sports that require a "touch," such as putting a golf ball, basketball shooting, and bowling

Activities to promote kinesthetic function include any activity that increases tension on the joints, muscles, and tendons. Selected activities that have proven useful in promoting kinesthetic function are:

1. Games involving pushing (or kicking) a large cage ball
2. Lying prone on a scooter, holding onto a rope, and being pulled by a partner
3. Using the hands and feet to propel one's self while seated on a gym scooter
4. Doing any type of activity while wearing wrist and/or ankle weights

Tactile System

The tactile receptors are located throughout the body and respond to stimulation of body surfaces. Some of the receptors lie close to the surface of the body; others are located more deeply. A well-functioning tactile system is needed for an individual to know where the body ends and space begins, and to be able to tactually discriminate between pressure, texture, and size. Children who are tactile defensive are believed to have difficulty processing sensory input from tactile receptors. Behaviors demonstrated by the tactile-defensive child include:

1. Low tolerance for touch (unless the person doing the touching is in the visual field of the student)
2. Avoidance of activities requiring prolonged touch, such as wrestling or hugging
3. Avoidance of toweling down after a shower or bath unless it is done in a vigorous fashion
4. Tendency to curl fingers and toes when creeping

Activities believed to stimulate the tactile system and promote sensory input processing should begin with coarse textures and progress (over time) toward finer texture stimulation. A sequence of such activities follows:

1. Present the child with a variety of different textured articles (nets, pot scrubbers, bath brushes). Have the child select an article and rub it on his or her face, arms, and legs. (Tactile-defensive children will usually select the coarsest textures to use for this activity.)
2. Using an old badminton net, play "capture me" while crawling around on a mat. The teacher should toss the net over the child as the child tries to crawl from one end of the mat to the other. When the child has been captured, rub the net over exposed parts of the body as the child struggles to escape. Repeat the activity with the child chasing and capturing the teacher.
3. Construct an obstacle course with several stations where the child must go through hanging textures (strips of inner tube, sections of rope) and/or squeeze through tight places.
4. Using a movement exploration teaching approach, have the students find various textures in the gym to rub a point or patch against (i.e., rough, smooth, wavy).

DOMAINS OF MOTOR ABILITIES

Abilities emerge after sensory input systems begin to stabilize, usually during the fifth through the seventh years of life. Development of these abilities requires not only intact information from the sensory input systems, but also the capacity to integrate those signals in the brain. When all sensory input systems are functioning and cortical reception and association areas are intact, domains of abilities and motor skills emerge and generalize with practice. Weakened, distorted, or absent signals from the sensory input systems will detract from the development of abilities as well as all other motor performance. This is not to say that specific abilities and motor performance cannot be taught in the absence of intact sensory information. Specific functions can be taught, but only as splinter skills. A *splinter skill* is a particular perceptual or motor act that is performed in isolation and does not generalize to other areas of performance. If hard neurological damage or age of the learner prevent development of the sensory input systems, it becomes necessary to teach splinter skills. In such cases the top, down approach (task analysis) is recommended. If however, it is believed that sensory input systems are fully functioning and cortical integration is possible, practice in the following activities should promote development of a wide variety of perceptual-motor abilities from which motor skills can emerge.

Balance

Balance is the ability to maintain equilibrium in a held position (static) or moving positions (dynamic). Balance ability is critical to almost every motor function. Some literature suggests that until balance becomes an automatic, involuntary act, the central nervous system must focus on maintaining balance to the detriment of all other motor and cognitive functions.[11,15] Balance development is dependent on vestibular, visual, reflex, and kinesthetic development. When these systems are fully functioning, high levels of balance development are possible. Clues to poor balance development include:

1. Inability to maintain held balance positions (e.g., stand on one foot, stand heel to toe) with eyes open
2. Inability to walk heel to toe on a line or on a balance beam
3. Tripping or falling easily
4. Wide gait while walking or running

Activities that can be used to promote static balance include:

1. Freeze tag—play tag; the child who is caught is "frozen" until a classmate "unfreezes" by tagging the child; "It" tries to freeze everyone.
2. Statues—each child spins around and then tries to make himself or herself into a "statue" without falling first.
3. Tripod—child balances by placing forehead and both hands on the floor; knees balance on elbows to form tripod balance.
4. Child balances bean bags on different parts of the body while performing balancing positions.

Activities that can be used to promote dynamic balance include:

1. Hopscotch
2. Various types of locomotor movements following patterns on the floor
3. Races using different types of locomotor movements
4. Walk forward heel to toe between double lines, on a single line, and then on a balance beam; make this more demanding by having the child balance a bean bag on different body parts (e.g., head, shoulder, elbow, wrist) while walking the balance beam

Laterality

Laterality is an awareness of the difference between the two sides of the body. Children who have not developed laterality often demonstrate balance problems on one or both sides. Delays in the development of laterality may be indicated by the following types of behavior:

1. Avoiding use of one side of the body
2. Walking sideways in one direction better than the other
3. Using one extremity more often than the other
4. Lacking a fully established hand preference

Laterality is believed to develop from intact kinesthetic and vestibular sensory inputs. If these two input systems are believed to be adequately functioning, then a child will benefit from activities that require differentiation between the two sides of the body. Examples include the following:

1. Wear ankle and/or wrist weights on the weak (unused) side of the body while climbing on apparatus, moving through obstacle courses, and kicking, bouncing, throwing, or catching a ball.
2. Walk a balance beam while carrying objects that weigh different amounts in each hand (i.e., carry a small bucket in each hand, with different numbers of bean bags in each bucket).
3. Push a cage ball with one hand only.
4. Use only one hand in tug of war.

Spatial Relations

Spatial relations concerns the ability to perceive the position of objects in space, particularly as they relate to the position of the body. Development of spatial relations is believed to depend on vestibular, kinesthetic, and visual development. Problems may be indicated by:

1. Inability to move under objects without hitting them or ducking way below the object

2. Consistently swinging a bat too high or low when attempting to hit a pitched ball
3. Inability to maintain an appropriate body position in relation to moving objects
4. Inability to position the hands accurately to catch a ball

If it has been determined that none of the prerequisite input systems are delayed, spatial relations can be facilitated by practice in the following activities:

1. Set up an obstacle course with stations that require the child to crawl over, under, and through various obstacles.
2. Place a 10-foot taped line on the floor. Give the child a bean bag and ask him or her to place the bean bag halfway down the line. If the child makes an error, ask him or her to walk from one end of the line to the other, counting the number of steps. Then have the child divide the number of steps in half, walk that far, and place the bean bag down at that point. The child should then stand to the side of the line and look from one end of the line to the bean bag. Continue practicing until the child is successful at estimating where, on several different lengths of line, the midpoint is.
3. Repeat Activity #2 with the child wearing ankle weights.
4. Place several chairs around the room with varying distances between them. Ask the child to point to the two chairs that are closest together, furthest apart, or a given distance from one another (i.e., 3 feet, 10 feet, 6 feet). If the child makes an error on any task, have him or her walk the distance between the chairs and/or measure the distance with a measuring tape.

Ocular-Motor Control

Ocular-motor control includes the ability to fixate on and to visually track moving objects as well as the ability to match visual input with appropriate motor response. Observed deficiencies might include:

1. Failure to visually locate an object in space

FIGURE 4-4. A child must have spatial relationship abilities to fit the body through the circular tunnel.

2. Failure to visually track a softball when attempting to hit it
3. Failure to visually track a fly ball or ground ball
4. Failure to keep a place when reading
5. Difficulty using scissors or tying shoelaces
6. Poor foot-eye coordination
7. Messy handwriting

Ocular control can be improved with practice if a child does not have serious orthoptic (depth perception) problems. If an individual does have depth perception problems, participation in ocular control activities can worsen their visual difficulties. Once it is ascertained that no depth perception problems exist, the following activities can be used to promote ocular control of the eyes:

Fixation

1. Child sits and rocks back and forth while keeping his or her eyes on a tape on the wall directly in front of him or her.
2. Child lies on back with eyes fixated on a point on the ceiling. Child then stands up (or does a series of stunts) while continuing to fixate on the spot.
3. Child is in a standing position fixating on a designated point on the wall. Child then jumps and turns 180 degrees and fixates on a designated point on the opposite wall.
4. Child is in a standing position fixating on a designated point on the wall. Child then jumps and turns completely around (360 degrees) and again fixates on the original point.

Convergence/divergence

1. Draw two X's on the chalkboard (at shoulder height of child) approximately 36 inches apart. Have the child stand centered about 2 inches in front of the board and move his or her eyes back and forth between the two X's.
2. Have the child sit at a table and look from an object on the table to an object on the wall directly ahead; continue back and forth 10 times. The table should be about 15 inches from the wall.
3. The child sits with arms extended and thumbs up, looking back and forth from one thumb to the other.
4. The child sits with one arm extended and the other flexed so that the hand is about 6 inches from the nose with thumbs up. Have the child look back and forth from one thumb to the other 10 times.

Visual tracking

1. The child lies on his or her back. Have the child visually track lines, pipes, or lights on the ceiling, without moving the head.
2. The child lies on his or her back. Attach a small ball to a string and swing the ball horizontally above the child's head. The child should track the swinging ball with his or her eyes and then point to it as it swings. (The ball should be suspended approximately 16 inches above the child's head.)
3. The child throws a ball up in the air and follows the path of the ball with his or her eyes until it hits the floor. Repeat several times, and encourage the child not to move his or her head while tracking the ball.
4. The child either sits or lies on his or her back, then hits a suspended ball with the hand and visually tracks the movement of the ball.

Cross-Lateral Integration

Cross-lateral integration is the ability to coordinate use of both sides of the body. It normally follows the development of balance and laterality. A child who has not developed cross-lateral integration by age 8 years is said to have a *midline problem* because there is difficulty using the hands efficiently at and across the center of the body. Teachers will note the following problems demonstrated by a child with a midline problem:

1. Difficulty using both hands to catch a ball
2. Tendency of eyes to jump when trying to visually track an object that is moving from one side of the body to the other
3. Inability to master a front crawl stroke with breathing while trying to swim
4. Inability to hop rhythmically from one foot to the other
5. Tendency to move the paper to one side of the body when doing paper and pencil tasks

Activities that will promote cross-lateral integration are as follows:

1. The child crawls down a rope or line on the floor, crossing hands back and forth over the line (rope) going forward, then crossing feet back and forth while crawling backward.
2. The child picks up objects (from right side of body) with the right hand and places them in a container on the left side of the body. This should be repeated using the left hand. Pick up one object at a time.
3. The child plays pat-a-cake.

FIGURE 4-5. Activities that contribute to the development of visual systems.

4. The child practices swimming the front crawl with breathing.

Body Awareness

Body awareness is a broad term that includes how a person pictures his body, his attitude toward his body, and his knowledge of personal bodily capabilities and limitations. Body awareness develops from all sensory input system information as well as from a person's experiences with his body. Indications of a poorly developed body awareness are:

1. Lack of knowledge of where body parts are located
2. Distorted drawings of self
3. Lack of knowledge about what specific body parts are for
4. Poor motor planning

Activities that can be used to facilitate a child's body awareness include:

1. Give verbal commands to the child (e.g., touch your knees, touch your ankles, touch your ears, touch your shoulders, etc.).

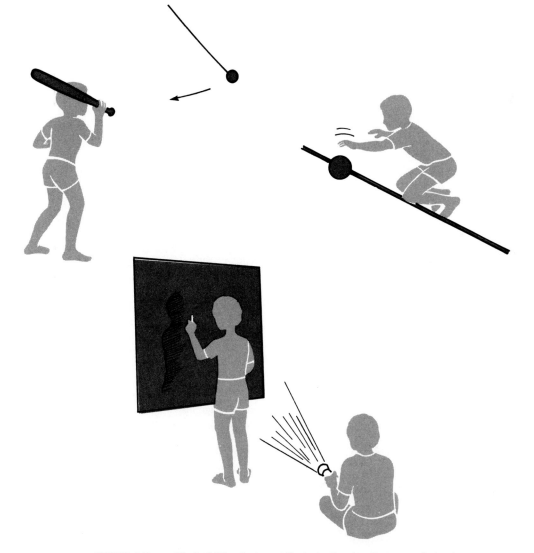

FIGURE 4-5, cont'd. Activities that contribute to the development of visual systems.

2. Have the child stand with eyes closed. The teacher touches various body parts, and the child identifies them. Then have the child touch the same part that the teacher touches and name the part.

3. Trace an outline of the child's body on a large piece of paper or with chalk on the floor. Then have the child get up and fill in the details (e.g., facial features, clothes, shoes). Perhaps make an "own self" body puzzle. After the child is finished drawing, laminate the body shape; cut it into pieces for the child to reassemble.

   a. Have the child name all the body parts.
   b. Leave out a part and see if the child notices it.
   c. Have the child trace around the teacher and name all the body parts.
   d. Have the child trace certain body parts on the drawing with different colors (e.g., yellow for feet, blue for arms, etc.).

4. Draw an incomplete picture of a person on the chalkboard and have the child fill in the missing parts.

SKILLS

Skills are motor acts that are necessary to perform a specific activity. Skills are categorized as functional or sport specific. Functional skills include locomotor patterns such as crawling, creeping, walking, running, jumping, hopping, sliding, and skipping. Sport skills include kicking a soccer ball or a football, shooting a basketball, serving a volleyball, and ice skating. As explained earlier in this chapter, content, prerequisite, and/or anatomical task analyses are conducted to determine which parts of a skill are lacking. Once the missing components are determined, skills are developed by directly teaching these components and by practicing the actual movement under a variety of conditions.

An example of using a content analysis of discrete taks to execute a lay-up shot in basketball was presented earlier in this chapter (see p. 69). After watching the student attempt the lay-up shot, the physical educator determines which components are contributing to the student's inability to successfully perform the task. If, for example, the student is performing all parts of the task correctly except timing the jump to occur just before the body reaches the area under the basket and directing the ball to the correct point on the backboard, those are the two components that require attention.

To correct the jump timing problem, it might be necessary to mark an area on the floor where the jump should be executed for a right hand lay-up. The student would practice approaching the mark and landing on it consistently with the left foot. When that movement becomes habitual, the student would practice the approach and add a jump off the left foot when reaching the mark on the floor. Then to direct the student's attention to the correct place to rebound the ball, an area could be marked on the backboard. The student then practices the correct approach, jump, and striking the outlined area on the backboard with the ball in one continuous motion. Minor adjustments may need to be added to modify the amount of force the student uses when releasing the ball.

Additional examples of teaching skill components are routinely included in regular physical education, motor learning, kinesiology, and techniques texts and curricula.

Instructional Strategies

Instructional strategies are the ways to arrange an educational environment so that maximum learning will take place. Factors that affect the type of instructional strategy selected include levels of performance demonstrated by individual students in the class, age of the learners, comprehension levels of the students, class size, and number of people available to assist the teacher. An instructional strategy that meets the needs of a wide range of learners and can be delivered by a limited number of personnel is more valuable for ensuring that individual needs are met than is a strategy that presumes homogeneous grouping. For learners with disabilities who have heterogeneous needs an instructional strategy that promotes individualized learning is not only desirable, but absolutely necessary.

Individualization of instruction can be realized through the use of programmed instruction. The major goals of programmed instruction are to promote students' abilities to direct their own learning and to develop a communication system between the student and teacher that enables them to become independent of each other. The teacher's primary goals are to guide and manage instruction according to the student's individual needs and learning characteristics. The programmed instruction approach enables a teacher to cope with heterogeneous groups of children and to accommodate large numbers of children in the same class without sacrificing instructional efficiency.

To implement such a program, however, three major factors must be taken into consideration: (1) programming must be constructed on the basis of scientific principles[1]; (2) learners must be trained in specific behaviors[9]; and (3) learning principles must be applied through the use of programmed curricula.

The most expeditious way to manage an average size class in a public school, using the individualized approach, is by means of instructional objectives that shift learning conditions to create task sequences. Prearranged instructional objectives take the form of self-instructional and self-evaluative programs appropriate for typical and atypical children. However, for the child who cannot self-instruct and self-evaluate, the teacher must assume the responsibility for directing instruction and monitoring progress. Task analysis and pattern analysis will facilitate development. A child functioning at a low level, like a child who strives to reach upper limits of development for competitive purposes, needs special types of programming and thus specific attention by instructors when the teacher-student ratio is low. Self-instructional and self-evaluative materials composed of prearranged objectives help students develop skills at their own rates.

Component Model of Functional Physical and Sport Activity Routines: An Assessment and Programming Strategy

Frequently persons with disabilities learn specific parts of sport skills (splinter skills) but do not possess the capability to put the parts together in a routine that enables them to participate in a recreational activity. Budoff[4] describes an integrated softball league in which many of the mentally retarded individuals had learned some of the softball skills; however, few had ever played the actual game. The players had to be taught how to use their skills in a game situation. Before participants can be taught to use their skills in a functional activity, a decision must be made about what must be learned to enable participation. One way to determine the skills necessary to perform in functional activity in the community (i.e., what individuals with disabilities need to learn to enable them to participate in community physical activities) is to use the component model of functional routines.[16] This model breaks down a person's daily sport and other physical activity into a series of routines that are composed of several skills. Each routine is comprised of a skill sequence that begins with natural cues needed in a playing environment and ends with the achievement of the specific sport behavior in a functional setting.[14] The focus of the physical play routines is the broad competencies needed to function in natural physical and sport environments in the community. Unlike the traditional ecological approach, the component model systematically divides sport and physical routines into structured subsets of physical skills and cues needed. Once these compo-

nents are identified, they can be assessed and programmed.

Generalization to community environments

Time spent teaching skills in physical education training settings is wasted if the individual with disabilities cannot demonstrate competency in sport settings other than the schools and in the presence of persons other than the original teachers.[2] To ensure that generalization to community environments and activities does occur, simulated training conditions need to be developed. Although there are few studies in physical education that have examined generalization of motor skill and sport performance from instructional to community environments, Budoff[4] indicates positive results of softball training of mentally retarded persons in integrated community environments. On the other hand, the review of literature on simulated settings versus training in the applied settings on non-physical education tasks is mixed. Browder, Snell, and Ambrogio[3] report successful generalization from simulated settings using vending machines while Marchetti et al.[13] found that training an individual in pedestrian skills was significantly more effective when done in the community rather than in a simulated training environment. The more severe the handicap, the more difficult it seems to be to generalize trained skills across environments.[17] It is critical that instruction not cease until the individual uses the new skills spontaneously and correctly in the community.

Principles of programmed instruction

An adapted list of characteristics for programmed instruction has been suggested by Lindvall and Bolvin[12]:

1. Definition of the objectives the students are expected to achieve must be clear and specific.
2. Objectives must be stated in behavioral terms.
3. Objectives must lead to behaviors that are carefully analyzed and sequenced in a hierarchical order so that each behavior builds on the objectives immediately preceding and is prerequisite to those which follow.
4. Instructional content of a program must consist of a sequence of learning tasks through which a student can proceed with little outside help and must provide a series of small increments in learning that enable the student to proceed from a condition of lack of command of behavior to a condition of command of behavior.
5. A program must permit the student to begin at the present ability level and allow him or her to move upward from that point.
6. A program must allow each student to proceed inde-

pendently of other students and learn at a rate best suited to his or her own abilities and interests.

7. A program must require active involvement and response on the part of the student at each step along the learning sequence.
8. A program must provide immediate feedback to the student concerning the adequacy of his or her performance.
9. A program must be subjected to continuous study by those responsible for it and should be regularly modified in light of available evidence concerning the student's performance.
10. A program must accommodate the ability range of many students, thus enabling continuous progress.

These principles can be applied when a hierarchical behavioral program is designed for each child. When using a hierarchical teaching sequence, a single task is broken down into small steps that are then arranged in order of difficulty. Pupils enter the sequence at their present level of performance and then advance at their own rate through the sequence. This sequencing of steps can be used for basic input systems abilities and skills. As children master one level of performance, they move on to the next. It is essential that the steps be arranged in a hierarchy or it will not be possible for the students to progress from simple to more difficult levels of performance.

Progressively more difficult performance standards are built into the program by shifting either the conditions under which the task must be performed or the criteria for success. Condition shifting alters the conditions surrounding performance of the task. For example, in bowling, conditions such as the performer's distance from the pins, the distance apart that the pins are set, and the size of the ball can be changed to make the task more or less difficult. Criterion shifting alters the level of acceptable performance by increasing the number of repetitions, the distance traveled, the speed, or the range of motion needed to accomplish the task. Examples of shifting criterion measures are building strength by increasing the number of repetitions or amount of weight lifted, building cardiovascular endurance by increasing the distance run, and building flexibility by increasing the range of motion at a specific joint.

Once the teacher has decided whether to use a criterion- or condition-shifting program (or a combination of both), the teaching sequence should be decided on. There are several different strategies for developing standard teaching sequences. A standard procedure often used is as follows:

1. Select a behavior that needs to be developed (identify a long-range goal).
2. Identify a way to measure the behavior objectively.
3. Select the conditions or criteria that will be used to make the task more difficult.
4. Write your short-term objectives.
5. Arrange the short-term objectives in a hierarchy from simple to difficult.
6. Identify the materials or equipment that will be needed in the teaching sequence.

Examples of two teaching sequences—one using a shifting criterion and one using a shifting condition—are found in Fig. 4-6. These examples focus on specific skills. The same type of teaching sequence can be developed for basic levels and for abilities. When programming to develop basic levels, such as vestibular function, activities believed to facilitate that system are selected and arranged in a hierarchy. For example, the teacher may decide to use activities such as rolling, turning, or spinning to stimulate the vestibular system. A technique for determining whether the activities have been useful for activating the system could be duration of nystagmus immediately after the activity. A sequence of short-term objectives might be 3 seconds of nystagmus after 30 seconds of spinning, 3 seconds of nystagmus following 25 seconds of spinning, 3 seconds of nystagmus after 20 seconds of spinning, and so on until the child demonstrates nystagmus for half the spinning time (i.e., 3 seconds of nystagmus after 6 seconds of spinning). The next step in the sequence would be to increase the amount of time nystagmus is demonstrated (i.e., 5 seconds of nystagmus following 30 seconds of spinning). The sequence is continued until the child reaches the normally expected duration of nystagmus (10 seconds of nystagmus after 20 seconds of turning at a speed of 180 degrees per second).

When programming for abilities, the same format is used. If the need to develop cross-lateral integration has been identified, an objective measure of this ability would be decided on, such as percent of time the student uses the right hand to pick up objects on the left side of the body. A criterion- or condition-shifting sequence would be constructed, and activities to promote the behavior would be selected.

Whenever possible, the teaching strategy should be as self-directed as possible. If children are not able to read written instructions, pictures or figures that represent the action to be performed should be included in the lesson.

Values of preplanned activities

The preplanned activities from task analysis and programmed instruction enable adequate monitoring

STANDARD TEACHING SEQUENCE

The system requires only that the teacher note the child's progress using the following symbols: **X** = the steps (activities) in the standard teaching sequence that can be mastered by the student, in this case step nos. 1, 2, 3, and 4; / = immediate short-term instruction objective, in this case no. 5;* = goal, in this case no. 18. All behaviors between the present level (/) and the goal (*) are potential objectives (6 to 18).

Walks unsupported (step no.): X̶ 2̶ 3̶ X̶ 5̶ 6 7 8 9 10 11 12 13 14 15 16 17 18* 19 20 21 22 23 24 25 26

Two-footed standing broad jump

Type of program: Shifting criterion
Conditions
    1. Both feet remain behind restraining line before takeoff.
    2. Takeoff from two feet.
    3. Land on two feet.
    4. Measure from the restraining line to the tip of the toe of the least advanced foot.
Measurement: Distance in inches.

Two-footed standing broad jump (inches)	60	62	64	6̶6̶	6̶8̶	7̶0̶	7̶2̶	74	76	78	80	82*	84
Date mastered				9/7	9/21	10/5							

The scoring procedure of the ongoing development of the person would be explained as follows. The program that the child is participating in is the two-footed standing broad jump. The child began the program at an initial performance level of 66 inches on September 7 and increased performance by 4 inches between September 7 and October 5. Thus the present level of educational performance is 70 inches (note the last number with an **X** over it). The child will attempt to jump a distance of 72 inches (immediate short-term objective) until he or she masters that distance. The child will continue to progress toward the goal, which is 82 inches (note the asterisk). It is a mistake in the applications of learning principles to ask the child to jump the 82 inches when it is known that the goal far exceeds the present level of educational performance. Unreasonable instructional demands from the learner by the teacher violate the principle of learning in small steps, which guarantees success for the child.

The same procedure could be used when teaching a child to throw a ball for accuracy. In the following example, a shifting condition program is used. For instance, two hierarchies that are known in throwing for accuracy are the size of the target and the distance between the thrower and the target. Thus a standard teaching sequence might be similar to the following sequence of potential objectives: demonstrate the ability to throw a 4-inch ball a distance of _____ feet and hit a target that is _____ feet square five out of five times.

Throwing for accuracy

Type of program: Shifting condition
Conditions
    1. Remain behind the restraining line at all times.
    2. Complete an overhand throw (ball released above the shoulder).
    3. If the ball hits any part of the target, it is a successful throw.

FIGURE 4-6. Standard teaching sequence.

Continued.

STANDARD TEACHING SEQUENCE—cont'd

The previous information would be contained in a curriculum book. However, the specific standard teaching sequence would be placed on a bulletin board at the performance area in the gymnasium. This would enable the performer to read his or her own instructional objective. The measurement of the performer's placement in the standard teaching sequence would be indicated on the prescription sheet.

Criterion for mastery: Three successful hits out of three.

DISTANCE OF THROW	SIZE OF TARGET	DISTANCE OF THROW	SIZE OF TARGET
Step 1. 6 feet	3 feet square	Step 10. 18 feet	2 feet square
Step 2. 9 feet	3 feet square	Step 11. 21 feet	2 feet square
Step 3. 12 feet	3 feet square	Step 12. 24 feet	2 feet square
Step 4. 15 feet	3 feet square	Step 13. 27 feet	2 feet square
Step 5. 18 feet	3 feet square	Step 14. 30 feet	2 feet square
Step 6. 21 feet	3 feet square	Step 15. 21 feet	1 foot square
Step 7. 24 feet	3 feet square	Step 16. 24 feet	1 foot square
Step 8. 27 feet	3 feet square	Step 17. 27 feet	1 foot square
Step 9. 30 feet	3 feet square	Step 18. 30 feet	1 foot square

The steps of the standard teaching sequence can be reduced and tasks can be added that are more or less complex as the situation requires.

STUDENT RECORDING SHEET

Throwing for accuracy (step no.)	1	2	3	4	5	6	7	8	9	10	11	12	13	14*	15	16	17	18
Date mastered																		

FIGURE 4-6, cont'd. Standard teaching sequence.

---

for a child's progress throughout the school year because of the specificity of what is to be taught. Furthermore, preplanned activities enable the parent to take part in the process. There are several distinct ways in which preplanned activities help children learn. Programmed instructional objectives function as follows:

□ They assist teachers with evaluation of the curriculum so that it may be revised to facilitate the child's learning at a subsequent time.

□ They structure behavior so that there are interrelationships between activities. This facilitates development.

□ They can introduce scientific validity to curriculum materials. This enhances accountability and assists refinement of measures that indicate the child's educational progress.

□ They enable employment of procedures that indicate limits of the child's current functioning on a specific task.

□ They provide opportunities for the child to become

a self-directed learner and to have an IEP in the regular class without undue attention.

□ They enable a comparison between where the child is in the sequence and where the child should be based on chronological age expectancies.

□ They provide information about the strengths and weaknesses of the child so that relevant instructional decisions can be made to meet unique needs.

□ They enable communication with the parents so that instructional programming may be continued in the home.

□ They free the teacher from curriculum construction so that he or she can manage individualized instruction.

□ They facilitate the monitoring of the instructional delivery system.

□ They enable evaluation of instructional technique through knowledge of measurable learning outcomes.

□ They enable the child to progress continuously

when the instructional setting is changed, and they facilitate the coordination of efforts between the physical educator and those who provide related services.

☐ They guide the revision process when changes are made in the IEP.

☐ They expedite the attainment of goals of the IEP.

☐ They assist with appropriate allocation of responsibility, time, facilities, and other resources among professionals.

☐ They enable placement of the child with a disability in a regular class where he or she can work independently on the IEP.

☐ They enable the systematic application of principles of learning to behavioral analysis.

EDUCATIONAL VALIDITY

A physical education program cannot be considered educationally valid unless it contributes to indepen-

dent recreational participation in sport and physical activity.[7] Evans and Meyer[6] identify two components of educational validity—social validity and empirical validity. *Social validity* requires evidence that as a result of instruction individuals with disabilities receive benefits that are meaningful to them in everyday life. In the case of physical education, meaningful activity is activity that, for the most part, has some immediate practical use or is a prerequisite that can be maintained and developed to use in physical activity for daily living or recreational sport activity. However, as Evans and Meyer[6] indicate, social validity is not a sufficient criterion for judging the importance of an outcome. Social validity must be supported with empirical evidence that the individual's accomplishments will contribute to the best possible long-term outcomes.

Empirical validity refers to the need to produce evidence that a particular accomplishment will make a difference in the ability of an individual to participate

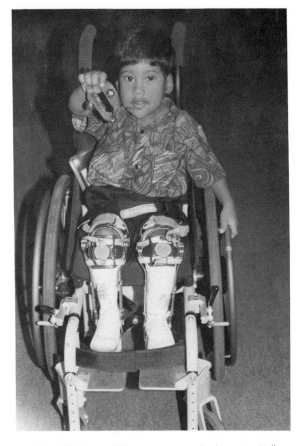

FIGURE 4-7. Every child can make music. (Courtesy Dallas Independent School District.)

FIGURE 4-8. An autistic child learns functional movement skills. (Courtesy Dallas Independent School District.)

in current and future environments and activities. Empirical validity can be established by demonstrating the usefulness of each learned skill. For example, learning to hit, catch, and throw a softball will eventually allow an individual to participate in a softball game independently with others. Empirical validity also can be supported by evidence that the goal attainment produces a ripple effect.[6] In the case of softball, the acquisition of the skills of throwing, catching, hitting, and fielding will enable an individual to play games such as catch with other persons so that opportunities for social de-

velopment are present. Empirical validity also refers to the long-term outcomes that might be established by gathering follow-up data on graduates of a physical education program (i.e., gathering evidence that graduates of the program participate in independent recreational sports programs, intramural sports programs, physical activities within the school, or special programs for persons with disabilities in the community). Table 4-5 includes questions that need to be answered to demonstrate the educational validity of instructional goals.

Three Essential Components of Educational Validity

There are three essential components that need to be verified to demonstrate educational validity of a goal or an individual program. (1) Is the planned behavior change, objective, or goal meaningful? (2) Has the change of behavior toward the goal occurred as a result of the intervention? (3) Did the educational intervention match the specification of the educational goal?

TABLE 4-5

Empirical and social validity evaluation questions

Normalization

1. Is the activity age-appropriate?
2. Will attainment of the skill be useful in integrated environments?
3. Will nonhandicapped peers view the learner positively if they see him or her engage in this activity?
4. Is this an activity the learner can access both when she or he is alone and with others?
5. Will the learner be able to access this activity, once taught, without direct supervision?
6. Will the activity be longitudinally appropriate, across the lifespan?
7. Do the learner's parents value this activity?
8. Is the activity accessible in a variety of places and throughout the year?

Individualization

1. Can this activity be used at both low and high skill levels?
2. Can any need for assistance on the activity be accomplished by involving nonhandicapped persons in the natural, community environment?
3. Can the activity be adapted or modified with needed prosthetic devices?
4. Does the learner enjoy this activity?
5. Does the activity involve the performance on one or more critical skills?
6. Will the activity enhance personal development (physical benefits)?

Environmental

1. Will this activity continue to be available to the learner in the future?
2. Is the activity reasonably safe?
3. Will this activity be noxious to others in the learner's environment?
4. Can the activity be accessed at reasonable cost?
5. Can instruction on this activity be provided in the relevant criterion situations and environments?
6. Will the learner's natural environment (home,etc.) continue to support the use of this activity?

From Evans IM, Meyer L: An educative approach to behavioral problems, Baltimore, 1985, Paul H Brookes Publishing.

FIGURE 4-9. A creative teacher helps a child with no fingers enjoy arts and crafts. (Courtesy Dallas Independent School District.)

Educational Integrity

Educational integrity refers to the value of the educational process. Physical education programs that result in measurable functional student performance improvement because of instruction have educational integrity. Numerous environmental variables can affect the disabled student's success in the pysical education program and compromise the educational integrity of the program. An effective physical education program might be rendered ineffective in a gymnasium that has distracting aspects. Teacher impact, physical arrangements, daily activities, and social conditions also influence the educational process.[6] Insufficient instructional time is another factor. If students do not have enough learning experiences, they cannot demonstrate progress. In addition, even the best teacher cannot be truly effective in a physical education class with more than thirty students. Large numbers of students make it impossible to provide vital, individual attention to students.

To determine whether a program possesses educational integrity it is important to accumulate evidence of the kinds of experiences that lead to gains by learners. Thus to demonstrate educational integrity a teacher must be able to accurately assess and select instructional activities that lead to improved student performance. To gather meaningful data requires, at the very least, that a baseline or initial present level of perforance be established. Once present level of performance is ascertained and desirable goals selected, short-term objectives that lead to each goal must be identified. Acquisition of short-term instructional performance objectives indicates positive movement toward the behavioral goals of the individual educational program. The value of the intervention is demonstrated by showing that whenever the intervention is not in effect, the acquisition rate or performance declines. To determine whether an intervention is successful requires the keeping of a systematic record of pupil performance during instruction. This information can then be shared with school authorities, parents and instructional staff to determine changes in the skill acquisition of the student withdisabilities.

FIGURE 4-10. A child learns to jump on a bouncing **board.** (Courtesy of Callier Center for Communicative Disorders, Dallas, Texas.)

Program Evaluation

To determine whether a physical education program is contributing positively to an individual's functional performance, the following questions must be answered[19]:

1. Frequency: Did the individual perform the activity during the last month?
2. Independence: Did the individual perform the physical activity independently?
3. Social integration: With whom did the individual do this activity during the last month?
4. Physical integration: Where has the individual done this activity during the last month?
5. Limitations: If the individual did not perform the activity, why not?
6. Opportunity: Has anyone else in the family done this activity during the last month?
7. Preference: How well does the individual like to perform the activity?
8. Perceived importance: Should the program work

FIGURE 4-11. Modified sports equipment opens the world to individuals with disabilities. (Courtesy RADVENTURES, Inc.)

to improve the individual's performance in this activity?

REPORTING THE RESULTS TO PARENTS

Parents should always be informed of their children's educational performance levels and the goals and objectives of the school curricula. P.L. 94-142 requires that the parents be apprised of the educational status of their children and approve the IEP that has been designed for them. When the procedures described in this chapter are followed by the teacher and the information shared with the parents, there will be no question about the educational process. Parents may question whether appropriate goals have been selected for their children; but usually, when evaluation results and the importance of their child achieving as normal a performance level as possible are explained, parents agree with the professional educator's opinion.

It is important to point out to the parents their child's specific deficiencies and how those deficiencies interfere with the child's functional ability. Wherever possible, basic level and ability deficiencies should be linked to skill performance. That is, the educator should explain not only what deficits exist, but how those deficits relate to the child's present and future levels of performance ability. Once parents understand these relationships, they usually endorse the school's efforts on behalf of their children. In addition to pointing out a child's deficiencies, it is important to tell the parent about areas of strength their child has demonstrated. Parents of children with disabilities need to hear positive reports as frequently as possible. Do not overlook that need.

SUMMARY

Present levels of educational performance are the functional capabilities of a student along a developmental continuum at a particular point in time. Determining present levels of performance is necessary before goals and objectives for the student can be determined. Standardized tests may be helpful in deciding whether a child is in need of a specialized program; however, content-referenced assessment such as task analysis or sensory input screening is necessary to determine the precise levels at which a student is functioning. Once a student's levels of functioning are determined, goals and objectives are agreed on and activities that lead to their attainment are selected. A teaching sequence that permits ongoing measurement is designed. Shifting criterion and condition programs that are carefully sequenced enable constant measurement of progress. All this information and the importance of this process should be explained to parents. Programs should be evaluated to determine their success in assisting students with disabilities to meet the physical demands of recreational and domestic environments in the community. This is called establishing educational validity. There is a greater chance of demonstrating educational validity if the physical education program includes functional routines of physical activity that are available in the community rather than promoting splinter skills, which may be difficult to express in environments away from the instructional setting.

REVIEW QUESTIONS

1. How are unique needs in physical education determined?
2. How are present levels of performance determined through administration of domain-referenced standardized tests?
3. How does one determine a present level of educational performance through task analysis of a skill that is to be taught to a student?

4. What is a prerequisite analysis and how is it used to determine present levels of performance for a child?
5. Provide examples of hierarchies in tasks that can increase or decrease difficulty of the task.
6. What are the types of measures that can be incorporated into the instructional process? Provide examples of each.
7. Describe the interrelationships of the components of the instructional process of the IEP.
8. Construct an instructional objective.
9. What are some possible developmental delays involving the sensory input systems?
10. What is one difference between primitive and equilibrium reflexes?
11. Provide an example of a deficient prerequisite that can be observed in a specific sport skill.
12. What is the difference between determining a present level of performance during skill acquisition and during the performance phase?
13. Evaluate the constructional effectiveness of a behavioral shaping program.
14. Find your present level of performance in a hierarchical behavioral shaping program.
15. What are the different types of behavioral programs in which present levels can be determined?
16. Describe a standard teaching sequence/hierarchical behavioral program.
17. How can behavioral programs of abilities be used with the top, down and bottom, up approaches?
18. Provide examples of educational validity.
19. List some standards for evaluating the effectiveness of the assessment and programming procedure.

STUDENT ACTIVITIES

1. Use a combination of domain-referenced and criterion-referenced data to develop an individualized program of activities to meet the unique needs of a hypothetical child.
2. With a hypothetical data base from domain-referenced tests that have norms, determine the specific activities that would constitute a physical education program.
3. Perform a task analysis of a sport skill.
4. Assess a real or hypothetical learner who has a deficient teachable component of a task-analyzed skill.
5. Use a hierarchical behavioral program to instruct a student and plot his or her progress.
6. Plot the progress of a learner in the acquisition phase of a skill that has been task analyzed.
7. Write an exercise prescription from present levels of performance for a person in a cardiovascular fitness program.
8. Using standards proposed by Wilcox and Bellamy (see Table 4-5) evaluate some goals of an individualized physical education program.
9. Identify a group of motor skills necessary to carry out a functional routine of sport activity in the community.
10. Administer the screening test included in this chapter to some students to determine if they have any developmental delays (see Table 4-2).
11. Simulate activity that would portray developmental delays in the vestibular, visual, kinesthetic, and tactile systems. Have a partner attempt to identify the delays.
12. Assess some children with disabilities and identify developmental delays in ocular control, reflexes, and kinesthetic functioning.
13. After using the screening test and identifying some developmental delays, design a physical education intervention program using activities included in this chapter.

REFERENCES

1. Bellamy T, Peterson L, Close D: Habilitation of the severely and profoundly retarded: illustrations of competence, *Educ Train Ment Retard* 10:174-186, 1975.
2. Billingsley F: Where are the generalized outcomes? An examination of instructional objectives, *J Assoc Persons Severe Handic* 9:186-192, 1984.
3. Browder D, Snell M, Ambrogio B: Using time delay to transfer stimulus control within the behavioral chain of vending machine use with a comparison of training sites, *Unpublished manuscript,* Department of Special Education, Lehigh University.
4. Budoff M: *The Massachusetts mixed softball league: a final report to Special Olympics International, Washington, DC,* Cambridge, Mass, 1987, Research Institute for Educational Problems, Inc.
5. Dunn JM, Frederick H: *Physical education for the severely handicapped: a systematic approach to a data based gymnasium,* Austin, Tex, 1985, PRO-ED.
6. Evans IM, Meyer L: *An educative approach to behavioral problems,* Baltimore, 1985, Paul H Brookes Publishing.
7. Evans IM, Wilson FE: *Behavioral assessment as decision making: a theoretical analysis.* In Rosenbaum M, Franks CM, Jaffe Y, editors: *A perspective of behavior therapy in the 80's,* New York, 1983, Springer Publishing.
8. Gaylord-Ross R, Halvoet J: *Teaching severely handicapped children and youth,* Boston, 1984, Little, Brown & Co.
9. Gold M: *Task analysis: a statement and example using acquisition and production of a complex task by the retarded blind,* University of Illinois at Urbana-Champaign, 1975, Institute for Child Behavior and Development.
10. Guess D, Noonan MJ: Curricula and instructional procedures for severely handicapped students, *Focus Except Child* 14:1-12, 1982.
11. Kohen-Raz R: *Learning disabilities and postural control,* London, 1986, Freund Publishing House.
12. Lindvall CM, Bolvin JD: *Programmed instruction in the schools: an application of programming principles in individually prescribed instruction,* Sixty-sixth Yearbook of the National Society of the Study of Education, Chicago, 1967, University of Chicago Press.
13. Marchetti AG et al: Pedestrian skill training for mentally retarded adults: a comparison of training in two settings, *Ment Retard* 21:107-110, 1983.
14. Neel RS et al: *Teaching autistic children: a functional*

analysis approach, Seattle, 1983, University of Washington, College of Education.

15. Quiros JB, Schrager OL: *Neuropsychological fundamentals in learning disabilities,* San Rafael, Calif, 1979, Academic Therapy Publications.

16. Snell M: *Systematic instruction of persons with severe handicaps,* Columbus, Ohio, 1987, Merrill Publishing.

17. Snell M, Browder D: Community referenced instruction: research and issues, *J Assoc Persons Severe Handic* 11:1-11, 1986.

18. Wessel JA, Kelly L: *Achievement-based curriculum development in physical education,* Philadelphia, 1986, Lea & Febiger.

19. Wilcox B, Bellamy GT: *Design of high school programs for severely handicapped students,* Baltimore, 1986, Paul H Brookes Publishing.

SUGGESTED READINGS

Dunn JM, Fredericks H: *Physical education for the severely handicapped: a systematic approach to a data based gymnasium,* Austin, Tex, 1985, PRO-ED.

Evans IM, Meyer L: *An educative approach to behavioral problems,* Baltimore, 1985, Paul H Brookes Publishing.

Pyfer J: Teachers, don't let your students grow up to be clumsy adults, *J Phys Educ Rec Dance* 59:38-42, 1988.

Seaman JA, DePauw K: *The new adapted physical education: a developmental approach,* Palo Alto, Calif, 1989, Mayfield Publishing.

Wessel JA, Kelly L: *Achievement-based curriculum development in physical education,* Philadelphia, 1986, Lea & Febiger.

CHAPTER

5

OBJECTIVES

Cite the procedures for planned behavioral intervention.

Collect data when observing behaviors.

Explain a variety of positive intervention strategies.

Describe techniques to eliminate behaviors using positive and negative methods.

Construct a contingency management program.

Apply principles of learning to instructional objectives.

Explain how to apply techniques of generalization.

Tell alternative modes to develop motor skills using task analysis.

State considerations for using cues and corrections procedures.

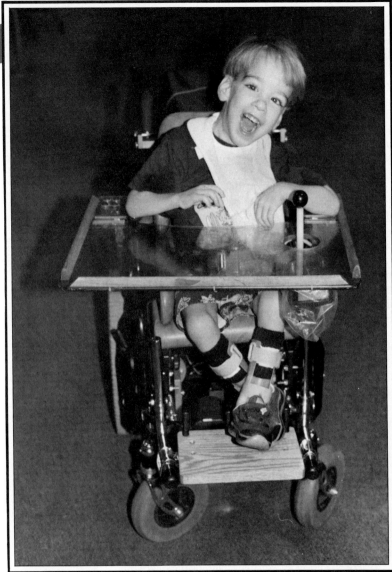

Courtesy Dallas Independent School District

Facilitating Learning

*T*he benefit of physical education programs can be maximized if acceptable principles of learning and development are applied to instruction. Teachers of children with disabilities bear the responsibility for ensuring that learning takes place. In the past, teachers often were assigned to children with disabilities on the basis of tolerance or because they enjoyed working with these children. The physical education programs that teachers designed often focused on the children's enjoyment of them. If the children appeared to be having a good time, the teacher was judged to be effective. Since the advent of the Education of the Handicapped Act of 1975, the qualifications for teachers of learners with disabilities have changed dramatically. Now these teachers not only must enjoy their work, but they also must be masterful at designing educational environments that promote maximum learning. Maximizing learning involves the ability to generalize skills from the instructional settings to functional use in natural integrated community environments.

Teachers of learners with disabilities must be able to test children, interpret test results, write appropriate long-range goals and short-term objectives that lead to those goals, and apply principles of learning, development, and behavioral strategies that contribute to classroom learning. In addition to these skills, the teacher provides patterns of behavior for the child to copy. From their teachers, immature children learn how the environment works and how persons cope with changing environments.

These teachers must be emotionally stable, flexible, and empathetic toward atypical behavior while encouraging learning. To best understand what the child with a disability is experiencing, teachers must be sensitive enough to perceive the importance of even the slightest change in the child's behavior. This degree of understanding provides a medium through which a child may better understand his or her own behavior and then modify it. This is no easy task. Being in contact with anxiety-provoking persons often stretches the teacher's emotional capacities. Some of the behaviors that teachers often tolerate are implied rejection from the child and conflicting demands from the child, which range from demanding that immediate needs be met to severe withdrawal, aggressive tactics, and immature behavior.

Teachers who work with normally developing children may be unaccustomed to the many behaviors demonstrated by students with disabilities. To succeed, teachers must understand and accept the behavior patterns of atypical children while designing and implementing programs that ensure learning progress. The best defense a teacher has is knowledge of what is occurring coupled with teaching and behavioral strategies to move the child beyond present levels of educational performance.

BEHAVIORAL TECHNOLOGY
Application and Use

Applying behavioral technology in the education of learners with disabilities involves use of learning the-ory, operant conditioning, and precise objectives.[17] Behavioral technology structures the environment to produce changes in pupil behavior; this allows maximum learning to take place. The strategies and procedures have two purposes: (1) to manage disruptive behavior and (2) to reach the objectives specified on the individual education program (IEP). The general process is the same in both instances; however, certain techniques are effective for managing disruptive behavior, whereas others are more beneficial in step-by-step learning of motor skills.

FIGURE 5-1. Time spent with a caring parent is a reward in and of itself.

Behavior Management

The physical education teacher should establish learning environments that permit students to be productive. The environment must be arranged to facilitate skill learning and discourage disruptive behavior. Disruptive behavior by one student interferes with that student's learning as well as that of the others in the class. In such cases the teacher must design a learning environment that makes each student feel accepted when following the guidelines for acceptable behavior. Usually, if students are informed of the guidelines for behavioral management, they will accept them if they are applied fairly, equally, and consistently.

There are several strategies physical education teachers can use to manage classroom behavior; however, the most effective intervention programs are based on student performance data. A data-based system helps students control their behavior, learn new behaviors, and maintain appropriate behaviors. The data-based system involves a systematic process that (1) identifies specific behaviors, (2) analyzes the student behavior to determine any discrepancy between present behavior and desired behavior, and (3) implements interventions when necessary.

A step-by-step strategy the teacher should follow to improve behavior is listed below:

1. Identify a specific (target) behavior.
2. Select an observation system and collect baseline data on the behavior.
3. Analyze the data to determine the need for an intervention program.
4. If data indicate the need for an intervention program, select or design an intervention program that uses the most positive approach.
5. Implement the intervention program.
6. Collect data on student performance.

Event Recording

EXAMPLE 1: SIMPLE FREQUENCY AND PERCENT DATA

Student ___ Sue ___ Observer ___ Ms. Smith ___
Behavior Observed: Objectives completed by Sue on recording sheet
Data Reported: Frequency and percentage of short-term objectives completed each day
Time of Observation: Individualized skill development and prerequisites; period of the class for 5 periods

Day	Number of expected objectives achieved	Number completed	Percentage completed
1	4	(3)	75%
2	4	(2)	50%
3	5	(5)	100%
4	5	(4)	80%
5	5	(3)	60%

EXAMPLE 2: SIMPLE FREQUENCY

Student ___ Jim ___ Observer ___ Mr. Jones ___
Behavior Observed: Talk-outs by Jim during instruction by teacher; talk-outs are verbalizations loud enough to be heard by the instructor
Data Reported: Frequency of talk-outs and rate of talk-outs per 5 minutes of instruction time
Time of Observation: Entire time teacher instructs

Day	Number of minutes	Number of talk-outs	Frequency
1	5	3	3
2	5	2	2
3	5	1	1
4	5	0	0
5	5	0	0

7. Analyze the data to determine the need to continue, modify, or terminate the intervention.
8. Take the required action.
9. When the behavior reaches the desired level and is no longer dependent on intervention, continue to collect maintenance data and return to step 4.

Identifying specific target behaviors

When identifying specific behaviors, observe students as they perform. Whether the behavior involves performance on learning tasks or disruptive actions, the data collected must be precise. Precision is accomplished when the behavior is carefully defined in objective terms that can be measured. If the behavior is clearly stated, two or more observers can agree on whether the student has performed the behavior.

Collecting baseline data

When collecting baseline data, it is necessary first to select a measurement system and then decide who will observe and how often. Several measuring systems are available for collecting and recording behavior. These systems include the following:

□ *Permanent product recording*—a system that involves counting actual products that are produced
□ *Event recording*—the number of times a specifically defined behavior occurs within a time interval (e.g., counting the number of times a student steps away from a line within one class period)
□ *Duration recording*—the length of time a behavior occurs (e.g., how long a student can stay on a specific task)
□ *Interval recording*—the occurrence or nonoccurrence of a behavior within a specific time interval (e.g., the teacher may observe that Jim was active only two of the five 1-minute observation periods)

The method selected depends on the type of behavior, the kind of data to be gathered, and the ease of implementation by the observer. The most common behavior measurement systems used in physical education are event, duration, and interval recordings.

Event recording produces frequency data that can be converted into percentages. Percentages and frequencies are appropriate measures for skill behaviors done in blocks of tasks. Percentages can be computed by counting the number of baskets made out of 10 shots, or the number of successful kicks out of 5 at a goal in soccer. Frequency data are simply the number of occurrences of the behavior. To compare frequencies, the observation periods should be equal in length

and the student should have the same opportunity to demonstrate the behavior during each observation period. Frequency data can be converted into rate information. Rate is simply the number of times a behavior occurs within a certain time limit, such as the number of times a student is able to set up a volleyball in 20 seconds.

Duration recordings are useful if the length of time a student engages in a behavior is of interest. For example, observers may note the amount of time a student requires to move from one activity to the next or how long a student is active or inactive. Duration can be recorded in actual time limits (e.g., Jack was on task for 5 minutes) or in a percentage (e.g., Ralph was active for 40% of the time) (see box below).

Interval recordings are particularly useful for the regular class teacher because they do not require that students be observed continuously. McLoughlin and Lewis describe advantages of this system and several of the different recording systems[10]:

This technique does not require counting or timing behaviors. Instead, the observer simply notes whether or not a behavior is present or absent during a specified time interval. For example, if a teacher is interested in observing staying on task, smiling, or swearing, the classroom day may be broken into short time periods, such as 15- or 5- or 3-minute intervals. One of several variations of interval recording can be used:

Duration Recording

DURATION AND PERCENT DATA

Student ___Sue___ Observer ___Jim___
Behavior Observed: Time working on self directing task
Data Reported: Amount of time (duration) on task; observer starts timing when child moves to learning stations
Time of Observation: Five-minute intervals for observational periods during a class session

Day	Time	Number of minutes	Percentage of time
1	9:00-9:05	1:00	20%
2	9:10-9:15	1:30	30%
3	9:00-9:05	1:15	25%
4	9:25-9:30	2:00	40%
5	9:20-9:25	3:00	60%

1. *Whole interval time sampling.* The observer notes whether the target behavior occurs continuously during the entire interval. That is, if 5-minute intervals are being used, the observer notes for each interval whether the behavior occurred *throughout the interval.*
2. *Partial interval time sampling.* The partial interval method requires only that the observer determines whether the behavior occurs at least once during the interval. That is, if the observation period has been broken down into 20-minute intervals, the observer notes for each interval whether the behavior has occurred at all during that time.
3. *Momentary time sampling.* Observation occurs only at the end of each time interval (see Example 2 in the box on p. 108). That is, if the observation period is broken down into 3-minute intervals, the teacher checks the student only at the end of each interval and notes if the target behavior is occurring at that moment.

Observers must be trained to evaluate and record data accurately and consistently. The most effective data collection system requires that the students be able to evaluate themselves as to whether they did or did not demonstrate that behavior. Peer teachers and aides also can be trained to assist in and monitor the data collection. Someone other than the performer (teacher, aide, tutor) observes for only a short period each day; however, it is long enough to obtain an accurate picture of the student's behavior (Table 5-1).

Analyzing the data

The collected data must be studied by the teacher to determine whether the behavior is effectively contributing to the learning process or deterring learning. If the behavior being observed relates to performance of a skill or learning task, the greater the number of successful occurrences the better. If the behavior being monitored is disruptive (undesirable), the fewer the number of occurrences the better (see Example 2 in the box on p. 105).

Efficient Ways of Collecting Data

It is imperative that data be collected while instruction is conducted. Three groups of persons can collect the data: physical education teachers, students who participate in activity, and peer teachers.

There are generally three types of data. One type indicates attainment of short-term objectives. Another involves observation and recording of positive social behavior that develops the individual or supports the instructional system. Disruptive behavior is the third type. Interval and time sampling techniques would be used to gather this type of information.

Data on acquisition of short-term objectives

The collection of data on the acquisition of short-term objectives should be done while the physical education class is in progress. The data sheets should be

---

TABLE 5-1

Measures of behavior

Measure	Derivation	Example	Application
Percentage	Number of correct trials out of a block of trials	Seven basketball goals made out of a block of 10 trials $$\frac{7}{10} \times 100 = 70\% \text{ accuracy}$$	A measure of accuracy without regard for time or proficiency
Frequency	$\dfrac{\text{Count of behavior}}{\text{Observation time}}$	Pupil tutor feeds back three times in 3 minutes $= \dfrac{3}{3}$	How often a distinct behavior occurs within a period of time
Duration	Direct measures of length of time	A child is off task for 45 seconds	The total length of time a continuous behavior occurs
Intervals	Number of fixed time units in which behavior did or did not occur	Children are observed for 20 seconds; then the observer records whether behavior occurred during the interval; observers then repeat the process (usually data are expressed in terms of percentage of intervals during which behavior occurred) $$\frac{4 \text{ intervals}}{10 \text{ intervals total}} \times 100 = 40\% \text{ of intervals}$$	When behavior occurs over a time frame

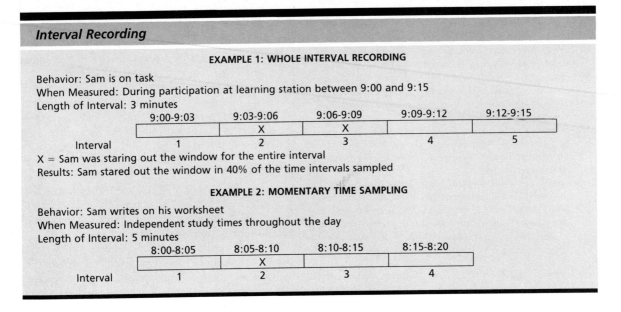

Interval Recording

EXAMPLE 1: WHOLE INTERVAL RECORDING

Behavior: Sam is on task
When Measured: During participation at learning station between 9:00 and 9:15
Length of Interval: 3 minutes

9:00-9:03	9:03-9:06	9:06-9:09	9:09-9:12	9:12-9:15
	X	X		
Interval 1	2	3	4	5

X = Sam was staring out the window for the entire interval
Results: Sam stared out the window in 40% of the time intervals sampled

EXAMPLE 2: MOMENTARY TIME SAMPLING

Behavior: Sam writes on his worksheet
When Measured: Independent study times throughout the day
Length of Interval: 5 minutes

8:00-8:05	8:05-8:10	8:10-8:15	8:15-8:20
	X		
Interval 1	2	3	4

prepared before class. Check marks should be made during class to indicate achievement. Time usually does not permit written comments. Once a child is familiar with a score sheet, a check can be made in 2 or 3 seconds. Time intervals for recording depend on the nature of the tasks and the learner. Three suggested ways of structuring the data sheets to indicate progress are (1) to have the measurement of the task on a data sheet, (2) to convert objectives that are communicated on posters in the physical education class to numbers on a data sheet, and (3) to have the objectives stated on a sheet that the learner carries while participating in different activities.

Measurement of the task on the data sheet

Objectives should have performance measures. Many objectives build on one another to form a hierarchy. For instance, if a child was attempting to increase the distance of the long jump, the data sheet would indicate a series of measures in inches. The pupil would then indicate present status in the jumping hierarchy by placing an X over the jumping level of current instruction. If the activity was throwing a ball, distance of the throw might be marked. If the activity was running endurance, the measure might be time elapsed to run a specified distance. In this data collection system there is direct information on performance of the pupil scored on the data sheet itself. A data matrix incorporates the same principle. However, with this system

several behaviors are placed in a hierarchy that forms the vertical axis of the matrix, and the performance measures of the objectives are indicated on the horizontal axis of the matrix. The student graphs or checks objectives attained with this system (see Fig. 5-2) and records personal data.

Conversion of objectives to numbers on a data sheet

The objectives may be written on a sheet from which the student receives instruction. In this system the pupil reads the objective from the sheet and checks the objective when mastered.

Data sheets can be numbers that represent tasks. A check mark over the number on the data sheet represents acquisition of the short-term instructional objective. In this system it is necessary to have the objectives on a poster in the class setting. The pupil identifies the number of the objective in question from the poster on a specific day. The number on the data sheet is matched with the number of the objective on the poster. The objective is performed by the pupil and checked on the data sheet if mastered. The posted objectives may be written or converted to stick figures or pictures to clarify the behaviors. Use of posters requires time to teach children to match objectives on the posters with objectives on the data sheet. However, once the poster objectives are learned, the children can collect data on one another or by themselves.

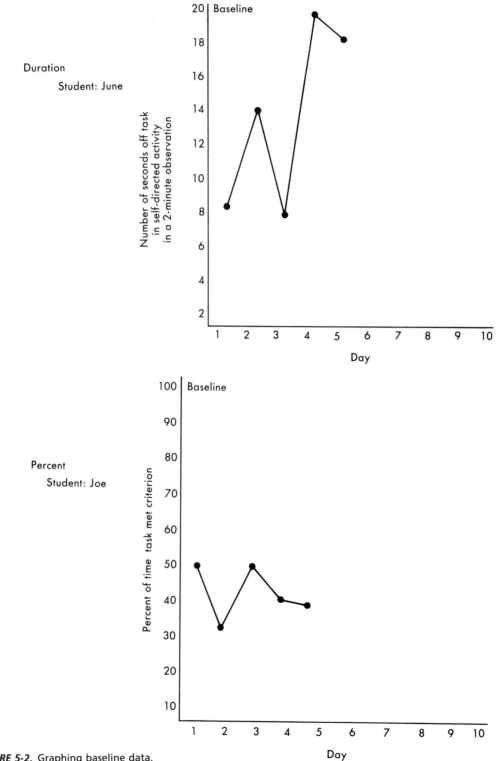

FIGURE 5-2. Graphing baseline data.

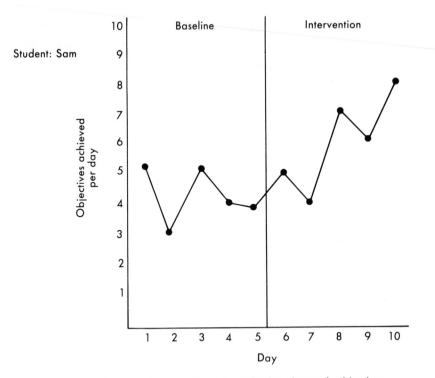

FIGURE 5-3. Graphing intervention data. Behavior observed: objectives achieved by Sam; intervention: reinforcement by peer teacher.

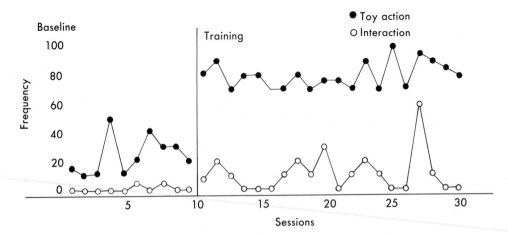

FIGURE 5-4. Graphing intervention data.

Recording Data on Social Behavior

The classic manner of data collection on social behavior is for the teacher to collect information by means of interval, time sample, or event recording sheets and then graph the results (see Figs. 5-3 and 5-4). But this system may distract the teacher from instruction. The problem may be overcome if the teacher places a piece of masking tape on the student's wrist and records data on the tape with a marking pen. Appropriate and inappropriate behaviors are identified. When the pupils conduct themselves appropriately, they are given marks of one color (red). When the behaviors are inappropriate, they are awarded marks on the wrist tape of another color (green). After the class is over, the pieces of masking tape are placed on a board beside their names. The data marks may be made by a teacher or peer teachers. The marks are usually delivered immediately, do not disrupt ongoing instruction, and enable the teacher or peer teacher to deliver a consequence that relates to desired behavior. If children have severe behavioral problems, an interval or time sample or duration records are to be made.

Determining need for an intervention program

The amount of productive behavior being demonstrated is the primary criterion for determining whether an intervention program is needed. To make this decision, the teacher must refer to the student's educational objectives and compare the behavior being demonstrated with those objectives. If a behavior to be learned or maintained is not being demonstrated consistently, an intervention program is needed. If disruptive behavior is occurring to the extent that meaningful learning is not occurring, an intervention program can decrease the undesirable behavior.

Selecting a positive intervention program

The central purpose of the physical education program is to develop positive physical and motor behaviors that result in improved health and recreational activity. Research has demonstrated the effectiveness of several intervention techniques that can be used to promote positive behaviors. These techniques involve communication of the target task to the learner, efficiently establishing the behavior so performance can be improved, and employing methods to enable density of relevant programming. Following is a list of techniques that can be used to promote learning of a task. (See p. 116 for techniques to eliminate disruptive behaviors.)

Purpose	Technique
Communication of a learning task	Modeling
Establishing behavioral performance	Priming, prompting, fading, and forward and backward chaining
Density of relevant programming	Cycle constancy
Developing new behavior	Shaping

Modeling

Modeling refers to demonstration of a task by the teacher or reinforcement of another student who performs a desirable behavior in the presence of the target student. When a teacher actually performs the desirable behavior, he or she is teaching the target student how the task is to be performed. When another student is used as the model and performs a task correctly, the teacher praises the behavior in the presence of the target student. For example, if a teacher wants all the children to maintain a curled back while doing a sit-up, those children who keep their backs curled would be pointed out by the teacher and praised while doing their sit-ups. All other children who then perform the task correctly would also be reinforced. Modeling can

FIGURE 5-5. Pet therapy is a creative, nurturing way to facilitate learning. (Courtesy Recreation Services, Division Care and Treatment Facilities, Department of Health and Social Services, Northern Wisconsin Center for the Developmentally Delayed.)

lead to a fairly close approximation of the desired response. Refinement of the response could be done at another time.

Physical priming (prompting)

Physical priming,[1] or prompting, involves physically holding and moving the body parts of the learner through the activity. Usually priming will enable a successful response or a close enough approximation so that shaping can be used to improve the performance level. Physical priming should be used with the idea of eliminating the primers as quickly as possible so that the learner can begin to function independently.

Prompting and fading

Prompting and fading involve providing just enough physical assistance so that the student realizes some success at the task and then gradually withdrawing the help. The rule for prompting is to provide the minimum prompt necessary for the learner to be successful. For example, if a student tries to stand on one foot but cannot, the teacher can place his or her hands under the student's arms to provide support. The prompt is sequentially faded by having the teacher gradually move his or her hands down the student's arm to the tip of the fingers and finally letting go.

Prompts are valuable if the tasks can be quickly learned. If the task is not performed in a relatively short time, the teacher probes through prerequisite components to determine which ones are missing and need to be learned before the skill can be performed.

Forward and backward chaining

Chaining is leading a person through a series of teachable components of a motor task. Each teachable component represents a discrete portion (link) in a task. When these portions or links are tied together, the process is known as chaining. Some skills can be broken into components and taught by the chaining process more easily than others. Self-help skills are easily broken into parts. Clearly, grasping a spoon is an essential link in the process of eating; however, it is a behavior distinctly different from scooping the food with the spoon or placing the food in one's mouth. Each of these components is a necessary link that must be tied together (chained) to accomplish the skill of self-feeding. Continuous physical skills do not break into discrete teachable components and are difficult to chain. Other physical skills, such as the lay-up shot in basketball, can be broken into discrete components that lend themselves to chaining (see Chapter 4).

When the last of the series of steps is taught first, the process is known as *backward chaining*. Teaching a basketball lay-up by means of backward chaining requires that the student (1) stand close to the basket, reach high with the arm, and shoot the basketball; (2) jump from the inside foot, reach high with the arm, and shoot the basketball; (3) run-jump from the inside

---

Examples of Skills Taught by Backward Chaining

Behavior	Task sequence
Pass receiving in football	(1) Catch pass, (2) run and catch pass, (3) make cut, run, and catch pass, (4) release from line, run, cut, and catch pass.
Tackling in football	(1) Tackle ball carrier, (2) run pattern to intersect and tackle ball carrier, (3) release blocker, run pattern to ball carrier, and tackle ball carrier, (4) administer technique to neutralize blocker, release blocker, run pattern to ball carrier, tackle ball carrier.
Shooting a soccer goal	(1) Shoot soccer goal, (2) dribble and shoot soccer goal, (3) receive a pass, dribble, and shoot soccer goal.
Passing a soccer ball	(1) Pass soccer ball, (2) bring ball under control and pass soccer ball, (3) dribble, bring ball under control, and pass the soccer ball.
Leg takedown in wrestling	(1) Take opponent to the mat, (2) secure the legs and take opponent to the mat, (3) shoot move for legs, secure the legs, and take the opponent to the mat, (4) set up move, shoot the move for the legs, secure the legs, and take the opponent to the mat.
Fielding a ball and throwing a player out at first base in softball	(1) Throw to first base, (2) field the ball and throw to first base.

foot, reach high with the arm, and shoot the basketball; and (4) dribble a ball while running, jump from the inside foot, reach high with the arm, and shoot the basketball. The value of backward chaining is that the individual is reinforced during each step by completing the task successfully.

Other skills that may be taught by backward chaining are those expressed in team play. Examples of the analysis of these tasks are shown in the box on p. 112.

Self-help tasks such as tying a shoe and dressing are easily and effectively taught by backward chaining.

When using *forward chaining,* the first step is taught first, the second step is taught second, and so on until the entire task is learned. Most teachers use forward chaining when teaching tasks.

Cycle constancy

Cycle constancy is the continual recurrence of a specific motor act within similar time periods. Gold[5] has indicated that cycle constancy positively affects some students' ability to learn motor tasks. The value of cycle constancy is that the learner is able to predict when stimuli will be presented and when consequences will be delivered. It is relatively easy to apply cycle constancy to behavioral programming of motor tasks. To promote learning, as tasks recur, either the conditions or the criteria are altered.

Cycle constancy is most frequently used when dealing with serious emotional disturbances. Children so affected are often disruptive if their attention is not focused intently on one task. Often, when this type of child is placed in a group situation that includes some activities beyond or less than his or her ability level, the child becomes inattentive and begins to act out. When one child becomes disruptive in group activity, there is a tendency for others to do the same. To prevent disruptive behavior or to bring it under control, Foxx and Azrin[4] propose that a high density of relevant programming be used. This simply means that attention should be focused on activities that have meaning for the student. When these activities are coupled with predictability of the tasks and their consequences (cycle constancy), the child will focus attention on the tasks and learning will occur.

Shaping

Shaping involves the reinforcing of small progressive steps that lead toward a desired behavior. The technique of shaping is used to teach new behaviors and is particularly valuable in the performance phase of acquiring a skill. When shaping a new motor response, the physical education teacher has the choice of wait-

ing for the learner to demonstrate the next small step toward the goal or helping the learner attain the objective through the use of a physical prompt. In either case the specifically defined task (step) must be reinforced. The procedures for shaping a behavior are as follows:

Procedure	Example
1. Define the behavior.	Balancing on one foot with eyes open for 10 seconds
2. Define a reinforcer.	Knowledge of task success
3. Determine the present level.	2 seconds on the task
4. Outline a series of small steps that lead to the desired behavior.	16 increments of ½ second each
5. Advance the learner on a predetermined criterion.	Each step three times in a row
6. Define the success level.	90%

Reinforcement

Reinforcement is a strategy that follows and strengthens a behavior. The discussion that follows focuses on positive reinforcers because they yield the most lasting results. Positive reinforcers include teacher or peer praise, material rewards, activities a student enjoys doing, and success on a task. Positive reinforcement is constructive because it helps individuals feel good about themselves.

Selecting reinforcers. There are intrinsic (internal) and extrinsic (external) reinforcers. Intrinsic reinforcement comes from within the learner. Often knowledge of success on a task or the satisfaction of participating is sufficient to reinforce oneself. Extrinsic reinforcement comes from outside the learner. Examples of extrinsic reinforcement are praise and other rewards from a person who acknowledges the learner's achievement. One objective of a reinforcement program is to move the learner from dependence on extrinsic reinforcers to seeking intrinsic reinforcers. Once learners no longer have to rely on teachers for feedback, they can direct their own learning. It is important that both the learner and the teachers agree on what the reinforcer will be and how the system of reinforcement will work.

Reinforcement procedures. Contingency management is a way of controlling the use of reinforcers. A *contingency* is an agreement between the student and the teacher that indicates what the student must do to earn a specific reward. A *token economy* is a form of contingency management in which tokens (external

FIGURE 5-6. Crowd support facilitates performance in some athletes. (Courtesy Adapted Physical Education Department, Jefferson Parish Public School System, Louisiana.)

reinforcers) are earned for desirable behavior. This type of a system can be used with a single student, selected groups of students, or with classes of students. Lewis and Doorlag[8] suggest the following procedure for setting up a token economy:

1. Specify the behaviors that earn tokens.
2. Use tokens that are appropriate for the student.
3. Pose a menu (a list) of the types of available reinforcers.
4. Allow students to suggest reinforcers for the list.
5. Revise the menu regularly.
6. Use a clear record system (of distributing the tokens) that is accurate.
7. Give students frequent opportunities to cash in their earned tokens.
8. The cash-in system should take a minimal amount of time.
9. Provide clear rules to staff and peer tutors for distribution of tokens.
10. Gradually reduce the value of the tokens to increase reliance on more natural reinforcers.

Token economy systems that have proven successful in the physical education program include those that allow students to "cash-in" their tokens to buy the following:

☐ A given number of minutes of supervised free play
☐ The right to lead class warm-up exercises
☐ The right to choose a class activity for 5 to 10 minutes on a given day
☐ The privilege of being the "assistant" teacher for a given class
☐ The privilege of 5 to 10 minutes of uninterrupted 1-1 play time with the physical education teacher
☐ The right to eat lunch with the physical education teacher
☐ A poster of a sports star
☐ Recreation and sport equipment

Relatively inexpensive recreation and sport equipment can be purchased to support the token economy system. Children love having the privilege to earn jump ropes, balls, juggling scarves, or hackey-sacs. Parent Teacher Associations often are willing to help with fund-raising to help provide the physical education teacher with this type of equipment. There are corporations that have fund-raiser/promotional campaigns

---
TABLE 5-2

Classroom reinforcers for use in a school setting

	Social-verbal	Manipulative	Token
Elementary students	Hug Positive comments ("Good job" "That was a nice play") Pat on the back	Helping teacher Being team leader Time in the game center Choosing a game Extra minutes of recess X minutes of free-time activity	Paper certificate Stars Positive note sent to parents Medal
Adolescents	Gesture of approval Handshake Positive comments ("Great job" "You did it" "Great effort")	Choosing class activity	Sports equipment Posters Positive note sent to parents T-shirt

(e.g. Campbell's Soups) that may help the physical education teacher secure this type of equipment without buying it out of an already small budget or an equally small personal salary.

Table 5-2 lists several examples of different types of reinforcers appropriate for use in school settings. Social and activity reinforcers have special appeal, since they are usually available at no cost to the teacher.

Frequency of reinforcement. The frequency of distributing reinforcers should be carefully controlled so that the student continues to strive toward desirable goals. The frequency that reinforcers are given is called the *reinforcement schedule* (see Table 5-3). Schedules of reinforcement should move from continuous (a reinforcer every time the desirable behavior occurs) to a fixed interval ratio (e.g., one reinforcer for every three instances of desirable behavior). The schedule should be changed eventually to a variable interval ratio (e.g., one reinforcer for every three instances of desirable behavior followed by one reinforcer for every five instances of desirable behavior, or one reinforcer every minute followed by one reinforcer every 3 minutes).

TABLE 5-3

Intermittent schedules on reinforcement

Name of schedule	Definition of schedule	Effects on behavior	
		Schedule in effect	Schedule terminated (extinction)*
Fixed ratio (FR)	Reinforcer is given after each **X** responses	High response rate	Irregular burst of responding; more responses than in continuous reinforcement, less than in variable ratio
Fixed interval (FI)	Reinforcer is given for first response to occur after each **X** minutes	Stops working after reinforcement; works hard just prior to time for next reinforcement	Slow gradual decrease in responding
Variable ratio (VR)	Reinforcer is given after **X** responses on the average	Very high response rates; the higher the ratio, the higher the rate	Very resistant to extinction; maximum number of responses before extinction
Variable interval (VI)	Reinforcer is given for first response after each **X** minutes on the average	Steady rate of responding	Very resistant to extinction; maximum time to extinction

From Walker HM: The acting-out child: coping with classroom disruption. Copyright © 1979 by Allyn & Bacon, Inc. Reprinted with permission.
*See p. 119 for discussion on extinction.

The variable interval ratio is the most effective because when students are unable to predict when they will be reinforced, they tend to persist at a task.

TECHNIQUES TO ELIMINATE DISRUPTIVE BEHAVIORS

Much of the previous discussion concerns the uses of reinforcement to increase efforts toward learning tasks. Very often reinforcement procedures are used to decrease undesirable behaviors. The undesirable behaviors must be eliminated or substantially reduced so that the student can focus attention and effort on positive learning habits.

Because of self-concept and attention deficits, children with disabilities may disrupt classrooms and make it difficult for themselves and others to learn meaningful motor skills. When behavioral technology is applied to classroom management, it must be systematic, consistent, and concerned with both preventing disruptive behavior and promoting positive behavior. There are two levels of classroom management, one for the group and another for individuals within the group.

Controlling Group Behavior

The single most effective method for controlling group behavior is prevention. The most significant technique for controlling behavior is to **"Catch 'em being good!"** This proactive teaching response, in which the teacher consistently and enthusiastically embraces "good" behavior, allows the teacher and the students to focus on "good" behavior. It must be noted that it is crucial that, when addressing the behavior of a child or children, the focus is on behavior. When praising a child for good behavior it is necessary that other children understand that it is the behavior that is being praised so those not being praised do not get the unintentioned message that they are somehow "bad." Examples of appropriate responses include the following:

- □ "Juan, thank you for being such a good listener."
- □ "I really like the way that Thelma is following directions."
- □ "Carlos, I'm really proud of you for putting your ball away."
- □ "Way to be, Jason! I like the fact that you shared your toy with Julianna."

This basic good teaching technique of "catch 'em being good," is one of the basic elements of preventive planning, which consists of establishing class rules and enforcing them in the least intrusive ways possible. Rules for class conduct should communicate to the students the behavior expected by the teacher. Effective class rules should be (1) few in number, (2) a state-

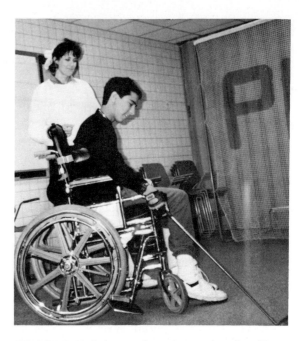

FIGURE 5-7. Verbal correction promotes learning. (Courtesy "Never Say Never," Kathy Corbin's Golf for the Physically Challenged.)

ment of behavior desired from the student, (3) simple and clearly stated in a positive way, and (4) guidelines that the teacher can enforce. For example, a well-stated rule is: "When lined up at the door waiting to pass to the next class, keep your hands to yourself."

Clearly stated expectations lead to appropriate classroom behavior. They provide learners with rules of conduct and identify behavior that will be rewarded. It is suggested that a list of rules be placed where students can observe it each day. The consequences for breaking rules should also be made clear to the students. These must be posted in the native languages of the children served. For example, if a school serves a large number of Hispanic students, rules and consequences should be posted in both English and Spanish.

When serving young children or non-readers, rules and consequences must be reviewed before each class period; in some situations, rules and consequences may need to be repeated periodically throughout the class.

Rules cannot take care of every situation; often there is disruptive behavior not covered by the rules. The difficult decision each teacher must make is whether to intervene and stop the disruptive behavior. Teachers have a responsibility to interfere with behaviors that:

☐ Present a real physical danger to self or others

☐ Are psychologically harmful to the child and others

☐ Lead to excessive excitement, loss of control, or chaos

☐ Prohibit continuation of the program

☐ Lead to destruction of property

☐ Encourage the spread of negativism in the group

☐ Lead to conflict with others outside the group

☐ Compromise the teacher's mental health and ability to function[15]

If the teacher does decide it is necessary to intervene to control disruptive behavior, several techniques are effective in controlling disturbances. Some specific techniques that have been identified by Redl[12] to manage disruptive students in a physical education setting are as follows:

☐ *Planned ignoring.* Much of children's behavior is designed to antagonize the teacher. If this behavior is not contagious, it may be wise to ignore it and not gratify the child.

☐ *Signal interference.* The teacher can use nonverbal controls such as hand clapping, eye contact, frowns, and body posture to indicate to the child disapproval and control.

☐ *Proximity control.* The teacher can stand next to a child who is having difficulty. This is to let the child know of the teacher's concern regarding the behavior.

☐ *Interest boosting.* If a child's interest is waning, involve the child actively in class activities of the moment and let him or her demonstrate the skill that is being performed or discussed.

☐ *Reduction of tension through humor.* Humor is often able to penetrate a tense situation, with the result that everyone becomes more comfortable.

☐ *Hurdle lesson.* Sometimes a child is frustrated by the immediate task. Instead of asking for help, the child may involve his or her peers in disruptive activity. In this event structure a task in which the child can be successful.

☐ *Restructure of classroom program.* If the teacher finds the class irritable, bored, or excited, a change in program might be needed.

☐ *Support from routine.* Some children need more structure than others. Without these guideposts they feel insecure. Structure programs for those who need it.

FIGURE 5-8. Competition may enhance performance in skilled performers. (Courtesy Adapted Physical Education, Jefferson Parish Public School System, Louisiana.)

□ *Direct appeal to value areas.* Appeal to certain values that children have internalized, such as a relationship between the teacher and the child, behavioral consequences, awareness of peer reaction, or appeal to the teacher's power of authority.

□ *Removal of seductive objects.* It is difficult for the teacher to compete against balls, bats, objects that can be manipulated, or equipment that may be in the vicinity of instruction. Either the objects have to be removed, or the teacher has to accept the disorganized state of the group.

□ *Verbal removal.* When a child's behavior has reached the point at which he or she will not respond to verbal controls, the child may have to be asked to leave the room (to get a drink, wash up, or deliver a message—not as punishment, but to distract the child).

□ *Physical restraint.* It may be necessary to restrain a child physically if he loses control and becomes violent.

Handling the Disruptive Student

The behavior problems of special students frequently contribute to their placement in special physical education programs. When special students return to the physical education class, teachers are often concerned that their problem behaviors will interfere with the operation of the classroom.

Behaviors that interfere with classroom instruction, impede social interaction with the teacher and peers, or endanger others are considered *classroom conduct problems.* Examples of inappropriate classroom behaviors are talking out, fighting, arguing, being out of line, swearing, and avoiding interactions with others. Breaking the rules of the game, poor sportsmanship, and immature and withdrawn behaviors also fall under this category. Behaviors that interfere with the special student's motor skill development are considered *skill problems.* Typical skill problems are poor attention and failure to attempt tasks with a best effort.

Problem behaviors are exhibited in one of three ways: (1) low rate of appropriate behaviors, (2) high rate of inappropriate behaviors, and (3) the appropriate behavior is not part of the student's repertoire. Knowing the characteristics of the behavior is important, since different management strategies are linked to each.

Low rate of appropriate behaviors

Students with low rates of appropriate behaviors do exhibit appropriate behaviors, but not as frequently as expected or required. For example, a student may be able to stay on task only 50% of the time. Also, students may behave appropriately in one setting but not another. For instance, the special student may work well on individual tasks but may find it difficult to work in group games. To alleviate these problems, the teacher sets up a systematic program to generalize on-task behaviors from one situation to another.

High rate of inappropriate behaviors

Inappropriate behaviors that occur frequently or for long periods are troublesome to teachers. Examples are students who do not conform to class rules 30 to 40 times a week, those who talk during 50% to 60% of class instruction, those who use profanity 5 to 10 times in one class period, and those who are off task 70% to 75% of the class period. To overcome these high rates of inappropriate behavior, the physical education teacher attempts to decrease the frequency or duration of the undesired behavior by increasing appropriate behaviors that are incompatible. For instance, to decrease the incidence of hitting a peer while in class, the teacher can increase the rate of performing tasks or decrease the time between tasks.

Appropriate behavior not part of student's repertoire

Students may not yet have learned appropriate behaviors for social interaction or classroom functioning. For instance, they may not know conduct of sportsmanship in class games. Teachers must provide instruction to help students acquire new behaviors. Behavior problems do not occur in isolation. Events or actions of others can initiate or reinforce inappropriate behaviors. To understand and manage classroom problems, the teacher should examine the student in relation to the target behavior. For example, classmates who laugh at clowning or wisecracks tend to reinforce that type of disruptive behavior; as a result, the disruptive student continues to exhibit the undesirable behavior.

Students show inappropriate behavior when they have not learned correct responses or have found that acting inappropriately is more rewarding than acting appropriately. These behavior problems do respond to instruction.

Methods for Decreasing Inappropriate Behavior

Several methods for decreasing inappropriate behavior are available. Walker and Shea[15] have proposed the following continuum of behavior modification interventions.

1. Reinforcement of behavior other than the target behavior: A reinforcer is given at the end of a

FIGURE 5-9. Attempting a new skill may require encouragement from a friend. (Courtesy Wisconsin Lions Camp Rosholt, Wisconsin.)

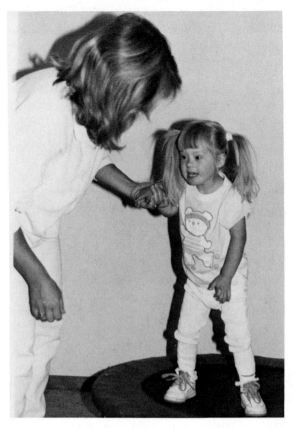

FIGURE 5-10. A well-designed home-based motor program greatly enhances motor development.

specified period of time provided that a pre-specified misbehavior has not occurred during the specified time interval.

2. Reinforcement of an appropriate target behavior: A reinforcer is given following the performance of a prespecified appropriate target behavior.

3. Reinforcement of incompatible behaviors: A reinforcer is given following the performance of a prespecified behavior that is physically and functionally incompatible with the target behavior.

4. Extinction: The reinforcer that has been sustaining or increasing an undesirable behavior is withheld.

5. Stimulus change: The existing environmental conditions are drastically altered to ensure that the target behavior is temporarily suppressed.

6. Nonexlusionary time-out:
   a. Head down on desk or table in work area in which target behavior occurred.
   b. Restriction to chair in a separate area of the classroom but able to observe classroom activities.
   c. Removal or materials (work, play).
   d. Reduction or elimination of room illumination.

7. Physical restraint.

8. Negative practice or satiation: The target behavior is eliminated by continued and increased reinforcement of that behavior.

9. Overcorrection: The repeated practice of an appropriate behavior in response to the exhibition of an inappropriate target behavior.

10. Exclusionary time-out:
    a. In-school suspension.
    b. Quiet room.

APPLICATION OF LEARNING PRINCIPLES TO INSTRUCTIONAL OBJECTIVES

Disruptive behavior by children in our public schools is a major public concern. This has escalated in recent years because of the increasing numbers of gangs in the schools and gang-associated weapons brought into and used in the schools. The application of behavior management techniques by teachers is one technique that may assist in bringing structure to the environment and lead to the alleviation of disruptive student behaviors.

There is consensus that successful schools have systems of firm, consistent management. Research confirms that clearly structured, secure environments permit students to master the objectives of the program. Haring[6] indicates that "teaching . . . necessitates finding a method of instruction which allows the child to learn."

The preconditions for the application of learning principles are that there must be a precisely defined short-term instructional objective, and there must be incentives for the learner to master the objective. If either of these preconditions is not satisfied, the effect of the program is minimized.

Effective learning is the result of mutual understanding between the student and the teacher. There is a contingency relationship between what a student must do with respect to a specific consequence. Homme[7] provides nine rules for developing contingency contracts. These principles also can be applied to the acquisition of any type of objectives by students.

1. Praise the correct objective.
2. Praise the correct objective immediately after it occurs.
3. Praise the correct objective after it occurs and not before.
4. Objectives should be in small steps so that there can be frequent praise.
5. Praise improvement.
6. Be fair in setting up consequences for achieving objectives.
7. Be honest and provide the agreed-on consequences.
8. Be positive so that the child may achieve success.
9. Be systematic.

Praise the Correct Objective

To implement this principle effectively, persons involved with instruction (teachers, school administrators, parents, and related service personnel) must know precisely the objective or behavior that the learner is to carry out. That behavior must be praised only if it is achieved. The application of this principle must be consistent among all persons who work with the child.

There are two ways that this learning principle can be violated by a teacher, parent, or school administrator. First, he or she may provide praise even though the objective has not been achieved; second, he or she may neglect to provide the praise even though the objective has been achieved. In the first case the learner is being reinforced for doing less than his or her best and consequently will have a lessened desire to put forth maximum effort on subsequent trials. In the second case, if the teacher does not deliver the agreed on consequence (explicit or implicit), the student's desire to perform the instructional task again will be reduced.

Praise Immediately after Completion of the Task

Learners need to receive feedback immediately after task performance. Homme[7] indicates that reinforcing feedback should be provided 0.05 second after the task for maximum effectiveness. Immediacy of feedback on task performance is particularly important with children functioning on a lower level. If there is a delay between task performance and feedback, the child may be confused as to what the praise is for. For example, if a child walks a balance beam correctly but confirmation of task mastery is provided late (for instance, as the child steps off the beam), the behavior of stepping off the beam may be strengthened to a greater degree than the desired objective of walking the beam. Thus the timing of the feedback (immediately after the task has been completed) is important.

Praise at the Appropriate Time

If a child is praised for performing an objective before it is completed, there is a good chance that he or she will expend less effort to meet the objective.

Objectives Should Be in Small Steps

If step size is small, there will be a greater rate of success. As has been indicated, disruptive behavior may be triggered by lack of success. The principle may therefore be applied in attempts to control disruptive behavior in the classroom. Thus if a child often exhibits many different types of disruptive behavior, objectives can be postulated to reduce the occurrence of these disruptive behaviors in small steps. For children with disabilities, learning by small steps permits much needed success.

Praise Improvement

The acquisition of skill toward an objective should be praised. Providing appropriate consequences for improvement may in some instances violate the principle of praising the correct objective. However, on tasks that cannot be broken into small steps it is necessary to praise improvement. To do so, the instructor must know precisely the student's present level of educational performance. When the performance reflects an improvement on that level, the student must be reinforced with praise. Improvement means that the learner is functioning on a higher level than before. Therefore it is unwise to praise or provide positive consequences to students who perform at less than their best effort, since to do so may encourage them to contradict their potential.

Be Fair in Setting Up Consequences

When there are specific objectives to be achieved to develop skill or appropriate classroom behavior, specific consequences can be arranged to support the development of these objectives. However, if such arrangements are to be made between the learner and the teacher, there must be equity between the task and the incentives. If the learner does not have sufficient incentive to perform the tasks or to behave appropriately, he or she is unlikely to do so. This learning principle operates at very early ages.

In our clinical experience we set up a target objective for an 18-month-old boy with Down syndrome to learn to walk. The task involved walking from one chair to another, which was placed 8 feet away. If the child walked the full distance, he was allowed to play for 15 seconds with the toys that were placed on top of the chairs. When this period elapsed, he would return to the task of walking a prescribed distance of 8 feet 1 inch, a short distance farther than the previous time. After a time the child refused to participate in the activity. The child's mother suggested that he be permitted to play with the toys for 30 seconds rather than for 15 seconds. This procedure was employed, and the child again engaged in the instructional task. It was inferred that the child would participate in tasks if the opportunity to play was commensurate with the effort put forth to master the objective. In our opinion, this is an example of equity between incentive and performance.

Be Honest

Agreements between teachers and learners must be honored by both. If there is an implicit or explicit arrangement between the teacher and the learner and the teacher does not follow through with the arrangement when the learner has upheld his or her end of the bargain, then the learning conditions will be seriously weakened. It is not uncommon for teachers to inadvertently forget the arrangements that have been made. Therefore it is important for teachers to have records

FIGURE 5-11. Immediate reinforcement can contribute to the competitive experience. (Courtesy Texas Special Olympics.)

of arrangements between themselves and the learner. Forgetting the preconditions between learner and teacher may have a negative impact on the pupil's learning at a subsequent time.

If the teacher requests that a learner perform a specific task, the teacher must not provide the desirable consequences unless the learner achieves the proper objective. Honest delivery of the agreed-on consequences is similar to praise for the correct behavior. However, praise for the correct behavior usually connotes a specific short-term task, whereas an agreed-on consequence may involve a contractual arrangement between two parties. Principals and teachers who set policies may achieve positive results with the application of this principle.

Be Positive

The objective should be phrased positively so that the learner can achieve the stated objective; for example,

"Walk to the end of the balance beam." An example of a negative statement is "Don't fall off of the balance beam." In the negative instance the child is avoiding failure, and there can be little value in mastering the desired behavior.

Be Systematic

To make the greatest positive impact on children with disabilities, it is necessary to apply all the learning principles all the time. Inconsistency confuses the learner with regard to the material to be learned and the type of behavior to maintain during class. The consistent use of modern behavioral technology enhances a child's ability to learn desirable behaviors. This learning principle is the most difficult one for teachers of emotionally disturbed children to master.

GENERALIZATION

In the past, generalization was an expected, yet unplanned, outcome of instructional programs.[14] Tradi-

FIGURE 5-12. #1. Courtesy Texas Special Olympics.

tionally, generalization has been left to chance; however, recently, particularly in the area of the education of severely and profoundly disabled populations, efforts are being made to assure that newly learned behaviors can be generalized to other settings, particularly to facilitate independent living in the community. Although basic research has documented generalization practices in the learning of motor skills, the process and the variables that control generalization of all types of behaviors are currently being developed to enhance carryover in applied settings (e.g., in the community).

For a skill to have value for improving the quality of life for individuals with disabilities it is necessary that it be functional for independent living. Thus a functional skill is one that is part of a daily routine of an individual who is living independently within a community. Two purposes of the adapted physical education program are (1) to build students' functional skills and (2) to promote the generalization of these skills in a variety of environments. Specific generalization goals should be incorporated into the severely disabled students' educational program.[13]

Although there are a number of considerations that are a part of the development and application of generalization techniques, there are two that are of paramount importance: (1) the techniques should support the generalization of functional motor skills to nontraining settings, such as recreational environments in the community and the home; and (2) the techniques should be reasonably efficient. *Efficiency* refers to the use of a skill in an applied setting with a minimum amount of training or assistance to produce the desired results.

Description of Generalization

The successful use of stimulus control technology and application of behavioral techniques and principles for teaching motor skills has made generalization of treatment effects a prominent issue in applied research in education.[16] Successful instruction of a new motor skill is a two-part process. The first step is to establish the target motor skill in an instructional situation. The second is to establish the day-to-day use of the new motor skill that has been acquired in a variety of appropriate circumstances in the natural environments. The technology for successful instruction in motor skills for individuals with disabilities has been demonstrated across many populations. The task now remains for both researchers and educators to develop a technology for ensuring that new motor skills will be maintained and extended outside of instructional settings and into physical activities in natural community and recreational environments. Such generalization will assist with independence and add to the quality of life for persons with disabilities.

Morris[11] describes three types of generalizations: (1) response maintenance, (2) situation or setting, and (3) response generalization.

- □ Response maintenance generalization are changes that are maintained even after the behavior modification has stopped.
- □ Situation or setting generalization are changes that occur from one environment to another, and/or from one person to another.
- □ Response generalization refers to changes in behavior that was not targeted for intervention.

There are two basic curriculum content forms of generalization in physical education: (1) the generalization of the acquired motor skills and (2) the generalization of the cognitive and social dimensions that enable participation with others. Clearly, if the skills of physical sports (e.g., basketball, soccer, and softball) are acquired, but the social skill is inappropriate for participation in culturally acceptable environments in the community, then the person with a disability will not have the opportunity to express the attained skills.[16]

Generalization Variables

When using generalization procedures, the adapted physical educator should consider the cognitive and social ability levels of the student, the acquired level of proficiency of the target skill, and the features of the natural environment. The range of cues and correction procedures that are present in the natural environment also will play a part in developing generalization strategies. Furthermore, the motivational level of the individual with disabilities and his or her attitude toward the skill are other dimensions of generalization. Ellis[2] indicates that the use of competitive goal structures in training could interfere with the generalization of strategy training. In competitive goal structures (e.g., team sports, games, and competition), the likelihood that a student will succeed is negatively related to the success of his or her peers.[9] These authors note that individual goal structures may not be profitable because individually evaluating and encouraging players to work harder at their own pace may be insufficient. They suggest that rewards should be contingent on combined achievements of the group. However, as Ellis[2] indicates, the demonstration of efficacy of generalization strategies awaits additional validation. Present theory may, however, serve as a basis for planning instruction that will carry over to community settings.

Considerations for Generalization

There are at least two different types of environments associated with the process of generalization. One is the instructional environment and the other is the natural environment. Instructional environments are settings where the education of students with disabilities is of explicit concern. On the other hand, natural environments are those settings where the actual performance of motor skills that occur in school are utilized in community environments. Natural environments are those in which individuals without disabilities function and in which individuals with disabilities should be taught to function. In each of these environments, cues and correction procedures are used to achieve objective behaviors. The differences in cues and correction procedures and in the different environments are essential considerations for the process of generalization. Basic principles that may help the physical educator employ strategies of generalization from instructional to natural environments are as follows: (1) instructional environments are preparatory for students with disabilities to function independently in a variety of current and subsequent natural environments; (2) the person with a disability may not necessarily perform specific motor skills in response to cues and correction procedures that are used in instructional environments when different cues and correctional procedures are used in other environments; (3) the students with disabilities should be taught to respond to only the most necessary cues and correction procedures in instructional and simulated or artificial environments; and (4) they should be taught to respond to as many cues and correction procedures as possible in current and subsequent natural environments.[3]

Warren et al.[16] suggest a process of generalization. It is as follows: (1) develop a management system to assess the generalized effect of the motor skill training program in nontraining environments; (2) determine the effects of training on motor function of persons with disabilities; (3) analyze the ecological variables (i.e., community situations in which the motor skills will be used); and (4) manipulate environmental variables to facilitate the generalization of the use of the motor skills.

Generalization is an important issue for students with severe disabilities because they typically do not learn motor skills to a sufficient enough performance level to enable participation in natural environments. Some persons with disabilities have difficulty generalizing newly learned motor behaviors to other settings, persons, and stimuli because of their limited motor capabilities. It is desirable to establish a comprehensive repertoire of motor behaviors that will permit not only sufficient immediate opportunities for participation in the community, but also motor skills that can be recombined to permit other opportunities to participate in an expanding number of recreational activities in the natural community. Fostering the ability to generalize across similar events in dissimilar settings is essential.

CUES AND CORRECTION PROCEDURES

Cues and correction procedures range from those that provide maximum assistance to those that offer minimum guidance, and those that occur exclusively in instructional environments to those that occur exclusively in natural environments.[3] There are three important considerations in the utilization of cues and correction procedures for generalization.

1. Know the cues and correction procedures that nondisabled persons typically use when performing a specific motor skill in the natural environment.
2. Know specifically the motor response required to perform the particular skill.
3. Know the cues and correction procedures of environments that are instrumental in shaping and developing motor responses.

All three component parts of the instructional process must be fully comprehended, and detailed attention must be given to these three essential aspects of instruction.

ALTERNATIVE MODES FOR DEVELOPMENT OF MOTOR SKILLS

The conventional procedure for the development of motor skills using instructional technology is the use of task-analyzed procedures, whereby knowledge of present level of performance is used to teach what is unlearned by the learner. However, there are alternative strategies that may facilitate the learning of students with disabilities. These include modeling, maintenance of behavior, and correction by errors.

Modeling

Modeling of generalizable skills is much the same as modeling of social behavior. It usually involves a demonstration of the behavior that the learner is to acquire. It serves to show the learner the "finished product" of his or her motor behavior. A model of hitting a ball could be a demonstration of someone hitting the ball in the same fashion that the child is to hit the ball. The model, particularly in motor tasks that are continuous and cannot be broken into component parts, is a very efficient way of promoting learning. The model cues and correction procedures provide students with disabilities with a demonstration of motor behavior that is expected of them. Still pictures, movies, or video tapes also may be used. The intent of the model is for the student to imitate the behavior that is demonstrated.

Maintenance

Maintenance is perpetuation of a trained behavior after all formal intervention has ceased. It can be assessed by either probes or by observing participation in natural environments. In the event that the individual does not maintain the desired behavior that is the focus of instruction, then instructional programming must be reintroduced at sufficient frequencies to reinstate the target behavior needed for participation in the natural environment. The evolution of scientifically validated maintenance programs is now the source of considerable research.

Learning by Correction

Another mode of teaching that is closely associated with modeling is learning by correction. In this scheme of instruction the assumption is that the feedback is provided after the student performs the motor skill. Feedback provided by an external source (e.g., the teacher) is of less value than self-correction. The most efficient learning by correction requires prerequisite cognitive ability and presupposes that the individual can reflect on his or her performance and determine where or how errors occurred. The ability to learn by correction varies according to the learner's cognitive capabilities and the complexity of the task being attempted.

SUMMARY

There is a technology based on research and demonstration that, if used in applied settings, facilitates the learning of motor skills by individuals with disabilities. These techniques include conducting procedures that facilitate generalization of trained skills from instructional to natural environments, controlling sensory inputs, providing appropriate consequences, and controlling environmental conditions to maximize learning. Planned procedures for intervention of programs require a systematic measurement system. This measurement system may be applied to positive learning or to decreasing inappropriate behavior. Positive and unobtrusive approaches should be used first. The levels of reinforcement of learning must be determined. The implementation of contingency management systems may be necessary in some situations. Application of behavioral learning principles can enhance the learning capabilities of children with disabilities. However, learning an instructional behavior in a school setting is only the first step of effective teaching. A motor behavior is not learned until it has been generalized across several environments or relevant tasks that are a part of recreational living in the community. Appropriate use of cues and correction procedures facilitates the process of generalization.

REVIEW QUESTIONS

1. What techniques can be applied to maximize student achievement in motor skill development?
2. What principles of learning can be applied to increase efficiency of training regimens that facilitate motor performance?
3. Name some techniques for providing consequences to behaviors to be learned that will facilitate motor proficiency.
4. What are some positive teacher techniques that can be used to adapt instruction to the needs of the learner?
5. What are the procedures for conducting applied behavioral programs?
6. Describe some techniques for recording data that extend present levels of performance.
7. Describe the different ways in which performance can be measured.
8. Name and describe some behavioral techniques for facilitating the development of positive behavior.
9. Indicate some principles for establishing class rules.
10. What are some techniques that can be used to manage disruptive classroom behavior?
11. List different types of reinforcers.
12. Provide examples of the application of learning principles that can be applied to the acquisition of positive behavior.
13. What are some of the characteristics of a teacher that can maximize the development of motor and social skills for individuals with disabilities?
14. What is generalization and how does it apply to independent recreational sport and physical activity in the community?
15. What are some principles that may guide the physical educator to generalize the physical education activities learned in a class setting to activity outside of class?
16. How does the appropriate utilization of cues and correction procedures assist a person with disabilities to generalize meaningful motor skills learned in physical education instruction?
17. Name three behaviors that teachers must address and stop.

STUDENT ACTIVITIES

1. Select a measurement technique, collect behavioral data on a child, and graph the results.

2. Observe a teacher who is instructing a child with a disability. Record techniques used that were discussed in this chapter.
3. Make a list of class rules that might minimize disruptive behavior.
4. Set up a contingency management system for a class. Indicate procedures for the administration of the system.
5. Evaluate a person who is instructing a child with a disability with the use of instructional objectives to determine effective use of the application of learning principles.
6. Conduct an ecological assessment of the community to determine what activities should be included in physical education programs for individuals with disabilities in your community.
7. Describe the differences in cues and correction procedures of tasks in the instructional setting and in a natural environmental setting.
8. Have the students develop a behavioral management checklist in class. Assign the students to use the checklist while observing a child with a disability participate in physical education class. Discuss the students' observations during the next class.

REFERENCES

1. Bellamy GT, Horner RH, Inman DP: *Habilitation of the severely and profoundly retarded,* Specialized Training Program Monograph, No. 2, Center on Human Development, University of Oregon, 1977.
2. Ellis ES: The role of motivation and pedagogy on the generalization of cognitive training by the mildly handicapped, *J Learning Disabilities* 19:66-70, 1986.
3. Falvey MA: *Community-based curriculum: instructional strategies for students with severe handicaps,* Baltimore, 1986, Paul H Brookes Publishing.
4. Foxx RM, Azrin NH: The elimination of autistic self-stimulatory behavior by overcorrection, *J Appl Behav Anal* 6:1-14, 1973.
5. Gold M: *Task analysis: a statement and example using acquisition and production of a complex assembly task by the retarded blind,* Institute for Child Behavior and Development, University of Illinois at Urbana-Champaign, 1975.
6. Haring N, editor: *Developing effective individualized programs for severely handicapped children and youth,* Washington, DC, 1977, US Office of Education, Bureau of Education for the Handicapped.
7. Homme L: *How to use contingency contracting in the classroom,* Champaign, Ill, 1970, Research Press.
8. Lewis RB, Doorlag DH: *Teaching special students in the mainstream,* Columbus, Ohio, 1983, Charles E Merrill Publishing.
9. Licht BC, Kistner JA: *Motivational problems of learning-disabled children: individual differences and their implications for treatment.* In Torgesen JK, Wong BYL, editors: *Psychological and educational perspectives on learning disabilities,* New York, 1986, Academic Press.

10. McLoughlin JA, Lewis RB: *Assessing special students,* Columbus, Ohio, 1981, Charles E Merrill Publishing.

11. Morris RJ: *Behavior modification with exceptional children,* Glenview, Ill, 1985, Scott, Foresman.

12. Redl F: *Managing surface behavior of children in school.* In Long HJ, editor: *Conflict in the classroom,* Belmont, Calif, 1965, Wadsworth.

13. Sailor W, Guess D: *Severely handicapped students: an instructional design,* Boston, 1983, Houghton Mifflin.

14. Stokes TF, Baer DM: An implicit technology of generalization, *J Appl Behav Anal* 10:349-367, 1977.

15. Walker J, Shea T: *Behavior management,* Columbus, Ohio, 1988, Merrill Publishing.

16. Warren SF et al: *Assessment and facilitation of language generalization.* In Sailor W, Wilcox B, Brown L: *Methods of instruction for severely handicapped students,* Baltimore, 1985, Paul H Brookes Publishers.

17. Winnick J: *Project UNIQUE,* Paper presented at the International Symposium, Year of the Disabled Child, New Orleans, 1981.

SUGGESTED READINGS

Falvey MA: *Community-based curriculum: instructional strategies for students with severe handicaps,* Baltimore, 1986, Paul H Brookes Publishing.

Kohen-Raz R: *Learning disabilities and postural control,* London, 1986, Freund Publishing House.

Lewis R, Doorlag DH: *Teaching special students in the mainstream,* Columbus, Ohio, 1983, Charles E Merrill Publishing.

Sailor W, Guess D: *Severely handicapped students: an instructional design,* Boston, 1983, Houghton Mifflin.

Seaman JA, DePauw KP: *The new adapted physical education: a developmental approach,* Palo Alto, Calif, 1989, Holt, Rinehart & Winston.

Walker JE, Shea TM: *Behavior modification,* Columbus, Ohio, 1988, Merrill Publishing.

PART THREE

PROGRAMMING FOR SPECIFIC DISABILITIES

IN THIS SECTION specific types of disabilities are described in

detail. Each condition is defined, characteristics are given,

means of testing are suggested, and specific programming and

teaching techniques are detailed.

OBJECTIVES

Describe the nature of infant mortality in the United States.

Explain the nature of drug abuse on children with and without disabilities.

Describe the nature of abuse and neglect on children with and without disabilities.

Explain the relationship of poverty and homelessness to inadequate psychosocial development in children.

Describe the changing nature of the schools and difficulties associated with teaching in these schools.

List the social benefits of play, games, and sports for children with and without disabilities.

State the instructional process needed to change social behavior through sports and games.

Describe the benefits of leisure and recreation, particularly outdoor/environmental based activity in the pychosocial develoment of individuals with disabilities.

Explain how to generalize social behavior used in play, games, sports, and leisure/recreation activities to the society at large.

Courtesy: Wisconsin Special Olympics

Psychosocial Development

Contemporary education must respond to the increased psychosocial needs of the infants, children, and adolescents it serves. Children with and without disabilities are entering the public school system unprepared, understimulated, abused, homeless, unloved, fearful, tired, hungry, and unkempt. Any and all of these factors have an impact on the psychosocial development of these children. In this chapter we discuss the psychosocial development and deficits of at-risk infants, children, and adolescents and the unique psychosocial developmental deficits of children with disabilities. In the first section we discuss the societal influences that have a negative effect on the pychosocial development of at-risk infants, children, and adolescents. In the second section we discuss the unique psychosocial needs of children with disabilities. In the third section, the role of well-designed physical education, leisure, recreation, and sport programs in the development of appropriate psychosocial behaviors is discussed.

AT-RISK INFANTS, CHILDREN, AND ADOLESCENTS

A growing number of infants, children, and adolescents in this society are at risk. The societal forces acting on these children are overwhelming. They include poverty, homelessness, prenatal maternal neglect, child abuse, violence, and racism. According to Geoffrey Cowley[11]:

> Children have never had it easy. A fair proportion have always been beaten, starved, raped or abandoned, and until quite recently even the loved ones faced daunting obstacles. . . Nearly one in four is born into poverty, a formidable predictor of lifelong ill health, and a growing number lack such basic advantages as a home, two parents, and regular access to a doctor. Every year thousands die violently from abuse or preventable accidents. Millions go unvaccinated against common childhood diseases. . . American children remain the most neglected in the developed world.

Infant Mortality

The most obvious indication of the neglect that Cowley describes is the fact that the United States ranks behind 19 developed nations in its infant mortality rate. The National Commission to Prevent Infant Mortality suggests the national rate may climb from its present level of 10.1 deaths per 1000 live births.[23] According to the National Commission to Prevent Infant Mortality, some cities in the United States are becoming "infant mortality disaster areas." The U.S. death rate equals those of some Third World nations as 105 infants die each day.[44]

Of the 105 infants who die in the United States each day, more black children die than white children. In fact, the death rate for black infants is 17.6 per 1000 live births as of 1988. That is more than twice the rate for white infants (8.5 per 1000).[11]

Almost as frightening as the infant mortality rate is the number of low birth weight infants born in the United States. According to the National Commission

to Prevent Infant Mortality, there has been an escalation in the number of low birth weight infants born in the United States. At issue is the fact that low birth weight infants are infinitely more likely to die than infants of normal weight. Infants with low birth weight (less than 5.5 pounds) are 40 times more likely to die within their first month and 20 times more likely to die within their first year than infants weighing more than 5.5 pounds at birth.[11]

Of equal importance is the fact that the immature and incomplete in utero development of these children causes them to be at serious risk for developmental disabilities throughout their lives. These low birth weight infants who survive have high risks of deafness, blindness, mental retardation and other disabilities.[23] It is frightening to note that in 1988 13% of all black children were born dangerously underweight,[11] making them more at-risk for developmental disabilities.

FIGURE 6-1. Special olympians celebrate their success with a friend. (Courtesy Texas Special Olympics.)

Alcohol and Other Drug Abuse

According to Greer[24]:

> We are facing the emerging of what some are now calling a 'bio-underclass;' a frightening proportion of the next generation of school children will have impairments which, in the words of Dr. Harold Nickens of the American Society of Addiction Medicine, may require the medical community 'to define an entirely new, organic brain syndrome' based on the physical and chemical damage done to fetal brains by drug-abusing mothers.

The escalation of the use and abuse of alcohol and other drugs has had a profound impact on the quality of life of millions of infants, children, and adolescents with and without disabilities.[50] Each day, 1000 babies are born to mothers who use drugs.[23] Estimates suggest that 1.2 million women in the United States who use and abuse alcohol, nicotine, marijuana, cocaine, or other drugs may give birth to babies with developmental delays.[7] Fetal alcohol exposure is the nation's leading known cause of mental retardation, surpassing both Down syndrome and spina bifida. The figures are staggering. Between 5000 and 10,000 children are born with severe fetal alcohol syndrome each year.[11] According to Dr. Ira Chasnoff, president of the National Association for Perinatal Addiction Research and Education, about 11% of all newborns, or 375,000 infants, were exposed to drugs in utero.[12]

Infants born in the inner cities have an increased chance of being effected by the drug culture. In New York's Harlem Hospital, reported cocaine use among pregnant women skyrocketed from 1% in 1980 to 20% in 1988.[11] At the Washington, D.C. General Hospital, 20% to 30% of pregnant women admitted to being users of cocaine, heroine, PCP (phencyclidine hydrochloride), or "poly drugs" (any combination of drugs not specifically prescribed for use) in 1988.[23] Wehling reported that 58% of women seeking obstetric care at the Family Center of Jefferson Medical College in Philadelphia's inner city tested positive for cocaine in 1990.[57]

Characteristics of infants exposed to drugs in utero

Greer[24] reported that children exposed to cocaine in utero—those born addicted to cocaine—face overwhelming odds. The results of early research suggest the cocaine-addicted infant may suffer from poor body-state regulation, tremors, chronic irritability, and poor visual orientation.[24] Crack-abusing women are giving birth to babies with small heads, missing bowels, and malformed genitals and who suffer strokes and seizures as infants.

Those infants exposed to drugs in utero who are able to survive the tenuous first year demonstrate the characteristics of any post-drug impairment syndrome, including difficult withdrawal experiences. Cratty noted that early observation of drug-stressed newborns indicates the presence of tremors, which may terminate or fade out in the third or fourth month of life.[14] In addition, the children demonstrate behaviors that will have an impact on their early education experiences. These are: poor abstract reasoning and memory, poor judgment, inability to concentrate, inability to deal with stress, frequent tantrums and violent acting-out behaviors, as well as a variety of other behavior problems.[23]

It is almost impossible to imagine the impact of this prenatal child abuse—women literally abusing their babies with alcohol, crack, heroin, PCP, and poly drugs when the infants are in utero. The child protective service agencies, child welfare agencies, and the foster care system are being bombarded. Not only have these infants been "abandoned" during the prenatal experience, but often these infants are subsequently abandoned on the streets and in the hospitals. The women who gave birth to these infants commonly continue to be drug abusers and often are unable to care for themselves, much less an infant.

Abandoned infants and children, without extended family willing to assume responsibility, generally are placed in protective custody of the state. The first placement is generally in a foster care home. A study of the foster care system in New York demonstrated an escalated need and increased demand on the child protective service system in recent years. In 1980, 19% of the children placed in foster homes were under the age of 5. In 1990, over 50% of children placed in foster homes were under the age of 5. Officials in the New York foster care system suggest that this dramatic increase is directly attributable to crack abuse.[1]

U.S. schools are facing the same overwhelming need. The Dallas Independent School District has an active "Drug Babies" Task Force seeking to devise strategies to meet the needs of these children. The Los Angeles Unified School District has developed a pilot preschool program designed to serve children exposed prenatally to crack. According to Wehling[57]:

> The pilot preschool program in the Los Angeles Unified School District is one of the first in the nation to tackle a problem that many educators fear is about to explode nationally: a surge in the number of drug-damaged children

entering public schools. These children present a variety of developmental, neurological, and behavioral challenges—including unusually short attention spans, hyperactivity, sudden temper flare-ups, speech and language delays, poor task organization, and an exaggerated need for structured routine."

The National Association for Perinatal Addiction Research and Education has led the nation in its efforts to examine the impact of in utero exposure to drugs. The research is scarce, however, for a number of reasons. The women and infants/children involved tend to be transient, and this makes it difficult to do research on the long-term effects of the in utero drug exposure on children as they grow. Research also is difficult because it is impossible to isolate the variables that may cause the child to have developmental delays—poverty, malnutrition, lack of medical intervention, and environmental deprivation from drug-related delays. It also is difficult to complete such research because each child appears to be affected differently, depending on the mother's drug(s) of choice. It is difficult, for example, to examine the effects of perinatal cocaine addiction on a newborn infant because most cocaine addicts tend to use other drugs (poly drugs, heroin, PCP, marijuana, and alcohol) as well. The National Association for Perinatal Addiction Research and Education, acknowledging difficulty with control of all variables, studied the long-term consequences of perinatal addiction in 263 children. The following findings were reported[57]:

□ Children of drug-using mothers were more likely to be born prematurely and generally weighed less, were shorter, and had smaller head circumferences. As infants, they were unusually irritable and had a low threshold for overstimulation.

□ By 3 months, the mean weight of drug-affected children had caught up with that of infants in a drug-free control group; by 12 months, the two groups were not significantly different in body length.

□ Through age 2, head circumference measurements remained smaller in drug-affected children.

□ Drug-exposed children scored within the normal range for cognitive development and are not considered to be brain-damaged. However, they require a structured learning environment and patient, one-on-one attention from teachers and caregivers.

Poverty and Homelessness

Dr. Lillian Parks, superintendent of the East St. Louis schools, said, "Gifted children are everywhere in East St. Louis, but their gifts are lost to poverty and turmoil and the damage done by knowing they are written off

FIGURE 6-2. Special olympians enjoy a few minutes between events. (Courtesy Texas Special Olympics.)

by their society."[38] The U.S. Census Bureau reported in 1990 that 13.5% of the population, or 33.6 million people, live in poverty. Cowley[11] suggested:

Kids under 5 suffer more poverty than any other age group in America. Roughly one in four is poor, versus one in eight adults, and the consequences are manifold. Poor children are more likely to suffer from low birth weight, more likely to die within the first year of life, more likely to suffer hunger or abuse while growing up and less likely to benefit from immunizations or adequate medical care.

Mayor Ray Flynn, chairman of the Conference of Mayors Task Force on Hunger and Homelessness, suggested that increases in hunger, homelessness, and poverty are "one of the most dramatic changes that swept across our country" in the 1980s.[48] Poverty is particularly threatening to families headed by single women. Such families are six times more likely to be poor than families headed by married couples.[48] Census Bureau figures released in 1989 indicate that women head 44% of black families, 23% of Hispanic families, and 13% of white families—an increase across race from the beginning of the decade.[61]

These single-parent families, headed by women, represent 34% of the homeless population.[3] The New York City Department of Health reported that in 1987 40% of homeless women studied had had no prenatal care at all. As a result these women are dangerously at risk for low birth weight babies and difficulties with pregnancy.

The picture of adults that comes to mind when the term *homeless* is mentioned must be erased. Many of the homeless are children. In fact, one in four homeless people is a child.[48] Bassuk[3] reported that between 65,000 and 100,000 homeless *children* (italics added) sleep in emergency shelters, welfare hotels, abandoned cars, or abandoned buildings every night.

Characteristics of homeless children

The U.S. Department of Education estimates that there are more than 220,000 homeless school-age children in America. Those that make it to school are frightened, exhausted, hungry, and disenfranchised. The children feel unempowered and overwhelmed by the uncertainty of their lives. According to Bassuk[3]:

> During critical, formative years, homeless children lack the basic resources needed for normal development. They undergo experiences resulting in medical, emotional, behavioral, and educational problems that may plague them forever . . . Homeless children experience more acute and chronic medical problems than do poor children who have homes. Health care workers find high incidences of diarrhea and malnourishment, as well as asthma and elevated blood levels of lead, in shelter children.

The Children's Defense Fund, an active child advocate agency, has reported that homeless children are three times more likely to have missed immunizations than are poor children with houses. Recent research has identified inner-city neighborhoods where 50% to 70% of preschool children are unvaccinated. As a result there has been an overwhelming resurgence of once rare childhood diseases. In fact, reported measles cases rose from 1500 in 1983 to an absurd 25,000 in 1990.[11]

Bassuk reported data from a 1985 study of homeless children. The researcher found[3]:

> . . . almost half of the homeless preschoolers manifested serious emotional and developmental delays. When compared with poor, housed children, homeless children were slower in language development, motor skills, fine motor coordination and personal and social ability.

Wood et al. assessed the health status of 196 homeless families living in shelters in Los Angeles, and 194 housed, poor families. They wrote[62]:

> Homeless children are at high risk for health and behavior problems because of the confluence of risks that accompany homelessness. In addition to being poor and experiencing family problems such as parental loss, violence, and drug use, homeless children frequently also experience loss of friends, loss of familiar neighborhood surroundings, school disruptions, exposure to many strangers, and threatening situations on the streets and in the shelters.

Wood et al.[62] concluded that homeless children have a significant risk of present and future developmental delays, behavior disorders, academic problems, and nutritional deprivation. Homeless children experience a great risk of present and future health problems that affect the quality of life.

Homeless children are among those most at risk for delays in psychosocial development. These children are denied the most basic of human rights—to be warm and protected and safe.

Child Abuse and Neglect

The National Center on Child Abuse Prevention Research indicated that in 1989-1990 an estimated 2,508,000 children were reported to child protective service agencies as victims of maltreatment. This is approximately 39 out of every 1000 children in the United States.[15]

In 1990, an estimated 1211 children died from abuse and/or neglect. According to Daro and McCurdy,[15] fatalities have increased in the United States by 38% since 1985. It is estimated that over three children die from abuse and neglect each day.[15] These data are frightening. But the data reflect the fact that most child abuse is an abuse of power. The most helpless, the children least likely to be able to defend themselves, are the victims. Reports from 30 states indicate that 89% of the victims of child abuse are less than 5 years old at the time of their death.[8] Data indicate that 53% of the children killed as a result of abuse are under the age of 1.[15]

The American Association for the Protection of Children (AAPC) reported the following distribution of cases reported to child protective service agencies: 27% physical abuse, 15% sexual abuse, 46% neglect, 9% emotional maltreatment, and 4% other.[15]

Rampant poverty, economic instability, unemployment, sanctioned societal violence ("spare the rod, spoil the child"), family history of abuse, and substance abuse are among the primary factors in the continued

FIGURE 6-3. Interaction with a gentle animal may lead to interaction with gentle human beings. (Courtesy Adapted Physical Education Department, Jefferson Parish Public School System, Louisiana.)

growth in child abuse reports and fatalities.[35] Children with disabilities are even more at risk for abuse than other children.[32] In fact, the very nature of children with some disabilities puts them in jeopardy. For example, Elizabeth Rahdert, a research psychologist in the division of clinical research at the National Institute on Drug Abuse suggested that:

> When you have infants and children fetally exposed to crack, they may be easily excitable, hyperarousable and do more crying. So if the child is impaired and the mother or care giver is impaired, the situation is even more explosive and dangerous.[13]

The research literature provides growing evidence that children who are abused or neglected are at greater risk of becoming emotionally disturbed, language-impaired, mentally retarded, and/or physically disabled, while children with disabilities may be at greater risk of abuse and neglect.[16,34,39,58]

Characteristics

Children with disabilities may have one or more of the following characteristics, which make them more susceptible to child abuse and neglect than children without disabilities:

□ Need for expensive medical intervention/therapy
□ Inability to follow expected developmental patterns in motor, speech, and social skills
□ Dependency on others to take care of basic daily living needs
□ Dependency on others to take care of social/friendship needs
□ Inability to take control of own life, which causes long-term need for caregiver
□ Inability to effectively communicate needs and wants
□ Inability to participate in reciprocal relationships
□ Lack of knowledge about sex and misunderstanding of sexual advances
□ Inability to differentiate between acceptable and nonacceptable touch
□ Inability to defend self [32,58]

Please refer to Chapter 16 for a more complete description of the types of child abuse and neglect.

PSYCHOSOCIAL DEFICITS OF CHILDREN AND YOUTH WITH DISABILITIES
At-Risk Children and Youth with Disabilities

It is important to note that the students receiving special education services in the United States are disproportionately at-risk minority children. The Public Education Association of New York reported:

> Classes for the emotionally handicapped, neurologically impaired, learning disabled and educable mentally retarded are disproportionately black. . . . Classes for the

FIGURE 6-4. Participation in competition with age and ability matched athletes provides a real self-testing opportunity. (Courtesy Texas Special Olympics.)

speech, language, and hearing impaired are disproportionately Hispanic.[33]

Kozol[38] wrote:

Nationwide, black children are three times as likely as white children to be placed in classes for the mentally retarded but only half as likely to be placed in classes for the gifted: a well-known statistic that should long since have aroused a sense of utter shame in our society.

Children with disabilities face even more problems than children without disabilities; this is particularly true of at-risk children, poor or homeless children, or abused children who happen to have disabilities. Their lives are more complex and more frightening because of an even more overwhelming sense of lack of power than that experienced by children facing only the disabilities.

Children and Youth with Disabilities

Children with disabilities may find it difficult to experience typical psychosocial development for a number of reasons. They may face rejection, overt or covert, by their parents, siblings, teachers, or peers. These rejections are generally borne of fear, guilt, pity, or the process of equating disability with illness. In ancient Greece and Rome, for example, infants with disabilities were perceived to be disgusting to the gods and were abandoned to die. In the Middle Ages, individuals with disabilities were believed to be possessed by "evil spirits." Unfortunately, some of this type of mentality persists. One has only to read about the treatment of children with acquired immunodeficiency syndrome (AIDS), for example, to understand the nature of prejudice toward children with disabilities.

The psychosocial development of children with disabilities may be seriously affected by the prejudice of others. In fact, the prejudice of others may predispose the child to have low self-esteem. Children with disabilities may be overprotected and, subsequently, prevented from developing age-appropriate play and interaction skills. Well-meaning parents and teachers may keep children with disabilities from participating in activities with their siblings and peers.

Individuals with disabilities generally experience more problems in individual and social development and adjustment than do their peers without disabilities.[19] Some of the problems with psychosocial development are a function of the prejudice and expectations of others. Some of the problems may be a function of the behaviors of children with disabilities. Some disabilities cause, by their very nature, serious difficulties in social interaction skills. The autistic child or the child with childhood schizophrenia, for example, is deemed to be disabled primarily because of the difficulties the child experiences in interacting with other people.

Some of the ways in which children with disabilities may differ socially from others are as follows:

1. They may have difficulty with basic communication skills and, as such, lack ability to relate to others and respond appropriately.
2. They may lack impulse control.
3. They may have significant difficulty following directions and following rules; in fact, they may be unable to follow directions/rules.
4. They may have difficulty in age-appropriate social interactions with peers and teachers, particularly in a structured school environment.
5. They may be verbally or physically aggressive toward self, peers, and teachers.

6. They may have difficulty taking turns and sharing equipment, particularly toys, balls, etc.
7. They may have difficulty understanding social cues and, subsequently, respond inappropriately to the advances or rebuffs of others.
8. They may exhibit difficulty processing and understanding gestures, facial expressions, and vocal inflections that are crucial to understanding the context of an interaction with another.
9. They may exhibit "out-of-control" behaviors or temper tantrums, particularly in response to overstimulation or change in routine.
10. They may exhibit developmental delays in play behaviors basic to the social development of children.

SOCIAL BENEFITS OF PLAY, GAMES, AND SPORTS FOR STUDENTS WITH DISABILITIES

Many educators view schools as the vehicle for transmitting social and cultural values to children. This may be done through an instructional process similar to that for teaching motor skills. It involves:

□ Identifying the social abilities and values to be transmitted
□ Identifying necessary prerequisites of social participation in play, games, and sport
□ Using procedures to assess the present level of participation in play, games, and sport
□ Using procedures to assess social skills exhibited in play, games, and sport
□ Determining social goals
□ Intervening with specific techniques and strategies to achieve the social goals in age and developmentally appropriate play, games, and sport

The development of social capability of children with disabilities is an important objective of the physical education program. Exhibiting socially appropriate skills improves the chance of social acceptance by others. Seaman and DePauw[49] and Oliver[47] indicate that physical education is an efficient medium through which these children can realize social and emotional growth. Some social benefits that might be outcomes of a physical education program follow:

□ It provides a controlled environment in which to learn socially appropriate play skills.
□ It provides an opportunity for the child to experience a variety of social experiences and interactions.[20]
□ It gives children with and without disabilities the opportunity to learn in a setting with "real-life" situations—winning, losing, succeeding, and not succeeding.

FIGURE 6-5. The development of trust is often difficult for children. (Courtesy Wisconsin Lions Camp, Rosholt, Wisconsin.)

□ It enables children with and without disabilities to learn their capabilities and limitations.[36]
□ It enables children to be contributors to team and group efforts.[18]
□ It enables children to become intelligent spectators in the sport activities in which they participate.

THE REGULAR EDUCATION INITIATIVE

More and more children with disabilities are being returned to regular education programs to receive the majority of services. One of the primary motivations for the regular education initiative is to allow children with disabilities to participate in programs and activities with children without disabilities. In fact, this return to the regular education program is often planned solely for the purpose of allowing the child with disabilities to have a social experience. This is being done, unfortunately, without regard to the child's academic or motor development needs.

Children with disabilities are often placed into the regular physical education program solely for the purpose of providing an opportunity for socialization. This decision may be made without regard for the motor needs of the child. The physical educator must be prepared to defend the motor and fitness components of the physical education program. Physical education cannot be regarded solely as an opportunity for the provision of play—children can "play" at recess.

If a child with a disability is to be educated in the regular physical education program, care must be taken to provide the child with an excellent motor and fitness program, within the context of a nurturing, caring environment for the development of psychosocial skills.

Children with disabilities, however, should not be returned to the regular physical education program without preparation. Regular physical education teachers and students need to be carefully educated to prepare them to accept and understand the unique needs of a child with disabilities. If this careful preparation, including empathy experiences, is not part of the total process of integrating children with disabilities into the regular physical education program, all the children may be set up to fail.

In school programs that do not abuse the concept of the regular education initiative, a decision regarding placement in the least restrictive physical education environment is based on the assessment of the child's motor, cognitive, and social skills. Placement in the least restrictive environment should be related to the social ability of the student with a disability.[25] That is, all of the demands of the physical education environment and the abilities of the learner should be matched. It should be noted that the physical education environment may be the single most socially demanding environment in the instructional program. In many schools, physical education classes are huge, teacher-student ratios are ridiculous, and there is limited personal space for each student.

A system that considers social ability for participation in physical education should include at least two main provisions. First, the system should provide assurance of progression of social skills in physical activities included in the regular school curriculum. This may facilitate the acquisition of behaviors that are similar to those demonstrated by students without disabilities in the public schools. Second, the system should attempt to accommodate the abilities of each student by altering the demands of the tasks and social situations so the students may be challenged while also experiencing success.

Physical Education for At-Risk Children and Youth

The physical educator is in a unique position to address some of the issues that plague at-risk children. In fact, in and through play, games, and sport, the physical educator can help children who have experienced psychosocial deprivation by providing the opportunity to develop social skills necessary to function within play, games, and sport. Many of the skills necessary to participate successfully in the physical education program are those necessary to participate successfully within the schools and within society at large. Hellison and his associates at the University of Illinois-Chicago Circle have piloted physical education and sports programs for at-risk children and youth.[28]

Hellison and his associates have based their programs on the notion that the physical education class, or a team within a class, is a microcosm of the greater society and that children can learn to develop values and behaviors in the often intense gymnasium experience. The intent of the program is to develop the child's self-responsibility and social responsibility. Hellison wrote[28]:

> . . . self-responsibility is conceptualized as empowering at-risk youth to take more control of their own lives, to learn how to engage in self-development in the face of a variety of external forces, including socialization patterns, peer pressure, self-doubt, lack of concepts and skills, and limited vision of their own options. Social responsibility is conceptualized as the development of sensitivity to the rights, feelings, and needs of others. Indicators include movement beyond egocentrism and ethnocentrism, recognition of the rights and feelings of others, caring and compassion, service to others, and concern for the entire group's welfare.

Their programs have been based on the notion that children, even those who are most seriously at risk, can learn the social and emotional skills necessary to function in play, games, and sport and, perhaps more important, can generalize those skills to participation in the larger society. Hellison suggests a four level model of behavior/value development for the physical education program[29]:

☐ Level 1: Sufficient self-control to respect the rights and feelings of others.

☐ Level 2: Participation and effort in program activities.

☐ Level 3: Self-direction with emphasis on independence and goal-setting.

☐ Level 4: Caring about and helping others.

SOCIALIZATION SKILLS NECESSARY TO PARTICIPATE IN PLAY, GAMES, SPORT, AND LEISURE AND RECREATION ACTIVITIES

Socialization is the process of learning how to behave appropriately in social settings—that is, how to interact with others.[49] At-risk children and children with disabilities often have difficulty interacting with others in a socially appropriate way.[4] Social skill instruction follows the same procedures as those for teaching motor skills. In the process the learner interacts within a social environment (the play, games, sport, or leisure/recreation activity), adapts to the characteristics of the environment, and thus changes actions so that he or she is better able to engage in the social process. Fos-

FIGURE 6-6. Special Olympics provides an opportunity for the development of self-esteem. (Photo by Jo Arms, Courtesy Texas Special Olympics.)

tering, nurturing, guiding, influencing, and controlling social behavior are possible in a designed environment with practical objectives structured by the physical educator. If the teacher is successful, children with and without disabilities move to higher levels of social skills.

Curriculum-Based Assessment and Programming

Curriculum-based assessment and programming is a system in which students are assessed and classified relative to the degree to which they are learning specific curriculum content.[31,55] Those who employ curriculum-based assessment and programming believe it is more important to assess students' acquisition of skills and knowledge included in the curriculum of the local school rather than the degree to which the students differ on normative performance measures. This approach has been used in academic areas; however, there is little information on curriculum-based assessment and programming in games in the physical education program that are designed specifically to facilitate the social development of children. The materials that follow represent an example of a process to construct a rudimentary system of curriculum assessment and programming for social development in physical education. The constructs of social development are based on prerequisites of social adaptive behavior from Grossman.[26] No claims are made as to the validity of the taxonomy or the sequence of games. Prerequisites for the development of curriculum-based assessment and programming are as follows:

1. Skill, physical, and cognitive prerequisites to participate in an activity
2. A taxonomy of social objectives/behavior
3. A sequence of environments where more elaborate social skills, which are task analyzed, are required
4. A procedure for assessing the present level of performance
5. Intervention strategies by the teacher
6. Skills to accommodate social and skill deficiencies
7. Management procedures to structure the social environments

Skill prerequisites

Children with disabilities, and at-risk children, must learn the skills necessary to participate in social play and recreational sport activity. In the event that the skill level of a person is very low compared with those of the group, there may be diminished opportunity for social facilitation. Therefore the skill levels must be assessed for each individual in comparison with persons with whom that individual might participate.

For example, an autistic child may need to be moved through a specially designed program in which the child evolves from onlooker to participatory behaviors. The stages include:

1. *Onlooker:* The child follows the movement/activity of other children/adults in the learning area.
2. *Parallel play:* The autistic child participates in individual play in the same space as another child participating in individual play.
3. *Parallel play:* The child participates in individual play in the same space as another child participating in individual play, and demonstrates an interest in the activity of the other child.
4. *Participatory:* The child engages in play, sharing a space and toys with another child.
5. *Cooperative:* The child cooperatively engages in play behavior to play accomplish a common goal.

To help the child develop the necessary terminal skills, the process of identifying and planning individual education program (IEP) goals and objectives is crucial. The process is outlined below:

1. Specification of terminal objectives in behavioral terms
2. Division of the terminal objective into a series of less and less complex responses
3. Sequencing the series of less complex responses
4. Verification of the student's ability to perform each response in the series
5. Teaching the student to perform each response in serial order
6. Recording performance during each training phase so that adjustments can be made during the teaching process

Cognitive prerequisites for playing games

Rules and strategies incorporated in games require cognitive comprehension. Many children without disabilities learn rules and strategies incidently, because of their experience in play and games. However, children with disabilities may have had a limited early play experience and, as such, struggle not only with a lack of social skills to engage in play and a difficulty with motor skills necessary for participation, but struggle with basic cognitive skills necesssary for participation in social events. Some of the basic cognitive abilities that a student must possess to play games effectively follow:

1. Respond to one's name.

2. Follow simple directions: line up, stop, throw the ball, etc.
3. Line up or remain in assigned areas of the classroom.
4. Respond to start and stop cues.
5. Be aware of the behavior of others in relation to one's own behavior.
6. Respond to modeling.
7. Respond to signs that cue behavior.
8. Understand the boundaries for games.
9. Understand winning and losing.
10. Understand signs that communicate movement (forward/backward, fast/slow, run, jump, throw, catch, etc.).

Social taxonomy

The ability of a person to adapt to the changing social environment is often a major criteria in the determination of disability. Before a person is classified as mentally retarded, for example, there must be impairment in adapted social behavior. This is also true for emotional disturbances and autism. Thus if the components of adapted behavior can be defined and behavior ascribed to each of these components, it may be possible to design intervention programs to develop behavior that can be generalized to social abilities. Play, games, sports, and leisure/recreation activities are usually microsocieties in which rules of interaction and behavior are required for successful participation.

There are two ways of developing social behavior. One is to treat the specific, operationally defined behavior (task-specific approach). The other is to develop social behavior that relates to a common ability and generalize the ability to other environments. For instance, if a child can be taught to cooperate while "making popcorn" with a parachute, the cooperative behavior may transfer to other situations if it is planned; transfer does not happen incidentally—it must be taught. Suggested lists of ability traits follow. Most games that involve social interaction generate behavior that can be classified in one of these categories of social ability.

Internal traits. These six social abilities are internal traits that are not necessarily expressed around other persons. They are assessed and can be developed individually as persons perform sport tasks.

1. *Delay of gratification:* The ability to control emotional responses so one's social status in the group is not jeopardized or the goals of the group are not deterred (exercising self-control, not losing one's temper or acting out). Common violations: (a) loses temper at a referee's deci-

sion, (b) does not attend to tasks, (c) does not participate with vigor in competition because of fatigue.

2. *Responsibility:* Carrying out the role that has been assigned by an authority figure as a member of the society. Common violations: (a) does not play assigned positions in a sport or game, (b) does not carry out assigned functions associated with participation in the game, (c) may withdraw from difficult assigned duties when the activity is underway.

3. *Reliability:* The consistency with which one carries out assigned responsibilities. This relates to the qualitative aspects of performance. Example: consistency in the successful execution of tasks for which one is responsible, such as (a) high batting and fielding averages in baseball, (b) high shooting percentages in basketball, (c) high percentages of successful execution of assignments in football.

4. *Pride in accomplishment:* Internal satisfaction of having completed a task to the maximum of one's capability. This requires assessment of one's capability and the efforts that one must put forth to achieve a desired outcome. Accomplishment is a function of effort. Examples: (a) meeting a standard in the physical education class as a result of hard practice, (b) winning a medal in the Special Olympics as a result of participation in a training program for the event.

5. *Control of personal feelings for the good of the group:* Reaching the goals of the group are primary. Persons cooperating together can achieve goals that the individual cannot. Therefore it may be necessary for persons to give up their own personal feelings to enhance the goals of the group. Example: cooperating with another person within the game, such as (a) passing to a teammate who has a better shot, even though the player wants to shoot, (b) playing a position that will make the team stronger but is not that person's choice.

6. *Long-range goals:* Delay of immediate needs and desires to reach a future goal. Examples: (a) working at physical fitness programs to improve sport skills, (b) practicing hard in an Achilles Track Club practice.

External traits. Each of these traits has a developmental structure that can be identified while students participate in games. If there is an inappropriate behavior, an intervention program can be implemented (see Chapter 5).

1. *Response to authority:* Abiding by the decisions of those in authority by virtue of office (official in a game, coach, physical education teacher, squad leader, peer teacher). Examples: (a) abiding by the decision of an official in a game, (b) following directions of the teacher in the organization of games, (c) appropriate responses to squad leaders and peer teachers.

2. *Cooperation:* The ability to work with other members of a group to achieve a common goal. Examples: (a) taking turns while participating in an activity, (b) participating in a dance activity, (c) participating as a team member, (d) fitting well into the group structure.

3. *Competition:* The willingness to enter into a game in which there can be only one winner, regardless of whether the competitors' abilities are equitable. Examples: (a) maximizing efforts when games are close, (b) maximizing efforts when behind, (c) maximizing efforts when the other person is the better player, (d) maximizing efforts when the individual is inferior.

4. *Leadership:* Recognition of group goals and determination of the way to achieve the goal; motivation of the group to undertake a plan of action to achieve the goal. Examples: (a) providing a role model for others, (b) providing a plan of action for others, (c) assuming roles such as captain or exercise leader for the group.

5. *Asocial behavior:* Not knowing the expected normative behavior of the group. Examples: (a) demonstration of any inappropriate behavior that can be corrected, (b) nonparticipation in or withdrawal from activity.

6. *Antisocial behavior:* Planned action to undermine the rules and strategies for achieving the social structure or the achievement of group goals. Examples: (a) disobeying rules of conduct of a game in a premeditated fashion, (b) breaking training rules set up by a coach.

Social sequence

There appears to be a developmental sequence of social behavior. The lowest form of development occurs when the person engages in social behavior through the initiative of another. The higher forms of social behavior require adaptation to environments with complex rules, skills, and judgment. These behaviors are required for participation in highly organized games, sport, and leisure/recreation activity. However, each activity might be placed on a social continuum that requires more or less complex social behavior.

The following is a hypothetical sequence of social behavior for which there are many subdivisions. Stages of social development with substages are described.

Adult-initiated activity. In this case the social activity is initiated by someone other than the individual. Social behavior depends on the teacher or a group leader. Individuals with severe disabilities may need to function, initially, at this level of social development. To advance from this stage of development, persons must have interests and skills to interact with the social environment.

Self-initiated activity. At this level of social development the person voluntarily chooses activity that is within his or her range of interest and capability. There are at least four distinct substages at the self-initiated level:

1. *Observer:* The individual is involved with activity but only as a spectator. The person does not interact with the environment but can learn about social behavior through observation.
2. *Nonpurposeful activity:* The individual becomes active in the exploration of self and the environment, but it is nonpurposeful. The activity usually involves objects or body parts.
3. *Purposeful solitary activity:* The activity has a definite purpose (bouncing a ball, kicking a ball, building blocks). There is usually an observable outcome of the activity.
4. *Elaborate solitary activity:* The self-initiated activity involves a wide range of activities and materials. It expands the existing repertoire of skills to prepare for later social interaction.

Parallel activity. This category involves play with objects. The activity takes place at the ability level of the individual in observable proximity to other persons. There is a tendency for persons to get closer together as they mature socially, which permits reciprocal modeling of one another's behavior. A considerable amount of learning can occur under these circumstances. Movement education is based on parallel activity.

Social interaction. At this stage of social development persons interact with one another. Its purpose is the achievement of mutual satisfaction. There are usually few, if any, rules to the interaction. The social situation is discontinued when either party is no longer interested in the activity. The social interaction level is usually spontaneous rather than planned activity.

Organized social games and sports

Organized social games and sports can be arranged on a continuum from low to high organization. The characteristics that make games more or less socially complex are as follows:

- *The level of skill:* The less skill, the simpler the game.
- *The number of social interactions with others:* The more interactions, the more socially complex the game. Examples: Hot Potato, rolling the ball to another person (simple); quarterback in football (complex) (1) snap from center, (2) handoff or fake to backs, (3) follow blockers who protect on a pass, (4) hand off to backs, (5) throw passes to receivers, (6) execute plays called by the coach, etc.
- *The number of rules to the game:* There are few in Hot Potato, but an extensive rulebook for football.
- *The complexity of strategies:* There are few strategies for Hot Potato and complex strategies for football.
- *The interdependency of persons in the group:* There are few interdependencies in Hot Potato but many in football; the center's snap to the quarterback must be proper, the quarterback's fake to a back and handoff to the ball carrier must be proper, the blockers must carry out assignments for the back, and the back must run the appropriate route of the designed blocking scheme.
- *The consequence of winning or losing:* There is no winning in Hot Potato, but there can be great social consequence for losing an important interscholastic game.
- *The structure of training regimens:* The more structure, the more complex the microsociety.

A hierarchy of social games can be developed so that persons can participate in games that meet their social needs. Under these conditions games and sports are not merely recreational but also have a valuable social purpose. Playing games also can be used to teach strategies and rules and to apply acquired skills from instruction. And perhaps as important, play, games, sport, and leisure/recreation activities provide a valuable framework in which to address the values and tenets basic to functioning in society as part of a group.[28,29]

Social adjustment requires adaptation to the rules of the microsociety. These basic rules may include "keeping hands to self," "call others only by names they like," etc. A child without adequate models may not know the rules basic to a society. And children may be confused by rules on the "street" that are very different from rules in school.

Constructing a game to develop social skills. There are many games designed for elementary children, but the rules and strategies are often not well defined.

Games of lower organization can be designed so that the structure permits analysis of social behavior. A procedure and format for construction of games for diagnostic-prescriptive programming follow:

NAME THE GAME

Each game should be labeled or named. This communicates to the students the rules, strategies, and formations of games that have already been learned.

OBJECTIVES OF THE GAME

Most games have objectives for the students and their teams. For instance, the objective of bowling is to knock down pins. The objective of miniature golf is to putt the golf ball into the hole. Groups of persons or individuals try to achieve the same objectives.

RULES OF THE GAME

Each game must have rules, just as does society at large. Breaking rules may be willful or accidental. Therefore the physical education teacher, to minimize accidents and rule breaking, must make the rules precise, enforce them during play, and watch for deficient social ability reflected in rule violation. Perhaps most important, the teacher must be actively engaged throughout in reinforcement of appropriate social behavior.

STRATEGIES

Many games have rules that require cooperative strategies among members of the team. The implementation of these strategies in some cases requires complex social behavior of students playing the game, which can be judged against the social abilities. A popular form of play which emphasizes cooperative behavior are those espoused in *The New Games Book* and in *More New Games*. The games described in these books allow children and adults, with and without disabilities, to participate in activities that require a common goal. For example, instead of playing traditional volleyball, the goal in Infinity Volleyball is for players on both sides of the net to keep the ball up in the air as long as possible. In the midst of tug-of-war if one side begins to win, a member of that team runs to join the other team to even the sides. The emphasis on cooperation rather than competition is particularly valuable when teaching values and human interaction skills.

ANALYZING THE GAME

Description of the Game

The description should include the formation required to play the game, how the game is started, what the opposing players do, how the game is terminated, how the game is scored, and the consequence for losing. Descriptions for Hot Potato follow:

1. Formation: circle formation, persons close enough so the ball can be handed to one another, one person in the center of the circle.

2. Start: ball is passed around the circle at the command of the person in the middle.
3. Participation: the ball is moved from one person to another as quickly as possible.
4. Termination: person in the middle says "Stop."
5. Consequence: person holding the ball on command "Stop" goes to the middle.

Procedures for Teaching the Game

The persons who teach the game must know the exact procedures so they can conduct the game. The specific procedures enable peer tutors to conduct the games. If peer and cross-age tutors can learn to conduct the games, then several different games may be played at the same time. This allows more students to participate at their social ability level. The procedures are step-by-step analysis of what the leader must do to teach the game. The teaching procedures for Hot Potato follow:

1. Instruct the children to form a circle by joining hands.
2. Identify one person for the middle to start the game.
3. Instruct the person holding the ball to pass it to the right and keep the ball moving.
4. Instruct the person in the middle to close his or her eyes.
5. Tell the person in the middle to say "Stop" within the next 10 seconds.
6. Tell the person who last held the ball to move to the center.
7. Keep track of the persons who have been in the center.
8. The person who has been in the center the fewest times wins.

Diagram of Starting Position

A diagram of the starting position is prerequisite information to initiate the game. The components of the diagram should include the different players, the formation, and permanent equipment.

Diagram of the Game While in Progress

There should be a diagram of the game while it is in progress. It is desirable to indicate movement of the players and equipment in relation to the formation of the game.

Variation of the Rules to Make the Game More Complex

The rules of a game can be varied to increase demands for higher skills or require more sophisticated social behavior. Below are variations of hot potato that may make the game more or less complex.

Use two balls	Improved perceptual skills are required because the visual mechanism must focus on two objects.
Clap hands before passing	There are three components to the task instead of two (i.e., receive-clap-pass versus receive and pass).
Smaller circle	The amount of movement necessary to pass the ball is reduced.

Relationship of game behavior with social abilities. The game should be analyzed to determine potential social traits that can be violated. These may be predicted by study of the desired behaviors of the rules and the strategies of the game. These two features of play tend to govern social interaction. An analysis of social abilities for playing Hot Potato follows. The positive and negative behaviors are linked with specific social abilities.

Ability	Positive behavior	Negative behavior
Cooperation	Passes ball to next person	Holds or throws the ball
Competition	Moves ball as fast as possible	Does not try to pass ball fast
Responsibility	Maintains proper position in formation throughout the game	Moves from the formation
Delay gratification	Attends to the game	Inattentive to the conduct of the game

Prerequisite skills. The prerequisite skills for game participation should be noted. This includes all of the skills that enable successful participation in the activity. For Hot Potato the prerequisite motor skills are receiving and passing (hand-to-hand). Any skill can be analyzed into skill components.

Prerequisite abilities. In the event a person cannot successfully perform the skills required for participation in the game, a prerequisite analysis is desirable. The analysis should be made in the perceptual-physical-psychomotor area. A prerequisite analysis for Hot Potato appears below. The ability trait is described in relation to the activity involved in the game.

Ability	Activity
Visual tracking	Following the ball with the eyes around the circle
Hand-eye coordination	Receiving and passing the ball
Speed of limb	Moving the ball fast so the person will not be "it"
Manual dexterity	Manipulation of the ball (physical)

Interrelationship skills and abilities and social behavior. Skills and abilities are prerequisites for acceptable social behavior in group play. To determine the present level of performance of a child in a social game, it is desirable to know the game thoroughly and then analyze the game in relation to skills and abilities for engagement in social behavior in the sport or game. The game should be designed with enough specificity

that peer or cross-age tutors can conduct it. The physical education teacher should be trained with the skills to analyze the behavior of the children as the game unfolds and to make prescriptive judgments of social needs for the children.

PSYCHOSOCIAL ASSESSMENT

There are several social assessment techniques.[25] Some of the techniques are (1) naturalistic observations, (2) sociometric measures, (3) teacher ratings, (4) norm-referenced social assessments, and (5) content-referenced social assessments. A brief description of each of the methods follows.

Naturalistic Observations

Naturalistic observations of a child's social behavior is a self-validating method of assessing children's social behavior.[2] Each child is observed interacting with others in a variety of natural social settings. Frequency of specific behaviors are observed and recorded. Observations collected across a variety of environments provide a fairly complete picture of the child's social behavior.[25] Naturalistic observations have been found to correlate moderately with sociometric measures.

Sociometric Measures

Peer ratings have been extensively researched.[2] To determine peer ratings, children are asked to specify which classmates they would prefer to interact with in a given situation (e.g., name two classmates with whom you like to play best). It might be feasible to use this type of measure to gather social data on children with and without disabilities.

Teacher Ratings

Teacher rating scales have been used for many years to gather social data. One instrument, the Social Behavior Assessment tool[53] analyzes 136 social skills necessary to perform a variety of environmental, interpersonal, self-related, and task-related behaviors. The essential question that is answered by the teacher is "whether each behavior is important for success in the class." This type of information can help identify which social skills a child must have to benefit fully from a specific classroom experience.

Normative-Referenced Social Assessment

Selected normative-referenced social assessment instruments are the Detroit, Brigance, Vineland Social Maturity Scale, the American Association on Mental Deficiency (AAMD) Adaptive Behavior Scales, and the Gesell Developmental Schedules. Most of these tests have subtests that represent domains of social behavior. Some of the domains on these tests are personal independence, socialization, self-direction, language development, number and time concepts, self-help, communication, and locomotion. Normative-referenced test results provide information about an individual's general social behavior. For the most part, these tests identify specific behavioral characteristics that generalize across persons, environments, and activities. Examples of some recent normative-referenced behavior tests are the Pyramid Scales,[10] the Vineland Adaptive Behavior Scales,[52] and the Scales of Independent Behavior.[5] Such tests may be useful to teachers of students with disabilities for two purposes: (1) the test results provide information about an individual's general behavioral characteristics and (2) the results may provide a global picture of an unfamiliar student's abilities, thereby giving direction for gathering more precise information. These tests are not designed to detect small changes in behavior, nor do they address all areas where instruction is likely. Thus normative-referenced tests of adaptive behavior do not indicate much more about the se-

Text continued on p.148.

Hot Potato (Seated)

Game classification: individual competition.
Materials needed for the game: 1. __8″ ball__ 2. _____ 3. _____ 4. _____ 5. _____

OBJECTIVE OF THE GAME

To hit the ball before the signal for termination of the game.

DESCRIPTION OF THE GAME

Circle formation, one child in the center with eyes closed. Ball is passed around the circle. Person in middle says "go" and then calls out "stop"; the person caught with ball in his hands or whoever touches it last must go to the center of the circle. Game is started over again.

RULES OF THE GAME

1. Must remain in the circle.
2. Must move the ball when the signal to begin game is given.
3. Ball must stay on the floor.

PROCEDURES FOR TEACHING THE GAME

1. Instruct them to form a circle by joining hands by the time the instructor counts to 10.
2. Identify one person to be in the middle.
3. Instruct the person holding the ball to pass it to his right (point).
4. Instruct person in center to close his eyes, start and stop the game.
5. Give the group a "do it" signal. Keep score as game proceeds.

VARIATION OF RULES TO MAKE THE GAME MORE OR LESS COMPLEX

1. Use two balls.
2. Before passing the ball, clap hands.
3. Count before passing the ball.
4. Form a smaller circle.

SOCIAL STRATEGIES ASSOCIATED WITH THE GAME

There are few social strategies.

Traits	Positive description	Description of social deficiency
Cooperation	Hits balls that are in his area	Refuses to participate
Competition	Tries to move the ball as fast as possible	Does not fully attend to the game at all times; moves ball slowly
Responsibility	Maintains proper position throughout game	Moves out of position when game is underway

Duck, Duck, Goose

Game classification: individual competition

Materials needed for the game: 1. ___none___ 2. _____ 3. _____ 4. _____ 5. _____

OBJECTIVES OF THE GAME

1. The runner avoids the tag of the person who is "it."
2. The person who is "it," the goose, must chase and tag the runner.

DESCRIPTION OF THE GAME

Group sits in circle with one person standing (goose). Goose walks around circle tapping sitters on the head and saying "duck." When goose gets to the person who is to chase, the command "goose" is given. The person tagged by the goose must chase her around the circle. If the chaser cannot tag the goose before she gets to the chaser's place, then he becomes the goose.

RULES OF THE GAME

1. Everyone sits in circle except one person, who is the goose. She must tap others on head and say "duck."
2. When she comes to the person who is to be "it," the runner taps him on the head and says "goose."
3. Person must chase tagger around circle: if chaser catches the goose, she's still "it."

PROCEDURES FOR TEACHING THE GAME

1. Hold someone else's hands.
2. Make a circle.
3. Back up as far as possible while still holding hands.
4. Sit on the floor.
5. Designate a "goose."
6. Say "Do what I do" (walk around circle and say "duck, duck").
7. Instruct those sitting that they are to run around the circle once and tag the goose before she sits on the spot where the chaser started.
8. Instruct the goose to walk around the circle and say "duck, duck."
9. If the child walks more than once around the circle, identify a chaser.

VARIATION OF RULES TO MAKE THE GAME MORE OR LESS COMPLEX

1. Run around circle twice.
2. Hop around circle.
3. Sitters raise arm when goose comes by and lower arm when chaser comes by.

SOCIAL STRATEGIES ASSOCIATED WITH THE GAME

There are no social strategies for this game.

Traits	Positive description	Description of social deficiency
Cooperation	Cooperates in the formation of the game	Does not hold hands during organization of the game
Competition	Competes against the other person	Runs for the sake of running; does not try if behind
Sportsman-ship	Tags persons of equal competition	Tags someone when the outcome is not in doubt
Responsibility	Maintains appropriate position throughout the game	Moves out of position in the circle

Jump the Brook

Game classification: individual competition
Materials needed for the game: 1. ropes (2)   2. _____   3. _____   4. _____   5. _____

OBJECTIVES OF THE GAME

1. Jump as far as one can.
2. Jump farther than everyone else.

DESCRIPTION OF THE GAME

Two ropes are laid parallel to each other. The players take turns jumping over the ropes. After all have gone through the first time, the ropes are moved farther apart and jumping is repeated. Jump until there is failure to make it over both ropes. This procedure goes on until one person is left. That person is the winner.

RULES OF THE GAME

1. Two ropes are placed parallel to one another, 1 foot apart.
2. All players line up behind the ropes.
3. The players attempt to jump over the two ropes.
4. Take off before the first rope and land after the second rope.
5. Widen the distance between the ropes 2 inches after each person in the group has jumped.
6. Jump until there is a miss. The last player who has made all attempts is the winner.

PROCEDURES FOR TEACHING THE GAME

1. Set the ropes parallel, 1 foot apart.
2. Line the pupils behind ropes.
3. Teach the rules of the game as it develops.

VARIATION OF RULES TO MAKE THE GAME MORE OR LESS COMPLEX

1. Shorten the running space.
2. Move the rope 6 inches each time.
3. Perform blindfolded.

SOCIAL STRATEGIES ASSOCIATED WITH THE GAME

There are no tactical social strategies associated with this game.

Traits	Positive Description	Description of social deficiency
Delay of gratification	Is under emotional control at all times	Does not want to participate
Sportsmanship	Engages in fair endeavor with others	Poor evaluation of self mastering the task; will not leave game on a miss
Pride in individual accomplishment	Puts forth effort	Does not value successful performance, misses early in the game without effort
Individual responsibility	Is considerate in giving other performers room to jump	Fails to stay behind the restraining line or wait turn in line to jump
Response to authority figures	Abides by the referee's decision on make or miss	Refuses to go out of game when the teacher indicates failure
Competition	Participates with intensity on each jump that challenges	Will not try when task is difficult

Circle Stride Ball

Game classification: competition between players
Materials needed for the game: 1. _volleyball_ 2. _____ 3. _____ 4. _____ 5. _____

OBJECTIVES OF THE GAME

1. The player in the center of the circle rolls the ball through the legs of players in the circle.
2. The players in the circle prevent the ball from being rolled through their legs.

DESCRIPTION OF THE GAME

There is a circle of players; "it" is in the center. The circle players take a stride-stand position with the feet touching those of the person beside them. The center player attempts to roll the ball through the legs of the players in the circle.

RULES OF THE GAME

1. Players in the circle can use only their hands to stop the ball.
2. Players in the circle cannot move their feet.
3. The player in the center of the circle must roll the ball underhand.
4. The player in the center of the circle must stay in the center.
5. If the ball goes through the legs of a player in the circle, places are traded with the player in the center.
6. Player returns ball to "it" when ball is stopped.

PROCEDURES FOR TEACHING THE GAME

1. Instruct the players to join hands and form a circle.
2. Designate one person as the center person.
3. Instruct the players in the circle to spread their legs so feet touch one another.
4. Instruct the center player to roll the ball through the legs of the circle players.
5. Clarify the rules as the game progresses.

VARIATION OF RULES TO MAKE THE GAME MORE OR LESS COMPLEX

1. Change the size of the balls.
2. Change the number of persons who are in the circle.

SOCIAL STRATEGIES ASSOCIATED WITH THE GAME

This is an individual game in which there is little interdependency among players.

Traits	Positive description	Description of social deficiency
Competition	Plays intensely at all times to win	Is sporadic in attempts to score
Sportsmanship	Gracious winner and loser	Ungracious winner and loser

Bowling

Game classification: cooperation; team responsibilities
Materials needed for the game: 1. __6 pins__ 2. __bowling ball__ 3. _____ 4. _____ 5. _____

OBJECTIVE OF THE GAME

1. To knock down more pins than the other team within a specified time.

DESCRIPTION OF THE GAME

There are three players on each team: one bowler, one ball retriever, and one pin setter-scorer. The bowler rolls the ball down and knocks as many pins over as possible, being sure not to cross the line. Retriever throws back ball as quickly as possible. Pins are reset, and score is kept by the pin setter. The bowler knocks as many pins over as possible in 15 seconds. At end of 15 seconds, players change places. This procedure is repeated until each person has bowled.

RULES OF THE GAME

1. Three players on a team: bowler, retriever, pin setter.
2. Ball must be rolled.
3. Count pins knocked over in a 15-second time frame.
4. Bowler may not cross the restraining line.

PROCEDURES FOR TEACHING THE GAME

1. Divide or instruct three persons to stand behind the bowling pins.
2. Ask no. 1's to raise their hands, then stand behind the bowling line.
3. Ask no. 2's to raise their hands, then be a pin setter and count the total number of pins knocked down.
4. Ask no. 3's to raise their hands, then tell them to retrieve the ball after it hits the pins.
5. Instruct them to knock down as many pins as possible in 15 seconds.

VARIATION OF RULES TO MAKE THE GAME MORE OR LESS COMPLEX

1. Bowl ball a different distance.
2. Increase or decrease time allowance.
3. Use smaller or larger ball.
4. Knock down more pins.

SOCIAL STRATEGIES ASSOCIATED WITH THE GAME

The strategies depend on the techniques an individual possesses in carrying out functions.

Traits	Positive description	Description of social deficiency
Cooperation	Develops a system to interrelate functions	Tends to perform independently of other teammates
Competition	Tries on all tasks all of the time	Does not get involved in the contest: performs poorly when behind
Objectivity in meeting team goals	Performs the function assigned to best ability	Overtly shows impaired performance in unappealing task
Sportsmanship	Is willing to abide by rules of fair competition	Gains undue advantage, violates restraining line
Reliability	Always performs the functions assigned	Sporadic in performing the assigned roles in the game
Responsibility	Understands the function that is to be performed and does it	Does not fulfill the roles assigned in the game

verity of a problem or its cause than do more simplified screening instruments.[19]

Content-Referenced Social Assessment

Content-referenced social assessment requires the acquisition of information about what an individual can and cannot do within the context of social sport and play activity of the specific physical education curriculum of a given school district. The information received from such an assessment may be used to make relevant instructional decisions to enhance social behavior. The prerequisites for such an assessment of individual social abilities within the context of sport and games are as follows:

1. Operationally defined social abilities to be developed
2. A sequence of games/play activities that progress from lower to higher demands for social skills of participants
3. Entry procedures to determine present level of sport/play ability of the learner and the specific deficient social behavior within a specific social context

Analyzing Play, Games, Sport, and Leisure/Recreation for Social Demands

It is difficult to structure spontaneous play; the sports and games social curriculum is a sequence of simple to complex activity. Some of the characteristics that make a sport or game more or less complex are skills required by the learner, rule complexity, strategy level, social responsibility for a function, and number of structured interactions. These characteristics are translated into more difficult social abilities that students must display to successfully participate in the games. The considerations for ordering games from less to greater complexity are as follows:

1. Ascribe a degree of difficulty for each social ability for each game on an arbitrary scale of 0 to 4.
2. Tabulate the total raw score for each game.
3. Order the games in sequence.

The box below shows a battery of 40 social games that have been arranged according to an arbitrarily assigned difficulty score. Keep in mind that when a game is expressed by a single score, there is no indication as to which specific social abilities contribute to the difficulty of the game. An ability analysis of 18 games of cooperation, responsibility, response to authority, and competition appears in Table 6-1. A comprehensive analysis of games would require an analysis of all abilities. With the profile of weighted traits for each game, activities can be selected according to specific social abilities needed by specific individuals. The problem of entry becomes one of determining which games are beneficial for the social development of each child.

Difficulty Rating of Social Games

1. Movement Imitation	3.2		21. Fish Net	7.6
2. Simon Says	3.8		22. Scooter Relay	7.7
3. Hot Potato	3.8		23. Round the World	8.0
4. Duck, Duck, Goose	3.8		24. Four Square	8.0
5. Drop the Handkerchief	3.8		25. Club Guard	8.5
6. One, Two, Three	4.3		26. Tag End Person	8.5
7. Musical Chairs	4.5		27. Tug of War	8.9
8. Movement Imitation II	4.6		28. Wheelbarrow Relay	9.0
9. Squirrels and Trees	4.9		29. Whiffle Baseball	10.1
10. Cat and Mouse	5.0		30. Bowling	
11. Hoop Tag	5.2		31. Air Ball	11.0
12. Jump the Brook	5.3		32. Kickball Soccer	11.9
13. Steal the Bacon	5.5		33. Scooter Basketball	12.4
14. Jump the Bean Bag	5.6		34. Scooter soccer	12.7
15. Streets and Alleys	5.9		35. Kickball	12.8
16. Run and Catch	6.0		36. Badminton	12.9
17. Crows and Cranes	6.1		37. Dodge ball	12.9
18. Running Bases	6.2		38. Keep Away	13.1
19. Sick Cat	6.6		39. Newcombe Volleyball	13.2
20. Circle Stride Ball	6.8		40. Basketball	14.4

TABLE 6-1

Social games developmental scale

Game	Total score	Competition	Responsibility	Response to authority	Cooperation
Hot Potato	2.7	0.0	1.5	0.5	1.0
Duck, Duck, Goose	2.0	0.0	0.5	0.5	1.0
Green Light	2.5	0.0	0.5	1.0	0.7
Squirrels and Trees	3.9	0.7	1.2	0.5	1.5
Hoop Tag	4.5	0.5	0.5	1.0	2.5
Steal the Bacon	4.8	0.3	0.5	1.0	3.0
Crows and Cranes	5.0	0.5	1.0	1.0	2.5
Scooter Relay	5.2	0.5	1.5	0.7	2.5
Streets and Alleys	6.3	2.0	2.0	1.0	1.3
Over and Under	7.5	1.5	2.0	1.5	2.5
Dodge Ball	7.5	1.0	1.3	1.7	3.5
Four Square	8.0	0.0	3.5	1.0	3.5
Tag End Person	9.3	2.5	2.5	1.3	3.0
Bowling	10.0	3.0	3.5	0.8	2.7
Newcombe Volleyball	12.5	3.5	3.0	2.5	3.5
Kickball	14.3	3.3	4.0	3.0	4.0
Scooter Soccer	15.5	4.0	4.5	3.0	4.0
Scooter Basketball	15.5	4.0	4.5	3.0	4.0

The sequence of social activity of games and sports enables rough judgments to be made on the nature of activity in which individuals may and may not be successful. Determining the social needs through games and sports requires two types of information. One is the complexity of games that are commensurate with the social abilities of the individual. The other is the specific social ability traits that may be deficient in a person for a specific activity.

Analysis Through Observation of Play

The placement of a person in the sequence of games is conducted by having children participate in the games and observing social deficiencies as they play. If the individual has little or no social deficiency in a specific game, it can be assumed that less difficult games also may be played with success. Of course, this is not always true, since the skills and specific social abilities for each game vary. Therefore a specific match between characteristics of the game and the child may be present in a more complex game and not in a less complex one. However, knowing which abilities are needed to participate in a game is valuable for selecting games on a social continuum.

The identification of social deficits observed as specific behaviors that link with ability traits requires documentation of specific behaviors as the game is being played. An inference must also be made as to the link of the behavior with the social ability trait. For instance, in the game of Hot Potato, if a child breaks formation and withdraws from the game momentarily, the teacher may infer, based on previous observation, that the child is defying authority of the teacher or is attending to more interesting stimuli in the environment and cannot delay the gratification until termination of the game. These are judgments that need to be made by the teacher. The professional judgment that links behavior with social abilities is important for generalization of the social ability rather than just for treating a social behavior. Therefore social assessment involves finding out which games can be played by the children and the specific nature of the deficit (if one exists).

It is important to standardize the administrational procedures for the games when entering persons in the sequence. This enables better control of the variables of the social situation. Those who conduct the games must practice implementation for consistency. A procedure for teaching the game is to present the game rules as succinctly as possible and engage the children in activity. They should see a model of the game when it is underway. Then prompt the behavior of the individuals into the activity and fade instructor assistance. Under these conditions every person has an opportunity to be successful. If children cannot perform the skills and social requirements of the games after the prompt and fade procedure, there is most likely a deficiency in social, skill, or prerequisite abilities.

Persons who provide instructional services to develop social abilities should have an extensive activity curriculum. Following are procedures for the selection and design of the social activities:

1. Identify the activities from the literature or make them up.
2. Pilot the activities in small groups.
3. Write the specifications for administration.
4. Play the game with other populations.
5. Finalize the administration procedures.
6. Conduct an analysis of the game and enter it into the sequence of social games.

DEVELOPMENT OF INCENTIVES FOR SOCIAL PARTICIPATION IN GAMES

There may be a developmental hierarchy of incentives for participation in social activity. Kohlberg[37] suggests the following sequence of psychosocial development. The range of social responsibility is from participation based on avoidance of punishment to maintaining the self-respect on a voluntary basis.

1. Obey rules to avoid punishment.	If there is no punishment, the rules will not be obeyed.
2. Conform to obtain rewards.	If there are no rewards, there may be inappropriate social behavior.
3. Conform to obtain approval from others.	If there is little recognition from the group, there is little incentive to maximize participation.
4. Conform to avoid censure by authority figures.	If there is no authority censure, there is insufficient incentive to participate.
5. Conform to maintain respect of social community.	If the social community cannot express respect, there is insufficient incentive to participate.
6. Conform to maintain self-respect and integrity.	If there is little desire to be a person of integrity, there is less incentive to participate.

An understanding of Kohlberg's hierarchy is crucial for the physical educator. A child who is unloved, unwanted, uncared for and in other ways neglected may not respond to the threat of punishment or may be unable to care about a potential reward. If the child comes from a situation in which cause-effect has not been addressed fairly, specifically if the child is treated differently for exhibiting the same behaviors on two different occasions (e.g., if mom is sober I can say

"hello," if mom is drunk and I say "hello," she'll hit me), the child comes to school either unwilling to act or acting out.

The nature of the child's life outside of school must be given serious consideration in the determination of appropriate rewards, for example. If the child is hungry, earning a "smiley face" sticker may have no meaning; earning an apple may reward behavior and meet the child's basic need—hunger.

If the child with spina bifida, for example, is "bribed" to do everything at home with money, the chances that a teacher can effect behavioral change at school without that reinforcement is remote. A significant parent-teacher conference is vital at this point to determine the value structure reinforced in the home.

WRITING SOCIAL GOALS

The standard procedure for developing social behavior is through application of behavioral principles to a behavior that is to be changed. This is usually directed toward disruptive or self-abusive behaviors, which are negative and should be brought under control. The development of positive social goals suggests a different approach. A goal that involves social development possesses the following characteristics:

□ It should contain a social ability that can be generalized from the microsociety of sport and games to a macrosociety.
□ It should be observable in the sports and games in physical education classes and in generalized environments.
□ It should be measurable to determine the effectiveness of the proposed strategies for intervention.
□ It must have the capability of being developed through classroom intervention.
□ It must represent a social ability concept as well as a specific behavior in the class.

For example, in Hot Potato the child will demonstrate the responsibility (1) of staying in circle formation (2) for three (3) 1-minute games. All the criteria for writing a social goal are met in this statement. No specific applied behavioral intervention would be planned. If one technique fails, another is attempted.

TECHNIQUES TO PROMOTE SOCIALIZATION
Peer Tutoring

The general process of socialization is one of children modeling an activity for their peers. Under such conditions, those who have appropriate social behavior can transmit it to those who possess inappropriate behavior. The persons who receive the most social benefit are those who learn from the group with appropriate social behavior. There is impressive evidence favoring the value of peer instruction.[54] To accommodate the needs of any children, it is desirable for peer tutors and cross-age peers to learn to administer social activity. Ideas for training peer tutors to administer the games are included in the following list:

1. Learn the rules, formation, and procedures of the game.
2. Define the teacher responsibilities in the game, such as getting the equipment, setting up the equipment, and keeping score.
3. Assign the responsibilities to specific peer teachers.
4. Train them to secure the equipment.
5. Train them to set up the instructional environment.
6. Teach them to score the game.
7. Teach them to conduct the game.
8. Teach them how to evaluate their performance in the conduct of the game.

FIGURE 6-7. Exploring the lake with a new friend. (Courtesy Dallas Independent School District.)

If peer tutors are to be used so that children without disabilities are put in the role of "tutor" for children with disabilities, it is vital that this process is reversed at some time during the week. The child with a disability cannot always be the recipient of tutoring. Whenever possible, the child with a disability should be given the opportunity to reciprocate and share skills and knowledges with a child without a disability. This is vital if the child with a disability is to ever evolve into independence.

Staff Skills

A team of persons may be involved with the conduction of social programming. Staff efforts should complement one another. The staff should know the games thoroughly and be consistent in the application of language cues and reinforcers of the correct social behavior. A list of guidelines for conduction of social instruction follows:

1. All staff should know thoroughly the social games.
2. All staff should be consistent in instruction.
3. Effective reinforcers should be applied expressively and immediately.
4. Language cues should be consistent, short, and relevant.
5. Extra visual and language cues should be provided if necessary.

Social Communication Skills

Individuals with disabilities must possess social prerequisites before they can enter into meaningful social interaction. Some of the prerequisites are as follows:

☐ *Verbalization:* This is the best means of communicating with another person. Signing is a substitute for the deaf, severely mentally retarded, or severely emotionally disturbed individual who cannot or does not speak.

☐ *Visual onlooking:* This is the ability to interpret the modeling process of another person.

☐ *Imitation:* This is the ability to reproduce behavior of another through the modeling process.

☐ *Smiling:* This communicates the approval of one person of the actions of another.

☐ *Token giving:* Giving something to another person establishes a commonality between them.

☐ *Affection:* Smiles, hugs, and kisses reinforce the behavior of another.

The social interaction process involves ways of receiving information from another person and also ways of feeding back to the other person approval for his or her behavior. Visual onlooking enables the assessment of social information from others. The other prerequisites of social interaction are means of initiating social activity or giving feedback on the appropriateness of another's social behavior.

- *Sharing materials (toys):* This involves materials of mutual interest to two persons when they share them and engage in social interaction.
- *Appropriate physical contact:* A "high-five" or another sign of approval of a behavior can be used.
- *Complimentary comments:* Say something nice about another person. This may be something that the person wears or has, but the most appropriate compliment involves something the person can do.
- *Peer reinforcement:* Reinforcing a peer for an appropriate behavior will strengthen that behavior. A compliment is not directed at strengthening any particular behavior.

Structuring Social Interactions

Social interactions between individuals with and without disabilities have a greater chance of success if instructors provide guidelines. When initial social contact is purposeful and well structured, positive social development is likely to occur. Techniques for structuring these interactions appear in the following sections.

Cooperative learning

In cooperative learning students work together on teams and carry out their responsibilities. *New Games* activities are particularly appropriate for the creation of cooperative learning experiences.[45,46] These teams are small groups of students with a wide range of abilities. Cooperative learning provides practice in learning motor skills and social interactions to promote social acceptance. The instructor establishes and guides the cooperation. Gottlieb and Leyser[22] suggest the following steps:

1. Teacher specifies instructional objectives on the learning task.
2. Teacher selects the group size most appropriate for the game.
3. Students are assigned to the teams or groups.
4. Roles are structured among the groups.
5. Requirements are made for each child.
6. The appropriate equipment is provided for each group.

FIGURE 6-8. Freedom to explore a beautiful natural environment may enhance the development of a sense of self-worth. (Courtesy Wisconsin Lions Camp, Rosholt, Wisconsin.)

7. The task and cooperative goal structure are explained.

8. Peers are trained if necessary.

As an example, consider bowling as the instructional task for the group.

Instructional objective	Group knocks a bowling pin down 15 times in a specified time
Group size	Three persons in each group
Group assignment	Heterogeneous
Structured roles	Bowler rolls ball from 10 feet to knock down the pin
	Pin setter sets the pin up each time it is knocked down
	Retriever rolls the ball back to the bowler
	Counter counts the number of pins knocked down
	Timer determines how long it took the group to knock down the pins 15 times
	Manager keeps the group informed as to whose turn it is to bowl (each person bowls until 5 pins are knocked down)
Requirements	Each person performs to the preceding specifications
Equipment	Ball and bowling pin
Explanation	Describe the game and the responsibility of each person

Group rewards

In a group reward system games are won not only by team score but also for appropriate social behavior. There are two winners—a social winner and a game winner. Class members pool their positive and negative points. This approach increases the number of positive social interactions during the play of the activity and helps improve the attitudes of all students.[25]

Cognitive Training

Another approach to the development of social skills is the use of cognitive behavior modification to develop skills that can be used in a variety of settings. Students are involved as active participants in sports and games. They are aware of the behaviors targeted for change and receive training in how behaviors change.[30] Cognitive training programs may teach self-evaluation and self-instruction strategies. In self-evaluation, students may record their own inappropriate behaviors and reinforce themselves for acceptable performance. This type of program requires that teachers reward students for accurate evaluation of their own

behaviors. Hellison and his associates suggested the use of student logs and/or diaries in which they explain behavior and indicate progress on skills at each of the four levels of social development.[28,29]

Cognitive training is an efficient approach with children with disabilities who have relatively high intellectual functioning. Teachers can train students to become responsible for their own behavior in the instructional program, and the teacher then assumes a monitoring role. Typical cognitive training includes:

☐ Problem definition
☐ Goal statement
☐ Impulse delay (stop and think before you act)
☐ Consideration of consequences (think of the different consequences that may follow each solution)
☐ Implementation
☐ Recycling (use self-evaluation and error-correcting options)[36]

TECHNIQUES TO CHANGE SOCIAL MISBEHAVIOR

There are several techniques that can be used by instructors to change social behavior of children with disabilities.[59] Each technique has different applications. A description of some of these techniques follows:

PROXIMITY CONTROL

This involves placing persons who are isolated from group activity closer to the activity. This may facilitate opportunity for peer modeling and social interaction. The strategy can be used when attempting to move a person from self-initiated activity to parallel or social interaction levels.

PEER-MEDIATED REINFORCEMENT

Peers are trained to reinforce specific social behaviors of a pupil. This procedure has powerful generalization effects.

PEER-MEDIATED REINFORCEMENT AND SELF-RECORDING

In this procedure peers reinforce the behavior, but the pupil makes records of the successful event. The pupil is actively involved in assessing his or her own behavior.

MUTUAL PEER REINFORCEMENT

Peers are trained to mutually reinforce one another.

MODEL-PROMPT-REINFORCE

The instructor models the appropriate behavior, physically prompts the pupil in the behavior, and then quickly reinforces the behavior. It is important that latency (time between model and prompt), prompt, and reinforcement be minimal.

STIMULUS PAIRING

This is a positive event paired with an opportunity to play or participate in an activity. Example: Isolated child of-

FIGURE 6-9. The out-of-doors provides the opportunity for the development of quality human interaction. (Courtesy Recreation Services, Division Care and Treatment Facilities, Department of Health and Social Services, Northern Wisconsin Center for the Developmentally Disabled, Chippewa Falls, Wisconsin.)

fered candy to playmates just before play period. There was over a 400% increase in the amount of play time of the isolated child with the peers.

FILM-MEDIATED MODELS

Observational learning includes both incidental and controlled interaction among children. Social patterns undergo modifications as a direct result of observing another's behavior and its consequences. In this case films depict appropriate peer interaction.

DIRECT SHAPING OF BEHAVIOR

This technique involves establishing or identifying a social behavior and then making it more or less frequent with a program of small steps.

DIRECT SHAPING OF PREREQUISITE BEHAVIOR

There are occasions when the desired social behavior cannot be emitted. Under these conditions it is necessary to shape the prerequisite behaviors, such as onlooking.

INCREASE NUMBER OF OBJECTS/MATERIALS FOR INTERACTION

The range of options for social activity may be limited. Therefore an increase in the number of objects and materials may provide the novelty for interaction. This technique can be used to move the person to the self-initiated social activity level.

LIMIT NUMBER OF OPTIONS FOR PLAY

There are times when the materials of the environment should be limited. If a person is repetitiously engaged with activity with a single object and purpose, this imposed limit may increase the range of skills and interests. The preferred objects can be removed to facilitate interaction with other materials. Specific strategies need to be paired with specific purpose.

ACTIVITIES OF SIMILAR STIMULUS CHARACTERISTICS

If a person has favored materials or activities, those of similar stimulus characteristics may be well accepted by the pupils. Example: If a person or group has a favorite game, the game can be altered so that the objectives, skills, and social interactions are different.

MATERIALS THAT REQUIRE TWO PERSONS TO PARTICIPATE

Certain activity requires the participation of two persons. Engagement in this activity facilitates social interaction. Examples: Teeter-totter, throwing and catching a ball, and tandem bicycle riding.

MIX HIGH AND LOW SOCIALLY DEVELOPED PERSONS

Persons who are to develop social behavior through modeling need to participate with those who can provide the models. This technique is effective for social development in games.

CONFEDERATE PEER INITIATES ACTIVITY

A peer is trained and integrated into a group to initiate activity.

TWO PEERS TRAINED BY ONE ADULT

The instructor structures the social interaction between two peers who are participating in an activity. The interaction capability of each peer must be determined. The specific social behaviors of each peer must be defined before this procedure is attempted.

RECIPROCALLY REINFORCING ACTIVITY TO PROMPT TAKING TURNS

The behavior of one child sets the stage for reinforcing a partner. Examples: Teeter-totter, play catch with a ball, and table games. A natural cue prompts a child to take turns and initiate interaction.

GENERALIZATION

Issues related to successful implementation of social programming are the generalization and maintenance of behavior outside of the play, sport, and game environments of instruction. The generalization of social behavior is a product of complex interactions between a number of factors, such as the following:

1. *The level of the behavioral disorder.* Data indicate that the more severe the behavior disorder, the more difficult the generalization process.
2. *Reduction of the discrepancy between the training and the generalization setting:* This refers to similarity of the stimulus characteristics of the environment, the similarity in response and reinforcement properties of the tasks of the training, and natural environments.

There are techniques for generalizing social behavior within and external to the instructional setting. The mission of generalization of social behavior within the instructional setting is to enable the behaviors to be demonstrated independent of the training staff. For low functioning persons it is often necessary to have staff and trained peers involved in the process of social development. Techniques for generalization involve fading (gradually eliminating) peers and trainers from the social activity. Some specific techniques for generalization of social behavior in the instructional setting are to (1) fade the number of trainers in a social game, (2) fade the number of higher functioning peers, (3) fade

the amount of time a trainer spends in activity, and (4) increase the number of peers and decrease the number of staff involved in the game. Once the social behavior in play and game activity is established in the instructional setting, attempts should be made to generalize the behaviors across other persons and environments. Some considerations for generalization of social behavior and abilities outside of the instructional setting are:

1. Practice the skills in different environments (intramurals, other facilities).
2. Practice the skills in the home with parents, siblings, and relatives.
3. Practice the skills in the neighborhood and community-based programs.

SOCIAL INTEGRATION OF THE PERSON WITH DISABILITIES IN LEISURE, RECREATION, AND SPORT ACTIVITIES

The Amateur Sports Act of 1978 (P.L. 95-606) encourages the integration of persons with and without disabilities in sport competition. The United States Olympic Committee provides assistance to amateur athletic programs for inclusion of individuals with disabilities into training and competition with individuals without disabilities. This theme is also expressed in the Rehabilitation Act of 1973 (P.L. 93-112) and the Education for All Handicapped Children Act of 1975.

In some cases integration requires creative strategies. Special Olympics International has developed several creative programs designed specifically to enhance integration of individuals with and without disabilities into sports programs. The Partner's Club Program is designed to encourage high school–age students to seek coaching certification and to be actively involved as coaches of mentally retarded athletes. The Unified Sports Program is designed to foster the integration of individuals with and without disabilities into training and competition programs by matching participants on the basis of age and ability. Then, children with and without disabilities can train and compete together, mutually dependent on each other for the outcome of the event. The concept is applicable in school settings. Students without disabilities could be mobilized to participate in integrated play with their peers with disabilities in public school physical education programs.

More and more community-based leisure and recreation programs are being made available to individuals with disabilities. The most promising of these are programs that encourage individuals with disabilities to participate with individuals without disabilities. Wilderness Inquiry II, Minneapolis, Minnesota has a model

FIGURE 6-10. Coaches and special olympians share a quiet moment. (Courtesy Texas Special Olympics.)

program that includes wilderness canoeing, backpacking and hiking, cross-country skiing, and dog sledding. Wachtel, a participant in Wilderness Inquiry II, described his experience:

> This type of trip is really at the cutting edge of recreational experiences. Most trips that include disabled peo ple are trips that do for people; decisions are made for disabled people, and disabled people are cared for and allowed to have an experience.
>
> This trip, as an integrated trip, was not a care for trip, it was a do with trip. It was a trip with disabled people.[56]

Part of the growth of leisure, recreation, and sports programs is due to an increased desire of individuals with disabilities to participate in leisure and recreation activities and to their willingness to serve as self-advocates in finding resources and programs that will address their needs.

One of the major developments in leisure and recreation programs nationally is the trend toward participation by individuals with and without disabilities in programs with an emphasis on outdoor, environmental experiences. The Breckenridge Outdoor Recreation Center in Breckenridge, Colorado is known for exceptional wilderness programming for challenged individuals. It is based on the philosophy that:

> There is therapeutic value in wilderness programming. Wilderness adventures can be strong tools for attitude changes and psychological growth . . . providing experiences that bring out the best of the human spirit . . . the real mission has to do with empowerment; instilling in participants the sense that who they are and who they can be is a product of their own hand, heart, and vision. Climbing, backcountry travel, and survival training are not ends in themselves. Rather, such activities are methods to attain other goals.[43]

The innovative program includes the following winter activities: downhill and cross-country skiing, sit-skiing, mono-skiing, helicopter skiing, ice sledding, winter camping, backpacking, solo trips, and ropes courses.

Camp ASCCA-Easter Seals, Adaptive Aquatics, Inc. has a recognized program that focuses on water skiing and includes special instruction in slalom, barefoot, jumping, and trick skiing. A new and exciting program has opened new vistas for individuals with physical disabilities. Gary Fagner, founder and executive director of Ocean Escapes, based in Oceanside, California has developed a program in which, "We offer renewed freedom to individuals who are mobility impaired through illness or accident. In a weightless environment, unencumbered by paralyzed legs, a disabled diver moves with the ease of a dolphin."[17] Ocean Escapes provides instruction/programming in scuba as a form of aquatic therapy. Becky McCafferty, a one-time Olympic swimming hopeful, survived a neck injury in a body surfing accident that left her a quadriplegic. She said, of the Ocean Escapes program, "I can't take a shower, but I can scuba dive. On land, I struggle with motion. But underwater, I have unbelievable fluidity. And it makes me realize that my fears can limit me more than my paralysis if I let them".[17] Desert Breezes, Balloon Adventures, Inc. has developed a balloon basket customized and certified to fly the passenger with a disability. The Vinland Center has developed a comprehensive program for children and adults with disabilities. Vinland's programs are whole person in nature and focus on wellness, positive lifestyles, fitness, and productivity.

The Wisconsin Lion's Camp focuses on the development of individual competency through the use of a challenging "in the trees" ropes course, rock climbing, and aquatic activities. Other camping-based programs focus on the unique needs of the chronically ill child. Camp John Marc Myers, for example, in Bosque County, Texas, has been designed to give children with special health needs the chance to learn new skills, form peer relationships, and develop greater independence and self-esteem. Camp John Marc Myers is based on the following philosophy:

> Chronic disease and physical disability can rob children of the chance to just be kids, leaving them to spend the precious years of their youth watching from the sidelines. In lives that are filled with doctors, hospitals, and the painful awareness that they are not like other children, the chance to be a 'normal' kid is rare. Going away to camp gives children with special health needs that chance. The feeling of freedom experienced through camping provides an invaluable opportunity for these children to overcome preoccupation with illness and feelings of isolation.[6]

Other programs offer children with disabilities the opportunity to learn more community-based leisure and recreation skills. Kathy Corbin's "Never Say Never" program is a nonprofit organization that teaches golf to physically challenged individuals. The National Amputee Golf Association will provide clinics in local schools/community centers to teach golf skills and golf teaching skills to those with amputations. The United States Tennis Association has a series of clinics that they will offer in the public schools to teach beginning tennis to children with and without disabilities. The American Wheelchair Bowling Association works in close cooperation with the American Bowling Association to develop integrated bowling leagues.

Some colleges and universities offer sport camps for children with physical disabilities. Ball State University in Muncie, Indiana, the University of Texas at Arlington, and the University of Wisconsin-Whitewater are known for their children's sports training camps.

SUMMARY

Children with and without disabilities in this society are at risk. Children are among the most neglected of our people. Children with and without disabilities are entering the public school system unprepared, understimulated, abused, homeless, unloved, fearful, tired, hungry, and unkempt. Any and all of these factors have an impact on the psychosocial development of these children.

At-risk individuals and individuals with disabilities sometimes demonstrate delayed psychosocial development. Factors that contribute to this delay include differences in appearance and behavior, over-protective environments, lack of opportunity to interact with others in play, and rejection by others.

Psychosocial development can be promoted through participation in play, games, sports, and leisure/recreation activities. To enable such growth it is necessary to determine which psychosocial skills are lacking, set clear-cut goals, and design instructional environments that favor development. Both internal and external social traits, as well as each individual's placement on a social continuum, must be determined. Once functioning levels are determined, clearly stated social goals are developed. Appropriate games and activities are selected and sequenced to promote specific goals. Peer tutoring, total staff involvement, prerequisite communication skills, cooperative learning, group rewards, and cognitive training facilitate psychosocial growth and development. Curriculum-based assessment and programming for social skill development is a system that can be used within the physical education program.

The use of specific techniques to change social misbehavior and knowledge of techniques to generalize social behavior contribute to the durability of appropriate behaviors and continued psychosocial development.

There are increasing opportunities for individuals with disabilities to participate in community-based leisure, recreation, and sport programs. The more innovative programs provide opportunities for individuals with and without disabilities to participate together.

REVIEW QUESTIONS

1. Describe the infant mortality rate in the United States.
2. Explain the relationship between maternal prenatal neglect and low birth weight infants.
3. List some of the reasons that children with disabilities are more at-risk for child abuse and neglect than other children.
4. Describe the impact of poverty and homelessness on infants and children.
5. Describe the turbulent nature of the schools in contemporary society.
6. What are some social benefits that can be derived from play, games, sports, and leisure/recreation activities?
7. Describe an instructional process for developing social skills of children.
8. List some specific social traits that may be generalized from the microsocieties of games to other aspects of social life.
9. What are the six stages of social development?
10. Construct a standardized social game from which social development can be measured.
11. What are some different methods of assessing social behavior?
12. Write a social goal, appropriate for a leisure/recreation activity in a community-based program.
13. What are the necessary steps to follow when constructing a game to develop social skills?
14. Suggest a procedure to structure cooperative learning.
15. Describe the nature of a "New Game."
16. What are some techniques that can be used to change social behavior?
17. How can social behavior be generalized from games and sports to other social environments?
18. How does curriculum-based assessment and programming differ from normative-referenced behavioral assessment in the conduct of physical education programs to develop social behavior?

STUDENT ACTIVITIES

1. Interview a physical education teacher working in the inner city. Interview a physical education teacher working in an affluent suburb. Compare and contrast their experiences. Ask specific questions regarding the "out-of-school" lives of their children.
2. Volunteer at a shelter for the homeless or at a shelter for abused women and children.
3. Observe a child with a disability at play with other children. Note whether the child demonstrates any delays in external social interaction traits. Note the student's reaction when responding to authority, cooperating and competing with others, and when given an opportunity to lead the group.
4. Observe three groups of children of different ages at play. Identify which stage of social development each group demonstrates (adult-initiated activity, self-initiated activity, parallel activity, or social interaction).
5. Analyze one game and one leisure activity. Determine what social strategies, physical skills, and cognitive skills are required for each game.
6. Write three social goals that include the five social goal characteristics given in this chapter.
7. Contact an organization that provides activities for persons with disabilities and gather information about their services. Report your findings to the class.

REFERENCES

1. Anderson J: What will happen when crack babies grow up? *The Dallas Morning News,* March 24, 1990.
2. Asher SR, Taylor AR: The social outcomes of mainstreaming: sociometric assessment and beyond, *Except Educ Q* 1:13-30, 1981.
3. Bassuk EL: Homeless families, *Sci Am* 265:66-72, 1991.
4. Box T: Long, heated summer feared as gangs' grip tightens in the area, *The Dallas Morning News,* May 20, 1990.
5. Bruininks RH et al: *Scales of independent behavior,* Allen, Tex, 1984, DLM Teaching Resources.
6. Camp John Marc Myers, Special Camps for Special Kids, Dallas, Tex.
7. Chasnoff IJ: *Perinatal addiction: consequences of intrauterine exposure to opiate and nonopiate drugs.* In Chasnoff IJ, editor: *Drug use in pregnancy: mother and child,* Boston, 1986, MTP Press.
8. Child abuse: Cycle of abuse must be broken, *The Dallas Morning News,* September 10, 1990.
9. Cohen S, Warren RD: *Child abuse, disability, and family support: an analysis of dynamics in England and the United States with references to practices in other European countries,* New York, 1987, World Rehabilitation Fund.
10. Cone JD: *The pyramid scales,* Austin, Tex, 1984, PRO-ED.
11. Cowley G: Children in peril, *Newsweek Special Issue,* Summer, 1991,
12. Crack children, *Newsweek,* February 12, 1990, pp 62-63.
13. Crack hurts parental instinct, *The Dallas Morning News,* March 17, 1990.
14. Cratty BJ: Motor development of infants subject to maternal drug use: current evidence and future research strategies, *Adapt Phys Act Q* 7:110-125, 1990.
15. Daro D, McCurdy K: *Current trends in child abuse reporting and fatalities: the results of the 1990 annual fifty state survey,* The National Center on Child Abuse Prevention Research, a working paper, 1991.
16. Diamond LJ, Jaudes PK: Child abuse in a cerebral-palsied population, *Dev Med Child Neurol* 1:12-18, 1997.
17. Fagner G: *Ocean Escapes pioneers advances in aquatic therapy,* Oceanside Cal, Ocean Escapes Incorporated, 1991.
18. Fait H, Dunn J: *Special physical education,* Philadelphia, 1984, Saunders College Publishing.

19. Gaylord-Ross RJ, Holvoet J: *Strategies for educating students with severe handicaps,* Boston, 1985, Little, Brown & Co.

20. Garcia J: Two Dallas schools get metal detectors, *The Dallas Morning News,* December 16, 1989.

21. Gibbs N: Shameful bequests to the next generation, *Time,* October 8, 1990.

22. Gottlieb J, Leyser Y: Facilitating the social mainstreaming of retarded children, *Except Educ Q* 1:57-70, 1981.

23. Green C: Infant mortality rate may rise: poverty, drug use, AIDS among factors cited in panel's report, *The Dallas Morning News,* February 27, 1990.

24. Greer JV: The drug babies, *Except Child,* February, 1990, 382-384.

25. Gresham FM: Social skills assessment as a component of mainstreaming placement decisions, *Except Child* 49:331-336, 1986.

26. Grossman HJ, editor: *Classification in mental retardation,* Washington, DC, 1983, American Association on Mental Deficiency.

27. Hellison D: Making a difference—reflections on teaching urban at-risk youth, *J Phys Educ Rec Dance* 61:33-45, 1990.

28. Hellison D: Physical education for disadvantaged youth, *J Phys Educ Rec Dance* 61:37, 1990.

29. Hellison D: Teaching PE to at-risk youth in Chicago—a model, *J Phys Educ Rec Dance* 61:38-39, 1990.

30. Heron TE, Harris KC: *The educational consultant: helping professionals, parents, and mainstreamed students,* Boston, 1982, Allyn & Bacon.

31. Howell K, Morehead MK: *Curriculum based evaluation in special education and remedial education,* Columbus, Ohio, 1987, Merrill Publishing.

32. Huettig C, DiBrezzo R: *Factors in abuse and neglect of handicapped children.* Paper presented at American Alliance of Health, Physical Education, Recreation and Dance National Convention, Las Vegas, April, 1987.

33. *I hated the school, barriers to excellence,* Boston, 1985, National Coalition of Advocates for Children.

34. Jaudes PK, Diamond LJ: The handicapped child and child abuse, *Child Abuse Negl* 9:341-347, 1985.

35. Kenyon R: The deceptive peace of the countryside, *Wisconsin: The Milwaukee Journal Magazine,* August 12, 1990.

36. Kneedler RD: The use of cognitive training to change social behavior, *Except Educ Q* 1:65-73, 1980.

37. Kohlberg L: *The cognitive-development approach to moral education.* In: *Values, concepts, and techniques,* Washington, DC, 1971, National Education Association.

38. Kozol J: *Savage inequalities: children in America's schools,* New York, 1991, Crown Publishers.

39. Lifka BJ: Hiding beneath the stairwell—a dropout prevention program for Hispanic youth, *J Phys Educ Rec Dance* 61:40-41, 1990.

40. Lincoln CA, Higgins NM: Making schools work for all children, *Principal,* September, 1990.

41. Luckner JL: Outdoor adventure and the hearing impaired . . . consideration for program development, *Palaestra* 4:40-51, 1988.

42. Meisgeier C: A social/behavioral program for the adolescent student with serious learning problems, *Focus Except Child* 13:1-13, 1981.

43. Mobley M, Marlow P: Outdoor adventure: a powerful therapy, *Palaestra* 3:16-19, 1987.

44. Moos B: We are failing our children, *The Dallas Morning News,* March 9, 1990.

45. *More new games . . . and playful ideas from the New Games Foundation,* Garden City, NY, 1981, A Headlands Press Book.

46. *New games,* Garden City, NY, 1976, A Headlands Press Book

47. Oliver J: *Physical activity and the psychological development of the handicapped.* In Kane JE, editor: *Psychological aspects of physical education and sport,* Boston, 1972, Routledge & Kegan Paul.

48. Rise in urban needy reported, *The Dallas Morning News,* December 21, 1989.

49. Seaman JA, DePauw K: *The new adapted physical education,* Palo Alto, Calif, 1989, Mayfield Publishing.

50. Seffrin JR: Adolescent health: national crisis poses challenge for American Alliance of Health, Physical Education, Recreation and Dance, Update, May/June 1991.

51. Songster T: *A model leisure sport skill integration process through Special Olympics,* Application submitted to the US Department of Education, Office of Special Education, Washington, DC, 1987.

52. Sparrow SS, Balla DA, Cicchetti DV: *Vineland adaptive behavior scales,* Circle Pines, Minn, 1984, American Guidance Service.

53. Stephens TM: *Social skills in the classroom,* Columbus, Ohio, 1978, Cedars Press.

54. Strain PS: Peer-mediated treatment of exceptional children's social withdrawal, *Except Educ Q* 1:93-105, 1981.

55. Tucker JA: Curriculum-based assessment: an introduction, *Except Child* 52:199-204, 1985.

56. Wachtel LJ: Thoughts on a wilderness canoe trip, *Palaestra* 3:33-40, 1987.

57. Wehling D: The crack kids are coming, *Principal,* May, 1991, 12-13.

58. Westcott H: The abuse of disabled children: a review of the literature, *Child Care Health Dev* 17:243-258, 1991.

59. Wheman P: *Helping the mentally retarded acquire play skills,* Springfield, Ill, 1977, Charles C Thomas, Publishers.

60. Williams W: Education: a desperate situation, *Denton Record-Chronicle,* April 25, 1990.

61. Women heading more families in '80's, *The Dallas Morning News,* December 7, 1989.

62. Wood DL, Valdez RB, Hayashi T, Shen A: Health of homeless children and housed, poor children, *Pediatrics* 86:858-866, 1990.

SUGGESTED READINGS

Fluegelman A, editor: *New games book,* Garden City, NY, 1976, A Headlands Press Book.

Howell K, Morehead MK: *Curriculum based evaluation in special education and remedial education,* Columbus, Ohio, 1987, Merrill Publishing.

Kozol J: *Savage inequalities: children in America's schools,* New York, 1991, Crown Publishers.

More new games...and playful ideas from the New Games Foundation, Garden City, NY, 1981, A Headlands Press Book.

Ramsey-Muselwhite C: *Adaptive play for special needs children: strategies to enhance communication and learning,* San Diego, 1986, College-Hill Press.

Courtesy Wisconsin Special Olympics

7

OBJECTIVES

Define mental retardation.

Explain the variability of characteristics among individuals who are mentally retarded.

Recognize the need for differential programming for severely mentally retarded individuals.

Select appropriate activities depending on the age and level of functioning of each retarded person.

Explain procedures for appropriate placement and programming of individuals in the least restrictive environment.

Mental Retardation

*I*t is now recognized that mental retardation is not a fixed, unalterable condition that condemns an individual to a static, deprived lifetime of failure to achieve. Rather, today we understand that cognitive, psychomotor, and affective behaviors are dynamic processes that, if properly stimulated, can be developed further than ever before imagined. Early concepts of mental retardation viewed the condition as an inherited disorder that was essentially incurable. This notion

161

resulted in hopelessness on the part of professionals and social and physical separation of persons who were mentally retarded. After years of research and innovative programming, it is now recognized that intelligence and other functions depend on the readiness and experience of the child, the degree and quality of environmental stimulation, and many other variables.

In the late 1960s and early 1970s institutions that served retarded persons began designing and implementing educational programs intended to develop independent living skills of retarded persons to enable them to function in community settings. As institutionalized retarded individuals rose to the challenge of these educational programs, a movement began to promote their placement in communities. Thousands of persons were removed from the institutions and allowed to take their rightful place as contributing members of communities.

As institutions began to develop viable educational programs, public schools took up their responsibility toward young mentally retarded children living in the communities. Professionals trained in appropriate teaching techniques were hired by the school systems to provide educational opportunities for retarded children. As a result of efforts by both institutions for retarded persons and public school systems, all except the most severely involved mentally retarded individuals are living, going to school, and working in the community. Thus mentally retarded persons today have more opportunities than ever before for optimum social interaction. However, the technical processes for arranging environments to maximize the social benefits for both the mentally retarded and non–mentally retarded persons is in its infancy.

DEFINITION AND CLASSIFICATIONS

The newest definition of mental retardation was adapted by the American Association on Mental Retardation (AAMR) in May 1992. The new definition is as follows:

> Mental retardation refers to substantial limitations in certain personal capabilities. It is manifested as significantly subaverage intellectual functioning, existing concurrently with related disabilities in two or more of the following applicable adaptive skill areas: communication, self-care, home living, social skills, community use, self-direction, health and safety, functional academics, leisure, and work. Mental retardation begins before age 18.[1]

The 1992 definition differs from past definitions in three ways:
1. Mental retardation refers to substantial limita-

tions in certain, but not all, personal capabilities. The personal capabilities identified include cognitive, functional, and social abilities.
2. Mental retardation is manifested as significantly subaverage intellectual functioning plus related disabilities in two or more specific adaptive skill areas. The inclusion of at least two specific adaptive skill areas assures the inclusion of individuals who are limited in fully accessing independent functioning in our society.
3. The fact that mental retardation must be evident before age 18 is clearly stated; however, the condition may not always be of lifelong duration. The recognition that mental retardation is not necessarily permanent speaks directly to a point many of us have argued for years. That is, with appropriate and timely intervention services, individuals who are born mentally retarded can be taught to perform to acceptable (normal) personal and social standards. Clearly, we must increase our efforts to use the most up-to-date information and technology to help mentally retarded individuals advance to the point where they can become fully functioning, independent citizens in society.

Levels of Retardation

The new classification system includes only two levels—mild and severe retardation. The diagnostic system is divided into six parts: (1) intellectual functioning and adaptive skills; (2) psychological and emotional considerations; (3) health and physical considerations; (4) etiological considerations; (5) environmental considerations; and (6) appropriate supports. Use of this diagnostic system yields an overall profile of each mentally retarded individual that should greatly facilitate programming for these students.

In applying the definition the following three assumptions are essential:
1. Specific adaptive disabilities often coexist with strengths in other adaptive skills or other personal capabilities.
2. The existence of disabilities in adaptive skills occurs within the context of community environments typical of the individual's age peers and is indexed to the person's individualized needs for support.
3. With appropriate supports over a sustained period, the life functioning of the person with mental retardation will generally improve.

According to the new definition mental retardation is environmentally determined, therefore IQ score will no longer be used to determine the severity of mental retardation. Instead individuals will be assessed in 10 adaptive skill areas:

1. Communication
2. Home living
3. Community use
4. Health and safety
5. Leisure
6. Self-care
7. Social skills
8. Self-direction
9. Functional academics
10. Work

Level of retardation (mild or severe) will be based on functioning in the adaptive skill areas and on the amount of support the individual needs. The four levels of support are:

1. No support needed—The person is either self-sufficient or can procure needed supports on his or her own.
2. Minimal support—The person needs intermittent help or support in areas such as case management, transportation, home living, physical health, employment, and self-advocacy.
3. Substantial/extensive support—The person needs regular ongoing support and includes instruction, assistance (such as attendant care), and/or supervision within a designated adaptive skill area.
4. Pervasive/consistent support—The person needs constant care on a 24-hour basis and may include the maintenance of life support function/systems.

The new definition adopted by the American Association on Mental Retardation will probably eventually effect classification techniques now being used in our public school settings. However, how and when that will occur is not known at this time. The important thing to keep in mind is that individuals considered to have mental retardation while in some environments (school) may not be so classified in other settings (work).

CHARACTERISTICS OF MENTALLY RETARDED INDIVIDUALS

Although research tends to generalize the characteristics of the mentally retarded, they are diverse in cognitive, social, and physical functions. The performance of mentally retarded athletes in the recent Special Olympics International games, where performance exceeded expectations, is testimony for their competence. On the other hand, some persons with mental retardation are unable to participate in regular sport events and

need modification of the activities to be successful in their efforts to play. Other persons with severe mental retardation may not be ambulatory.

The cognitive capabilities of the mentally retarded may vary greatly. In addition to the considerable variability in intelligence as measured by standardized tests, there are aspects of intelligence that may be superior to many with so-called "normal" intelligence. For instance, some persons with mental retardation have phenomenal memories. There is also considerable variance in cognitive functioning with respect to the decision making process. Some persons with mental retardation may be able to make decisions that enable independent functioning in the community while others may be totally dependent on others for cognitive decisions.

The social characteristics of the mentally retarded also vary greatly. Some persons with mental retardation are dependable, cooperative, and can delay their gratification, while others are self-centered and impulsive.[44]

The mentally retarded population is comprised of a diverse group of individuals. Thus it is difficult to generalize a set of characteristics to the total population. However, there are general characteristics that are representative of the group. The cognitive and physical characteristics of this population provide basic guidelines and alert the physical educator to the potential nature of the physical education programs they need. Sherrill[46] and Fox et al.[22] indicate that over 22% of the mentally retarded youngsters between the ages of 5 and 15 years are obese. However, as these individuals become older, and if they are living in institutions, there is evidence that the incidence of obesity raises to 45% in males and over 50% in females.[30] The low fitness levels of Down syndrome youngsters ages 6 to 21 years fall below the 10th percentile on all items of the American Alliance for Health, Physical Education, Recreation, and Dance (AAHPERD) 1980 Health Related Physical Fitness Battery. This would be expected if these individuals have inactive lifestyles and a preponderance for obesity.

Cognitive Characteristics Related to Skill

As a group, mentally retarded persons are not as adept in perceptual attributes that relate to motor skills as are comparable nonretarded individuals. They may be clumsy and awkward and lack balance, which would affect their ability to perform motor tasks efficiently. Newell[38] suggests that there may be more specific concerns about a small range of motor skills than the problems of learning. A review of the literature reveals that there are many perceptual and cognitive characteristics that may inhibit the learning of motor skills. Examples are less preparation and slower actual movement time[50] and a delay in developing postural reflexes.[39] Also, when compared to other persons they are less able to spontaneously predict changing conditions of a motor task.

Competition

Competition is an important motivator to bring out the best efforts of athletes. While evidence exists that mentally retarded persons can benefit through competition such as Special Olympics, some mentally retarded youngsters may not understand the concept of competition. The more severely mentally retarded athlete may not comprehend "run as fast as you can,""jump as high as you can," and "score more points than your opponent."

Attention to Task and Memory

Two important aspects to learning motor skills are the attention that one gives to the instructional task and the ability to remember and respond to movement cues. According to Kerr and Blais[31] individuals with Down syndrome tend to process components of a complex task and deal with them independently. However, they can learn a task by practicing the isolated component parts. DePauw and Ferrari[16] indicate that nondisabled individuals have a more difficult time performing tasks when some interference occurs than do mentally retarded subjects. Thus once retarded individuals are on task, they are not distracted by extraneous cues and information. Furthermore, Newell[38] found no difference between mentally retarded subjects and nonretarded groups on adopting memory strategies for the recall of movement cues on a motor task. Thus it would seem that mentally retarded persons could make improvements in their movement accuracy equal to the improvements of their nonretarded counterparts if the retarded individuals are helped to understand and remember essential movement information.

Developmental Delays

Another characteristic of mentally retarded populations is developmental physical and motor delays. Because of these inherent delays, good physical education programs are critical for facilitating development. Growth and development is a continuous process in all types of populations. Yabe et al.[55] reported that as subjects with IQs of 40 and above increased in chronological age, their reaction times and individual variability decreased. Thus it is reasonable to expect retarded individuals to continually grow and develop. Physical education programs can promote this growth.

Cardiovascular Development

The cardiovascular system is less well developed in many mentally retarded individuals.[46] Poor respiration and susceptibility to respiratory infections may accompany the underdeveloped cardiovascular system. However, there is evidence that the cardiovascular system can be developed through training regimens. Wright and Cowden[54] report the development of cardiovascular endurance through participation in Special Olympics' swimming training programs. Thus mentally retarded persons may not need a specific cardiovascular training program if they are given the opportunity to participate in sports training programs.

Postural Development

Many mentally retarded individuals have postural abnormalities that include malalignment of the trunk or the legs. One of the most obvious postural deficiencies is that of the protruding abdomen because of lack of abdominal strength. In addition, there may be malalignment of the legs and pronated ankles.[46] Delays in postural reactions development accommpany delays in motor milestones.[25] Postural alignment of retarded students should be assessed and followed by specific programming to correct postural abnormalities.

Promoting Motor Development

Knowledge of the characteristics of mentally retarded populations provides information about the types of programs that need to be implemented to serve them. However, designing whole physical education programs around these characteristics for the purpose of teaching groups of mentally retarded persons may not meet the needs of individuals within the group. Clearly, the assessed needs of each individual must be taken into consideration when designing the individual physical education program.

It is true that mentally retarded individuals have developmental lags in intellectual quotients and usually have parallel lags in motor and social development. Table 7-1 shows the mental and chronological ages of retarded individuals with a conversion of motor behaviors one would expect from individuals with delayed mental ages. Low mildly mentally retarded children with a chronological age of 2 to 5 years would be expected to attempt locomotor patterns. Those between 6 and 9 years would be attempting to learn to jump and balance on one foot briefly, as well as learning to

TABLE 7-1

Conversion of behavior in physical education activity adjusted for mental age of the moderately mentally retarded

Chronological age	Activities for normal children by chronological age	Activities of low mildly mentally retarded adjusted for mental age	Mental age
4 to 8 years	Generalization of running, jumping as sub-routines into play activity; low organized games (i.e., Follow the Leader, Tag).	Learning to run; balance on one foot; manipulate objects; engage in activity that requires simple directions.	2 to 4 years
8 to 12 years	Can play lead-up games to sport skills that involve throwing and catching. Can play games of competition where there is team organization. Can learn rules and play by them.	May be able to generalize running and locomotor skills into play activity. May be able to play games of low organization and follow simple direction. May socially interact in play; may play by self; or may play in parallel.	4 to 6 years
12 to 17 years	Can play games of high organization. Can further develop skills that involve racquet sports and balls and require high levels of skill. Can participate in team games and employ strategies in competitive activity.	Can participate in modified sport activity. Is better in individual sports (e.g., swimming, bowling and track) where there is a minimum of social responsibility. Can throw and catch balls, but it is difficult to participate in meaningful competitive activity.	6 to 8 years
Over 17 years	Can participate independently in recreational activities in their choosen community.	Can participate in community recreational sport and physical activity in special programs and with assistance from others.	Over 10 years

throw. This information provides a good basis for constructing curricula for group activity because it is simple and straightforward. However, full assessments of the physical education needs of mentally retarded persons will reveal deviations from behaviors indicated in Table 7-1.

Every effort must be made to provide each mentally retarded student with an appropriate physical education program that will promote the motor growth and development of that child. Children under the age of 9 years will benefit from a bottom, up physical education program that focuses on promoting sensory input and perceptual-motor integration. Older students should be taught to perform culturally relevant community-based recreational skills that can be used throughout their lives to promote and maintain a healthy lifestyle in social settings.

TESTING TO DETERMINE FUNCTIONING LEVELS

Development of the individual education program (IEP) requires that present functioning levels be determined. Several formal tests that can be used with mentally retarded students are listed in Table 3-1 of this text. Other acceptable ways to evaluate the functioning levels of this population are task analysis and observation of the students as they perform a hierarchical sequence of activities. These techniques have been described in Chapter 5.

One of the most difficult problems of testing mentally retarded individuals is deciding whether poor comprehension or poor motor development is the reason for their inability to perform a specific task. Because it is difficult to determine whether a mentally retarded student understands directions given during test situations, the following suggestions may help the evaluator elicit the best performance possible:

1. If after the student has been told what to do the response is incorrect, demonstrate the position or movement.
2. If demonstration does not elicit the correct performance, manually place the student in or through the desired position or pattern.
3. Use positive reinforcement (praise, tokens, free play) to encourage the student.

When severely mentally retarded students are tested, it may be necessary to use an anatomical task analysis (see Chapter 4) to determine their level of capability.

TEACHING STRATEGIES

Physical education programs should be based on the nature and needs of the learner. As mentioned previously there is great variability among the mentally retarded population. This is attributable to inherent differences between mild and more severe retardation, causes, and the many other disorders that accompany mental retardation.

Disorders associated with mental retardation may be sensory impairments such as blindness, being hard-of-hearing, or deafness; emotional disturbances; and neurological disorders such as cerebral palsy, muscular dystrophy, and problems in perception. It becomes apparent that physical education programs for mentally retarded persons must meet a multitude of needs at all age levels and all levels of intellectual and physical development.

The mentally retarded are a very heterogeneous group. Many techniques of instruction are necessary to elicit a desired response. Therefore it is difficult to make generalizations that may be helpful in the instruction of physical education activities for mentally retarded persons. However, as a guide, some teaching hints follow:

1. Consider individual differences when selecting the activities. There are many games that allow for differences in abilities among class members.
2. Select activities according to the needs of the mentally retarded.
3. Select activities to meet the students' interest levels. However, precaution should be taken against participation in one particular activity to the exclusion of others. Be aware of the retarded student's tendency to favor the single activity with which he or she is most familiar.
4. Do not underestimate the ability of mentally retarded students to perform skilled movements. There is a tendency to set goals too low for these children.
5. Select sensory-perceptual-motor activities to promote specific and general development of the young retarded child and develop recreational skills of older students to make it possible for these individuals to integrate socially with peers and members of their families now and in later life in community activity.
6. Select activities primarily on the basis of the development of motor skills. However, chronological ages should bias your selection of activities; whenever possible, the activities should be age-appropriate, as well.

7. Structure the environment in which the activity takes place so that it challenges the students yet frees them from the fear of physical harm and gives them some degree of success.
8. Analyze tasks involved in activities to be sure you are clear about all the components of the skill you are about to teach.
9. Remember that mentally retarded children with lower functioning must be taught to play. This means that physical education programs are responsible for creating the play environment, developing basic motor skills that are the tools of play, identifying at what play level (self-directed, onlooker, solitary, parallel, associative, or cooperative) the child is functioning, and promoting development from that point.
10. Create a safe play environment, but do not necessarily provide security to the extent that the children are unduly dependent on you for physical safety.
11. Use manual guidance as a method of instruction. The proprioceptors are great teachers of movement. Manual guidance is more important for the younger and more severely mentally retarded children. The less ability the child has to communicate verbally, the more manual guidance should be considered as a tool for instruction.
12. Work for progression in skill development. For preschool retardates use sensorimotor activities that contribute to skills found on motor development scales; for mentally retarded children functioning above the preschool level, use task analysis and progression methods commonly employed for nonretarded children.
13. Work for active participation on the part of all mentally retarded children. Active involvement contributes more to neurological development than does passive movement.
14. Modify the activity so that each child can participate up to his or her ability level.
15. Convey to mentally retarded persons that they are persons of worth, reinforcing their strengths and minimizing their weaknesses.
16. Be patient with smaller and slower gains in more severely retarded persons. Often gains that seem small when compared with those of nonretarded children are tremendous for the more severely mentally retarded.
17. Use strong visual and auditory stimuli for the more severely retarded children, since these often bring the best results.

FIGURE 7-1. A mentally retarded adolescent experiences the challenge of an "in-the-trees" ropes course. (Courtesy Wisconsin Lions Camp, Rosholt, Wisconsin.)

18. Use demonstration as an effective instructional tool. It is particularly effective to use a peer demonstrator.
19. Have many activities available, because attention span is short.
20. Keep verbal directions to a minimum. They are often ineffective when teaching more severely retarded children.
21. Use distributed rather than massed practice.
22. Provide a broad spectrum of activities that have recreational and social significance for later life.
23. Analyze physical activity into component parts and teach through common instructional techniques such as modeling, behavioral research, graduated prompt levels, and contingent descriptive praise with subsequent fading procedures.[14]

24. Utilize effective maintenance and generalization programs to assure that the skills attained in physical education are utilized in community settings.[14] If possible, teach the skills within the community-based setting that will be used for leisure, recreation, or sport participation.
25. Teach specific social skills that are meaningful within a specific social environment so that the behavioral change results in functional social performance.[35]
26. Assist mentally retarded persons to develop sound self-management procedures so they can learn to plan and complete tasks independently, evaluate their own performance, compare their performance to a standard, and make adjustments.[36]
27. Use a systematic style of instruction where the behaviors are defined, measured, modeled, and monitored for acquisition within a sructure that is best for the individual learner.[8,27]

Adaptations for Mildly Retarded Students

The most apparent difficulty for persons with the mildest forms of mental retardation is comprehension of complex playing rules and strategies. Often the mildly retarded student who is placed in the mainstream is accused inappropriately of trying to cheat, when in reality, he or she honestly does not understand what the rule or proper move is. Such accusations by peers or teachers often lead to momentary or prolonged rejection of the retarded child. Rejection leads to feelings of low self-esteem, which contribute directly to withdrawal or retaliation on the part of the retarded student. Acting out then becomes an everyday occurrence, and before long they are perceived by peers or teachers as troublemakers. The vicious cycle can be avoided if the teacher anticipates comprehension difficulties and acts to counter them before they occur. Some suggestions for dealing with lack of understanding of rules or playing strategies are as follows:

1. Place the student in a less demanding position.
2. Overteach and constantly reinforce cognitive aspects of each game.
3. Help the other students in the class develop an understanding and sensitivity toward the retarded student's learning difficulties.

If the mildly retarded child has a propensity toward excessive body fat, this problem will be detected when the AAHPERD Health Related Fitness Test or a similar assessment is given early in the school year to all students. Every child identified as having excessive body fat should be provided with appropriate aerobic activities and, possibly, nutritional counseling to reduce body fat stores. There is a need for routine health-related testing of all students in all schools, at every level. The sooner children learn the importance of controlling body fat levels through diet control and exercise, the better the chance that these good habits will carry over to adulthood.

Should other types of testing (motor skills, balance, coordination) be deemed necessary by the physical educator, developmental delays may be found in mildly retarded students. The reader may refer to Table 3-1 for appropriate tests to use with this population. Appropriate intervention strategies such as direct teaching of the specific basic motor components found to be deficient in a variety of abilities and skills will benefit these students greatly.

To enhance the probability that mentally retarded children will interact with their families and peers in healthful leisure time pursuits, care must be taken to teach the retarded student to play games and sports that are typically pursued in community settings. The child who finds success and enjoyment in vigorous activity at a young age will continue participation as an adult.

Students with more significant levels of mental retardation exhibit performance ranges from very poor motor skill and physical fitness levels to quite acceptable performance ability. Traditional studies done by Hayden,[26] Cratty,[12] and Rarick[40] showed the motor development of children with IQs between 36 and 52 to lag 2 to 4 years behind that of children with normal intelligence. However, the performance level of these mentally retarded persons may indeed reflect the type of motor development programs afforded them.

Numerous studies have demonstrated that mentally retarded individuals benefit from physical fitness training coupled with reinforcement.[13,42,52] Appropriate motivation, high teacher expectations, and carefully designed learning sequences appear to be the keys to promoting learning among the mentally retarded population.

It is true that these youngsters often demonstrate delayed motor development milestones early in life and learn at about one-half the rate of normal children. However, the early childhood intervention programs that are gaining in popularity may help offset the marked motor delays more involved retarded children demonstrate when they reach school age.

FIGURE 7-2. Adult special olympians participate in a "new games" clinic. (Courtesy Wisconsin Special Olympics.)

The physical educator is cautioned against generalizing about the motor functioning level and learning capability of the mentally retarded student. As in all cases of students with disabilities, the mentally retarded child should be thoroughly tested for motor skill functioning level and physical fitness before decisions are made as to what type of physical education program is needed. If testing shows a mentally retarded student to be deficient in areas of motor behavior performance, a thorough task analysis should be completed before the student's program is determined.

Physical Education for the Severely Retarded Student

A relatively recent trend in the field of special education is the development of instruction for children with severe disabilities. With the development of new instructional technology in the late 1970s, it was possible to demonstrate the competence of severely mentally retarded individuals. The Data Based Gymnasium is an excellent example of a physical education program developed specifically for severely retarded persons.[18] The Association for Persons with Severe Handicaps is a professional and parent group that has developed instructional procedures based on research and demonstration, and provided opportunities for severely mentally retarded persons.[39] The severely mentally retarded segment of the population numbers over 30,000 people. Through implementation of the available information from research and demonstration (i.e., best practice), it has been demonstrated that it is possible to maximize the potential of this group of individuals for meaningful participation in society. Physical education, which develops the motor capabilities of this group, is an integral and important part of their education.

Characteristics

Persons with severe mental retardation most likely will have adverse performance in social, cognitive, language, and motor development. Many severely mentally retarded students will have difficulty interacting with others. This may stem from abnormal behavior, which may include self-abusive acts as well as behavior that is injurious to others. Furthermore, stereotyped behaviors and bizarre acts such as rocking back and forth, waving the hands in front of the eyes, and making strange noises may also adversely affect social interaction with others. In addition, many severely mentally retarded persons may have problems with self-help skills such as dressing, feeding, and basic motor functioning.

Severely mentally retarded persons frequently have impaired cognitive and language development. Many

FIGURE 7-3. Stable paddle boats allow freedom and independence for severely mentally retarded adolescents. (Courtesy Wisconsin Lions Camp, Rosholt, Wisconsin.)

are unable to respond to simple commands. Thus it is difficult for them to grasp instruction. Furthermore, they may lack the ability to generalize skills learned in one setting to another setting. They often have problems with language. This further makes communication during instruction difficult.

Motor delays are very common among severely mentally retarded persons. Difficulty in walking and performing such basic tasks as sitting down, standing up, grasping objects, or holding the head up is common. In addition, these deficits, to varying degrees, may reflect on their motor and physical capabilities. They may be less capable in areas of strength, flexibility, agility, coordination, and balance. Whereas the characteristics of severely retarded individuals may suggest grim prospects for development, there is, however, impressive evidence that through quality instruction severely mentally retarded individuals can improve their motor skills and make great strides in becoming self-sufficient persons.[37]

Principles of instruction

Every student, regardless of disability, can learn.[17] However, for severely mentally retarded individuals there are instructional procedures that should be followed to maximize motor development. These include: (1) assess the present level of the student in defined target skills, (2) arrange the skills in an appropriate sequence so that objectives can be identified, (3) provide clear cues during the instructional process, (4) provide precise feedback immediately after the task is completed, (5) include strategies to promote generalization of skills to meaningful community environments, and (6) measure and evaluate the performance gains to enable appropriate subsequent instructional decisions.

Behavior modification coupled with task analysis is usually recommended when teaching the severely mentally retarded student.[3] This system involves selecting a signal or a request to cause the desired behavior. After selecting the skill to be taught, divide it into its component parts. Teach the parts using backward or forward chaining. If the task is a continuous one (such as running or jumping), shaping, rather than task analysis, is more appropriate. Once the physical skill has been performed, reinforce the student (see Chapter 5).

Motor activities for severely mentally retarded persons

Special Olympics International has developed training materials for use with severely mentally retarded

individuals.[48] This motor development curriculum promotes improvement in coordination and control of the body when performing a variety of motor activities. It is designed to develop age appropriate sport and recreation skills as well as physical fitness, sensory awareness, and the sense of being part of a group. Included in the curriculum is a motor activities assessment instrument that should be used to evaluate mobility, dexterity, striking, kicking, and aquatic activity, as well as manual and electric wheelchair mobility skills. Also included are Special Olympics activities specifically adapted for severely mentally retarded athletes. These include aquatics, track and field, basketball, bowling, gymnastics, softball, volleyball, and weight lifting. Each sport is task analyzed for inclusion of the motor activities in the guide. Criteria and standards are identified to inform the teacher as to when the skill or the task has been mastered. Furthermore, data sheets on which to record types of instruction used (physical assistance, physical prompts, demonstration, verbal cues, and visual cues) are included. Spaces are also provided for recording the type of reinforcement used (i.e., edible, social, token, etc.) as well as the schedule of reinforcement (continuous, fixed, or intermittent).

Activities. Activities in the motor development manual are broken down into the following components: dexterity, reaching, grasping, releasing, posture, head control in prone and supine positions, sitting in a chair, rolling, crawling, use of an electric wheelchair, sensory awareness, visual-motor, auditory-motor, and tactile awareness. Each of these activities are sequenced to maximize the potential for learning.

When designing the adapted physical education program, the physical educator should work closely with both the physical and occupational therapists, who often test severely retarded students to determine range of motion and level of reflex development. Consultation with the therapists and creative modification of traditional physical education activities will benefit severely mentally retarded students. Some common activities used by physical and occupational therapists with this population follow*:

1. To stretch hip and knee flexors remove the non-ambulatory severely mentally retarded student from a sitting position and allow him or her to stretch out on a mat.
2. To improve range of motion encourage the indi-

---

*An excellent resource to use when working with this population is *Gross Motor Management of Severely Multiply Impaired Students* by Fraser, Galka, and Hensinger (see Suggested Readings at the end of this chapter).

vidual to reach for an object held just a few degrees beyond the range of capability. To hold interest, permit the person to reach the object occasionally.

3. Place the student face down on the mat and place a pillow or bolster under the upper chest. Encourage the student to look up (lift head) from this position as often as possible.
4. Place the severely mentally retarded student face down on a long scooter. Pull the scooter and encourage the individual to try using hands and feet to propel himself or herself.
5. Place the student in a supine position on an air mat or trampoline. Gently bounce the surface around the student.
6. Praise every attempt the severely mentally retarded student makes to initiate movement.
7. Hook a lightweight Theraband strip or an elastic loop around each of the student's limbs (one at a time) and encourage him or her to pull against the loop.

Atlantoaxial Instability

The Atlantoaxial segments of the cervical spine of children with Down syndrome may have a tendency for development of localized anomalies that are in danger of atlantoaxial dislocation. As a result of this potential danger, in 1983 a group of physicians, including experts in sports medicine and the Surgeon General of the United States, met at the Joseph P. Kennedy, Jr., Foundation to discuss the perceived dangers of atlantoaxial instability among individuals with Down syndrome. Of particular concern were the thousands of athletes in Special Olympics with Down syndrome.

Atlantoaxial instability is a greater than normal mobility of the two upper cervical vertebrae—C1 and C2—at the top of the neck. The condition exposes the victims to possible serious injury if they forcibly flex the neck, because the vertebrae may shift and thereby squeeze or sever the spinal cord. A dislocation involves an actual displacement of the bone from the normal position in the joint. Awareness of the significance of the atlantoaxial instability can aid in the prevention of injuries at the upper cervical spine level. The instability is due to (1) the laxity of the transverse ligament that holds the odontoid process of the axis (C2) in place against the inner aspect of the inner arch of Atlas (C1) and (2) abnormalities of the odontoid. These conditions allow some leeway between the odontoid and the atlas, especially during flexion and extension of the neck. This results in an unstable joint. The atlantoaxial instability can be gradual and progressive.

Incidence

Incidence of atlantoaxial instability is in question. The range of incidents is reported from 10% to 30% of the Down syndrome population. However, the public health department reports 10%.[2]

Symptoms

The two types of symptoms of atlantoaxial dislocation are observable physical symptoms and neurological signs. Some of the behavior symptoms are:
- Deterioration in ambulatory skills
- Changes in bowel or bladder function
- Changes in neck posturing, neck pain, or limitations of neck movement
- Weakness of any of the extremities
- Progressive clumsiness and loss of coordination[11]

Some of the neurological signs associated with atlantoaxial dislocation are:
- Hypersensitivity
- Hyperreflexiveness
- Cloneness (there are certain abnormalities that are present in neurological examinations)
- Extensor plantar responses (i.e., abnormalities detected in the neurological examination)[11]

Precautionary measures

Special Olympics has taken the lead in the formulation of policies for the participation of athletes with Down syndrome who may have atlantoaxial instability. Tens of thousands of mentally retarded individuals with Down syndrome have participated in Special Olympics over the past 20 years. However, officials of Special Olympics International believe that none have suffered injury related to atlantoaxial instability while participating in Special Olympics training or competition. However, as a precaution, Special Olympics has developed a policy concerning participation in Special Olympics by individuals with Down syndrome.

Implications for adapted physical education

Professionals in adapted physical education need to be aware of the potential injury-inducing activities and situations for persons with atlantoaxial instability. The adapted physical educator should be aware of the student's medical status, including the condition of the atlantoaxial joint. Hopefully, results of medical examinations will be kept in the student's permanent health file at the school. The following guidelines from Special Olympics policy and the Committee on Sports Medicine[10] should be followed:

1. Check the medical files to determine which individuals have the atlantoaxial instability condition

2. Restrict participation in gymnastics, diving, the butterfly stroke in swimming, the diving start in swimming competition, the high jump, soccer, and any warm-up exercises that place pressure on the muscles of the neck
3. Discuss the medical options and the situation with the parents or guardians of the student
4. Have the parents sign a consent form allowing the child to participate in the physical education program
5. Design a physical education program with activities that are not contraindicated for those with atlantoaxial instability
6. Watch for the development of the symptoms indicating a possible dislocation
7. Adhere to the physician's recommendations
8. Contact the parents and explain the importance of screening

Further considerations

Davidson[15] has studied the recommendations for implementation of sport programs for students with Down syndrome at risk for atlantoaxial instability. His analysis of scientific information of the risk factor of permanent injury as a result of atlantoaxial instability requires consideration. He notes that the published papers on the issue indicate that there are no data with which to determine the incidence of atlantoaxial dislocation in contrast to instability among individuals with Down syndrome, and that there is little or no evidence that indicates that instability constitutes a predisposition to dislocation. He also notes that there is no evidence that the current roentgenogram criteria of atlantoaxial instability are predictive of a tendency to dislocation. Furthermore, in as much as the evidence provided by Special Olympics indicates no knowledge of accidents in a 17-year history, he questions policies that would potentially exclude tens of thousands of individuals with Down syndrome every year from many sports on the basis of the evidence published to date.

THE PHYSICAL EDUCATION PROGRAM

If at all possible, mentally retarded children should be integrated with their peers in regular physical education classes. If they cannot participate successfully in regular classes, they should be given special developmental physical education commensurate with their capacity and needs. It is recognized that the regular physical education class may not provide adequate placement for all mentally retarded children. These children have social and motor deficits that make it difficult for them to participate equally with members of the regular class. Consequently, they often are found on the periphery of activity and do not involve themselves in the games and activities of the physical education class. An effort must be made to integrate mentally retarded persons into regular class activities; however, if this is not possible, special physical education programs should be adapted to the particular needs of the children.

It also is suggested that any mentally retarded children who can be successfully integrated socially in the unrestricted physical education program, but who have physical or motor deficiencies, receive supplementary physical education to remedy or ameliorate the particular diagnosed motor deficiency. Erroneous assumptions often are made relative to the physical abilities of a person labeled mentally retarded. In many instances mentally retarded children from special classes are proficient in interscholastic athletics.

THE INTEGRATION PROCESS

The literature on the integration of individuals with and without disabilities describes the types of interactions, the values of such interactions, and the techniques for facilitating integration.[20,35,36] However, there is little information in the literature that describes ways to develop specific recreational sports skills that would advance the individual through a series of community environments leading to independent recreation in sport activity. It could be that an effective integration process would generalize to different sport skills. For the most part, integrated activity is easier to manage in individual sport skills (e.g., bowling, physical fitness training, marathon running, and bicycle riding) than in team sport skills. This is probably true because the social rules for participation in individual sports are relatively simple when compared with the rules for team sports, and team sport skills are usually more complex than the skills needed for participation in individual sports. Therefore the degree of successful integration of individuals with and without disabilities may depend on (1) the physical and social complexity of the activity and (2) the social and physical capabilities of the athletes. Thus strategies for inclusion of mentally retarded persons into integrated activity may involve adapting the complexity of the activity to the present ability level of the learner and structuring the social environment of play so that mentally retarded individuals can enjoy participation in the game. However, every effort should be made to retain the original characteristics of the game as much as possible so that participating nondisabled players have the opportunity to enjoy culturally relevant recreational activity.

When mentally retarded individuals can participate

in sport activity independent of other support systems, they are integrated. In recent years, there have been specific techniques developed for integration and systematic procedures for movement of individuals with disabilities along a continuum of lesser restrictive environments. However, these continua have been structured, primarily, in the areas of domestic living and vocational placements. There are few, if any, descriptions of community-based continua of lesser restrictive environments structured to integrate mentally retarded individuals toward independent functioning in community sport activities. One goal of Special Olympics is to develop and provide such opportunities.

Previous Integration Research

The ultimate goal of sports and physical activity for mentally retarded persons is participation in integrated physical activity in natural community environments. For the most part, integration models for acquiring physical skills for persons with mental retardation in the public schools is to offer a choice of participation in regular or special physical education programs. It is becoming increasingly apparent that routinely exposing persons with mental retardation to students without mental retardation in regular physical education class (mainstreaming) may have a detrimental effect on the mentally retarded student.[3,41,49] Without systematic attention to the needs of the mentally retarded individual during the integration process in physical activity, the self-esteem and social interaction capabilities of many mentally retarded persons may be adversely affected.

Individuals with disabilities have a basic right to be provided opportunities that will lead to their full integration into community recreational settings. (Special Olympics has initiated several such integration programs, which will be detailed later in this chapter.) To achieve this integration, the process should include the following opportunities:

1. There should be a continuum of lesser restrictive environments in both instructional settings in the schools and in community recreational environments; and they should be coordinated for the benefit of each individual.
2. Persons with mental retardation should be placed in the most appropriate environment that is commensurate with the individual's social and physical abilities.
3. Persons with mental retardation should be provided with a support system commensurate with their needs to adapt to present restrictive environments and advance to lesser restrictive environments.

When this procedure to achieve integration is utilized, individuals with disabilities will have a much greater opportunity to interact successfully in community recreational settings than they now have. Just placing mentally retarded students in a regular physical education class and hoping they gain all that is needed has not been successful. The current mainstreaming practice of chance placement must be replaced by a carefully planned integration process.

The Regular Education Initiative

As explained in Chapter 17, nationwide there is an effort to integrate all students regardless of disability into classrooms with nondisabled students. Advocates of the single placement option argue that placing all children in a "normal" environment is the best way to promote understanding and socialization of individuals with disabilities. Opponents of the movement caution that until cognitive, behavioral, and social disparities between children with and without disabilities are ameliorated, the regular classroom setting is not "normal" for a student with a disability. The question those of us who work with disabled populations ask is "how can the student with a disability best be served?" Regardless of placement, our role is to ensure the maximum growth possible for each of our disabled students. Because the vast majority of students with disabilities are now being served in the regular class,[19] techniques for providing adequate instruction must be implemented.

Some models for accommodating different levels of performance in motor activities exist. In 1990, approximately 10% of young children with disabilities were served in preschool programs designed primarily for children without disabilities.[51] Block and Krebs[4] have proposed a procedure for developing support systems for disabled students assigned to the regular physical education class. Special Olympics has developed a process to move the mentally retarded individual through a continuum of lesser restrictive environments into competitive sports in the community.[47]

Techniques for preparing regular classroom teachers to effectively deal with students with disabilities have proven helpful in facilitating the development of both motor and social skills of mentally retarded students.[24] Gains in peer interaction and social development of disabled students have been reported in integrated early childhood programs[23] and outdoor education programs for older children.[43] However, in spite of advances in techniques for facilitating integration of all students, there is still the question of how to best serve each child with a disability.[53] Klein, Gilman, and Zigler[32] and others continue to contend that promoting the regular education initiative to "normalize" and integrate all students should not overshadow meeting the specific needs of individuals and promoting the optimum development of each mentally retarded person.

Continuum of Lesser Restrictive Environments in the Community

To enable individuals with disabilities to progress toward integration into community recreation programs, a continuum of lesser and lesser restrictive environments is needed. Three major environments that would promote participation of individuals with disabilities in a sport activity are (1) a training environment restricted to individuals with disabilities, (2) a mixed or integrated athletic competition, and (3) a normal community environment (see Fig. 7-4). A disabled-persons-only training/playing environment, where athletes receive special training from teachers and trained peer tutors, is a critical starting place for many mentally retarded individuals. They need opportunities to learn basic fundamental movement skills before being placed with nondisabled persons. The next most appropriate environment is mixed or integrated athletic competition, where the composition of the team is at least 50% nondisabled athletes. This step is important because to facilitate functioning in natural settings, mentally retarded athletes need exposure to non-mentally retarded peers who have specific training in principles of integration. The next step would be participation in integrated settings with nontrained, nondisabled peers who are willing to assist with the integration process. In the fourth step, mentally retarded individuals would participate in integrated leisure, recreational, and sport activities with the assistance of nonparticipants. The ultimate goal is to participate without assistance in natural community, school, and recreation environments such as churches, YMCAs, and community recreation programs. Modifications of the major integration environments may be made to serve the unique needs of each mentally retarded athlete. It is most important that the thrust of integration be a process to move the students through the continuum of restrictive environments in specific sports to lesser restrictive environments to independent recreational functioning in sport activities that occur in communities.

Physical skill is one variable to consider for placement of persons with mental retardation in integrated settings with non-mentally retarded students. The ability to adapt to others when participating in activity is critical for successful integration of mentally retarded students into leisure, recreation, and sport activity. The ability to cooperate and work harmoniously with others, compete, display sportsmanship, respond to coaching and instruction, and control one's emotions are necessary social behaviors if a mentally retarded student is to participate successfully in an integrated leisure, recreation, or sport activity. In addition to considering the physical and social abilities of mentally retarded students, the social complexity and the entry level of skill required to participate need to be considered. Individual sports such as track and field, bowling, or swimming require less social ability than team sports with complex rules such as basketball or soccer. It is more difficult to integrate the mentally retarded individual into complex team sports.

Specific examples of integration techniques follow.

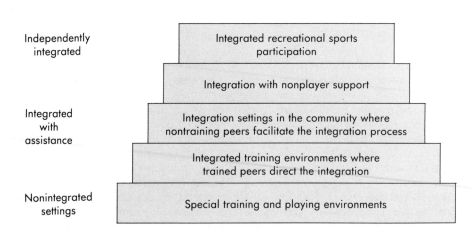

FIGURE 7-4. A continuum of lesser restrictive environments that enable progression toward independent recreational participation in a specific sport activity.

Marathon Running Integration

A project was designed to integrate mentally retarded Special Olympics' athletes into 5- and 10-kilometer marathons. This project was conducted by a committed volunteer who was a marathon runner and coach of Special Olympics' track athletes. The athletes participated in a series of training and competitive environments. The first environment was an *all* mentally retarded Special Olympics' track environment where the athletes were trained for distance running. However, to advance to a lesser restrictive environment, it was necessary for the athletes to acquire greater skill. To achieve this, Special Olympics' runners were given additional training with marathon runners who were also mentally retarded. After additional skill and higher performance levels were achieved, the prime athletes were integrated in training with nonretarded adult marathon runners. The final step of the integration process was competition with the non-mentally retarded runners in a regular marathon. Thus athletes progressed through three training environments—Special Olympics' training, extended Special Olympics' training conducted by a parent, and integrated training with non-mentally retarded competitors in 5- and 10-kilometer races.

Softball Integration

There is a concept in the integration process that is known as reverse mainstreaming.[46] In this procedure, non-mentally retarded persons are integrated into activities designed for mentally retarded participants. Modification of this technique was initiated in the development of the Massachusetts Special Olympics' softball integration project.[7] Special Olympics International subsequently funded the Research Center for Education Achievement to study the effects of Special Olympics' softball integration on coaches and mentally retarded and non-mentally retarded players. (The integrated softball game is composed of teams that are at least 50% non-mentally retarded players.) Reverse mainstreaming can be used with individuals with any type of disability.

Integrated softball is a lesser restrictive environment than traditional Special Olympics, where a different social support system is provided to produce positive results. Through construction of social networks of lesser restrictive environments in which nonretarded and retarded individuals participate on the same team, impressive social and physical gains can be made.

Budoff[7] has conducted research on integrated (Special Olympics) softball. In this activity, the nonretarded individuals participate on the same team as an equal number of mentally retarded players. Budoff, in comparing the play of the mentally retarded players in inte-

grated softball with all other mentally retarded softball games, makes the following comments: "The contrast between the mixed (integrated) and all-mentally retarded teams is so stark as to make the same slow-pitch softball game look like a dramatically different game." As a result of a 3-month season of integrated softball, the mentally retarded athletes demonstrated lateral movement and intelligent positioning for the ball as it was coming toward them. There were few "dead spots" where players were immobile and did not move when a ball was directed to them. The team members worked well together. To explain this phenomena, Budoff comments that "it seems that playing alongside of non-handicapped players helped to steady their (‹mentally retarded players›) game, even when there were no overt signs of instruction."

An integrated team promotes the mentally retarded players' development in playing and understanding because (1) the coach and the non-mentally retarded players are commited to teaching and supporting the retarded players and (2) the non-mentally retarded players serve as models on the field. According to Budoff, "There seems to be no doubt of the individual development observed in the play and sense of the game among handicapped players during this past season on the integrated (mixed) teams."[7] Thus there are strong indications that an integrated environment in sport activity is a critical factor that benefits mentally retarded individuals.

Integrated Basketball with Severely Mentally Retarded Adolescents

The previous descriptions of integrated activity with the non-mentally retarded participants were based on modeling procedures and intuitive coaching techniques of non-mentally retarded players and coaches. Many of the athletes in both the marathon running and integrated softball projects had the potential for integrated activity without a highly technical support system. However, there are persons with mental retardation who may always need support systems for integrated play in sports.

Pilot research has been done in integrated basketball play with severely retarded individuals.[3] In this activity an equal number of college students preparing for professional roles in human service served as player-coaches. The rules of the basketball game were modified so that the mentally retarded athletes were required to perform the basic skill aspects of the game. The modified rules were (1) a mentally retarded player could travel and double dribble, (2) nonretarded persons could not dribble, shoot the ball, or pass to a nonretarded teammate, and (3) only mentally retarded players could shoot. To increase scoring, another modification to the game was to award one point when the ball hit the rim. This modification provided more reinforcement to the conditions of play.

Each nonretarded player was paired with a specific athlete with mental retardation. The nonretarded athlete-coach then provided direct instruction as to when and to whom the ball was to be passed, when to dribble, and when to pass. These specific behaviors were reinforced. Thus play and technical instruction were combined. It is to be emphasized that when using this procedure the stimulus cues and reinforcing properties by peer player-coaches are withdrawn as the mentally retarded athlete improves social and physical skills and can perform tasks without the cues. The limitations to this type of integrated play are that the desirable ratio of player-coach volunteers is one to one. Furthermore, prerequisite training is needed for direct instruction by player-coaches.

Role of Player-Coaches

The roles assumed by the player-coaches in the complex social interactive game (e.g., basketball and softball), which may require direct coaching of social and cognitive strategies, appear to be critical to the integration process. The complexities of the social and cognitive judgment of the athletes in marathon running were not as great as basketball and softball. Therefore the demand on the coaches was not as great. Nevertheless, attention by the coach was necessary to adapt integrated environments and training regimens commensurate with the ability of the mentally retarded athletes.

In all three integration environments there was commitment by those who conducted the coaching. The attitudes of the coaches involved in all three projects support the notion that in an educational setting with teachers who favor integrating individual with disabilities, mainstreaming has a reasonable chance of success. On the other hand, the evidence also suggests that where teachers oppose integration, the prognosis for success is not good. Thus because Special Olympics is a volunteer activity for coaches, it is logical to assume that volunteers bring with them good attitudes toward the integration process in which they are involved.

Competition and Integration

The evidence from these integration programs is that they were beneficial to the performance of athletes with mental retardation. Inasmuch as there is some debate on the values of competition for mentally retarded persons as compared with play, the preliminary findings from these studies would indicate support for the findings of Karper, Martinek, and Wilkerson.[29] Their study investigated the effects of competitive and noncompetitive learning environments on motor performance in mainstreamed physical education classes. They found performance of the mentally retarded students dropped during noncompetitive treatment following a competitive one. Although there is no way of knowing whether competition was the cause for behavioral changes, the effects of competition on the performance of mentally retarded athletes may be a significant and fruitful avenue for future research.

Causal Relationships Between Integration and Improved Performance

There has been considerable concern about the nature of the integration, the need for social interaction, causative factors during integration, and functional outcomes.[5,33] For the most part, research of functional outcomes resulting from integration of persons with disabilities has been speculative.[6] Furthermore, little research activity has involved direct measurement, particularly of social interaction of individuals with severe disabilities[5,33] When the research has been of direct measures of social interaction, few studies have linked reproducible interventions to performance outcomes[46] or how social interaction competence generalizes to different social environments. The study of the process of integration with mentally retarded participants in Special Olympics was an exploratory effort that may lead to designs of reproducible treatments that demonstrate functional causal relationships with behaviorally defined social and physical outcomes that can be generalized to other environments.

OPPORTUNITIES BEYOND FORMAL EDUCATION

Opportunities to learn motor skills and participate in leisure and recreation using learned skills should be available to all persons beyond the normal years of public-sponsored education. After leaving school, individuals must be able to find recreation using the skills and activities taught during the formal years of schooling. Opportunities for such recreation should be available to mentally retarded persons of all ages. Those who have been deprived of opportunities to participate and to learn motor skills should be provided with opportunities to learn these skills and ways of using leisure time for physical activity. The desired aspects of physical fitness for the particular age and characteristics of a retarded person should be a part of the extended physical education program.

Recreation

Mentally retarded children need to be taught to play regardless of their level of retardation. Fine, Welch-Burke, and Fondario[21] propose a three-dimensional model designd to enhance leisure functioning of individuals with mental retardation. Levels of social play are autistic, solitary, parallel, cooperative, and competitive. Levels of cognitive play are functional, constructive, dramatic, and games with rules. Areas of skill development range from acquisition of prerequisite fine and gross motor skills and functional play to toy-play, art, simplified table games, exposure to the community, self-initiated play, and leisure education. Following is the 5-step model designed to promote achievement of higher levels of play:

1. Assessing current levels of skill and play
2. Setting goals consistent with individual needs
3. Teaching goal behaviors
4. Generalizing newly learned skills to higher levels of skill and to other environments
5. Teaching individuals to apply skills in natural environments

Recreational opportunities for mentally retarded children should be provided after the school day terminates, during school vacations, and after formal educational training. There should be adequate provision in the recreation program for vigorous activity such as sports, dancing, active games, swimming, and hiking. Intramural and community sports leagues should be provided to reinforce skills developed in the instructional program. In addition, winter snow games should be made available. Camping and outdoor education programs are other ways of affording expression of skills and interests.

In conjunction with the recreation program, special events scheduled throughout the school year serve to stimulate interests, motivate the children, and inform the community about the progress of the physical education program and about the abilities of mentally retarded children. Examples of such events are demonstrations for PTA meetings, track and field meets, swimming meets, play days, sports days, pass-punt-kick contests, hikes, and bicycle races.

Programs

Severely mentally retarded children often require individual attention. Volunteers trained in specific duties can be of assistance to the instructional program as well as to after-school and vacation recreation programs. Parents of retarded children, members of high school and college service clubs, and scouting groups are becoming increasingly active as volunteers. Instruc-

tors can seek out these people and ask them to become involved with the programs for the mentally retarded. A 1- or 2-hour training session can be planned to teach these volunteers what needs to be done, how to do it, what to expect from retarded individuals, and how to deal with behavior problems.

THE HOME PROGRAM

The amount of time that the physical educator will be involved personally with the mentally retarded children is relatively small. If maximum benefits are to be derived from programs, it is necessary to have a follow-up of activities taught in the form of a home program. Therefore an educational program for parents describing the children's program and its purpose should be provided for implementation in the home. Parents should receive direction and assistance in methods for involving their children in physical activity taking place in the neighborhood and the home. The "Let's-Play-to-Grow" materials published by the Joseph P. Kennedy, Jr., Foundation are an excellent source of information for parents of handicapped children.[28]

SPECIAL OLYMPICS

Probably no single program has done as much to foster the participation of retarded individuals in physical activities as has the Special Olympics program. This program, which is now international in scope, was begun in 1968 by the Joseph P. Kennedy, Jr., Foundation.* The program includes training in physical fitness and sports and provides competition for mentally retarded children and adults at the local, district, state, national, and international levels. As was discussed earlier, Special Olympics also has been instrumental in developing integration programs for mentally retarded athletes.

Twenty-two official sports are offered—alpine and Nordic skiing, basketball, bowling, diving, Frisbee throwing, floor hockey, gymnastics, figure skating, field hockey, physical fitness and weight training, rhythmic movements, softball, speed skating, walking, poly hockey, soccer, swimming, track and field events, volleyball, and wheelchair events.

Competition is conducted according to the following age groupings: 8 to 9 years, 10 to 11 years, 12 to 13 years, 14 to 15 years, 16 to 17 years, 18 to 19 years, 20 to 29 years, and 30 years and older. To qualify for

---

*Information about Special Olympics can be obtained by writing to Special Olympics, Inc., Joseph P. Kennedy, Jr., Foundation, 1350 New York Ave., Washington, D.C. 20006.

competition, students' records of performance levels during practice must be submitted (in most cases) on an entry form. Assignment to a division by the meet director is based on these scores. Girls and boys compete separately, and every participant is recognized in some way.

SUMMARY

Mental retardation refers to substantial limitations in certain personal capabilities. It is manifested as significantly subaverage intellectual functioning, existing concurrently with related disabilities in two or more of the following adaptive skill areas: communication, self-care, home living, social skills, community use, self-direction, health and safety, leisure, functional academics, and work. Mental retardation begins before age 18 but may not always be of lifelong duration. The prevalence of mental retardation in the population is approximately 3%. Two levels are recognized—mildly retarded and severely retarded. Persons with mental retardation can be expected to learn and develop.

Physical educators can expect to be called on to serve mentally retarded students in the public school system. Carefully selected teaching strategies and program adaptations will yield positive motor development results. Retarded students should be tested to determine their specific motor strengths and weaknesses, as is true for most performance abilities. Physical education programs should be designed around these test results. Outside recreation, home programs, and participation in Special Olympics should be encouraged. Physical education programs in the public schools should provide assistance for transition of the recreational skills acquired in physical education classes to independent, integrated recreational activity in the community. Special Olympics has taken the lead in developing programs to include mentally retarded individuals in integrated sports activity.

REVIEW QUESTIONS

1. What is the history of the social perception of mentally retarded persons as contributing members of the community?
2. What are the essential concepts for determination of who is mentally retarded?
3. What are the intellectual and adaptive response levels of mental retardation classifications?
4. What is reverse mainstreaming?
5. What are five specific teaching strategies that can be used with mentally retarded persons?
6. How are adaptations for physical activity different for mildly and severely mentally retarded persons?
7. What is the need or lack of need for supplemental programs outside of school and beyond formal education for mentally retarded individuals?
8. What are the activities and participation age ranges of the Special Olympics program?
9. What is necessary to conduct a successful process of integration of mentally retarded persons with nonretarded individuals in community sports activities?

STUDENT ACTIVITIES

1. Interview parents of mildly and severely mentally retarded adults. Determine differences on the following:
   a. When did mental retardation first become apparent?
   b. What problems did each person in the family have with adapting to the neighborhood?
   c. What was the nature of the schooling at each level?
   d. What services are being provided at present?
   e. What are the prospects for future or continued self-sufficiency in the community?
2. Learn more about agencies and organizations in your community that provide services for the mentally retarded. In most areas there are agencies of both state and local governments that service mentally retarded adults. Most communities have associations for retarded citizens. Many mentally retarded persons have multiple disabilities and have access to services for the physically disabled, deaf, blind, and emotionally disturbed.
   a. What services do these agencies provide?
   b. How does one go about receiving these services?
3. Locate one of the journals that deals with mental retardation. (Some of these journals are *Adapted Physical Education Quarterly; Palaestra: The Forum of Sport, Physical Education and Recreation for the Disabled; Exceptional Children; Retardation; Education and Training of the Mentally Retarded;* and *American Journal of Mental Deficiency.*) Look through recent issues for articles that present teaching techniques that might be applied to conducting physical education programs for the mentally retarded.
4. Visit classes in which mentally retarded children are mainstreamed. Compare the progress of these children with that of children in special, segregated, adapted physical education classes. Compare the following factors for each class:
   a. The nature of the activity

b. The interaction with peers and with the teacher

c. The degree to which there is active participation

d. The steps that should be taken to improve instructional efficiency

5. Visit classes of mildly and severely mentally retarded children. Describe the physical, intellectual, and behavioral characteristics of each group.

6. Talk with a physical education teacher who has worked with mentally retarded children and ask which teaching strategies have proven successful with specific types of learners on specific tasks.

7. Observe a Special Olympics meet. Describe how the meet was conducted to accommodate the different abilities of the participants so all could engage in meaningful competition.

8. Assess a mentally retarded person to determine what social support systems would be needed for the person to become integrated into a specific physical activity or sport.

REFERENCES

1. American Association on Mental Retardation: Classification in mental retardation, Washington, DC, 1992.

2. Antony RM: Atlantoaxial instability: why the sudden concern, *Adapt Phys Act Q* 3:320-328, 1986.

3. Auxter DM et al: *Prediction of playing basketball and basketball skills among persons with severe mental retardation,* Unpublished paper, Special Olympics International, Washington, DC, 1987.

4. Block ME, Krebs PL: An alternative to the continuum of least restrictive environments: a continuum of support to regular physical education, *Adapt Phys Act Q*, 1992 [in press].

5. Brinker RP: Interactions between severely mentally retarded students and other students in integrated and segregated public school settings, *Am J Ment Defic* 89:587-594, 1984.

6. Brinker RP, Thorpe MD: Integration of severely handicapped students and the proportion of IEP objectives achieved, *Except Child* 51:168-175, 1984.

7. Budoff M: *The evaluation of the mixed teams softball in Massachusetts Special Olympics—coaches' views,* Cambridge, Mass, 1987, Research Institute for Educational Problems, Inc.

8. Christenson SL, Ysseldyke JE, Thurlow JL: Critical instructional factors for students with mild handicaps: an integrative review, *Remed Spec Ed* 10:21-31, 1989.

9. Combs C, Jansma P: The effects of reinforcement-based fitness training on adults who are institutionalized and dually diagnosed, *Adapt Phys Act Q* 7:156-169, 1990.

10. Committee on Sports Medicine, Atlantoaxial instability in Down syndrome, *Pediatrics* 74:152-154, 1984.

11. Cooke RE: Atlantoaxial instability in individuals with Down's syndrome, *Adapt Phys Act Q* 1:194-196, 1984.

12. Cratty BJ: *Motor activity and the education of retardates,* ed 2, Philadelphia, 1974, Lea & Febiger.

13. Curtis CK: Are education students being prepared for mainstreaming? *Educ Canada,* Summer 1985.

14. Danforth DS, Drabman RS: *Community living sills.* In Matson JL, editor: *Handbook of behavior modification with the mentally retarded,* New York, 1990, Plenum Press.

15. Davidson RG: Atlantoaxial instability in individuals with Down syndrome: a fresh look at the evidence, *Pediatrics* 81:857-865, 1988.

16. DePauw K, Ferrari N: The effect of interference on the performance on a card sorting task of mentally retarded adolescents, *The Phys Educ* 43:32-38, 1986.

17. Dunn JM, Fait H: *Special physical education: adapted, individualized, developmental,* Dubuque, Iowa, 1989, Wm C Brown.

18. Dunn JM, Morehouse JW, Fredericks HD: Physical education for the severely handicapped: a systematic approach to a data based gymnasium, Austin, Tex, 1986, PRO-ED.

19. Epstein ME et al: Mild retardation, student characteristics and services, *Educ Train Ment Retard* 24:7-16, 1989.

20. Falvey MA: *Community based curriculum: instruction strategies for students with severe handicaps,* Baltimore, 1986, Paul H Brookes Publishing.

21. Fine A, Welch-Burke C, Fondario L: A developmental model for the integration of leisure programming in the education of individuals with mental retardation, *Ment Retard* 23:289-296, 1985.

22. Fox RA et al: Incidence of obesity among retarded children, *Educ Train Ment Retard* 20:175-181, 1985.

23. Fuchs D et al: Prereferral intervention: a prescriptive approach, *Except Child* 56:493-513, 1990.

24. Guralnick MJ: Major accomplishments and future directions in early childhood mainstreaming, *Top Early Childhood Spec Ed* 10:1-17, 1990.

25. Haley S: Postural reactions in infants with Down syndrome: relationship to motor milestone development and age, *J Am Phys Therapy* 66:17-22, 1986.

26. Hayden F: *The nature of physical performance in the trainable retardate,* Paper presented at the Joseph P. Kennedy, Jr., Foundation Third International Scientific Symposium on Mental Retardation, Boston, 1966.

27. Jansma P et al: A fitness assessment system for individuals with severe mental retardation, *Adapt Phys Act Q* 5:223-232, 1988.

28. Joseph P. Kennedy, Jr., Foundation: *Let's-play-to-grow,* Washington, DC, 1978, The Foundation.

29. Karper WB, Martinek TJ, Wilkerson JD: Effects of competitive/non-competitive learning on motor performance of children in mainstream physical education, *Am Correct Ther J* 39:10-15, 1985.

30. Kelley LE, Rimmer JH, Ness RA: Obesity levels in institutionalized mentally retarded adults, *Adapt Phys Educ Q* 3:167-176, 1986.

31. Kerr R, Blais C: Down syndrome and extended practice of a complex motor task, *Am J Ment Defic* 91:591-597, 1987.

32. Klein T, Gilman E, Zigler E: *Special Olympics: an evaluation by professionals and parents,* Special Olympics International, Washington, DC, 1992.

33. Low LG, Teasdale GR: An observational study of the social adjustment of spina bifida children in integrated settings, *Br J Educ Psychol* 5:81-83, 1985.

34. Marchetti AG, Campbell VA: *Social skills.* In Matson JL, editor: *Handbook of behavior modification with the mentally retarded,* New York, 1990, Plenum Publishing.

35. Martin JE et al: *Consumer-centered transition and supported employment.* In Matson JL, editor: *Handbook of behavior modification with the mentally retarded,* New York, 1990, Plenum Publishing.

36. Monroe H, Howe C: The effects of integration and social class on the acceptance of retarded adolescents, *Educ Train Ment Retard* 6:21-24, 1971.

37. Naganuma G: Early intervention for infants with Down syndrome: efficacy research, *Phys Occup Ther Pediatr* 7:81-92, 1987.

38. Newell R: *Motor skill orientation in mental retardation: overview of traditional and current orientation.* In Clark JH, Humphrey J, editors: *Motor development: current selected research, vol I,* Princeton, NJ, 1985, Princeton Book Co.

39. Patton J, Payne J, Smith M: *Mental retardation,* Columbus, Ohio, 1986, Charles E Merrill Publishing.

40. Rarick GL: *The factor structure of the motor domain of trainable mentally retarded children and adolescents,* Unpublished study, Berkeley, 1977, University of California.

41. Rarick GL, McQuillan J, Beuter A: *The motor, cognitive and psychosocial effects of the implementation of P.L. 94-142 on handicapped children in the school physical education programs,* grant no. G007901413, Berkeley, 1981, University of California.

42. Rimmer J, Kelly L: Effects of a resistance training program on adults with mental retardation, *Adapt Phys Act Q* 8:146-153, 1991.

43. Rynders JE, Schleien SJ, Mustonen T: Integrating children with severe disabilities for intensified outdoor education: focus on feasibility, *Ment Retard* 28:7-14, 1990.

44. Schroeder SR et al: *Self-injurious behavior.* In Matson JL, editor: *Handbook of behavior modification with the mentally retarded,* New York, 1990, Plenum Publishing.

45. Sherrill C: *Adapted physical education and recreation, ed 3,* Dubuque, Iowa, 1986, Wm C Brown Publishing.

46. Sherrill C: *Adapted physical education and recreation, ed 2,* Dubuque, Iowa, 1982, Wm C Brown Publishing.

47. Songster T: *A model leisure sport skill integration process through Special Olympics,* grant application submitted to the US Department of Education, Office of Special Education, Washington, DC, 1987.

48. Special Olympics International: Adapted pysical education sports skill assessment resource manual, *Special Olympics Bulletin,* Washington, DC, 1991.

49. Stein J: Physical education and sports as required by P.L. 94-142 and section 504, *Am Correct Ther J* 32:145-151, 1978.

50. Surburg PR: The influence of task incompletion of motor skill performance of mildly retarded adolescents, *Am Correct Ther J* 40:39-42, 1986.

51. US Department of Education, Thirteenth Annual Report to Congress on the Implementation of the Individuals with Disability Education Act, 1991.

52. Weber R, French R: Downs syndrome adolescents and strength training, *Clin Kines* 42:13-21, 1988.

53. Whitman L, Hantula DA, Spence BH: *Current issues in behavior modification with mentally retarded persons.* In Mason JL, editor: *Handbook of behavior modification with the mentally retarded,* New York, 1990, Plenum Publishing.

54. Wright J, Cowden JE: Changes in self concept and cardiovascular endurance of mentally retarded youth in Special Olympic swim training program, *Adapt Phys Educ Q* 3:177-183, 1986.

55. Yabe K et al: Developmental trends of jumping reaction time by means of EMG in mentally retarded children, *J Ment Defic Res* 29:137-145, 1985.

SUGGESTED READINGS

Fraser B, Galka G, Hensinger R: *Gross motor management of severely multiply impaired students,* Baltimore, 1980, University Park Press.

Hardman ML, Drew CPJ, Egan MW: *Human exceptionality, society, school and family,* Boston, 1987, Allyn & Bacon.

Horner RH, Meyer LH, Fredericks HD: *Education and learners with severe handicaps,* Baltimore, 1986, Paul H Brookes Publishing.

Wheman P, Renzaglia A, Bates P: *Functional living skills for moderately and severely handicapped individuals,* Austin, Tex, 1985, PRO-ED.

8

OBJECTIVES

Name the three forms of autism.

Describe the type of physical education setting that is appropriate for autistic students.

Indicate how peer tutors should be prepared to assist autistic children.

Give examples of activities appropriate for autistic children at various stages of development.

Explain simple strategies to encourage appropriate behavior in autistic children.

Courtesy Dallas Independent School District

Autism

*F*or the last 10 years school personnel have reported increasing numbers of students with autistic behaviors. National awareness of the growing prevalence of autism was evidenced when the condition was first listed as a disability in P.L. 101-476, the Individuals with Disabilities Education Act (IDEA), which became effective October 1, 1990. Three different forms of autism are described in the literature—classic autism, Asperger's syndrome, and Rett syndrome. Together these forms afflict 5 in 10,000 newborns. The common and unique characteristics of each form are discussed in this chapter.

CLASSIC AUTISM

Classic autism, originally known as Kanner's syndrome, was first described by Dr. Leo Kanner in 1943.[11] The principle characteristics of classic autism are global language disorder, abnormal behavior patterns (commonly referred to as "bizarre" behaviors), social isolation, and usually but not always, mental retardation. The severity of symptoms varies widely. Reports of incidence range from 4 in 10,000 to 21 in 10,000 births,[3] and males evidence the condition 3 to 5 times more frequently than females.[8]

Characteristics

The two primary formal clasification systems used to identify autism are the DSM-III-R system developed by the American Psychiatric Association (1987)[1] and the ICD-10 system developed by the World Heath Organization (1987).[20]

For a formal diagnosis of autism the DSM-III-R system requires that at least 8 of the following behaviors be demonstrated:

1. Qualitative impairment in reciprocal social interaction as manifested by at least two of the following:
   A. Marked lack of awareness of the existence of feelings of others
   B. No or abnormal seeking of comfort at times of distress
   C. No or impaired imitation
   D. No or abnormal social play
   E. Gross impairment in ability to make peer friendships
2. Qualitative impairment in verbal and nonverbal communication, and in imaginative activity, as manifested by at least one of the following:
   A. No mode of communication, such as communicative babbling, facial expression, gesture, mime, or spoken language
   B. Markedly abnormal nonverbal communication, as in the use of eye-to-eye gaze, facial expression, body posture, or gestures to initiate or modulate social interaction
   C. Absence of imaginative activity, such as play acting of adult roles, fantasy characters, or animals, lack of interest in stories about imaginary events
   D. Marked abnormalities in the production of speech, including volume, pitch, stress, rate, rhythm, and intonation
   E. Marked abnormalities in the production of speech, including stereotyped and repetitive use of speech
3. Markedly restricted repertoire of activities and interests, as manifested by at least one of the following:
   A. Stereotyped body movements (e.g., hand flicking or twisting, spinning, head banging, complex whole body movements)
   B. Persistent preoccupation with parts of objects
   C. Marked distress over changes in trivial aspects of environments (e.g., insisting that exactly the same route always. be followed when shopping)
   D. Markedly restricted range of interests and a preoccupation with one narrow interest (e.g. interested only in lining up objects, in amassing facts about meteorology, or in pretending to be a fantasy character)
4. Onset during infancy or childhood

The World Health Organization (1987) criteria for autism are less descriptive and impose a time limitation on the onset of the condition. Specific criteria are:

☐ Qualitative impairments in reciprocal social interaction
☐ Qualitative impairments in communication
☐ Restricted, repetitive, and stereotyped patterns of behavior, interests, and activities
☐ Developmental abnormalities must have been present in the first 3 years for the diagnosis to be made

In addition to formal classification systems, early identification instruments have been developed for use in school settings. Teachers find these instruments useful for identifying autistic behaviors and referring students for diagnostic testing. These instruments vary in length and sophistication. For example, the Autism Behavior Checklist (ABC)[14] is a 57-item questionnaire that requires yes/no answers. The Behavioral Summarized Evaluation (BSE) is a 20-item paper/pencil scale developed for use by professionals and paraprofessionals. It appears to be most effective in the identification of severely affected autistic children with mental retardation.[2] A simpler instrument is presented in Fig. 8-1. This Autism Prescreening Checklist, which was developed by the Dallas Independent School District Autism Task Force, includes 14 behavioral signs and symptoms of autism.[5] Preschool and elementary teachers are taught to use this instrument so that children with au-

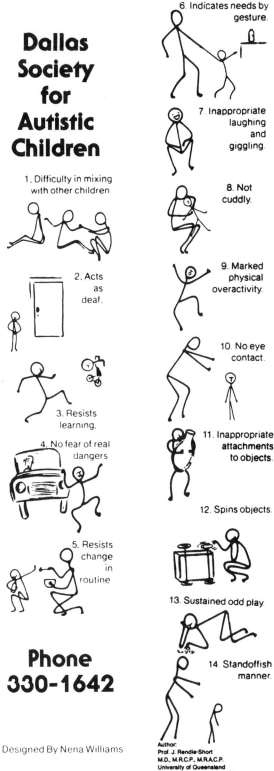

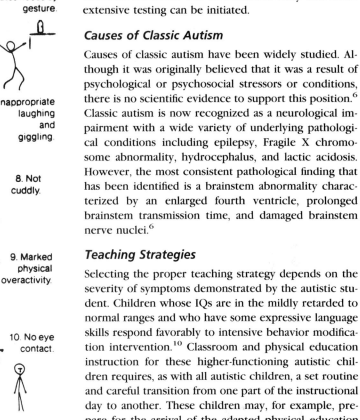

FIGURE 8-1. Behavioral signs and symptoms of autism. (Courtesy Dallas Independent School District.)

tistic-like behaviors can be identified early and more extensive testing can be initiated.

Causes of Classic Autism

Causes of classic autism have been widely studied. Although it was originally believed that it was a result of psychological or psychosocial stressors or conditions, there is no scientific evidence to support this position.[6] Classic autism is now recognized as a neurological impairment with a wide variety of underlying pathological conditions including epilepsy, Fragile X chromosome abnormality, hydrocephalus, and lactic acidosis. However, the most consistent pathological finding that has been identified is a brainstem abnormality characterized by an enlarged fourth ventricle, prolonged brainstem transmission time, and damaged brainstem nerve nuclei.[6]

Teaching Strategies

Selecting the proper teaching strategy depends on the severity of symptoms demonstrated by the autistic student. Children whose IQs are in the mildly retarded to normal ranges and who have some expressive language skills respond favorably to intensive behavior modification intervention.[10] Classroom and physical education instruction for these higher-functioning autistic children requires, as with all autistic children, a set routine and careful transition from one part of the instructional day to another. These children may, for example, prepare for the arrival of the adapted physical education teacher by selecting an appropriate "task" card from their "daily task chart." The task card may simply say, "PE," or may be a photograph of the adapted pysical education teacher. These children may prepare for a supervised walk or jog by selecting a laminated picture of a person walking or jogging.

Most physical education instruction for even mildly autistic children occurs in a self-contained setting. This setting, like the child's classroom setting, must be very structured and include transitions between activities. Each child should have a designated exercise spot to begin the class, to perform stationary exercises, and to serve as a "home base." There should be a definite, predictable routine during each class session. Each class session should start with the same set routine. This may simply be saying "good morning" to each child individually and then waiting for/prompting a greeting in return. If warm-ups are to be done to music, the physical education teacher should use the same songs over and over; a new song may be introduced after others have been mastered. If laps are to be run, the children should always run on the same path and in the same direction. If a given motor skill is to be practiced, the same class organization and equipment should be used. If the class is working on catching, for example, the teacher should use the same size and color ball. Exchanging a red playground ball for a yellow nerf ball could be a terrible distraction. When using terms to describe a given activity or motion, the teacher should use the same terms. For example, if each child is assigned a plastic dot to serve as his home base, the teacher should refer to the plastic dot by calling it a "dot" and not use interchangeable terms like circle or spot. This type of consistency is crucial if the teacher is to maximize learning and avoid acting-out behaviors.

The Physical Education Program

The types of activities included in the autistic student's physical education program depends on the age of the child and the severity of his/her disability. The older the student, the more important it is to develop functional skills. The younger the student, the greater the focus on more basic motor components.

Vigorous, aerobic exercise two or three times daily is critical because it effectively reduces self-stimulatory behaviors and increases time on academic tasks.[12,15] However, physical education programs for autistic children of all ages should include exercise that promotes the development of cardiovascular endurance.

Kindergarten to third grade

The physical education program for young autistic children, kindergarten to third grade, should emphasize cardiovascular-respiratory endurance activities, "whole body" movement, rhythms, activities to foster primary body part identification, and the development of onlooker and parallel play skills. Cardiovascular-respiratory endurance activities should be the basis of the program. The child should be engaged in vigorous, cardiovascular-respiratory activities with heart rate in target heart rate zone for at least 20 minutes per day. A general approximation of target heart rate zone is 60% to 75% of maximum heart rate. The maximum heart rate is calculated by subtracting the child's age from 220. For example, a 5-year-old child would have a maximum heart rate of 215 beats per minute. This child's training heart rate zone would be 129 to 161 heart

FIGURE 8-2. The development of functional gross motor skills is vital to the child with autism. (Courtesy Dallas Independent School District.)

beats/minute ($.60 \times 215 = 129$; $.75 \times 215 = 161$). Cardiovascular-respiratory endurance activities for young autistic children may include aerobic walking, stationary cycling, and structured aerobic dance.

The development of equilibrium responses is a fundamental component of the physical education program of young autistic children. These equilibrium activities include the following:

SCOOTER BOARD ACTIVITIES

Depending on the child's level of development, the child should assume a supine, prone, sitting, or kneeling position on a scooter board. Initially, the activity will be teacher-initiated and teacher-controlled. Gradually, the teacher should fade out involvement so that the scooter-spinning activity is child-initiated and child-controlled.

CRAZY SIDEWALK

Place a mat, or series of mats, over the top of other, pliable objects. Then, depending on the child's developmental level, ask the child to crawl, creep, walk, or run over the top of the ever-shifting surface.

MAGIC CARPET RIDE

Have the child assume a supine lying, prone lying, sitting, all-fours, or kneeling position on a mat or blanket. Hold the edge of the mat or blanket and pull the child about the room.

"Whole body" movement is also a curricular priority for the young autistic child. This includes "wrap-em-ups" (roll the child in a sheet or blanket, grasp the edge and lift, rolling the child out of the sheet/blanket), log rolls, egg rolls, shoulder rolls, and forward/backward rolls.

In addition, simple songs and dances may be used to encourage the development of primary body part identification skills and rhythmic responses, as well as to provide an ideal opportunity for the child to be engaged in parallel play with peers. At the least, the child is sharing the same music with classmates. Songs and dances for young autistic children should have the following characteristics: (1) simple, clear, and often repeated directions; (2) repetitive phrasing; (3) even beat; (4) dominant rhythm instrument; and (5) nonintrusive "background" accompaniment.

Fourth to sixth grade

The physical education curriculum for autistic children in the fourth through sixth grades continues to emphasize cardiovascular-respiratory endurance activities. These activities may include aerobic walking, stationary cycling, aerobic dance, jogging/running, and stationary rowing.

The development of "functional" locomotor skills is a vital part of the physical education curriculum for children in these grades. The autistic child should be given the opportunity to develop walking, running, and jumping skills in the following situations:

1. Ask the child to move over different surfaces:
   A. Sidewalk – grass – sidewalk
   B. Grass – sand – grass
   C. Dry sidewalk – icy sidewalk – dry sidewalk
   D. Dry linoleum – wet linoleum – dry linoleum
2. Ask the child to move over, around, and through objects/obstacles:
   A. Step in and out of holes
   B. Walk around puddles
   C. Jump over puddles
   D. Step over an object or series of objects
   E. Walk up and down inclines
   F. Walk up and down stairs
   G. Vary number of stairs
   H. Vary height of stairs
   I. Vary surface of stairs (carpeting, linoleum, wood)
   J. Walk through a revolving door
3. Ask the child to move carrying an object(s):
   A. Walk carrying a bag of groceries
   B. Walk carrying an umbrella
   C. Walk with a backpack
   D. Run with a ball tucked under the arm
4. Ask the child to push/pull an object:
   A. Walk, pulling a wagon
   B. Walk, pushing a wheelchair
5. Ask the child to lift an object of varying size/weight from different levels—off the floor, from a cupboard, etc.

More sophisticated equilibrium activities are also an important part of this program. These include self-testing balance activities. The child moves, for example, on a tapered balance beam. Or the child steps from one stone to another as the stones get smaller. Bouncing activities are also emphasized. Using a mini-trampoline, an air mattress, or a gym mat placed on top of a tire, help the child "bounce" while sitting, kneeling, or standing.

Rhythm activities and low-organization games are important to children in this age range. Rhythms and games may be used particularly well to develop body image. In addition, these activities may be used to teach skills like taking turns and sharing equipment.

Middle through high school

In the middle school and high school the primary curricular emphasis continues to be cardiovascular-respiratory endurance. In addition, there is an emphasis on the development of leisure and recreation skills. These include bowling, fishing, horseshoes, bocci, horseback riding, roller skating, skateboarding, and one-on-one basketball.

Decisions regarding the activities that are taught should be based on the child's need to function within the community and the accessibility of leisure and recreation facilities to the child. For example, it is unfair to foster a love of horseback riding in a child from a poor family if the child's only access to a horse involves expensive rental. It would seem much more humane to help the child develop the skills needed to participate in activities with other children in the neighborhood, like one-on-one basketball. IDEA mandates that every child over the age of 16 must have a transition plan included as part of the individual education program (IEP). It is important that the adapted physical education IEP include plans to help the child use leisure/recreation skills within the community.

Management of Behavior

The physical educator working with an autistic child must, if possible, adopt the behavior management system used by the child's classroom teacher. This consistency is vital if the child is to make the transition from the classroom to the physical education setting. One of the most successful strategies for the management of behavior of autistic children is to redirect inappropriate behavior. Since the autistic child does not understand cause-effect relationships, it is ineffective to scold the child for misbehavior or to say "no." It is much more effective to redirect existing behavior. For example, if the child is kicking furniture, replace the furniture with a ball. If the child is biting his fingers, replace the fingers with a cracker. If the child is spinning about the room, place the child on a scooter board and encourage the child to spin in an appropriate play activity.

Another technique for managing behavior is to simplify the task if the child is misbehaving while attempting a task. Often, an autistic child "acts out" as a result of frustration. Simplifying the task at hand may allow the child to succeed at the task while reducing inappropriate behaviors.

If the child is acting out or is "out of control," moving the child to a less stimulating area may allow the child to regain control of his behavior. For example, the child may be asked to return to a seat in the classroom or may be separated from the rest of the children to reduce noise levels, confusion, and distractions, which over-stimulate the autistic child.

Perhaps most important, whenever possible the autistic child should be encouraged to communicate instead of "act out." For example, if the child does not wish to participate in a given activity, the teacher should be delighted if the child says "no," or shakes his head instead of striking out or biting or pinching or tantrumming. The child should be rewarded, then, by being allowed not to participate in the activity.

Physical Education Placement

Only the most highly functioning autistic child is capable of placement within the regular physical education setting. For most autistic children the physical education setting is extremely restrictive; that is, the very nature of the physical education experience often includes large numbers of children making a great deal of noise in an unstructured setting. A large number of variables need to be considered before a decision is made to place an autistic child into the regular physical education setting. The box below describes the *only* type of setting that may be appropriate for a mildly autistic child.

More severely involved youngsters respond favorably to a "top, down" task analytic instructional model that includes physical, visual, and verbal prompts to guide learning.[4] These students must receive physical education instruction within a self-contained setting. Once again, the class must be very structured. This structure may include limiting opportunity for "out-of-seat" activity for all but the one child taking a turn. For example, all the children in the class may be physically and verbally prompted to remain in their respective

---

Characteristics of a regular physical education setting appropriate for mildly autistic children

CLASS DYNAMICS

The teacher-student ratio must be less than 1:20.
The class must be highly structured.
The class routine must be consistent.

INSTRUCTIONAL STAFF

The physical education teacher must be willing to create an environment that will facilitate learning for the autistic and the non-autistic child.
A physical education aide or special education aide must be present.
The physical education staff must be willing to work closely with special education personnel to learn strategies for managing the instructional environment.

INSTRUCTIONAL PROGRAM

The focus of the instructional program must be individual skills rather than group games and team sports.

GYMNASIUM AND/OR PLAYGROUND

The gymnasium must be relatively free of distractions—fans, standing equipment, etc.
The playground must be surrounded by a fence.

"cubies" (chairs) while one child is "spotted" in the performance of a forward roll.

Peer Tutors

Use of peer tutors to assist the autistic child in attending to specific tasks may be very beneficial. In addition to helping the autistic student focus attention on specific tasks, the use of peer tutors also promotes social interaction skills.[18] The use of peer tutors must be part of a carefully designed instructional program. Peer tutors must be well trained for their role. They must be given specific instruction about the nature of autism and the behaviors they should expect from their autistic peers. The peer tutors must be very mature children who can accept the atypical interaction skills, the inability to play, and the inability to form meaningful peer relationships, characteristic of autistic children. The peer tutor may function best in the role of "demonstrator."

ASPERGER'S SYNDROME

In 1944 Hans Asperger introduced an autistic disorder that is now widely known as Asperger's syndrome.[19] This condition, known as "high level autism" shares many of the same symptoms as classic autism; however, distinguishing characteristics include motor clumsiness and a family history of Asperger traits.[6] Estimates of incidence range from 2.6 to 3 in 10,000 births with males being affected 10 times more frequently than females.[8]

Diagnostic criteria include the following:
- ☐ Severe impairment in reciprocal social interaction
- ☐ All-absorbing, circumscribed interest
- ☐ Imposition of routine or interest
- ☐ Speech and language problems in spite of superficially excellent expressive language skills
- ☐ Nonverbal expressive language skills
- ☐ Motor clumsiness[8]

Teaching Strategies

No studies suggesting teaching strategies are reported in the literature. However, because Asperger's syndrome is believed to be a form of autism, it is reasonable to assume that an intensive behavior modification program using the "top, down" task analytic instructional model would be appropriate for this population.

RETT SYNDROME

Rett syndrome is a neurological disorder first described in 1966 in Germany by A. Rett.[16] The condition is characterized by normal development during the first 6 months of life followed by loss of acquired fine motor

FIGURE 8-3. The development of leisure and recreation skills is a vital and integral part of each student's individual education transition plan. (Courtesy Wisconsin Lions Camp, Rosholt, Wisconsin.)

skills, impaired language skills, gait apraxia, and stereotypic hand movements.[17] Prevalence is estimated at 1 in 10,000 to 1 in 15,000 female births.[9]

Diagnostic criteria are as follows:
1. Necessary criteria:
   A. Apparently normal prenatal and perinatal periods
   B. Apparently normal psychomotor development through the first 6 months
   C. Normal head circumference at birth
   D. Deceleration of head growth between ages 5 months and 4 years
   E. Loss of acquired purposeful hand skills between ages 6 and 30 months, temporally asso-

ciated with communication dysfunction and social withdrawal

F. Development of severely impaired expressive and receptive language, and presence of apparent severe psychomotor retardation

G. Stereotypic hand movements such as hand wringing/squeezing, clapping/tapping, mouthing, and "washing"/rubbing automatisms appearing after purposeful hands skills are lost

H. Appearance of gait apraxia and truncal apraxia/ataxia between ages 1 and 4 years

I. Diagnosis tentative until 2 to 5 years of age

2. Supportive criteria:

A. Breathing dysfunction
   i. Periodic apnea during wakefulness
   ii. Intermittent hyperventilation
   iii. Breath-holding skills
   iv. Forced expulsion of air or salivation

B. Electroencephalography (EEG) abnormalities
   i. Slow waking background and intermittent rhythmical slowing (3-5 Hz)
   ii. Epileptiform discharges, with or without clinical seizures

C. Seizures

D. Spasticity, often with associated development of muscle wasting and dystonia

E. Peripheral vasomotor disturbances

F. Scoliosis

G. Growth retardation

H. Hypotropic small feet

3. Exclusive criteria:

A. Evidence of intrauterine growth

B. Organomegaly or other signs of storage disease

C. Retinopathy or optic atropohy

D. Microcephaly at birth

E. Evidence of perinatally acquired brain damage

F. Existence of identifiable metabolic or other progressive neurological disorder

G. Acquired neurological disorder resulting from severe infections or head trauma.[20]

The cause of Rett syndrome is unknown; however, because only females are affected, it is assumed that it is a result of a dominant mutation of an X-linked gene, which would be lethal in a male fetus.[13] Because individuals with Rett syndrome demonstrate many autistic-like behaviors, inaccurate diagnosis is common.[7] One distinguishing characteristic that has been reported is lack of nystagmus after spinning.[7] Lack of nystagmus strongly suggests a brainstem-vestibular abnormality;

however, the technology to validate this hypothesis has not yet been developed.

Teaching Strategies

No studies involving teaching strategies for Rett syndrome have been reported to date in the literature. However, because of the similarities between Rett syndrome and autism, it is assumed that the female with Rett syndrome would benefit from the same structured physical education program suggested for other autistic students. A "top, down" task specific teaching approach that includes physical, visual, and verbal prompts using peer tutors should be attempted. Gait apraxia and breathing dysfunction may prohibit the inclusion of cardiovascular endurance training. Also, the possible presence of brainstem-vestibular abnormality would negate the use of vestibular stimulation activities.

SUMMARY

Because of the increasing numbers of children with autism, the condition is now included as a disorder that qualifies affected students for special education services. Forms of autism are classic autism, Asperger's syndrome, and Rett syndrome. Characteristics common to all forms of autism are communication difficulties, abnormal behaviors, and poor social skills. Physical education programs require set routines and careful transition between each part of the instructional day. Students with classic autism or Asperger's syndrome should participate in daily vigorous physical exercise. Students with Rett syndrome will benefit from a structured top, down, task specific teaching approach. Behavior modification techniques and use of peer tutors will be beneficial in helping the student focus on each physical education task.

REVIEW QUESTIONS

1. Name some characteristics of a regular physical education setting appropriate for mildly autistic children.

2. Name the three forms of autism.

3. What types of activities should be included in classic autistic and Asperger's syndrome children's adapted physical education classes?

4. Give some examples of equilibrium activities that could be included in young autistic children's physical education class.

5. Give some examples of behaviors autistic children might demonstrate.

6. Describe three strategies a teacher could use to manage the behavior of autistic children in a physical education class.

7. What types of instruction do peer tutors need before assisting with autistic children?
8. Explain how Asperger's syndrome and Rett syndrome differ.

STUDENT ACTIVITIES

1. Observe a physical education class comprised of autistic children. Afterwards list the specific modifications the teacher utilized to accommodate the children.
2. As part of a small group project, using the teaching suggestions included in this chapter, develop one 30 minute physical education class for autistic learners.
3. Read and report on one article on autism.

REFERENCES

1. American Psychiatric Association:*DSM-III-R Diagnostic and statistical manual of mental disorders (revised),* Washington, DC, 1987.
2. Barthelemy C et al: The behavioral summarized evaluation: validity and reliability of a scale for the assessment of autistic behaviors, *J Autism Dev Disord* 20:189-203, 1990.
3. Batshaw M, Perret Y: *Children with handicaps: a medical primer,* Baltimore, 1986, Paul H Brookes Publishing.
4. Collier D, Reid G: A comparison of two models designed to teach autistic children a motor task, *Adapt Phys Act Q* 4:226-236, 1987.
5. *Dallas Independent School District Autism Task Force: Autism prescreening checklist,* 1988, Adapted with permission of Randal- Short, University of Queensland, Brisbane Children's Hospital, Australia.
6. Gillberg C: Autism and pervasive developmental disorders,*J Child Psychol Psychiatry* 31: 99-119, 1990.
7. Gillberg C: The borderland of autism and Rett syndrome: five case histories to highlight diagnostic difficulties,*J Autism Dev Disord* 19:545-559, 1989.
8. Gillberg I, Gillberg C: Asperger syndrome—some epidemiological considerations: a research note, *J Child Psychol Psychiatry* 30:631-638, 1989.
9. Hagberg B: Rett's syndrome: prevalence and impact on progressive severe mental retardation in girls, *Acta Paediatr Scand* 74:405-408, 1985.
10. Howlin P, Rutter M: *Treatment of autistic children,* New York, 1987, John Wiley & Sons.
11. Kanner L: Autistic disturbances of affective contact, *Nervous Child* 2:217-250, 1943.
12. Kern L et al: The effects of physical exercise on self-stimulation and appropriate responding in autistic children,*J Autism Dev Disord* 12:399-419, 1982.
13. Killian W: On the genetics of Rett syndrome: analysis of family and pedigree data, *Am J Med Genet* 24:369-376, 1986.
14. Krug D, Arick J, Almond P: Autism behavior check-list for identifying severely handicapped individuals with high levels of autistic behavior, *J Child Psychol Psychiatry* 21:221-229, 1980
15. Quill K, Gurry S, Larkin A: Daily life therapy: a Japanese model for educating children with autism, *J Autism Dev Disord* 19:625-635, 1989.
16. Rett A: Uber ein eigenartiges hirnatrophisches syndrom bei hyperammonamie im kindersalter, *Weiner Med Wochenschrift* 116:723 -726, 1966.
17. The Rett Syndrome Diagnostic Criteria Work Group: Diagnostic criteria for Rett syndrome, *Ann Neurol* 23:425-428, 1988.
18. Schleien S, Heyne L, Berken S: Integrating physical education to teach appropriate play skills to learners with autism: a pilot study, *Adapt Phys Act Q* 5:182-192, 1988.
19. Shopler E: Convergence of learning disability, higher level autism, and Asperger's syndrome, *J Autism Dev Disord* 15:359, 1985 (editorial).
20. World Health Organization: Mental disorders: glossary and guide to their classification in accordance with the tenth revision (draft) of the International Classification of Diseases, 1989.

SUGGESTED READINGS

1. Batshaw M, Perret V: *Children with handicaps: a medical primer,* Baltimore, 1986, Paul H Brookes Publishing.
2. Denckla M, James L, editors: An update on autism: a developmental disorder, *Pediatrics* (Suppl) 87, May 1991.
3. Howlin P, Rutter M: *Treatment of autistic children,* New York, 1987, John Wiley & Sons.

Define the term *specific learning disability.*

Explain the contemporary controversy about the importance of motor development to the functioning of individuals with specific learning disabilities.

Cite the variety of motor development delays demonstrated by individuals classified as having specific learning disabilities.

List at least five teaching strategies to use when working with specific learning disabled students.

Describe the relationship between sensory motor integration and perceptual motor training programs.

Courtesy Callier Center for Communicative Disorders, Dallas, Texas

Specific Learning Disabilities

Probably no handicapping condition has proven to be more controversial nor has undergone more name changes than what we now call *specific learning disability.* Confusion about the condition is reflected in the number of terms associated with disability. Over the past 30 years individuals with these disabilities have been classified as perceptually handicapped, brain injured, brain damaged, minimal brain dysfunctionate, dyslexic, and/or developmentally aphasic. In every case each term has been selected in an attempt to convey the fact that persons with a specific learning disability have normal intelligence but fail to demonstrate the same academic competencies as do the majority of individuals whose IQs fall within the normal range.

Estimates of the prevalence of the condition range from 3% to 20% of the population, depending on the number of characteristics included in the definition.[17,58] Regardless of which characteristics are included, it is widely accepted that 70% to 90% of the children identified as having a specific learning disability are male. We do not know why this is the case.

What is known is that children who were once believed to be daydreamers, inattentive, mischievous, or just plain "dumb" in school do indeed have an organic basis for their behaviors.[40] However, the true reasons for their learning problems are far from proven. The best we can do at this point is to describe the condition and postulate reasons why persons with specific learning disabilities do not learn cognitive information as adeptly and easily as do others.

DEFINITION

Specific learning disability was defined in the Individuals with Disabilities Education Act (IDEA) of 1990. It is a disorder in one or more of the basic psychological processes involved in understanding or using language, spoken or written, which may manifest itself in the imperfect ability to listen, think, speak, write, spell, or perform mathematical calculations. Such disorders include such conditions as perceptual disabilities, brain injury, minimal brain dysfunction, dyslexia, and developmental aphasia. The term does not include children who have learning problems that are primarily the result of visual, hearing, or motor disabilities; mental retardation; emotional disturbance; or environmental, cultural, or economic disadvantage.[22]

At the onset of the Education for All Handicapped Children Act in 1977 (now known as the Education of the Handicapped Act), there were approximately 800,000 learning disabled individuals. However, by 1990, the incidence of learning disability had more than doubled (i.e., more than 2 million). As would be expected, research on this disability has greatly increased in recent years. At this writing, specific learning disability is the most prevalent disabling condition of individuals in the United States.

A serious problem surrounding this condition is its lack of clear-cut characteristics.[45] Some educators believe that individuals with a true specific learning dis-

ability do not demonstrate any visual, hearing, or motor handicaps. In truth, the individual who has a specific learning disability may indeed demonstrate any one or all of these conditions. The difficulty rests with sorting out whether the visual, hearing, or motor handicaps are causing the learning difficulty or whether the problem is one of processing information that has arrived at the brain relatively intact.

It is easier to determine the presence of visual and hearing factors than it is to distinguish motor involvement. As visual specialists become more adept at evaluating orthoptic visual problems that interfere with an individual's ability to fixate on the printed word and smoothly track a series of written words, individuals with visual problems can be distinguished from those with specific learning disabilities.[9] As hearing specialists learn to use sophisticated equipment that actually determines where, neurologically, the auditory signal is being thwarted, the truly hearing impaired also can be identified. Distinguishing motor impairment, however, from imperfect ability to listen, think, speak, write, spell, and understand mathematical concepts will not be accomplished as easily, because of the complexity of neural interactions between sensory and motor components that may indeed contribute directly or indirectly to cognitive functioning and the difficulty in measuring basic sensory and motor components.

COGNITIVE-MOTOR RELATIONSHIPS

No attempt is made in this text to resolve the controversy concerning whether specific learning disabilities have a direct relationship with sensory-perceptual-motor functioning; however, it is important that the physical educator be aware of the historical perspectives surrounding the controversy. Initially, the reason many special educators took such a firm stand against the position that motor impairments may affect cognitive processing dates back to the 1960s. During that decade the perceptual-motor theories of Kephart[38] and Frostig and Maslow[25] were emerging. These pioneers proposed that the basic "stuff" from which cognitive information was constructed included perceptual and motor components. Special educators with little or no background in motor development seized on these theories as the possible answer to resolving the academic learning problems manifested by learning disabled populations. In an attempt to "cure" the learning disabled individuals, Kephart's and Frostig and Maslow's programs of activities were tried on groups of learning disabled students. Almost without exception, the wholesale application of these theories proved disappointing. In most cases the learning disabled student improved in motor function but demonstrated no immediate change in reading or mathematical ability. As a result, many special educators abandoned the notion that there could be a causative relationship between motor and cognitive functioning.

Kavale and Mattison,[36] in a thorough review of studies on the effectiveness of perceptual-motor programs, concluded that such programs were not effective and should be questioned as a feasible intervention technique for exceptional children. Myers and Hamill's[46] reviews tended to support these conclusions. They recommended that perceptual-motor programs be carefully reevaluated and suggested that when these programs are implemented in the schools, they be considered highly experimental, nonvalidated services that require careful scrutiny and monitoring. Researchers with extensive knowledge about neurological functioning, however, have not been so quick to rule out the possibility of a very real and powerful relationship between the basic sensory and motor components and cognitive functioning.

Prominent advocates of a definitive relationship between the domains are Ayres[4,5] and deQuiros and Schrager.[19] Ayres, a well-known researcher in the area of sensory integration therapy, has for many years advocated that "learning and behavior are the visible aspects of sensory integration"[4] and that sensory integration results from sensory stimulation and motor activity. Schrager and deQuiros continue to propose that primary learning disabilities have their bases in vestibular dysfunctions, perceptual modalities, and cerebral dysfunctions. They advocate the use of sensory-perceptual-motor activities to assuage vestibular and perceptual problems. A third researcher, Buckley,[12] proposes that the hyperkinetic child will sometimes demonstrate clumsiness and problems with writing, reading, spelling, and mathematical concepts. However, the "pure" learning disability type will exhibit writing, reading, and spelling disabilities but rarely demonstrate poor motor coordination. Children who are both hyperkinetic and learning disabled usually will exhibit poor motor coordination and writing, reading, and spelling disabilities.

Obviously, the controversy will not be easily settled. Carefully designed research studies that delineate specific types of motor components and their possible effect on cognitive functions will need to be completed and replicated. Longitudinal studies that follow individuals who have been exposed to contemporary sensory-perceptual-motor intervention programs will need to be carried out. Dialogue among educators, neurologists, visual and hearing specialists, and researchers will need to be initiated and fostered. The questions to be answered must be approached with open minds, honest and critical analysis, and persistence.

NEUROPHYSIOLOGICAL ASPECTS OF SPECIFIC LEARNING DISABILITY

Most of the research and theory on learning disability has been done by cognitive theorists. However, recently there has been increased emphasis on neurophysiological functioning of the brain as it relates to learning disability. Studies of the brains of individuals with specific learning disabilities have been done using electroencephalography (EEG), auditory brainstem-evoked response (ABER), and regional cerebral blood flow (rCBF). The purpose of this research is to determine whether any significant differences exist between the brain structure and function of normal and learning disabled individuals. Some differences have been reported.

Using EEG, Johns[33] demonstrated that the evoked potentials of groups of learning disabled students were significantly different from students with no learning problems. Other investigators have reported significant differences in regions of blood flow[43] and brainstem-evoked responses during speech processing tasks.[27] Neurophysiological tools such as these show great promise for early identification of children with specific learning disabilities. Once unique brain structure and function profiles are identified and correlated directly to specific learning difficulties, we can begin to develop educational intervention strategies specific to each child's individual needs.

Instruction and Language

The physical education teacher should recognize individual language usage differences among learning disabled children.[21] Such knowledge can be used to modify teaching strategies that involve comunication through language. There are at least three language categories. They are (1) receptive language, (2) expressive language, and (3) inner language.

Receptive language involves the ability to comprehend the meaning associated with language. Deficits in receptive language may be either visual or auditory. Visual deficits are reflected by the inability to organize and interpret visual information appropriately. For example, a child may be unable to interpret facial gestures appropriately. Auditory receptive language deficits may be reflected in failure to follow directions, or inability to discriminate between sounds.

Expressive language involves the ability to communicate through either audition or the visual mechanism. Auditory deficits are expressed through impaired speech, whereas visual expressive language deficits refer to problems in writing. Problems in visual expressive language are inability to reproduce simple geometric forms, persistent reversal of letters, rotation or inversion of letters, or reversed sequence of letters.

Inner language processes refer to the ability to transform experience into symbols. This of course is dependent on experiences. Inasmuch as young children gain much of their experience with the world through play and motor activity, environmental exploration with the body is an important aspect of the development of inner language.

PSYCHOMOTOR, COGNITIVE, AND BEHAVIORAL CHARACTERISTICS

All children differ in their psychomotor, cognitive, and behavioral characteristics. Likewise, learning disabled children differ from one another, and there is considerable overlap in abilites between the learning disabled child and the nondisabled child. However, there are some similar group characteristics that differentiate learning disabled individuals from nondisabled individuals.

Children can differ in motor performance for many reasons, including (1) attention deficits, (2) inability to receive information that tells the body what to do, (3) problems in processing information needed to express motor acts, (4) deficits in the physical and motor abilities to perform the desired skills, and (5) social skill deficits.

Attention Deficit Disorders

Over the years many terms have been used to describe inatttentive and impulsive behaviors demonstrated by some children. Although originally identified in the 1930s,[8] research did not focus on this continuum of behaviors until the 1960s,[59] when the term *hyperkinetic impulse disorder* surfaced[42.] This was replaced by the term *hyperactive child syndrome* in the 1970s, and *attention deficit disorder* (ADD) in the 1980s.[57]

Three distinct forms of ADD have been identified: (1) attention deficit disorder with hyperactivity (ADHD), (2) attention deficit disorder without hyperactivity (ADD-WO), and (3) attention deficit disorder—residual (ADD-R).

Behaviors common to all three forms of the disorder are short attention span, distractibility, and incompleted tasks. Specific behaviors demonstrated in each form include:

☐ ADHD—short attention span, easy distractibility, poor listening skills, incompleted tasks, impulsiveness, restlessness, and inappropriate excessive motor activity.[39]

☐ ADD-WO—loss of thought patterns, shifts from ini-

FIGURE 9-1. The development of functional independent leisure skills can enhance the quality of life. (Courtesy Wisconsin Lions Camp, Rosholt, Wisconsin.)

tial impressions, delays in delivering responses, delays in recalling names and descriptions.[39]

□ ADD-R—identifies the adolescent child or young adult who hasn't outgrown the syndrome. (Approximately 20% of all ADD individuals do not outgrow the problem.[34])

Estimates of prevalence of all forms of the disorder are diffficult to locate because some authors include various forms of learning disabilities and/or conduct disorders in their counts. Others, particularly those in the medical profession, focus specifically on the ADHD population. It is probably safe to estimate that 10% to 20% of the school-age population experience some form of ADD, with or without concomitant problems.[54]

Inability to Receive Information

An analysis of perceptual attributes important to skilled motor performances indicates that exteroceptors (e.g., eyes, ears, and tactile receptors) and proprioceptors (e.g., vestibular and kinesthetic receptors) are important avenues for receiving information from the environment. Deficits in information from these senses may result in deficits in performance of physical activities.

There is evidence that learning disabled persons may be impaired in their ability to balance. Good balance depends on accurate information from the vestibular system as well as normal reflex and depth perception development. When vestibular information is not received or processed efficiently, impaired balance results. In addition, persisting primitive reflexes and/or a delay in development of postural (equilibrium) reflexes also inhibit a person's ability to achieve and maintain balance. Depth perception deficiencies interfere with an individual's ability to use visual cues in the environment to assist in balancing. Impaired balance interferes with postural and locomotor efficiency as well as foot-eye and hand-eye coordination.

Learning disabled children also may possess deficits in kinesthetic perception. These deficits limit knowledge of precise position and rate of movement of body parts in space. Kinesthesis is an essential prerequisite for sophisticated, refined sport skills that require precise movements, such as putting a golf ball, shooting a basketball, setting a volleyball, and any other movements that require qualitative forces for success. Most physical education activities require an awareness and control of body parts in space (i.e., kinesthetic perception). Thus kinesthesis is considered an important prerequisite for movement control, which generalizes to many other physical and sport activities.

Many learning disabled children are uncoordinated and lack control of motor responses. Individuals with poorly developed balance and kinesthetic systems tend to have problems in changing directions or body positions. As a result, these individuals commonly have difficulty learning to perform efficient specific sport and motor skills.

Problems Processing Information

There is evidence that many learning disabled persons may differ from the nondisabled as a result of their inability to process information efficiently.[11] Information processing relates to how one retains and manipulates information. It refers to how information is acquired, stored, selected, and then recalled. Although there appears to be agreement that as a group the learning disabled population has problems in information processing, the specific locus of the problem is disputed. Cermak[14] indicates that processing deficits appear in the speed of rehearsal strategies. On the other hand, Karr and Hughes[35] indicate that the problem with the learning disabled individual may not be a processing deficit. They indicate that this population is able to handle information associated with increased task difficulty in the same manner as nondisabled persons; however, a problem may exist in the very early input stages of the processing mechanism (i.e., getting information into the processing system). Learning disabled individuals often demonstrate motor performance behaviors that provide clues about inappropriate receipt or use of information received through the visual and auditory mechanisms.

For instance, the six extraocular motor muscles of the eye must be controlled in such a way that objects of attention are fixated at the same points on each retina. If one or more sets of the extraocular muscles of the eye are weakened, one or both eyes will misalign and depth perception will be impaired. Individuals with impaired depth perception will misjudge where objects are in space. As a result they will be unable to catch and kick balls, will descend stairs one at a time, and will avoid climbing apparatus. Figure-ground perception involves the ability to distinguish an object from its background. It requires selecting and attending to the appropriate visual cue among a number of other cues that are irrelevant to that task at a particular moment. If the visual object to which the individual is to respond is not well defined, then chances are the motor task will be less proficient than desired. Individuals with poor depth perception almost always demonstrate deficits in visual figure-ground perception.

Another visual characteristic that may be impaired in learning disabled individuals is ocular saccadical abilities, which permit the learner to refix the eye on differing targets accurately and quickly. The ocular saccadical ability is required in those sports in which an individual must concentrate on a moving ball as well as a moving target (e.g., in football, when a quarterback throws a ball to a second receiver after seeing that the first potential receiver is covered; in basketball, when focusing on a rebounding ball and then refocusing vision to find an outlet player to pass to). Any visual deficiency that interferes with visual discrimination needed for proficient performance of a given sport will impair the performance in that sport.

The auditory mechanism may not be as critical in performance of sport activity as the eye; however, impaired ability of the individual to utilize auditory information may result in performance that is below normative expectations. Some of the sport activities requiring auditory discrimination and perception are dancing and floor routines in gymnastics. Auditory figure-ground discrimination is important to skill proficiency. Anytime there are extraneous auditory sounds, auditory figure-ground perception is needed (e.g., when players participating in a noisy gym must attend closely to hear the coaches' instructions and officials' calls).

Many learning disabled individuals also have deficits in long-term and short-term memory. Four steps are necessary for learning to occur: (1) a stimulus must be registered in the brain, (2) that stimulus must be maintained while its relevance is determined, (3) the stimulus must be processed in light of material present in long-term storage, and (4) the stimulus must be placed in long-term storage.[51] Thus deficits in either short-term or long-term memory limit the benefits of prior experiences and practice.

Memory is also a prerequisite for closure. *Closure* is the ability to recognize a visual or auditory experience when only part is presented. An example of visual closure occurs when a baseball player is batting. The batter must make inferences as to where the ball will be when it crosses the plate. If a batter is not able to estimate where the ball will cross the plate, it is impossible to determine where the bat should be swung.

Learning disabled individuals also may be deficient in cue selections. *Cue selection* is the ability to attend to relevant cues and block out irrelevant stimuli. Individuals with memory, visual, or auditory deficits will not make efficient cue selections.

Ayres[4] suggests that learning disabled individuals may have deficits in motor planning. Eichstaedt and Kalakian[23] describe motor planning as the ability to execute behaviors in a proper sequential order. Sport skill tasks require the integration of discrete component parts in sequence for task success. When learning a motor task, each component part of the skill must be planned and carried out in sequence before the skill can be executed correctly. With practice, the skill becomes a subroutine that is stored in long-term memory, and motor planning requirements are lessened. However, when learning new skills that are composed of component parts that must be sequenced, each component part must be present for the skill to be learned. Learning disabled individuals who demonstrate difficulty with motor planning may not have the necessary components (e.g., vestibular, kinesthetic, or visual information) available to them.

Social Skill Deficits

Learning disabled children may improperly perceive the social intent of others. Such circumstances make it difficult for them to comprehend the social meaning of their actions as well as others' actions. Sometimes they are unable to interpret social expressions such as gestures and body language. Consequently, their social behavior may be inadequate because of lack of understanding of their actions and those with whom they associate. Carlton and Rainey[13] suggest that social problems may be reduced by establishing routines of the child at home and at school. In both settings the child should be encouraged to focus on relevant social cues.

DEFICITS IN PHYSICAL AND MOTOR ABILITIES

As mentioned earlier, during the 1960s and 1970s, many professionals who served students with specific learning disabilities associated the disorder with impaired motor functioning. The activities of the Optometric Extension Program[26] provided the basis for the ongoing research in this area. In the 1960s optometrists observed many children age 10 and older who had no refractory errors of vision yet could not read efficiently nor do other forms of academic work. Because vision is believed to mature by age 10 years, they began to question what prerequisites might be missing in children with academic difficulties. They believed that efficient ocular motor control was an essential prerequisite to efficient vision and to many forms of learning. Ocular motor control was essential for the eye to obtain visual information from the environment. They then began to theorize about components that contribute to ocular motor development. They recognized that "special motor systems" where activities involving the hands and feet were coordinated with vision were essential for determining the substance of the world. They then identified general locomotor systems of running, jumping, hopping, leaping, skipping, and other locomotor tasks as prerequisite to development of the special motor systems. Basic to the general motor systems was the development, inhibition, and interweaving of reflexes. Thus they concluded that the foundation on which the visual mechanism is based is good posture.[6] As a result, proponents of optometric theory utilized considerable physical activity to develop the assumed prerequisites for good vision. Getman[26] was a prolific writer who promoted optometric theory. Kephart[38] was a psychologist who worked with the brain injured early in his career and promoted the optometric theory in educational circles for slow learners. Barsch[6] extrapolated the theory into a movagenic curriculum. Ayres[4,5] advanced the theory in the field of occupational therapy. Today, behavioral optometrists continue to expand, refine, and utilize the theory first introduced almost 30 years ago.[7]

Deficiencies that reflect the optometric extension theory of visual development can be found in many children with learning disabilities. Some of these deficiencies may be observed when these children exhibit difficulty in:

1. Catching a ball with their hands (manipulative deficiency)
2. Positioning the hands in the path of the ball (spatial relationships)
3. Tracking the ball into the hands and catching it
4. Coordinating the hands with each other
5. Coordinating the hands and feet such as punting a ball out of the hands (football, soccer goalie)
6. Standing with good posture
7. Maintaining rhythm while walking or chaining motor movements together
8. General motor coordination
9. Maintaining good balance
10. Initiating and continuing smooth and coordinated movements
11. Being aware as to where the body parts are in space

Several authors[14,55,58] agree that the specific learning disabled student may demonstrate cognitive processing problems, perceptual difficulties, hyperactivity, and clumsy motor performance. Cermak and Henderson[15] estimate that 60% to 95% of learning disabled children have poor static and dynamic balance, coordination problems, low muscle tone, poor spatial orientation, and delayed acquisition of equilibrium reactions. Morrison, Hinshaw, and Corte[44] also report this population demonstrates significantly more primitive reflexes and vestibular and equilibrium delays than children without disabilities. However, another researcher found that learning disabled children who demonstrated poor coordination or clumsiness demonstrated normal peripheral vestibular function, but poor static and dynamic balance and bilateral integration function.[31]

Any one or all of these factors will affect the design and success of the adapted physical education program. Children with cognitive processing problems may not understand or remember instructions. Perceptual difficulties lead to spatial awareness or body image problems. Hyperactivity interferes with a student's ability to attend to instructions about, or persistence at, a task. Clumsy motor performance directly influences a student's ability to master basic movement tasks and to combine those tasks into complicated patterns necessary to succeed in sports or leisure time activities. Researchers who have tested children with specific learning disabilities agree that their motor problems include equilibrium problems, difficulty with controlled visual-motor movements, fine motor coordination delays, and delayed bilateral coordination.[10,30]

It is, however, difficult to group all specific learning disabled children together when trying to determine precisely what movement difficulties they will demonstrate. In an attempt to determine whether there is a clear-cut motor profile demonstrated by this population, Pyfer and Alley[50] administered a wide variety of tests to 263 children with specific learning disabilities. Pyfer[49] later repeated the study with an additional 126 children. The results of these two studies revealed three very distinct groups of learning disabled children. Approximately 12% demonstrated no motor delays, 75% scored average on some tests but below average on other tests, and the remaining 13% were severely delayed in all areas tested. When all of the subjects were analyzed together to determine what type of motor performance characterizes specific learning disabled children, it was found that when these students have developmental delays, they tend to be in the perceptual-motor (body image, visual-motor control, spatial awareness), balance, and fine motor areas of performance. Although these findings agree with those of the studies cited earlier in this chapter, it must be pointed out that no one performance profile characterizes all specific learning disabled children. These children constitute a heterogeneous group and as such they need to be treated as individuals. Haubenstricker[29] proposes that before appropriate prescriptive activities are selected, efforts must be made to determine particular movement characteristics of the students with specific learning disabilities. He proposes that the earlier the problem is identified and the longer the remediation is carried out, the better the chances for eliminating the problems.

TESTING TO DETERMINE MOTOR FUNCTIONING LEVELS

Appropriate tests to use with this population include the Purdue Perceptual Motor Survey, the Frostig Developmental Test of Visual Perception, and the Bruininks-Oseretsky Test of Motor Proficiency. If time or expense only permits one test to be administered, the Bruininks-Oseretsky Test (entire battery) will probably provide the greatest number of clues as to the motor functioning level of the child with a specific learning disability.

INTERVENTION PROGRAMS

Two types of intervention commonly used with specific learning disabled students are perceptual-motor programs and sensory integration programs. Some research studies support the value of these programs, and others give reasons to question their value.[52] Until more evidence is available it is reasonable to conclude that each of these programs has some value for some specific learning disabled children.

Perceptual-Motor Program

A perceptual-motor program usually is made up of activities believed to promote development of balance, body image, spatial awareness, laterality, directionality, cross-lateral integration, and so on. Sometimes intact perceptual-motor programs such as those developed by Kephart[38] or Frostig and Maslow[25] are used. Other times physical educators select perceptual-motor activities from a variety of sources. Activities used include balance beam tasks, making forms and shapes with the body, hand-eye coordination tasks, and moving through obstacle courses. Very often these activities are taught via an indirect approach such as movement education. Such activities can benefit the specific learning disabled child if the child has been assessed as deficient in any one or more of these areas and if there are no underlying deficiencies (e.g., vestibular, kinesthetic, visual, or reflex delays). However, if underlying deficiencies are found, the physical education program should include activities to promote development of the deficient systems (see Chapter 4).

Although there is controversy about the benefits of perceptual motor training, the development of cognitive behaviors in learning disabled children can affect their performance in physical education. Studies by Keogh and Sugden,[37] and Sage,[53] although not intended specifically for the learning disabled population, dem-onstrate that learning can take place through movement.

Sensory Integration Program

A sensory integration program is made up of activities believed to promote processing of sensory stimuli. The activities used are based on Ayres' theory of sensory integration.[4] This theory, which has been evolving over the past 25 years, proposes that sensory input systems such as the kinesthetic, vestibular, and tactile systems must be fully developed and integrated before an individual can build cognitive structures needed to accurately interpret the environment. Selection of appropriate intervention activities is determined from results of the Southern California Tests of Sensory Integration (see Chapter 3). Usually only occupational or physical therapists are trained and certified to administer and interpret these tests. Activities included in a sensory integration program include rolling, spinning, turning, balancing on unstable bases, rubbing the body with different textures, and many activities with scooter boards.[4]

The question has been raised as to the efficacy of sensory motor integration among various subgroups. Densem et al.[18] indicated that the students making the least progress with sensory motor integration were children with epilepsy, those from single parent low income families, or those with behavioral problems.

The primary criticism of use of the sensory integration tests and program concerns the tendency of some therapists to decide that every specific learning disabled child they test has developmental delays and needs a sensory integration program. Therapists well schooled in the use of the theory and tests are less adamant about every child needing the program. If a sensory integration program is being used in a school, the physical educator should discuss with the therapist how best to coordinate the adapted physical education program with the therapies being used.

The Relationship Between Sensory Integration and Perceptual-Motor Development

Perceptual-motor training requires an individual to direct attention to performance of a specific task. On the other hand, sensory integration emphasizes activities to promote functioning at subcortical levels. Neural impulses arising from reflexes, postural reactions, and senses (i.e., tactile, kinesthetic, vestibular, auditory, and visual) must be integrated if efficient movement is to occur. Sensory-motor integration practices are rooted in neurodevelopmental approaches. Proponents of these approaches contend that sensory integration is a

FIGURE 9-2. Students must be given the opportunity to practice safety skills before participating in water sports. (Courtesy Wisconsin Lions Camp, Rosholt, Wisconsin.)

prerequisite to higher ordered perceptual-motor performance.

Approaches to Perceptual-Motor Training

There is controversy among physical educators as to whether a bottom, up developmental approach or a task specific top, down approach should be utilized in the instruction of motor skills for the learning disabled. A bottom, up approach to facilitate movement efficiency would begin with sensory stimulation to provide prerequisite components for meaningful culturally relevant skills. With such an approach there would be extended periods during which children would be engaging in specific activities to facilitate basic sensory and reflex systems. Proponents of this approach believe that once the basic sensory and reflex systems are functioning, and those stimuli are integrated, perceptual-motor development as well as learning of specific mo-

tor skills will occur. Admittedly the number of components of sensory input systems as well as perceptual-motor functions are considerable. All of the senses, the integration of each of the senses, the perceptual-motor characteristics of the individual, the way in which information is processed, and associative and organizational structures of perceptual skills that can be linked with each of the sensory modes are taken into consideration. Thus systematic attention requires development of each of the deficient prerequisites necessary for acquisition of many skills. Effective utilization of this approach requires extensive knowledge on the part of the teacher and the willingness to delay instruction in what many consider culturally relevant skills.

The top, down approach to facilitating movement efficiency would start with the culturally relevant skills and work down toward prerequisite components when it becomes apparent a learner is not benefiting from direct instruction of a specific task. Which approach to use can be determined through thorough evaluation and interpretation of results. When evaluation results clearly indicate no sensory or reflex deficits, the most economical method would be the top, down approach. Also, the older the learner, the less appealing the bottom, up approach becomes.

TEACHING STRATEGIES

Regardless of what type of program a physical educator favors, tests should be administered to determine the motor functioning level of the child with a specific learning disability. After areas of deficiency have been identified, activities can be selected to promote development in these problem areas. If appropriate activities are selected and carefully taught, the prognosis for the motor development of these students is quite good. At least one study reported that once perceptual and motor deficiencies of specific learning disabled children were resolved through a well-designed bottom, up motor development program, the children developed motor ability along age-expected levels.[41]

Specific activities to use with students with specific learning disabilities can be found in Chapter 3. General points to keep in mind when working with these students follow:

- To reduce interference from hyperactive (hyperkinetic) tendencies, select a larger number of different activities and spend less time on each than you would with other children the same age.
- Use a positive behavior modification program to get the students to finish tasks (e.g., use tokens or let them select their favorite activity once each day if they stay on task).

□ Incorporate 3 to 5 minutes of conscious relaxation instruction/practice into each class period (preferably at the end of the lesson).

□ Use a very structured, one-on-one teaching/learning arrangement whenever possible. Do not permit these students to participate in group activities that are beyond their capabilities. Such practices only reinforce the feeling that the children are different from their nondisabled peers.

□ Design your programs to promote sensory input functioning before concentrating on perceptual-motor integration or motor output behaviors. The greatest amount of carryover will occur if you "fill in the blanks" of missing sensory and perceptual components before teaching motor output behaviors.

□ Give brief instructions and ask the children to repeat those instructions before starting an activity. By doing this you prevent problems that arise from the limited memory some of the children demonstrate.

□ To enhance the children's self-concept, use very small learning steps and praise every legitimate effort the students make.

TEACHING TECHNIQUES

Controlling attention: One of the methods for controlling attention is to establish routines that are repeated day after day. This enables the child to develop a pattern of activities. The teaching techniques, behavior modification program, and organizational patterns should be kept as structured and consistent as possible.

Control extraneous stimuli in the environment: In addition to stable routines, the environment should appear relatively the same from one day to the next. Positioning of equipment and systematic procedures to store equipment should be established and maintained.

Control of desired behaviors: There should be instructionally relevant stimuli to focus the attention of learning disabled students (e.g., designate specific spots on the floor where students are to begin class each day). Visual cues can be used that indicate where the hands are to be placed for a push-up or for a forward roll. Specific visual or auditory information can be introduced that indicates to the individual specifically what to do with body parts to enhance motor control.

Control methodology: If the learner has a tendency to disassociate visually or auditorially, use the whole-part-whole method of teaching. Later, attention to details of performance can be emphasized.

Differentiate between activities: Many learning disabled children perseverate (i.e., possess the inability to shift easily from one component of a task to another or to differentiate tasks). They repeat what they have al-

FIGURE 9-3. A teenager prepares for the challenge of an above-the-ground (30 feet) ropes course. (Courtesy Wisconsin Lions Camp, Rosholt, Wisconsin.)

ready done. To minimize perseveration, planned sequences of activities in which one is distinctly different from the other in terms of formation, starting the activity, skills used, rules, and strategies should be used.[58]

Use more than one sensory modality: In addition to verbally describing the task to be performed, use visual stimuli (e.g., a picture, drawing, or demonstration). In this way, if the learning disabled student has either visual or verbal deficits, another sensory avenue can be used to comprehend the instruction. Kinesthetic aids such as manually moving a child through sequences also can be used.

DRUG THERAPY

Drug therapy is a common medical intervention technique used in the treatment of behavioral, emotional, and attention deficits associated with the education of learning disabled children.[24] Although the reported use of drug treatment with children with specific learning disabilities varies, Aman and Rojahn[1] suggest that 10% of these children may be taking prescribed psychotropic drugs.

There are numerous behavioral and cognitive symptoms associated with specific learning disabilities. As a result, there are a variety of drugs used with this population. These include (1) neuroleptics (antipsychotics, "major tranquilizers"), 2) anticonvulsants, (3) sedative-hypnotics, (4) antidepressant/antimanic drugs, (5) central nervous system stimulants, and (6) miscellaneous drugs.[2] Drug treatment of a child with a specific learning disability will depend on his/her physician's assessment. However, by far, the most frequent drugs prescribed are methylphenidate (Ritalin) and dextroamphetamine (Dexadrine), which are both central nervous stimulants. Because of the increasing use of stimulant drugs by learning disabled populations,[56] physical educators should be aware of the major effects of drug treatment.

Effects of Drug Treatment

Chandler, Gualtieri, and Fahs[16] suggest that most drugs produce substantial behavioral changes in children with specific learning disabilities when properly prescribed and managed. There are reports that stimulant drugs that lessen hyperactivity and improve short term memory improve academic learning performance of learning disabled children. However, much of the literature does not support long term academic gains due to the use of stimulants.[1]

Assessment and Management of Drug Treatment

Observations made at home and school are extremely helpful in assessing the value of drug treatment. Because single observation of the behavior of children taking drugs is rarely sufficient, Atkins and Pelham[3] suggest that multiple classroom measures involving formal teacher ratings, peer ratings, and direct observations should be made. With such assessments it is easier to determine how the drugs effect learning and social behaviors. Direct observations in the gymnasium and on the playground are helpful in determining the effects of drug treatment and management of behavior.

The side effects of drug treatment vary depending on the individual, the nature or type of drug, the length of time the student has been taking the medication, strength of the dose, and other variables. Negative side effects from drugs that should be reported immediately are nausea, vomiting, rapid breathing, hearing problems, drowsiness, increased appetite, increased eupho-

ria, weight loss, anemia, menstrual irregularities, insomnia, psychic disturbances, sweating, visual disturbances, weakness, fatigue, reduced heart rate, headaches, coma, convulsions, skin rashes, feeling of urinary urgency, dehydration, loss of balance, hyperactivity, fainting, and inability to concentrate.[48]

Medication Policies

It is reported that slightly less than one half of the public schools have medication policies.[24] Even when there are policies, there is little consistency across schools. Epstein et al.[24] suggest that schools should organize a multidisciplinary team to develop procedures for labeling, storing, administering, monitoring, and reporting medication.

USE OF INSTRUCTIONAL MODELS

There are a number of different interventions that have been developed to promote cognitive functioning of specific subtypes of learning disabled populations. The main purpose of these programs is to build students' skills so there is a more promising potential in later school programs. These interventions may involve tutoring by an outside agency, assistance from personnel with specialized training, or placement in a disabled-only educational setting. Each approach reflects the severity of the difficulty, the area of the deficiency, and the resources and attitudes of those involved (e.g., parents and school districts).[32] As would be expected, controversies about these approaches have emerged.[28]

An alternative to developing different interventions for specific population subtypes is to develop a comprehensive model that can be systematically tested and evaluated. Paine, Bellamy, and Wilcox[47] agree that models should be used for conducting instruction. They define a model as a collection of reproducible techniques that are effective, based on research and demonstration to enhance behavioral changes in target skills. Models usually involve reproducible procedures that enable the generalization to other tasks and environments. Deshler, Scumaker, and Lenz[20] suggest a model for learning disabled populations that is composed of the following seven components: (1) motivation, (2) detailed specific instruction targeting skills, (3) generalization of mastered skills to other content areas and settings, (4) a content that needs mastery, (5) communication enabling coordinated services to the student from various professions, (6) transition from secondary school to postschool life, and (7) evaluation of the obtained intervention. Model development in adapted physical education is rare and awaits further development.

SUMMARY

Specific learning disability is a condition that is manifested through disabilities in listening, thinking, writing, speaking, spelling, and mathematical calculations. The majority of children with this disability also demonstrate sensory-perceptual-motor problems. There is widespread disagreement about the relationship between the cognitive and psychomotor problems demonstrated by children with specific learning disabilities. The controversy does not dismiss the reality of poor perceptual and motor coordination displayed by many of these children. Before an appropriate physical education program can be developed for the person with a specific learning disability, testing must be done to determine type and extent of the perceptual and motor disabilities. Activities should be selected on the basis of test results and carefully sequenced to produce optimum results. There are two types of programs that may assist students who have learning disabilites: (1) a bottom, up approach that would focus on facilitating deficit sensory input and reflex systems, and (2) a top, down perceptual-motor approach that would focus on instruction in specific performance tasks.

REVIEW QUESTIONS

1. What is the relationship between perceptual-motor abilities and cognitive functioning?
2. What are some psychomotor, cognitive, and behavioral characteristics of children with specific learning disabilities?
3. What are some positive effects of drug therapy?
4. What are the ways in which learning disabled children may differ as the result of perceptual-motor testing?
5. What are some teaching strategies that can make learning more effective for children with specific learning disabilities?
6. What is the relationship between sensory-motor integration and perceptual-motor training programs?
7. What is the difference between utilization of models and traditional program designs?

STUDENT ACTIVITIES

1. Select a journal that focuses on learning disabilities or a physical education and recreation journal that discusses learning disabled persons. Some are *Journal of Health, Physical Education, Recreation, and Dance; Adapted Physical Activity Quarterly; Palaestra: The Forum of Sport, Physical Education and Recreation for the Disabled; Journal of Learning Disabilities; Learning Disability Quarterly;* and *Academic Therapy.* Look through articles that discuss the relationship between perceptual-motor activity and learning disability. Discuss the implications of the findings.
2. Talk with physical education teachers who have worked with learning disabled children. Discuss the strategies they used to enable participation at the children's ability levels in the physical education class.
3. Observe a class with learning disabled persons. List some of the characteristics of these children as they participate in physical activity. Describe the social and physical-motor characteristics. Describe differences among the learning disabled persons.
4. Observe a perceptual-motor program. Describe the types of activities in which the class participated.
5. Visit with an adult who has learning disabilities. Discuss the physical-motor and social problems this person had in school, community, physical education, and sports programs. List the specific strategies employed to accommodate the person's specific needs by teachers and those who conducted the programs.
6. Compare and contrast a sensory-motor integration test and a perceptual-motor test. How would programming from test results differ for each test?
7. Ask a special education classroom teacher how he or she assesses and programs for perceptual-motor deficiencies that affect academic performance.
8. List the strengths and weaknesses of treating motor skill deficiencies with a bottom, up (developmental) or top, down (task specific) approach. Indicate your preference.

REFERENCES

1. Aman MJ, Rojahn J: *Pharmacological intervention.* In Singh NN, Beale LL, editors: *Learning disabilities: nature, theory and treatment,* New York, 1992, Springer-Verlag.
2. Aman MJ, Singh NN: *Psychopharmacology of the developmental disabilities,* New York, 1988, Springer-Verlag.
3. Atkins MS, Pelham WE: School based assessment of attention-deficit hyperactivity disorder, *J Learn Disab* 24:197-204, 1991.
4. Ayres AJ: *Sensory integration and the child,* Los Angeles, 1980, Western Psychological Services.
5. Ayres AJ: *Sensory integration and learning disorders,* Los Angeles, 1972, Western Psychological Services.
6. Barsch R: *Movagenic curriculum,* Seattle, 1968, Special Child Publications.
7. Bowan MD: *Mental gymnastics,* Vernon, Penn, 1990, The Learning Clinic.
8. Bradley C: The behavior of children receiving benzedrine, *Am J Psychiatry* 94:577-585, 1987.
9. Broxterman J, Stebbins AJ: The significance of visual training in the treatment of reading disabilities, *Am Correct Ther J* 35(5):122-125, 1981.
10. Bruininks VL, Bruininks RL: Motor proficiency and learning disabled and nondisabled students, *Percept Mot Skills* 44:131-137, 1977.
11. Brunt D, Magill R, Eason R: Distinctions in variability of motor output between learning disabled and normal children, *Percept Mot Skills* 57:731-734, 1983.
12. Buckley RE: The biobasis for distraction and dyslexia, *Acad Ther* 16:289-301, 1981.
13. Carlton G, Rainey D: Teaching learning disabled children to help themselves, *Dir Tchr* 6:8-9, 1984.

14. Cermak LS: Information processing deficits in children with learning disabilities, *J Learn Disab* 16:599-605, 1983.

15. Cermak S, Henderson A: *Learning disabilities.* In Umphred D, editor: *Neurological rehabilitation, ed 2,* St Louis, 1990, Mosby—Year Book.

16. Chandler M, Gualtieri CT, Fahs JJ: *Other psychotropic drugs: stimulants, antidepressants, and anxiolytics, and lithium carbonate.* In Aman MJ, Singh NN, editors: *Psychopharmacology of the developmental disabilities,* New York, 1988, Springer-Verlag.

17. Cratty BJ: *Adapted physical education for handicapped children and youth,* Denver, 1980, Love Publishing.

18. Densem JA et al: Effectiveness of a sensory integrative therapy program for children with perceptual-motor deficits, *J Learn Disab* 22:221-229, 1989.

19. deQuiros JB, Schrager OL: *Neuropsychological fundamentals in learning disabilities,* Novato, Calif, 1979, Academic Therapy Publications.

20. Deshler DD, Scumaker JB, Lenz BK: Academic and cognitive interventions for learning disabled adolescents, *J Learn Disab* 17:108-117, 1984.

21. Dunn JM, Fait H: *Special physical education,* Dubuque, Iowa, 1989, Wm C Brown Publishers.

22. EDLAW, Inc: *Individuals with disabilities education act,* Potomac, Md, 1991.

23. Eichstaedt CB, Kalakian LH: *Developmental/adapted physical education,* New York, 1987, Macmillan Publishing.

24. Epstein MH et al: Psychopharmacological intervention. II. Teacher perceptions of psychotropic medication for students with learning disability, *J Learn Disab* 24:477-483, 1991.

25. Frostig M, Maslow P: *Movement education: theory and practice,* Chicago, 1970, Follett Publishing.

26. Getman GN: *The visuomotor complex.* In Hellmuth K, editor: *Learning disorders I,* Seattle, 1965, Special Child Publications.

27. Grant D: *Brainstem level auditory function in specific dyslexics and normal readers,* University of Michigan, 1980, DAI 3376-B.

28. Hallahan DP, Kauffman JM, Lloyd JW: *Introduction to learning disabilities, ed 2,* Englewood Cliffs, NJ, 1985, Prentice-Hall.

29. Haubenstricker JL: Motor development of children with learning disabilities, *J Phys Educ Rec Dance* 53(5):41-43, 1983.

30. Haubenstricker JL: *The efficiency of the Bruininks-Oseretsky test of motor proficiency in discriminating between normal children and those with gross motor dysfunction.* Paper presented to the Motor Development Academy at the annual convention of the American Alliance for Health, Physical Education, Recreation, and Dance, Boston, 1981.

31. Horak F et al: Vestibular function and motor proficiency of children with impaired hearing or with learning disability and motor impairments, *Dev Med Child Neurol* 30:64-79, 1988.

32. Houck CK: *Learning disabilities: understanding concepts, characteristics, and issues,* Englewood Cliffs, NJ, 1984, Prenticc-Hall.

33. Johns ER: *Neurometric evaluation of brain function in normal and learning disabled children,* Ann Arbor, Mich, 1991, University of Michigan Press.

34. Jordan DR: *Attention deficit disorder: ADD syndrome,* Austin, Tex, 1988, PRO-ED.

35. Karr R, Hughes K: Movement difficulty and learning disabled children, *Adapt Phys Act Q* 5:72-79, 1987.

36. Kavale K, Mattison PD: One jump off the balance beam: meta analysis of perceptual-motor training program, *J Learn Disab* 16:165-173, 1983.

37. Keogh J, Sugden D: *Movement skill development,* New York, 1985, Macmillan Publishing.

38. Kephart N: *The slow learner in the classroom,* Columbus, Ohio, 1971, Charles E Merrill Publishing.

39. King KJ: The attention deficit disorder (ADD) child, *KAPPAN,* December 22-26, 1989.

40. Leary PM, Batho K: The role of the EEG in the investigation of the child with learning disability, *S Afr Med J,* June 1981, pp 867-868.

41. McLaughlin E: *Followup study on children remediated for perceptual-motor dysfunction at the University of Kansas perceptual-motor clinic,* Eugene, 1980, University of Oregon.

42. Menkes M, Rowe J, Menkes J: A twenty-five year follow-up study on the hyperkinetic child with minimal brain dysfunction, *Pediatrics* 39:393-399, 1967.

43. Millay K, Grant D, Pyfer J: *Structural and functional differences in brain organization in developmental dyslexics.* Unpublished paper, Denton, Tex, 1991, Texas Woman's University.

44. Morrison D, Hinshaw S, Corte E: Signs of neurobehavioral dysfunction in a sample of learning disabled children: stability and concurrent validity, *Percept Mot Skills* 61:863-872, 1985.

45. Murphy V, Hicks-Stewart K: Learning disabilities and attention deficit-hyperactivity disorder: an interactional perspective, *J Learn Disab* 24:386-388, 1991.

46. Myers PI, Hamill DD: *Learning disabilities: basic concepts, assessment practices and instructional strategies,* Austin, Tex, 1983, PRO-ED.

47. Paine S, Bellamy GT, Wilcox B: *Human services that work,* Baltimore, 1984, Paul H Brookes Publishing.

48. Patton JR et al: *Exceptional children in focus,* New York, 1990, Macmillan Publishing.

49. Pyfer JL: *Sensory-perceptual-motor characteristics of learning disabled children: a validation study.* Unpublished paper, Denton, Tex, 1983, Texas Woman's University.

50. Pyfer JL, Alley G: *Sensory-perceptual-motor dysfunction of learning disabled children.* Paper presented at the First World Congress of the Council for Exceptional Children, Stirling, Scotland, 1978.

51. Rapin J: *Children with brain dysfunction,* New York, 1982, Raven Press.
52. Rimmer J, Kelly L: Gross motor development in preschool children with learning disabilities, *Adapt Phys Act Q* 6:268-279, 1989.
53. Sage GH: *Motor learning and control: a neuro-psychological approach,* Dubuque, Iowa, 1984, Wm C Brown Publishing.
54. Schacher R: Childhood hyperactivity, *J Child Psychol Psychiatry* 32:155-191, 1991.
55. Seaman JA, DePauw KP: *The new adapted physical education: a developmental approach,* Palo Alto, Calif, 1989, Mayfield Publishing.
56. Shaywitz SE, Shaywitz BA: Introduction to the special series on attention deficit disorder, *J Learn Disab* 24:68-74, 1991.
57. Shaywitz SE, Shaywitz BA: Attention deficit disorder: current perspectives, *Pediatr Neurol* 3:129-135, 1987.
58. Sherrill C: *Adapted physical education and recreation, ed 3,* Dubuque, Iowa, 1986, Wm C Brown Publishing.
59. Stewart M et al: The hyperactive child syndrome, *Am J Orthopsychiatry* 35:861-867, 1966.

SUGGESTED READINGS

Ayres AJ: *Sensory integration and the child,* Los Angeles, 1980, Western Psychological Services.
Eichstaedt CB, Kalakian LH: Developmental/adapted physical education, New York, 1987, Macmillan Publishing.
Hardman ML, Drew CJ, Egan MW: *Human exceptionality: society, school and family,* Boston, 1987, Allyn & Bacon.
Hallahan DP, Kaufman JM, Lloyd JW: *Introduction to learning disabilities, ed 2,* Englewood Cliffs, NJ, 1985, Prentice-Hall.
Seaman JA, DePauw K: *The new adapted physical education: a developmental approach,* Palo Alto, Calif, 1989, Mayfield Publishing.

10

Describe the scope and types of emotional disturbance.

Explain the characteristics of emotionally disturbed persons.

Describe the techniques used for conducting programs of physical education for the emotionally disturbed.

Explain the relationship among the teacher, services, and programming for the emotionally disturbed.

Describe a process for making appropriate decisions to control excessive behavior displayed by emotionally disturbed students.

Select appropriate activities for emotionally disturbed students.

Classify problem behaviors.

Courtesy Dallas Independent School District

Emotional Disturbances

There are several terms in the literature that have parallel meaning to the term *emotionally disturbed*. Some of these terms are *emotionally disordered, behaviorally disordered, behaviorally disabled, emotionally handicapped, psychologically disordered,* and *mentally ill.* For the purposes of this discussion, the term *emotionally disturbed* incorporates all of these terms.

According to the Education of the Handicapped Act, Section 121a.5(b)(8), serious emotional disturbance is defined as follows[36]:

1. The term means a condition exhibiting one or more of the following characteristics over a long period of time and to a marked degree, which adversely affects educational performance.
   A. Inability to learn, which cannot be explained by intellectual, sensory, or health factors.
   B. An inability to build or maintain satisfactory interpersonal relationships with peers and teachers.
   C. Inappropriate types of behavior or feelings under normal circumstances.
   D. A general pervasive mood of unhappiness or depression
   E. A tendency to develop physical symptoms or fears associated with personal or school problems.
2. The definition includes children who are schizophrenic. The term does not include children who are socially maladjusted, unless it is determined that they are seriously emotionally disturbed.

CONTINUUM

Emotional functioning may be viewed as a continuum of demonstrated behavior from normal to abnormal and socially unacceptable. Usually, the greater the deviance from the norm, the greater the need for resources to maintain or provide remedial services. French and Jansma[14] describe a continuum of emotional disturbance based on the percentage of inappropriate behavior.

The severity of the emotional disturbance is another important variable that reflects placement on a continuum. When acts that result from an emotional disturbance present a danger to self and to others, such behavior is said to reflect deep-seated emotional problems.

Kalakian and Eichstaedt[18] make a distinction between having an emotional disturbance and being emotionally disturbed. Having an emotional disturbance in response to frustration is expected and normal. The state of being emotionally disturbed is characterized by behavior that is disordered to a marked degree and that occurs over a protracted period.

INCIDENCE

There is disagreement among authorities as to the incidence of emotional disturbance. During 1989-90, 0.9% of all school children were classified as having serious emotional disturbance.[35] However, a conservative estimate of school-age populations of seriously emotionally disturbed children is 2%. It also is estimated that 3% of these students are labeled juvenile delinquents.[9]

Other estimates indicate that 10% to 15% of school-age children need some form of psychiatric help to function optimumly.[31] When short-term and long-term disturbances of varying extremes are counted, the incidence of emotional disturbance would perhaps be between 7% and 15%. These figures would include delinquents who often exhibit characteristics of the emotionally disturbed, such as defiance, impertinence, uncooperativeness, irresponsibility, antisocial behavior, hyperactivity, and restlessness. In addition, they may display characteristics of shyness, hypersensitivity, and high levels of anxiety. A common ratio given in the literature of the incidence of emotional disturbance in boys and girls is 4 to 1.

CAUSES

When working with emotionally disturbed children, teachers sometimes find it helpful to know the causes of the emotional disturbances. This may help them form prognoses and be aware of circumstances that may aggravate existing conditions.

There is disagreement among authorities as to the cause of behavioral disorders in young people. However, hereditary, organic, and functional causes are reported to exist. Meyen[24] has recognized the importance of both predisposing factors (a condition that may cause disturbance) and precipitating factors (a specific condition, a stressful moment) as they relate to the cause of emotional disturbance. An *organic* cause might be brain involvement resulting from disease, trauma, injury, infection, neurological degeneration, poor nutrition, chemical imbalances, or glandular dysfunctions. *Environmental* or *functional* causes are behavioral disorders caused by real or imagined pressures from peers, parents, teachers, or other authority figures, as well as child abuse, poverty, discrimination, peer pressure, breakdown in the family unit, or perception of self as being of limited value. Many clinicians place emphasis on locating a hypothesized environmental source of the disturbance. It is suggested that additional environmental causes of emotional blocks to learning might be parental ambitiousness, awareness of the impending birth of a sibling, or inability to adapt to a change in surroundings.

There are differing points of view regarding the predominant cause of the more severe emotional disturbances of childhood. Many authorities trace the cause of emotional disturbance to environmental circumstances that occur early in life. Faulty parental relationships, in particular, are believed by some authorities to account for the cause of a great portion of emotional disturbance in children. Some authorities estimate that

75% of the children who are disruptive in school come from "broken" homes.[20]

Hardman, Drew, and Egan[15] list five theoretical causal factors of behavior disorders on which treatments are based. These theoretical positions may be described as (1) biological, (2) psychoanalytical, (3) behavioral, (4) phenomological, and (5) sociological/ecological.

Biological

The biological position is based on the belief that emotional disorders arise from abnormalities of the central nervous system that may be inherited or occur after birth. Biochemical imbalances or genetic abnormalities are believed to be the cause of the disease. Physicians often support the biological orientation. Treatment to improve emotional behavior includes drugs to restore biochemical balance and to have a favorable impact on the physiological functions of the nervous system.

Psychoanalytical

The psychoanalytical position is based on the theoretical notions of Freud. According to Freud and his followers, behavior is driven by subconscious processes that develop early in life. Remedies to the disorders are sought by gaining insight and resolution of psychic conflicts by means of psychotherapy. In children, play therapy is used to identify and resolve inner conflicts.

Behavioral

The behavioral model is based on the belief that undesirable behaviors result from developing unacceptable responses to environmental stimuli. The undesirable behaviors are changed by identifying acceptable goals and using behavior modification techniques to direct the person toward those goals (see Chapter 5). The ultimate objective is to replace undesirable behaviors with those that are more appropriate.

Phenomological

The phenomological position views abnormal behavior as a result of past events that link a person's self-concept, feelings, and thoughts to behavior. The advocate of the phenomological approach believes accurate perceptions of one's feelings are necessary for mental health. Psychotherapy that helps an individual develop satisfactory self-perceptions is used to remedy abnormal behaviors.

Sociological/Ecological

The sociological/ecological model proposes that behavioral disorders are caused by a variety of cultural interactions with other people. Undesirable behavior may be perpetuated as a result of labeling (i.e., labeling a youngster as a juvenile delinquent may motivate the youth to behave in that fashion).

MEDICAL VS. EDUCATIONAL MODEL

Medical and educational models differ in their perception of disorders. The medical model stresses identification of a set of symptoms that can be traced to a specific pathological factor. The symptoms are used to identify an underlying disorder, but do not lead to suggested solutions to the problem. Therefore medical diagnoses alone usually are not very useful to educators.[16]

The educational model is more concerned with managing the behavior of children so that learning can occur.[6] The individual is evaluated and an educational intervention program is designed so that the child can benefit from his or her school experience regardless of the disability. It is, however, important that educators and the medical profession communicate with one another.[11] The child whom the physical educator recognizes as having emotional problems could have any of the following personality disorders: (1) schizophrenia, (2) delusional (paranoid), (3) psychotic (schizophreniform or schizoaffective), (4) mood, (5) anxiety, (6) somatoform, (7) dissociative, or (8) sexual.

Schizophrenia

Schizophrenia is the most prevalent type of personality disorder demonstrated by school-aged children. This disorder involves abnormal behavior patterns with personality disorganization. There is usually less than adequate contact with reality.

Diagnostic criteria for schizophrenia as defined by the American Psychiatric Association[1] are as follows:

A. Presence of characteristic psychotic symptoms in the active phase: either (1), (2), or (3) for at least 1 week (unless the symptoms are successfully treated)
1. Two of the following:
   a. Delusions
   b. Prominent hallucinations (throughout the day for several days or several times a week for several weeks, each hallucinatory experience not being limited to a few brief moments)
   c. Incoherence or marked loosening of associations
   d. Catatonic behavior
   e. Flat or grossly inappropriate affect
2. Bizzarre delusions (i.e., involving a phenomenon that the person's culture would regard as totally implausible, [e.g., thought broadcasting, being controlled by a dead person])
3. Prominent hallucinations (as defined in 1,b, above)

of a voice keeping up a running commentary on the person's behavior or thoughts, or two or more voices conversing with each other

B. During the course of the disturbance, functioning in such areas as work, social relations, and self-care is markedly below the highest level achieved before onset of the disturbance (or, when the onset is in childhood or adolescence, failure to achieve expected level of social development).

C. Schizoaffective disorder and mood disorder with psychotic features have been ruled out (i.e., if a major depressive or manic syndrome has ever been present during an active phase of the disturbance, the total duration of all episodes of a mood syndrome has been brief relative to the total duration of the active and residual phases of the disturbance).

D. Continuous signs of the disturbance for at least 6 months. The 6-month period must include an active phase (of at least 1 week, or less if symptoms have been successfully treated) during which there were psychotic symptoms characteristic of schizophrenia (symptoms in A), with or without a prodromal or residual phase, as defined below.

Prodromal phase: A clear deterioration in functioning before the active phase of the disturbance that is not due to a disturbance in mood or to a psychoactive substance use disorder and that involves at least two of the symptoms listed below.

Residual phase: Following the active phase of the disturbance, persistence of at least two of the symptoms noted below, these not being due to a disturbance in mood or to a psychoactive substance use disorder.

1. Marked social isolation or withdrawal
2. Marked impairment in role functioning as wage-earner, student, or homemaker
3. Markedly peculiar behavior (e.g., collecting garbage, talking to self in public, hoarding food)
4. Marked impairment in personal hygiene and grooming
5. Blunted or inappropriate affect
6. Digressive, vague, overelaborate, or circumstantial speech, or poverty of speech, or poverty of content of speech
7. Odd beliefs or magical thinking, influencing behavior and inconsistent with cultural norms (e.g., superstitiousness, belief in clairvoyance, telepathy, "sixth sense," "others can feel my feelings," overvalued ideas, ideas of reference)
8. Unusual perceptual experiences (e.g., recurrent illusions, sensing the presence of a force or person not actually present)
9. Marked lack of initiative, interests, or energy

    Examples: Six months of prodromal symptoms with 1 week of symptoms from A; no prodromal symptoms with 6 months of symptoms from A; no prodromal symptoms with 1 week of symptoms from A and 6 months of residual symptoms.

E. It cannot be established that an organic factor initiated and maintained the disturbance.

F. If there is a history of autistic disorder, the additional diagnosis of schizophrenia is made only if prominent delusions or hallucinations are also present.

Five types of schizophrenia have been identified. Diagnostic criteria for each follow[1]:

Catatonic type

A type of schizophrenia in which the clinical picture is dominated by any one of the following:

1. Catatonic stupor (marked decrease in reactivity to the environment and/or reduction in spontaneous movements and activity) or mutism
2. Catatonic negativism (an apparently motiveless resistance to all instructions or attempts to be moved)
3. Catatonic rigidity (maintenance or a rigid posture against efforts to be moved)
4. Catatonic excitement (excited motor activity, apparently purposeless and not influenced by external stimuli)
5. Catatonic posturing (voluntary assumption of inappropriate or bizarre postures)

Disorganized type

A type of schizophrenia in which the following criteria are met:

1. Incoherence, marked loosening of associations, or grossly disorganized behavior
2. Flat or grossly inappropriate affect
3. Does not meet the criteria for catatonic type

Paranoid type

A type of schizophrenia marked by:

1. Preoccupation with one or more systematized delusions or with frequent auditory hallucinations related to a single theme
2. None of the following: incoherence, marked loosening of associations, flat or grossly inappropriate affect, catatonic behavior, grossly disorganized behavior

Specify stable type if schizophrenic criteria A and B, listed above, have been met during all past and present phases of the illness.

Undifferentiated type

A type of schizophrenia in which:

1. There are prominent delusions, hallucinations, incoherence, or grossly disorganized behavior
2. The criteria for paranoid, catatonic, or disorganized type are not met

Residual type

A type of schizophrenia marked by:
1. Absence of prominent delusions, hallucinations, incoherence, or grossly disorganized behavior
2. Continuing evidence of the disturbance, as indicated by two or more of the residual symptoms listed in criterion D of schizophrenia, above.

USE OF TEST INFORMATION TO LABEL

Psychological tests are required to establish the presence of emotional disturbance. However, the psychological data and the label associated with the data do not provide specific information to assist the physical education teacher in planning instruction. Without a behavioral assessment and programming relevant to skills that are a part of the physical education program, the label is of limited value. Once a pupil is placed in a class as emotionally disturbed, a correlation should be made among behavioral activity, diagnostic data concerning functional activity, and instructional strategies.

Classifying Problem Behaviors

When the adapted physical educator encounters a student who demonstrates disruptive behavior, several questions need to be answered before an appropriate intervention program can be planned. A list of important questions that may prove useful when analyzing the need to change specific behaviors follows[29]:
1. *Intensity:* Is intensity of the behavior such that it disrupts the activity of the child or others?
2. *Appropriateness:* Is the behavior a reasonable response that is acceptable to others in the same environment?
3. *Duration:* Does the behavior last only a short time, or does it generalize to other activities or environments?
4. *Acceptance by peers:* Is the behavior accepted or rejected by peers?
5. *Concomitant behavior:* Are there other behavioral problems associated with the central behavior?
6. *Comparison with the norm:* Is the behavior below normative expectations for the group?
7. *Behavioral circumstances:* Is the event that triggers the behavior identifiable?
8. *Manageability:* Can the behavior be readily managed so that the outcomes are identifiable?

The information provided from answering these questions may assist the teacher in making judgments as to whether intervention should be used. This information may also assist in making judgments as to whether the behavior can be managed by the adapted physical education teacher or whether someone with specialized training in modifying behavior should be brought in to control the student's behavior.

CHARACTERISTICS OF THE EMOTIONALLY DISTURBED

The physical education teacher may identify emotionally disturbed children as they participate in activity through observation of adverse performance or abnormal behavior. Identifying emotional disturbance during the initial stages is difficult because behavior is similar to that of nondisturbed persons. However, timeliness in identification of emotional disturbance is essential for effective treatment. A list of characteristics that can be observed by physical education teachers and that can be used to assist with early identification of emotional disturbance follows. A child is considered emotionally disturbed if he or she exhibits one or more of the following characteristics over a long period of time to a marked degree:[36]

☐ An inability to learn that cannot be explained by intellectual, sensory, or health factors. Emotional factors play a part in the learning of the child. Inability to learn is a readily observable characteristic among all emotionally disturbed children. A child's inability to learn at the expected rate might indicate some disability, one of which may be emotional disturbance.

☐ An inability to build and maintain satisfactory interpersonal relationships with peers and teachers. The result of an emotional disturbance may thus be some type of antisocial or asocial behavior, which has an adverse effect on the child's interaction with others at school. Unsatisfactory personal relationships of children with one another and the teacher are easily observed.

☐ Inappropriate types of behavior or feelings under normal circumstances. Such characteristics indicate that an individual reacts to the environment differently than do others. Emotionally disturbed children may act aggressively or totally withdraw from activity.

☐ A general and pervasive mood of unhappiness or depression. Such persons display characteristics of unhappiness.

☐ A tendency to develop physical symptoms or fears associated with personal and school problems. This may be due to long-term anxiety, excessive or unrealistic fears, or anxieties stemming from perceived stress.

Other parts of the definition that are critical are:
over a long period of time: Means the behavior must be chronic. Many symptoms must be observed for at least 6 months, however, other symptoms may be of considerably less duration.[1] For instance, school phobia may be apparent for only 2 weeks.

to a marked degree: Refers to the level of seriousness and interference with the child's total life. To qualify as a serious behavioral problem, the behavior must impair the child's ability to function in different environments rather than just isolated situations.

which adversely affects educational performance: Means that the condition results in lowered educational achievement. Applied to performance in physical education, this means the emotionally disturbed child fails to make reasonable progress in sport skills or physical fitness development.

Emotionally disturbed children constitute a heterogeneous group. This becomes apparent when a person compares the behavior of an emotionally disturbed child who is hyperactive with the behavior of an emotionally disturbed child who is withdrawn. There are many behavioral characteristics that are prevalent among the emotionally disturbed; however, all emotionally disturbed children do not possess all of these characteristics.

Characteristics that may interfere with the learning of motor skills and the management of physical education classes are the following:

1. Learning
   A. Poor work habits in practicing and developing motor skills and aspects of physical fitness
   B. Lack of motivation in achieving goals not of an immediate nature
   C. Disruptive class behavior on the part of students who are hyperactive
   D. Lack of involvement on the part of students who are withdrawn
   E. Inability to follow directions or seek help despite demands for constant attention
   F. Short attention span
   G. Poor coordination
   H. Development of physical symptoms (stomachache, headache, etc.) when confronted with physical activities with which the person is not secure
   I. Overactivity
   J. Restlessness
   K. Distractibility
   L. Amnesia
   M. Forgetfulness
   N. Impaired memory span
   O. General and specific disability
   P. Daydreaming
2. Interpersonal relationships
   A. Lack of conscience
   B. Loss of emotional control
   C. Formation of superficial relationships
   D. Shyness
   E. Sensitivity
   F. Detachment
   G. Unsocialized aggressiveness
   H. Hostility
   I. Quarrelsomeness
   J. Destructiveness
   K. Temper tantrums
   L. Hostile disobedience
   M. Physical and verbal aggressiveness
   N. Holding group values of delinquency
   O. Fear
   P. Flight reaction
   Q. Apprehension
   R. Anxiety
   S. Tension habits[21]
   T. Inferiority feeling
   U. Inadequacy feeling
3. Inappropriate behavior under normal conditions
   A. Unhappiness or depression
   B. Inconsistencies in responses
   C. Rigid expectations of everyday life
   D. Carelessness, irresponsibility, and apathy
   E. Immaturity
   F. Timidity
   G. Feelings of rejection
   H. Feelings for restitution and retribution
   I. Aggressive behavior
   J. Withdrawal and self-isolation
   K. Negativism
   L. Non-cooperation and contrariness
   M. Undisciplined
   N. Incorrigible
   O. Impulsive
   P. Repetitious behavior
   Q. Aimless behavior
   R. Disorderly
   S. Unplanful
4. Physical and motor characteristics
   A. Poor physical condition caused by withdrawal from activity
   B. Retardation of motor skill development caused by withdrawal from activity
   C. Disorientation in space and time

Identification

The early identification of children who are emotionally disturbed is extremely important. It is recognized that the earlier educators and mental health specialists can attack this problem, the greater the prospect for ameliorating or remedying it. In many instances the treatment and education of emotionally disturbed persons involve the unlearning of behavioral patterns. If identification is made early, less unlearning is necessary.

Assessment of Undesirable Behavior

There are very few school systems that engage in systematic screening of behavior disorders.[33] For the most part behavior is not questioned until a child exhibits a problem in class. Before a referral is made, several parent conferences are held to discuss the child's behavior. When these conferences do not resolve the child's behavior problems, a professional assessment by a school psychologist usually is sought. There are a number of standardized instruments that have been developed that are used by these professionals. Which one is selected depends on the philosophical orientation of the evaluator.

Information gathered by school psychologists may or may not be helpful to the adapted physical education teacher. School psychologists use standardized personality inventories or projective techniques to identify students' strengths and weaknesses. However, the information from such an assessment does not always differentiate between students with and without disabilities. Furthermore, the information provided is difficult for the physical education teacher to use for specific programmming of an individual.

It is also important that teachers know their role in screening. The purpose of screening is to determine which children are not functioning properly, not to determine what caused the difficulty. The purposes of identifying children with emotional disturbances are as follows:

□ To identify children with emotional problems that impair their learning
□ To identify children with emotional problems that disrupt classroom management and prevent others from learning
□ To permit intervention to control the disturbance with remedial services (special or adjunctive physical education services)
□ To place children in the educational environment in which they can best develop their potential

It is not easy to determine which children have problems that require special educational services. Usually, a problem in physical education class is manifested by disruption of the student's work, the desirable cooperation of the group, or the individual's ability to function adequately. Buhler, Smitter, and Richardson[5] describe the following sequence of behavioral patterns that lead to a severe disturbance, which may assist educators in identifying the severity of a disturbance:

1. Trivial everyday disturbances such as giggling or the lack of concentration that teachers cannot study in detail; action can be met with counteraction to eliminate this form of disturbance
2. Repetitious behavior that must be interpreted as a sign of deeper underlying tension
3. Repetitious behavior accompanied by a serious single disturbance, a tantrum, or breaking into tears
4. A succession of different disturbances on different days such as talking when roll is taken, poking the person standing nearby, and staring into space; indicates deep-seated tension and requires the experience of a psychologist or a psychiatrist

The other characteristics previously listed also will provide assistance in identifying emotionally disturbed children. More often than not, the teacher makes the initial identification of the disturbance and then refers the case to the school psychologist. There is a great need to develop sensitivity to the characteristics of emotionally disturbed children in teacher training programs so that these children may be better served in a public school setting.

Emotionally disturbed children possess a multitude of traits. Consequently, the label *emotionally disturbed* tells little about a particular person.

It has been traditional to classify emotionally disturbed children with a label describing their behavior. Suggested categories that may be of significance to the physical educator of emotionally disturbed children follow:

□ *Dimension of personality afflicted:* Personality characteristics associated with emotional disturbance may be immaturity of physical, emotional, social, or psychological traits. Each trait has implications for physical education programming. Social immaturity limits the child's participation in a hierarchy of social games requiring team play and adherence to discipline with regard to obeying rules. The psychological problems are often perceptual in nature, making it difficult to match perception with motor skills that are associated with many sport activities. In many instances the child's emotional instability may affect his or her physical development.
□ *Overt behavior patterns:* Emotionally disturbed children tend to be on a continuum from hyperactivity to withdrawal. Children at each end of this continuum pose different types of problems to the physical educator.
□ *Degree of emotional disturbance:* Neurosis is a less

severe form of emotional disturbance than psychosis. The psychotic child loses touch with reality and poses a more difficult problem for the physical educator than does the neurotic child.

□ *Associated deficiencies:* In some instances emotional disturbance is accompanied by other disorders such as mental retardation, sensory deterioration, perceptual problems, epilepsy, and obesity.

THE TEACHER

The teacher of an emotionally disturbed child bears great responsibility. The teacher organizes physical activities, directs play, and, what is more critical, provides patterns of behavior for the child to emulate. It is from the teacher that immature children learn how the environment works and how persons cope.

The teacher of an emotionally disturbed child must be stable, flexible, and understanding toward atypical behavior and must be able to perceive what the child is experiencing. Such a teacher provides a medium through which the child may better understand his or her own behavior and modify it. This is no easy task. Being in contact with anxiety-provoking persons often stretches a teacher's emotional capacities. Some of the child's behaviors that the teacher often must tolerate are implied rejection, conflicting demands ranging from demands that immediate needs be met to severe withdrawal, aggressive tactics, and immature behaviors. Regular classroom teachers may be unaccustomed to these behaviors. However, to succeed in working with these children, teachers must understand and accept their atypical behavior patterns and be able to establish a good working relationship with these students. It may be necessary for teachers to receive special guidance and support to prevent reaching an emotional breaking point.

COORDINATION OF SERVICES

Several different persons including psychological support service personnel usually provide services to emotionally disturbed children. The physical education teacher often has a better opportunity to contribute to the solution of these children's problems because of the universal appeal of play to school-aged children. Appropriate use of the appeal of activity can result in a successful program that the child finds interesting. However, it must be noted that the physical education teacher or program content may have either positive or negative influences on emotionally disturbed children. Thus it is suggested that all changes in behavior, for better or worse, be closely observed. Consultation with other personnel involved with the child, includ-

ing those in psychological services, should be on a regular basis.

BENEFITS OF SPORT ACTIVITY

Sport and physical activities are important for emotionally disturbed persons because there is potential for the development and restoration of physical and emotional characteristics. Sport and physical activities provide a wide variety of opportunities to meet the interest of these students. Some of the benefits of programs of sport and physical activities for the emotionally disturbed are as follows:

□ The program may provide incentive for acceptable modes of conduct during sport activity.

□ Aggressive tendencies may be expressed in socially acceptable ways because of controlled rules.

□ Games and activities may provide opportunities for the development of social characteristics such as co-operation and competition.

□ Activities requiring continuous movement tend to dissipate pent up emotions.

THE PHYSICAL EDUCATION PROGRAM
Approach of the Adapted Physical Education Teacher

Although there has been considerable emphasis in the past on identifying causes before alleviating disruptive behavior, Kauffman[19] states that "the first or ultimate cause of behavior disorders almost always remains unknown . . . the focus of the educator should be on those contributing factors that can be altered by the teacher." Under most conditions, the physical education teacher cannot control the cause of abnormal behavior even if it is known. Thus it is essential that the adapted physical education teacher plan for developing skills included on the individual education program (IEP) through the use of appropriate behavioral strategies.

Objectives

The objectives of a physical education program for emotionally disturbed children are the same as those for children without disabilities. The program for emotionally disturbed children should stress the development of motor skills and physical fitness, social competence, and personal adequacy. The objectives should be to develop personal and social competencies that will make the students aware of their own resources and potential for self-development. Physical activities fostering desirable relationships between self and both peers and persons in authority should be provided. Physical activities should also provide constructive and

FIGURE 10-1. Equine therapy can be valuable in the development of psychosocial skills. (Courtesy Texas Special Olympics.)

positive new experiences that enhance the concept of self and provide a feeling of worth.

The approach to the education of emotionally disturbed individuals is a central problem needing resolution. The difference between medical and educational models for emotionally disturbed children is adequately described by Hobbs,[17] who indicates that education places the emphasis on health rather than on illness, on teaching rather than on treatment, on learning rather than on fundamental personality reorganization, on the present and future rather than on the past, and on the operation of the total social system of which the child is a part rather than on the intrapsychic processes exclusively. The primary purpose of the physical educator is to deal with the process of education, not with therapeutic treatment, when implementing programs.

Intervention Strategies

Hardman, Drew, and Egan[15] indicate four different types of intervention approaches that may be applied with emotionally disturbed children. These are (1) insight-oriented therapy, (2) play types of interventions, (3) behavioral interventions, and (4) the use of drugs to control behavior.

Insight-oriented therapy

Insight-oriented therapy involves relieving symptoms by treating causes of behavior. Furthermore, it attempts to develop a therapeutic relationship between the teacher and the child. Insight-oriented therapies usually use a nondirective, client-centered or psychoanalytic approach to relieve symptoms.

Play therapy

Development of the individual through play is the central mission of this approach. Development of social relationships with others and playing out emotional problems as well as developing positive peer relationshps are important. Through the play process, the emotionally disturbed child becomes aware of his or her own unconscious thoughts and the behaviors that result from these thoughts. In group play, the development of problem-solving skills can occur and be used to resolve problems in social situations. Small play groups may be formed to assist in developing social and problem-solving skills. Structured situations that involve (1) modeling, (2) role playing, (3) performance feedback, and (4) transfer of training have proven successful.[23]

Behavior therapy

The purpose of behavior therapy is to develop positive peer relationships as well as adequate physical and motor skills. This intervention strategy can be used to eliminate disruptive behavior that interferes with management of classes and learning of the individual. It is useful for the control of excessive and unusual behavior as well as for control of aggressive behavior. Behavioral interventions are usually designed to decrease undesirable behavior and increase rates of desirable behavior. Contingency contracting and other motivational systems are used to encourage children to engage in normal behavior.

Drug therapy

Drugs to relieve symptoms and to control unusual aggressive behaviors or other types of behaviors that interfere with learning are frequently prescribed for active, inattentive, and impulsive children. Drugs also may be used to control disorganized or highly erratic behavior. The decision of whether to prescribe drugs usually depends on several factors, including the severity of the disorder, the type of the disorder, and the side effects of the drug. A balance between the side effects that interfere with learning and the control of the behavior must be weighed by professionals.

Medication. It is estimated that 25% of students with disabilities are receiving medication for school-related problems.[28] Estimates of the incidence of drug use for the emotionally disturbed that are in need of medication to control behavior are high. Safer and Krager[28] estimate that in the elementary school, the duration of drug treatment is an average of 2 years; in the middle school, 4 years; and in the high school, 7 years. The Drug Enforcement Agency[10] reports a doubling of the rate of medication for hyperactive students every 4 to 7 years. Therefore knowledge of the effects of drugs may be helpful to the physical educator in planning and conducting programs for this group of children.

Types of drugs. Psychoactive drugs produce behavioral, emotional, and/or cognitive changes. Amen and Singh[2] list 100 psychoactive drugs that are prescribed in this country. They clasify these drugs as:

1. Neuroleptics (antipsychotic "major" tranquilizers)
2. Anticonvulsants
3. Sedative-hypnotics
4. Antidepressant/antimanic drugs
5. Central nervous system stimulants
6. Antiparkinson drugs
7. Miscellaneous drugs

FIGURE 10-2. A child demonstrates solitary play skills. (Courtesy Dallas Independent School District.)

The categories of drugs that are most commonly used with emotionally disturbed children are antipsychotic, sedative-hypnotic, antidepressant, and stimulant drugs.

Drug treatment. Emotionally disturbed children who are under medication often present behavioral problems that interfere with the learning of motor and physical skills, as well as with social interaction with others. It may be of interest to the physical educator to understand the effects of medication on specific behaviors that have an impact on the physical education class. Thus once the target behaviors that interfere with learning in the classroom are observed, and there is knowledge of a drug intervention, the physical educator is in a position to assess the effectiveness of the drug on that behavior and modify accommodations that need to be made in physical education class for a specific child. However, antipsychotic, antidepressant, antianxiety, antimanic, and stimulant drugs often are not therapeutically specific,[2] but often have a generalizing effect or a side effect. Thus the physical educator may not be able to evaluate the total effectiveness of a drug, but may be able to observe specific behaviors relevant to instruction.

Evaluation of drug treatment programs. Despite the prevalent use of psychoactive drugs to treat emotionally disturbed individuals, there are several problems in the administration of such drug programs to students who may take part in physical education classes.[22] First, the doses may be high and thus may produce side effects; medical supervision has been less than exemplary.[2] Second, there is a need for more attention to defining specific clinical requirements and therapeutic goals. Third, the efficacy of certain drugs to modify specific behaviors that disrupt learning or the class needs further examination. Fourth, Schroeder[30] indicates that there is tremendous variability in the use of drugs from one setting to another. This may indicate the need for uniform practices in the profession for managing behavior through drug treatment programs. Fifth, the percentage of emotionally disturbed students who are responders to the drugs as compared to those who do not respond needs to be clarified.

Medical reduction. Inasmuch as there are often side effects associated with medication, it is desirable that those prescribing the medication reduce it to a minimum to lessen the side effects. Briggs et al.[3] call for medication reduction programs that involve objective identification of the student's undesirable behaviors, the collection of baseline data of the behaviors, and regular multidisciplinary assessment of the effectiveness of the medication. The physical educator

could contribute to such a program in the event the target behaviors were displayed in a particular class. The behaviors that disrupt learning of the student or other members of the class could be documented.

Whereas some drugs may control the behavior and conditions for which the medication is targeted, there are occasions where drugs that are effective in decreasing behavioral symptoms may have adverse effects on cognition and learning.[34] The majority of studies indicate that drug treatment by itself does not result in maintaining long-term academic achievement gains even though such drugs may control undesirable behavior and improve attention.[13] It is reasonable to suggest that the prescription of medication be guided by clinical experience and the collective wisdom of colleagues in practice with subsequent feedback to those who prescribe medication.[7] There is currently a strong movement to reduce the use of psychoactive drugs.[2] This has, in part, been facilitated by court decisions that restrict the use of antipsychotic medications[4] until there is evidence that the particular drugs are effective in treating specific problems demonstrated by an individual.

Treatment uncertainties. Werry[37] suggests attention to overall quality of life should be the most important measure of effects of drugs. He further states that the quality of life of the patient is too important to be left solely to the medical profession. Perhaps through observation of emotionally disturbed individuals involved in physical activity, the physical educator may contribute to such decisions.

Principles of Teaching

To conduct a developmental curriculum in physical education for emotionally disturbed children, it is necessary to understand their learning characteristics in the development of motor skills and to apply principles taking these characteristics into consideration. The principles of good teaching of emotionally disturbed children in physical education are as follows:

1. Provide the appropriate stimulation. Many emotionally disturbed children need a strong prompt to focus their attention on the activity at hand. Use tactile stimulation in teaching if the child does not attend to the task. However, avoid overstimulation of the hyperactive emotionally disturbed child.
2. Remove distracting objects. The attention span can be increased if seductive objects are removed from the environment because the possibilities of involvement in other activity are reduced. Bats, balls, and other play equipment should be kept out of sight until the time of use, if possible.

FIGURE 10-3. Aquatic experiences open a new world. (Courtesy Wisconsin Lions Camp, Rosholt, Wisconsin.)

3. Provide manual guidance when teaching basic skills to some emotionally disturbed children. This is not necessarily a good procedure for all disturbed children. A rapport must first be built between the child and the instructor before use of manual guidance or the kinesthetic method of teaching motor skills becomes effective. Manual guidance is less effective with hyperactive children than with those who are withdrawn.

4. Impose limits with regard to conduct and use of equipment and facilities. Undue expectations with regard to developmental level of emotions should not be made. However, each child should adhere to behavioral limits within his or her capabilities. Responsible behavior in the use of equipment and facilities involved in play activity affords opportunities for the development of positive attitudes.

5. Do not necessarily strive for control in all situations. One major goal of education for persons who are emotionally disturbed is to affect adequate social adjustment. This does not imply strict obedience to authority but the ability of the individual to adjust to situations independently of supervision. Control should be of such a nature that the preconceived goals of the IEP are being achieved.

6. Discourage inappropriate interaction among the children. Such interaction may result in conflicts that disrupt the whole class. It may be necessary to separate children who interact in a disruptive manner.

7. Identify specific disruptive behaviors that can be brought under control. If disruptive behaviors can be identified and defined, intervention strategies from applied behavioral analysis can be used to control the disruptions (see Chapter 5 for the application of these principles).

8. Expect aggressive behavior during specific periods. Depending on specific conditions, aggressive and disruptive behaviors may fluctuate. It is important that trends of the strength and frequency of the aggressive or disruptive behavior be monitored and linked with specific behavioral techniques and strategies.

9. Do not stress elimination of neurotic behavior but build positive behavior.[8] It may be difficult to build positive behavior and extinguish neurotic behavior at the same time. Careful strategies must be developed to ensure that attempts are not made to bring too much behavior under control at one time. Eventually, neurotic behavior can be reduced within the context of a carefully thought out plan and strategies.

It is recognized that the emotionally disturbed population is an extremely heterogeneous group that possesses varying traits. Therefore the principles mentioned above are obviously not applicable to all emotionally disturbed children. They are to serve only as a guide to the implementation of programs of physical education for the emotionally disturbed.

Successful Activities for Emotionally Disturbed Students

The physical and motor capabilities of emotionally disturbed individuals and their ability to adapt to instructional procedures vary widely. For this reason it is difficult to suggest specific activities that will benefit all emotionally disturbed students. However, children with emotional disturbances may demonstrate similar problems with learning that can be alleviated through the application of behavioral strategies, and as a result, benefit physical activity performance. The very nature of physical activities must be carefully studied to determine which behavioral control strategies can be most beneficial. Some general suggestions that may assist with the selection and implementation of activities include the following:

1. Games of social interaction should be at the social level and skill level of the emotionally disturbed child. However, if support systems for integrating students into the activity are used, then the individual's social abilities can be a little below the level normally expected for participation.
2. There should be immediate feedback provided either intrinsically from the task or extrinsically by the instructor or peers. Positive reinforcement tends to motivate the emotionally disturbed student to participate in tasks more readily. The more attention that is provided to a successful outcome of a task, the more apt the behavior is to be controlled. Tasks that provide intrinsic, immediate knowledge of results as to the correctness of the task should be provided (i.e., hitting a ball, catching a ball, hitting a target with a ball).
3. Activities selected for the emotionally disturbed learner must be at the present level of performance. Select activities that can be modified so the demands of the task will match the ability level of the learner.
4. The activity should be individualized according to the assessed needs of the child. In the event there is little opportunity for individualized instruction, you should teach at the level that will reach all of the students in the group even though using this "common denominator" approach may be detrimental to some students (e.g., below the level that would benefit them most).
5. Peer tutors provide the support system for emotionally disturbed students, and successful activities are often those that can be easily learned by these tutors. Use of peer tutors is one of the best ways to really individualize physical education programs to benefit the physical and social development of emotionally disturbed students.
6. Use activity and a variety of games that will accommodate the students' different physical, social, and emotional developmental levels. The short attention span of these children makes it necessary to have several games on hand so that their interest can be recaptured when an initial activity is no longer productive. Novelty in activities is a great aid in holding attention.
7. Work with motor skills and games that allow some degree of success.[31] Every satisfying experience makes for decreased anxiety and increased confidence.
8. Know when to encourage a child to approach, explore, and try a new activity or experience. A new experience is often met with resistance. In such instances it is wise to build guarantees of success into the new experience. Subsequent involvement becomes much easier for the emotionally disturbed child. The child who witnesses peers participating successfully in activities sometimes receives impetus to participate with them.
9. Discourage stereotyped play activities that develop rigid behavioral patterns. Emotionally disturbed children often tend to respond to the same objects or activities day after day. After a skill has been mastered, it may deter initiation of other activities.
10. Use activities that provide immediate consequences of the child's performance. The child should receive some feedback as to the limit of capability and the degree of success that was achieved on the task.

Teaching Strategies

Physical activity in the form of play and dance has traditionally been used by mental health specialists both as a tool in diagnosis and as therapy for emotionally disturbed persons. The qualitative aspects of play and the development of motor skills in disturbed persons have not always received a great deal of attention in the past. However, educators of emotionally disturbed children now recognize that play is not an intermittent freedom from the discipline of academic tasks but is of educational value.

There is a qualitative aspect to the nature of physical activity in play that can contribute to the well-being of disturbed children. Constructive play of a higher order implies the socialization of children. Usually, emotionally disturbed children must be taught how to play and enjoy physical activity. Once constructive play is learned, it provides a medium through which the children may experiment with self-control and with the control of the environment. Play also offers opportunity for social learning and tension release. Because emotionally disturbed children strain the educational program, they are often left out of the extracurricular and intramural activities of a regular school. This is in reverse order of their basic needs for experience in community living.

To enable successful classroom participation of the emotionally disturbed student, a primary consideration is that of managing behavior during instruction. To manage behavior efficiently, it is often necessary to highly structure environments. Such structure, in and of itself, may control hyperactive and aggressive behaviors. When emotionally disturbed children are "on task," disruptive behavior is incompatible with the activity. However, when emotionally disturbed children are not performing tasks, there is opportunity for behavior that may disrupt instruction.

The management of a classroom can be improved if there are designated spots on the floor or specific locations where the children are to be when they are not performing a learning task. Such an arrangement enables greater behavior control during the slack times when the occurrence of disruptive behavior is probable. Pupils may be placed so that they are spread over an area or are close together.

Signals that indicate the beginning and end of activity and movement of the children from one part of the play area to another part increase the structure of the play environment. The characteristics of signals for providing structure to the instructional environment are as follows:

1. The command signals should be short and concise.
2. The signals should be no stronger than needed to elicit the response.
3. Signals may be needed to secure attention (such commands as "listen" and "look" may be needed to secure the attention of the more severely emotionally disturbed persons).
4. Feedback signals about task mastery are needed to provide information to the learner; through the use of these signals, the teacher should indicate to the student the level of success he or she is experiencing.

Undesirable behavior can sometimes be reduced through the use of time out from reinforcement, which involves taking away reinforcement opportunities. This approach is used when some feature of the instructional environment is reinforcing (appealing) to the student. There is a considerable difference between time out from reinforcement and removal from an instructional setting solely for the purpose of enabling scheduled activity to continue without interruption. Using a time out from reinforcement usually involves restricting the environment in which learning occurs. Examples of time-out procedures ranging from the least restrictive to the most restrictive are as follows:

1. Time the individual out from reinforcement but permit participation in activity. This form of time out from reinforcement is, however, only effective if the individual is responsive to the reinforcements associated with the activity (e.g., interacting with friends, being aggressive). If the task itself (e.g, playing football, softball, basketball) is reinforcing, this form of time out may not be effective.
2. A more restrictive type of time out from reinforcement would be removing the student from the game for very brief periods. When removal is used, the student should be able to observe and acquire information through observing peers as the game unfolds. Under these conditions, there may still be a beneficial educational outcome.
3. More severe forms of restrictiveness in timing an individual out from reinforcement would be taking the individual farther away from the activity without total separation from one's peers.
4. The most severe form of time out involves actual removal from the instructional setting for sequentially longer periods.

Analytical techniques for applying tentative principles of behavior to improve behavior are well understood and widely practiced. The application of applied behavioral analysis requires objective definition of the behavior to be changed, an intervention procedure, and a design or schedule to follow during the intervention. Treatment decisions are based on observable behavior that is to be changed, not on medical data.

Conscious decision making

Traditional training of physical education teachers to work with disabled populations requires them to link basic theory with management of behavior. However, there are few research data in the literature that indicate teachers can make the thoughtful transition from theory to practice. Rather, it is suggested that in

FIGURE 10-4. A child develops eye-hand coordination skills in a level-up activity. (Courtesy Dallas Independent School District.)

most cases it is only through the use of modeling, demonstrations, and being taught techniques based on research that teachers of physical education will learn to effectively change the behavior of disabled students in their own classrooms.[27]

There is a move toward training teachers of special populations to deal with behavioral problems through conscious decision making.[12] To promote conscious decision making it is necessary that teachers in training be taught to examine ever-changing sets of environmental conditions before making decisions for specific individuals. These decisions must be based on the changing developmental capabilities and trends of excessive behavior demonstrated by the emotionally disturbed student. The process of changing behavior is ongoing and dynamic; therefore pat answers and solutions will not be effective in the long run. Aspiring teachers must be taught to analyze learning environments and student reactions so that the solution they select is appropriate to the situation confronting them. The basic techniques and procedures for applying behavioral management principles for all types of students appear in Chapter 5.

Intervention

Students with behavior problems usually need to be taught to "own" their behavior. That is, they need to learn to discriminate between unacceptable and acceptable behaviors. In the well-managed educational environment the behaviors that will be permitted and those that are inappropriate are clear and available.[25] That is, the teacher and, when appropriate, the students determine what the rules of conduct will be and the rules are posted where everyone can see them. Examples of rules appropriate for a pysical education setting include:

☐ No swearing
☐ Keep hands to yourself
☐ Take your turn when it is your turn
☐ No talking while the teacher is talking
☐ Follow the rules of the sport
☐ No arguing with the official
☐ Take care of the equipment
☐ Pay attention when being given instructions
☐ No running in the shower
☐ Arrive before the roll is taken
☐ Participate in all class activities unless excused by the teacher
☐ Promptly report any injuries to the teacher

The rules of conduct and consequences for not following these rules should be explained at the beginning of each semester, and any time during the year a new student enters the class. They should be kept posted in a clear place in the gymnasium.

Developing Socialization Skills

There are specific techniques and procedures that physical education teachers can use to develop socialization skills of the emotionally disturbed. Severely emotionally disturbed persons may have impaired ability to relate to persons and may choose, instead, to relate to inanimate objects. To facilitate interpersonal relationships during play, another person can be paired with the inanimate object that is the focus of the emotionally disturbed pupil's attention. In some cases there may be positive transfer from the inanimate object to the person paired with the object. Such a transfer could constitute the beginning of an interpersonal contact for the emotionally disturbed person.

It should also be noted that team membership in sports may place social controls on behavior to such an extent that unsocialized behavior is curbed. However, the composition of the membership of the team is important. When emotionally disturbed children are grouped together, it is extremely difficult to predict group behavior. In fact, it is not uncommon to see that emotionally disturbed children who have been grouped together contribute to one another's problems as they infect one another with inappropriate behavior.[18]

If emotionally disturbed children are placed in groups of persons with emotional maturity, group behavior becomes more predictable, especially if the students without disabilities are sensitive regarding accommodation of the emotionally disturbed students in the play environment. Also, good role models may be of value for social development of the emotionally disturbed children. Thus social development through games for disturbed children can best be accomplished in play with their nondisabled peers where planned strategies between the teacher and nondisabled peers occurs. It is important to foster sport skill development and basic levels of social skills because they are prerequisites for play in organized sport activity.

Development of Self-concept

Emotionally disturbed persons often possess poor self-concepts. This may be due to previous failure on physical education tasks, which creates anxiety. Levels of anxiety and failure can be lessened through individualization of instruction and provision of activity in small steps that slightly extend (shape) present levels of performance (see Chapter 5). Through this procedure, failure can be controlled and learning measured. Such successful experiences may alleviate anxiety and improve the self-concept.

Decisions for Controlling Behavioral Disorders

To control excessive behavior of emotionally disturbed students, adapted physical education teachers must make decisions based on many factors. Commercial materials and teacher training approaches that deemphasize the decision-making processes of the teacher have been developed. Examples include computerized models for making curriculum decisions for disabled students, lists of published interventions, all-inclusive packages that classify behaviors with descriptive deficits paired with interventions, and even individualized physical education programs. In the last analysis, a specific teacher needs to make a specific decision based on the behavior of a specific learner in a specific environment performing a specific task at a specific time. Thus the all-inclusive packages and other such predetermined approaches leave a great deal to be desired. Dependence of teachers on packages and general suggestions may be detrimental to the development of generalized principles involved in the decision-making process that all teachers must follow.

There are at least two decisions that need to be made to control excessive inappropriate behavior of emotionally disturbed students. These decisions are based on (1) assessment as to whether intervention is appropriate and (2) strategies for controlling disruptive and excessive behavior if a decision is made to intervene.

Appropriateness of the need to intervene

There are several considerations that must be taken into account before a decision is made to develop a strategy to control the disruptive or excessive behavior of an emotionally disturbed student. Some of the questions that need to be answered before making such a decision are as follows:

1. Is the excessive behavior a danger to other students in the class?
2. Is the excessive behavior a danger to the student (i.e., does the student engage in self-abusive behavior or risk taking that may lead to injury)?
3. Has the problem existed over a period of time? There often is a remission of many behaviors without an intervention.
4. Is the behavior such that it is acceptable in the community? If the behavior is unacceptable, its existence may stigmatize the individual and interfere with social development.
5. Would learning of instructional behaviors be improved if the excessive behaviors were reduced? Many excessive behaviors do not interfere with the learning of curriculum objectives.
6. Is the excessive behavior a concern to the teacher and other personnel who interact with the child?
7. Would the intervention be in the child's best interest? The intervention should not be a deterrent to the acquisition of goals and objectives of the individual physical education program.

Instructional strategy decision making

Once the decision has been made to intervene with a program to control excessive behavior, there are at least four components that should be considered: (1)

the type of reinforcement procedures to be used, (2) whether the environment needs to be modified, (3) curriculum modifications that need to be made, and (4) the appropriate punishment procedures to be used.

Reinforcement procedures

Reinforcement procedures have been described in Chapter 5. In review, they involve collecting baseline data on the problem, determining an appropriate reinforcer to use, and then subsequently reassessing to make judgments as to whether the reinforcers are effective. Reinforcement procedures that deal specifically with excessive behavior may involve the treatment of the target behavior with differential reinforcement of others. If the individual is reinforced by the situation that controls the excessive behavior, then different treatments with lower-density reinforcers may be required to gain control over the excessive behavior.

Environmental procedures

Decisions must be made on environmental (ecological) components that relate to excessive behavior. Some of the components of the environment that need to be controlled are (1) an increase or decrease in the space available to perform activiites; (2) an increase in the number and type of activities, materials, and equipment; and (3) regulation of light and noise and other students in the immediate vicinity of instructional activity. Decisions need to be made as to how each of these components effect the behavior of the individual.

Curriculum procedures

Controlling excessive behavior and achieving predetermined instructional objectives at the same time may not be possible. It is desirable to identify skills that can be taught while behavior is being brought under control. Frequently activities that provide high-density reinforcement of the target behavior will override the excessive behavior. Well-planned curricula include tasks of short duration and enjoyable activities that provide high-density reinforcement.

Punishment procedures

Punishment techniques are used when positive reinforcement techniques fail. Considerations for the selection of punishment techniques must be based on principles of least obtrusiveness to the child (for further detail see Chapter 5).

SUMMARY

Emotionally disturbed children may exhibit unsatisfactory relationships with teachers and peers, inappropri-

ate types of behavior, or a pervasive mood of depression, or may even develop physical symptoms or fears associated with school problems. These characteristics result in inability to learn.

Emotional disturbance may be viewed on a continuum of demonstrated behavior from normal to abnormal and socially unacceptable, where the pupil is a danger to himself or herself and others.

The program objectives for emotionally disturbed children are similar to those for nondisabled children. They can benefit equally with nondisabled peers in sport activities and physical activities designed to meet their interests and needs.

The central problem that needs to be addressed by physical educators working with emotionally disturbed persons is management of abnormal behavior in the classroom. There are several techniques and procedures that can be used to manage fear, withdrawal, aggressiveness, and hyperactivity. Among these are accepted principles of classroom management, desensitization to alleviate fears, and shaping with a success/failure ratio of 90% to 10%, which may build self-concept and counter withdrawal from activity caused by previous failure.

There are appropriate principles for selection of activities that may enable greater success of emotionally disturbed students in the physical education program. Appropriate selection of activities may decrease excessive behaviors that interfere with learning. When a student engages in excessive behavior, a process should be undertaken to control the behavior so it does not interfere with the goals and objectives in the individual physical education program.

REVIEW QUESTIONS

1. What are some causes of emotional disturbance?
2. What are the personal-social and physical-motor characteristics of the emotionally disturbed?
3. What are some behavioral patterns of children that may indicate the severity of emotional disturbance?
4. When is it important to identify persons who are emotionally disturbed?
5. What are some characteristics of a physical education teacher of emotionally disturbed students?
6. What are some benefits of sport for emotionally disturbed students?
7. What are the objectives of a physical education program for persons with emotional disturbances?
8. What are some teaching principles for instructing the emotionally disturbed students?
9. What are some principles for selecting activities for emotionally disturbed students that may facilitate learning in physical education?

10. What decisions should be made by the adapted physical education teacher to control excessive behavior?

STUDENT ACTIVITIES

1. Observe a physical education teacher who conducts programs for students with emotional disturbances. Describe the following:
    a. The nature of the class (special or integrated class).
    b. The manner of instruction (individual, small groups, or as a total class).
    c. The ways in which the physical and motor needs were met.
    d. Strategies the teacher employed during instruction.
    e. Disruptive pupil behaviors.
2. There are several organizations designed to serve emotionally disturbed persons. Identify the local chapters of such groups in your area. Contact a local or national office of such an organization. Inquire about the services they render for specific clientele.
3. Read two articles that discuss techniques for working with students with emotional disturbances. The *Journal of Applied Behavioral Analysis* and *Behavioral Disorders and Behavior Therapy* are journals in which such articles often appear. In addition, articles about physical education for students with emotional disturbances can be found in the *Adapted Physical Activity Quarterly* and *Palaestra: The Forum of Sport, Physical Education and Recreation for the Disabled.* Describe how these techniques may be applied to a physical education program with children who have emotional disturbances.
4. Talk with teachers or other professionals from different schools about ways to improve social acceptance of emotionally disturbed children in special and integrated classes. Indicate their suggestions and methods they have tried in the past that have worked. Indicate the activities they provide for parents, classroom teachers, students, and others.
5. Interview an adult person with mental health problems. Try to determine the following:
    a. The nature of the person's physical education program
    b. Whether the person was taught in an integrated setting
    c. The person's perception of how teachers and peers view him or her
6. Interview a person from psychological services or a school counselor. Determine the relationship of responsibilities between the services provided by this person and a physical education teacher.
7. Visit a recreational facility where emotionally disturbed individuals participate. Conduct a case study on one or two individuals to determine their recreational play capability and limitations.

REFERENCES

1. American Psychiatric Association: *Diagnostic and statistical manual DSM III-R, ed 4,* Washington, DC, 1987.
2. Amen MG, Singh NN: *Psychopharmacology of developmental disabilities,* New York, 1988, Springer-Verlag.
3. Briggs R et al: *A model for evaluating pychoactive medication with mentally retarded persons.* In Mulick J, Mallany B, editors: *Transition in mental retardation: advocacy, technology and science,* Norwood, NJ, 1985, Ablex Publishers.
4. Brooks AD: The right to refuse antipsychotic medication: law and policy, 1987, *Rutgers Law Rev* 39:339-376, 1987.
5. Buhler C, Smitter F, Richardson S: *What is a problem?* In Long HJ, editor: *Conflict in the classroom,* Belmont, Calif, 1965, Wadsworth Publishing.
6. Center DB: *Curriculum and teaching strategies for students with behavioral disorders,* Englewood Cliffs NJ, 1989, Prentice Hall.
7. Chandler M, Gualtieri CT, Fahs JJ: *Other psychotropic drugs: stimulants, antidepressants, anxiolytics, and lithium carbonate.* In Amen MG, Singh NN, editors: *Psychopharmacology of developmental disabilities,* New York, 1988, Springer-Verlag.
8. Cratty BJ: *Adapted physical education for handicapped children and youth,* Denver, 1980, Love Publishing.
9. Craven RS, Ferdinand TM: *Juvenile delinquency, ed 3,* New York, 1975, Harper & Row, Publishers.
10. Drug Enforcement Administration: In the matter of methylphenidate production quotas-1986, decision of the administrative Law Judge, Docket No. 86-52, 1987, p 29.
11. Dunn JM, Fait H: *Special physical education,* Dubuque, Iowa, 1989, Wm C Brown Group.
12. Evans IM, Meyer PL: *An educative approach to behavioral problems—a practical decision model for intervention with severely handicapped learners,* Baltimore, 1985, Paul H Brookes Publishing.
13. Famularo R, Fenton T: Effect of methyphenidate on school grades in children with attention deficit disorder without hyperactivity: a preliminary report, 1987, *J Clin Psychiatry* 48:112-114.
14. French RW, Jansma P: *Special physical education,* Columbus, Ohio, 1982, Charles E Merrill Publishing.
15. Hardman ML, Drew CJ, Egan MW: *Human exceptionality,* Boston, 1987, Allyn & Bacon.
16. Heward WL, Orlansky MD: *Exceptional children,* Columbus, Ohio, 1988, Charles E Merrill Publishing.
17. Hobbs N: *How the Re-ED plan developed.* In Long HJ, editor: *Conflict in the classroom,* Belmont, Calif, 1965, Wadsworth Publishing.
18. Kalakian LH, Eichstaedt CB: *Developmental/adapted physical education,* Minneapolis, 1982, Burgess Publishing Co.
19. Kauffman JN: *Characteristics of behavior disorders of children and youth, ed 4,* Columbus, Ohio, 1989, Charles E Merrill Publishing.
20. Klein C: A summary of remarks at the House-Senate education committee hearing, Senator Reibman, chairperson, Senate Bill 1214, Harrisburg, Pa, 1978.
21. Langone J: *Teaching students with mild and moderate learning problems,* Boston, 1990, Allyn & Bacon.

22. Lewis MH, Mailman RB: *Psychotropic drug blood levels: measurement and relation to behavioral outcomes in mentally retarded persons.* In Amen MG, Singh NN, editors: *Psychopharmacology of developmental disabilities,* New York, 1988, Springer-Verlag.

23. McGinnis E et al: *Skill streaming the elementary school child: a guide for teaching pro-social skills,* Champaign, Ill, 1984, Research Press.

24. Meyen EL: *Exceptional children and youth,* Denver, 1978, Love Publishing.

25. Morgan SR, Reinhart JA: *Interventions for students with emotional disorders,* Austin, 1990, PRO-ED.

26. Morse WC: The helping teacher/crisis teacher concept, *Focus Except Child* 8:1-11, 1976.

27. Paine SC, Belamy GT, Wilcox B: *Human services that work,* Baltimore, 1984, Paul H Brookes Publishing.

28. Safer DJ, Krager JM: A survey of medication treatment for hyperactive inattentive students, *JAMA* 260:2256-2258, 1988.

29. Sailor W, Wilcox B, Brown L: *Methods of instruction for severely handicapped students,* Baltimore, 1985, Paul H Brookes Publishing.

30. Schroeder SR: *Neuroleptic medications for persons with developmental disabilities.* In Amen MG, Singh NN, editors: *Psychopharmacology of developmental disabilities,* New York, 1988, Springer-Verlag.

31. Seaman JA, DePauw KP: *The new adapted physical education,* Palo Alto, Calif, 1989, Mayfield Publishing.

32. Sherrill C: *Adapted physical education and recreation, ed 3,* Dubuque, Iowa, 1985, Wm C Brown Group.

33. Smith CR: Identification of handicapped children and youth: a state agency perspective on behavior disorders, *Remedial Spec Educ* 6:34-41, 1985.

34. Sokol MS, Campbell M: *Novel psychoactive agents in the treatment of developmental disorders.* In Amen MG, Singh NN, editors: *Psychopharmacology of developmental disabilities,* New York, 1988, Springer-Verlag.

35. US Department of Education: *Thirteenth annual report to Congress on the implementation of the Individuals with Disabilities Education Act,* Washington, DC, 1991.

36. US Department of Health, Education, and Welfare: Regulations for the Education for All Handicapped Children Act of 1975, *Fed Reg,* vol 4, Aug 23, 1977.

37. Werry JS: *Conclusions.* In Amen MG, Singh NN, editors: *Psychopharmacology of developmental disabilities,* New York, 1988, Springer-Verlag.

SUGGESTED READINGS

Evans IM, Meyer LH: *An educative approach to behavior problems,* Baltimore, 1985, Paul H Brookes Publishing.

Kauffman JM: *Characteristics of children and youth behavior disorders, ed 4,* Columbus, Ohio, 1989, Charles E Merrill Publishing.

Sailor W, Wilcox B, Brown L: *Methods of instruction for severely handicapped students,* Baltimore, 1984, Paul H Brookes Publishing.

Courtesy Iron Horse Productions, Inc.

OBJECTIVES

Describe a variety of physical disabilities.

List which physical activities are recommended for individuals with specific types of disabilities.

Explain variations of physical characteristics among persons with neurological and orthopedic disabilities.

Adapt activity to maximize participation in sports and games.

List sports organizations that serve individuals with neurological and orthopedic disabilities in the community.

Neurologically and Orthopedically Disabling Conditions

There are many different types of neurologically and orthopedically disabling conditions. Afflictions can occur at more than 500 anatomical sites. Each person who has a disabling condition has different physical and motor capabilities.

223

Thus each person must be treated in such a manner that his or her unique educational needs are met. In this chapter we suggest a procedure to accomplish this task. The goals of this procedure are to (1) identify the specific clinical condition of the child, (2) determine which activities are contraindicated based on medical recommendations, (3) determine functional motor skills needed, (4) determine the activities that will assist the development of the desired motor skills, and (5) determine aids and devices that will enable the child to secure an education in the most normal environment.

There are two broad aspects of the physical education program. In one portion of the program the student engages in activity to develop skills and abilities. In the other portion the student expresses the skills attained through instructions in the playing of games. A student may develop individual skills during play, but because of the lack of control of specific conditions, skill acquisition may be due to chance. The primary values of playing a game are to learn rules and strategies and to benefit from the social interaction with teammates.

Accommodations must be made for individuals with physical disabilities so they may participate in games and sports. It is desirable to include a program of modified games and sports for these students for many reasons:

1. Students with disabilities need activities that have carryover value. They may continue exercise programs in the future, but they also need training in sports and games that have recreational potential that will be useful to them in later life.
2. Modified sports have therapeutic value if they are carefully structured for the students.
3. Modified sports and games should help physically disabled persons learn to handle their bodies under a variety of circumstances.
4. There are recreational values in games and sport activities for students who are facing the dual problem of getting a good education and overcoming a disability.
5. A certain amount of emotional release takes place during play, and this is important to students who are physically challenged.
6. The modified sports program, regardless of the frequency with which it is provided, tends to relieve the boredom of a regular exercise program. No matter how carefully a special exercise program is planned, it is difficult to maintain a high

level of interest if the students participate in this kind of activity on a daily basis.

Included in this chapter are definitions and descriptions of specific types of neurologically and orthopedically handicapping conditions, types of medical treatment used for each condition, and suggestions for physical activity programs that will benefit persons with specific conditions.

DEFINITION AND SCOPE

There are several specific physically disabling conditions that are the result of neurological or orthopedic conditions. Neurological disabilities are chronic debilitating conditions that result from impairments of the central nervous system. Neurological disabilities discussed in this chapter include cerebral palsy, muscular dystropy, multiple sclerosis, epilepsy, Parkinson's disease, amyotrophic lateral sclerosis, and Bell's palsy. By federal definition the term *orthopedic impairment* means a severe orthopedic impairment that adversely affects a child's educational performance. The term includes impairments such as arthritis, hip disorders, coxa plana, coxa vara, coxa valga, Osgood-Schlatter condition, clubfoot, spina bifida, brittle bone disease, curved joints, osteomyelitis, poliomyelitis, spinal cord injuries, and amputations.

Disabilities affect the use of the body as a result of deficiencies of the nerves, muscles, bones, and/or joints. The three main sources of disabilities are neurological impairments, musculoskeletal conditions, and trauma. Musculoskeletal conditions are so diverse in character that individual programming is required for persons with such conditions. However, some of the conditions focus on a specific part of the anatomy and have similar characteristics, which permits broad recommendations to be made for pairing appropriate types of activity with conditions.

CONTINUUM OF PHYSICAL DISABILITY

The effects of physical disability on the performance of physical education tasks are considerable. Thus persons with physical disabilities have diverse abilities to perform motor tasks.

INCIDENCE

Federal agencies report that 1% of school-aged children are physically disabled.[52] About half of the physically disabled children have cerebral palsy or other crippling conditions. The other half have chronic health problems or other diseases. An increase in physical disabilities during the recent decades has been reported by some health agencies.[58] This may be because many severely and profoundly disabled individuals in the past would not have survived or would not have been kept alive.[55]

CAUSES

There are two principal causes of neurological and orthopedic disabilities—congenital defects, in which children are born with a disability, and trauma, which damages muscles, ligaments, tendons, or the nervous system and results in physical impairment.

TESTING FOR IDENTIFICATION

Both physicians and physical educators test children to determine degree of impairment. The physician may use numerous tests to determine the specific neurological, physiological, and anatomical aspects of the condition. Medical techniques such as electroencephalography, electromyography, x-ray examination, and reflex testing, as well as other procedures, can be used.

The physical educator, on the other hand, assesses the child's performance on the specific motor tasks inherent in the physical education curriculum. A mild orthopedic disability may be the reason for poor performance. Some physical disabilities are obvious because the child cannot participate in physical tasks that are part of an unrestricted program.

NEUROLOGICAL DISORDERS

CEREBRAL PALSY

Cerebral palsy is a condition rather than a disease. The term *cerebral palsy* is used to denote conditions that stem from brain injury, including a number of types of neuromuscular disabilities characterized by disturbances of voluntary motor function. It is the result of a permanent brain injury and is therefore a lifelong condition.[25]

Statistical estimates indicate that approximately 1 in 14,000 births in the United States results in severe brain injury. Conditions that give rise to these disorders may be operative during the prenatal, natal, or postnatal period. Authorities believe that approximately 30% of the cases are due to prenatal causes, 60% to natal causes, and the remaining 10% to postnatal causes. Prenatal causes include maternal infection such as rubella, syphilis, and toxoplasmosis; metabolic malfunction; toxemia; diabetes; placental abnormalities such as fetal anoxia; and excessive radiation.

Certain groups of infants including those with prolonged birth anoxia, very low birthweight, and abnor-

mal neurological symptoms are possible candidates for cerebral palsy.[10] Many children with cerebral plasy possess poor postural adjustment. As a result, simple gross motor movements (e.g., kicking, throwing, and jumping) are difficult to perform effectively.[57]

Characteristics and Types

The degree of motor impairment of children with cerebral palsy may range from serious physical disability to little physical disability.

Since the extent of the brain damage that results in neuromotor dysfunction varies greatly, diagnosis is related to the amount of dysfunction and associated motor involvement. Severe brain injury may be evident shortly after birth. However, cases of children with cerebral palsy who have slight brain damage and little motor impairment may be difficult to diagnose. In the milder cases developmental lag in the motor and intellectual tasks required to meet environmental demands may not be detected until the children are 3 or 4 years old. As a rule, the clinical signs and symptoms of cerebral palsy reach maximum severity when the children reach the age of 2 to 4 years.

Individuals with cerebral palsy usually demonstrate persistence of primitive reflexes and frequently are slow to develop equilibrium (postural) reflexes. It is difficult for most performers to execute simple gross motor movements effectively unless appropriate postural adjustments occur to support such movements[57] and the individual is given additional time to plan and execute the movements.

Some of the secondary impairments that may accompany cerebral palsy are mental retardation, hearing and vision loss, emotional disturbance, hyperactivity, learning disabilities, loss of perceptual ability, and inability to make psychological adjustments. Healy[25] reports that 60% of all children with cerebral palsy have seizures.

There are differences in kinesthetic properties of individuals with and without cerebral palsy and among those with different types/severities of cerebral palsy. When Opila-Lehman, Short, and Trombly[43] compared children with quadriplegic cerebral palsy with nondisabled children, the children with cerebral palsy had more absolute errors on a perceptual motor task than the nondisabled group. In addition, those with spastic cerebral palsy had significantly more absolute errors than did those with athetoid cerebral palsy.

Various authors agree that more than 50% of children with cerebral palsy have oculomotor defects. In other words, children with brain injury often have dif-

FIGURE 11-1. Ocean Escapes, a pioneer in aqua therapy for wheelchair-bound individuals, offers weightlessness through scuba diving to individuals who, on land, are trapped by gravity. (Courtesy Ocean Escapes.)

ficulty in coordinating their eye movements. The implications of this for physical activities that involve a great deal of oculomotor tracking of projectiles point to a need for programs that train for ocular control.

Emotional disturbances constitute another concomitant to cerebral palsy. Children with cerebral palsy are often afflicted with significant impairment that may deprive them of opportunities for ordinary social experience and thus restrict normal social maturation. An interrelated maldevelopment in the physical and social spheres may be retarded emotional development. The basic needs of the child with cerebral palsy—recognition, esteem, and independence—all require fulfillment and are an integral part of the experiences of childhood.

Hard signs of neuromotor disorders

The different clinical types of cerebral dysfunction involve various obvious motor patterns, commonly known as hard signs. There are six clinical classifications—spasticity, athetosis, rigidity, ataxia, tremor, and atonia. Of persons with cerebral palsy, 50% are clinically classified as spastic, 25% as athetoid, and 13% as rigid; the remaining 12% are divided among ataxic, atonic, tremulous, and mixed and undiagnosed cerebral palsy conditions.

Spasticity. Muscular spasticity is the most prevalent type of hard sign among persons with cerebral palsy. One characteristic of spasticity is that muscle contractures that restrict muscular movement give the appearance of stiffness to affected limbs. This makes muscle movement jerky and uncertain. Spastic children have exaggerated stretch reflexes that cause them to respond to rapid passive stimulation with vigorous muscle contractions. Tendon reflexes are also hyperactive in the involved part. When the spastic condition involves the lower extremities, the legs may be rotated inward and flexed at the hips, knees may be flexed, and a contracted gastrocnemius muscle holds the heel off the ground. Lower leg deficiency contributes to a scissors gait that is common among persons with this type of cerebral palsy. When the upper extremities are involved, the characteristic forms of physical deviation in persons with spastic cerebral palsy include flexion at the elbows, forearm pronation, and wrist and finger flexion. Spasticity is most common in the antigravity muscles of the body. Contractures are more common in children with spastic cerebral palsy than in children with any of the other types of cerebral palsy. In the event contractures are not remedied or addressed, permanent contractures may result. Consequently, good posture is extremely difficult to maintain. Because of poor balance among reciprocal muscle groups, innervation of muscles for functional motor patterns is often difficult. Mental impairment is associated with spasticity more than with any other clinical type of cerebral palsy, so the incidence of mental retardation among this group is high.

Athetosis. Athetosis is the second most prevalent clinical type of severe cerebral palsy. The distinguishing characteristic of the athetoid individual is recognizable incoordinate movements of voluntary muscles. These movements take the form of wormlike motions that involve the trunk, arms, legs, or tongue or muscle twitches of the face. The unrhythmical, uncontrollable, involuntary movements seem to increase with voluntary motion and emotional or environmental stimuli. Because of the athetoid individual's inability to control muscles and the presence of primitive reflexes, posture is unpredictable and poses a problem. Impairment in the muscular control of hands, speech, and swallowing often accompanies athetosis.

Rigidity. A central feature of the rigid type of cerebral palsy is the functional incoordination of reciprocal muscle groups. There is great resistance to slow motion, and the stretch reflex is impaired. Mental retardation often accompanies this clinical type of cerebral palsy.

Ataxia. A primary characteristic of the ataxic type of cerebral palsy is a disturbance of equilibrium, which impairs the ability to maintain balance. This impairment in balance becomes evident in the walking gait. The gait of the person with ataxic cerebral palsy is unstable, which causes weaving about during locomotion. Standing is often a problem. Kinesthetic awareness seems to be lacking in the individual with ataxia. Also, muscle tone and the ability to locate objects in three-dimensional space are poor in persons with ataxic cerebral palsy.

Tremor. Tremor is evidenced by a rhythmic movement that is usually caused by alternating contractions between flexor and extensor muscles. Tremors appear as uncontrollable pendular movements.

Atonia (flaccidity). Atonia is characterized by a lack of muscle tone. The muscles of the atonic person are often so weak that the activities of daily living are severely hampered. Indeed, the child with atonia may be unable to sit without assistance, unable to lift the hands, and/or to hold the head in alignment.

Alternate systems

Another means of classifying persons with cerebral palsy concerns the limbs that are affected. The classifications are as follows:

□ *Paraplegia:* Legs only
□ *Diplegia:* Legs mainly, arms slightly
□ *Quadriplegia:* All four extremities
□ *Hemiplegia:* One half of the body or the limbs on one side of the body
□ *Triplegia:* Both legs and one arm, or both arms and one leg
□ *Monoplegia:* One extremity

A third way in which individuals with cerebral palsy are classified is based on the anatomical part that contributes to the palsy. There are three primary classifications:

□ *Pyramidal cerebral palsy,* usually characterized by spasticity
□ *Extrapyramidal* or *basonuclear cerebral palsy,* characterized by athetosis, tremors, and rigidity
□ *Cerebellar cerebral palsy,* characterized by ataxia

Medical Treatment

Increasingly the medical community and society at large have come to understand that the focus of medical intervention should be on the prevention of disabilities through appropriate prenatal care and early intervention with at-risk children. The four procedures prevalent in medical treatment of individuals with existing physical disabilities are bracing, drug therapy, operation, and rehabilitation. Braces are important as an aid in teaching joint function as well as in assisting in the locomotion of patients who are severely disabled. Another use for bracing is the prevention of deforming contractures. Drug administration usually serves two functions—aiding in relaxation of muscle groups when neuromuscular exercise therapy is attempted, and controlling epileptic seizures through the use of anticonvulsant drugs.

There are various opinions as to the value of orthopedic surgery for persons with cerebral palsy. Certain types of operative procedures have met with considerable success, especially with particular types of cerebral palsy. The physical growth of children affects the efficiency of muscle and tendon surgery; however, surgical operation, for the most part, is not curative but rather assists the functional activities of daily living. Tenotomy (tendon cutting) of the hip adductor and hamstring muscles seems to be the most valuable surgical procedure for adults with cerebral palsy.

Physical Activity Program

There is no treatment for the repair of a damaged brain. However, the portion of the nervous system that remains intact can be made functional through a well-managed training program. Intervention by the physical educator and other personnel is needed to build

FIGURE 11-2. Celebrating the victory. (Courtesy Texas Special Olympics.)

functional developmental motor patterns with the operative parts of the body. Each child should be evaluated closely, and programs that foster those functional abilities should be formulated. Developmental programs should be constructed to correct deficiencies that respond to treatment. The specific child should be considered when determining the exercise regimen. Because of their numerous involuntary muscular activities, children with athetosis are much more active than children with spasticity, ataxia, and rigidity, who are inhibited regarding physical activity.

There is growing evidence that some of the perceptual characteristics can be improved through training. Perceptual training techniques are developed primarily through visuomotor and sensorimotor training programs. The aspects of such a program include reducing primitive reflex involvement, developing locomotor patterns, balancing, performing actively to rhythm, developing ocular control, and using devices that detect form perception. All of these perceptual activities are inherent in most physical education programs. However, the quality of physical education programs could be improved by implementation of programs of activities that might enhance these particular perceptual characteristics.

The individual education program (IEP) is designed to meet the unique needs of each child. Therefore special physical education and related services include many types of physical activity. Some of the therapeutic activities and techniques include the following:

1. Muscle stretching to relieve muscle contractures, prevent deformities, and permit fuller range of purposeful motion
2. Gravity exercises that involve lifting the weight of the body or body part against gravity
3. Muscle awareness exercises to control specific muscles or muscle groups
4. Neuromuscular reeducation exercises that are performed through the muscles' current range to stimulate the proprioceptors and return the muscles to greater functional use
5. Reciprocal exercises to stimulate and strengthen the action of the protagonist
6. Tonic exercises to prevent atrophy or to maintain organic efficiency
7. Relaxation training to assist in the remediation of muscle contractures, rigidity, and spasms
8. Postural alignments to maintain proper alignment of musculature
9. Gait training to teach or reteach walking patterns

10. Body mechanics and lifting techniques to obtain maximum use of the large muscle groups of the body

11. Proprioceptive facilitation exercises to bring about maximum excitation of motor units of a muscle with each voluntary effort to overcome motor functioning paralysis

12. Ramp climbing to improve ambulation and balance

13. Progressive, resistive exercise to develop muscle strength

There is impressive evidence that motor skills, muscular endurance, and strength can be developed in children with cerebral palsy through progressive exercise. Pitetti, Fernandez, and Lanciault[45] indicate that adults with cerebral palsy who exercised regularly demonstrated improvement in functional capacity. Holland and Steadward[29] have identified Nautilus weight lifting exercises that develop the neck, chest, and arms. The authors conclude that persons with cerebral palsy can participate in intense strength training programs without sacrificing flexibility or increasing spasticity.

Failure to provide children with cerebral palsy the opportunity to participate in progressive exercise may leave them short of their potential development. The opportunities for adapted physical education to maximize the physical development of these children are great. Furthermore, children with cerebral palsy frequently do not develop adequate basic motor skills because of their limited play experiences.

A variety of intervention approaches has been utilized with cerebral palsied children. Laskas et al.[38] support neurodevelopmental treatment, which has two fundamental premises: (1) motor development occurs in a sequential order that both nondisabled and disabled children follow and (2) through controlled sensorimotor experiences, normal patterns of motor behavior can be elicited in the child with a damaged nervous system.

When a child with cerebral palsy participates in group activity, it may be necessary to adapt the activity to the child's abilities or modify the rules or environment. A child with quadriplegic spastic cerebral palsy may be given the opportunity to play the bells during a rhythm activity, instead of being asked to dance with his/her feet. A wheelchair-enabled child with rigid cerebral palsy may "hold" one handle on the parachute with the edge of his/her chair. A child with ataxia may play a sitting circle game with classmates while propped in teacher's lap or propped against a wall.

In addition to adaptation of activity, the capabilities of each individual must be considered. Children with spasticity, athetosis, and ataxia differ greatly in function. For instance, the spastic child finds it easier to engage in activities in which motion is continuous. However, in the case of the athetoid child, relaxation between movements is extremely important to prevent involuntary muscular contractions that may thwart the development of skills.

Ataxic children have different motor problems—they are usually severely limited in all activities that require balance. The motor characteristics of the basic types of cerebral palsy, as well as of each individual child, are important variables in the selection of activities. Rest periods should be frequent for children with cerebral palsy. The length and frequency of the rest periods should vary with the nature of the activity and the severity of the disability. The development of a sequence of activities varying in degree of difficulty is important. This sequencing provides an opportunity to place each child in an activity that is commensurate with his or her ability and proposes a subsequent goal to work toward.

Physical activities described under the definition of physical education in the Education of the Handicapped Act are appropriate for children with cerebral palsy. At the early elementary level, the focus should be on the development of sensory-motor function, body image, and rhythmicity. Appropriate motor activities might include fundamental motor patterns such as walking, running, and jumping and fundamental motor skills such as throwing, kicking, and catching. Aquatics is a vital part of the curriculum for children with cerebral palsy. The buoyancy of the water frees the child from gravity-imposed restrictions encountered on dry land. Rhythm activities are also a vital part of the quality physical education program for children with cerebral palsy; expressive dance may prove vital in the development of language and comunication, as well as motor skills. If possible, the physical education program for children with cerebral palsy at the elementary school level should include age-apppropriate, geographically appropriate leisure and recreation skills. Horseback riding is a particularly effective intervention activity for even the most severely involved child. Other leisure and recreation skills are an important part of the total program, as well. The child should be introduced, for example, to skills needed to participate in bowling, including the use of automatic grip release balls and ramps, if necessary. If geographically appropriate, the child should learn the skills necessary to sled with family and friends.

The junior high school level curriculum should focus on the development of physical fitness, body mechanics, and relaxation techniques. Once again, aquatics is a vital component of the curriculum. Increased focus should be placed on exposing the student to community-based leisure and recreation activities and, where appropriate, competitive sports programs.

In the high school program, it is important that students with cerebral palsy maintain adequate levels of physical fitness, practice body mechanics, and develop more sophisticated relaxation techniques. The student's IEP must address techniques that will allow the student to make the "transition" from school-based to community-based leisure and recreation programs. For example, the IEP may address the skills necessary for the student to register for and participate in an adult bowling or archery league. These skills may include independent management of a ramp, for example. In addition, these students should be made familiar with the activities and programs of the United States Cerebral Palsy Athletic Association.

MUSCULAR DYSTROPHY

Muscular dystrophy is a disease of the muscular system characterized by weakness and atrophy of the muscles of the body. Weakness often afflicts the muscles that enable breathing and results in major complications including congestive heart failure and pneumonia.[30] Although the exact incidence of muscular dystrophy is unknown, estimates place the number of persons with the disorder in excess of 200,000 in the United States. It is estimated that more than half of those cases known fall within the age range of 3 to 13 years.

The etiological factors of muscular dystrophy are not known. Speculation regarding the exact cause includes faulty metabolism (related to inability to utilize vitamin E), endocrine disorders, and deficiencies in the peripheral nerves. There is some indication that an inherited abnormality causes the body's chemistry to be unable to carry on proper muscle metabolism.

Characteristics and Types

The physical characteristics of persons with muscular dystrophy are relevant to the degenerative stage as well as type of muscular dystrophy. In the late stages of the disease connective tissue replaces most of the muscle tissue. In some cases deposits of fat give the appearance of well-developed muscles. Despite the muscle atrophy, there is no apparent central nervous system impairment.

The age of onset of muscular dystrophy is of impor-

FIGURE 11-3. An elite athlete. (Courtesy United States Cerebral Palsy Athletic Association.)

tance to the total development of the children. Persons who contract the disease after having had an opportunity to secure an education, or part of an education, and develop social and psychological strengths are better able to cope with their environments than are those who are afflicted with the disease prior to the acquisition of basic skills.

Although the characteristics of patients with muscular dystrophy vary according to the stage that the disease has reached, some general characteristics are as follows:

1. There is a tendency to tire quickly.
2. There may be a tendency to lose fine manual dexterity.
3. Intelligence is normal, but there is a lack of motivation to learn because of isolation from social contacts and limited educational opportunities.
4. Progressive weakness tends to produce adverse postural changes.
5. Emotional disturbance may be prevalent because of the progressive nature of the illness and the resulting restrictions placed on opportunities for socialization.

There are numerous classifications of muscular dystrophy based on the muscle groups affected and the age of onset. However, four main clinical types of muscular dystrophy have been identified: pseudohypertrophic (Duchenne), facioscapulohumeral, juvenile, and mixed.

Pseudohypertrophic type

The pseudohypertrophic type is the most prevalent type of muscular dystrophy and is usually recognized when the child is between the ages of 4 and 7 years. It occurs primarily in males. Symptoms that give an indication of the disease are the following:

1. Decreased physical activity as compared with activity of children of commensurate age
2. Delay in the age at which the child walks
3. Poor motor development in walking and stair climbing
4. Little muscular endurance
5. A waddling gait with the legs carried far apart
6. Walking on tiptoe
7. Moving to all fours and then "climbing up the legs" when changing from a prone to a standing position (Gowers' sign)
8. Weakness in anterior abdominal muscles
9. Weakness in neck muscles, which makes it difficult to hold head in alignment
10. Pseudohypertrophy of muscles, particularly in the calves of the leg, which are enlarged and firm on palpation
11. Pronounced lordosis and gradual weakness of lower extremities

The progressive nature of muscular dystrophy is perhaps best illlustrated by the stages of functional ability outlined by Worden and Vignos[60] in Table 11-1.

As the disease progresses, imbalance of muscle strength in various parts of the body occurs. Deformities develop in flexion at the hips and knees. The spine, pelvis, and shoulder girdle also eventually become atrophied. Contractures and involvement of the heart may develop with the progressive degeneration of the disease. In general, the later the age at which the disease is observed, the slower the disease progresses. Consequently, persons who are affected later in life may perform functional activities longer.

The advent of the motorized wheelchair has increased independence of children in the advanced stages of muscular dystropy. Though unable to perform activities of daily living, the child using a motorized wheelchair retains a measure of mobility that promotes independence and allows integration into many school-based and community-based programs.

Facioscapulohumeral type

The facioscapulohumeral type of muscular dystrophy is the second most common type. The onset of symptoms or signs of the facioscapulohumeral type is usually recognized when the person is between the ages of 3 and 20 years, with the most common age of onset between 3 and 15 years. Both genders are equally subject to the condition.

This form of muscular dystrophy affects the shoulder and upper arm, and the person may have trouble in raising the arms above the head. There is also a weakness in the facial muscles; the child may lack the ability to shut the eyes, close the eyes completely when sleeping, whistle, or drink through a straw. A child with this type of disease often appears to have a masklike face that lacks expression. Later, involvement of the muscles that move the humerus and scapula will be noticed. Weakness usually appears later in the abdominal, pelvic, and hip musculature. The progressive weakness and muscle deterioration often lead to scoliosis and lordosis. This type of muscular dystrophy is often milder than the pseudohypertrophic type, and some persons with it have been able to live long, productive lives. Facioscapulohumeral muscular dystrophy usually progresses slowly, and pseudohypertrophy of the muscles is rare.

Juvenile type

The juvenile type of muscular dystrophy begins in late childhood, adolescence, or early adulthood. Mus-

---

TABLE 11-1

The stages of functional ability

1. Walks and climbs stairs without assistance.
2. Walks and cimbs stairs with aid of railing.
3. Walks and climbs stairs slowly with aid of railing (over 25 seconds for 8 standard steps.)
4. Walks, but cannot climb stairs.
5. Walks unassisted but cannot climb stairs or get out of chair.
6. Walks only with assistance or with braces.
7. In wheelchair. Sits erect and can roll chair and perform bed and wheelchair activities without assistance.
8. In wheelchair. Sits erect. Unable to perform bed and chair activities without assistance.
9. In wheelchair. Sits erect only with support. Able to do only minimal activities of daily living.
10. In bed. Can do no activities of daily living without assistance.

From Worden DK, Vignos PJ: *Pediatrics* 29:968-977, 1962.

cle atrophy is more general, with the muscles of the shoulder girdle being affected first. The progression is usually slower than the types mentioned previously, and persons afflicted with this type live longer.

Mixed type

The mixed version of muscular dystrophy may occur between the ages of 30 and 50 years. Effects are most likely to appear in the area of the scapula and pelvis. Persons with this type may take on many of the characteristics of the pseudohypertrophic type.

Medical Treatment

Muscular dystrophy is one of the most serious disabling conditions that can occur in childhood. Although not fatal in itself, the disease contributes to premature death in most known cases because of its progressive nature. Particularly if a child is affected by the pseudohypertrophic type, the progress is cruel and relentless as the child loses function and moves toward inevitable death. However, it is worth noting that scientific research may be close to solving unanswered questions regarding the disease, and eventually the progressive deterioration may be halted.

Physical Activity Program

An individually designed activity program may significantly contribute to the quality of life of the individual affected by muscular dystrophy. Inactivity seems to contribute to the progressive weakening of the muscles of persons with muscular dystrophy. Exercise of muscles involved in the activities of daily living to increase strength may permit greater functional use of the body. Furthermore, exercise may assist in reducing excessive weight, which is a burden to those who have muscular dystrophy. Movement in warm water— aquatic therapy—may be particularly beneficial for the child with muscular dystropy. It aids in the maintenance of muscle tonus, flexibility, and encourages circulation.

The child's diet should be closely monitored. Prevention of excess weight is essential to the success of the rehabilitation program of persons with progressive muscular dystrophy. For individuals whose strength is marginal, any extra weight is an added burden on ambulation and on activities of daily living.

A great deal can be done to prevent deformities and loss of muscle strength from inactivity. If a specific program is outlined during each stage of the disease, it is possible that the child may extend the ability to care for most daily needs for many additional years. In addi-

tion to the administration of specific developmental exercises for the involved muscles, exercises should include development of walking patterns, posture control, muscle coordination, and stretching of contractures involved in disuse atrophy. However, it should be noted that all exercises should be selected after study of contraindications specified by a physician. Rusk and Taylor[46] have stressed that variations in prognosis determine the ambulatory activities and restrictions that should help educators and therapists in program planning. It may be desirable to blueprint the activities around the remaining strengths so that enjoyment and success can be achieved.

Adapted Sports Program

One must recognize that all the types of muscular dystrophy cannot be considered the same; therefore the physical and social benefits that children can derive from physical education and recreation programs are

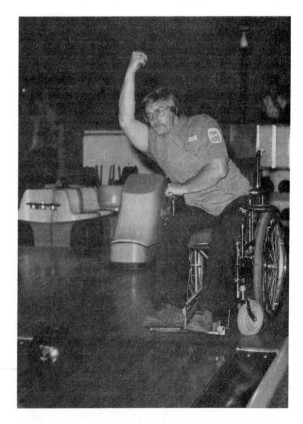

FIGURE 11-4. An athlete goes for the strike. (Courtesy American Wheelchair Bowling Association, Inc.)

different. However, all children with muscular dystrophy can profit from a well-designed program to enhance the quality of life. The focus of the program, particularly for children with the pseudohypertrophic form of muscular dystropy, is on the development of leisure and recreation skills that will be appropriate as the child progressively loses function. For example, a child with Duchenne's muscular dystrophy should be taught to fish. That is a skill that child can use and enjoy throughout the lifespan. A child with Duchenne's muscular dystrophy should be taught to play bocci; and the child should be given the opportunity to learn board and videogames that will provide entertainment and joy throughout the lifespan.

One focus of the program should also be the development of relaxation techniques. The progressive loss of functional skills causes a great deal of stress, as does facing the inevitability of an early death; and the quality of the child's life can be enhanced if the child has learned conscious relaxation skills.

Perhaps more important, a significant dance, music, and art therapy program should be a part of the child's total program. Movement and dance, even dance done in a motorized wheelchair, can help the child/adolescent express his emotions—grief, rage, frustration and, we hope, love and joy. Music and art therapy provide vital avenues of expression as the child loses motor capabilities. In addition, a trained therapist can be of value as the child moves through the stages of grief. The intent of the program is to enhance the quality of the child's life and, with professional support, allow the process of dying to be as humane, caring, and ennobling as possible.

MULTIPLE SCLEROSIS

Multiple sclerosis is a chronic and degenerative neurological disease primarily affecting older adolescents and adults. It is a slowly progressive disease of the central nervous system leading to the disintegration of the myelin coverings of nerve fibers, which results in hardening or scarring of the tissue that replaces the disintegrated protective myelin sheath.[40] The cause of multiple sclerosis and other related diseases, such as amyotrophic lateral sclerosis (Lou Gehrig disease), is not known.

Physical Symptoms

The symptoms of multiple sclerosis include sensory problems, tremors, muscle weakness, spasticity, speech difficulties, dizziness, mild emotional disturbances, partial paralysis, and motor difficulties.

Prognosis

Multiple sclerosis generally appears when the person is between the ages of 20 and 40 years and results in loss of function and eventual death.

Physical Activity Program

There is no treatment that can repair the damage to the nervous system caused by degeneration. However, each person should be evaluated individually and programs of resistive exercise administered to maintain maximum functioning. The goal of these programs is to maintain functional skills, strength of muscles, and range of motion. It is particularly important to teach the skills necessary for functional use of walkers, crutches, and/or wheelchairs. In addition, the individual should be given the opportunity to develop compensatory skills—skills needed to function given changes in central nervous system function. These include skills to compensate, for example, for disequilibrium.

Inactivity may contribute to the progressive weakening of the muscles needed for daily activity. Individuals should be encouraged to participate in an exercise program that maintains cardiovascular respiratory functioning and sufficient muscle strength to allow participation in activities of daily living as long as possible. Braces may be introduced at the later stages of the disorder to assist with locomotion.

EPILEPSY

Epilepsy is a disturbance resulting from abnormal electrical activity of the brain. It is not a specific disease, but a group of symptoms that may be associated with several conditions. The estimated incidence of epilepsy is 2% of the population. Many persons with epilepsy experience their first attack during childhood. No cause can be found in many children who have epilepsy. However, some authorities believe that some forms of epilepsy are due to a microscopic scar in the brain as a result of birth trauma or other head injury.[3]

Characteristics and Types

There are several types of epilepsy and each type has a particular set of characteristics. Although there are several methods of classifying various types of epilepsy, the one most commonly used includes four categories: grand mal, petit mal, focal, and psychomotor seizures.

Grand mal

The grand mal, French for "big illness," is the most severe type of seizure. The individual often has an "aura" that immediately precedes the seizure and may give the individual some warning of the imminence of the seizure. The aura is usually a somatosensory flash—a particular smell, a blur of colors, or an itching sensation, for example. The seizure itself usually begins with bilateral jerks of the extermities, followed by convulsions and loss of consciousness. The student may be incontinent during the seizure, losing control of the bowels and bladder. After the seizure, the individual is usually confused, often embarrassed, and exhausted.

Petit mal

The onset of the petit (little) mal seizure is sudden and may last for only a few seconds or for several minutes. Usually the individual appears to simply stare into space and have a lapse in attention. It is often characterized by twitching around the eyes or mouth. There is a loss of consciousness, but no collapse. The individual remains sitting or standing. Seizures of this type usually affect children between the ages of 5 and 12 years and may disappear during puberty.

The student with petit mal seizures may experience serious learning difficulties. It is not uncommon for a child to have hundreds of petit mal seizures in a day. If a child has 100 seizures and each lasts only 30 seconds, the child will have lost a full 50 minutes of learning time.

Focal

The focal seizure is similar to the grand mal seizure. It is characterized by a loss of body tone and collapse. The student usually remains conscious during the attack, but speech may be impaired. In jacksonian focal seizures there is a localized twitching of muscles in the extremities, which move up the arm or leg. If the seizure spreads to other parts of the brain, generalized convulsions and loss of consciousness result.

Psychomotor

A psychomotor seizure is characterized by atypical social-motor behavior. The behaviors may include uncontrollable temper tantrums, hand clapping, spitting, swearing, or shouting. The individual is unaware of the activity during and after the seizure. Psychomotor seizures may occur at any age.

There are several factors that may cause seizures. Some of these factors are (1) emotional stress such as fear, anger, or frustration; (2) excessive amounts of alcohol; and (3) menstruation.

Medical Treatment

Anticonvulsant drugs are the preferred medical treatment for approximately 95% of individuals with epilepsy. The major antiepileptic drugs are phenytoin (Di-

lantin), usually the drug of choice, phenobarbital, primidone (Mysoline) for complex partial seizures, and ethosuximide (Zarontin) and clonazepam (Klonopin) for petit mal seizures. Which type of drug and optimum dosage is difficult to determine and highly individualized. Teachers should be sensitive to the side effects of these drugs that may impair motor performance. Dilantin, for example, may produce dizziness and mental confusion in some students. These side effects may be detrimental to the student's safety in certain activities. Information about the student's drug treatment program should be discussed during the IEP meeting.

Physical education teachers should be familiar with procedures for handling seizures. Perhaps the most significant procedure for handling a seizure is to educate the student's class members regarding the nature of epilepsy. If the child's classmates are knowledgable about seizures, the child will not have to suffer from post-seizure embarrassment.

In the event a child has a grand mal seizure, the physical educator should do the following[22]:

1. Place the student on the floor in a back-lying position.
2. Move all objects away from the student so he/she will not bang the head or limbs against objects.
3. Loosen all restraining clothing, such as a belt or shirt collar.
4. If the student is experiencing breathing difficulty, tilt the student's head back to open the airway.
5. Once the convulsion has stopped, place a blanket or towel over the student to eliminate embarrassment if the student lost bowel or bladder control.
6. Allow the student to rest.
7. Report the seizure to the appropriate school official.

A grand mal seizure is not a life-threatening event and should be treated as a routine event. The seizure process is dangerous only if the student moves into status epilepticus—has a series of grand mal seizures without a break. If this happens, emergency medical personnel must be contacted immediately.

If the student experiences a focal or psychomotor seizure, the child should be removed to an isolated part of the gymnasium, if possible. If the student experiences a petit mal seizure and the teacher is aware of it, the teacher should repeat any instructions given previously.

Physical Activity Program

If medication is effective and the child's seizures are under control, the student should be able to partici-

FIGURE 11-5. Part of men's F.I.T.A. line, International Wheelchair Archery Championship, Hershey, Pa 1987. (Photo Credit Pennsylvania Game Commission, Courtesy The American Wheelchair Archers.)

pate in an unrestricted pysical education program. However, activities that involve direct blows to the head should be avoided. Boxing or heading a soccer ball, for example, are contraindicated. Activities that are performed while a considerable height from the floor should be avoided. Rope climbing, diving, horizontal and uneven parallel bar activities, and high balance beam activities are contraindicated. Swimming should be carefully supervised. Underwater swimming, snorkeling, and scuba diving are contraindicated, as is swimming in cold water.

PARKINSON'S DISEASE

Parkinson's disease is a slow, progressive disorder that results in physical debilitation. The disease usually appears gradually and progresses slowly. It may progress to a stage where there is difficulty with routine activities of daily living. The condition may be aggravated by emotional tension or fatigue.

Characteristics

The observable characteristics of Parkinson's disease are tremor of the resting muscles, a slowing of voluntary movements, muscular weakness, abnormal gait,

and postural instability. These motor characteristics become more pronounced as the disease progresses. For instance, a minor feeling of sluggishness may progress until the individual is unable to get up from a chair. The walking gait becomes less efficient and can be characterized by shuffling of the feet for the purpose of postural stability. In addition, voluntary movements, particularly those performed by the small muscles, become slow, and spontaneous movements diminish.

Medical Treatment

In general, most persons require lifelong management consisting of physical therapy and drug therapy. Physical therapy consists of heat and massage to alleviate muscle cramps and relive tension headaches that often accompany rigidity of the muscles of the neck.

Physical Activity Program

Parkinson's disease is a degenerative condition that results in inefficient movement, tremors, muscular rigidity, and postural instability. Because of the degenerative nature of the disease, the goals of physical activity programs are to preserve muscular functioning for purposive movement involved in the activities of daily living and required for the performance of leisure and recreation skills. The general types of physical activities that may be of value are general coordination exercises to retard the slow deterioration of movement, as well as relaxation exercises that may reduce muscular incoordination and tremors.[41] In addition, balance activities and those that teach compensation for lack of balance should be included. Exercises directed at maintaining postural strength and flexibility should be a part of the program plan.

AMYOTROPHIC LATERAL SCLEROSIS

Amyotrophic lateral sclerosis (ALS) is a progressive neurological disorder that results in degeneration of the muscular system.[41] The disease is infrequent in school-age populations and is more common in adulthood. It affects men two to three times more than women. Lou Gehrig, the hall-of-fame first baseman of the New York Yankees, who finally missed a game after more than 2000 successive starts, was forced to retire as a result of the disease. It has since been named the "Lou Gehrig" disease.

Characteristics

The central feature of the disease is atrophy and muscle wasting resulting in marked weakness in the hands, arms, shoulders, and legs and in generalized weakness, as well. Muscular weakness may also cause problems with swallowing, talking, and respiration. Concomitant spinal conditions may include ruptured intervertebral disks, spinal cord tumors, and spinal malformations.

Medical Treatment

There is no specific medical treatment for ALS. Although there may be periods of remission, the disease usually progresses rapidly with death ensuing within an average of 2 to 5 years.[41]

Physical Activity Program

The major goals of the ALS physical education program are to maintain physical capability as long as possible. It may be desirable to focus attention on activities that would maintain efficient movement of the body for activities of daily living. Leisure skills should be taught that have functional use at present or in the near future. The nature of the physical activities will depend on the physical capabilities of the individual at each point in time.

BELL'S PALSY

Bell's palsy is a pathological condition resulting in the paralysis of the muscles of the face.[3] The cause is unknown but it is presumed to involve swelling of a nerve caused by a viral infection.

Characteristics

Paralysis of the facial muscles result in loss of control, usually of one side of the face. The student has sagging on one side of the mouth, which makes eating difficult and drooling common. Pain behind the ear may precede the facial weakness after which paralysis may develop within hours.

Medical Treatment

The disorder is treated with medication. Physical therapy can be applied only to provoke motion and prevent contractures of the paralyzed muscles. Recovery within several months follows partial facial paralysis. The likelihood of complete recovery is 90%.[3]

Physical Activity Program

Students with Bell's palsy, for the most part, can participate in an unrestricted physical education program. Bell's palsy would not usually, in and of itself, qualify a student for special education services. However, at the onset of the disorder, when the student may be medicated, it is desirable to observe the student for side effects of the medication. Precaution must be taken to diminish the risk of a blow to the afflicted facial area during physical activity.

ORTHOPEDIC DISABILITIES
ARTHRITIS

The term *arthritis* is derived from two Greek roots— *arthro-,* meaning joint, and *-itis,* meaning inflammation. It has been estimated that more than 12 million people in the United States are afflicted with some form of arthritic disease. Since arthritis inflicts a low mortality and high morbidity, the potential for increasing numbers of those afflicted and disabled is great.

It is assumed that a great many factors may predispose one to arthritis. Major contributors could be infection, hereditary factors, environmental stress, dietary deficiencies, trauma, and organic or emotional disturbances.

Characteristics and Types

In most cases arthritis is progressive, gradually resulting in general fatigue, weight loss, and muscular stiffness. Joint impairment is symmetrical, and characteristically, the small joints of the hand and feet are affected in the earliest stages. Tenderness and pain may occur in tendons and muscular tissue near inflamed joints. As the inflammation in the joints becomes progressively chronic, degenerative and proliferative changes occur to the synovial tendons, ligaments, and articular cartilages. If the inflammation is not arrested in its early stages, joints become ankylosed and muscles atrophy and contract, eventually causing a twisted and deformed limb.

The American Rheumatism Association indicated that the three most prevalent forms of arthritis are arthritis from infection, arthritis from rheumatic fever, and rheumatoid arthritis. Arthritis after trauma and degenerative joint disease of the elderly (osteoarthritis) also have a high incidence among the general population.

Infectious arthritis

Arthritis from infection is usually caused by staphylococci and streptococci. The disease appears as an acute inflammatory condition with joints becoming swollen, hot, red, and painful. Associated muscle tendons may also become inflamed, resulting in contractures, inactivity, and, subsequently, muscle atrophy. Uncontrolled infection eventually results in bone deterioration.

Arthritis from rheumatic fever

Arthritis caused by rheumatic fever involves many joints but does not involve the chronic effect of degeneration of articular tissue. The highest incidence of rheumatic fever occurs in children. After a general systemic reaction of sore throat and fever, a transitory polyarthritis travels from one joint to another. Carditis may later be manifested by the appearance of murmurs, tachycardia, and chest pain.

Rheumatoid arthritis

Rheumatoid arthritis represents the nation's number one crippling disease, afflicting more than 3 million persons. It is a systemic disease of unknown cause. Seventy-five percent of the cases occur between the ages of 25 and 50 years and in a ratio of 3:1, women to men. A type of rheumatoid arthritis called Still's disease, or juvenile arthritis, attacks children before the age of 7 years. Approximately 250,000 children in the United States are afflicted with rheumatoid arthritis, making it a major crippler among young children.[50]

Medical Treatment

Medical treatment of patients with rheumatoid arthritis involves proper diet, rest, drug therapy, and exercise. Because of its debilitating effect, prolonged bed rest is

FIGURE 11-6. A quality athletic experience can enhance life throughout the lifespan. (Courtesy Texas Special Olympics.)

discouraged, although daily rest sessions are required to avoid undue fatigue. A number of drugs may be given to the patient, depending on individual needs; for example, salicylates such as aspirin relieve pain, gold compounds may be used for arresting the acute inflammatory stage, and adrenocortical steroids may be employed for the control of the degenerative process.

There are drugless techniques of controlling arthritis pain, such as biofeedback, self-hypnosis, behavior modification, and transcutaneous nerve stimulation. Such techniques are often used as an adjunct to other more traditional types of treatment.

The majority of persons afflicted with rheumatoid arthritis recover almost totally with only minor residual effects. However, it has been estimated that about 10% to 15% of persons become crippled to the point of invalid status. For the most part, the course of the disease is unpredictable, with spontaneous remissions and exacerbations.

Physical Activity Program

Physical therapy is primarily concerned with preventing contracture deformities and muscle atrophy by the use of heat, massage, and graded exercise. The exercises required by arthritic patients fall into three major categories: exercises that prevent deformity, exercises that prevent muscle atrophy, and exercises that maintain joint range and basic function. The physical educator can use gradual or static stretching, isometric muscle contraction, and graded isotonic exercises to advantage.

Preventing deformity is a major concern of the arthritic patient. In the acute stage, when muscle contractures are prevalent, splinting is a common practice. The patient is encouraged to engage in muscle tensing exercises numerous times during the day while lying in bed and splinted. Such a program tends to prevent general weakness and maintains a balance of strength.

Preventing muscle weakness from inactivity is important if the arthritic patient is to maintain joint function. Muscle-setting exercises, isometrics, and isotonic exercises must be employed throughout the patient's convalescence. Particular emphasis is paid to the gluteus and knee extensor muscles, which are extensively used in ambulation.

Maintenance of normal joint range of movement is of prime importance for establishing a functional joint. Stretching is first employed passively.

An individual with arthritis may need rest periods during the day. These should be combined with a well-planned exercise program. Activity should never increase pain or so tire an individual that normal recovery is not obtained by the next day.

Because of the nature of arthritis, an activity program must be based on the particular requirements of the individual. If the disease has been arrested from the acute stage, a variety of sports and game activities may be initiated; however, abnormal physical stress or injury must be avoided at all costs. Swimming and/or aquatic exercise is an excellent activity for the arthritic person; however, the water should be warm to enhance circulation and avoid muscle tightness. Additional sports might include archery, golf, badminton, tennis, and weight training. Exercises that improve joint range of movement should be conducted daily. Posture training and good body alignment must be stressed in all aspects of the arthritic person's daily living.

HIP DISORDERS

Developmental hip dislocation, commonly called congenital hip dislocation, refers to a partially or completely displaced femoral head in relation to the acetabulum (Fig. 11-7). It is estimated that it occurs six times more often in females than in males; it may be bilateral or unilateral, occurring most often in the left hip.

The cause of congenital hip dislocation is unknown, with various reasons proposed. Heredity seems to be a primary causative factor in faulty hip development and subsequent dysplasia. Actually, only about 2% of developmental hip dislocations are congenital.

Characteristics

Generally, the acetabulum is shallower on the affected side than on the nonaffected side, and the femoral head is displaced upward and backward in relation to the ilium. Ligaments and muscles become deranged, resulting in a shortening of the rectus femoris, hamstring, and adductor thigh muscles and affecting the small intrinsic muscles of the hip. Prolonged malpositioning of the femoral head produces a chronic weakness of the gluteus medius and minimus muscles. A primary factor in stabilizing one hip in the upright posture is the iliopsoas muscle. In developmental hip dislocation, the iliopsoas muscle serves to displace the femoral head upward; this will eventually cause the lumbar vertebrae to become lordotic and scoliotic.

Detection of the hip dislocation may not occur until the child begins to bear weight or walk. Early recognition of this condition may be accomplished by observ-

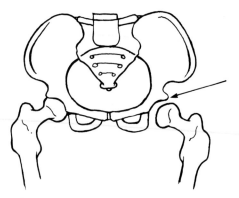

FIGURE 11-7. Developmental hip dislocation.

ing asymmetrical fat folds on the infant's legs and restricted hip adduction on the affected side. The Trendelenburg test will reveal that the child is unable to maintain the pelvis level while standing on the affected leg. In such cases, weak abductor muscles of the affected leg allow the pelvis to tilt downward on the nonaffected side. The child walks with a decided limp in unilateral cases and with a waddle in bilateral cases. No discomfort or pain is normally experienced by the child, but fatigue tolerance to physical activity is very low. Pain and discomfort become more apparent as the individual becomes older and as postural deformities become more structural.

Medical Treatment

Medical treatment of the developmental hip dislocation depends on the age of the child and the extent of displacement. Young babies with a mild involvement may have the condition remedied through gradual adduction of the femur by a pillow splint, whereas more complicated cases may require traction, casting, or operation to restore proper hip continuity. The thigh is slowly returned to a normal position.

Physical Activity Program

Active exercise is suggested along with passive stretching to contracted tissue. Primary concern is paid to reconditioning the movement of hip extension and abduction. When adequate muscle strength has been gained in the hip region, a program of ambulation is conducted, with particular attention paid to walking without a lateral pelvic tilt.

A child in the adapted physical education or therapeutic recreation program with a history of developmental hip dislocation will, in most instances, require specific postural training, conditioning of the hip region, continual gait training, and general body mechanics training. Swimming is an excellent activity for general conditioning of the hip, and it is highly recommended.

Activities should not be engaged in to the point of discomfort or fatigue.

COXA PLANA (LEGG-PERTHES DISEASE)

Coxa plana is the result of osteochrondritis dissecans, or abnormal softening, of the femoral head. It is a condition identified early in the twentieth century independently by Legg of Boston, Calve of France, and Perthes of Germany. Its gross signs reflect a flattening of the head of the femur (Fig. 11-8), and it is found predominantly in boys between the ages of 3 and 12 years. It has been variously termed *osteochondritis defor-*

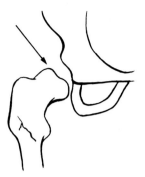

FIGURE 11-8. Coxa plana.

mans juvenilis, pseudocoxalgia, and *Legg-Calve-Perthes disease.*

The exact cause of coxa plana is not known; trauma, infection, and endocrine imbalance have been suggested as possible causes.

Characteristics

Coxa plana is characterized by degeneration of the capital epiphysis of the femoral head. Osteoporosis, or bone rarefaction, results in a flattened and deformed femoral head. Later developments may also include widening of the femoral head and thickening of the femoral neck. The last stage of coxa plana may be reflected by a self-limiting course in which there is a regeneration and an almost complete return of the normal epiphysis within 3 to 4 years. However, recovery is not always complete, and there is often some residual deformity present. The younger child with coxa plana has the best prognosis for complete recovery.

Medical Treatment

The first outward sign of this condition is often a limp favoring the affected leg, with pain referred to the knee region. Further investigation by the physician may show pain upon passive movement and restricted motion upon internal rotation and abduction. X-ray examination will provide the definitive signs of degeneration. The physical educator or therapist may be the first person to observe the gross signs of coxa plana and bring it to the attention of the parents or physician.

Whatever the mechanism of injury, the individual with coxa plana experiences progressive fatigue and pain upon weight bearing, progressive stiffness, and a limited range of movement. A limp is apparent, which reflects weakness in the hip abductor muscles and pain referred to the region of the knee. With displacement

FIGURE 11-9. Sling and crutch for hip conditions.

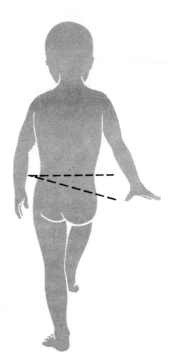

FIGURE 11-10. Trendelenburg test.

of the epiphyseal plate, the affected limb tends to rotate externally and to abduct when flexed.

Treatment of coxa plana primarily entails the removal of stress placed on the femoral head by weight bearing. Bed rest is often employed in the acute stages, with ambulation and non–weight-bearing devices used for the remaining period of incapacitation. The sling and crutch method for non-weight bearing is widely used for this condition (Fig. 11-9).

Weight-bearing exercise is contraindicated until the physician discounts the possibility of a pathological joint condition.

Physical Activity Program

The individual with an epiphyseal affection of the hip presents a problem of muscular and skeletal stability and joint range of movement. Stability of the hip region requires skeletal continuity and a balance of muscle strength, primarily in the muscles of hip extension and abduction. Prolonged limited motion and non-weight bearing may result in contractures of tissues surrounding the hip joint and an inability to walk or run with ease. Abnormal weakness of the hip extensors and abductors may cause shortening of the hip flexors and adductors and lead the individual to display the Trendelenburg sign (Fig. 11-10).

A program of exercise must be carried out to prevent muscle atrophy and general deconditioning. When movement is prohibited, muscle-tensing exercises for muscles of the hip region are conducted, together with isotonic exercises for the upper extremities, trunk, ankles, and feet.

When the hip becomes free of symptoms, a progressive, isotonic, non–weight-bearing program is initiated for the hip region. Active movement emphasizing hip extension and abduction is recommended. Swimming is an excellent adjunct to the regular exercise program.

The program of exercise should never exceed the point of pain or fatigue until full recovery is accomplished. A general physical fitness program emphasizing weight control and body mechanics will aid the student in preparing for a return to a full program of physical education and recreation activities.

Principles described in the opening section of this chapter may be applied to persons with coxa plana to include them in games and sports. To the greatest extent possible, children with coxa plana should be taught activities that parallel those of nondisabled children.

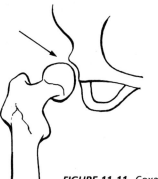

FIGURE 11-11. Coxa vara.

COXA VARA AND COXA VALGA

In adults the normal angle of inclination of the femoral head, or neck of the femur, is about 128 degrees. An abnormal increase in this angle is called coxa valga and a decrease is called coxa vara (Fig. 11-11).

The acquired type of coxa vara is, by far, the most prevalent and occurs most often in adolescent boys between 10 and 16 years of age. It is commonly termed *adolescent coxa vara.*

The pathological mechanics of coxa vara and coxa valga result from the combined stresses of an abnormal increase or decrease in weight bearing. A variation of more than 10 to 15 degrees can produce significant shortening or lengthening of an extremity.

Coxa valga and coxa vara can be caused by many etiological factors—for example, hip injury, paralysis, non-weight bearing, or congenital malformation. Coxa vara and coxa valga are described according to where the structural changes have occurred in the femur— that is, neck (cervical), head (epiphyseal), or combined head and neck (cervicoepiphyseal).

Adolescent coxa vara is found in boys who have displacement of the upper femoral epiphysis. Boys who are most prone to adolescent coxa vara have been found to be obese and sexually immature, or tall and lanky, having experienced a rapid growing phase. Trauma such as hip fracture or dislocation may result in acute coxa vara. More often, through constant stress, a gradual displacement may take place.

Characteristics

Coxa vara and coxa valga are disturbances in the proximal cartilage or epiphyseal plate of the femur that result in alteration in the angle of the shaft as it relates to the neck of the femur. Two types of conditions have been recognized—the congenital type and the acquired type. The congenital type may be associated with developmental hip dislocation.

Medical Treatment

Management in the early stages of coxa vara involves use of crutches and the prevention of weight bearing to allow revascularization of the epiphyseal plate. Where deformity, displacement, and limb shortening are apparent, corrective surgery may be elected by the physician.

Physical Activity Program

The severity of the condition of the hip will determine the nature of the physical activity program. In many cases, the degree of involvement is such that the student with coxa vara or coxa valgus can participate in an unrestricted regular physical education program. However, if modification in the program is needed, attention should be given to modifying the amount of stress on the hip. When the condition is severe, walking and running will be limited, and strength and cardiovascular endurance may suffer. If this is the case, other ways should be found to improve the student's physical fitness levels. Swimming is an excellent activity for students with coxa vara and coxa valgus.

OSGOOD-SCHLATTER CONDITION

Many terms have been applied to the Osgood-Schlatter condition; the most prevalent are *apophysitis, osteochondritis,* and *epiphysitis of the tibial tubercle.* It is not considered a disease entity, but rather the result of a separation of the tibial tubercle at the epiphyseal junction.

The cause of this condition is unknown, but direct injury and long-term irritation are thought to be the main inciting factors. Direct trauma (as in a blow), osteochondritis, or an excessive strain of the patellar tendon as it attaches to the tibial tubercle may result in evulsion at the epiphyseal cartilage junction.

The Osgood-Schlatter condition usually occurs in active adolescent boys and girls between the ages of 10 and 15 years who are in a rapid growth period. Antich and Lombaro[2] indicate that 72% of the patients diagnosed in their study were males. Furthermore, the condition occurred more frequently in the left knee (twice as frequently) than in the right knee. Basketball was cited as a sport in which the condition was most likely to occur.

Characteristics

Disruption of the blood supply to the epiphysis results in enlargement of the tibial tubercle, joint tenderness, and pain upon contraction of the quadriceps muscle. The physical educator may be the one to detect this condition from the complaints of the student, who should be immediately referred to a physician.

Medical Treatment

If the Osgood-Schlatter condition is not properly cared for, deformity and a defective extensor mechanism may result; however, it may not necessarily be associated with pain or discomfort. In most cases, the Osgood-Schlatter condition is acute, is self-limiting, and does not exceed a few months' duration. However, even after arrest of symptoms, the Osgood-Schlatter condition tends to recur after irritation.

Local inflammation is accentuated by leg activity and ameliorated by rest. The individual may be unable to kneel or engage in flexion and extension movements without pain. The knee joint must be kept completely immobilized when the inflammatory state persists. Forced inactivity, provided by a plaster cast, may be the only answer to keeping the overactive adolescent from using the affected leg.

Physical Activity Program

Early detection may reveal a slight condition in which the individual can continue a normal activity routine, excluding overexposure to strenuous running, jumping, and falling on the affected leg. All physical education activities must be modified to avoid quadriceps muscle strain while preparing for general physical fitness.

While the limb is immobilized in a cast, the individual is greatly restricted; weight bearing may be held to a minimum, with signs of pain at the affected part closely watched by the physician. Although the Osgood-Schlatter condition is self-limiting and temporary, exercise is an important factor in full recovery. Physical education activities should emphasize the capabilities of the upper body and nonaffected leg to prevent their deconditioning.

After arrest of the condition and removal of the cast (or relief from immobilization), the patient is given a graduated reconditioning program. The major objectives at this time are re-education in proper walking patterns and restoration of normal strength and flexibility of the knee joint. Strenuous knee movement is avoided for at least 5 weeks, and the demanding requirements of regular physical education classes may be postponed for extended periods depending on the physician's recommendations. Although during the period of rehabilitation emphasis is placed on the affected leg, a program also must be provided for the entire body.

The criteria for the individual to return to a regular physical education program would be as follows:

1. Normal range of movement of the knee
2. Quadriceps muscle strength equal to that of the unaffected leg
3. Evidence that the Osgood-Schlatter condition has become asymptomatic
4. Ability to move freely without favoring the affected part

After recovery, the student should avoid all activities that would tend to contuse, or in any way irritate again, the tibial tuberosity.

Principles described in the opening section of this chapter may be applied to persons with the Osgood-Schlatter condition to include them in games and sports. To the greatest extent possible, children with the Osgood-Schlatter condition should be taught activities that parallel those of children without disabilities

CLUBFOOT

One of the most common deformities of the lower extremity is clubfoot. This deformity is characterized by plantar flexion or dorsiflexion and inversion or eversion of the foot. The clubfoot deformity, if not corrected, would force the individual to walk on the side of the foot or on the ankle rather than on the sole of the foot (Fig. 11-12).

Characteristics

Clubfoot can be acquired or congenital. The acquired type of clubfoot can develop from a spastic paralysis,

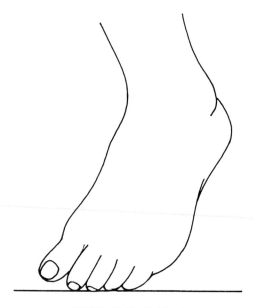

FIGURE 11-12. Clubfoot.

as in cerebral palsy or other neuromuscular diseases, which may eventuate in bone and soft tissue changes. Congenital clubfoot is by far the most prevalent type. Talipes equinovarus has the highest incidence, amounting to 70% among the congenital forms of clubfoot.

If talipes equinovarus is not corrected early in life, the individual develops an awkward gait and walks on the outside of the foot and ankle.

Medical Treatment

If the deformity is recognized soon after birth, a plaster cast is employed to retain the foot in an overcorrected position. Special clubfoot shoes with a rigid steel pole may be employed for the prewalker to help maintain the proper position of the foot. Various corrective shoes may be worn and splints applied to continue the development of proper foot alignment until amelioration is achieved.

Physical Activity Program

The pupil's limitations and capabilities will depend on the extent of residual derangement and deformity. A child with a severe malformation may be restricted from standing for long periods or may be unable to walk without fatigue. Activities requiring running and jumping must be modified. Team and individual sport activities are beneficial for the pupil with clubfoot, but they have to be adapted to prevent the deleterious effects of extensive running, jumping, and kicking.

Exercise cannot be considered a means for correcting a clubfoot. However, a graded program should be given to the pupil that will maintain or improve muscle tone, ambulation, body mechanics, posture, and physical and motor fitness.

SPINA BIFIDA

Spina bifida is the most common congenital defect occurring to the spine. It has replaced poliomyelitis as the major cause of paraplegia in young children.[20] Spina bifida implies congenital malformation of the posterior aspects of the spinal column, in which some portion of the vertebral arch fails to form over the spinal cord (Fig. 11-13).

Spina bifida occulta is the unfused condition of vertebral arches without any cystic distension of the meninges. The National Information Center for Handicapped Children and Youth[42] estimates that approximately 40% of all people in the United States have spina bifida occulta, but few even know it. The incidence of spina bifida is estimated at 0.02%, making it one of the most common birth defects causing physical disability.

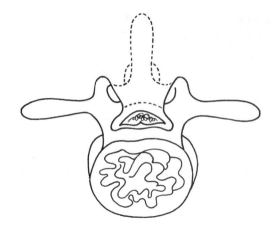

FIGURE 11-13. Spina bifida occulta.

Characteristics

In any type of spina bifida, spinal cord defects may produce varying degrees of neurological impairment ranging from mild muscle imbalance and sensory loss in the lower limbs to complete paraplegia. In almost half the children with spina bifida, a hydrocephalic condition also exists. In these cases, shunting is mandated to prevent irreversible brain damage. However, neurological disturbances may be completely absent in cases of spina bifida occulta or may not become symptomatic until later in life.

Children who are paraplegic from spina bifida are often able to move about with the aid of braces and crutches. There may or may not be changes in the overlying skin, neurological signs, or pathological changes in the spinal cord.

Medical Treatment

Activities that could distress placement of any shunts or put pressure on sensitive areas of the spine must be avoided. Of considerable concern is the prevention of contractures and associated foot deformities (e.g., equinovarus) through daily passive flexibility exercises.

Physical Activity Program

No particular program of physical education or therapy can be directly assigned to the student with spina bifida. Some students have no physical reaction and discover the condition only by chance through x-ray examination for another problem. On the other hand, a person may have extensive neuromuscular involvement requiring constant medical care. A program of physical education or therapeutic exercise based on the individual needs of the person should be planned.

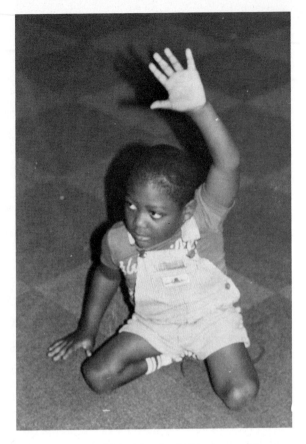

FIGURE 11-14. A child with spina bifida dances. (Courtesy Dallas Independent School District.)

Class activity (song/dance:)	Modifications for child in wheelchair
"Warm-up Time"	
Clap hands	None
Swing arms	None
Bend knees	Child lifts knees with hands
Stamp feet	Child slaps feet with hands
"What a Miracle"	
Clap hands	None
Stamp feet	Child slaps feet with hands
Swing arms	None
Bend and stretch legs	Child lifts knees with hands
Twist and bend spine	None
One foot balance	Child pushes into push-up position
"Swing, Shake, Twist, Stretch"	
Swing	Child swings arms or head
Shake	Child shakes hands, elbows, or head
Twist	Child twists trunk
Stretch	Child stretches arms
"Bendable, Stretchable"	
Stretch to sky, touch floor	Child stretches to sky, touches toes
"Run, Run, Run in Place"	
Run in place	Child spins chair in circle
"Simon Says Jog Along"	
Jog	Child rolls chair in time to music
Walk	Child rolls chair in time to music

Adapted physical education programming is often not required for pupils with spina bifida occulta or meningocele acquired at infancy. However, children with myelomeningocele need programs that are modified to their needs and that stress intensive development.

The child with spina bifida meningocele is often able to participate in a regular physical education program more effectively in a wheelchair than if the child uses a walker or crutches and braces. While the child with spina bifida meningocele should be encouraged to walk whenever possible, it may be difficult for the child to participate in activities safely in a crowded gymnasium.

Simple modifications can be made to allow the child with spina bifida meningocele, using a wheelchair, to participate actively in regular physical education. Following is an example of modifications that can be made in a typical warm-up session for a kindergarten or first grade class.

The emphasis in the physical education program should be on functional movement skills. The child, if wheelchair-enabled, should be given every opportunity to move in the chair. The child should practice moving in the chair with activities that modify the movment variables of time, space, force, and flow. For example, the child should be able to do the following:

1. Time
   a. Wheel fast, then slow
   b. Wheel to a 4/4 beat
2. Space
   a. Wheel up and down inclines
   b. Wheel on cement, linoleum, grass, a gymnasium floor, etc
   c. Wheel around obstacles
   d. Wheel over sticks
   e. Wheel, holding a glass of water
   f. Wheel, holding a ball on lap
3. Force
   a. Wheel with buddy sitting on lap
   b. Wheel while pulling partner on scooterboard

c. Push hard and see how far the chair will roll
4. Flow
    a. Roll forward, spin in a circle, roll forward
    b. Roll forward, stop, roll backward, stop

The same type of movement activities should be made available to the child with spina bifida moving with crutches and braces.

Social Problems

Many social problems result from spina bifida. In addition to the physical disability, there are often problems associated with control of bowels and bladder, which draw further attention to the children as they function in a social environment. In many cases, this has a negative social impact on the children. Often, children with spina bifida need catheterization. If someone must do it for them, the attention of others is drawn to these circumstances. However, in many cases older children may be taught to catheterize themselves. The physical disability and the associated physiological problems stress social situations where groups must adapt to the needs of spina bifida children. Social circumstances can be made more favorable if these children are integrated into regular classes in the early grades and if social integration strategies are employed (see Chapter 6).

OSTEOGENESIS IMPERFECTA (BRITTLE BONE DISEASE)

Osteogenesis imperfecta is a condition marked by both weak bones and elasticity of the joints, ligaments, and skin. It is apparently inherited, although at times it seems to be caused by spontaneous changes in the genes (mutation).

There are two main types of osteogenesis imperfecta. One is evident at birth (congenital) and the other occurs after birth. Children with the congenital type are born with short, deformed limbs; numerous

FIGURE 11-15. Dick Traum, PhD, above knee amputee, running the 100K; time 25 hours, 16 minutes, Achilles Track Club. (Photo Credit Leszek Sibiski, October, 1988, Kalish, Poland.)

broken bones; and a soft skull, which if they live, tends to grow in a triangular shape, broad at the forehead and narrow at the chin. Many babies with this condition die at birth, however.

Characteristics

The bones of children with this defect are in many ways like those of the developing fetus, and the immaturity is caused by reduction in bone salts (calcium and phosphorus) rather than any defect in the calcification mechanism. The underlying layer of the eyeball (choroid) shows through as a blue discoloration.

As growth occurs in individuals with either type of the disease, the limbs tend to become bowed. The bones are not dense, and the spine is rounded backward and often evidences scoliosis. The teeth are in poor condition, easily broken, discolored, and prone to cavities. The joints are excessively mobile, and the positions that the children may take show great flexibility.

Medical Treatment

No known chemical or nutrient has been shown to correct osteogenesis imperfecta, and the most satisfactory treatment is the surgical insertion of a steel rod between the ends of the long bones. This treatment, plus bracing, permits some youths to walk.

Many persons with brittle bone disease need a wheelchair at least part of the time, and those with severe cases require a wheelchair exclusively.

Physical Activity Program

Some authorities have suggested that physical activities are to be ruled out for this population, while others suggest that persons who have undergone surgical insertion of the steel rods may participate in specialized programs of aquatics and activities taking place in special facilities. The condition of children who have undergone operation tends to stabilize as the children grow older; they incur fewer fractures, and they may attend a regular school.

Mild activity, or even attempts to stand or walk, can cause fractures throughout the bony framework. Many children with osteogenesis imperfecta are unable to walk. Pillows are kept around both sides of the bed as well as at the head and feet. Heavy books and toys are not allowed.

Adapted physical education teachers should be sensitive to the presence of older children with this condition in their classes and to the presence of other children whose bones may be highly susceptible to injury, trauma, or breakage because of this and related conditions. The child who approaches normalcy in other areas continues to require a highly adapted physical education program that is limited to range of motion exercises. Although the diagnosis of osteogenesis imperfecta is assigned only to severe cases, many children seem to have a propensity for broken bones. Physical educators should take softness of bones into consideration when developing the physical education prescriptions for children.

ARTHROGRYPOSIS (CURVED JOINTS)

Arthrogryposis is a condition of flexure or contracture of joints (joints of the lower limbs more often than joints of the upper limbs). When several limbs are in contracture, the condition is referred to as multiple congenital contracture. Sherrill[47] reports that each year approximately 500 children are born in the United States with arthrogryposis. The cause is unknown, and the contractures may be observed relatively early in fetal life because of either a primary

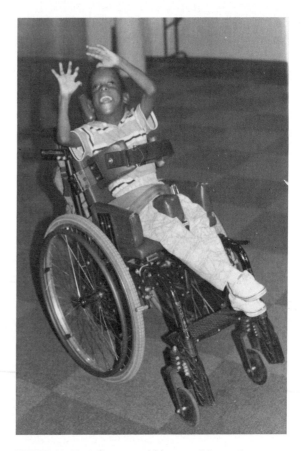

FIGURE 11-16. A five-year-old boy participates in creative dance. (Courtesy Dallas Independent School District.)

muscle disease or a spinal cord disease of cells controlling muscle contraction.

Characteristics

The limbs may be fixed in any position. However, the usual forms are with the shoulders turned in, elbows straightened and extended, forearms turned with the palm outward (pronated), and wrists flexed and deviated upward with the fingers curled into the palms. The hips may be bent in a flexed position and turned outward (externally rotated), and the feet are usually turned inward and downward. The spine often evidences scoliosis, the limbs are small in circumference, and the joints appear large and have lost their range of motion.

Several physical conditions are associated with arthrogryposis, including congenital heart disease, urinary tract abnormalities, respiratory problems, abdominal hernias, and facial abnormalities. Children with arthrogryposis may walk independently but with an abnormal gait, or they may depend on a wheelchair.

The literature states that articular surfaces do deteriorate with age. Therefore developmental exercises may assist in amelioration of deficient motor ability.

Medical Treatment

Surgery often is used to correct hip conditions as well as knee and foot deformities and is sometimes used to permit limited flexion of the elbow joint as well as greater wrist mobility.

Physical Education Program

The awkwardness of joint positions and mechanics cause no pain, and therefore children with arthrogryposis are free to engage in most types of activity.

OSTEOMYELITIS

Osteomyelitis is an inflammation of a bone and its medullary (marrow) cavity. This condition is occasionally referred to as *myelitis*. It is caused by *Staphylococcus, Streptococcus,* or *Pneumococcus* organisms.

In its early stages osteomyelitis is described as acute. If the infection persists or recurs periodically, it is called chronic. Since chronic osteomyelitis may linger on for years, the physical educator should confer with the physician about the nature of an adapted program.

Characteristics

The bones most often affected in osteomyelitis are the tibia, femur, and humerus. Pain and tenderness are present, and heat is felt through the overlying skin. Soft tissues feel hard, and neighboring joints may be distended with clear fluid.[47] There are limited effects on range of joint movement. The child may limp because of the acute pain.

Medical Treatment

If medical treatment is delayed, abscesses work outward, causing a sinus (hole) in the skin over the affected bone from which pus is discharged. This sinus is covered with a dressing that must be changed several times daily. The medical treatment is rest and intensive antibiotic therapy. Through surgery, the infected bone may be scraped to evacuate the pus.

Physical Activity Program

Rehabilitation activity can restore motor functions so that normal activity can be resumed. However, under certain conditions the child with osteomyelitis can participate in most developmental and recreational activities that allow the affected limb to be mobilized.[50] Exercise is always contraindicated when infection is active in the body.

POLIOMYELITIS

Poliomyelitis (polio) is a disease that causes damage to the central nervous system. An inflammation affects the motor cells in the spinal cord, which in turn affects the muscles. Polio is caused by a filterable virus that attacks the anterior horn of the spinal cord. It has seen a resurgence in this country because of large numbers of children who do not receive the polio vaccine.

Characteristics and Types

There are three prevalent classifications of poliomyelitis—abortive, nonparalytic, and paralytic.

The symptoms of abortive poliomyelitis are headache, fever, and nausea.

Nonparalytic poliomyelitis involves the central nervous system but does not damage the motor cells permanently. In addition to the symptoms of abortive poliomyelitis, the victim might experience general and specific pain and acute contractions of one or more muscle groups located in the upper and lower extremities, neck, and back.

Paralytic poliomyelitis includes three afflictions: spinal poliomyelitis, which involves upper limbs, lower limbs, respiratory muscles, and trunk muscles; bulbar poliomyelitis, which affects the muscles of the respiratory center; and, spinal-bulbar poliomyelitis, which involves a combination of voluntary and involuntary muscles (the most serious of the three paralytic forms).

Approximately 4% of those who contract polio die, 21% have severe paralysis, 25% suffer mild aftereffects, and 50% recover completely.

Medical Treatment

Tendon transplants and arthrodesis are commonly performed during the chronic stage of poliomyelitis.

Physical Activity Program

Exercise programs should focus on motor tasks that develop strength, endurance, flexibility, and coordination. Orthopedic deformities do not totally restrict movement. Children learn quickly to compensate for the inconvenience of an impaired foot or arm. At the elementary school level, many children with polio can achieve considerable athletic success. However, as they progress through school life, accumulated developmental lags as a rule influence skill development. Wheelchair sports are popular for polio victims who cannot walk.

SPINAL CORD INJURIES

Spinal cord injuries usually result in paralysis or partial paralysis of the arms, trunk, legs, or any particular combination thereof depending on the locus of the damage. The spinal cord is housed in the spinal or vertebral column. Nerves from the spinal cord pass down into the segments of the spinal column. Injury to the spinal cord affects innervation of muscle. The higher up the vertebral column the level of injury, the greater the restriction of body movement. Persons with spinal cord injuries are usually referred to as *paraplegics* or *quadriplegics*. A paraplegic is one who has the legs paralyzed. The quadriplegic has both the arms and legs affected.

Characteristics

Spinal cord injuries are classified according to the region of the vertebrae affected. The regions affected are cervical, thoracic, lumbar, and sacral. A description of the movement capability at each level of the lesion appears below.

Fourth cervical level: There is use of only the neck muscles and the diaphragm. Upper limb function is only possible with electrically powered assistive devices. The student needs complete assistance moving to and from the wheelchair.

Fifth cervical level: There is use of the deltoid muscles of the shoulder and the biceps muscles of the arm. The arms can be raised; however, it is difficult to engage in manipulative tasks. Persons with this level of involvement can perform many activ-

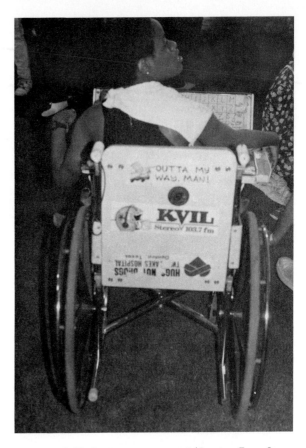

FIGURE 11-17. Outta my way, man! (Courtesy Texas Special Olympics.)

ities with their arms. However, they need assistance with transfer to and from the wheelchair.

Sixth cervical level: There is use of the wrist extensors and the student can push the wheelchair and make use of an overhead trapeze (a bar hung overhead to be grasped). Some persons afflicted at this level can transfer the body to and from the wheelchair.

Seventh cervical level: There is use of the elbow and wrist extensors. Movement of the hand is impaired. However, the person afflicted at this level may be able to perform pull-ups, push-ups, and participate in activities that involve the grasp release mechanism.

Upper thoracic levels: There is total movement capability in the arms, but none in the legs. There is some control in the muscles of the upper back. The student can control a wheelchair and may be able to stand with the use of long leg braces.

Lower thoracic levels: There is control of the abdominal musculature that rights the trunk. The use of the abdominal muscles makes it possible to walk with the support of long leg braces.

Lumbar levels: There is control of the hip joint and there is a good possibility of walking with controlled movement.

Sacral level: There is muscular functioning for efficient ambulation. The functional level of the bladder, anal sphincters and external genitals may be impaired.

The physical fitness characteristics of persons with spinal cord injury have been suspected as being related to the level of their lesion. Kofsky et al.[36] found significant differences between the aerobic power as predicted by submaximal ergometer tests between classifications of spinal column lesions at levels 2, 3, and 4. However, Winnick and Short,[59] who studied children aged 10 to 17 classified as levels 2 to 5, found that when comparing skinfold measures, grip strength, arm-hand pull-ups, speed in the 50-yard dash and shuttle run, and distance in the softball throw, significant differences were not found among levels nor ages. Collectively, the physical characteristics are as follows:

1. Inappropriate control of the bladder and digestive organs
2. Contractures (abnormal shortening of muscles)
3. Heterotopic bone formation, or laying down of new bone in soft tissue around joints (during this process the area may become inflamed and swollen)
4. Urinary infections
5. Difficulty in defecation
6. Decubitus ulcers on the back and buttocks (caused by pressure of the body weight on specific areas)
7. Spasms of the muscles
8. Spasticity of muscles that prevent effective movement
9. Overweight because of low energy expenditures

Physical Activity Program

The physical activity program for persons with spinal cord injury should be based on a well-rounded program of exercises for all the usable body parts, including activities to develop strength, flexibility, muscular endurance, cardiovascular endurance, and coordination. Cardiovascular development may be attained through arm pedaling of a bicycle ergometer, pushing of a wheelchair over considerable distances, and agility maneuvers with the wheelchair.

DiCarlo[19] reported that male quadriplegics with lesions at the fifth to seventh cervical level were able to increase their wheelchair propulsion endurance and cardiopulmonary function by engaging in arm cycle ergometry exercises three times a week for 8 weeks. Hardison, Isreal, and Somes[24] demonstrated the same types of gains with quadriplegic males with lesion levels ranging from T4 to T12. They demonstrated improved oxygen utilization with a training program consisting of a 70 rpm ergometer cranking rate at 60% of the subject's maximum VO_2.

Movement and dance therapies have been used successfully in rehabilitation programs for persons who have spinal cord injuries. Berrol and Katz[4] indicate that the focus of outcomes is goal oriented and there is considerable similarity between dance therapy, movement therapy, and those activitites that traditionally are included in adapted physical education programs. Once treatment goals are established, the disciplines appear to conduct their programs in a similar manner.

Paraplegics can perform most physical education activities from a wheelchair. For younger children, fundamental motor skills such as throwing, hitting, and catching are appropriate. Once these skills are mastered, games that incorporate these skills may be played. Modifications of games that have been previously described are appropriate for children in wheelchairs. Children in wheelchairs can participate in parachute games and target games without accommodation. They can maintain fitness of the upper body through the same type of regimens as do the nondisabled. Strengthening of the arms and shoulder girdle is important for propulsion of the wheelchair and for changing body positions when moving in and out of the wheelchair. Swimming is a particularly good activity for the development of total physical fitness. The emphasis should be on the development of functional movement skills. (Please refer to the section on spina bifida in this chapter.)

Several organizations promote competition for persons in wheelchairs. These include archery, bowling, basketball, table tennis, wheelchair racing, and track events. Classification systems based on the levels of injury and physical functioning ability have been developed for equitable competition. A comparison of three such systems is presented in Table 11-2.

SPONDYLOLYSIS AND SPONDYLOLISTHESIS

Spondylolysis and spondylolisthesis result from a congenital malformation of one or both of the neural arches of the fifth lumbar vertebra or, less frequently, the fourth lumbar vertebra. Spondylolisthesis is distinguished from spondylolysis by anterior displacement of

TABLE 11-2

Comparison of wheelchair classification systems

NWBA			NWAA	ISMGF (except basketball)
C-5		IA	Triceps 0-3	IA
C-6		IB	Triceps 4-5	IB
C-7			Wrist flexion/extension present	
		IC	Finger flexion/extension 4-5	IC
C-8			No useful hand intrinsics	
			No useful abdominals	
T-1	I	II	No lower intercostals	II
T-2	Motor loss at T7 or above			
T-3				
T-4	Sitting balance poor			
T-5				
T-6			Upper abdominals good. No useful lower abdominals. No useful lower trunk extensors.	
T-7		III		III
T-8	II			
T-9	Abdominal and spinal extensor muscle strength 3-5		Poor to fair sitting balance	
T-10				
T-11	Sitting balance fair to good	IV	Good abdominals and spinal extensors. Some hip flexors/adductors.	IV
T-12				
L-1	Hip flexors ≤4		Fair to good balance	Good balance
	Hip adductors ≤3		Quad strength <3	1-20 points traumatic
	Quadriceps ≤2		Includes bilateral hip disarticulation amputees	1-15 points postpolio
L-2	Includes bilateral hip disarticulations			Amputees not included
L-3	III	V		
	Trunk control, pelvic control		Normal balance	
			Quad strength ≥3	
L-4	Sitting balance good to normal		<40 points	V
			Most amputees AK & BK	Normal balance
L-5	Quads 3-5		In V/VI	21-40 points traumatic
S-1	All other amputees		VI (Swimming only)	16-35 points polio
			≥40 points	Amputees not included
				VI (Swimming only)
				41-60 points traumatic
				36-50 points polio
				Not eligible >61 points traumatic
				>51 points polio

(From Weiss M, Curtis KA: Controversies in medical classification of wheelchair athletes. In Sherrill C: Sport and disabled athletes—the 1984 Olympic Scientific Congress proceedings, volume 9, Champaign, Ill, 1986. Copyright by Human Kinetics Publishers.)

the fifth lumbar vertebra on the sacrum. Both conditions may be accompanied by pain in the lower back.

Forward displacement may occur as a result of sudden trauma to the lumbar region. The vertebrae are moved anteriorly due to an absence of bony continuity of the neural arch, and the main support is derived from its ligamentous arrangement. In such cases, individuals often appear to have severe lordosis.

Characteristics

Many individuals have spondylolysis, or even spondylolisthesis, without symptoms of any kind, but a mild

twist or blow may set off a whole series of low back complaints and localized discomfort or pain radiating down one or both sides.

Medical Treatment

The pathological condition eventually may become so extensive as to require surgical intervention.

Physical Activity Program

Proper therapy may involve a graduated exercise program that may help prevent further aggravation and, in some cases, remove many symptoms characteristic of

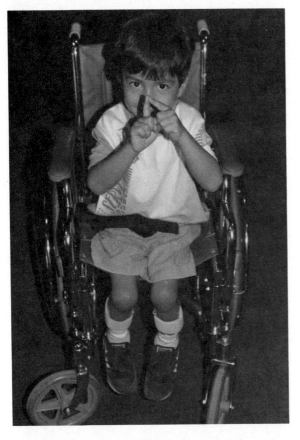

FIGURE 11-18. A child participates in creative story telling at camp. (Courtesy Dallas Independent School District.)

the condition. A program should be initiated similar to that for ameliorating the postural malalignment of lordosis (with primary concentration on the strengthening of abdominal muscles, the lengthening of lower back muscles, and the segmental realigning of legs, pelvis, and spine).

Games and sports that overextend, fatigue, or severely twist and bend the lower back should be avoided. In most cases, the physician will advise against contact sports and heavy weight lifting.

AMPUTATIONS

Amputation is the loss of part or all of a limb. Amputation may be performed to arrest a malignant condition caused by trauma, tumors, infection, vascular impairment, diabetes, or arteriosclerosis. Amputees in the United States exceed 300,000 in number.

Characteristics and Types

Amputations can be classified into two categories—acquired amputation and congenital amputation. The amputation is acquired if one has a limb removed by operation; it is congenital if the child is born without a limb.

Congenital amputations are classified according to the site and level of limb absence. When an amputation is performed through a joint, it is referred to as a disarticulation.

Medical Treatment

Medical treatment for amputation involves the design of a prosthetic appliance. The purpose of the prosthetic device is to enable the individual to function as normally as possible. The application of a prosthetic device may be preceded by surgery to produce a stump. After the operation the stump is dressed and bandaged to aid shrinkage of the stump. After the fitting of the prosthesis, the stump must be continually cared for. It should be checked periodically and cleaned to prevent infection, abrasion, and skin disorder.

The attachment of a false limb early in a child's development will encourage the incorporation of the appendage into natural body activity more than if the prosthesis is introduced later in life.

Physical Activity Program

Amputees must develop skill to use prostheses; effective use demands much effort. Training should be directed toward daily living skills such as eating, drinking, dressing, and recreational skills that can be taught in physical education. Lower limb prostheses often result in problems of ambulation. These problems vary with the specific level of amputation.

Gait training

Most gait deviations result from problems with the alignment of the lower limb prosthesis. Deviations may include rotations of the foot at heel strike, unequal timing, side-walking base, abducted gait, excessive heel ride, instability of the knee, excessive knee flexion, hyperextension of the knees, excessive pronation of the foot, foot slap, and rotation of the foot with continuing whip.[14]

Persons with amputations below the knee can learn ambulation skills well with a prosthesis and training. Persons with amputation above the knee but below the hip may have difficulty in developing efficient walking gaits. Amputations at this level require alteration of the gait pattern. Steps are usually shortened to circumvent lack of knee function.

Aids

Aids may be designed to assist prostheses of the legs or the arms. Assistive devices may be used to aid locomotion when the legs are debilitated. Some assistive devices are canes and crutches. A major problem for students who use canes and crutches is the need to learn balance to free one hand for participation in activity. Use of the Lofstrand crutches, which are anchored to the forearms, enables balance to be maintained by one crutch. This frees one arm and enables participation in throwing and striking activities.

Although it is difficult to substitute for the human hand and fingers, it is possible to achieve dexterity with the use of a utility arm and split hook. These aids enable the use of racquets for paddle games if both arms are amputated. Persons who have lost a single arm can play most basic skill games and participate in more advanced sport activity without modifications. Special devices can be built by an orthotist to fit into the arm prosthesis to hold sports equipment such as gloves.

Amputees are often exposed to beneficial exercise through the use of the prosthesis. Exercises should be initiated to strengthen muscles after a stump heals. Training also enhances ambulation, inhibits atrophy and contractures, improves or maintains mechanical alignment of body parts, and develops general physical fitness.

Adapted Sport Activity

Authorities agree that children with properly fitted prostheses should engage in regular physical education activities. Amputees have considerable potential for participation in adapted sports and games. The National Amputee Golf Association, for example, provides clinics nationwide to introduce children and adults with disabilities to the sport of golf and to train teachers and coaches to adapt methods/instruction to meet the needs of amputees. There are opportunities for persons with prostheses to participate in official sports competition. Persons with above-knee amputations can walk well and engage in swimming, skiing, and other activities with the proper aids. Arm amputees who have use of their feet can participate in activities that require foot action such as soccer and running events, as well as other activities that involve exclusively the feet.

There are several adaptations of physical activity that can be made for children with impaired ambulation. For these children the major disadvantages are speed of locomotion and fatigue to sustained activity. Some accommodations that can be made are shorten-

ing the distance the player must travel and decreasing the speed needed to move from one place to another.

Physical fitness of amputees should be an important part of a physical education program. Strength and flexibility and power of the unafflicted limbs are important. Furthermore, Lasko and Knorph[39] stress the importance of developing and maintaining the amputee's level of cardiovascular efficiency.

BRACES AND WHEELCHAIRS

Many physically challenged children who participate in physical education programs use a wheelchair for locomotion or wear braces, and some children require both devices. The physical educator should have a working knowledge of the care and maintenence of lower extremity braces and wheelchairs. One of the teacher's responsibilities is daily observation of the student's use and care of ambulation equipment. In conjunction with related services, the child's classroom teacher, family, and physical educator should develop a program to maximize the use of ambulation devices in

FIGURE 11-19. An athlete competes in the motorized wheelchair obstacle course. (Courtesy Texas Special Olympics.)

the physical education setting and beyond the school boundaries. In addition, any problems that arise with the ambulation devices should be communicated to the special or regular class teacher or the parents.

Leg Braces

Leg braces are metal or plastic support frames that are strapped to the body above and below specific joints to assist with ambulation. The main purposes of lower extremity braces are to support the weight for ambulation, control involuntary movements, and prevent or correct deformities.

In general, there are three classifications of lower leg braces—short leg braces, long leg braces, and hip braces.

Short leg brace

A short leg brace is appropriate when the disabling condition occurs at the ankle joint. Although there are several different types of short leg braces, the simplest form consists of a single metal upright bar attached to the shoe with a cuff around the calf of the leg (Fig. 11-20). When more stability is needed, double upright bars are used. The design of this type of brace should facilitate the control of four movements of the ankle joint. Leather straps attached to the metal uprights and strapped around the ankle assist with control of the ankle joint.

Long leg brace

The long leg (knee-ankle-foot) brace assists with control of the ankle and knee joint (Fig. 11-21). The fundamental purpose of the long leg brace is to pre-

vent hyperextension of the knee caused by weak extensor muscles. The brace must be in different positions when the student is sitting as compared to standing. To accommodate the different positions of the knee, various types of locks are placed at the knee joints, the most common of which is a sliding metal lock that is easily locked and unlocked by hand. The knee joint of the long leg brace is locked when the individual is sitting in a chair. Locking devices also may be used to control the ankle when this type of brace is used.

Long leg brace with pelvic band

The long leg brace may extend from below the ankle to above the hip. Such a brace is called a hip-knee-ankle-foot long leg brace. The purpose of such a brace is to control movements of the hip joint as well as the knee and the ankle. To assist with the control of the hip joint, a pelvic band is attached to the top of the upright bar.

The physical education teacher should have a work-

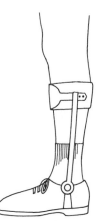

FIGURE 11-20. A short leg brace.

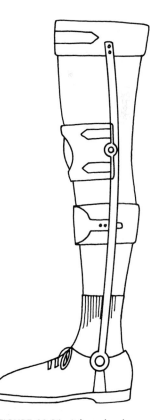

FIGURE 11-21. A long leg brace.

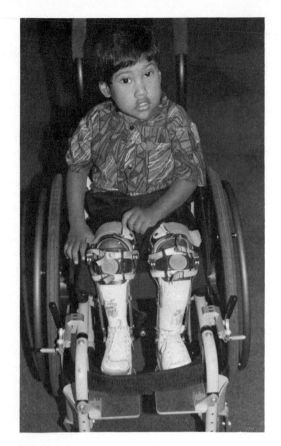

FIGURE 11-22. A three-year-old child with long-leg braces. (Courtesy Dallas Independent School District.)

ing knowledge of the functions of leg braces. Some of the characteristics that can be observed are as follows: (1) brace joints work easily, (2) brace and anatomical joints coincide, (3) upright conforms to the leg, (4) brace is of correct length, and (5) upright coincides with the midline of the leg.

Wheelchairs

The purpose of wheelchairs is to provide a means of locomotion for persons who lack strength, endurance, or flexibility of muscles prerequisite for ambulation. Persons who can walk but cannot rise from a seated position to a standing position or those who need to transport objects but cannot do so may also need a wheelchair.

There are several types of wheelchairs. However, the most common are made of metal and have four wheels. The two back wheels are large, and the two front wheels are small and mounted on casters that pivot freely. Two or more separate rims that can be grasped to propel the chair are mounted to the back wheels.

Wheelchair design is a continuous process, the goal of which is to make the wheelchair more functional. Many special features can be added to make a wheelchair more functional or comfortable, including armrests, footrests, legrests, and headrests, all of which can be removed. Leg spreaders have also been incorporated into some wheelchairs to prevent the scissoring of legs. Analog devices for aligning the rear wheels have been developed to maximize efficiency in propelling the wheelchair.[11] Many wheelchairs can be folded for easy storage. There are motorized wheelchairs to accommodate persons who have severe afflictions of the upper extremities. Some other features of a wheelchair are unique folding mechanisms that allow it to double as a stroller or car seat, adjustable Velcro fasteners, pads, and attachable trays. The boxed material on pp. 256-257 contains a checklist that will enable physical education teachers to assess wheelchairs and braces as they relate to optimum functioning and comfort of the individual.[54]

Specialized Adapted Seating

Adapted seating for severely disabled individuals has been a subject of increasing concern. Inappropriate seating of severely afflicted individuals can result in severe scoliosis with vertebral rotation. Severe contractures may result from fixed postures in a wheelchair. To avoid this, extensive adaptations of the chair may be necessary. Hundertmark[33] indicates that the anterior and posterior tilt of the pelvis and the vertical angle of the backrest are important considerations in achieving therapeutic seating for the severely multihandicapped person.

Wheelchair propulsion

Wheelchair competitive sports are becoming more and more popular. Interest in improving performance has spurred researchers to study ways to increase the efficiency of propelling wheelchairs. Gehlsen, Davis, and Bahamonde[23] indicate that a forward lean of the trunk may allow the student to increase the range of hand-handrim contact. Hedrick et al.[26] indicate that a wheelchair racer's speed can be increased when they rotate the upper torso sideways or maintain a flexed position while coasting. Alexander[1] describes a technique to increase propulsion of the wheelchair in which the back of the hands propel the wheelchair by drawing the hands up and over the wheel and finishing

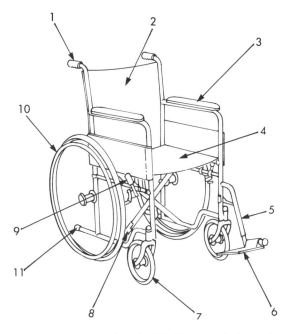

FIGURE 11-23. Parts of a wheelchair. 1, Handgrips/push handles; 2, back upholstery; 3, armrests; 4, seat upholstery; 5, front rigging; 6, footplate; 7, casters; 8, crossbraces; 9, wheel locks; 10, wheel and handrim; 11 tipping lever.

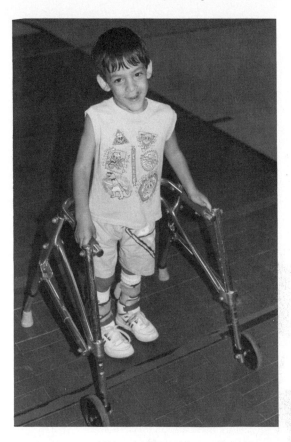

FIGURE 11-24. A child ambulates with a walker. (Courtesy Dallas Independent School District.)

the power stroke with lower arms in supination. Pads are used to increase friction between the hands and the wheelchair, and allow the student a longer power phase. In addition, Burd and Grass[8] describe procedures for strapping students in wheelchairs to correct posture deviations that diminish the full propulsive stroke on the handrim of the wheelchair.

In addition to improved techniques for wheelchair propulsion, research has been conducted on motivational variables that may facilitate competition in wheelchairs. Dummer et al.[21] suggest that teaching students the right strategies that are compatible with their abilities, and helping them enjoy the activity and competition enhances their desire to compete. Brasile and Hedrick[7] suggest that intrinsic task-related reasons for participation are important motivators for success in physical activity for students with orthopedic and neurologic disabilities.

Physical Activity Program

Persons with physical disabilities should develop skills that can be expressed in leisure and recreational activity in the community. One of the desired outcomes of

the acquisition of sport skills is participation in competitive sports. Therefore the instruction in the physical education program should match opportunities for sports participation in the community. The generalization of the sport skills acquired by the physically challenged in the instructional phase of the physical education program requires close study of several variables. Some considerations might be the nature of the specific disability, the equipment required for participation (wheelchairs and ancillary equipment), and ways of structuring competition to maximize fulfillment for the individual.

Opportunities for participation

Persons with physical disabilities need opportunities to express attained sport skills in competition. Many public schools have limited numbers of physically challenged children of similar ages and ability. This makes organized competition difficult. Therefore

SHORT LEG (ANKLE-FOOT) BRACE

A. With the brace off the student
1. Do joints work easily?
2. Can shoes be easily removed?
3. Is the workmanship good?
   a. No rough edges
   b. Straps secure
   c. Leather work stitched properly
B. Student standing with brace on
1. Are the sole and heel flat on the floor?
2. Are the ankle joints aligned so that they coincide with the anatomical joints?
3. Is there ample clearance between the leg and the brace (one finger width)?
4. Does the T strap exert enough force for correction without causing deformity?
5. Do the uprights conform to the contour of the leg?
6. Do the uprights coincide with the midline of the leg when viewed from the side?
7. Is the brace long enough?
   a. It should be below the bend of the knee so the student can bend the knee comfortably to 120°.
   b. It should not be lower than the bulky part of the calf muscle.
C. Student walking with brace on
1. Is there clearance between the uprights and the leg?
2. Are there any gait deviations?
3. Is the brace quiet?

LONG LEG (KNEE-ANKLE-FOOT) BRACE

A. With the brace off the student
1. Do joints work easily?
2. Can shoes be easily removed?
3. Is the workmanship good?
   a. No rough edges
   b. Straps secure
   c. Leather work stitched properly
B. Student standing with brace on
1. Are the knee joints aligned at the approximate anatomical joints?
   a. There should be no pressure from the thigh band when knee is bent (if so joints are too high).
   b. There should be no pressure from calf band when knee is bent (if so joints are too low).
   c. There should be no pressure on calf (if so joints are too far forward).
   d. There should be no pressure on shin or knee cap (if so joints are too far backward).
2. Are locks secure and easy to work?
3. Is the brace long enough?
   a. Medial upright should be up into groin region but should not cause pain.

b. Lateral upright should be 1 inch longer.
4. Are the thigh bands and calf bands about equal distance from the knee?

LONG LEG BRACE WITH PELVIC BAND (HIP-KNEE-ANKLE-FOOT ORTHOSIS)

A. With the brace off the student
1. Do joints work easily?
2. Can shoes be easily removed?
3. Is the workmanship good?
   a. No rough edges
   b. Straps secure
   c. Leather work stitched properly
B. Student with brace on
1. Is the pelvic band located below the waist?
2. Is the student comfortable sitting and standing?
3. Are the hip joints in the right place and do the locks work easily?

OTHER POINTS TO CHECK

A. Do the shoes fit and are they in good repair?
B. Do reddened areas go away after the brace has been of 20 minutes?
C. Is the student comfortable?
D. Is the brace helping the student?

PLASTIC BRACES

A. Does the brace conform to and contact the extremity?
B. Is the student wearing a sock between foot and brace?
C. Does the brace pull away from the leg excessively when the student walks?
D. Do reddened areas go away after the brace has been off 20 minutes?

LOWER EXTREMITY PROSTHETICS

A. Is the student wearing prosthesis (frequency)?
B. Does the student use assistive devices with prosthesis (crutches, canes, one can, other)? If so, what does he or she use and how often?
C. Is the prosthesis on correctly?
1. Is the toe turned out about the same as the other foot?
2. When the student sits is the knee in alignment?
D. Does the leg appear the same length as the normal leg?
1. Does the student stand straight when bearing weight on the prothesis?
2. Are the shoulders even when leg is bearing weight (one shoulder does not drop)?
3. When the student walks does the knee stay straight without turning out or in?

From Venn J, Morganstern C, Dykes MK: Teach Except Child, Winter 1979, pp 51-56. Copyright 1979 by The Council for Exceptional Children. Reprinted with permission.

GAIT DEVIATIONS

A. Does the student stand straight when bearing weight on the prosthesis?
B. Does the artificial leg swing forward without turning in or out?
C. Does the student swing the artificial leg through without rising up on the foot of the normal leg?
D. When the student walks does the leg swing straight forward? (It should not swing out in an arc.)
E. When the student stands are the feet a normal distance apart? (The stance should not be too wide.)
F. Does the knee bend and straighten like a normal leg?

CONDITION OF THE PROSTHESIS

A. Do the suspension joints appear to be in good condition (leather, joint, band)?
B. Does the leg stay in place when the student is standing and sitting?
C. Does the knee bend appropriately?
D. Are the joints quiet when moved?
E. Do the foot and ankle appear to be in one piece?
F. Is the shoe in good condition (heel, sole)?

WHEELCHAIR

A. Arms
 1. Are the armrests and side panels secure and free of sharp edges and cracks?
 2. Do the arm locks function properly?
B. Back
 1. Is the upholstery free of rips and tears?
 2. Is the back taut from top to bottom?
 3. Is the safety belt attached tightly and not frayed?
C. Seat and frame
 1. Is the upholstery free of rips and tears?
 2. Does the chair fold easily without sticking?
 3. When the chair is folded fully are the front post slides straight and round?
D. Wheel locks
 1. Do the wheel locks securely engage the tire surfaces and prevent the wheel from turning?
E. Large wheels
 1. Are the wheels free from wobble or sideplay when spun?
 2. Are the spokes equally right and without any missing spokes?
 3. Are the tires free from excessive wear and gaps at the joined section?
F. Casters
 1. Is the stem firmly attached to the fork?
 2. Are the forks straight on sides and stem so that the caster swivels easily?
 3. Is the caster assembly free of excessive play both upward and downward as well as backward and forward?
 4. Are the wheels free of excessive play and wobble?
 5. Are the tires in good condition?
G. Footrest/legrest
 1. Does the lock mechanism fit securely?
 2. Are the heel loops secure and correctly installed?
 3. Do the foot plates fold easily and hold in any position?
 4. Are the legrest panels free of cracks and sharp edges?

WITH STUDENT SITTING IN WHEELCHAIR

A. Seat width
 1. When your palms are placed between the patient's hip and the side of the chair (skirtguard), do the hands contact the hip and the skirtguard at the same time without pressure?
 2. Or, is the clearance between the patient's widest point of either hips or thigh and the skirtguard approximately 1 inch on either side?
B. Seat depth
 1. Can you place your hand, with fingers extended, between the front edge of the seat upholstery and to the rear of the knee with a clearance of three or four fingers?
 2. Or, is the seat upholstery approximately 2 to 3 inches less than the student's thigh measurement?
C. Seat height and footrest
 1. Is the lowest part of the stepplates no closer than 2 inches from the floor?
 2. Or, is the student's thigh elevated slightly above the front edge of the seat upholstery?
D. Arm height
 1. Does the arm height not force the shoulders up or allow them to drop significantly when the student is in a normal sitting position?
 2. Is the elbow positioned slightly forward of the trunk midline when the student is in a normal sitting position?
E. Back height
 1. Can you insert four or five fingers between the patient's armpit area and the top of the back upholstery touching both at the same time?
 2. Is the top of the back upholstery approximately 4 inches below the armpit for the student who needs only minimum trunk support?

WITH STUDENT PUSHING OR RIDING IN WHEELCHAIR

A. Is the wheelchair free from squeaks or rattles?
B. Does the chair roll easily without pulling to either side?
C. Are the large wheels and casters free of play and wobble?

cooperative efforts need to be made among schools to provide opportunities for competition among the athletes. Special Olympics, in some states, provides this opportunity. Wheelchair sports events are staged for competition. Several colleges and universities have intercollegiate wheelchair sports programs. The University of Illinois has developed one of the best intercollegiate wheelchair sports programs. Several other universities also have well-developed intercollegiate athletic programs.

There are two national organizations for wheelchair sports—the National Wheelchair Athletic Association and the National Wheelchair Basketball Association. Competition is open to both men and women.[49] The mission of both of these organizations is to promote competition in which persons confined to wheelchairs may participate. These organizations provide a forum and incentive to maximize proficiency in sports for competition. Wheelchair sports competitions have been held primarily at national and international levels.

FIGURE 11-25. An Olympian ready for the victory dance. (Courtesy Texas Special Olympics.)

There is a movement for the organization of games for individuals with generic disabilities at the state level. Project GUMBO in Louisiana is a good example of games organized for the pysically challenged at the state level.[12] More sophisticated competition is held by the International Sports Organization for the Disabled. Competitions are intense. As a result, training camps are being developed to improve performance at international games.[15] Not only have international games developed in the intensity of competition, but also in the magnitude of participation. Thus opportunities exist for many individuals with physical disabilities to participate in competitive sports at their ability level with incentive to increase skills to a world-class level.

Nature and scope of program

Wheelchair sports are designed to accommodate persons with significant, permanent physical disability of the lower extremities that prevents full participation with able-bodied peers. Persons who may be included in this group are those with cerebral palsy, muscular dystrophy, or spinal cord injuries. Many of these persons may not use wheelchairs but qualify for competition because of inability to engage in full participation with able-bodied peers.

The sport activity program involves sports that do not require use of the legs and can be performed from the wheelchair. Some of the sport activities of the National Wheelchair Athletic Association are target archery, table tennis, swimming, weight lifting, and selected field events. Other activities for which adaptation can be made are fencing, bowling, badminton, volleyball, floor hockey, and miniature golf.

In addition, competitions at the international level have been organized for the sports of snow skiing,[13] tennis,[34] racquetball,[27] and aquatic events such as water skiing, rowing, and kayaking.[35] There is also a movement to enable persons with disabilities to participate with nondisabled athletes in major sporting events. For example, wheelchair athletes participate at the classic running event, the Boston Marathon.[32]

Differences in abilities

Official wheelchair sports competition is based on a medical classification system (see Table 11-2). As will be noted when reviewing Table 11-2, sports organizations for athletes with disabilities use sightly different systems for classifying athletes for competitive purposes. In Table 11-2 three classification systems are described in relation to muscular involvement and spinal level of impairment.

The National Wheelchair Basketball Association

(NWBA) uses three categories for competition purposes: I, which encompasses impairments of the cervical and thoracic spine through T7 (seventh thoracic vertebra); II, which includes impairments from T8 (eighth thoracic vertebra) through L2 (second lumbar vertebra); and III, which includes all impairments to vertebra below the second lumbar area.[51] The National Wheelchair Athletic Association (NWAA) and the International Stoke-Mandeville Games Federation (ISMGF) use similar classification systems. These two organizations categorize athletes with cervical level impairments as IA, IB, or IC depending on the level of impairment: category II includes T1 through T6 impairments; category III encompasses T7 through T10 vertebral impairments; category IV includes T11 through L2 impairments; and category V includes all impairments from the third lumbar vertebra down.

The purpose of the classification system is to allow for fair competition. Tests are administered to determine the level of muscular function. Such tests do not take into account the proficiency of the athletes in competition. Several writers have questioned the validity of existing classification systems.[5,6,28] Clearly, children in wheelchairs do not have equal abilities. Therefore to provide equitable competition in school-based wheelchair activities, it may be necessary to test skill performances and group the participants according to ability in the individual sports.

Amputees are considered to possess a lesser disability when compared with other athletes confined to wheelchairs. In some instances they play sports such as volleyball standing up.[56] In efforts to equate competition they are classified according to the number of amputations and the location and the length of the stumps. Amputations may occur on one or both sides of the body, above or below the knees.

Another group of persons in wheelchairs have severe impairment of the upper appendages. They may have spasticity or contractures. It is not uncommon for these children to adopt unique throwing patterns to maximize performance. Their physical structure rules out the teaching of mechanically sound sport skill patterns. Specific techniques must be determined for each child.

Adaptation of equipment

The physical limitations of children with physical disabilities are related to opportunity for participation in play and games. It may be necessary to adapt equipment to include children in sport activity. For instance, there are several commercially available pieces of equipment that enable persons with physical disabili-

ties to participate in bowling. Some of the adaptations are a bowling bowl with handles, a fork that allows the person to push the bowling ball as in shuffleboard, and a ramp that enables gravity to act on the ball in place of the force provided by movement. Each of these adaptations in equipment accommodates for a specific physical problem related to bowling. The adapted equipment for bowling is paired with the nature of the physical problem.

Equipment	Accommodation of disability
Handles	Needs assistance with the grip but has the use of the arm and wrist
Fork	Has the use of the arm but has limited ability to control the wrist and an underhand throwing pattern
Ramp	Has limited use of the arm, wrist, and fingers as they apply to an underhand movement pattern

FIGURE 11-26. Abu Yilla, an elite wheelchair athlete, participates in a year-round weight training program. (Courtesy Texas Special Olympics.)

Assessment of skills needed for participation

Many children with severe physical disabilities can engage in games and sports with few adaptations. Most can enjoy swimming activities. However, persons restricted to wheelchairs should be appraised to determine their functional movement capabilities. Motor programs should then be developed to meet their unique needs. The assessment should provide information about the potential for movement of each action of the body. This would involve knowledge of strength, power, flexibility, and endurance of specific muscle groups. In addition, there should be information about which movement actions can be coordinated to attain specific motor outcomes. For instance, several throwing patterns that children with severe impairments use when participating in the Special Olympics can help circumvent movement problems of the arms and hands. The desired throwing pattern is one of extension of the arm and elbow and flexion of the wrist. If either of these actions is impaired, alternate throwing patterns need to be found. Some throwing patterns developed to circumvent extreme disability of arm, elbow, and wrist are underhand movement, horizontal abduction of the arm/shoulder, flexion of the arm and elbow (over the shoulder), horizontal abduction of the arm (side arm), and overhand movement with most of the force from a rocking motion of the trunk. To maximize the potential of each of these types of throwing patterns, it is necessary to conduct training programs that will consider each child's assets and develop them fully. However, another option is to provide therapeutic exercise for each of the desired actions and then teach it as a functional, normalized movement pattern.

The ability prerequisites of strength, flexibility, endurance, power, and coordination can be applied to many wheelchair activities. Some of these activities involve (1) basic mobility skills, (2) transfer skills from and to the wheelchair, (3) performance on mats, (4) performance on gymnastics apparatus, (5) ability to maneuver vehicles, (6) motor capabilities in a swimming pool, (7) walking with aids, and (8) the ability to push and pull objects. The ability prerequisites for each fundamental movement pattern should be studied to identify specific problems so that appropriate intervention can be undertaken. Examples of the categories of activities or abilities follow.

1. Basic mobility skills[61]
   a. Moving up and down ramps
   b. Moving from a wheelchair to another chair
   c. Transporting objects
2. Transfer skills
   a. Standing from a wheelchair
   b. Moving from a wheelchair to another chair
   c. Moving from a wheelchair to mats
   d. Moving from a wheelchair to different pieces of equipment
3. Performance on mats
   a. Forward and backward rolls
   b. Partner activity
   c. Climbing on low obstacles and elevated mats
4. Performance on gymnastics apparatus
   a. Rings
   b. High bar
   c. Parallel bars
5. Ability to maneuver vehicles
   a. Floor scooters
   b. Hand-propelled carts
   c. Tricycles
   d. Upright scooters with three wheels
6. Swimming pool activity
   a. Getting into and out of the pool
   b. Use of the railing for resting
   c. Swimming
7. Walking with aids
   a. Different types of canes
   b. Crutches
   c. Walkers
8. Ability to push and pull objects
   a. Throw a ball or push a ball
   b. Propel scooters with the hands
   c. Push a cage ball

Each of the above-mentioned behaviors should be analyzed to see if the student's strength, flexibility, endurance, power, and coordination are sufficient for acquisition and proficiency of these functional activities.

One of the most common concerns of students and athletes who use wheelchairs is efficient propulsion. Van der Woude, Veeger, and Rozendal[53] conducted an extensive review of the literature to determine which variables effect the ease, comfort, safety, and efficiency of wheelchair use. They reported that considerable research is needed before enough is known to optimumly fit wheelchairs to their users.

ADAPTING ACTIVITY FOR NEUROLOGICALLY AND ORTHOPEDICALLY DISABLED LEARNERS

Many games and sports in which students regularly participate in physical education classes can, with minor modification, be made safe and interesting for persons with physical disabilities. In general, the rules, techniques, and equipment of a game or activity should be changed as little as possible when they are modified for students wtih disabilities. Some of the ways that regular physical education and sport activities can be modified are the following:

1. The size of the playing area can be made smaller, with proportionate reduction of the amount of activity.
2. Larger balls or larger pieces of equipment can be introduced to make the game easier or to slow down the tempo so physical accommodations can be made.
3. Smaller, lighter balls or striking implements (plastic or styrofoam balls and plastic bats) or objects that are easier to handle (a beanbag) can be substituted.
4. More players can be added to a team, which reduces the amount of activity and the responsibility of individuals.
5. Minor rule changes can be made in the contest or game while as many of the basic rules as possible are retained.
6. The amount of time allowed for play can be reduced via shorter quarters, or the total time for a game can be reduced to allow for the onset of fatigue.
7. The number of points required to win a contest can be reduced.
8. Free substitutions can be made, which allows the students alternately to participate and then rest while the contest continues.

These modifications can be made in a game or contest whether the student participates in a segregated or integrated physical education class. If the child with a disability participates in a segregated class, it is possible to provide activities similar to those of regular physical education classes by practicing many of the culturally accepted sport skills in drill types of activities. An example would be playing such basketball games as "twenty-one" and "around the world" or taking free throws as lead-up activities to the sport. Pitching, batting, throwing, catching, and games such as "over the line" can be played as lead-up activities for softball. Serving, stroking, volleying, and the like can be practiced as lead-up activities for tennis. Such activities can be designed to accommodate physical limitations (see Table 11-3). Students with temporary injuries may become more skillful in various activities so that when they return to an unrestricted class they may participate in the whole game or sport with a reasonable degree of success.

Procedure for Adapting Sports and Games

Teachers who include children with disabilities in games and sports in the regular physical education

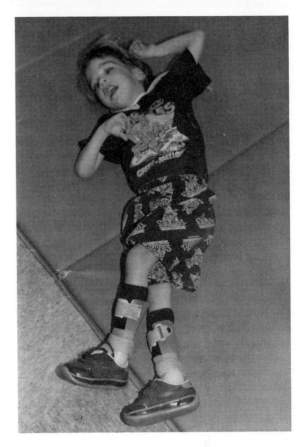

FIGURE 11-27. A child develops independent rolling skills.

class must be able to apply principles of adapting the sports and games to each child. It is beyond the scope of this book to compile adaptations of games for a wide range of disabilities for specific activities. Following is a suggested procedure for adapting a sport or game for a child with a disability:

1. Select and analyze the play, game, or sport
2. Identify the problems the individual child will have in participating in the play, game, or sport
3. Make the adaptations
4. Select principles of adaptation that may apply to the specific situation

Adaptations for Children with Limited Movement

There are several options to accommodate individual problems for children with limited movement. First, play and games may be selected that circumvent the

TABLE 11-3

Principles for adapting physical activity

Activity	Modification	Consequence
Reduce size of playing area		
Soccer	Reduce size of field	Less distance to cover; ball moves from one end of field to other faster
Soccer	Reduce size of goal commensurate with student's movement ability	Less distance to cover
Badminton	Reduce size of court	Less distance to cover; accommodation can be made to equate movement capability of disabled student with that of nondisabled student
Softball	Shorten distance between bases when disabled person bats	Disabled student has equitable amount of time to reach base
Introduce larger pieces of equipment		
Softball	Use balloon or beach ball	Speed of the object and tempo of game are reduced
Softball	Use larger ball	Chance of success is enhanced and tempo of game is reduced
Soccer	Use larger ball	Area where ball can be propelled successfully is increased
Volleyball	Use beach ball	Area of contact is increased, enhancing success and requiring less finger strength to control ball
Introduce lighter equipment		
Softball	Use lighter bat	Bat can be moved more quickly so there is greater opportunity to strike ball
Soccer	Use lighter ball	Speed is reduced and successful contact is more likely
Bowling	Use lighter ball	Weaker person has greater control of ball
Archery	Use lighter bow	Weaker person can draw bow
Tennis	Use aluminum racquet	Weaker person can control racquet
Modify size of team		
Volleyball	Add more players	Less area for each person to cover
Soccer	Add more players	Distance each person must cover in team play is reduced
Softball	Add more players	Less area for each person to cover
Handball/tennis	Play triples	Less area for each person to cover
Make minor rule changes		
Wrestling	Use physical contact on takedown for blind persons	Blind person will always be in physical contact with opponent, enables him or her to know where opponent is at all times
Volleyball	Allow person with affliction in arms/hands to carry on a volleyball hit	Opportunity for success is greater
Soccer	Reduce size of goal	Opportunity for success is greater
Gymnastics	Strap legs of paraplegic together	Strap controls legs when body moves
Reduce playing time		
Basketball/soccer	Substitute every 3 or 4 minutes	Accommodation is made for fatigue
Swimming	Swim beside pool edge and rest at prescribed distances of travel or time intervals	Accommodation is made for fatigue
Reduce number of points required to win contest		
Handball/paddleball/tennis	Lessen number to fatigue level of individual	Physical endurance will not be factor in outcome of game
Basketball	Play until specified number of points are made	

inability to move. This enables children with disabilities to participate in a normal environment with their peers. However, it is obvious that such activity will comprise but a small part of the play, games, and sports of the total physical education program. Second, in team sports it is not uncommon for specific positions of a sport to require different degrees of movement; thus children who have limited movement capability should assume positions that require less movement. Third, the rules of the game can be modified, enabling equitable competition between persons with and without disabilities. Fourth, aids can be introduced that accommodate inability so that adjustments can be made to the game. Any one or a combination of these principles of adaptation may be employed to enable children with disabilities to participate in regular classes.

Physical Fitness Testing for Neurologically and Orthopedically Disabled Persons

Physical fitness testing for persons with neurological and orthopedic disabilities has been done primarily for two purposes: (1) to assess their physical fitness levels and (2) to classify disabled athletes for competition. Winnick and Short[59] have done extensive testing and have normative-referenced the performance of physically disabled persons on physical fitness tests (see Chapter 3). Horvat et al.[31] have studied ways to modify the treadmill so that it can be used to measure cardiovascular function of persons with orthopedic disabilities. Burkett et al.[9] have developed an apparatus for testing paraplegic and quadriplegic individuals for cardiovascular fitness. The apparatus uses weights placed in a tin can. The frequency, speed, and amount of weight that can be lowered is recorded for each individual. The instrument was reported as being a valid physiological measure for maximum work with spinal cord injury populations. Furthermore, its design could enable progressive resistance exercises for persons in wheelchairs. A more recent advance in cardiovascular equipment design for indiviudals using wheelchairs is the "Saratoga Cycle," a bicycle ergometer that can be propelled by the hands or the feet, which enables the student to exercise without asistance when he or she desires.[16]

Competitive sports for athletes with physical disabilities have been organized on the basis of etiological factors of the disability. This theory is based on the belief that equitable competition of individuals in wheelchairs is dependent upon the disability level. However, Labonowich et al.[37] and Brasile[6] indicate less emphasis should be placed on disability levels of wheelchair basketball participants and more emphasis should be

FIGURE 11-28. A three-year-old boy develops basic eye-hand coordination skills. (Courtesy Dallas Independent School District.)

placed on developing functional assessment tools that could be used in judging performance of athletes with disabilities.[55]

Computer-Controlled Movement of Paralyzed Muscles

In the past it was thought that paralyzed muscles could not contract to produce purposeful movement. The development of electrical stimulation procedures to muscles and computer technology have opened a new era for the prospect of functional movement for persons who are paralyzed.[44]

The application of robotic technology to prosthesis is not new; however, the application of computer technology to electrical stimulation of paralyzed muscles is currently being developed. The Research Institute for Biomedical Engineering at Wright State University is in the process of designing microprocessors to control the stimulation of paralyzed muscles. The research at the institute has followed a logical evolution to develop techniques that will make paralyzed muscle functional, thereby allowing paralyzed persons to achieve proficiency on motor skills needed for self-sufficient living. The steps that led to computer-controlled functional walking of paralyzed persons required the synthesis of several techniques. The basis of computer-controlled ambulation is artificial stimulation of muscle. Once this technique was established to contract muscle, the problem was one of controlling the stimulation so that functional movement of paralyzed muscles would occur. The application of computer technology to control muscle function has led to the possibility of useful movements to enhance self-sufficient living. Microprocessors are now being used to control stimulation of the muscles that are used for walking. Computers to control functional movement of paralyzed muscles are currently in the early stages of development.[44]

ORGANIZATIONS THAT DEVELOP POLICIES FOR SPORTS COMPETITION

The Committee on Sports for the Disabled (COSD), a standing committee of the United States Olympic Committee, functions as a coordinating body for amateur sports for persons with disabilities in the United States. A subcommittee of this group compiled a Disabled Sport Research Directory and serves as a clearinghouse for disabled sport research information.[18]

In the United States, summer sports are governed by the United States Amputee Athletic Association (USAAA), and winter sports are conducted under the auspices of the National Handicapped Sports and Recreation Association (NHSRA). Annual and national competitions are held by these organizations. National competitions of these groups are governed by the International Sports Organization for the Disabled (ISOD). The National Wheelchair Athletic Association (NWAA) offers competition to persons with spinal cord injury and other spinal neuromuscular conditions in archery, track and field, fencing, slalom, swimming, table tennis, weight lifting, pistol shooting, and riflery. To prepare youth with spinal cord injuries for the real world of sports and recreation, these sports should be embodied in the curriculum.[47] A similar organization has been developed for the individuals with cerebral palsy—The United States Cerebral Palsy Athletic Association. The membership in this organization continues to grow as individuals with cerebral palsy find the joys and rewards inherent in athletic training and competition.[48]

SUMMARY

There are many different types of neurologically and orthopedically disabling conditions. Afflictions can occur at more than 500 anatomical sites. Each student with a disability has different physical and motor capabilities and is to be provided with special accommodations that enable participation in modified games and sport activity.

There are certain fundamental considerations that teachers must make to meet the unique physical education needs of the child. When developing programs for physically disabled persons, the teacher must avoid contraindicated activity, as identified by medical personnel.

Furthermore, physical educators must address two types of program considerations to meet the physical education needs of the orthopedically and neurologically disabled. One is to develop therapeutic programs that enhance sport skills, prerequisite motor patterns, and physical and motor fitness. The other is to structure the environment so that children with disabilities can derive physical benefits through expression of their skills in adapted sport activity (this may be facilitated by the use of aids for specific types of activities and disabilities).

The physical educator should be ready to accommodate the individual program needs of physically disabled persons by adapting activity and environments in integrated classes, segregated classes, and special settings.

There are organizations that have been developed in the community that enable orthopedically and neurologically disabled persons to participate in sports competition. The focus of testing this population is changing from one of assessing disability to one of assessing functional ability to participate in recreational sports and physical activity.

REVIEW QUESTIONS

1. What are some principles for adapting physical activity for students with physical disabilities?
2. Apply these principles for adapting physical activity for a specific disability in a specific activity.
3. What are some motor and nonmotor characteristics of individuals with cerebral palsy?
4. What are the clinical classifications of cerebral palsy?
5. What are the physical characteristics of persons with muscular dystrophy?
6. Describe different types of muscular dystrophy.
7. What are the physical characteristics of arthritis, the prognosis for the disorder, and physical activities that would benefit individuals with arthritis?

8. What are the physical characteristics of developmental hip dislocations? Describe physical activity concerns.
9. What are some orthopedic conditions of the lower extremity? Describe the physical characteristics, medical prognosis, contraindications, and the application of principles for adapting physical activity.
10. Describe two spinal column malformations. Indicate the physical characteristics, medical prognosis, contraindications for physical activity, physical activities, and principles for adapting physical activity for individuals with a spinal column malformation.
11. Describe some organizations in the community that may assist individuals with physical disabilities with participation in sport activity.
12. Describe modifications of tests that enable the assessment of physical fitness levels of persons with orthopedic or neurological disabilities.

STUDENT ACTIVITIES

1. Arrange a visit with a physical education teacher who has physically challenged children in a class. Inquire about the types of activities the teacher provides and about whether the class is a special adapted class or an integrated regular class. What is the relationship with the physical therapist and other medical services?
2. Select one or two major journals in the field of physical or special education. Some of these journals are *Journal of Health, Physical Education, and Recreation; Exceptional Children; Adapted Physical Activity Quarterly; Palaestra: The Forum of Sport, Physical Education and Recreation for the Disabled;* and *Sports n' Spokes.* Look through the issues from the past few years for articles that present useful suggestions for adapting instruction for students with physical disabilities. Make a file of these suggestions.
3. There are several organizations designed to serve parents of children with neurological and orthopedic disabilities. Some of these are Easter Seals, Association for Muscular Dystrophy, and United Cerebral Palsy Associations, Inc. Contact a local or national office to learn the purpose of these groups. Do they provide information about these disabilities or serve as advocates for parents? What should physical education teachers know about these organizations?
4. Talk to an adult with a physical disability. Ask about the ways in which the physical disability affects recreational activity and activity in the domestic and community environments. If the person was physically disabled as a child, ask about school experiences. Were adapted physical education services available? What were the effects of the services or lack of services on adult life?
5. Visit a school, shopping center, or municipal building. Are there architectural barriers that would deny access to some individuals? Watch for stairs, curbs, and steep inclines. What types of activities might enable persons with physical disabilities to gain access to these facilities through therapeutic programming?
6. Conduct a case study of an athlete with a physical disability. Determine how that athlete's interest was developed, training regimens followed, obstacles to participation, and benefits from participating in the activity.
7. Discuss the pros and cons of conducting separate sports programs for individuals with physical disabilities. When are separate sports programs appropriate and under what conditions?

REFERENCES

1. Alexander MJ: New techniques in quadriplegic wheelchair marathon racing, *Palaestra* 3:13-16, 1987.
2. Antich TJ, Lombaro SJ: Clinical presentation of Osgood-Schlatter disease in the adolescent population, *J Orthop Sports Phys Ther* 7:1-4, 1985.
3. Berkow R: *The Merck manual of diagnosis and therapy,* Rahwey, NJ, 1987, Merck Sharpe Dohme Research Laboratories.
4. Berrol CF, Katz SS: Dance-movement therapy in the rehabilitation of individuals surviving severe head injuries, *Am J Dance Ther* 8:46-66, 1985.
5. Brasile F: Performance evaluation of wheelchair athletes more than a disability classification level issue, *Adapt Phys Act Q* 7:289-297, 1990.
6. Brasile F: Wheelchair basketball proficiencies versus disability classification, *Adapt Phys Act Q* 3:6-13, 1986.
7. Brasile F, Hedrick BN: A comparison of participation incentives between adult and youth wheelchair basketball players, *Palaestra* 7:40-46, 1991.
8. Burd R, Grass K: Strapping to enhance athletic performance of wheelchair competitors with cerebral palsy, *Palaestra* 3:28-32, 1987.
9. Burkett LN et al: Construction and validation of a hysteresis brake wheelchair ergometer, *Adapt Phys Act Q* 4:60-71, 1987.
10. Cambell SK, Wilhelm IJ: Development from birth to three years of age of 15 children at high risk for central nervous system dysfunction, *Phys Ther* 65:463-469, 1985.
11. Cooper RA: A new racing wheelchair rear wheel alignment device, *Palaestra* 4:8-11, 1988.
12. Cowden JE: Project GUMBO...games uniting mind and body, *Palaestra* 4:13-27, 1988.
13. Cummings KC: Spring skiing in Snowmass...the handicapped nationals, *Palaestra* 4:20-22, 1988.
14. Daniels L, Worthingham C: *Muscle testing, ed 4,* Philadelphia, 1980, WB Saunders.
15. Davis RW: Elite wheelchair training camp, *Palaestra* 4:48-52, 1988.
16. DeGraff AH: Accessible aerobic exercise: the Saratoga Cycle, *Palaestra* 5:30-32, 1989.
17. DePace PM: World wheelchair weightlifting championships, *Palaestra* 7:47, 1991.
18. DePauw K: Research on sport for athletes with disabilities, *Adapt Phys Act Q* 3:292-299, 1986.
19. DiCarlo S: Effect of arm ergometry training on wheelchair propulsion endurance of individuals with quadriplegia, *Phys Ther* 68:40-44, 1988.

20. Dumars KW: Approach to genetic disease. In Conn RB, editor: *Current diagnosis,* ed 7, Philadelphia, 1985, WB Saunders.

21. Dummer GM et al: Attributions of athletes with cerebral palsy, *Adapt Phys Act Q* 4:278-292, 1987.

22. Dunn JM, Fait H: *Special physical education,* Dubuque, Iowa, 1989, Wm C Brown Publishers.

23. Gehlsen GM, Davis RW, Bahamonde R: Intermittent velocity and wheelchair performance characteristics, *Adapt Phys Act Q* 7:219-230, 1990.

24. Hardison GT, Isreal RG, Somes G: Physiological responses to different cranking rates during submaximal arm ergometry in paraplegic males, *Adapt Phys Act Q* 4:94-105, 1987.

25. Healy A: *Cerebral palsy in medical aspects of developmental disabilities in children birth to three,* Rockville, Md, 1984, Aspen Publishers.

26. Hedrick B et al: Aerodynamic positioning and performance in wheelchair racing, *Adapt Phys Act Q* 7:41-51, 1990.

27. Higgs C: Wheelchair racquetball: a preliminary time motion analysis, *Adapt Phys Act Q* 7:370-384, 1990.

28. Higgs C et al: Wheelchair classification for track and field events: a performance approach, *Adapt Phys Act Q* 7:22-40, 1990.

29. Holland LJ, Steadward RD: Effects of resistance and flexibility training on strength, spasticity/muscle tone and range of motion of elite athletes with cerebral palsy, *Palaestra* 6:27-31, 1990.

30. Hopkins LC: Muscular dystrophies. In Conn RB, editor: *Current diagnosis, ed 7,* Philadelphia, 1985, WB Saunders.

31. Horvat NA et al: A treadmill modification for wheelchairs, *Res Q Exer Sport* 55:297-301, 1984.

32. Huber JH: Wheelchair division of the 93rd Boston Marathon: new world records, issues, trends, *Palaestra* 5:44-46, 1989.

33. Hundertmark LH: Evaluating the adult with cerebral palsy for specialized adapted seating, *Phys Ther* 65:209-212, 1985.

34. Kaus T: Upsets abound at the National Wheelchair Table Tennis Championships, *Palaestra* 2:29, 1986.

35. Kegel B, Peterson J: Summer splash—a water sports symposium for the physically challenged, *Palaestra* 5:17-19, 1989.

36. Kofsky P et al: Fitness classification tables for lower limb disabled individuals. In Sherrill C, editor: *Sport and disabled athletes,* Champaign, Ill, 1985, Human Kinetics Publishers.

37. Labanowich S et al: The principles and foundations for the organization of wheelchair sports, *Sports n' Spokes* 9:25-32, 1984.

38. Laskas CA et al: Enhancement of two motor functions for the lower extremity in a child with spastic quadriplegia, *Phys Ther* 65:11-16, 1985.

39. Lasko PM, Knorph KG: *Adapted and corrected exercise for disabled adults,* Dubuque, Iowa, 1984, Eddie Bowers Publishing.

40. Meyen EL: *Exceptional children and youth,* Denver, 1978, Love Publishing.

41. Miller BF, Keane CB: *Encyclopedia and dictionary of medicine nursing and allied health,* Philadelphia, 1987, WB Saunders.

42. National Information Center for Handicapped Children and Youth: *Spina bifida,* Washington, DC, 1983, Department of Education.

43. Opila-Lehman J, Short M, Trombly C: Kinesthetic recall of children with athetoid and spastic cerbral palsy and of nonhandicapped children, *Dev Med Child Neurol* 27:223-230, 1985.

44. Petrofsky JS, Phillips CA: Computer controlled walking in the paralyzed individual, *IEEE NAECON Rec* 2:1162-1165, 1983.

45. Pitetti KH, Fernandez JE, Lanciault MC: Feasibility of an exercise program for adults with cerebral palsy: a pilot study, *Adapt Phys Act Q* 8:333-341, 1991.

46. Rusk HA, Taylor EJ: Rehabilitation medicine, ed 4, St Louis, 1977, Mosby–Year Book.

47. Sherrill C: *Adapted physical education and recreation,* ed 3, Dubuque, Iowa, 1986, Wm C Brown Publishing.

48. Sherrill C, Mushett CA: Fourth national cerebral palsy games: sports by ability . . . not disability, *Palaestra* 1:24-27, 1984.

49. Smith RW: Deja vu: the 40th Annual National Wheelchair Basketball Tournament, *Palaestra* 4:21, 1988.

50. Spencer CH: Juvenile rheumatoid arthritis. In Conn RB, editor: *Current diagnosis, ed 7,* Philadelphia, 1985, WB Saunders.

51. Strohkendl H: The new classification system for wheelchair basketball. In Sherrill C, editor: *Sports and disabled athletes,* Champaign, Ill, 1986, Human Kinetics Publishers.

52. US Department of Education: Thirteenth Annual Report to Congress on the Implementation of the Individuals with Disabilities Act, Washington, DC, 1991.

53. van der Woude L, Veeger D, Rozendal R: Ergonomics of wheelchair design: a prerequisite for optimum wheeling conditions, *Adapt Phys Act Q* 6:109-132, 1989.

54. Venn J, Morganstern L, Dykes MK: Checklist for evaluating the fit and function of orthoses, prostheses, and wheelchairs in the classroom, *Teach Except Child,* Winter 1979, pp 51-56.

55. Verhaaren P, Connor H: Physical disabilities. In Kaufman JM, Hallahan DP, editors: *Handbook of special education,* Englewood Cliffs, NJ, 1981, Prentice Hall.

56. Vodola T: *Motor disabilities or limitations,* Oakmont, NJ, 1976, Project Active.

57. Williams HG, McClenaghan B, Ward DS: Duration of muscle activity during standing in normally and slowly developing children, *Am J Phys Med* 64:171-189, 1985.

58. Wilson MI: Children with crippling and health disabilities. In Dunn LM, editor: *Exceptional children in the schools, ed 1,* New York, 1973, Holt, Rinehart, & Winston.

59. Winnick J, Short F: *Physical fitness testing of the dis-*

abled, Project UNIQUE, Champaign, Ill, 1985, Human Kinetics Publishers.

60. Worden DK, Vignos PJ: Intellectual function in childhood progressive muscular dystrophy, *Pediatrics* 29:968-977, 1962.

61. Wright J: *Project C.R.E.O.L.E.: wheelchair sports and mobility curriculum,* Harvey, La, 1989, Jefferson Parish Public School System.

SUGGESTED READINGS

Brasile FN: Wheelchair basketball: proficiencies versus dis... ity classifications, *Adapt Phys Act Q* 3:6-13, 1986.

Conn RB: *Current diagnosis,* Philadelphia, 1985, WB Saunders.

Eichstaedt C, Kalakian L: *Adapted/developmental physical education,* New York, 1987, Macmillan.

Sherrill C, editor: *Sports and the disabled,* Champaign, Ill, 1986, Human Kinetics Publishers.

12

OBJECTIVES

List the physical, psychological, and social characteristics of persons with hearing impairments.

Explain how to determine hearing loss through informal assessment.

State instructional techniques and methods for communicating with the hearing-impaired individual.

Apply principles for adapting instruction and activity for the hearing-impaired student.

Describe a process of integration that would permit hearing-impaired children to participate with non–hearing-impaired children.

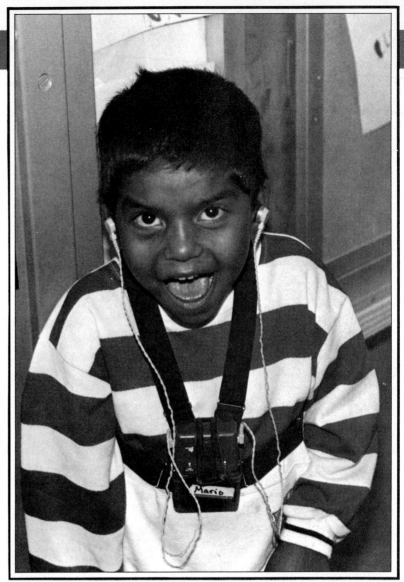

Courtesy Callier Center for Communicative Disorders, Dallas

Hearing Impairments

*H*earing is one of the strongest lines of communication between persons and the world in which they live. Children who have permanent hearing impairment are afflicted with disabilities that often have an impact on their total development, adjustment, and personality. The purpose of this chapter is to provide a background into the nature of hearing impairments and the needs of persons who are deaf and hard of hearing and to discuss the role of physical education in meeting these needs as part of the total educational process. Formal and informal tests, classifications of hearing loss, characteristics of hearing-impaired individuals, and teaching techniques and principles are discussed.

DEFINITION

According to The Education of the Handicapped Act,

'Deaf' means a hearing impairment which is so severe that the child is impaired in processing linguistic information through hearing, with or without amplification, which adversely affects educational performance (Section a.5.b.3) . . . . 'Hard of hearing' means a hearing impairment whether permanent or fluctuating, which adversely affects a child's educational performance but which is not included under deaf in this section (Section 121a.5.b.3).[34]

This definition is useful to physical educators because it requires focus on the child as he or she participates in tasks in physical education. If there is performance deficiency, the question can be asked, "Is the deficiency the result of hearing loss?" If the answer is "Yes" special accommodation for the child should be made.

CONTINUUM OF DISTURBANCE

The continuum of degree of hearing loss and ability to understand speech ranges from that of little significance to that of extreme disability, whereby an individual cannot understand amplified speech. Table 12-1 indicates the relationship between decibel loss, degree of disability, and ability to understand speech.

Children classified as having a marked disability may be educationally deaf in academic subjects. *Intensity* (decibel) is one measurable attribute of sound. Others are *frequency*, which refers to perception of high and low pitch, and *spectrum* or *timbre*, which encompasses different tonal qualities ranging from a tone of single frequency to complex tones such as speech.

INCIDENCE

There are approximately 76,000 to 90,000 students between the ages of 5 and 17 years in the United States who are classified as hearing impaired.[10] Furthermore, one out of eight hearing-impaired students is classified as deaf (a 91-decibel loss or more).

CAUSES

There are two general categories of hearing loss—congenital defects, whereby children are born deaf or with a hearing loss, and deafness or hearing loss acquired after birth. Some individuals with congenital hearing defects have hereditary causes. Many can be traced to some form of disease. Rubella (German measles) in the

TABLE 12-1

Continuum of hearing impairment

Degree of impairment	Range of decibel loss	Label
Not significant	0-26	Normal hearing
Slight	27-40	Hard-of-hearing
Mild	41-55	Hard-of-hearing
Marked	56-70	Hard-of-hearing
Severe	71-90	Hard-of-hearing, deaf
Profound	>90	Deaf

mother has been recognized as the largest nongenetic cause of deafness in school-age children in the 1980s.[23] Venereal disease is also a prenatal cause of hearing loss.

There are several causes of acquired deafness, including the following:

1. The presence of foreign objects in the external ear (paper, pins, crayons, etc.)
2. Tumors of the external auditory canal
3. Excessive buildup of ear wax
4. Perforation of the eardrum from a blow to the head or excessive pressure in the middle ear
5. Infections that spread to the middle ear from the eustachian tube (otitis media)
6. Allergies that make the eustachian tube swell
7. Viral infections such as mumps and measles
8. Bacterial infections such as meningitis and encephalitis

There is a relationship between the cause of hearing impairment and the degree of hearing loss. The most devastating losses occur because of meningitis, maternal rubella, and hereditary factors.[12]

TESTING FOR IDENTIFICATION

There are two purposes in the assessment of hearing loss—to determine how well the person's hearing serves the process of communication and to determine what can be done in terms of auditory rehabilitation. The educator is mainly concerned with hearing tests for the purposes of communication. It is desirable to have children diagnosed at the earliest possible age so that correctable defects may be treated adequately. If this is done, the impairment will not interfere greatly with the child's development. Knobloch and Pasamanick[17] have suggested the following list of signs of hearing loss:

1. Hearing and comprehension of speech
   a. General indifference to sound

b. Lack of response to the spoken word

c. Response to noises as opposed to words

2. Vocalization and sound production
   a. Monotonal quality
   b. Indistinct speech
   c. Lessened laughter
   d. Meager experimental sound play
   e. Vocal play for vibratory sensation
   f. Head banging, foot stamping for vibratory sensation
   g. Yelling, screeching to express pleasure or need

3. Visual attention
   a. Augmental visual vigilance and attentiveness
   b. Alertness to gesture and movement
   c. Marked imitativeness in play
   d. Vehement gestures

4. Social rapport and adaptation
   a. Subnormal rapport in vocal games
   b. Intensified preoccupation with things rather than persons
   c. Puzzling and unhappy episodes in social situations
   d. Suspiciousness and alertness, alternating with cooperation
   e. Marked reaction to praise and affection

5. Emotional behavior
   a. Tantrums to call attention to self or need
   b. Tensions, tantrums, resistance, due to lack of comprehension
   c. Frequent obstinance, irritability at not making self understood

French and Jansma[9] cite additional behavioral characteristics that might indicate referral to an audiologist for a hearing test. They are poor speech, leaning toward the source of sound, request for repeated statements, recurring earaches, fluid draining from the ear, inattention, and poor balance.

Informal Methods

The electronic audiometer is the most refined instrument for the detection of hearing loss. However, informal methods still may be of use for the rough appraisal of a child's hearing. Some of the tests are as follows:

☐ Watch tick test: A watch is brought progressively closer to the child's ear until he or she acknowledges the sound of the watch.

☐ Coin click test: A coin is brought in contact with a hard surface that is placed progressively closer to the child's ear to detect hearing loss of high-frequency sounds.

☐ Conversational test: The child is placed 20 feet from

FIGURE 12-1. Friends at play. (Courtesy Callier Center for Communicative Disorders, Dallas.)

the teacher and is spoken to in a regular conversational tone. In the event the child cannot hear the teacher, the teacher moves closer and closer. If the child has difficulty hearing at 10 or 20 feet, he or she should be referred for a more thorough examination.

☐ Whisper test: The whisper test is administered in a manner similar to the conversational test except that the teacher uses a whisper.

CLASSIFICATION

The acquisition of speech and language skills is basic to the subsequent development of the individual. Therefore the time of onset of deafness is a critical factor in determining the effects that it may have on the learning situation. According to Meyen,[20] if hearing loss occurs before or at birth, there is no chance for language to be heard normally or for incidental learning to occur. A child who is afflicted with a hearing loss early in development progresses more slowly than does one who is afflicted with a loss later in the developmental process.

Persons whose sense of hearing is nonfunctional for the ordinary purposes of life may be grouped in two distinct classes according to time of onset. They are the congenitally deaf and the adventitiously deaf. Congenitally deaf persons are born deaf. Adventitiously deaf persons are born with normal hearing but incur the hearing loss after birth.

Proper diagnosis of hearing disabilities may provide assistance for development of physical education programs. Each type of deafness, accompanied with the uniqueness of each deaf child, requires individualized treatment by teachers. Categories of hearing loss that should be considered in the educational planning for the student are the following:

☐ Conductive hearing impairments: Typically, a condition in which the intensity of sound is reduced before reaching the inner ear, where the auditory nerve begins. A conductive hearing loss can also result when the membranes in the inner ear undergo physical changes that reduce the transfer of energy to the hair cells.

☐ Sensorineural hearing impairments: A condition caused by an absence or malfunction of a sensory unit. The damage may be present in the cochlea, the auditory nerve, or the central auditory system.

☐ Mixed hearing impairments: A condition that results from a combination of sensorineural and conductive disorders.

☐ Central hearing impairments: A condition that involves damage to the auditory nerve pathways from the brain stem to the auditory cortex. This condition

can occur concurrently with sensorineural impairments.[26]

The most prevalent cause of conductive hearing loss is infection of the middle ear, which is called *otitis media*. Another infection that may cause conductive hearing loss is *mastoiditis*. Mastoiditis occurs when there is chronic inflammation of the middle ear that spreads into the air cells of the mastoid process within the temporal bone. Other causes of conductive hearing loss are cerebral tumors or abscesses, arterial sclerosis, cerebral hemorrhage, and multiple sclerosis.

Sensorineural hearing loss is a dysfunction of the inner ear in which the main problem is discrimination among speech sounds. Sound can be heard, but persons often cannot derive meaning from high-frequency sounds. Hearing aids are of limited value to remedy this type of hearing loss.

PSYCHOLOGICAL AND BEHAVIORAL CHARACTERISTICS

Hearing loss can have profound consequences on a person's behavior. Hearing loss affects language and speech development, intellectual ability, and social adjustment. The areas most affected by hearing impairment are those of comprehension and production of the English language. Jensema, Karchmer, and Trybus[16] have indicated that of the hearing-impaired persons they studied, 15.4% were very intelligible, 29.4% were intelligible, 21.9% were barely intelligible, 20.5% were not intelligible, and 12.8% would not speak. Three reasons that may account for language deficit are that (1) hearing-impaired persons do not receive adequate auditory feedback when they make sounds, (2) they receive inadequate verbal reinforcement from adults, and (3) they are unable to hear adequately an adult language model.

The intellectual ability of hearing-impaired children has been the subject of controversy over the years. The once popular view that hearing-impaired individuals are somewhat deficient intellectually has been challenged. Several intelligence tests rely heavily on verbal skills. Many professionals hold the view that IQ tests do not assess the hearing-impaired child's true capability. The results of nonverbal tests favor the view that hearing-impaired children are not intellectually retarded.

Social personality development in the general population is dependent on communication. Social interaction is the communication between two or more people, and language is the most important means of communication. Therefore the personality and social characteristics of hearing-impaired persons often differ from those of people who have normal hearing ability.

Hoeman and Briga[14] indicate that hearing-impaired persons develop behavioral problems based on how well or poorly others in the environment accept their disability. Hearing-impaired children frequently grow up in isolation from others. The physical education program has the potential through games and sports to provide opportunity for much-needed social interaction.

Developmental Factors

Hearing loss that afflicts youngsters in the early phases of development impairs the total developmental process. One of the effects of deafness is to limit the children's play experience with other children. Play in the preschool years is important for learning of social skills and for development of motor skills. In play situations deaf children are often uncertain as to the part they should play in the game, and therefore they often withdraw from participation. Thus the role of play, which is important to the social, psychological, and motor aspects of development in typical children, is usually limited for deaf children.

The social benefits of play experienced by typical children are not experienced to the same degree by deaf children. Consequently, social development occurs more slowly in deaf children. It is in social maturation that the disability of deafness is most apparent. This retardation is probably partially caused by language inadequacy that results from the hearing loss.

Because of their impaired ability to function socially with their peers and because of their restricted developmental experiences, deaf children are likely to be subjected to more strain than are hearing children. Therefore young deaf children may be less emotionally mature than hearing children of the same age.

MOTOR CHARACTERISTICS OF HEARING-IMPAIRED INDIVIDUALS

Impairment of the semicircular canals, vestibule of the inner ear, and/or vestibular portion of the eighth cranial nerve has a negative effect on balance. Siegel, Marchetti, and Tecclin[31] reported significantly depressed balance performance by children with sensorineural hearing loss of below 65 decibels. Another study that did not examine etiological factors evaluated motor performance and vestibular function of a group of hearing impaired children. The vast majority (65%) of the studied group demonstrated abnormal vestibular function, but normal motor proficiency except for balance; whereas 24% had normal vestibular function and motor proficiency, including balance. Eleven percent had normal vestibular function but poor motor proficiency

and balance.[5] Butterfield and Ersing[3] found that the cause of hearing-impairment may have an impact on balance proficiency. In their study a group of hearing-impaired persons with acquired deafness performed significantly better than a group with congenital deafness. Thus it is important to point out that the balancing deficit associated with some hearing-impaired children cannot be generalized. The individual education program must be based on the needs of each child.

One characteristic that may be negatively affected by a hearing impairment is motor speed (i.e., the time it takes the child to process information and complete a motor act).[2] Beyond that characteristic there is disagreement about the physical abilities of hearing-impaired individuals.

Fait and Dunn[8] have suggested that physical fitness of persons with auditory impairments may be lower than that of their hearing peers. However, according to Winnick and Short,[35] on only one test item did hearing

FIGURE 12-2. A child develops play skills. (Courtesy Callier Center for Communicative Disorders, Dallas.)

subjects surpass the performance of auditorially impaired adolescents. Although Minter and Wolk[21] indicated that deaf children may appear hyperactive, Hattin[13] reported that deafness does not stimulate hyperactivity and that deaf children could profit from more endurance exercise to raise their levels of fitness. It appears that further research is needed to resolve these issues.

IMPORTANCE OF CASE HISTORY

Case histories often provide valuable information about children with limited hearing. The following information may be of relevance to the educational process:

1. Type, degree, cause, and age of onset involved in hearing impairment
2. Psychological impact of the onset of hearing loss on the student and the family
3. Major modes of communication and problems arising from the student's communication limitations
4. Effects of the disability in the social, educational, recreational, and domestic spheres
5. Behavior, attitudes, achievements, and aspiration of the student
6. History of diagnostic experiences and rehabilitative measures, including special education
7. Attitudes, motivations, and problems concerning education
8. Presence of other disabilities (visual defects and organic brain damage)
9. Health and medical problems

These data, if obtainable, should provide comprehensive information and may assist the future educational and rehabilitative program.

COMMUNICATION SYSTEMS

The two prevalent philosophies in the education of hearing-impaired persons in this country are known as the Oral method and the Total Communication method. With the Oral method (also known as the Oral-Aural method) children are provided amplification of their residual hearing and are taught through speechreading (lipreading). They express themselves through speech. The use of signs and fingerspelling are prohibited. The Total Communication method combines the Oral method with use of signs and fingerspelling. Children are provided amplification of sound, and are taught through speechreading, fingerspelling, and signs. They express themselves through speech, fingerspelling, and signs.[23]

The term *total communication* refers to both a method of instruction and a philosophy of education. As a philosophy it refers to the right of every hearing-impaired person to select whatever form of communication that is preferred. That is, depending on the circumstances, the hearing-impaired person should have the right to choose to communicate through speech, signs, gesture or writing. If they are taught through a total communication system, they have the option to comunicate in a way that best suits their need.[29] Since 1975, classroom instruction of the hearing-impaired in this country has been predominantly through the Total Communication method.[23] A variety of forms of manual comunication systems may be incorporated into the Total Communication method.

Manual Communication Systems

The manual comunication systems range from simple homemade gestures to fingerspelling. Signing systems between these two extremes include Pidgin Sign Language, American Sign Language, Manually Coded English, and fingerspelling. A description of each follows:

□ Homemade gestures: A primitive gestural system developed to communicate between individuals or among small groups.

□ Pidgin Sign Language: A mixture of English and American Sign Language. Key words and phrases are signed in correct order; prepositions and articles are usually omitted.[29]

□ American Sign Language: A visual-gestural language that is governed by rules. The visual-gestural language involves executing systematic manual and nonmanual body movements simultaneously. Manual movements involve shapes, positions, and movements of the hands; nonmanual gestures involve the shoulders, cheeks, lips, tongue, eyes, and eyebrows. The rules that govern this language relate to how the language works (e.g. functions of the language, meaning, structure and organization of sentences, and the sound or phonetic system).[26]

□ Manually Coded English: Signs are produced in English order and fingerspelling is used for words and concepts that do not have a sign equivalent. Forms of Manually Coded English include Seeing Essential English, Signing Exact English, and Signed English. All are variations of American Sign Language that attempt to model the vocabulary and syntax of the English language.[26]

□ Fingerspelling: Spelling each word letter by letter using a manual alphabet that consists of 26 letters. The hand is held in front of the chest, and letters are formed by using different single hand configurations.[23] Fingerspelling is also known as the Rochester method because it originated at the Rochester

School for the Deaf in the late nineteenth century.[26] Although many educators of the hearing impaired argue that it is in the best interest of hearing-impaired students to be educated using some form of Manually Coded English [26], the most widely used signing system used by deaf adults in this country is American Sign Language.[23]

Effective and efficient communication with hearing-impaired persons is a great challenge to teachers. Physical education teachers may improve their instructional ability by learning to communicate in a variety of ways to accommodate a wide range of pupils. Communication through hand signals may assist in communication with hearing-impaired persons. Fig. 12-3 indicates ex-

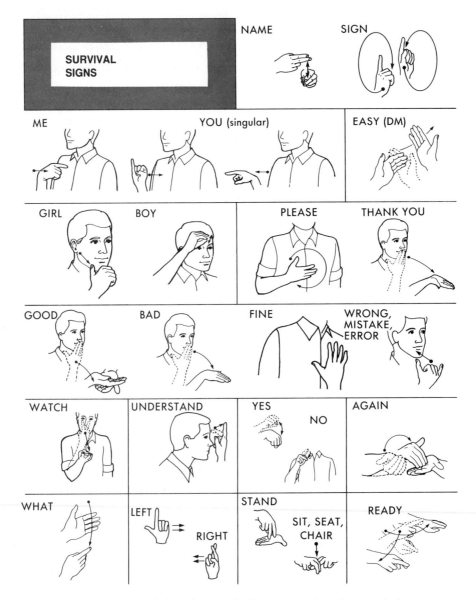

FIGURE 12-3. Survival signs. (Reprinted with permission from the Journal of Physical Education, Recreation, and Dance.)

amples of some of the basic survival signs needed by physical education teachers to communicate with hearing-impaired persons.

Most signs are for concepts and ideas rather than for words. Pointing, motioning, demonstrating, and signaling are perfectly acceptable.[7] A foundation for communication with hearing-impaired individuals can be developed through study of *The ABC's of Signing.*[25] Fig. 12-4 indicates some specific signs for physical education.

Stewart, Drummer, and Haubenstricker[32] caution that researchers involved with evaluating motor skills of deaf populations should be aware of the communication needs of their subjects and be willing to use ex-

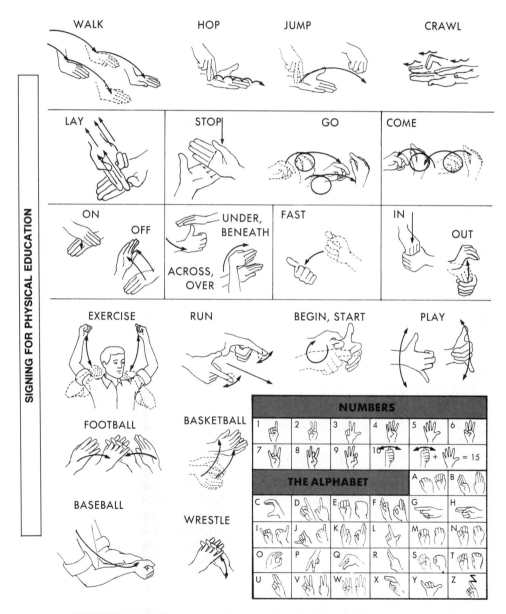

FIGURE 12-4. Specific signs for physical education. (Reprinted with permission from the Journal of Physical Education, Recreation, and Dance.)

perts familiar with their linguistic and communication needs to both design and administer the tests.

Hearing Aids

Hearing aids amplify sound and are effective for conductive deafness. They can be worn in one or both ears. Some of the modern hearing aids are wireless transmitter receivers that operate on the same principle as a walkie-talkie and may be worn on the chest.

A number of hard-of-hearing children are enrolled in regular physical education classes, and adaptation in instructional techniques should be made for optimum learning. Many hard-of-hearing children wear hearing aids. If this is the case, it may be best to remove the aid(s) when vigorous physical activity is scheduled. However, once the hearing aid is removed, the student is disabled in audition and learning, particularly through the verbal medium, so instructional adjustments are necessary. Judgment should be made concerning the removal of the hearing aid. The nature of the activity is usually the basis of such judgment. Active games involving body contact may require the removal of the hearing aid.

Excessive moisture corrodes batteries that operate hearing aids. Therefore they should not be placed in damp grass or places of high humidity such as indoor swimming pool areas.

One adjustment that can be made easily is to place the child close to the instructor so that greater amplification of speech is received. A second adjustment that may help is for the instructor to keep the face in view of the hard-of-hearing child.

When one sensory avenue to gathering of information is impaired, it is necessary to rely more on other senses. In the case of children with learning loss, visual aids are of great significance in instruction. Visual demonstrations, blackboard work, films, and slides are important instructional aids for the deaf. To get the attention of the hearing-impaired child, waving the hands or turning off and on lights has proven effective in some instances.

Deaf persons, because of an inability to comprehend information through auditory means, must rely mainly on visual and kinesthetic information during physical education instruction. Therefore when residual hearing is insufficient for communication, these sensory media should be utilized. According to Ling,[18] no single method can meet the individual needs of all children with hearing disorders, and whenever possible a total communication system should be used. Verbal instructions that describe movements are ineffective for deaf individuals who cannot read lips. When teaching motor

skills, temporal-spatial relationships of movement components must be synthesized. It is critical that precise visual models be presented to deaf individuals. To promote kinesthetic feedback, it is also helpful to move a child through the desired movement pattern. Moving the child in this fashion helps the student feel the temporal-spatial relationship of movements associated with a skill. Using both visual and kinesthetic instruction provides opportunities for two avenues of sensory information. A quick visual model followed by a physical prompting of the behavior may facilitate learning.

Some deaf children can read lips and thus receive directions through verbal means. If the child has residual hearing or is skilled at lip reading, the physical educator should make the environment conducive to reception of the spoken word. Instruction must be given close enough to the child so that precise movement of the lips and tongue can be deciphered. The instructor

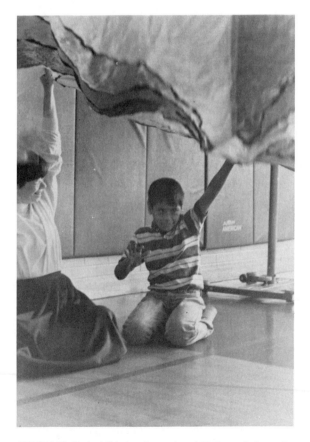

FIGURE 12-5. A child develops play skills in and through parachute play. (Courtesy Dallas Independent School District.)

should be in front and in clear view of the deaf student. When movement of a game requires the child to perform an activity at a distance where lips cannot be read, it is then necessary to use some combination of signing to communicate. Eichstaedt and Seiler[7] have devised 45 signs specific to physical education to communicate with the deaf (see Fig. 12-4 for some of these). Use of these signs will assist the physical education teacher in communicating with the deaf student. Another source of communication to these students may come from trained hearing paraprofessionals (teacher aides) or peers who can facilitate instruction by gaining the attention of the hearing-impaired child and then relaying instructions through either visual models, signs, or tactual inputs that guide the hearing-impaired child into class activities.

TEACHING STRATEGIES

The ability to effectively communicate is important in instructional settings as well as while participating in sporting events. When there is effective communication and the learning environment is properly managed, there may be little need to modify the demands of the physical activity.[3] However, when comunication impairments are present the student may perform motor and social skills less well, solely because of the communication problem. The physical educator who works with hearing-impaired students must do everything possible to ensure effective comunication. Techniques for enhancing communication with hearing-impaired students follows:

1. Position yourself where the hearing-impaired child can see your lips and maintain eye contact; do not turn your back on the child and talk (e.g., writing on the blackboard).
2. When out of doors, position yourself so that you, rather than the hearing-impaired child, face the sun.
3. Use only essential words or actions to transmit messages.
4. Use visual attention-getters.
5. Make sure that the teaching environment has adequate lighting.
6. Allow the child to move freely in the gymnasium in order to be within hearing and sight range.
7. Encourage the use of residual hearing.
8. Coordinate the method (oral, total communication) that your school uses.
9. Present games with straight-forward rules and strategies.
10. Familiarize the hearing-impaired student with the rules and strategies of a game before introducing the activity.
11. Learn some basic signs and use them during instruction (e.g., good, bad, okay, better, worse, line up, start, go, finish, stop, help, thank you, please, stand, sit, walk, run).
12. Use visual materials to communicate body movements (e.g., lay out footprints to indicate the foot placements required of a skill).
13. Refrain from having long lines and circle formations when presenting information to the class. This facilitates interpretation of lip movements.
14. Keep objects out of your mouth when speaking.[22]
15. Use body language, facial expression, and gestures to get an idea across.[22]
16. Avoid verbal cues during the game or activity. It is important that the hearing-impaired student fully understands his or her role prior to the beginning of the game or activity and that the role does not change.[22]
17. Inside facilities should be equipped with special lighting systems eaily turned on and off by the instructor to get the students' attention.[22]
18. Flags or bright objects can be useful in getting the attention of students out-of-doors. However, it must be made clear to the student that it is his or her responsibility to be aware of the teacher's presence throughout the lesson. Under no circumstances should the hearing-impaired student be allowed to manipulate the teacher by ignoring attempts to gain attention.
19. Captioned videotapes, loop films, and other visual aids can be helpful in explaining strategies.
20. Demonstrate or have another student demonstrate often. It may help the student form a mental picture of how to perform a particular skill correctly.
21. Keep instructions simple and direct.
22. Emphasize action rather than verbal instruction.
23. Stand still while giving directions.
24. Correct motor errors immediately.[22]
25. Select activities that allow all the children to be actively involved throughout; avoid activities that require children to spend a great deal of time sitting and waiting to participate.

Considerable individual differences exist among the deaf and hard-of-hearing regarding their response to various stimuli, and these differences must be taken into consideration. For example, persons with tinnitus (ringing in the ears) are highly sensitive to noise and vibration and may not perform well in a noisy facility such as the gymnasium. Deaf children with impaired semicircular canals, which affect balance, should not climb to high places. Also, some children with hearing loss should not participate in activity where there is excessive dampness, dust, or change in temperature.

The physical education program should be challenging to the hearing impaired and meet their needs and interests. To meet the needs and interests of this group it is important to assess motor development and design a program that is meaningful to the student. Instruction should be directed toward motor and social skills that will enable the student to participate in leisure, recreation, and sport activity in the community.[27] To encourage maximum participation, the skills and attitudes of the instructor are important. Following is a list of instructor activities that will enhance the hearing-impaired student's learning environment:

1. Provide immediate and enthusiastic acceptance of the hearing-impaired child because this relationship can be observed by other students.[2]
2. Plan activities that constantly challenge the students, but allow success.
3. Assess hearing-impaired students for possible balance problems. The equilibrium mechanism may be impaired.[2]
4. Provide the hearing-impaired student with opportunities to participate in out-of-school activities, particularly on weekends and in the summer.
5. Facilitate peer interaction by planning activities that encourage turn-taking and allow the students to work together in pairs and in small groups.
6. Plan activities that require group cooperation to achieve a goal.
7. Place the hearing-impaired students in close proximity to one another during activity to facilitate peer interaction.
8. Since many hearing-impaired students may not have a strong command of English, or their native language, it is advisable not to depend on printed materials for conveying information.[19]
9. Praise all students when it is deserved.[22]
10. The program should meet the needs and interests of the participants and should reflect the needs and interests of the community in which they will participate in leisure, recreation, and sport activities.

Principles of Adapting Physical Activity

The principles for adapting physical activity for the hearing impaired include: (1) use of residual hearing and senses, (2) modification of the instructional environment, (3) use of special aids, (4) use of special

FIGURE 12-6. Kayaking on an inland lake provides an opportunity to develop fitness and an appreciation of nature. (Courtesy Wisconsin Lions Camp, Rosholt, Wisconsin.)

techniques, (5) use of special feedback, and (6) use of peer assistance. The chart below outlines the application of those principles to the hearing impaired.

1. Use of residual senses
   a. Use visual signing.
   b. Use visual demonstration of skills to be taught.
   c. Use tactile and kinesthetic cues if necessary.
   d. Use the residual hearing.
   e. Provide audiovisual feedback.
   f. Provide visual cues that pair with audition in dance activities.
2. Use and care of aids
   a. Have student remove hearing aids before entering the pool area.
3. Instructional environment
   a. Avoid excessive noise in the instructional environment.
4. Special instructional techniques and considerations
   a. Use a special system of communication.
   b. Remind the student to keep the head above water when swimming.
   c. Underwater swimming is usually contraindicated.
   d. Diving, which involves an impact between the water surface and the hearing mechanism, should be avoided.
5. Feedback
   a. Provide audiovisual feedback.

Greater specificity for the modification of tasks to specific individuals can be developed within the context of these principles.

Implications for Physical Education

There are obvious social benefits that result when hearing-impaired students interact with others in leisure, recreation, sport, and physical education activities.[33] Communication, whether verbal or nonverbal, promotes unity and stability in those who are involved in sport and movement-based cooperative activities. It is in these settings that hearing-impaired children and hearing children interact naturally. This is an important step in fostering social interaction skills.

The objectives of a physical education program for hard-of-hearing children are the same as those for non–hearing-impaired children. However, loss of hearing, which impairs the ability to communicate effectively with others, is a great social disability. Therefore an objective that should be given priority is the provision of opportunity for social interaction through games with other students. Activities in physical education for deaf and hard-of-hearing persons are similar to those in the regular program, and although deaf and hard-of-hearing persons may function well in regular programs, there is an obvious need for special and compensatory attention to those who are deaf to fulfill the objectives of the physical education program.

At the preschool and early elementary school levels, suggested activities for the deaf are those that develop basic motor skills and rhythm activities. Percussion instruments such as cymbals, triangles, drums, and tambourines are valuable for rhythm activities, because they are capable of producing vibrations to which the deaf child can respond.

Deaf and hard-of-hearing children do not, as a rule, need a set of activities that differs from that of other children. However, assessment should be conducted to determine possible physical underdevelopment and poor motor coordination. If some children have these deficiencies, the program should be designed to remedy or ameliorate them. The physical education program for persons who are deaf or hard of hearing should provide for developmental activities.

PHYSICAL ACTIVITIES FOR THE HEARING-IMPAIRED STUDENT

Hearing-impaired youth need individual assessments and programs that will meet their unique needs. Activities that relate directly to leisure, recreation, and sport opportunities available within their community should be selected.

There are many physical and motor prerequisites for efficient functioning in community activities. One such prerequisite for hearing-impaired individuals is balance, and many hearing-impaired children may be deficient in this area. Balance activities that may be included in a program are (1) standing on one foot so that the other foot can be used for kicking and trapping, (2) walking a balance beam to develop leg, hip, and trunk strength, and (3) drills that build balance skills for chasing, stopping, starting, and dodging. If the student has neurological impairment that prevents vestibular information from reaching the central nervous system, direct instruction in each activity is necessary (i.e., the top, down approach). If vestibular processing is not impaired and balance is poor, the child's depth perception and level of vestibular function should be evaluated. Vestibular functioning can be facilitated with the bottom, up approach by using activities found in Chapter 4.

Activities that enhance vision and kinesthetic development and that are popular among hearing-impaired populations are the martial arts (karate, kung fu, t'ai chi).[30] The physical education program may focus primarily on prerequisites for performance such as vestibular, kinesthetic, and visual stimulation, or it may use specific activities that will carry over to community involvement. Probably the best approach is to begin with sensory input stimulation activities (see Chapter 4) and work toward instruction in specific tasks.

INTEGRATING THE HEARING-IMPAIRED STUDENT

Some seriously hearing-impaired individuals prefer to enroll in residential or day schools that provide segregated programs. These schools are preferred because they have a higher percentage of deaf teachers and workers, and the students have greater opportunities to participate in extracurricular activities such as sports.[30] Gallaudet University provides evidence of the success of segregated school programs. This well-known university for the deaf routinely competes successfully against hearing competitors in baseball and soccer.[22]

The Wisconsin School for the Deaf in Janesville, Wisconsin is nationally kown for not only academic excellence but athletic excellence as well. Athletes from the Wisconsin School for the Deaf make regular appearances in the Wisconsin Interscholastic Athletic Association post-season tournament play in football, wrestling, and track and field.

It should no longer be assumed that all deaf persons should or want to fit into and function in the hearing world. In some large cities there are whole communities of deaf citizens. This has occurred because deaf individuals have their own culture, which they value.[23] Requiring hearing-impaired individuals to meet the demands of the hearing population's culture may not always be in their best interest.[23] For example, Grimes and Prickett[11] argued that insisting deaf children only use what hearing people consider "proper" English (or Spanish, Vietnamese, or Thai) may lead to feelings of inferiority and inadequacy. For this and other reasons, the issue of placement of deaf children in a mainstreamed environment is a highly emotional and controversial issue with the deaf population. Moores[23] suggests that with the emphasis on individualized instruction there should be less concern for mainstreaming all children and a greater emphasis on identifying the proper match of program and child at each step in the child's development. Physical educators can make a major contribution to a deaf child's education by being sensitive to their individual needs and providing an appropriate and acceptable physical education program.

The Regular Education Initiative suggests that physical education instruction for deaf and hearing-im-paired students should, whenever possible, take place in an integrated setting so the hearing-impaired participant can learn socialization skills from his or her hearing peers.

Social success within the hearing community requires the ability to communicate effectively. Hearing loss makes social communication difficult. Physical educators are challenged to assist hearing-impaired students to develop normal behaviors through participation in integrated settings. Because the majority of hearing-impaired children in the elementary years possess near-average motor ability, they can participate successfully in regular physical education classes.[6] If denied participation in physical activities during childhood, motor deficiencies may develop. Organized sport and physical activity in natural community environments are critical for hearing-impaired youth.

There are certain physical education activities that enable the integration process to be accomplished with minimum support systems. Activities that require less social interaction and communication skills are individual sports such as bowling, archery, and weight

FIGURE 12-7. Children develop strength in parallel play activity. (Courtesy Dallas Independent School District.)

lifting. More complex team sports such as basketball, which requires frequent response to whistles and verbal communication involved in strategical situations among teammates, are more difficult to integrate. Hearing-impaired students have differing needs for support systems. Therefore a list of activities that need support systems and a list of those that do not should be compiled for each hearing-impaired individual. Activities that best meet the students' needs and levels of functioning can be selected from this list.

Complex team sports in which constant communication with teammates is vital are perhaps the most difficult activities in which to integrate the deaf. Organized football is perhaps the most difficult because of the need for ongoing information exchange between coaches and players while the game is in progress. The task is not, however, impossible. Kenny Walker, a deaf football player, was outstanding at the University of Nebraska and later played in the National Football League with the Denver Broncos.[28] Through his interpreters, he was integrated into the game of football at the highest levels of competition. He is an excellent example of how a deaf person can be successfully integrated into a complex sport with the use of supplemental aids and services.

Peer Tutors

The introduction of the hearing-impaired child into a regular class without prearranged support systems may be devastating. It is important to provide a peer support system where hearing peers give guidance to assist with the communication that is needed to successfully participate in the activities. A rule of any support system is to provide the least amount of assistance necessary for the individual to experience success.

DEAF-BLIND CHILDREN

Deaf-blind children have loss of both vision and hearing. They are considered to have less than 20/20 vision for a field of 20 degrees or less. In addition, they have a loss of hearing of 25 decibels or more. Thus they are often unable to be educated in class for the deaf or the blind.

Deaf-blind children have problems similar to those of the blind child and the deaf child. However, their problems are exponential rather than additive. There is practically no foundation for communicative skills. Residual sight, hearing, or both can be the basis of communication. If there is no residual sight or hearing, communication is then made kinesthetically through the hands.

ATHLETIC OPPORTUNITIES FOR DEAF PERSONS

Physical activity and sports available in the community are important recreational outlets for persons with hearing impairment. However, there are also organized opportunities for high-level national and international competition among hearing-impaired athletes. The criterion for participation in sports for deaf athletes is a hearing loss of 55 decibels or more in the better ear. In the United States, the American Athletic Association for the Deaf (AAAD) has a membership of approximately 20,000 and promotes state, regional, and national events for basketball and softball tournaments and prepares athletes for the World Games for the Deaf. In 1985 over 2500 athletes from more than 40 countries competed in 13 different sports in the World Games for the Deaf.

PARENT EDUCATION

Parent participation is important in the education of a child who has a hearing loss. Many parents who face rearing a child with a severe hearing impairment have little knowledge of what they can do. After the child is in school, it is important for the parents to know how the child's hearing is developing, how skills in physical education are progressing, and how certain aspects of the school program can be extended to the home. There is general agreement that parent educational programs are necessary and that orientation is an essential part of any program for the child with impaired hearing.

STATUS OF PHYSICAL EDUCATION FOR THE HEARING IMPAIRED

Under the Education of the Handicapped Act, all hearing-impaired children should receive an appropriate physical education program. Although there is scanty evidence on the status of physical education for this population, it may be that the status of education for the hearing impaired in general applies to physical education. Benderly[1] indicates that many old obstacles still bar the way to advancement of the hearing impaired. Many old prejudices and misconceptions endure within the larger hearing society. In a message to Congress by the Commission on Education of the Deaf,[4] it was reported that in the United States appropriate education for the hearing impaired means not too costly and not too troublesome. In fact, education for the hearing impaired is usually a education in the "mainstream," with children who can hear, without support. In this environment, the hearing-impaired child is often confronted with a teacher who has preconceived notions of the child's limits, a teacher who focuses on the nature of the disability rather than the child's ability. Unfortunately, the child is allowed "in the school door," but little is done to ensure that the hearing-impaired child is provided an appropriate education.

SUMMARY

Physical educators are concerned primarily with the extent to which the hearing loss affects ability to participate in physical and sport activity. Classification of hearing loss is often based on the location of the problem within the hearing mechanism. Conductive losses interfere with the transferral of sound. Central hearing impairments occur between the brain stem and the auditory cortex. Sensorineural problems are usually confined to the inner ear.

The electronic audiometer is the most refined instrument for the detection of hearing loss. However, informal methods such as the watch tick test, coin clink test, and whisper test may be used in the absence of sophisticated equipment and for survey purposes. The results of formal testing are measured in decibel loss. Loss of 0 to 25 decibels is not significant, while loss of more than 90 decibels represents a severe disabilty.

Methods of communication may be oral or total. Hearing aids amplify sound and are effective for conductive deafness. Considerations for effective communication by teachers of the deaf during instruction are teacher-learner position, intensity of the commands, interaction with hearing aids, and special attention to the environment. Other considerations for adapting activity for hard-of-hearing children are appropriate use of residual hearing, care of hearing aids, adaptation of the instructional environment, visual feedback, and other special instructional techniques. Athletic opportunities should be provided for the hearing impaired so that attained skills may be expressed to further develop motor skills, physical fitness, and personal and social characteristics outside of the physical education class.

REVIEW QUESTIONS

1. What are the different categories of deafness?
2. What are the indicators of hearing loss that can be observed by the physical education teacher while teaching a class?
3. List informal methods that a physical educator might use to determine whether a student has a hearing loss.
4. What are some behavioral characteristics of hearing-impaired children?
5. Discuss two different methods of communicating with deaf persons.

6. Discuss the practical application of signing to communicate with hearing-impaired persons.
7. What are some teaching strategies that can be used with deaf persons?
8. What specific application of principles for the hearing impaired can be made in physical activity?
9. What is the process to be followed to integrate hearing-impaired individuals into community environments?
10. What competitive sport opportunities for hearing-impaired and deaf individuals are available in your community?

STUDENT ACTIVITIES

1. Impaired hearing can be found in persons of any age. Survey your community to locate agencies that provide services to persons who have hearing impairments. What types of services are available? How do these differ from services provided by the public schools?
2. Simulate an interaction with a deaf person. Communicate to the person, through signs, the method of performing a physical education task.
3. Talk to a teacher of the deaf to determine the method of communicating with the deaf. Has the teacher used more than one method? Which method has been most effective with specific groups of deaf persons?
4. Observe hearing-impaired children participating in a physical education class. What teaching strategies were employed by the teacher? What adaptations were made to accommodate the hearing-impaired children in activity? What were the behavioral characteristics of the hearing-impaired children?
5. Talk with two physical educators from two different schools about how to improve the social acceptance of children with impaired hearing. What suggestions did they offer? What have they tried in the past that has worked?
6. Simulate a hearing loss by using ear plugs. Attempt to learn a new physical activity under these conditions.
7. Write a paper on the different types of hearing aids. Indicate any special implications for the conduction of physical education programs for these children.

REFERENCES

1. Benderly BL: *Dancing without music,* Washington, DC, 1990, Gallaudet University Press.
2. Butterfield SA: Deaf children in physical education, *Palaestra* 4:28-30, 1988.
3. Butterfield SA, Ersing WF: Influence of age, sex, etiology and hearing loss on balance performance by deaf children, *Percept Mot Skills* 62:659-663, 1986.
4. Commission on Education of the Deaf, *Toward equality-education for the deaf, Report to the United States Congress,* February, 1988.
5. Crowe T, Horak F: Motor proficiency associated with vestibular deficits in children with hearing impairments, *Phys Ther* 68:1493-1499, 1988.
6. Eichstaedt CB, Kalakian LH: *Developmental/adapted*

physical education, New York, 1987, Macmillan Publishing.

7. Eichstaedt CB, Seiler P: Communicating with hearing impaired individuals in a physical education setting, *J Health Phys Educ Rec Dance,* May 1978, pp 19-21.

8. Fait HF, Dunn JM: *Special physical education,* Philadelphia, 1984, Saunders College Publishing Co.

9. French R, Jansma P: Special physical education, Columbus, Ohio, 1982, Charles E Merrill Publishing.

10. Gallaudet Research Institute: *Today's hearing impaired children and youth: a demographic and academic profile,* Washington, DC, 1985, Center for Assessment and Demographic Studies.

11. Grimes UK, Prickett HT: Developing and enhancing a positive self-concept in deaf children, *Am Ann Deaf* 133:4, 1988.

12. Hallahan DP, Kaufman JM: *Exceptional children,* Englewood Cliffs, NJ, 1982, Prentice Hall.

13. Hattin H: Are deaf children usually fit?: a comparison of fitness between deaf and blind children, *Adapt Phys Educ Q* 3:268-275, 1986.

14. Hoeman HW, Briga JS: Hearing impairments. In Kaufman JM, Hallahan DP, editors: *Handbook of special education,* Englewood Cliffs, NJ, 1981, Prentice Hall.

15. Hottendorf D: Mainstreaming deaf and hearing children in dance class, *J Health Phys Ed Rec Dance* 60: 54-55, 1989.

16. Jensema CJ, Karchmer MA, Trybus RJ: *The rated speech intelligibility of hearing impaired children: basic relationships and detailed analysis,* Washington, DC, 1978, Gallaudet College Office of Demographic Studies.

17. Knobloch H, Pasamanick B: *Developmental diagnosis,* New York, 1974, Harper & Row, Publishers.

18. Ling D: *Early total communication intervention: an introduction in early intervention for hearing-impaired children: total communication options,* San Diego, 1984, College Hill Press.

19. Luckner JL: Outdoor adventure and the hearing impaired-...consideration for program development, *Palaestra* 4:40-43, 1988.

20. Meyen EL: *Exceptional children and youth,* Denver, 1978, Love Publishing.

21. Minter M, Wolk S: Knowledge and demonstration of physical fitness among a hearing-impaired postsecondary population: preliminary implications for curriculum, *Phys Ed* 44:363-367, 1987.

22. Minter MG: Factors which may prevent full self-expression of deaf athletes in sports, *Palaestra* 5:36-38, 1989.

23. Moores D: *Educating the deaf: psychology, principles and practices, ed 3,* Boston, 1987, Houghton Mifflin.

24. Moores DF, Meadow-Orlans KP: *Educational and developmental aspects of deafness,* Washington, DC, 1990, Gallaudet University Press.

25. O'Rourke IJ: *ABC's of signing,* Silver Springs, Md, 1987, National Association of the Deaf.

26. Paul P, Quigley S: *Education and deafness,* New York, 1990, Longman.

27. Reagan T: Cultural considerations in the education of deaf children. In Moores DF, Meadow-Orlans KP, editors: *Education and development of aspects of deafness,* Washington, DC, 1990, Gallaudet University Press.

28. Reed WF: Kenny Walker, *Sports Illustrated* 73:10,110, 1990.

29. Scott P: Certified Educator of the Deaf, Texas Woman's University, Denton, Tex, *Personal communication,* October, 1991.

30. Sherrill C: *Adapted physical education and recreation, ed 3,* Dubuque, Iowa, 1986, Wm C Brown Publishing.

31. Siegel J, Marchetti M, Tecclin J: Age-related balance changes in hearing-impaired children, *Phys Ther* 71:183-189, 1991.

32. Stewart D, Dummer G, Haubenstricker J: Review of administrative procedures used to assess the motor skills of deaf children and youth, *Adapt Phys Act Q* 7:231-239, 1990.

33. Stewart DA: Social factors influencing participation in sport for the deaf, *Palaestra* 3:23-29, 1987.

34. US Department of Health, Education, and Welfare: Regulations for the Education for All Handicapped Children Act of 1975, *Fed Reg* 4:42476, Aug 23, 1977.

35. Winnick JP, Short FX: *Physical fitness testing of the disabled,* Champaign, Ill, 1985, Human Kinetics Publishers.

SUGGESTED READINGS

Eichstaedt CB, Kalakian LH: *Developmental/adapted physical education,* New York, 1987, Macmillan Publishing.

Kirk SA, Gallagher JJ: *Educating exceptional children,* Boston, 1986, Houghton Mifflin.

Riekehof LL: *The joy of signing: the new illustrated guide for mastering sign language and the manual alphabet,* Springfield, Missouri, 1978.

Ross M, Calvert DR: Semantics of deafness revisited: total communication and the use and misuse of residual hearing, *Audiology* 9:127-145, 1986.

13

OBJECTIVES

Describe the nature of visual defects.

List the general characteristics of children with limited vision.

Explain the principles and methods for adapting physical activity for the blind.

Design and manage the instructional environment.

Select appropriate activities for the blind.

Integrate physical education instructional programs with recreational opportunities in the community.

Describe a process for integrating blind and sighted individuals.

Courtesy Wisconsin Lions Camp, Rosholt, Wisconsin

Visual Impairments

Visual disorders include both permanent and functional conditions. Children with visual disorders represent a unique challenge to the physical educator, because in addition to their visual impairments they usually demonstrate developmental lags. Many of these children have not had opportunities to physically explore the environment during their early years. As a result, intact sensorimotor systems are not stimulated adequately and motor development and physical fitness levels suffer. Low vitality and perceptual-motor development lags often prevent the children from participating in activities not contraindicated by the primary visual disorder.

For a child to qualify under the law for special services in physical education, the visual disability must adversely affect the child's physical education performance. Children with visual disorders who qualify for adapted/developmental physical education programs demonstrate one or both of the following:

1. A visual disability that, even with correction, adversely affects the child's educational performance; the term *visual disability* includes both partially sighted and blind children.
2. Concomitant hearing and visual impairments, the combination of which causes such severe communication and other developmental and educational problems that the child cannot be accommodated in special educational programs solely for deaf or blind children.

Other aspects of vision not covered by law include fixation and eye movement abilities, accommodation (eye focusing), convergence (eye aiming), and binocularity (eye teaming).

CONTINUUM OF DISABILITY

Children with visual disabilities must be approached in accordance with their own unique educational needs. All blind and partially sighted children should have a full evaluation as to the degree of visual loss.

A child who has a loss of vision also may be impaired in the function of mobility and may be less able than nonimpaired children in motor abilities. There is a great need for blind children to be provided with opportunities, through adapted physical education, that will compensate for their movement deficiencies.

Children with loss of vision are, for educational purposes, classified as blind (those who are educated through channels other than visual) or partially sighted (those who are able to be educated, with special aids, through the medium of vision, with consideration given to the useful vision they retain). Blindness is determined by visual acuity and is expressed in a ratio with normal vision in the numerator and actual measured vision in the denominator; for example, 20/30 vision means that the eye can see at the distance of 20 feet what a normal eye can see at 30 feet. The legally blind are described as those who have a visual acuity of 20/200 or less in the better eye after maximum correction or who have a visual field that subtends an angle of 20 degrees or less in the widest diameter.

There are varying degrees of blindness. If a person is not totally blind, it is still possible to make functional use of whatever vision remains. Some blind persons have little residual vision and are unable to perceive motion and discriminate light. These individuals are at the upper end of the continuum of blindness. Some blind persons, however, are capable of perceiving distance and motion, whereas others possess these capabilities and are also able to travel with the use of residual vision.

The point to be stressed is that when a person is considered blind, it does not necessarily mean that the majority of the activities in a typical physical education program must be ruled out. Rather, a person's capacity for specific activity depends on the degree of blindness as well as available skill.

The term *partially sighted* refers to persons who have less than 20/70 visual acuity in the better eye after correction, have a progressive eye disorder that will probably reduce vision below 20/70, or have peripheral vision that subtends an angle less than 20 degrees. The visual acuity of a child is one consideration for participation in physical activity. Physical and psychological adjustments should be made for persons who lose sight as a result of injury or operations. Such injury may result in eye anomalies that necessitate reeducation of abnormal eyes. Functional conditions not covered under the law have an impact on depth perception, eye-hand coordination, visual form perception, visual memory, visual-spatial development, and visual-spatial integration. Each child must be considered according to his or her ability to function, regardless of the nature or degree of the visual disability. In some instances a child's vision may fall within the normal range, but the child may have progressive eye difficulties or a disease of the eye or body that seriously affects vision.

The residual vision of blind and partially sighted disabled athletes may be related to the amount of assistance they need to participate in physical activity. It also may be related to the quality of performance. Therefore to provide equity in competition, classification of these competitors is based on the amount of sight. The United States Association for Blind Athletes (USABA) classification system of legally blind athletes is as follows:

1. Class A—totally blind; possess light perception only, have no visual acuity or see less than 3 degrees in the visual field
2. Class B—visual acuity no better than 20/400 or those with 3 to 10 degrees in the visual field; can see hand movement
3. Class C—visual acuity 20/399 through 20/299 or those with 10+ to 20 degrees in the visual field

INCIDENCE

It is difficult to assess the incidence of blindness and partial vision because of the differing definitions of blindness and the problems that exist in identification. Consequently, dependable statistics on the incidence of blindness in the United States are lacking, although there is a growing awareness that a greater incidence of blindness and vision impairment exists than had been believed previously. It is estimated that 0.1% of the population is visually disabled. A considerable number of children with visual dysfunctions are not categorized as either blind or partially sighted. Estimates indicate that approximately 20% of elementary school children and 30% of high school students have some functional visual defect.

CAUSES

The underlying causes for visual loss include diabetes, accidents and injuries, poisoning, tumors, and prenatal influences such as rubella and syphilis. Several defects may cause degeneration of vision, such as the following:

□ Refractive errors such as hyperopia, myopia, and astigmatism
□ Structural anomalies such as cataracts
□ Infectious diseases of the eyes
□ Orthoptic errors such as strabismus and nystagmus

VISUAL DISORDERS

Refractive errors are a result of inaccurate bending of light rays as they enter or pass through the eye. *Hyperopia,* or farsightedness, is a condition in which the light rays focus behind the retina, causing an unclear image of objects closer than 20 feet from the eye. The term implies that distant objects can be seen with less strain than near objects. *Myopia,* or nearsightedness, is a refractive error in which the rays of light focus in front of the retina when a person views an object 20 feet or more away. *Astigmatism* is a refractive error caused by an irregularity in the curvature of the cornea, so that portions of the light rays from a given object fall behind or in front of the retina. As a result, vision may be blurry.

Nystagmus involves rapid movement of the eyes from side to side, up and down, in a rotatory motion, or a combination of these.

In addition to the internal muscles of the eye mentioned previously, there are six muscles attached to the outside of each eyeball that control movement. Singular binocular vision involves coordinating the separate images that enter each eye into a single image in the visual cortex of the brain. When the two eyes function in unison and are coordinated in the brain, the images entering each eye are matched in the visual cortex, and binocular fusion results. If, however, the supply of energy to the extraocular muscles is out of balance and the images are not coordinated in the brain, the eyes do not function in unison. When this occurs, the images from one eye deviate from those of the other eye, and the images do not match in the visual cortex. The amount of visual distress experienced because of mismatched images *(strabismus)* depends on the degree of deviation of the eyes and the ability of the central nervous system to correct the imbalance. *Amblyopia* results when the image from an eye has been suppressed by the brain for a long time because a conflict exists between the two eyes. The eye with amblyopia does not function because the brain will not accept the deviant image.

The two most prevalent dysfunctions of external visual muscle control are heterotropias and heteropho-

FIGURE 13-1. An athlete uses guide wire in 25-meter dash. (Courtesy Texas Special Olympics.)

rias. *Heterotropias* are manifest malalignments of the eyes during which one or both eyes consistently deviate from the central axis. As a consequence, the eyes do not fixate at the same point on the object of visual attention. When the eyes turn inward, such as with crossed eyes, the condition is called *esotropia;* when one or both eyes turn outward, it is called *exotropia.* *Hypertropia* is the name given to the condition when one or both eyes swing upward; the term *hypotropia* is used when one or both eyes turn downward. Tropias always create depth-perception difficulties.

Heterophorias are tendencies toward visual malalignments. They usually do not cause serious visual distress because when slight variations in binocular fusion occur in the visual cortex, the central nervous system tends to correct the imbalance between the pull of the extraocular muscles. However, after prolonged use of the eyes, such as after reading for several hours, the stronger set of muscles overcomes the correction and the eyes swing out of alignment. An individual becomes aware of the malalignment when the vision of the printed page begins to blur. Phorias, like tropias, are named for the direction the eye tends to swing (*eso-* means in, toward the nose; *exo-* is a lateral drift; *hyper-* means up; and *hypo-* refers to down). Phorias create depth perception difficulties only after the correction is lost.

Term	Description
Amblyopia	A type of strabismus that causes the affected eye to be non-functional
Astigmatism	Refractive error caused by an irregularity in the curvature of the cornea of the lens; vision may be blurred
Esophoria	A tendency for an eye to deviate medially toward the nose
Esotropia	A condition in which the eye(s) turns inward (cross-eyed)
Exophoria	A tendency for an eye to deviate laterally away from the nose
Exotropia	A condition in which the eye(s) turns outward
Hyperopia	A condition in which the light rays focus behind the retina causing an unclear image of objects closer than 20 feet from the eye (farsighted)
Hyperphoria	A tendency for an eye to deviate in an upward direction

Term	Description
Hypertropia	A condition in which one or both eyes swing upard
Hypophoria	A tendency for an eye to deviate in a downward direction
Hypotropia	A condition in which one or both eyes swing downward
Myopia	A condition in which the light rays focus in front of the retina when a person views an object 20 feet or more away from the eye (nearsighted)
Nystagmus	Rapid movement of the eyes from side to side, up and down, in a rotatory motion, or in a combination of these motions
Ophthalmologist	Licensed physician specializing in the treatment of eye diseases and optical defects
Optician	Technician who grinds lenses and makes glasses
Orthoptic vision	The ability to use the extraocular muscles of the eyes in unison
Orthoptician	Person who provides eye exercises to refine control of the eye (e.g., visual behavioral specialist)
Refractive vision	The process by which light rays bend as they enter or pass through the eyes
Strabismus	Any orthoptic condition interferring with the ability to use the extraocular muscles of the eyes in unison

Several visual abnormalities are acquired or hereditary.

Term	Description
Albinism	A hereditary condition in which there is a lack of pigment in the eyes; may include light sensitivity and require dark glasses
Cataract	Opacity of the normally transparent lens
Glaucoma	Increased pressure of the fluid inside the eye, which causes visual loss; associated with decreasing peripheral vision
Retinitis pigmentosa	Degeneration of the retina that produces gradual loss of peripheral vision

Term	Description
Retrolental fibroplasia	Visual impairment caused by oxygen during incubation of premature babies

TESTING VISUAL IMPAIRMENT

Vision tests are extremely important to identify and remedy vision disorders and to facilitate the education of visually disabled persons. A widely used test of vision is the Snellen test, which is a measure of visual acuity. This test can be administered with expediency to a child by nonprofessional personnel and is applicable to young children. The Snellen chart can aid detection of myopia, astigmatism, higher degrees of hyperopia, and other eye conditions that cause imperfect visual images. However, the chart primarily measures central distance visual acuity. It does not give indications of near-point vision, peripheral vision, convergence ability, binocular fusion ability, or oculomotor dysfunctions. A thorough vision screening program must include tests supplementary to the Snellen test. Other visual screening tests that may provide additional information are the Massachusetts Vision test, the Keystone Telebinocular test, and the Orthoptor test.

Limitations in peripheral vision constitute a visual disability, particularly in some activities involving motor skills. Consequently, knowledge of this aspect of vision may assist the physical educator in determining methods of teaching and types of activities for the visually impaired child. Peripheral vision is usually assessed in terms of degrees of visual arc and is measured by the extent to which a standard visual stimulus can be seen on a black background viewed from a distance of about 39 inches when the eye is fixed on a central point.[9]

It is difficult to evaluate the results found on a given test of vision because two persons with similar vision characteristics on a screening test may display different visual behavior physically, socially, and psychologically. Although objective screening tests of vision are important, it is suggested that daily observations be made to supplement the screening tests. Daily observation for symptoms of eye trouble has particular importance in the early primary years. Detection of visual disabilities early in development enables early intervention, which maximizes skill development. Symptoms that might indicate eye disorders and might be observed by the physical educator are included in the following list:

1. Eyelids that are crusted and red, on which sties or swelling appears

2. Discharge from the eyes
3. Lack of coordination in directing vision of both eyes
4. Frequent rubbing of the eyes
5. Inattention when sustained visual activity is required or when looking at distant objects
6. Body tension
7. Squinting
8. Forward thrust of the head
9. Walking overcautiously
10. Faltering or stumbling
11. Running into objects not directly in the line of vision
12. Failure to see objects readily visible to others
13. Sensitivity to normal light levels
14. Inability to distinguish colors
15. Difficulty in estimating distances
16. Bloodshot eyes
17. Going down steps one at a time
18. Avoidance of climbing apparatus

Some blind persons have accompanying mental retardation. These individuals may exhibit self-stimulatory behavior, or *blindisms,* such as rocking the body or head, placing fingers or fists into the eyes, flicking the fingers in front of the face, and spinning the body around repetitiously. These behaviors provide vestibular, tactile, or visual stimulation.

New techniques for evaluating vision and assisting individuals with visual disorders are available through low vision clinics. Generally, people whose best corrected vision is 20/70 or less or whose visual field is restricted to 30 degrees or less are considered to have low vision and are most likely to benefit from low vision services.

VISION THERAPY

Vision therapy or vision training is defined as "the teaching and training process for the improvement of visual perception and/or the coordination of the two eyes for efficient and comfortable binocular vision."[18] The purpose of vision therapy is to treat functional deficiencies in order for the person to achieve optimum efficiency and comfort.[2] Although the value of this type of therapy has long been debated, when carried out by well-trained visual behavioral specialists there is strong scientific support for its efficacy in modifying and improving oculomotor, accommodative, and binocular system disorders.[2]

CHARACTERISTICS

There are widespread individual differences among visually limited persons. However, certain characteristics

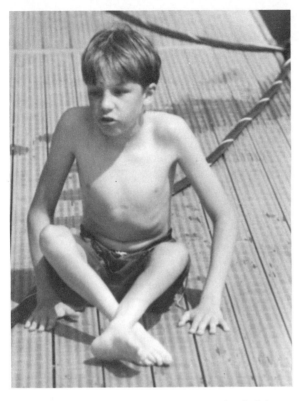

FIGURE 13-2. A totally blind child explores the deck before entering the water. (Courtesy Wisconsin Lions Camp, Rosholt, Wisconsin.)

appear more often than in sighted persons. Some of the characteristics that have implications for physical education are the following:

☐ There is loss of vision but wide variations of residual vision.

☐ There are significant problems in mastering complicated movement patterns.

☐ Physical fitness scores are below those of sighted peers.

☐ Posture is often poor; there is no visual model to emulate.

☐ Physical growth and maturation may be impaired because of limited opportunities for movement.

☐ There is a tendency toward obesity caused by a sedentary lifestyle.

☐ Development of the ability to balance is impaired.

☐ Fundamental motor patterns and skills are below normative performance.

☐ A person's vision may fluctuate depending on health

and environmental conditions such as lighting or stress.

Differences Between Acquired and Congenital Visual Disorders

There are two basic types of visual disorders: (1) congenital, or present at birth, and (2) adventitious, or acquired after birth. The onset of blindness will have an impact on the development of the child. It is obvious that depending on when blindness occurred, the adventitiously blind child will have some opportunities to explore environments and receive environmental information through the visual senses for development. The congenitally blind child will lack visual information upon which motor reponses may be built.

Congenital blindness

Overprotection may hamper the development of the congenitally blind individual. Frequently, parents and teachers tend to restrict the activity of blind children. The overprotection complicates development because the child is not permitted to explore environments necessary for the development of motor responses.

The child with normal sight makes judgments as to where objects are in space by pairing sensory information from vision with movement information received when moving to and from objects. Because congenitally blind persons cannot visually compare objects at varying distances in the environment, they are unable to formulate visual judgments.

The blind child is often unaware of the movement potential of body parts. The lack of awareness of potential may restrict movements, which in turn retards the development of muscles and balancing mechanisms needed for the development of complex motor skills. The congenitally visually disordered child may have more difficulty with social situations than the adventitiously blind individual. Any limitation in observing and interpreting gestures of individuals as they talk results in less information about what a person is attempting to communicate. Lack of opportunity to read body language and assess the social surroundings in terms of what is appropriate may limit social development of blind individuals.

Adventitious blindness

Previous sight experience impacts favorably on the physical and motor development of adventitiously blind persons. However, they may be despondent over a recently acquired condition of sight loss and find adjustment difficult. Thus there is a need for immediate

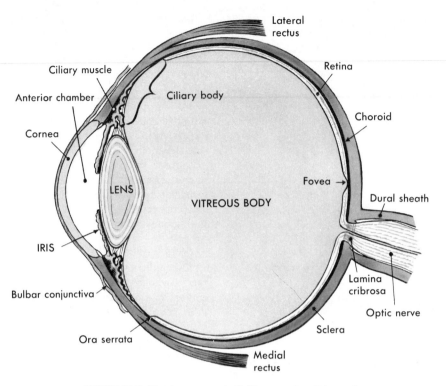

FIGURE 13-3. The human eyeball. (Courtesy Bess Schwarz.)

intervention with the adventitiously blind person when onset occurs.

Developmental Factors

Vision loss has serious implications for the general development of motor, academic, intellectual, psychological, and social characteristics. The blind infant has little motivation to hold the head up because of lack of visual stimulation, so in the formative stages of postural development (head control) blind children are behind normative expectations. In many instances intervention with training programs and adaptive measures is necessary to meet the developmental needs of the maturing child with a loss of vision. It is important to have some knowledge of how the child with vision loss may develop physically, socially, and psychologically so that the physical educator can be alert to cope with needs that may arise.

Evidence indicates that blind pupils in the public schools are educationally retarded as compared with their sighted peers of the same chronological age.[3] One possible reason is that adventitiously blind children may have a maladjustment at the onset of blindness, making it difficult to stay abreast of sighted peers. Physical educators must be alert to detect educationally retarded blind children. They must not be misguided by grade placement but must assess and meet the physical, motor, and social needs of each child.

Physical activity is essential for optimum child growth and development. Through movement experiences children with vision losses acquire a better understanding of themselves, others, and the world around them. However, limited vision restricts physical motor activity, which in turn limits the range and variety of experiences the children may encounter. They then become less effective in meeting the demands of the environment. Opportunities for manipulating toys and objects are extremely important in the early life of blind children because it is through touch and feeling, rather than through vision, that they learn about the physical world.

Providing an environment in which children with vision impairments can develop optimumly is a great challenge. Blind children are often slower to learn skills such as walking, talking, prehension, feeding, and socialization unless they are given help in developing these traits.

Norris and Brody[14] found that blind children showed delayed mastery of motor responses in tasks requiring fine motor coordination. There is impressive evidence that fine motor coordination develops with fluency only after the children have had experiences in gross motor activity. This indicates a need to provide environmental experiences for both gross and fine motor activities. Planned physical experiences are required for young blind children to counter slower rates of motor and physical development as compared with children who have normal vision.

Perceptual Development

Children with limited vision use other sensory abilities better as a result of increased attention to them in attempts to learn about and cope with the environment. A sighted person might be unaware of particular auditory stimuli, whereas a blind person might attach great significance to them.

FIGURE 13-4. A sighted partner makes it possible for a visually impaired adult to enjoy bicycling. (Courtesy Wisconsin Lions Camp, Rosholt, Wisconsin.)

These children need to use full proprioceptive, auditory, haptic, and space perception. Each form of perception contributes to the ability of the blind child to adapt to the environment. The proprioceptors can enable a blind person to maintain balance. Balance experience is acquired through different and unusual body positions. The proprioceptors are stimulated if the tasks become sequentially more difficult.

Interrelationship between balance and proprioceptive information in vision

The role of vision as it relates to balance and movement has been the focus of much research. Visual information that assists with performing specific motor skills is integrated with information from the vestibular apparatus and proprioceptive signals resulting from reflex and voluntary movements. Organization of these sensory inputs plays a central role in successfully maintaining posture and executing movement. Sensory organization is responsible for determining the timing, direction, and amplitude of movement based on information from vision, proprioception, and the vestibular sense. Nashner and McCollum[13] maintain that the information necessary to control movement is provided by visual images as well as by proprioceptive information about the specific positions of the eyes. Thus the execution of static and dynamic balance frequently requires a combination of several senses, one of which is vision.

Space Perception

Early visual experience of spatial relations establishes a method for processing information that affects cognitive and motor learning. Blind persons often cannot perceive the relationship of objects to each other in space. They also have an impaired ability to relate themselves to objects in space. Therefore the auditory, vestibular, kinesthetic, and tactile senses are used to establish spatial relationships.

Characteristics of Blind Individuals

Blind and visually disabled persons for the most part perform less capably on physical fitness tests than do their sighted peers.[19] Lack of fitness may contribute to a more passive lifestyle, which could cause increased obesity.[22] Ribadi, Rider, and Toole[16] indicate that congenitally blind individuals are less capable on static and dynamic balance tasks than are their sighted peers. There is evidence that even among elite blind athletes, their performance is different than sighted persons.

Gordon and Gavron[5] studied 28 running parameters of sighted and blind runners. As a group, the blind runners did not have a sufficient forward lean while running. There was insufficient hip, knee, and ankle extension at takeoff, which placed limits on power, and there was incomplete range of motion of the hip and the ankle. Furthermore, patterns of movement of blind and sighted runners may be different, just as there are differences among blind persons. Therefore single descriptive measures of performance of blind athletes give little information on how to train specific athletes. Clearly, studies indicate that each individual must be evaluated and provided individual training regimens based on his or her specific needs at a given time.[5] Thus normative data on patterns of locomotion of groups classified on a single characteristic (i.e., blindness) provide little information about the needs of a specific individual. Descriptive patterns of normative groups may not provide productive information for training regimens. The evidence is scanty that there are predictable relationships between running patterns and performance outcome. Thus it would seem that training regimens should be used to promote performance of specific skills.

Psychological and Social Adjustment

The emotional and social characteristics of the visually limited vary according to the individual. Blind students may have personality problems as well as physical incapacities. Research available regarding the social maturity of blind children reveals that, in general, they receive significantly lower social maturity scores than do sighted children.[7] Physical education programs may well be an important medium for enhancing the social maturity of blind children.

Psychological and social adjustment of the blind cannot be separated from the attitudes with which the nondisabled view them. The lack of respect from one's peers may create a need for a disproportionate amount of social and emotional adjustment of the blind not only to blindness, but also to their peers. The correlates of maladjustment are to be found in deficiencies of respect accorded the individual, rather than a lack of visual experience.

The uphill battle for social adjustment of the blind requires special attention; sighted persons acquire social habits through imitation, but the blind need direct instruction in everyday social adjustment. The emotional and social climate of the physical education class can be structured so that blind children are able to function comfortably at their own levels and establish wholesome social relationships. Lack of individualized instructional procedures can contribute to frustration by creating situations that accentuate, rather than minimize, differences.

Mobility

One of the greatest problems caused by blindness is impeded mobility. Success in school and at work in later years depends on mobility. By contributing to the independence of blind persons, mobility leads to opportunities for physical, social, and psychological development.

A mobility training program in a gymnasium or playing area greatly increases independence and thus the ability to perform in a physical education program. Orientation and training programs should help the blind person cope with physical surroundings effectively. Training programs should also foster successful interaction with peers as well as with the physical facilities and equipment. It must be remembered that some blind persons have enough vision to travel about—known as *travel vision*. The individual capabilities of each child should be assessed to determine the extent of the mobility training program.

THE PHYSICAL EDUCATION PROGRAM

The physical education teacher may be requested to instruct a class in which visually limited children are integrated with the regular class, to instruct a class

FIGURE 13-5. A child develops equilibrium and posture. (Photo by Jo Arms. Courtesy Albuquerque, New Mexico Public Schools.)

composed solely of visually limited children, or to instruct classes of multidisabled children.

There is a growing awareness that similarities are greater than differences when visually limited children are compared with sighted children. Therefore integration of visually limited children with their nondisabled peers should be instituted to meet the federal mandates of placement of all disabled children in the least restrictive environment (regular class, if possible). Such placement emphasizes the positive aspects of the children and minimizes differences.

In the past it was not uncommon for children with limited vision to be referred to and placed in residential schools. However, with the implementation of The Education of the Handicapped Act a countertrend has grown to bring instructional aids into resource rooms and regular classrooms of community schools. This practice has created a number of service delivery alternatives for least restrictive placement. According to Reynolds and Birch,[15] the following cascade system for placement of children with visual disabilities should be applied:

1. Regular class
2. Regular class with assistance by vision consultant
3. Regular class with consultation and itinerant instruction (orientation and mobility training)
4. Adapted physical education conducted by specialist; children attend part time
5. Self-contained adapted physical education class
6. Residential schools for the blind

The itinerant teacher is a specialist who possesses specific skills to work with children of limited vision. This teacher teams with the regular classroom teacher on behalf of visually disabled children. For more information concerning the duties of this type of teacher, refer to Moore and Peabody.[12]

The Teacher

The physical education teacher must be able to respect individuals who have atypical vision. Furthermore, attention should focus on the abilities, as well as the deficits, of visually disabled children for the purpose of creating an environment conducive to optimum growth. An assessment of the needs, abilities, and limitations of visually limited children is necessary, with subsequent program development according to defined needs. This is a challenging task for a teacher; however, it has been pointed out by many good teachers that instructing the visually limited has enabled them to do a better job with typical children because it was necessary to plan more carefully when working with the former group.

Some suggested considerations prerequisite to effective education of visually limited child are as follows:

1. Skilled observation of motor performance and behavioral characteristics of individuals and of group participants
2. Recognition of differences in the manner in which the visually limited child learns, as compared with the typical child, followed by appropriate adaptive methodology
3. Understanding of the growth and development of physical and social competence
4. Knowledge of appropriate curricula and methods in physical education for the visually limited

Physical Education Needs

Loss of vision, by itself, is not a limiting condition for physical exercise. A considerable amount of developmental exercises of muscular strength and endurance can be administered to such children. Through developmental exercise the visually limited child develops qualities such as good posture, graceful body movement, and good walking and sitting positions. Furthermore, physical education programs develop and maintain a healthy, vigorous body with physical vitality and good neuromuscular coordination. In addition to physical benefits, the physical education program contributes to social-emotional outcomes such as security and confidence and acceptance of the disabled by their sighted peers.

The ultimate goal of the class atmosphere for children with vision losses is to provide experiences that will help them adjust to the seeing society in which they live. The selection and method of experiences in the physical education program are critical. These experiences should not be overprotective to the extent that growth is inhibited; rather, the experiences should provide challenge yet remain within the range of the children's capabilities for achieving skill objectives.

The problems that confront the teacher regarding successful emotional and psychological adjustment of the visually limited involve both visually limited children and nondisabled children. Teacher guidelines for achieving the goal of adjustment for these children follow:

☐ Provide opportunities for participation and enjoyment in new experiences
☐ Provide individual education programs (IEPs) in which the children are free to grow and develop at their own rates
☐ Find ways in which the children can best contribute to the groups that are satisfying to them
☐ Help the children become acquainted with their physical surroundings

Physical education teachers working with children who are visually disabled should attempt to minimize the stereotyped manner in which the visually limited child receives an education and should encourage nondisabled children to accept their blind peers on a personal basis. The development of such attitudes of the nondisabled supports the principle of normalization of the disabled.

Adapting Methods and Activities

Children with limited vision are capable of participating in numerous activities; however, the degree of participation possible depends on each child's particular abilities. Broad curriculum areas should be available at appropriate levels of development to accommodate each child. Visually disabled children may represent a cross section of any school population with regard to motor abilities, physical fitness characteristics, and social and emotional traits. The purpose of adapting methods and activities for the visually limited is to provide many experiences that sighted children learn primarily through visual observation. A goal of group activity in which a child with limited vision participates is to assign a role to the child that can be carried out successfully. It is undesirable for the child to be placed in the position of a bystander.

Adaptation of the physical education program for visually limited individuals should promote confidence in them to cope with their environment by increasing their physical and motor abilities. It should also produce in them a feeling of acceptance as individuals in their own right. To achieve these goals, the program should include adaptation of the general program of activities, when needed; additional or specialized activities, depending on the needs of the child; and special equipment, if needed.

The physical educator who administers activities to children with limited vision should take special safety precautions. Some considerations that may enhance the safety factor in physical education programs for the visually limited are:

1. To secure knowledge, through medical records and observation, of the child's limitations and capabilities
2. To orient the child to facilities and equipment
3. To provide special equipment indicating direction, such as guide lines in swimming and running events, as well as deflated softballs

TEACHING STRATEGIES

The visually limited child must depend on receiving information through sensory media other than vision. Audition is a very important sensory medium of instruction. Another sensory medium that can be used is kinesthesis through manual guidance and movement of the body parts administered by an instructor or another student. This provides comprehension of body position and body action. The blind child has little understanding of spatial concepts such as location, position, direction, and distance; therefore skin and muscular sensations give meaning to body position and postural change in motor activity. The manual guidance method (accompanied by verbal corrections) is often effective in the correction of faulty motor skills, since two senses are used for instruction. A technique that has met with some success in the integrated class is for the teacher to use the blind child in presenting a demonstration to the rest of the class by manually manipulating the child through the desired movements. This enables the visually limited child to get the tactual feel of movement, and instruction to the sighted class

FIGURE 13-6. Returning from a distance bicycle ride.
(Courtesy Wisconsin Lions Camp, Rosholt, Wisconsin.)

members is not deterred. Providing information, rules, and tests in braille for advance study of a class presentation may enable the visually limited child to better understand the presentation.

Blind persons need concrete experiences with objects and events for learning to occur. To promote participation with sighted players, Richardson and Mastro[17] suggest that audible balls be used for relay and to play such games as "Steal the Bacon." With the audible ball, blind players can know where the ball is most of the time. For bowling, Stanley and Kindig[21] suggest that improvised rope guide rails in conjunction with a carefully placed carpet can be used to identify foot positions and distance traveled during instruction of a four-step approach. The carpet may replace the permanence of a guide rail and enable lesser restricted participation in bowling alleys; also the carpet can be rolled and transported conveniently. Visually disabled individuals can participate in alpine skiing with the help of a guide who stays within 5 to 8 feet of the blind skier. The guide and the skier ski independently; however, the guide keeps an eye on both the course and on the visually impaired skier.

Both guide wires and guide runners have been shown to be effective for runners. Guide wires are ropes or heavy string stretched 36 inches above the lane markers; they help runners feel the perimeters of the lane. A guide runner is a person who runs alongside the visually impaired runner and verbally describes the distance to the finish. In competition the guide runner is also permitted to touch the visually impaired runner's elbow to indicate any off-step laterally.[11]

Developing Socialization Skills

One of the chief problems to be confronted in the social and psychological adjustment of the visually limited person is the lack of opportunity for social participation with sighted persons. Recreational opportunities are a possible outlet for making social contact with the sighted population and also provide self-expression for the visually limited individual (see Chapter 6).

Because of the great visual content included in the components of certain games, some skill activities are more difficult to adapt to the visually limited than are others. In the case of the more severely disabled, participation in the more complex activities may be extremely difficult to modify. However, the skills comprising a game can be taught, and lead-up games with appropriate modifications are usually within the child's grasp. Some adaptations of basic sports skills follow:

Activity	Modification
Aerobic dance	Include verbal description of movement with demonstration
Archery	Beeper affixed to center of target
Bicycling	Child assumes rear seat position on tandem bicycle with sighted partner in front seat
Bowling	Beeper attached above pins at end of lane
Canoeing	Child assumes bow position, with sighted partner in stern
Frisbee	A frisbee with beeper attached
Horseshoes	Beeper affixed to stake
Horseshoes	Path to horseshoe pit made of wood chips or sand
Running	Ropes for guidance (guide wire)
Swimming	Lane lines that designate the swimming lanes
Swimming	Swimming pool with nonslip bottom
Swimming	Pool decks with nonslip surface
Swimming	A constant sound source for orientation
Swimming	Small bells suspended near gutters, activated by waves as person approaches end of pool
Softball	Sand or wood chips for base paths
Softball	T-stand for batting, instead of batting from pitcher
Softball	Different texture of ground or floor when near a surface that could result in serious collision
Weight training	Equipment and weights in the same place
Class management	Environment that is ordered and consistent
Class management	Reference points that indicate the location of the child in the play area
Class management	Auditory cues to identify obstacles in the environment
Class management	Tactile markings on the floor
Class management	Boundaries of different texture

Cognitive Instruction

Communication of information and testing of knowledge are part of physical education instruction. Accommodations must be made for the visually impaired during the communication of the physical education program:

□ Large print letters and numbers can be perceived by many partially sighted persons.

□ Use braille, a shorthand for tactile reading. Dots in a cell are raised on paper to indicate letters, numbers, punctuation, and other special signs.

□ Make better use of listening skills and position visually impaired students where they can hear instructional information best. This may be directly in front of the instructor.

□ Substitute kinesthetic (manual) guidance for vision when components of skills are to be integrated in space and time.

□ Encourage the use of residual vision during the cognitive communication process between instructor and visually impaired student.

□ Arrange seats to accommodate range of vision.

□ Design appropriate light contrasts between figure and ground when presenting instructional materials.

□ Be alert to behavioral signs and physical symptoms of visual difficulty in all children.

There are several considerations that physical educators must make to effectively accommodate blind children in the diverse activities and environments where instruction takes place. It is beyond the scope of this book to compile all these adaptations. The application of principles of accommodation may help the physical educator teach a wide variety of activities. Some suggested principles follow:

□ Design the instructional environment to accommodate the individual.

□ Introduce special devices, aids, and equipment to assist the individual.

□ Use special instructional techniques to accommodate the individual.

□ Introduce precautionary safety measures to meet the individual's needs.

□ Provide special feedback for tasks to facilitate learning.

□ Employ nondisabled peers to assist with instruction.

□ Train the individual for mobility and understanding of the environment.

□ Allow the visually impaired person to decide if assistance is needed or wanted.[10]

□ Keep equipment and objects in the same place. Moving objects without telling the visually impaired person can be frustrating.

□ Assist with the initiation of social interactions with peers.

Instructional Environment

The instructional environment for the blind should be safe and familiar and possess distinguishing landmarks. As a safety precaution, play areas should be uncluttered and free from unnecessary obstructions.[1] Blind children should be thoroughly introduced to unfamiliar areas by walking them around the play environment before they are allowed to play.

Environmental characteristics can be amplified. For instance, gymnasiums can be well lighted to assist those who possess residual vision. Boundaries for games can have various compositions, such as a base or path of dirt and concrete or grass for other areas. Brightly colored objects are easier to identify. Also, equipment may be designed and appropriately placed to prevent possible injuries. For instance, two swings on a stand are safer than three. A third swing in the center is difficult to reach without danger when the other two swings are occupied. Attention to the safety and familiarity of the environment specifically designed for the blind represents some degree of accommodation.

There are two parts to the management of safe environments. One is the structure of the environment, and the other is the teacher's control of the children as they participate in the environment. Following are suggestions to ensure safe play.

□ Alter the playing surface texture (sand, dirt, asphalt); increase or decrease the grade to indicate play area boundaries.

□ Use padded walls, bushes, or other soft, safe restrainers around play areas.

□ Use brightly colored objects as boundaries to assist those with residual vision.

□ Limit the play area.

□ Limit the number of participants in the play area.

□ Play in slow motion when introducing a new game.

□ Protect the eyes.

□ Structure activities commensurate with the blind child's ability.

□ Protect visual aids such as eyeglasses.

□ Select safe equipment.

□ Structure a safe environment.

□ Instruct children to use the environment safely.

The following material indicates the application of safety principles:

Principle	Safety measure
Protection of aids	Protect all body parts; spotting in gymnastics
Protect eyeglasses	

Principle	Safety measure
Safe equipment	Use sponge ball for softball, volleyball, many projectile activities
Structure of safe environment	Check play areas for obstacles and holes in ground
Activity according to ability	Avoid activities that require children to pass each other at high speeds
Close supervision of all potentially dangerous activity	

Designing a safe environment is important. Equally important is instructing children with limited vision to use the environment safely. Sherrill[19] has suggested some techniques for teaching safe use of playground equipment. Safety instruction in play environments for young blind children is particularly important because of their unawareness of the distance from the ground when on elevated play apparatus. The children should demonstrate safe play on all the equipment by (1) pumping a swing while sitting, (2) walking a hand ladder, (3) climbing to the top of an 8- to 14-foot slide and sliding down feet first, (4) playing simple games on the jungle gym, and (5) using the seesaw safely with a companion.

Auditory Aids

Distance in space for the visually limited is structured by auditory cues. Therefore it is desirable to structure space with these cues. For instance, a sighted partner may ride a bicycle with a piece of cardboard attached to the bike wheel. A noise is made when it touches the spokes.

Auditory aids can be built into the equipment that is a part of the game. For instance, in the game "Jump the Shot," "It" rotates a flat piece of metal attached to a rope from the center of a circle composed of players. The piece emits a sound as it travels along the ground and thus informs the participants of its whereabouts.

Audible balls emit beeping sounds for easy location. They may be the size of a basketball, soccer ball, softball, or playground ball.[6]

Audible goal locators are motor-driven noisemakers. They can indicate the position of backboards in basketball, targets in archery, pins in bowling, and stakes in horseshoes. Furthermore, they can be used to identify dangerous objects in the environment and boundaries.

Activities that can be conducted to develop space perception through the use of auditory aids in the environment are to:

1. Walk a straight line. Measure the distance of deviations over a specific distance. Use an audible device to provide initial assistance for direction and then fade the device.
2. Face sounds made at different positions. The intensity and duration of the sound can make the task more or less difficult.
3. Reproduce pathways and specific distances just taken with a partner.

Auditory information in the environment is invaluable for positioning children with limited vision appropriately in activity environments.

Special Devices, Aids, and Equipment

Equipment, aids, and devices that enhance participation of the blind in physical activity should provide information about the environment. Beep baseball and goal ball are two competitive sports for the blind. Each sport requires special equipment that enables knowledge of the whereabouts of the ball. The beep baseball is a regular softball with a battery-operated electronic sound device. This special equipment tells the blind person where the ball is at all times because of continuous sound. Other special equipment is the bases, which are plastic cones 60 inches tall with a speaker that makes continuous sound installed in each base.

A goal ball is constructed with bells inside it. When the ball moves, the bells help the players locate the ball. One of the skills of the game is to roll the ball smoothly to reduce auditory information (less sound from the bells) to make it more difficult for blind players to locate it. Following are other devices, aids, and techniques that can be used to accommodate the blind in physical activity:

Activity	Device, aid, or equipment
Swimming	Flotation to increase buoyancy
Gymnastics	Safety belt
	Soft mat to protect the performers

Special Instructional Methods

The application of special methods requires astute observation of the characteristics of each blind student. A list of special methods follows:

☐ Give clear auditory signals with a whistle or megaphone.

☐ Instruct through manual guidance.

- Use braille to teach cognitive materials before class.
- Encourage tactual exploration of objects to determine texture, size, and shape.
- Address the child by name.
- Individualize instruction and build on existing capabilities. Do not let the child exploit visual limitations to the extent of withdrawing from activity or underachieving in motor performance.
- Use the sensory mode that is most effective for specific learners (tactile, kinesthetic, haptic, auditory).
- Manage the instructional environment to minimize the need of vision. Use chains where children touch one another. Participate from stationary positions. Establish reference points where all persons return for instruction.
- Instructional strategies should match the nature of the task. Games of low organization are an important part of elementary school physical education programs. The games that require the least modification are those in which there is continuous contact with the participants, such as tug of war, parachute activity, end man tag, ring around the rosy, hot potato, over and under relay, wheelbarrow races.

Fundamental motor skills and patterns are essential prerequisites for successful and enjoyable participation in recreational sport activities. Some of these activities are running, jumping, throwing, and striking. They involve coordinated movements. Traditional instruction involves presentation of a visual model through demonstration of the whole task. Pupils then attempt to reproduce this task. However, children with limited vision must receive information from other senses.

Special Task Feedback

Blind children need to know the effects of their performance on physical tasks because they receive little or no visual feedback. Task feedback must come from other sensory modes. For example, buzzers or bells can be inserted inside a basketball hoop to inform the person when a basket is made. Gravel can be placed around the stake for horseshoes to indicate accuracy of the toss. Peers can also give specific verbal feedback on tasks that involve projectiles. Effective feedback is an important reinforcing property to be incorporated into physical activity for the blind.

Peer Assistance

Nondisabled peers can assist the disabled child with instruction in integrated settings. The nature of the assistance depends on the nature of the task. Peer assistance in providing feedback to task success is one application of peer assistance. Blind persons may choose to have sighted guides. According to Kalakian and Eichstaedt,[7] for safety in travel skills, a blind person should grasp the guide's upper arm, above the elbow, with the thumb on the outside and the fingers on the inside of the guide's arm. Both student and guide hold upper arms close to the body. When approaching doorways or objects, the guide moves the entire arm behind the back so blind students understand to walk directly behind the guide. Verbal cues inform the blind student when there are stairways and curbs. When nondisabled children provide such assistance, it is necessary to manage their time so as not to impede their own education.

Variable Adaptation

Physical activities need varying amounts of adaptation for blind participants. Considerations for selection of activities for blind players are as follows:

1. Activities that require a considerable amount of vision are most difficult.
2. Activities that require great amounts of movement in the environment are usually the most difficult to adapt.
3. The greater the number of visual cues required for participation, the more difficult the accommodation.
4. Environments in which there is continual change of visual cues rather than stable visual cues are most difficult (e.g., team games such as basketball, football, and soccer).
5. The more modifications that have to be made in the environment, the more difficult the accommodation for the blind player.
6. The more equipment that needs to be modified, the more complex the accommodation of the motor task for the learner.

Team sports that are highly loaded with visual information require considerable accommodation. Such games include basketball, soccer, and football because the ball as well as the offensive and defensive players continually move. Activities that require mimimum amounts of vision for participation are (1) wrestling (the only modification is contact with an opponent at a takedown), (2) individual fitness exercises, and (3) gymnastics or tumbling.

In many instances, equipment must be modified to accommodate the visual mechanism. Examples include: (1) beep baseball (i.e., the ball and the base locators), (2) goal ball (i.e., bells in the balls so that the blind player knows where the ball is at all times), and (3) raised boundaries.

Mobility Training

Mobility refers to the ability to move from one point to a second point. *Orientation* refers to the ability to relate body position to other objects in space. Obviously these abilities are related and required for efficient movement in a variety of environments.

Mobility training is an adaptive technique that applies to blind children and children with limited vision. It enables them to learn about their physical play areas. Mobility training increases their confidence in moving with greater authority and provides greater safety while they are participating. It is a valuable way to enhance participation in the physical education program.

There are several prerequisites to efficient mobility training. Some of these are (1) sound discrimination, (2) sound location, (3) concentration, (4) memorization, (5) retention of information, and (6) physical skill. These prerequisite skills provide environmental awareness needed for travel. Deficits in these prerequisites may be a deterrent to proficient performance.

Although specific techniques are employed by professionals for mobility training, physical educators may reinforce many of the concepts that are a part of sophisticated mobility training programs. Goodman[4] suggests that routes be learned for both indoors and outdoors. Routes are organized in units and are purposely chosen courses from a starting to finishing point for which a strategy is developed. Routes are selected according to the blind student's skills, interest, and needs. Usually routes progress in difficulty from simple straight-forward routes to more complicated ones. Activities in the physical education class that would reinforce professional mobility training programs are (1) practice walking straight lines while maintaining good posture,[8] (2) locate sounds in the environment, (3) follow instructions where movements have to be made that conform to instruction (memory), (4) practice reproduction of specific walking distances with respect to time, (5) find one's way back to starting points on different surfaces, and (6) practice changing body positions.

Orientation and training programs should help visually impaired persons cope with physical surroundings effectively. Training programs should also assist successful interaction with peers as well as with the physical facilities and equipment. The teacher should remember that some blind persons have travel vision. The individual capabilities of each child should be assessed to determine the extent of the mobility training program.

FIGURE 13-7. A child develops age-appropriate playground skills. (Photo by Jo Arms. Courtesy Albuquerque, New Mexico Public Schools.)

COMMUNITY-BASED ACTIVITIES

Several activities and equipment contribute to physical and motor fitness of children with limited vision: weight lifting, Universal gym equipment, isometric exercises, stationary running, the exercise bicycle, and the rowing machine. All these require simple environments and can easily be generalized to physical fitness programs in the home and community.

One of the purposes of physical education for the blind is development of skills that can be used in interscholastic athletics, intramurals, or for leisure in the community after formal schooling. Therefore activity should be community based. Such considerations for program development are sanctioned by Section 504 of the Rehabilitation Act of 1973 and the Individuals with Disabilities Education Act of 1990. Clearly, there are to be equal opportunities for participation in extracurricular activities for the disabled and the nondisabled. Therefore opportunities for sports participation outside the schools should be integrally linked with the physical education program in the public schools. Such considerations for extension of extracurricular activities to the blind involve identification of activities that are available in the community.

USABA Activities

The United States Association for Blind Athletes (USABA) sponsors national championships every year. Such high-level competition is an incentive for blind persons to engage in training regimens from which there are personal and physical benefits. Blind persons who participate in competitive activities such as those sponsored by the USABA may reach goals in both sport and personal development.

Several activities sponsored by USABA are related to leisure activities. Thus the competition can serve participants in two ways—for athletic competition and for participation in leisure activities in the community. Some of the activities that are a part of international competition and that can be expressed as a recreational skill in the community are listed below:

Activity	Skill
Track running event	Physical fitness program
Cycling	Physical fitness and recreational program
Weight lifting	Physical fitness programs and body building
Sailing	Recreational aquatics
Crew rowing	Rowing a boat for fishing and boat safety
Competitive diving	Recreational swimming and diving

Activity	Skill
Archery	Recreational shooting at archery ranges
Swimming	Recreational swimming in community pools
Downhill and cross-country skiing	Recreational skiing in selected communities where the resources are appropriate

Other activities that are less community-based recreational activities but provide opportunities to develop personal and social skills through participation are field events in track, wrestling, and gymnastics. Specific events in gymnastics and track and field are floor exercise, balance beam, uneven bars, vaulting, all-around competition, 60- or 100-meter dash, 200-, 400-, 800-, 1500-, 3000-, and 10,000-meter runs.

Goal Ball

Goal ball is a game that originated in Germany for blind veterans of World War II to provide gross motor movement cued by auditory stimuli (a bell ball). It is now played under the rules of the International Sports Organization for the Disabled.

The purpose of the game is for each team of three persons to roll the ball across the opponent's goal, which is 8.5 m (9¼ yards) wide for men and 7.5 m (about 8 yards) wide for women. A ball is rolled toward the opponent's goal. The entire team attempts to stop the ball before it reaches the goal by throwing the body into an elongated position. The ball is warded off with any part or the whole body. Games last 10 minutes with a 5-minute halftime. All players are blindfolded.

Many of the principles of accommodating visual impairment have been incorporated into this game. Examples of the application of these principles follow:

Instructional environment to accommodate the individual	The boundaries are made of rope so they can be detected by the players.
Special aids and equipment	Elbow and knee pads are provided to the players so they are not hurt when the body hits the floor or lunges to stop the ball. Bells are placed in the ball so the rolling ball can be heard en route to the goal.
Special instructional techniques	Kinesthetic movement of the body is required to instruct the players how to lunge to block the ball.

Precautionary safety measures	Pads and mats can be placed at the end of the gym where the goals are. The sidelines should be clear of objects.
Special feedback to facilitate learning	A piece of tin or materials that make sounds can be placed at the goal so players know when a goal has been scored rather than successfully defended.
Nondisabled peers to assist instruction	Nondisabled persons can provide feedback as to whether the movements of the game have been successfully achieved.
Train the players to understand the environment	The players should be trained to know where the goal ball training area is within the gym and how to enter and leave the gymnasium.

Beep Ball

Beep ball is a game played throughout the United States that is designed to encourage blind and sighted players to compete in softball. Each team has its own sighted pitcher and catcher. The catcher sets the target where the batter normally swings the bat and the pitcher attempts to hit the target with the ball. Equipment required to play beep ball is available through the Telephone Pioneers of America. Equipment includes a buzzing base and a ball 16 inches in circumference with a battery-operated electronic sound device inside. Specifications of the equipment and playing area are (1) a regulation bat, (2) a beep ball, (3) bases that are 48-inch, pliable plastic cones with a 36-inch bottom and a 10-inch long cylinder of foam-rubber top, (4) the bases are placed 90 feet down respective lines, and 5 feet off of the lines, and (5) sounding units that give off a buzzing sound when activated are fixed 20 feet from bases.

Specific rules of beep ball are as follows: (1) the umpire activates one of the bases when a ball is hit; (2) the runner must identify the correct base and run to it before a play is made by the defense; (3) a run is scored if the runner reaches the base before the fielder plays the ball and the beeper is turned off (there is no running from one base to another); (4) the batter is allowed five rather than the traditional three strikes (the fifth strike must be a total miss); (5) a hit ball must travel at least 40 feet to be considered fair (otherwise, it is considered foul); (6) games are 6 innings in duration with 3 outs per inning. There is only a first and third base, which are 90 feet apart.[1] Teams are usually comprised of both males and females.

Restrictive Environments for Blind Individuals

The mission of physical education programs for blind persons is to enable these pupils to engage in independent recreational sport and physical activity in the community. To achieve this, it is usually necessary to move individuals from more restrictive to lesser restrictive training environments. Restrictiveness of an environment is determined by the amount of special support systems that are needed for an individual to participate or learn. Movement to lesser restrictive environments usually involves withdrawal of support systems so the individual gradually learns to function with greater independence. At least two considerations need to be studied for the placement of blind persons in integrated sport activity: (1) whether it is possible to integrate an activity and (2) the need for support systems to enable integration.

Support systems for integration of disabled individuals have been suggested by Fait and Dunn.[3] These involve (1) design of the game in which the nonsighted and sighted players play together (e.g., in beep ball the pitcher and the catcher need to be sighted), (2) the use of peer tutors for activity play, and (3) a variety of environments where support for integrated activity is gradually withdrawn so the individual eventually can independently participate in recreational skills in the community. There are currently many educational integration models; however, in the last analysis, blind individuals must participate in the lesser restricted environment in the community. What is needed are educational models that match activities available in the community. Songster and Doherty[20] have identified a formal process for integration of disabled individuals, including blind players, into sport activity. The process involves (1) selection of the activity around which the integration process will take place, (2) development of a system of sequential supports in environments that enable greater independent functioning of the athletes among their normal peers, (3) placement of the individuals in appropriate environments commensurate with their social and physical abilities, (4) provision of needed supports to the individual, and (5) fading of the support systems of the individual through the lesser restrictive environments. It is to be emphasized that before the integration process is attempted, the sequential environments and support systems must be fully designed.

SUMMARY

Children with visual disorders vary in functional ability to participate in physical activity. Partially sighted persons have less than 20/70 acuity, and a blind person has 20/200 or less. There are several abnormalities of vision. Some associated with curvature of the light rays as they enter or pass through the eye are myopia, hyperopia, and astigmatism. Nystagmus, tropias associated with difficulties in depth perception, and heterophorias concern distorted visual integration.

Visual impairments may be identified by the Snellen test or other visual screening tests. They also may be identified by observing abnormal eye conditions, motor movements, and visual discrimination. Low vision clinics offer comprehensive evaluations and assistance to individuals with visual disorders.

Vision loss has serious implications for motor, intellectual, psychological, and social development. Vision loss early in life may delay mastery of motor responses, which can affect other areas of development. Planned physical experiences may counter maldevelopment in other areas.

Training programs in mobility increase the degree of independence of the blind. Accompanying direct instruction to develop travel vision and motor skills are techniques for adaptation. This may be accomplished by modifying activity and instructional environments and introducing special aids, devices, or equipment.

Persons with visual disorders should be trained with self-help or recreational skills that can be used in the community. This may enable participation in some of the community sports programs for the blind and visually limited.

There is a process that will integrate blind players into physical activity. The process involves assessment of the social and physical skill level of the individual to assure success in the activity, appropriate placement in a continuum of environments with the appropriate nondisabled support systems, and sequential withdrawal of support systems and movement to lesser restrictive participation environments that are commensurate with improved motor and social skills.

REVIEW QUESTIONS

1. Compare the movement capabilities of a child with slight loss of vision with that of a child who is totally blind.
2. List the classification system for severity of blindness used by the United States Association for Blind Athletes.
3. Indicate the estimated incidence of visually disabled persons.
4. List some causes for loss of vision.
5. Discuss the consequence of loss of vision on the development of physical and social skills.
6. List some general characteristics of persons with limited vision that impair physical performance of skills.
7. Discuss problems and solutions for the social adjustment of the visually disordered in integrated and special physical education classes.

8. List ways in which activities and environments could be modified to include the visually impaired in physical activity.
9. Describe how lack of vision may effect motor capability.
10. Discuss the essential components for integration of blind with sighted players in physical activity.
11. List some considerations for adapting activity so blind individuals may participate.

STUDENT ACTIVITIES

1. There are organizations designed to serve parents of blind children. Contact a local or a national organization to learn the purpose of these groups. Do they provide information about the blind? Do they serve as advocates for parents? What should physical education teachers know about these organizations?
2. Talk with an adult who is blind. Ask about the ways in which blindness affects physical activity. Ask about the person's school experiences in physical education. Ask what the person would like as an outcome of a physical education program. Was the person mainstreamed into regular physical education classes?
3. There are several ways of adapting instruction and the environment to accommodate persons with visual disorders. Select three activities and indicate how you might modify the activity, environment, or equipment.
4. Talk with a physical education teacher who has taught blind children. Ask how the visual disorders were identified.
5. Presume you are blind. Design an instructional program for yourself. Simulate the blindness with a blindfold and make the necessary adaptations.
6. Simulate being blind for one day and describe the accommodations that you needed to make to carry out daily activities.
7. Play a game of goal ball blindfolded. Comment on the limitations that you experienced while playing the game.
8. Visit a residential facility for the blind. Describe the accommodations made for the lack of vision in daily living and sport and physical activities.

REFERENCES

1. American Foundation for the Blind, *Creative recreation,* New York, 1988.
2. American Optometric Association: The efficacy of optometric vision therapy: special report, *Am Optom* 59:95-105, 1988.
3. Fait H, Dunn J: *Special physical education,* Philadelphia, 1984, WB Saunders.
4. Goodman W: *Mobility training for people with disabilities,* Springfield, Ill, 1989, Charles C Thomas Publishers.
5. Gordon B, Gavron SJ: A biomechanical analysis of the running pattern of blind athletes in the 100 meter dash, *Adapt Phys Act Q* 4:192-203, 1987.
6. Greaves JR: Helping the retarded blind, *Int J Blind* 5:164, 1953.
7. Kalakian LH, Eichstaedt CB: *Developmental adapted*

physical education, Minneapolis, 1982, Burgess Publishing.

8. Klee K, Klee R: Group training and basic orientation mobility and hearing skills, *J Visual Impair Blindness* 79:100-103, 1985.

9. Luria A: *Higher cortical functions in man,* ed 2, New York, 1980, Basic Books.

10. Mastro JV, Canabal MY, French R: Psychological mood profiles of sighted and unsighted beep baseball players, *Res Q Ex Sport* 59:262-264, 1988.

11. McGuffin K, French R, Mastro J: Comparison of three techniques for sprinting by visually impaired adults, *Clin Kines* 44:97-99, 1990.

12. Moore MW, Peabody RL: *A functional description of the itinerant teacher of visually disabled children in the Commonwealth of Pennsylvania,* Pittsburg, 1976, School of Education, University of Pittsburg.

13. Nashner LM, McCollum G: The organization of human postural movements: a formal basis and experimental synthesis, *Behav Brain Science* 8:135-172, 1985.

14. Norris MS, Brody RH: *Blindness in children,* Chicago, 1957, University of Chicago Press.

15. Reynolds M, Birch J: *Teaching exceptional children in all America's schools,* Reston, Va, 1977, Council for Exceptional Children.

16. Ribadi H, Rider RA, Toole T: A comparison of static and dynamic balance and congenitally blind and sighted blindfolded adolescents, *Adapt Phys Act Q* 4:220-225, 1987.

17. Richardson MJ, Mastro JV: So I can't see, I can play and I can learn, *Palaestra* 3:23-32, 1987.

18. Rouse M: Management of binocular anomalies: efficiency of visual therapy, *Am J Optom Physio Optics* 64:391-392, 1987.

19. Sherrill C: *Adapted physical education and recreation, ed 3,* Dubuque, Iowa, 1986, Wm C Brown Publishing.

20. Songster T, Doherty B: The Special Olympics integration process, Washington, DC, Special Olympics International Research Monograph [in press].

21. Stanley SM, Kindig EE: Improvizations for blind bowlers, *Palaestra* 2:38-39, 1986.

22. Weitzman DM: An aerobic walking program to promote physical fitness in older blind adults, *J Visual Impair Blindness* 79:97-99, 1985.

SUGGESTED READING

Buell C: *Physical education for blind children, ed 2,* Springfield, Ill, 1984, Charles C Thomas Publishing.

Dunn J, Fait H: Special physical education, Philadelphia, 1989, WB Saunders.

OBJECTIVES

Explain the values of good posture.

Assess postural deviations of the foot and ankle, knee, pelvis, upper back, lumbar region of the spine, scapula, and head and neck.

Select appropriate activities to ameliorate diagnosed postural deficiencies.

Describe the relationship between postural efficiency and age.

List potential postural abnormalities that may be associated with specific disabling conditions.

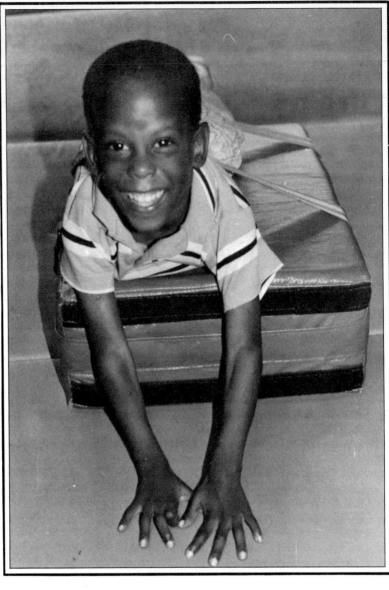

Courtesy Dallas Independent School District

Posture and Body Mechanics

Postural disorders impair the health and quality of life of millions of people in the United States. Low back pain alone is a major problem in today's society. It has been estimated that 8 out of 10 people will suffer from low back pain at one time or another in their lives.[14] The cost of medical care and lost job time is estimated to be in the billions of dollars annually.[15] Furthermore, a significant number of students from the public schools are reaching colleges/universities with postural asymmetries; nearly half are unaware of these problems.[1] According to Francis,[12] a high percentage of college women possess scoliosis.

Physical activity programs that include exercises to strengthen and stretch postural muscles should help prevent problems in later life. However, for maximum benefit individuals need to continue those exercises throughout the lifespan. According to Fisher, Domm, and Wuest,[11] the inability to maintain an ongoing exercise program is the major reason individuals suffer long-term problems associated with back and joint pain. They note that the difference between those who achieve and do not achieve their program goals are: (1) level of self-motivation, (2) tolerance of pain, and (3) ability to adapt their schedules to include regular exercise sessions.

Good posture might be defined as a position that enables the body to function to the best advantage with regard to work, health, and appearance. An individual's posture, in a large measure, determines the impression that he or she makes on other persons. Good posture is socially valued, whereas poor posture is socially devalued.[23] Good posture gives the impression of enthusiasm, initiative, and self-confidence, whereas poor posture often gives the impression of dejection, lack of confidence, and fatigue. We know that faulty posture does not necessarily indicate illness; however, we also know that good posture and body mechanics help the internal organs assume a position in the body that is favorable to their proper function and that allows the body to function most efficiently. Good posture should not be confused with the ability to assume static positions in which the body is held straight and stiff and during which good alignment is achieved at the sacrifice of the ability to move and to function properly. Possibly, good *body mechanics* would be a better term to use in describing the proper alignment and use of the body during both static and active postures.

Body mechanics is the proper alignment of body segments and a balance of forces so as to provide maximum support with the least amount of strain and the greatest mechanical efficiency.[13] There is general agreement that the human body operates best when its parts are in good alignment while sitting, standing, walking, or participating in a variety of occupational and recreational types of activities. There is no such thing as a normal posture for an individual. Certain anatomical and mechanical principles have been developed over the years that aid physicians, therapists, and physical educators in the identification of faulty body mechanics and posture.[10] Application of these principles helps individuals keep their bodies in proper balance with as small an expenditure of energy as possible and with the minimum amount of strain.

The center of gravity of the human body is located at a point where the pull of gravity on one side is equal to the pull of gravity on the other side. This center of gravity (higher in men than in women) falls in front of the sacrum at a point ranging from approximately 54% to 56% of the individual's height when standing. The center of gravity is changed any time the body or its segments change position.

In the upright standing position, the human body is relatively unstable. Its base of support (the feet) is small, whereas its center of gravity is high; and it consists of a number of bony segments superimposed on one another, bound together by muscles and ligaments at a large number of movable joints. Any time the body assumes a static or dynamic posture, these muscles and ligaments must act on the bony levers of the body to offset the continuous downward pull of gravity.

Whenever the center of gravity of the body falls within its base of support, a state of balance exists. The closer the center of gravity is to the center of the base of support, the better will be the balance or equilibrium. This has important implications for the individual both in terms of good posture and as it relates to good balance for all types of body movement. The body is kept well balanced for activities in which stability is important, whereas it may be purposely thrown out of equilibrium when movement is desired, speed is to be increased, or force is to be exerted on another object.[9,13]

As the human being matures, balance for both static and dynamic positions becomes more automatic. An individual develops a feel for a correct position in space so that little or no conscious effort is needed to regulate it and attention can be devoted to other factors involved in movement patterns. This feeling for basic postural positions, as well as for dynamic movement, is controlled by certain sensory organs located throughout the body. The eyes furnish visual cues relative to body position. The semicircular canals of the inner ear furnish information on body equilibrium. Receptors in the tendons, joints, and muscles also contribute to the individual's ability to feel the body's position in space. The loss or malfunction of any of these sense organs requires that major adjustments be made by the individual to compensate for its loss.

Some individuals with disabilities develop poor posture because they are unable to integrate sensory impulses critical to achieving and maintaining good posture.[31] Persons who do not have the ability to provide their muscles with information necessary for good posture frequently experience balance problems. Lack of appropriate information interferes with both their automatic balance reactions as well as their voluntary balance adjustments.[24] In addition to the physical and sensory prerequisites that enable the disabled to maintain and facilitate appropriate movement, posture is the ability to integrate the sensory and motor aspects of motor patterns. There is evidence that some individuals may have breakdowns in correlation of the amplitude of muscular responses during postural movement.[31] These movement breakdowns may jeopardize balance as a result of lack of speed and adroitness necessary to ensure recovery of stability. Inappropriate use of visual and/or somatosensory inputs may have a negative effect on balance, which relates to moving posture. Persons who have movement problems involving postural efficiency may have slower voluntary, as opposed to reflexive, mechanisms for correcting postural disturbances.[24]

CAUSES OF POOR POSTURE

There are many causes of poor posture and poor body mechanics, including environmental influences, psychological conditions, pathological conditions, growth handicaps, congenital defects, and nutritional problems. Any of these may have an adverse effect on the posture of the growing child, the adolescent, or the adult. Extended periods are needed to establish good body mechanics.[17] The habits of poor posture cannot be overcome with a few minutes of daily exercise. The neuromuscular system must be reeducated so that positions and movements become conscious and subconscious routines.

Poor posture that contributes to incorrect muscle development, tension, spinal deviations, lower back disorder, poor circulation, and unattractive appearance can be overcome through specific muscle training and reorientation of postural habits.

Pathological conditions often lead to functional and structural posture deviations. Some of these conditions are faulty vision and hearing, various cardiovascular conditions, tuberculosis, arthritis, and neuromuscular conditions resulting in atrophy, dystrophy, and spasticity. Disabilities related to growth include weaknesses in the skeletal structure and in the muscular system, growth divergencies, fatigue, and glandular malfunctions. Congenital defects include amputations, joint and bone deformities, spina bifida, and clubfoot. Nutritional problems include underweight, overweight, and poor nourishment.

POSTURE DEVELOPMENT

Growing children do not demonstrate the same posture that adults do. Children who are in the early stages of development have insufficient muscular strength to enable the anatomical parts of the body to be appropriately aligned. Body parts most frequently malaligned in young children are the legs and the spine.

Children between the ages of 18 months and 24 months often appear to have mild cases of bowlegs.[6] However, the condition usually corrects itself by 2 years of age. Furthermore, during the preschool years, the knees may not be properly aligned, and some children may have severely pronated feet. This is not considered a major problem unless it persists beyond the age of 8 years.[8] Treatment of pronated feet as prescribed by a physician usually consists of an inner-wedge support worn in the shoes. Stretching exercises and isometric strengthening activities may be employed to correct leg and foot positions.

As a result of improper alignment of the knees during preschool years, children may develop deficient walking patterns. One of the walking patterns identified in children 12 to 16 months of age is the pronated foot accompanied by external rotation at the hip. A study in which a young child was required to walk faster and at sequentially greater degress of incline on a treadmill resulted in proper alignment of the feet and legs.[3] Having the young child walk fast on a gradual incline increased muscle activity at the ankle, knee, and hip. Apparently the need to generate additional force to keep pace with the speed of the treadmill caused the child to properly align the legs and feet.

Typically young children under the age of 5 years have a protruding abdomen ("pot belly"). Their appearance may be one of postural abnormality, but in reality there is not maldevelopment. Normal play activities usually firm the abdominal muscles eventually; such activities also allow the pelvis to assume its correct position.

Scoliosis is a prevalent postural disorder. One out of every 10 persons has some degree of scoliosis and 3 in every 100 have a progressive condition.[27] Scoliosis is an abnormal condition that can develop at any age. If the curvature develops during the first 3 years of life, it is termed *infantile.* If it is developed between the third and twelfth years in girls and after age 14 (but before maturity) in boys, it is called *adolescent scoliosis.* It is desirable for the physical educator to know not only deficiencies in posture in children but also whether the deficiency of a given child is a function of normal devlopment or an abnormality that will affect future alignment of the body.

POSTURAL CONDITIONS AMONG PERSONS WITH DISABILITIES

There are many prerequisites for efficient posture. Among these are strength of the postural muscles, flexibility of the joints, vitality and muscular endurance to maintain appropriate positioning of anatomical parts, and kinesthetic and visual orientations that enable proper alignment and sufficient balance to erect the body and stabilize it over its base of support. If any one of these prerequisites is not fulfilled, postural disorders may result. Children with disabilities may have poor posture because of deficient prerequisites. For instance, an individual with an orthopedic impairment may have muscle imbalances due to muscular weakness or lack of joint flexibility. Mentally retarded individuals often do not generalize their postural mechanism through varying positions. The blind person may lack the necessary visual orientation to maintain efficient upright posture. Other health-impaired persons may lack the strength and vitality to maintain adequate efficient posture over extended periods.

Orthopedically Disabled

Because of the nature of their disability, individuals with orthopedic problems often lack postural muscle strength and joint flexibility. There may be differences in muscle strength on the two sides of the body because of an impairment on one side of the body (e.g., one leg may be shorter than the other). Orthopedically disabled individuals who use wheelchairs may have weak trunk muscles that cause them to lean to one side of the wheelchair. When this condition occurs, the possibility of developing scoliosis is increased. Therefore precautions should be taken to ensure that children in wheelchairs have enough strength and endurance of the musculature of the abdominal and postural muscles to maintain upright sitting postures so that they do not tilt sideways or forward. Some persons in the later stages of muscular dystrophy may have weakened abdominal and hip muscles. When this happens, excessive tightening of the lumbar extensors frequently causes lordosis. Some children with orthopedic disabilities walk on their toes. This tends to tighten the heel cords. If the condition is a result of habit, strengthening the dorsal flexors and stretching the reciprocal plantar flexors should alleviate the condition. If the toe walking is a result of persisting extensor thrust or positive support primitive reflexes, activities to promote integration of the reflexes should be used.

Mentally Retarded

Many mentally retarded individuals have poor posture. Although there are few studies that describe the postural alignment of mentally retarded populations, observation would suggest that the more severe the retardation, the greater the possibility of postural problems. If a mentally retarded individual does not generalize lo-comotor patterns to gait, or has poorly developed vestibular and/or kinesthetic systems, or has a depth perception problem, he or she will walk with the head down. Thus, over time an abnormal posture may develop. The abnormalities of locomotion may be transferred to posture in a general sense. Mentally retarded individuals with deficient balance and/or depth perception problems walk with a wide shuffling gait and descend stairs one step at a time. In addition to specific strengthening and stretching activities of postural muscle groups, kinesthetic awareness of head and trunk alignment, along with improvement in balance and depth perception, may contribute to more efficient postures.

Blind

Blind persons frequently have postural abnormalities. Visual cues in the environment provide information to the body as to where parts should be aligned. Blind individuals are without external visual aids and must rely more on the kinesthetic awareness of where the body parts are in relationship to one another. These individuals should receive specific instruction in the proper alignment of the body to enable them to develop the "feel" of good posture.

PROCEDURES FOR POSTURAL DEVELOPMENT

There are specific procedures that can be employed to improve posture. The six components involved in a program designed for postural development are[2]:

1. Introduction and explanation of the use of the postural analysis form
2. Posture screening
3. Explanation of the screening results
4. Referral to persons who will individualize instruction
5. Practice time for postural exercises
6. Evaluation of progress after 8 weeks

POSTURAL ASSESSMENT

After the postural analysis form has been introduced and explained, the next step in development of a postural education program is to assess each person to determine whether there is a need for postural programs. There are two major types of screening. One is group screening, and the other involves individual assessment. Group screening may be done by having a group of children move in a circle and then respond to changes in direction while the teacher observes from the center of the circle.[22] Group techniques also may be used to assess sitting posture. The other major type of screening involves individual assessment of each child by the teacher. There are several types of individual postural assessment. The focus of our discussion is on individual assessment techniques.

Plumb Line Test

The plumb line test is used to assess posture because it allows comparison of body landmarks with a gravity line. The plumb line can be hung so that it falls be-tween the person being examined and the instructor. The vertical line is used as a reference to check the student's anteroposterior and lateral body alignment. Certain surface landmarks on the body that align with a gravity line of the human body have been located by kinesiologists and engineers. These surface landmarks can be used as points of reference in conducting exam-

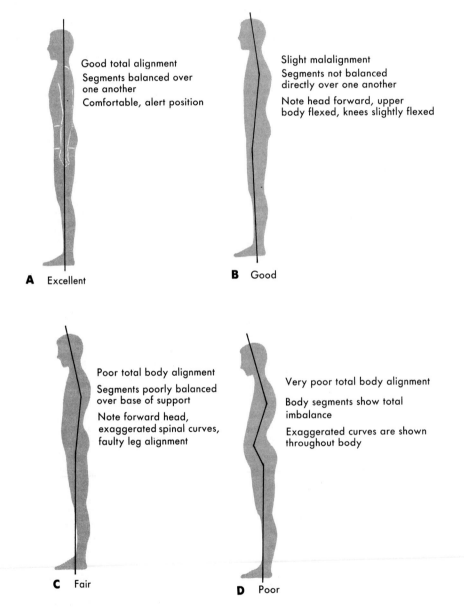

Good total alignment
Segments balanced over one another
Comfortable, alert position

A Excellent

Slight malalignment
Segments not balanced directly over one another
Note head forward, upper body flexed, knees slightly flexed

B Good

Poor total body alignment
Segments poorly balanced over base of support
Note forward head, exaggerated spinal curves, faulty leg alignment

C Fair

Very poor total body alignment
Body segments show total imbalance
Exaggerated curves are shown throughout body

D Poor

FIGURE 14-1. Four-figure system for rough assessment of posture is used to identify students in need of a more discriminating type of posture examination.

inations designed to see how well the body is balanced and how well its segments are aligned in the upright position.

Lateral view

From the lateral view (showing anteroposterior deviations), starting at the base of support and working up the body, the gravity line should fall at a point about 1 to 1½ inches anterior to the external malleolus of the ankle, just posterior to the patella, through the center of the hip at the approximate center of the greater trochanter of the femur, midway between the chest and back, through the center of the shoulder (acromial process), and through or just behind the earlobe.

Viewed from the front or rear, the spinal column should be straight. However, when the spine is viewed from the side, or lateral view, curves normally exist in various vertebral segments. The cervical spine is slightly hyperextended, stretching from the base of the skull to about the top of the thoracic vertebrae. The spine is flexed throughout the area of the thoracic vertebrae and hyperextended throughout the area of the lumbar vertebrae, and the sacral curve is flexed. These curves are present in the spinal column to help the individual maintain balance and to absorb shock, and they should be considered normal unless they are exaggerated.

Anterior view

From the anterior view (showing lateral deviations), the gravity line should fall an equal distance between the internal malleoli and between the knees; it should pass through the center of the symphysis pubis, the center of the umbilicus, the center of the linea alba, the center of the chin, and the center of the nose; and it should bisect the center of the upper portion of the head.

Posterior view

The landmarks to be checked in the posterior examination (showing lateral deviations) would include the same points as those checked in the anterior examination in the region of the ankle and knee, the cleft of the buttocks, the center of the spinous processes of the spinal column, and the center of the head.

Recording data

There are several ways in which data from a plumb line test can be recorded. A widely accepted assessment system has been adopted in the New York State Physical Fitness Test. Three sets of pictures represent three different and sequential levels of postural fitness. One sequence of pictures represents model posture, a second sequence represents deviant posture, and a third sequence represents marked discrepancies from normal posture. The observer views the student according to plumb line testing procedures and for each picture on the evaluation sheet asks the question, "Which picture does the person being tested most look like?" The posture profile has various numbering systems. Some are ranked on a 10, 5, 1 scale, with 10 being good/model, 5 deficiency, and 1 marked deficiency. Other grading scales are 5, 3, 1 and 7, 5, 3. The scoring system is used to assign a number to the postural condition of the person observed. These numbers can be totaled for a postural index. However, the treatment plan must be derived from an evaluation of the specific anatomical parts of the body that are malaligned. Usually, diagnosed deficiencies reflect a clinical postural disorder that is caused by tight or weak muscles. The target muscle groups must be identified and specific types of activity must be assigned to meet the unique problem of the specific postural deficiency.

A posture examination is much more meaningful to the student and far more useful to the teacher if the findings are carefully recorded by the examiner (especially during review of the material obtained in the examination prior to setting up an exercise or activity program or when doing a reevaluation of the pupil sev-

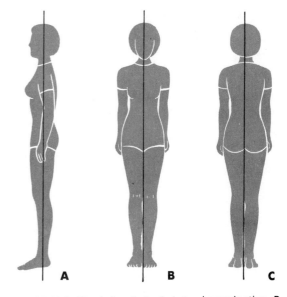

FIGURE 14-2. Plumb line tests. **A,** Lateral examination. **B,** Anterior examination. **C,** Posterior examination.

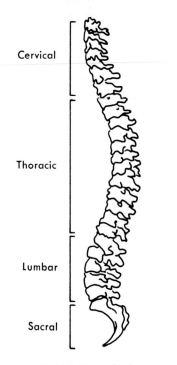

Cervical

Thoracic

Lumbar

Sacral

FIGURE 14-3. Normal spine.

eral months after the original examination). The examination form must provide space for the instructor to record the findings of the examination quickly and accurately. Provisions should be made for recording the severity of each of the conditions identified in the examination. The findings of successive examinations also can be recorded on the same form.

Posture Screen

Another form of posture testing may be done with a posture screen. The posture screen is a grid of vertical and horizontal lines that can be used as reference points to evaluate all segments of the body in relationship to each other. It consists of a rectangular frame mounted on legs so that it stands upright and laced with string so that a 2-inch-square grid pattern (4- and 6-inch squares are recommended by some) crosses the frame. The vertical lines are parallel to a center (gravity) line and the horizontal lines are exactly at right angles to the gravity line. The color of the center line usually differs from that of the other strings. This makes the center line easy to identify and to use in comparison with the landmarks described previously.

The posture screen should be checked for proper alignment with a plumb line to be sure that the gravity

line is true and that the screen is also plumb when viewed from the side. It is then necessary to locate a point about 18 inches from the posture screen where the student will be centered properly behind the gravity line. The instructor determines this point moving to a position 10 to 15 feet away from the posture screen and standing in alignment with the center string while holding a plumb line out in front. Sighting through the plumb line and the center line of the screen, the examiner then marks a point on the floor 18 inches behind the screen. This point is in alignment with the instructor and the center line itself. Thus when the student stands behind the screen it is possible to evaluate the posture from the anterior, posterior, and lateral views in relation to the center line of the screen.

A posture screen may be used to give quick, superficial screening examinations to identify students in need of special posture correction programs or it may be used to give very thorough examinations to students who have already been identified as requiring such programs. An example showing a three-way figure with the proper labels and with numbers to indicate the severity of the conditions discovered is shown in Fig. 14-7. With this kind of prepared examination form, the instructor can quickly identify deviations observed through the posture grid and can record them by drawing a diagonal line through the number that indicates the severity of the condition (first degree, slight; second degree, moderate; and third degree, severe). No other writing is necessary unless the instructor identifies a problem that does not appear on the chart or wishes to record special information. The same posture form can be used for successive examinations with different colored pencils used to indicate second, third, or fourth examinations. In this way, improvement can be shown through the use of the cumulative record.

Anterior view

The student is instructed to stand directly behind the posture screen with the internal malleoli of the ankles an equal distance from the mark on the floor. This will place the student in the proper position so that the surface landmarks of the body will fall in correct alignment in relation to the center (gravity) line of the screen. The student is then instructed to stand as he or she would normally. The instructor should take a position about 10 to 15 feet away from the posture screen and in direct line with the center line. The posture examination record can be mounted on a clipboard held by the examiner, or a lectern can be used to hold the forms to facilitate recording the findings. Since the feet

POSTURE RATING CHART

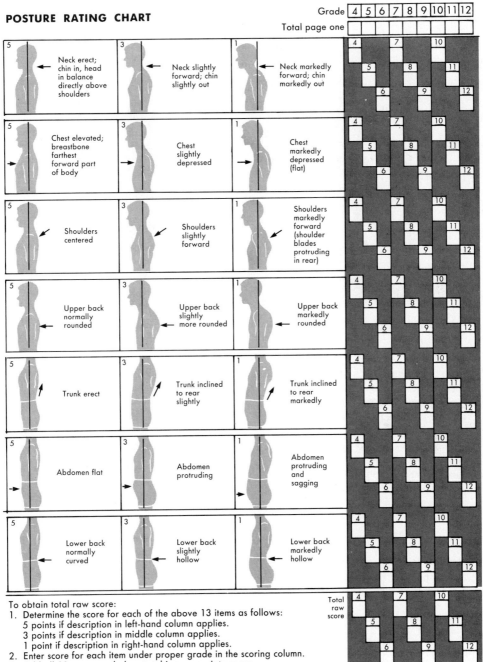

To obtain total raw score:
1. Determine the score for each of the above 13 items as follows:
   5 points if description in left-hand column applies.
   3 points if description in middle column applies.
   1 point if description in right-hand column applies.
2. Enter score for each item under proper grade in the scoring column.
3. Add all 13 scores and place total in appropriate space.

FIGURE 14-4. A lateral postural survey chart. (Courtesy New York State Education Department.)

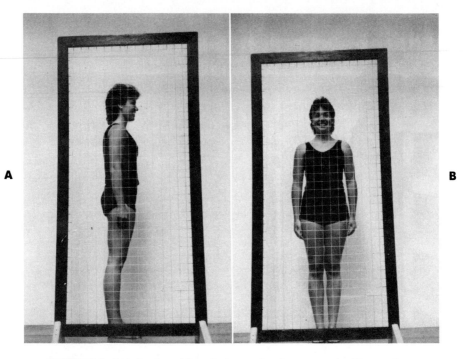

FIGURE 14-5. A, Lateral, and **B,** anterior, postural assessment with use of a screen.

serve as the base of support, it is important to examine the student from the feet upward in checking for proper body alignment. Specific examinations for the foot, ankle, and leg are covered in later sections of the chapter.

The feet should be checked to see if they are pointed straight forward or are toeing in or out. The longitudinal arch should be higher on its medial side than on its lateral side. The inner and outer malleoli should be about equal in prominence. The ankles and knees should be straight, with the kneecaps facing directly forward when the feet are held in the straight forward position. The height of the kneecaps should be even. The gravity line passes midway between the ankle bones, between the knees, and directly through the umbilicus, the linea alba, the center of the chin, and the center of the nose.

The symmetry of the sides of the body must then be

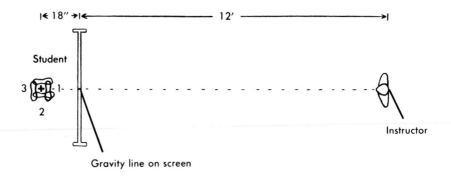

FIGURE 14-6. Alignment of posture as viewed from above. *1,* Anterior; *2,* lateral; *3,* posterior.

POSTURE EXAMINATION USING POSTURE SCREEN WITH 2-INCH GRIDS

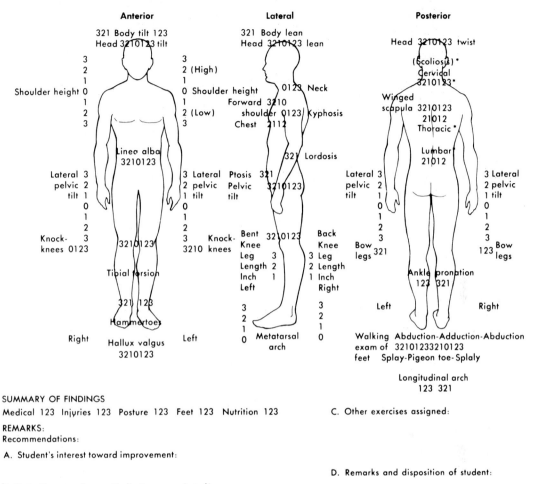

Anterior

321 Body tilt 123
Head 3210123 tilt

3
2
1
Shoulder height 0
1
2
3

Lineo alba
3210123

Lateral 3
pelvic 2
tilt 1
0
1
2
Knock- 3
knees 0123

3210123

Tibial torsion

321 123

Hammertoes

Right   Hallux valgus
               3210123

Lateral

321 Body lean
Head 3210123 lean

3
2 (High)
1
0 Shoulder height
1   Forward 3210
2 (Low)   shoulder 0123
3   Chest 2112

0123 Neck

Kyphosis

321 Lordosis

3 Lateral Ptosis 321
2 pelvic Pelvic 3210123
1 tilt tilt
0
1
2
3 Knock- Bent 32 0123
3210 knees Knee
       Leg   3
       Length 2
       Inch 1
       Left

Back
Knee
3 Leg
2 Length
1 Inch
Right

3   3
2   2
1   1
0 Metatarsal 0
  arch

Left

Posterior

Head 3210123 twist

(Scoliosis)*
Cervical
3210123*

Winged
scapula 3210123
        21012
     Thoracic*

Lumbar
21012

Lateral 3   3 Lateral
pelvic 2   2 pelvic
tilt 1   1 tilt
0   0
1   1
2   2
3   3
Bow 321   123 Bow
legs   legs

Ankle pronation
123 321

Left   Right

Walking Abduction-Adduction-Abduction
exam of 32101233210123
feet   Splay-Pigeon toe- Splaly

Longitudinal arch
123 321

SUMMARY OF FINDINGS
Medical 123 Injuries 123 Posture 123 Feet 123 Nutrition 123

REMARKS:
Recommendations:

A. Student's interest toward improvement:

B. Corrective exercises: (indicate nos. assigned)
1 2 3 4 5 6 7 8 9 10 11 12 13 14 15 16
17 18 19 20 21 22 23 24 25 26 27 28 29
30 31 32 33 34 35 36 37 38 39 40

C. Other exercises assigned:

D. Remarks and disposition of student:

FIGURE 14-7. Data recording sheet for use with postural grid.

checked. Any abnormal curvature or creasing on one side of the trunk (not found on the other side) should lead to more careful examination to determine whether a lateral sway or tilt of the body or a lateral curvature of the spine exists. Lateral spine curvature must be checked if any deviations in the position of the umbilicus exist or if there are any apparent differences in the depth of the sides of the chest (Fig. 14-8). With boys, the nipple levels are compared, and with both boys and girls the heights of the creases made where the arms join the body should be checked to be sure that the two creases on either side are symmetrical. It is also necessary to check to see if one arm hangs closer to the trunk than the other (Fig. 14-9). The shoulder height must be checked to see if the shoulders are level. If the pelvis is found to have a lateral tilt or if a high or low shoulder is noted, the student is then checked for lateral curvature of the spine. Although lateral curvatures do not occur with all the previously noted conditions, these types of conditions

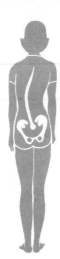

FIGURE 14-8. Lateral pelvic tilt.

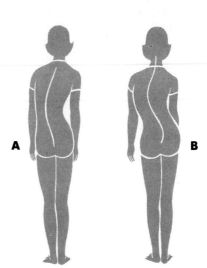

FIGURE 14-9. Scoliosis. **A,** Total left C curve. **B,** Regular S curve.

may serve as possible indicators of such a problem. The examiner next checks the head position to be sure that it aligns with the gravity line and to determine if there is any twisting of the head and neck. Finally, the total body should be viewed to determine whether it is being held in good alignment and balance and whether any lateral tilts of the total body exist.

Posterior view

For posterior examination, the student is instructed to assume the same position in relation to the posture screen as in the anterior examination, except that the back is now turned to the screen—that is, with the inner ankle bones over the marker on the floor. The posterior examination gives the instructor an opportunity to double-check many of the conditions noted from the anterior view and to make an evaluation of certain other conditions that cannot be checked during the anterior view examination.

The gravity line passes directly up through the center of the spinous processes of each of the vertebrae, bisecting the head through its center. The posterior view is the best view for detecting scoliosis (rotolateral curvature). If a lateral curvature exists, further examinations should be made to see if there is any rotation or torque in the pelvic girdle. The degree of lateral deviation and the amount of rotation should be checked. The posture card indicates all the areas where lateral deviation of the spine could be present and provides a place to record the degree of severity. If scoliosis is suspected, the examiner can make the eval-

uation of the spinal column more meaningful by marking the posterior surfaces of the spinous processes of the vertebrae with a skin pencil so that the curves can be observed more accurately. The sides of the trunk also are checked as they were in the anterior view for any abnormal unilateral curvatures and for any creases or bulges on one side only, which would indicate the presence of a tilt or of a lateral spinal curve.

The shoulder blades (or scapulae) are viewed from the posterior aspect to determine whether they are flat against the rib cage, whether the medial borders have been pulled laterally in abduction, and whether the medial borders and the inferior angles project outward from the back of the rib cage (this condition is called *winged scapula*).

Lateral view

For the lateral (side) view, the student stands with the left side to the screen (the side facing the screen is the one shown on the posture examination form). One foot is placed on either side of the mark on the floor, with the inner malleolus about 1½ inches behind its center. Deviations in alignment and posture can readily be observed through the screen. Abnormalities in flexion and extension of the toes may be easier to see from the side than they were from the front. The lateral examination is used to verify conditions noted in other phases of the examination.

If the student has a total forward or backward lean of the body, alignment is basically correct at all joints

FIGURE 14-10. Posterior overhang.

except the ankle, where he or she is leaning too far forward or backward. In this case, the examiner will find that the reference points become progressively farther out of alignment with each segment from the foot to the head. If the alignment is correct at the ankle and at the shoulder, but the center of the hip is too far forward, the individual has a total body sway. If the hips are too far back, the individual has a distorted position of the low back and buttocks. If the alignment is correct at the ankle, knee, and hip but the shoulder and the head are positioned too far back, the student has what is called a posterior overhang (Fig. 14-10). It is quite easy to identify these various conditions when the body landmarks are viewed in relation to the gravity line of the posture screen (see Fig. 14-5). The amount of deviation is ascertained by judging the distance the affected body parts are out of alignment against one of the vertical lines. It is usually easier to evaluate these landmarks if the student places a finger on each of them so that the examiner can see them more easily.

The vertebral spine should then be checked throughout its length for what would be termed its *normal curvatures.* The two conditions that are noted in the region of the lower back are excessive hyperextension in the lumbar spine, a condition called lordosis, and too little curve in the lumbar spine, known as flat low back. When the lumbar spine goes into a flexion curve, it is called lumbar kyphosis. This is not observed frequently, however. Usually associated with these lower back conditions are a forward pelvic tilt (with lordosis) and a backward pelvic tilt (with a flat low

back). Abdominal ptosis is often associated with these conditions, especially lordosis. Ptosis refers to a relaxation of the lower abdominal muscles with forward sagging of the abdomen often accompanied by misplacement of the pelvic organs. The degree of severity of this deviation must be judged subjectively.

In the region of the chest and shoulders, the normal curvature of the spine is one of mild flexion. The abnormal condition that would be looked for in the thoracic spine is an excessive amount of flexion, which in its severest form is called humpback. Any abnormal increase in flexion is known as kyphosis. Kyphosis is often associated with flattening of the chest and rib cage and, frequently, with deviations in the alignment of the shoulder girdle, called forward shoulders and winged scapula. Although these four conditions are often found in the same individual, they do not necessarily occur together. The winged scapula, mentioned in the discussion of the posterior examination, should be checked again from the lateral position to determine whether the inner border projects to the rear and whether the inferior angle projects outward from the rib cage. The degree of deviation in forward (round) shoulders is judged subjectively and is related to how far forward of the gravity line the center of the shoulder falls.

The most common condition found in the region of the neck is a forward position of the cervical vertebrae accompanying a forward head. An abnormal amount of hyperextension in the cervical or neck vertebrae exists when the individual has attempted to correct a faulty head position by bringing the head back and the chin up.

In all the examinations described previously, the instructor must be alert to the possibility that one postural deviation often leads to or is the result of another. It is a pattern of the human body to attempt to keep itself in some semblance of a state of balance (homeostasis). Therefore, when one segment or various segments of the body become malaligned, it is customary for the body to attempt to compensate for this by throwing other segments out of alignment, thus obtaining a balanced position. An example of this would be the individual with lordosis who compensates with kyphosis and forward head. The individual with a simple C-shaped scoliosis curve in the spine may compensate for this with a complex S-shaped curve (an effort to return the spine and thus the body to a state of balance).

Tests for Functional or Structural Conditions

There are two types of postural conditions. One is functional and the other is structural. Functional postural deficiencies result from muscular imbalances.

Functional postural deficiencies can be corrected by strengthening the antigravity postural muscles and stretching out the opposing muscle groups. On the other hand, structural postural deficiencies involve abnormalities in the bones and joints and are usually not responsive to exercise programs. When the condition is structural, procedures usually are required to alter the postural alignment.

Several tests may be used to determine whether spinal curvatures are functional (involving the muscles and soft tissue) or structural (involving the bones). Postural deviations that are the result of muscle and soft tissue imbalance often disappear when the force of gravity is removed. Structural posture deviations, which have gone beyond the soft tissue stage, with involvement of the supportive bones and connective tissue, are not eliminated by the removal of gravitational influences.

Prone lying test

The prone lying test is designed to check anteroposterior or lateral curves of the spine. Functional curves disappear or decrease when the student assumes the prone position on a bench, a table, or the floor.

Hanging test

The hanging test has the same uses as the prone lying test. The individual hangs by the hands from a horizontal support. Functional curves disappear or are decreased in this position (Fig. 14-11, *B*).

Adam test

The Adam test is used to determine whether a lateral deviation of the spine (scoliosis) is functional or structural. The student assumes a normal standing position, then gradually bends the head forward, continuing with the trunk until the hands hang close to the toes. The instructor stands a short distance behind the student and observes the student's spine and the sides of the back as the student slowly bends forward. If the spine straightens and if the sides of the back are symmetrical in shape and height, the scoliosis is considered functional (Fig. 14-11, *C*). Corrective procedures should be started under the direction of a physician.

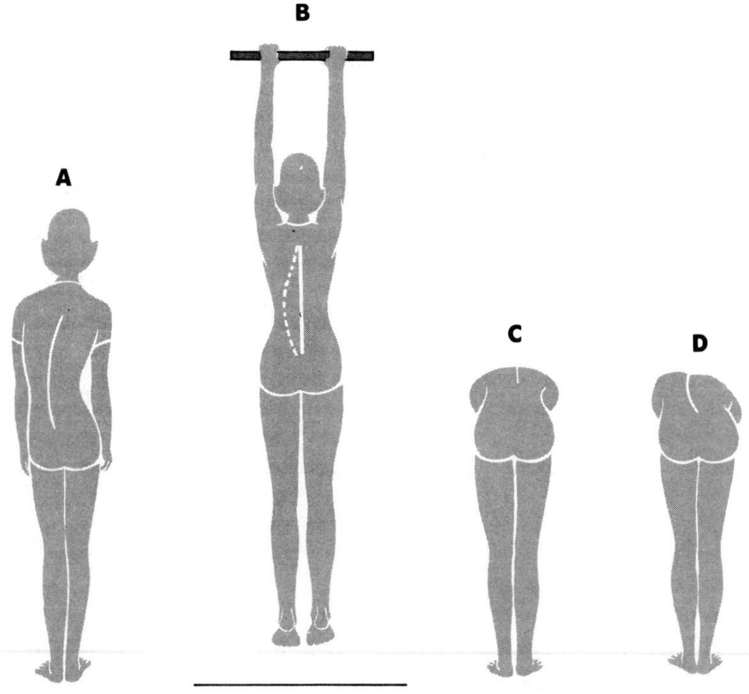

FIGURE 14-11. Test for functional-structural scoliosis. **A,** Left C-curve scoliosis. **B,** Hanging test for scoliosis. Note straight line indicates spinal position during hanging test. **C,** Adam's test showing functional scoliosis. **D,** Adam's test showing structural scoliosis.

If the spine does not straighten and if one side of the back (especially in the thoracic region) is more prominent (sticks up higher) than the other as the student bends forward, the scoliosis is judged to be structural (Fig. 14-11, *D*). In structural cases, the rotation of the vertebrae accompanying the lateral bend of the spine causes the attached ribs to assume a greater posterior prominence on the convex side of the curve. This curve does not disappear in the Adam test after changes occur in the bones of the spinal column. Structural cases must be cared for by an orthopedist.

Sitting Posture

The position of the body while sitting is similar to the position of the body while standing—that is, the head is held erect, the chin is kept in, normal anteroposterior curves are maintained in the upper and lower back, and the abdomen is flat. The hips should be pushed firmly against the back of the chair. The thighs should rest on the chair and help support and balance the body. The feet should be flat on the floor or the legs comfortably crossed at the ankles. The shoulders should be relaxed and level with the chest kept comfortably high.

Moving Posture Tests

Many persons have been critical of static posture evaluations for the following reasons:
1. Students are likely to pose in this type of examination.
2. Students may use it to obtain visual cues to correct faulty posture.
3. It does not indicate the student's habitual standing posture.
4. No attention is given to dynamic posture and alignment as they would relate to student's movements in activities.

For these reasons it is wise to include, as a part of the total posture examination, certain phases in which the students are actually in motion and during which they may or may not know that they are being examined. This may be accomplished in several different ways. One is to observe a class as they perform during an exercise session and when they are standing or sitting between exercises. To enable the examining teacher to identify students with major deviations and to record this, either the instructor must know all the students by name or by a number or the students must be removed from the group as posture deviations are noted. Their names should then be taken so that the posture deviations noted are recorded for the proper students.

Another technique that can be used to evaluate posture and body mechanics during movement is to have the students gather in a large circle (with the teacher standing at the center or periphery of the circle) and then walk, run, or do various kinds of activities as they move continuously around the circle. The teacher or therapist identifies the children who are in special need of posture correction and records their names along with the appropriate information regarding their posture deviations. As a part of each of these two types of examinations, especially if they are given in lieu of any type of static examination, the students should also assume a normal standing position with the teacher evaluating posture from the front, lateral, and rear views.

Walking posture

The basic position of the body in walking is similar to that of the standing posture, but all parts of the body are also involved in moving through space. The toes face straight ahead or toe out very slightly as the leg swings straight forward. The heel strikes the ground first, with the weight being transferred along the lateral side of the bottom of the foot. The weight is then shifted to the forward part of the foot and balanced across the entire ball of the foot. The step is completed with a strong push from all the toes. The upper body should be held erect with the arms swinging comfortably in opposition to the movement of the legs. The head is held erect with the chin tucked in a comfortable position. The chest is held high, the shoulder blades are flat against the rib cage, and the shoulders are held even in height.

Persons with deviations in their sitting, standing, or moving posture and body mechanics should receive special attention so that programs may be designed for correction of these problems. Suggestions for correc-

FIGURE 14-12. Good sitting posture.

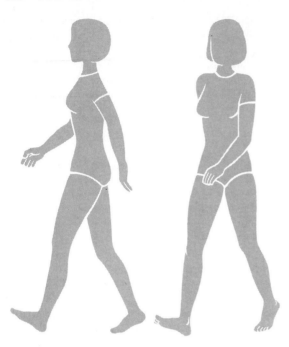

FIGURE 14-13. Good walking posture.

tion and prevention, for measurement, and for program adaptations are presented in this chapter as a part of the discussion of each deviation.

GUIDELINES FOR TESTING POSTURE

Gathering information on the postural characteristics of students requires many decisions. Some guidelines for testing posture follow:

1. Determine the method of posture evaluation (group or single subject).
2. Select a feasible assessment instrument (posture screen, comparative checklist, plumb line).
3. Determine a data collection procedure (notes, numerical scoring system).
4. Require children to wear as little clothing as possible during the examination.
5. Keep posture assessment equipment in correct working condition.
6. Use the correct testing procedures.
7. Have the same person administer the test on successive occasions.
8. Record all information accurately and indicate the date the test was given.
9. Determine accurately the location of landmarks used in measurement if they are a part of the evaluation process.

10. Standardize evaluation procedures and provide a written description of these procedures so that they can be followed on each occasion by any examiner.
11. Determine whether disorders are functional or structural.

Beattie, Rothstein, and Lamb[4] have listed advantages and disadvantages of commonly used posture asessment tools. An important aspect of a measuring tool is its validity (e.g. how truthful is the tool). For instance, frequently the sit-and-reach test is used to measure low-back functioning. However, the results should be interpreted with caution,[21] because that test actually measures flexibility of multiple joints (e.g. the entire back and hips). Excessive flexibility in one area may mask inflexibility in another area. Other things to consider when selecting posture assessment tools are (1) expense of the equipment, (2) reliability (constancy) of the measure, (3) requirements of the student, (4) limitations in the movement capability or intelligence of the students, and (5) precision of the instrument.

POSTURAL DEVIATIONS: CAUSES AND CORRECTIONS

The first step for conducting a postural education program is assessment of the present level of postural functioning. If there is need of intervention, activities need to be selected to remedy specific postural disorders. Usually weakening or tightening of specific muscle groups contributes to a specific postural disorder. Correction then involves strengthening the weak muscles and stretching the tight muscles. Daniels and Worthingham[9] have provided detailed procedures for assessing the functional level of muscles that may contribute to poor posture. Exercise regimens for strengthening weak muscles are described in Chapter 15. Levels of exercise from the least taxing to the most demanding are performance of the movement with gravity, without gravitational pull, against gravity, and against gravity with resistance. Garrison and Read[13] have suggested that stretching for tight muscles is enhanced under the following conditions:

1. The stretch is carried out to the point of moderate pain.
2. There is application of increased effort at regular intervals.
3. The stretch is done slowly and under control without development of momentum.
4. Movement of the body part proceeds through the full range.

The following sections include discussions of specific conditions as well as exercises to assist with the

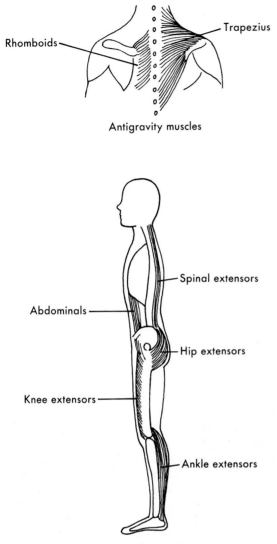

Antigravity muscles

FIGURE 14-14. Antigravity muscles involved in maintaining erect posture.

remediation of each condition. This should provide adequate information for teachers and therapists to plan programs for participants (with and without disabilities) in their programs.

Foot and Ankle

Postural deviations of the foot and ankle can be observed while the student is standing, walking, or running. The evaluation of the foot should be made by ob-servation from the anterior, lateral, and posterior views and should involve examination of both walking and static positions. The number of persons with deviations of the foot is large at all age levels, and the number of persons who have foot pain increases with increasing age. Muscles and joints of the foot and ankle become weakened from age and misuse. Pain associated with faulty mechanics in the use of the feet also begins to occur with increased age. The good mechanical use of the feet throughout life plus other factors such as good basic health, maintenance of a satisfactory level of physical fitness, proper choice of shoes and socks, and proper attention to any injury or accident to the foot should serve as preventive measures to the onset of weakness of ankles and feet in later life.

The foot consists of a longitudinal arch that extends from the anterior portion of the calcaneus bone to the heads of the five metatarsal bones. The medial side of the longitudinal arch is usually considerably higher than the lateral side, which, as a general rule, makes contact throughout its length with the surface on which it is resting (Fig. 14-15, *A* to *C*). This is particularly true when the body weight is being supported on the foot. The longitudinal arch is sometimes described as two arches, a medial arch and a lateral arch, extending from the anterior aspects of the heel to the heads of the metatarsal bones. However, it is most frequently described as one long arch that is dome shaped and higher on the medial side than on the lateral side. On the forepart of the foot, in the region of the metatarsal bones, a second arch can be distinguished that runs across the forepart (ball) of the foot. This arch, called the transverse or metatarsal arch, is slightly dome shaped, being higher at the proximal ends of the metatarsal bones than at the distal ends. It often is considered a continuation of the dome-shaped long arch described previously, and thus we have just one dome-shaped arch of the foot (Fig. 14-15, *D* and *E*).

There is substantial agreement about the need for correct structures and placement of the bones, the importance of the strong ligamentous bands that help hold the bones in place to form the arches of the foot, and the need for good muscular balance among the antagonist muscles that support the foot. All these factors have an important effect on the position of the foot under both weight-bearing and non–weight-bearing conditions. A foot is considered strong and functional when it has adequate muscle strength (especially the anterior tibial muscle and the long flexor muscles of the toes) to support the longitudinal arch, when the bones have strong ligamentous and fascial bindings, and when the small intrinsic muscles are developed

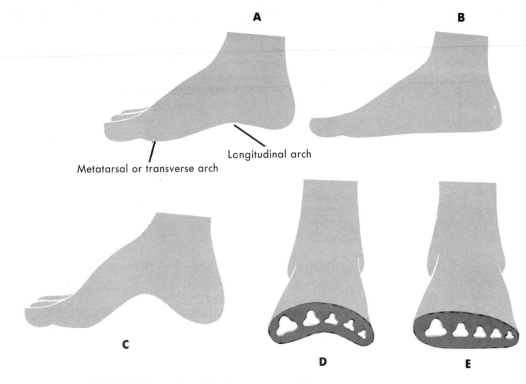

FIGURE 14-15. Arches of the foot. **A,** Normal foot. **B,** Pes planus. **C,** Pes cavus. **D,** Cross section of normal metatarsal arch. **E,** Flat metatarsal arch.

sufficiently to maintain proper strength of the arch in the metatarsal region.

In addition to considering the structure of the foot and ankle, it also is necessary to consider other factors such as the range of movement in the foot and ankle, the support of the body by the foot and ankle, and the effect that various positions of the foot, ankle, knee, and hip have on the mechanics of the foot itself. A consideration of the various movements possible in the foot and ankle, together with a description of the terms used to describe these movements, should help clarify the discussion of deviations of the foot and ankle.

The ankle joint is a hinge joint, therefore only dorsiflexion and plantar flexion are possible. The numerous articulations between the individual tarsal bones and between the tarsal and metatarsal bones allow for inversion, eversion, abduction, and adduction of the foot.

Movements of the foot are as follows:

□ *Dorsiflexion:* Movement of the top of the foot in the direction of the knee

□ *Plantar flexion:* Movement of the foot downward, in the direction of the sole

□ *Inversion:* Tipping of the medial edge of the foot upward, or varus (walking on the outer border of the foot)

□ *Eversion:* Tipping of the lateral edge of the foot upward, or valgus (walking on the inner border of the foot)

□ *Adduction:* Turning of the whole forepart of the foot in a medial direction (toeing-in)

□ *Abduction:* Turning of the forepart of the foot in a lateral direction (toeing-out)

□ *Pronation:* Combination of tipping of the outer border of the foot and toeing-out (eversion with abduction)

□ *Supination:* Combination of tipping of the inner edge of the foot upward and toeing-in (inversion with adduction)

It also should be remembered that it is possible to turn the foot into toed-in and toed-out positions by rotating the lower leg when the knee is bent and by rotating the whole leg at the hip when the knee is straight. Thus when an individual toes-in or toes-out while walking or standing, the examiner must determine whether this is the result of a foot deviation or a

TABLE 14-1

Postural abnormalities

Abnormalities	Description
Ankle pronation	Position of the ankle resulting in lowering the medial aspect of the foot (eversion) and turning the foot inward (abduction)
Ankle supination	Position of the ankle resulting in lowering the lateral aspect of the foot (inversion) and turning the foot outward (adduction)
Anti-gravity muscles	Dorsal muscles that keep the body in an upright posture
Barrel chest	Abnormally rounded chest
Coxa plana	Flattening of the head of the femur
Coxa valga	Increase in the angle of the neck of the head of the femur to more than 120 degrees
Coxa vara	Decrease in the angle of the neck of the head of the femur to less than 120 degrees
Genu recurvatum	Hyperextension of the knee joint
Genu valgum	Knock-knee
Genu veram	Bowlegs
Hallux valgus	Displacement of the great toe inward
Kyphosis	Exaggerated thoracic spinal curve
Kypholordosis	Exaggerated thoracic and lumbar spinal curvatures
Lordosis	Exaggerated lumbar curve (swayback)
Pes cavus	Exaggerated height of the longitudinal arch of the foot (hollow arch)
Pes planus	Extreme flatness of the longitudinal arch of the foot
Pigeon chest	Abnormal prominence of the sternum
Ptosis	Weakness and prolapse of an organ (i.e., prominent abdomen)
Round shoulders	Postural condition whereby the scapulae are abducted and the shoulders are forward
Scoliosis	Lateral and rotational deviation of the vertebral column
Talipes equinus	Walking on the toes or the interior portion of the foot
Talipes valgus	Walking on the inside of the foot (pronated)
Talipes varus	Walking on the outside of the foot (supinated)
Tibial torsion	Medial twisting of the lower leg on its long axis
Torticollis (Wry neck)	Contraction of neck muscles resulting in drawing the head to one side
Valgus (Valgum)	Angling of a body part in a direction away from the midline of the body (bent outward)
Varus	Angling of a body part in the direction of the midline of the body (bent inward)
Wing scapula	Vertebral border of the scapula wings outward because of weakness of the serratus anterior, middle and lower trapezius, and/or rhomboid muscles

rotation of the leg. Many foot and ankle deviations are closely linked to alignment problems occurring in the leg above the ankle.

On many occasions physicians will prescribe orthotic longitudinal arch supports to improve proper foot positionings. In addition, appropriate exercises are needed to build muscle strength and increase joint flexibility for optimum functioning.[25] Exercises should be progressive to build on the present levels of specific muscle group function.

Pes planus

Pes planus, or flatfoot, is a lowering of the medial border of the longitudinal arch of the foot. The height of this side of the longitudinal arch may range from the extremely high arch known as *pes cavus* to a position in which the medial border lies flat against the surface on which the individual is standing. When this side of the foot is completely flat, the medial border of the foot may even assume a rather convex appearance (Fig.

14-15, *A* to *C*). Pes planus may be the result of faulty bony framework, faulty ligamentous pull across the articulations of the foot, an imbalance in the pull of the muscles responsible for helping hold the longitudinal arch in its proper position, or racial traits. The specific cause often may be linked to improper alignment of the foot and leg and to faulty mechanics in the use of the foot and ankle.

When the foot is held in a toed-out (abducted) position while standing and walking, there is a tendency to throw a disproportionate amount of body weight onto the medial side of the foot, thus causing stress on the medial side of this arch. Over a period of time, this stress may cause both a gradual stretching of the muscles, tendons, and ligaments on the medial aspect of the foot and a tightening of like structures on the lateral side. When the individual walks with the foot in the abducted position, these factors are again accentuated and there is a tendency for the individual to rotate the leg medially in order to have it swing in alignment

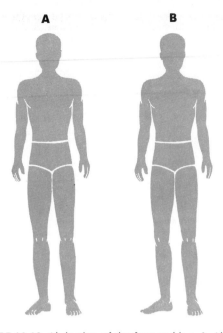

FIGURE 14-16. Abduction of the foot and leg. **A,** Abduction of the foot. **B,** Toeing-out resulting from outward rotation of the hip joint. Note difference in position of patella.

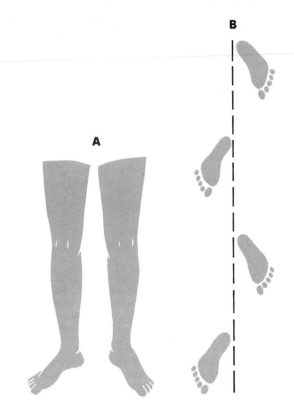

FIGURE 14-17. Improper walking. **A,** Toeing-out and walking across medial border of the foot. **B,** Footprints show outward rotation, or splayfoot position, while walking.

with the forward direction of the step. When the leg is swung straight in line with the direction of travel and with the foot toed-out, the individual walks across the medial side of the foot with each step (Fig. 14-17). This not only weakens the foot but also predisposes the individual to a condition called tibial torsion. Since the individual is walking with the leg in basically correct alignment but with the foot abducted, malalignment results. Thus it will be found that when the legs and kneecaps face straight forward, the feet are in the abducted position, and when the feet are parallel to one another, the kneecaps are facing in a slightly medial direction (tibial torsion). This may produce strain and possibly cause a lowering of the medial side of the longitudinal arch.

Correction of pes planus must involve a reversal of the factors and conditions just described. The total leg from the hip through the foot must be properly realigned so that the weight is balanced over the hip, the knee, the ankle, and the foot itself. The antagonist muscles involved must be reoriented so that those that have become stretched (tibial muscles) are developed and tightened and those that have become short and tight (peroneal muscles) are stretched; thus the foot is allowed to assume its proper position. The muscles on the lateral side of the foot must be stretched (peroneal group). The gastrocnemius and soleus muscles, which sometimes become shortened in the case of flatfoot, exert an upward pull on the back of the calcaneus bone, thus adding to the flattening of the arch. These muscles must also be stretched whenever tightness is indicated. The major muscle group that must be shortened and strengthened is the anterior tibial muscle group, which is extremely important in terms of supporting the longitudinal arch, along with help from the long and short flexor muscles of the toes. The individual also must be given foot and leg alignment exercise in front of a mirror to observe the correct mechanical position of the foot while exercising, standing, walking, and otherwise using the feet (Figs. 14-18 to 14-20).

Such activities as walking in soft dirt, on grass, or in sand with the foot held in the proper position can do

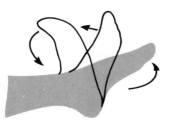

FIGURE 14-18. Foot circling.
Specific for: Metatarsal arch and toe flexors
Beneficial in: Flexibility and strength of the foot and ankle and longitudinal arch
Starting position: Sitting on bench with knees extended, shoes off, and toes pointed
Actions
1. Circle foot inward; toes extended.
2. Circle foot upward; toes extended.
3. Circle foot outward; toes extended.
4. Circle foot downward; toes flexed.
5. Repeat actions 1-4.

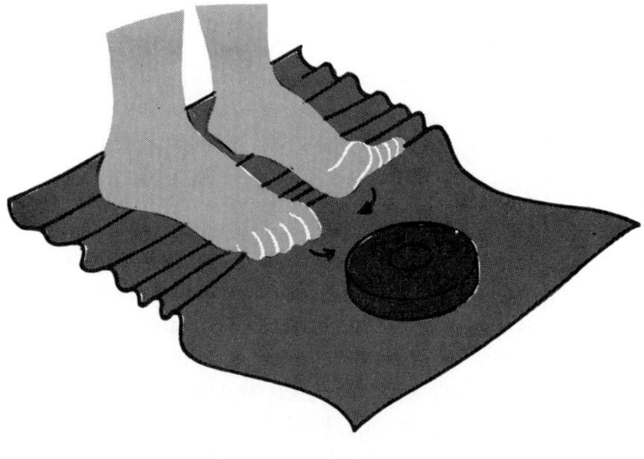

much to help strengthen the foot and realign it with the ankle and hip. Emphasis here should be on walking straight over the length of the foot and placing the heel down first, with the weight being transferred along the outer border of the foot and with an even and equal push-off from the forepart of the foot and the five toes. In actual practice, the great toe should be the last toe to leave the surface on the push-off.

Pes cavus

Pes cavus is a condition of the foot in which the longitudinal arch is abnormally high. This condition is not found as frequently in the general population as is pes planus. If the condition is extreme, the student is usually under the special care of an orthopedic physi-

FIGURE 14-20. Foot curling.
Specific for: Metatarsal arch and toe flexors
Beneficial in: Flexibility and strength of foot and ankle and longitudinal arch
Starting position: With no shoes or socks, sitting on a bench, knees straight, heels rest on bench/mat/floor
Actions
1. Circle foot inward with toes flexed.
2. Circle foot upward with toes extended.
3. Circle foot outward; extend toes.
4. Circle foot downward while flexing toes.
5. Repeat, making full circles with the feet.
Contraindications: Should never be used for students with hammer toes
Measurement: Circumference of the circle and repetitions over time

FIGURE 14-19. Building mounds.
Specific for: Metatarsal arch and toe flexors
Beneficial in: Strength of intrinsic muscles of the feet
Starting Position: Sitting on a bench, feet directly under the knees, toes placed on the end of a towel
Actions
1. Grip the towel with the toes
2. Pull toward the body; both feet work together and build mounds; heels remain on floor.
3. Repeat movements until the end of the towel is reached.
Measurement: The amount of weight that is placed on the towel and the distance over time the weight travels

cian. Special exercises are not usually given for the high arch unless the person has considerable associated pain, requiring special corrective procedures recommended by the physician (see Fig. 14-15, *C*).

Pronation of the foot

Since the ankle joint is a hinge joint allowing only plantar flexion and dorsiflexion, pronation of the ankle—as it is sometimes called—is actually a condition of pronation of the foot. As described previously, this is a combination of abduction and eversion of the foot. Since pronation involves eversion, the medial border of the foot is lowered because it is in the flat longitudinal arch. The forward part of the foot is also abducted, a condition caused by a shifting of the calcaneus bone downward and inward. (The reverse of this condition, one that involves inversion and adduction of the forepart of the foot, is called supination of the foot.) Correction of pronation of the foot is similar to that described for pes planus or flatfoot.

Metatarsalgia

Two types of metatarsalgia may be recognized in a thorough foot examination. The first is a general condition involving the transverse (metatarsal) arch, in which considerable pain is caused by the pressure of the heads of the metatarsal bones on the plantar nerves. The second type, Morton's toe, is more specific.

General metatarsalgia. General metatarsalgia may be caused by undue pressure exerted on the plantar surface of the foot. This pressure ultimately causes inflammation and therefore pain and discomfort. Its causes relate to such factors as wearing shoes or socks that are too short or too tight, wearing high-heeled shoes for long periods, and participating in activities that place great stress on the ball of the foot. The mechanism of injury may result in stretching of the ligaments that bind the metatarsophalangeal joints together, therefore exerting pressure on the nerves in this area. Correction involves the removal of the cause, if this is possible, and the assignment of special exercises to increase flexibility of the forepart of the foot. Exercises are then assigned to strengthen and shorten the muscles on the plantar surface, which may aid in maintaining a normal position in the metatarsal region. The physician may prescribe special shoes or suggest that an arch support or metatarsal bar be worn to support the metatarsal region of the foot to help reduce pain.

Morton's toe. Morton's toe, often called true metatarsalgia, is more specific than the general breakdown of the metatarsal arch described previously. The onset

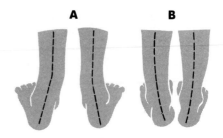

FIGURE 14-21. Faulty foot and ankle positions. **A,** Foot and ankle pronation. **B,** Supinated foot.

of true metatarsalgia is often abrupt, and the pain associated with it may be more intense than that found in general metatarsal weakness. In true metatarsalgia the fourth metatarsal head is severely depressed, sometimes resulting in a partial dislocation of the fourth metatarsophalangeal joint. The abnormal pressure on the plantar nerve often produces a neuritis in the area, which in turn causes intense pain and disability. Treatment consists first of the removal of the cause of the condition. The orthopedic physician will advise which procedure will follow this. Another type of Morton's toe is characterized by the presence of a second metatarsal bone longer than the first metatarsal bone.

Hammer toe

In hammer toe the proximal phalanx of the toe is hyperextended, the second phalanx is flexed, and the distal phalanx is either flexed or extended. The condition often results from congenital causes or from having worn socks or shoes that are too short or too tight over a prolonged period (Fig. 14-22). Tests must be made to determine whether the condition has become structural. If the condition is functional in nature and the affected joints can be stretched and loosened, corrective measures may be taken to reorient the antagonist muscle pull involved in this deviation. The first step, however, must be the removal of the cause, and in severe cases an orthopedic physician should be consulted relative to special bracing, splinting, or surgery for correction of this condition.

Hallux valgus

A faulty metatarsal bone or shoes or socks that are too short, too narrow, or too pointed can cause a deviation of the toe known as hallux valgus. In this condition the great toe is deflected toward the other four toes at the metatarsophalangeal joint (Fig. 14-23). Correction of this condition must involve consultation with a physician. If the foot is not properly aligned and

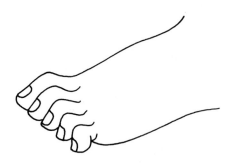

FIGURE 14-22. Hammer toe.

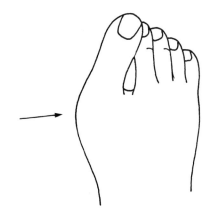

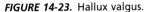

FIGURE 14-23. Hallux valgus.

A　　　**B**　　　**C**

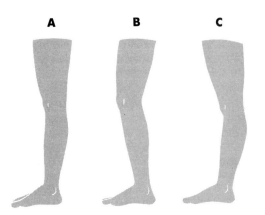

FIGURE 14-24. The knee. **A,** Normal. **B,** Bent (flexed). **C,** Hyperextended.

is toeing-out excessively, remedial measures should be taken to correct this alignment and prevent a further aggravation of hallux valgus.

Knee and Leg

Three conditions involving the knee and the upper and lower leg may be noted when a student is examined from the anterior or posterior view. Bowlegs and knock-knees are recognized from either of these two views, whereas tibial torsion is more easily identified from the anterior view.

Other common deviations of the knee consist of hyperextension (genu recurvatum) and hyperflexion. The normal position of the knee is straight but not stiff. The student can correct forward or backward knee by realigning the pull of the muscles that control its flexion or extension and by readjusting to the proper position of the leg (Fig. 14-24). Bent knee and backward knee are often associated with flat lower back and lordosis of the lumbar spine, respectively.

Bowlegs (genu varum)

Bowlegs can be identified by examining a student with a plumb line, by comparing alignment of the leg with one of the vertical lines of the posture screen, or by having the student stand with the internal malleoli of the ankles touching and the legs held comfortably straight. In the last of these three tests, if a space exists between the knees when the malleoli are touching, the individual may be considered to have bowlegs. Unless this is either a functional condition in the young child (which may be outgrown) or a condition related to hyperextension of the knees and rotation of the thighs in order to separate the knees, corrective measures ordinarily must be prescribed by an orthopedic physician. The student can correct hyperextension and rotation of the knees by assuming the correct standing position and developing proper balance in the pull of the antagonist muscles of the hip and leg (Fig. 14-25, *C*).

Knock-knees (genu valgum)

Knock-knees can be identified as described in the section on bowlegs; however, in this case, when the inner borders (medial femoral condyles) of the knees are brought together, a space exists between the internal malleoli of the ankles. Knock-knees may be related to pronation of the ankle and weakness in the longitudinal arch. Correction involves realignment of the antagonist muscles of the leg and foot, which control proper alignment (Fig. 14-25, *B*). This usually involves development of the outward rotators of the thigh and stretching the internal rotators of the thigh. Correction

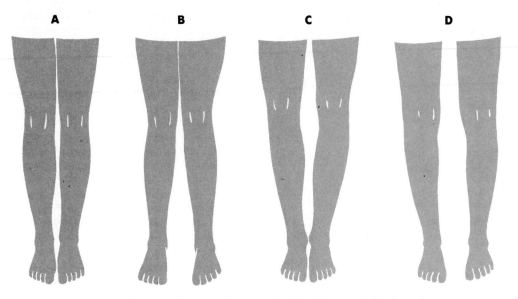

A **B** **C** **D**

FIGURE 14-25. Leg alignment. **A,** Normal. **B,** Knock-knees. **C,** Bowlegs. **D,** Tibial torsion.

of this condition also involves realignment of the foot, ankle, and hip. Knock-knees also may be related to tibial torsion.

Tibial torsion

Tibial torsion, or twisting of the tibia, is identified by examination of the student from the anterior view. When the feet are pointed straight ahead, one or both of the kneecaps face in a medial direction, or when the kneecaps are facing straight forward, the feet are rotated in a toed-out position (Fig. 14-25, *D*). Correction of this condition involves realignment of the total leg, with emphasis being placed on the regions of the ankle, knee, and hip. The outward rotators of the hip and the thigh must be developed, whereas muscles on the medial and lateral sides of the foot and ankle must be stretched to obtain proper alignment.

Trunk, Head, and Body
Pelvic tilt

The normal pelvis is inclined forward and downward at approximately a 60-degree angle when a line is drawn from the lumbosacral junction to the symphysis pubis. Any variation in this angle with the pelvis tipping (tilting) downward and forward usually results in a greater curve of the lumbar spine; by the same token, a variation in the angle with the pelvis tipping upward and backward tends to produce a flatness in the lumbar

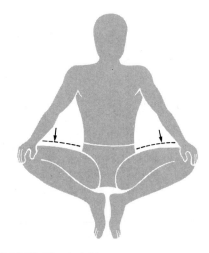

FIGURE 14-26. Hip stretching.
Specific for: Hip adductors
Beneficial in: Knock-knees
Starting position: Sitting, soles together, hands on inner surface of abducted knees
Actions
    1. Push the knees toward the floor
    2. Release the pressure.
    3. Repeat 1 and 2.
Measurement: The distance between the outer portion of the knee and the floor

FIGURE 14-27. Hip stretching.
Specific for: Hip adductors
Beneficial in: Knock-knees
Starting position: Lying on back, legs at right angle to trunk, and resting against a wall, arms reverse T
Actions
   1. Lower the legs (abduct) as far as possible, with the knees straight.
   2. Return the legs to the original position.
Measurement: The distance between the inner portion of the heels

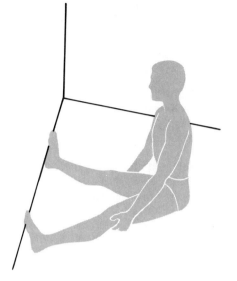

FIGURE 14-28. Hip stretching.
Specific for: Hip adductors
Beneficial in: Knock-knees
Starting position: Sitting, facing a wall, legs adducted, feet propped against the wall at right angle, hands beneath knees, knees straight
Actions
   1. Bend forward with spine extended; pull trunk with arms.
   2. Relax and return to starting position.
   3. Repeat 1 and 2.

area. Since the sacroiliac joint is basically an immovable joint and only a minimum amount of motion takes place at the lumbosacral joint, pelvic inclination and lumbar spinal curves are closely linked (Fig. 14-29). Since exaggerated spinal curves may limit normal motion in the lower back, both lordosis and flat low back require special attention.

A lateral pelvic tilt, in which one side of the pelvis is higher or lower than the other side, can be observed during anterior and posterior posture examinations. The examiner can evaluate these conditions by marking either the anterosuperior iliac spines or the posterosuperior iliac spines of the ilium and then observing their relative height through the grids of a posture screen. The examiner can also evaluate the height of the pelvis by placing his or her fingers on the uppermost portion of the crest of the ilium and by observing the relative height of the two sides of the pelvis. A lateral pelvic tilt may result from such things as unilateral

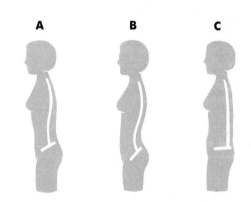

FIGURE 14-29. Pelvic positions. Note position of spine as pelvic position changes. **A,** Normal. **B,** Forward (downward) pelvic tilt. **C,** Backward (upward) pelvic tilt.

ankle pronation, knock-knees, bowlegs, a shorter long bone in either the lower or upper portion of one leg, structural anomalies of the knee and hip joint and deviations in the pelvic girdle, or scoliosis. Before an exercise program for lateral pelvic tilt is initiated, the cause of the condition must be determined by a physician, who may then suggest either symmetrical or asymmetrical exercises to realign the pelvic level. The position of the pelvic girdle as viewed from the anterior or posterior view has definite implications for the position of the spinal column as it extends upward from the sacrum. A lateral tilt of the pelvis will be reflected in the spinal column above it, since the sacroiliac and the lumbosacral joints are semi-immovable. The resulting lateral spinal curvatures are discussed in the next section of this chapter. Lateral tilt of the pelvis may also be related to a twisting of the pelvic girdle itself. This is a complicated orthopedic problem involving both hip joints, the legs, and the vertebral column. Such cases should be referred to the orthopedic physician for treatment and for advice relative to a special exercise program.

Lordosis

Lordosis is an exaggeration of the normal hyperextension in the lumbar spine. It is usually associated with tightness in the lower erector spinae (sacrospinalis), iliopsoas, or rectus femoris muscle group and either weakness or stretching of the abdominal muscles. Correction of this condition would therefore necessitate stretching and loosening of the lower erector spinae (Figs. 14-30 to 14-35), the iliopsoas (Figs. 14-36 to 14-38), and the rectus femoris muscles, together with assignment of exercises designed to shorten and tighten the abdominal muscle group (Figs. 14-39 to 14-43). It also may be important to develop control of the gluteal and hamstring muscle groups, which can exert a downward pull on the back of the pelvis. The development of the gluteal and hamstring muscle groups can help the individual assume a correct position while stretching, exercising, and even while in the static standing position; but these muscles must be relaxed when the individual wishes to walk, move, or run. It is then necessary for the abdominal muscles to hold the front of the pelvis up and to maintain the desired curvature in the lower back. A condition called ptosis (visceroptosis) is often associated with a forward pelvic tilt and lordosis. This condition is characterized by sagging of the lower abdominal muscles and protrusion of the lower abdominal area. It can also be corrected by

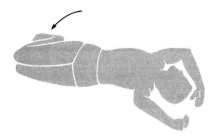

FIGURE 14-30. Spine mobilization.
Specific for: Mobilize the lower spinal area
Beneficial in: Lordosis
Starting position: Hook-lying, arms reverse T, knees flexed fully
Actions
1. Raise both knees until thighs are vertical and shoulders flat.
2. Lower knees to one side until they touch the floor.
3. Repeat actions 1 and 2; legs do not fall but are controlled throughout movement.
Measurement: Repetitions over time
Sequence: Increase the distance below the hip where knees are to touch floor/mat; the closer to the hips the more difficult

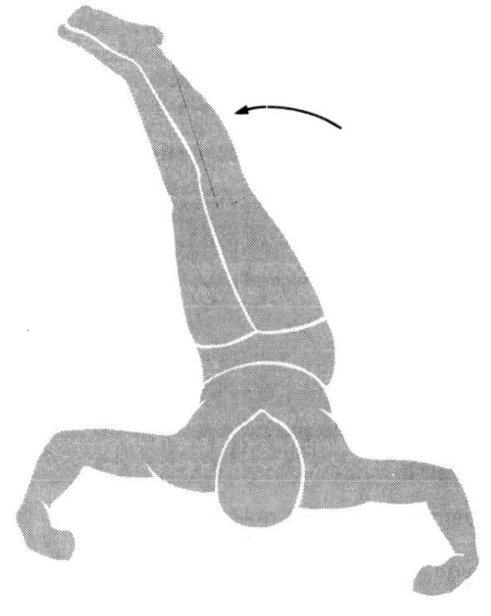

FIGURE 14-31. Spine mobilization.
Specific for: Mobilize the lower spinal area
Beneficial in: Lordosis
Starting position: Lying on back
Actions
1. Flex the knees to the chest.
2. Straighten the knees, extending the legs as high as possible.
3. Return knees to chest
Measurement: Repetitions over time

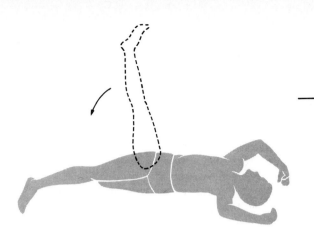

FIGURE 14-32. Spine mobilization (single leg).
Specific for: Mobilize the lower spinal area
Beneficial in: Lordosis
Starting position: Lying on back, arms reverse T
Actions
    1. Flex one leg to a right angle.
    2. Move the flexed leg so foot touches the floor on the opposite side of the body at *hip level.*
    3. Return the leg to a vertical position; keep thorax as flat as possible.
    4. Lower the leg to the original position.
Measurement: Repetitions over time
Sequence: Foot hits floor at lower levels down the leg

FIGURE 14-33. Knee-chest curl.
Specific for: Ptosis, lordosis, and developing abdominal strength
Beneficial in: Development of hip flexors and stretch of spinal extensors
Starting position: Lying on back with knees bent at right angles, feet flat on floor, arms straight out from shoulders, elbows bent 90 degrees, palms up
Actions
    1. Bring knees toward chest by pulling with the abdominals. Curl spine segment by segment off the mat; knees touch chest or shoulders.
    2. Return to starting position, keeping legs as close to floor as possible.
    3. Repeat 1 and 2.
Measurement: Number of repetitions and distance the knees are from the chin

FIGURE 14-34. Mad cat.
Specific for: Lordosis and abdominal muscles
Beneficial in: Dysmenorrhea, arms, shoulders, shoulder girdle, and low back stretch
Starting position: Kneeling on all fours
Actions
    1. Hump low back by tightening abdominal and buttocks muscles.
    2. Lean forward by bending arms until forehead touches the floor.
    3. Repeat 1 and 2.
Measurement: The number of repetitions and the height of the middle of the lumbar region of the spine from the floor

FIGURE 14-35. Arm windmill.
Specific for: Mobilizing the spine
Beneficial in: Lordosis
Starting position: Sitting position, arms out
Actions
    1. Rotate the trunk at the lumbar region.
    2. Rotate the trunk in the opposite direction.
Measurement: The number of degrees of rotation.

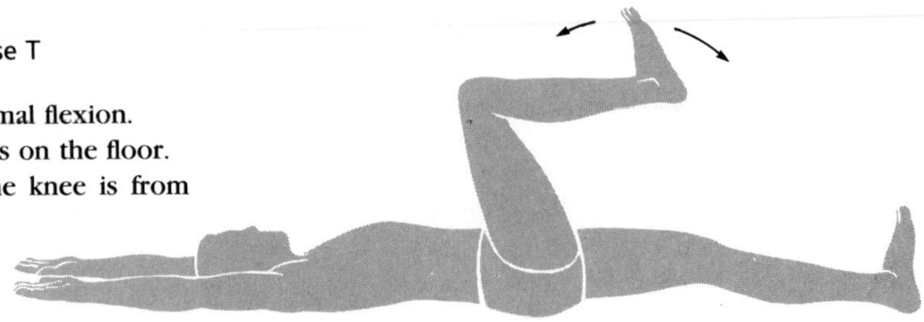

FIGURE 14-36. Hip and knee flexion (single leg).
Specific for: Hip flexors
Beneficial in: Lordosis
Starting position: Hook-lying, arms reverse T
Actions
    1. Flex one knee to the chest; maximal flexion.
    2. Extend the opposite leg so it rests on the floor.
Measurement: Distance the back of the knee is from the floor

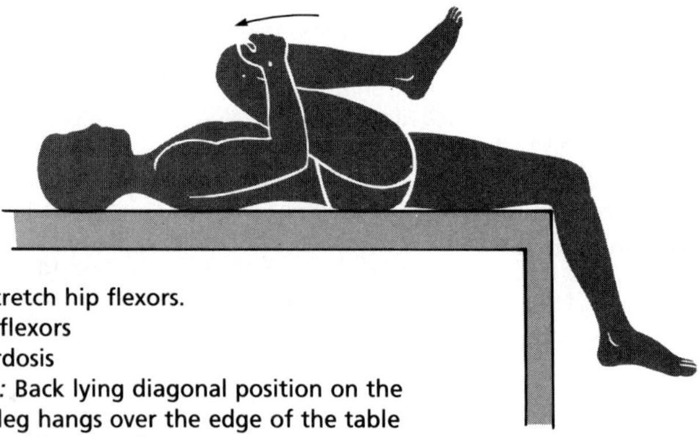

FIGURE 14-37. Stretch hip flexors.
Specific for: Hip flexors
Beneficial in: Lordosis
Starting position: Back lying diagonal position on the table, outside leg hangs over the edge of the table
Action: Hold flexed knee to chest
Measurement: Distance heel is from the floor; program should be built with a table a specified distance from the floor

shortening, tightening, and strengthening of the abdominal muscle groups. Clinically it has been assumed that there is a relationship among abdominal muscle strength, pelvic tilt, and lordosis. Strengthening the abdominal musculature and stretching the lumbar extensors are presumed to assist in controlling the position of the pelvis and relieving the lordotic condition. However, recent research is challenging the assumed relationships of these muscle groups to lordosis.[30]

Flat lower back

A flat lower back condition can develop when the pelvic girdle is inclined upward at the front, thereby decreasing the normal curvature of the lumbar spine. Often associated with this condition are tightness in the hamstring and gluteus maximus muscles, stretching of iliopsoas and rectus femoris muscles, and weakness in the lumbar section of the erector spinae muscle

FIGURE 14-38. Lunges.
Specific for: Hip flexors
Beneficial in: Lordosis
Starting position: Kneeling, hip and knee of one leg flexed
Actions
    1. Lean trunk forward against thigh.
    2. Slide resting knee back as far as possible.
Measurement: The distance between heel of flexed leg and knee of rear leg; height of hip from the floor

FIGURE 14-39. Knee circles.
Specific for: Abdominals
Beneficial in: Lordosis
Starting position: Hook-lying, arms reverse T
Actions
1. Flex the knees until the thighs are vertical and shoulders flat.
2. Make circles with the knees, keeping heels close to the thighs.
Measurement: Repetitions
Sequence: Increase the radius of the circle to make the task more difficult

FIGURE 14-40. Abdominal curl.
Specific for: Ptosis (protruding abdomen), lordosis, and developing and shortening abdominals
Beneficial in: Forward pelvic tilt
Starting position: Lying on back, elbows at side of body and bent at 90 degrees, knees flexed, feet flat on floor
Actions
1. Curl body forward: back flat on mat, elbows at side bent 90 degrees.
2. Uncurl slowly and with control.
Measurement: Repetitions; the height of the nose from the floor on the sit-up
Note: In all leg raising or trunk raising from the backward lying position, the student should exhale or count aloud as legs or trunk are raised to relieve intraabdominal pressure and strain.

FIGURE 14-41. One-legged curl.
Specific for: Abdominals
Beneficial in: Lordosis
Starting position: Hook-lying, hands behind neck
Actions
1. Simultaneously flex one thigh toward chest and touch knee with opposite elbow so they contact at waist level.
2. Repeat to other side.
Sequence: Reach farther with the elbow and less with the opposite knee
Measurement: Repetitions over time

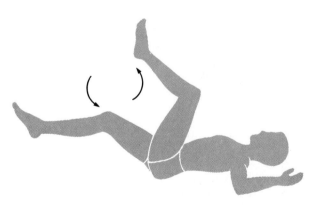

FIGURE 14-42. Bicycle.
Specific for: Abdominals and lumbar extensors
Beneficial in: Lordosis
Starting position: Hook-lying, arms in reverse T
Actions
1. Move knees to chest with low back and neck flat.
2. Extend legs upward with knees straight.
3. Alternately flex knees and move to chest.
4. Lower flexed knees to table.
Increase difficulty: Abduct and adduct the legs when they are in extended positions.
Measurement: Repetitions over time

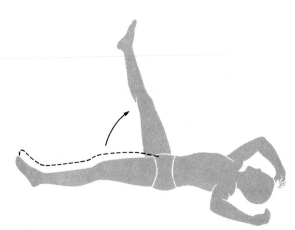

FIGURE 14-43. Leg raise (straight).
Specific for: Abdominals
Beneficial in: Lordosis
Starting position: Hook lying, back flat on floor
Actions
1. Raise the leg with knee straight to a height of 6 inches.
2. Lower raised leg to floor 10 times.
3. Repeat with other leg.
Measurement: Number of repetitions

group. The student can correct a flat back by stretching and increasing the length of the hamstring (Figs. 14-44 and 14-45) and gluteal muscles and by developing, shortening, and tightening the iliopsoas, rectus femoris, and erector spinae muscle groups.

In the correction of both lordosis and flat low back, the individual student must learn to feel what it is like to stand with the body in the correctly aligned position. It is helpful for the student to stand sideways to a regular or three-way mirror and observe the body in the correct mechanical position. A gravity line painted on the mirror or a plumb line hung down the length of the mirror will assist the student in realigning the body.

Lower back pain

Within the last 10 years there has been an increase in the prevention, treatment, and management of low back pain, primarily because of its high cost to the health care system. Even though it is estimated that 90% of normal individuals wih low back pain will improve within 6 weeks with[24] or without intervention,[7] there is a need for physical educators to understand low back pain prevention and treatment techniques.

Low back pain is generally not a comon cause for activity limitations during the school years, and therefore physical educators might easily overlook the importance of this concern for their disabled students.[21]

From a medical perspective, low back pain has long been a difficult problem. A major reason for this difficulty has been the inability of medical practitioners to accurately diagnose the specific cause of the condition.[26] Nachemson[18] reported an inability to find an objective cause for pain in 18% of his low back pain patients. However, others propose that the very structure of the joints and surrounding musculature in the back could be major factors in the cause of low back pain.[28] The argument is made that programs designed to strengthen and therefore stabilize the lower back will prevent future low back problems. As a result, "healthy back schools" for the prevention and management of low back problems are growing in popularity in this country.[29]

Programs advocated by healthy back schools vary in nature, however, all provide information and exercises believed to activate muscles related to low back problems. Such exercises have been shown to enhance the strength of muscles related to posture (e.g., lumbar extensors).[19] In addition to providing exercises to strengthen specific groups of muscles, most programs include postural reorientation exercises.[5]

The growing number of back schools has resulted in empirical studies of their effectiveness. Linton and Kamwendo[16] reviewed a number of these studies and concluded that there is limited evidence low back schools have a positive impact on number of health care contacts, amount of sick leave, work status, pain intensity or duration, activity level, or medication consumption. They believe that critical issues that need to be examined to demonstrate effectiveness are the extent to which patients comprehend the instructions and comply with the exercise regimen.

Perhaps what is critical for the physical educator is sensitivity to the growing problem of low back pain. Awareness of the magnitude of the problem should lead to instruction of students in proper lifting and carrying techniques as well as inclusion of general postural-enhancing exercises in the physical education program.

Kyphosis

Kyphosis (Fig. 14-46, *A*) is an abnormal amount of flexion in the dorsal or thoracic spine. An extreme amount of kyphosis is called humpback. This condition ordinarily involves weakening and stretching of the erector spinae and other extensor muscle groups in

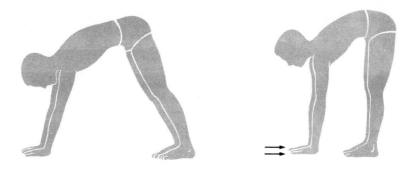

FIGURE 14-44. Walk hands to feet.
Specific for: Hamstrings
Beneficial in: Flat back
Starting position: Standing
Movement to desired position: Lean forward and rest weight on the hands with knees straight.
Action: Move the hands toward the feet; heels of hands on the floor/ ground and knees straight; heels on floor.
Measurement: Distance between the heel of the hands and the toes

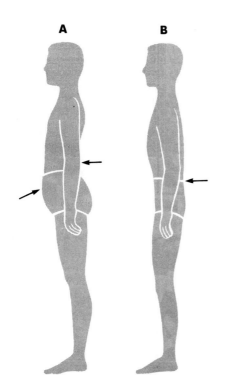

FIGURE 14-45. A, Ptosis and lordosis. **B,** Flat back.

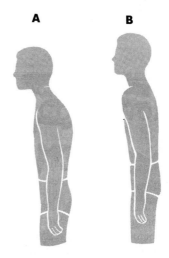

FIGURE 14-46. A, Kyphosis. **B,** Forward or round shoulders.

the dorsal or thoracic regions, along with shortening and tightening of the antagonist (pectoral) muscles on the anterior side of the chest and shoulder girdle. Its correction is effected primarily through stretching of the anterior muscles of the chest and shoulders, which allows the spinal extensor and shoulder girdle adductor muscle groups to be developed, strengthened, and shortened and thus to pull the spine back into a more desirable position. Forward (round) shoulders, flat chest, and winged scapula are often associated with kyphosis.

Forward (round) shoulders

Forward shoulders (Fig. 14-46, *B*) is a condition involving an abnormal position of the shoulder girdle. This condition usually exists when the anterior muscles of the shoulder girdle (pectoral muscles) become shortened and tightened and the adductor muscles of the shoulder girdle (rhomboid and trapezius muscles) become weak and stretched. It is often associated with a flat chest and kyphosis. The basic means of correction of this condition is to stretch and loosen the anterior muscles of the chest shoulder girdle and to develop, strengthen, and shorten the adductor muscles of the shoulder girdle.

The student with kyphosis or forward shoulders should also practice standing and sitting in good alignment in front of a mirror to get the feeling of what it is like to hold the body comfortably in proper balance. When the correct position becomes easy and natural, the student will no longer have to rely on the mirror and the visual cues associated with its use.

Kypholordosis

Kypholordosis is a combination of kyphosis in the upper back and lordosis in the lower portion of the spine. Often one of these deviations is a compensation for the other and involves the body's attempt to keep itself in balance. Correction of kypholordosis consists of the same basic principles involved in correcting the individual conditions described previously; however, time often can be saved in the exercise program by assigning certain exercises that are beneficial for the correction of both conditions.

Flat upper back

A flat upper back is the opposite of a kyphotic spine and involves a decrease or absence of the normal anteroposterior spinal curve in the dorsal or thoracic region. Stretching of the posterior muscles of the upper back allows the antagonist muscles on the anterior side of the body to be developed and shortened and thus is beneficial for this condition.

Winged scapula

Winged scapula is a condition that involves the abduction or protraction of the shoulder blades (the medial border of the affected scapula being farther from the spinal column than normal). Projection of the medial border of the scapula posteriorly and protrusion of the inferior angle are other concomitants of this condition (Fig. 14-47). Winged scapula is very common among children, who exhibit it especially when their arms are raised forward to the shoulder level. This results from lack of shoulder girdle strength; ordinarily, the condition will be outgrown as the children begin to participate in hanging and climbing activities for the development of the muscles of the shoulder girdle. In adolescents and young adults the condition involves unequal pull on the antagonist muscles of the shoulder girdle; corrective measures may be necessary. In general, the procedure would be to stretch and loosen the anterior muscles of the shoulder girdle and to develop the adductors of the scapula, involving both the trapezius and the rhomboid muscles. Developmental exercises for the serratus anterior muscle also are necessary, since it has a major responsibility for keeping the scapula in the correct position flat against the rib cage.

Forward head

Forward head is one of the most common postural deviations. It often accompanies kyphosis, forward shoulders, and lordosis. Two factors are involved in analyzing the causes of forward head and correcting it. The extensors of the head and neck are often stretched and weakened because of the habitual malposition of the head (Fig. 14-48). Correcting this condition involves bringing the head into proper alignment, with the chin tucked so that the lower jaw is basically in line with the ground and so that it is not tipped up when the head is drawn back. This involves reorientation of the head and neck so that the individual knows what it feels like to hold the head in the correct posi-

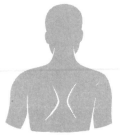

FIGURE 14-47. Winged scapula.

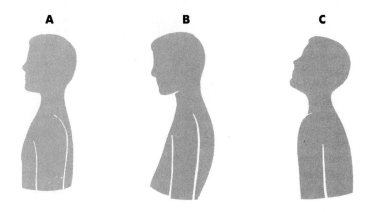

FIGURE 14-48. A, Normal head position. **B,** Forward head. **C,** Cervical lordosis.

tion. The antagonist muscles involved must be reeducated to hold the head in a position so that the lobe of the ear approximates a position in line with the center of the shoulder.

Cervical lordosis

Cervical lordosis may result from an attempt to compensate for other curves occurring at a lower level in the spinal column or from incorrect procedures in attempting to correct a forward head. The spinal extensors are often tight and contracted so that the head is tilted well back and the chin is tipped upward (Fig. 14-48, *C*). As in the case of forward head, a reeducation of the antagonist muscles and the proprioceptive centers involved is necessary so that the lower jaw is held in line with the ground. In the correction of cervical lordosis and forward head, the student must learn to assume the proper position and must exercise in front of a mirror in order to recognize this position.

Posterior overhang (round swayback)

In posterior overhang, the upper body sways backward from the hips so that the center of the shoulder falls behind the gravity line of the body. To compensate for this position, the hips and thighs may move forward of the gravity line, the head may tilt forward, and the chest may be flat. Correction of posterior overhang involves reorientation of the total body so that its several parts are returned to a position of alignment. The student is instructed to work in front of a mirror and align the body with a gravity marker on the mirror. As an alternative, the instructor may check and correct the student's posture. The exercise program includes reeducation of the antagonist muscles to enable the student to return the body to a position of balance.

The muscle groups needing special attention are the abdominal muscles, the antagonist muscle groups responsible for anteroposterior alignment of the tilt of the pelvis, the adductor muscles of the shoulder girdle, and the extensor muscles of the upper spine. The student must stand tall, with chin tucked and abdomen flat, to correct this condition.

Scoliosis

Ten percent of the population has some degree of scoliosis. Two to three percent have a progressive condition.[27] The symptoms of scoliosis initially are usually slight lateral curvatures of the back with no accompanying pain. Often they may go unnoticed for some time. The curves may be aggravated during adolescence and in adulthood. If the condition remains untreated, scoliosis can cause pain, arthritic symptoms, and obvious physical deformity resulting in heart and lung complications that limit activity.[27]

Scoliosis is rotolateral curvature of the spine. When viewed from the front or from the rear, a scoliotic spine has a curvature to one side; in advanced stages it may curve both to the left and to the right. Scoliotic curves are ordinarily described in relation to their position as the individual is being viewed from the rear. A curvature is described as a simple C curve to the left or right. In a more advanced stage compensation above or below the original curve may occur, and the resulting curvature is described as a regular S curve or a reverse S curve. Examples of scoliotic curves are shown in Fig. 14-57.

Initially, a lateral deviation of the spine may involve only a simple C curve to the left or right in any segment of the spine, depending on the cause of the problem, the resulting change in soft tissues, and the pull of

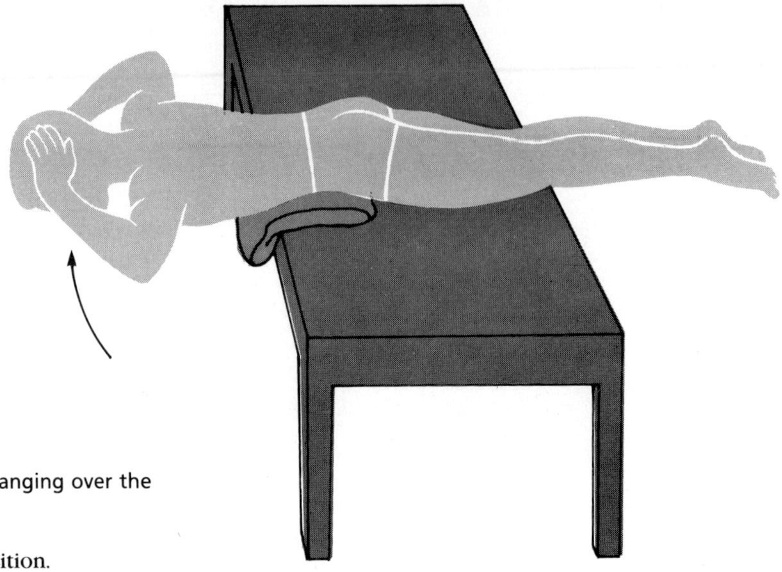

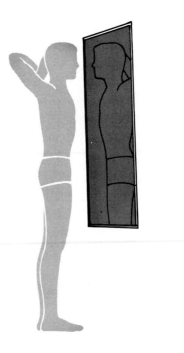

FIGURE 14-49. Trunk raises.
Specific for: Thoracic extensors
Beneficial in: Kyphosis
Starting position: Prone lying, trunk hanging over the
  edge of a table, hands behind neck
Actions
  1. Raise trunk to a horizontal position.
  2. Lower the trunk so head is supported on a chair.
  3. Repeat.
Measurement: (1) number of repetitions, (2) amount
  of weight placed on head, (3) distance of the repetition (distance between chair and table)

FIGURE 14-50. Neck flattener at mirror.
Specific for: Forward head, kyphosis, forward shoulders,
  lordosis, and shoulder development
Beneficial in: Total anteroposterior postural deviations
Starting position: Standing tall in front of mirror, head
  up, chin in, elbows extended sideward at shoulder
  level, fingertips behind base of head
Actions
  1. Draw head and neck backward vigorously as fin-
     gers are pressed forward for resistance and el-
     bows are forced backward (flattening upper
     back). Inhale.
  2. Flatten low back by tucking the pelvis by tighten-
     ing the abdominals and hip extensors.
  3. Hold; exhale; return to starting position. (Student
     can stand facing the mirror or with side of body
     toward mirror to check body position and to
     correct either anteroposterior or lateral posture
     deviations.)

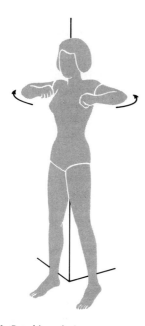

FIGURE 14-51. Breaking chains.
Specific for: Forward shoulders
Beneficial in: Kyphosis, flat chest, forward head, lordosis, and shoulder development
Starting position: Standing, with back against corner of post or sharp edge of corner of a room, feet 6 inches apart; place fists together in front of chest with elbows at shoulder level
Actions
1. Pull fists apart, keeping elbows at shoulder level; pinch shoulder blades together.
2. Inhale.
3. Tuck pelvis and press low back to wall as close as possible.
4. Hold position for 10 seconds.
5. Repeat

Measurement: Repetitions

Caution: Keep abdomen and buttocks tight and maintain body in starting plane during the exercise; when lordosis is present, the exercise may be done in sitting position with legs crossed in tailor's position.

FIGURE 14-52. Neck, back, and shoulder flattener.
Specific for: Forward head, cervical lordosis, kyphosis, forward shoulders, and lordosis
Beneficial in: Pelvic tilt
Starting position: Lying on back, knees drawn up, arms at sides with palms down
Actions
1. Inhale and expand chest as nape of neck is forced to mat by stretching tall and pulling chin toward chest.
2. Flatten small of back to mat by tightening abdominal and buttocks muscles.
3. Neck and back are flat on mat. Fingers cannot pass under neck. As it becomes easier to flatten back, the exercise may be made more difficult and more beneficial by gradually extending legs until the low back cannot be maintained in a flattened position.

FIGURE 14-53. Pectoral stretch (wand).
Specific for: Pectorals
Beneficial in: Round shoulders
Starting position: Sitting, grasp wand with hands, arms extended overhead
Actions
1. Lower the wand to the shoulders; good extension of neck and spine by flexing arms.
2. Return the wand to the starting position with arms straight.

Measurement: Distance between the inner portions of the hands

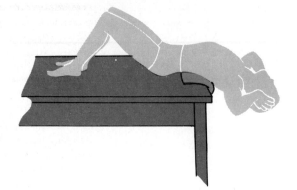

FIGURE 14-54. Pectoral stretch (lying).
Specific for: Pectorals
Beneficial in: Kyphosis
Starting position: Back-lying, hands behind the neck,
  edge of a table across the base of the scapula
Actions
  1. Simultaneously lean trunk back and down toward
     the floor, adduct the scapula, and extend the cer-
     vical spine.
  2. Relax to the starting position.
  3. Repeat.
Measurement: The distance the elbows are from the
  floor; the program should be developed with specific measurement of the height of the table

FIGURE 14-55. Pectoral stretch (sitting).
Specific for: Pectorals
Beneficial in: Kyphosis
Starting position: Sitting in a chair, hands behind the
  neck (touch head)
Actions
  1. Simultaneously lean trunk backward, extend up-
     per spine, adduct the scapula, and pull arms
     backward.
  2. Relax to starting position.
Measurement: The distance the elbows are from the
  ground/floor

the antagonist muscles. These curves are often functional in nature and thus are correctable through properly assigned stretching and developmental exercises
under the guidance of a physician. Untreated spines often become progressively worse, involving permanent
structural changes.

Scoliosis is often caused by asymmetry of the body.
Lateral pelvic tilt, low shoulder, asymmetrical development of the rib cage, or lateral deviation of the linea
alba may be a cause or effect of rotolateral curve of the
spine. Evidence of this would be found in one or more
of the following body changes:

  1. When the thoracic vertebral column is displaced
     laterally, the rotation of the vertebral bodies is in
     the direction of the convexity of the curve.
  2. Lateral bending of the spine is accompanied by a
     depression and protrusion of the intervertebral
     discs on the concave side, with a greater separa-
     tion between the sides of the vertebrae on the
     convex side of the lateral curve.
  3. There is an imbalance in the stability and pull of
     the ligaments and muscles responsible for hold-

FIGURE 14-56. Fatigue slump with kypholordosis.

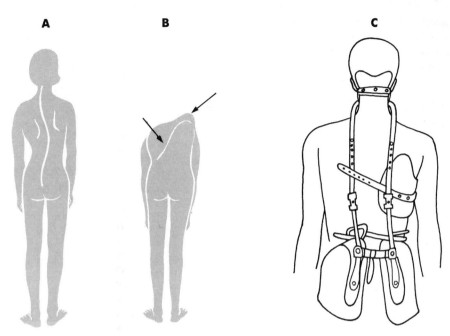

FIGURE 14-57. Scoliosis. **A,** Rotolateral curve. **B,** Rotation viewed from Adam's position. **C,** Milwaukee brace.

ing the vertebral column in its normal position. Muscles and ligaments on the concave side become tight and contracted, whereas those on the convex side become stretched and weak. Muscle atrophy may occur.

4. Changes in the rib cage involve flattening and depression of the posterior aspects of the ribs on the concave side, with a posterior bulging of the ribs on the side of the convex spinal curve. The opposite is true of the anterior aspect of the chest. There the ribs on the concave side are prominent, whereas they are flattened or depressed on the convex side.

During the past several years, orthopedic physicians have stressed the importance of identifying and treating scoliosis in young children between the ages of 9 and 14 years. Early detection by physical education teachers, therapists, and nurses and immediate referral to a physician who specializes in scoliosis treatment may prevent permanent deformity in many of these young persons.

The treatment of scoliosis is rather specific, depending on the cause of the condition and the resulting changes in the spinal column. Students with scoliosis must be referred to an orthopedist for examination and recommendations relative to stretching and developmental exercises, which may be either symmetrical or asymmetrical in nature. Some orthopedic physicians believe that the treatment of scoliosis should be very specific and indicate the types of asymmetrical exercises to be performed by the student. Others subscribe to the theory that the cause of scoliosis should be eliminated if possible, but that only symmetrical types of exercise should be assigned for this condition.

Since scoliosis is complicated and difficult to diagnose and treat, it is necessary for the adapted teacher or therapist to rely on the advice of the physician concerning the types of activities and exercises that should be prescribed for the student. Since lateral spinal curves are accompanied by a certain amount of rotation of the spine, a great deal of skill is required to diagnose and treat the condition correctly. Recommendations relative to types of games, sports, and activities should therefore be made by the examining physician.

Treatment may consist of use of casts or braces (Fig. 14-57, *C*) combined with a special exercise program assigned by the physician. Exercise programs without the cast or brace are not usually recommended. Cases that are not discovered early may require operation with spinal fusion or the insertion of rods along the

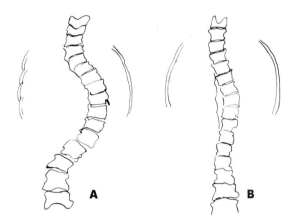

FIGURE 14-58. Severe scoliosis. **A,** Before surgery. **B,** After surgery and corrective procedures.

vertebral column to straighten the severely curved spine (Fig. 14-58).

Physicians at the Los Angeles Orthopedic Hospital and the Orange County Orthopedic Hospital in California have successfully treated large numbers of children and have spearheaded campaigns to provide for early diagnosis of this serious problem.

Treatment of patients with severe scoliosis may include any or all of the following:

1. Removal of the cause, if possible
2. Assignment of symmetrical exercises, especially for the abdomen, back, and hip regions
3. Mobilization of tightness in soft tissue in the trunk, shoulder girdle, and hip region
4. Assignment of asymmetrical exercises to strengthen muscles on the convex side of the curves on the recommendation of an orthopedic physician
5. Recommendation of traction of the spine by the physician
6. Assignment of exercises to increase the strength, anteroposterior balance, and alignment of the spine
7. Specific prescription of any derotation exercises by the physician

Physical educators who specialize in adapted physical education and specialists in therapeutic recreation should inform those teaching regular physical education, the school nurse, and other health-related personnel of the importance of early screening of young persons to detect scoliosis and other body mechanics problems. The students can then be involved in preventive programs under the guidance of a physician who specializes in the diagnosis and care of scoliosis and other serious orthopedic problems.

Shoulder height asymmetry

It is rather common for an individual to have one shoulder higher or lower than the other. This condition usually results from asymmetrical muscle or bone development of the shoulder girdle or lateral curvature in the spinal column. Correction of an abnormal curve in the spine may result in the return of the shoulders to a level position, although special exercises may be required in the process. When the cause is faulty muscle development, correction is a relatively simple matter of developing the strength of the weaker or higher side and stretching the contracted side. This also involves a reorientation of the student's feeling for the correct shoulder and body alignment. Exercises for a low or high shoulder should be performed in front of a regular or three-way mirror to enable the student to recognize the position of the body when it is being held in proper alignment.

Head tilt or twist

When viewed from the anterior or posterior view, the head may be either tilted directly to the side or tilted to the side with a concomitant twisting of the neck. In either case, it is necessary to reorient the student to the proper position of the head. Often, deviations in the position of the head and neck are compensatory for other postural deviations located below this area. The correction of these conditions involves reorientation to the proper position of the head. This entails reeducating the antagonist muscles responsible for holding the head in a position of balance, plus reorienting the student in terms of holding the head in the correct position, which will activate the appropriate proprioceptive centers and balance organs. The exercise program for correction of the condition should be rather specific in terms of the muscle groups that are stretched and developed. Moreover, the student should practice the exercise program standing in front of a mirror so that he or she can visualize the correct position and develop the feeling of holding the head in correct alignment.

Body tilt

Another deviation that may be noted in the anterior and posterior posture examinations is a problem of body alignment in which the total body is tilted to the left or right of the gravity or plumb line (Fig. 14-59). Standing with the body tilted to the side causes increased strain on the bones, joints, and muscles and may result in compensation being made to bring the body back into a position of balance over its base of support. Often this compensation results in the hips and shoulders being thrown out of alignment, leading

FIGURE 14-59. Body tilt.

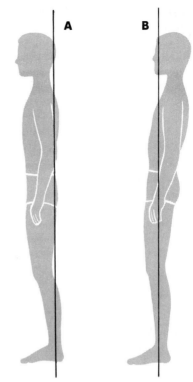

FIGURE 14-60. Total body forward **(A)** and backward **(B)** leans (plumb line test).

to the development of lateral curvature in the spine. Correction of this condition involves an analysis of the causative factors of the tilt, such as unilateral flatfoot, pronated ankle, knock-knee, or short leg. On the other hand, standing out of balanced alignment may be habitual with the student. Before correction of the lateral body tilt can be accomplished, unilateral deviations must be corrected. Specific suggestions for the correction of a weak foot, ankle, or knee are contained in another section of this chapter. Together with these specific corrective measures, exercises should be given to the student for body tilt. Exercises and activities that involve the symmetrical use of the total body and that will help the student learn to stand with body in correct alignment and balance are needed. Exercising in front of the mirror will give the student a visual concept of the feeling of standing with the body in a balanced position, which should help effect a correction of a lateral tilt of the body.

Postural sway

Standing balance is a dynamic process of maintaining stable, upright posture. Postural sway results when individual movements of different joints create oscilla-

tions of the body. Control over postural sway is a desirable goal of a postural education program. Ratcliffe et al.[20] have reported the use of a therapeutic technique called approximation (compression of joints), which decreases postural sway of healthy subjects and stabilizes standing balance.

Body lean

When viewed from the side, the total body may lean a considerable distance either forward or backward of the line of gravity. When the total body is in good alignment but leans forward or backward from the ankle so that the lobe of the ear is positioned either anterior or posterior to the gravity line, the condition is considered to be a total body lean (Fig. 14-60). If the body lean is not corrected, as the individual attempts to compensate for the lean and bring the body back into a balanced standing position, the body often will be transferred into one or more of the postural conditions discussed previously. Correction of the forward or backward lean of the total body is primarily a matter of reorientation of the proprioceptive centers of the body to enable the individual to feel when the body is in correct alignment in the standing position. Checking the forward or backward deviation of the body against a gravity line or a plumb line hung vertically before a three-way mirror is an excellent way for the student to recognize the feel of standing with the body in the correct position. Symmetrical exercises can then be assigned so that the student can develop the flexibility and strength necessary to hold the body in correct alignment.

SUMMARY

Good posture contributes to the well-being of the body and gives the impression of enthusiasm and self-confidence. There are good postures for sitting, standing, and walking. Antigravity muscles that are weak and stretched and reciprocal muscles that shorten are often the functional causes of poor posture. The procedure for ameliorating poor posture is as follows: (1) know the model of good posture, (2) assess the individual against the model of normal posture for deficiency, (3) identify the specific muscles that need to be strengthened or stretched, and (4) conduct programs to develop the deficient muscles. The specific areas to be assessed for postural abnormalities are the foot, ankle, leg, hips, anteroposterior aspect of the spinal column, lateral aspect of the spinal column, shoulders, and head and neck.

Tests and measurements can be used in adapted physical education to evaluate improvement, aid in instruction, determine whether body parts are properly aligned, and motivate students to work toward correction of body malalignment. Some of the tests and measurements traditionally used in adapted physical education programs are not highly valid or reliable but may still be of some use in identifying deviations, helping the instructor explain malalignments to students, and motivating students to work toward self-improvement. If any or all of these values are obtained from testing, it should be a worthwhile part of the total program. The data thus obtained are used to formulate specific performance objectives for each person.

The physician and the physical educator may diagnose and prescribe physical activity for school-aged children with postural disorders. If a physician diagnoses a postural disorder and prescribes treatment, this should be noted in the child's school health record. All activity that has been contraindicated by the physician should be noted by the physical educator. Under these conditions there should be close communication between the physical educator and the physician.

When postural conditions are of structural origin,

surgical techniques can usually improve mechanical alignment. Thus remedies for postural conditions that are structural in nature are under the jurisdiction of the medical profession. On the other hand, postural conditions caused by soft tissue and functional defects may respond to physical fitness programs to increase strength and flexibility of specific muscles as directed by physical educators. Postural education regarding functional disorders requires specially designed instruction to meet the postural needs of children. In accordance with regulations for engaging "related services," if children do not respond or benefit from the postural education programs, they should be referred to a physician.

Although there is optimum mechanical body alignment, children at young ages may have mechanical malalignments of body parts and still have normal posture for their age. There are apparent postural deficiencies among people with orthopedic disabilities because of muscular involvement associated with the disorders. Mentally retarded populations with neurological involvement have postural problems associated with vestibular and kinesthetic delays and depth perception problems. Other disabling conditions that affect strength and vitality may also have an impact on their postural alignment. The growing incidence of low back pain in the United States should alert the physical educator to the need to provide students with low back information and stabilizing exercises.

REVIEW QUESTIONS

1. What are the values of a postural education program?
2. What are the positions from which posture may be evaluated?
3. Can you list some deviations of the foot and the ankle? What activities might be used to ameliorate the conditions?
4. What are some disorders of the legs? How would one go about correcting the deficiencies?
5. Can you describe lordosis and identify activities that may remedy the condition?
6. Can you describe postural deviations of the upper back and scapula and indicate activities that may assist in correcting the muscles that contribute to the deficiencies?
7. How would you treat abnormal postural conditions of the head and neck?
8. Can you describe the different scoliotic curves and suggest activities to treat the disorders?
9. Can you describe tests to determine deviations of the foot and ankle, leg, pelvis, and spine?
10. How would you determine whether a postural deviation is structural or functional?
11. Provide examples of postural malalignment in young chil-

dren that may be regarded as normal with respect to their chronological age.

12. What disabling conditions have the greatest prevalence of postural deficiencies?

STUDENT ACTIVITIES

1. Examine a peer for postural deficiencies and indicate activities that may assist the individual to better his or her posture.
2. Visit a home for the aged and assess the posture of some of the clients. Analyze each segment of the body in terms of good alignment and indicate appropriate activities for the individual.
3. Teach your peers some postural activities. Specify the manner in which the activities are to be performed and identify the muscles that are to benefit from the activity.
4. Visit a teacher who conducts a postural education program. Are there individual postural education programs and postural objectives for each child? Do the activities that children are performing match the assessment information?
5. Have three persons evaluate an individual's postural fitness. Indicate differences and agreement on the evaluation of each of the areas of the postural assessment.
6. Study young children from 1 to 4 years of age to determine postural malalignments that are considered normal for their chronological age.

REFERENCES

1. Althoff SA, Heyden MS, Roberson LD: Back to basics—whatever happened to posture? *J Health Phys Educ Rec Dance* 59: 20-24, 1988.
2. Althoff SA, Heyden MS, Roberson LD: Posture screening: a program that works, *J Health Phys Educ Rec Dance* 59(8): 26-32, 1988.
3. Auxter DM et al: *Correcting hip retroversion in walking gait of an infant,* Final report to the US Department of Education, Project no. 029AH50223, 1986.
4. Beattie P, Rothstein JM, Lamb RL: Reliability of the attraction method for measuring lumbar spine backward bending, *Phys Ther* 67:364-369, 1987.
5. Biering-Sorenson F: Physical measurements as risk indicators for low back trouble over a one year period, *Spine* 9:106-109, 1984.
6. Blackman JA, editor: *Medical aspects of developmental disabilities in children birth to three,* Rockville, Md, 1984, Aspen Systems Corporation.
7. Bracker D, Gargen SR, Singer SA: Low back pain in a tennis player, *Phys Sports Med* 16:75-83, 1988.
8. Cailliet R: *Low back pain syndrome,* Philadelphia, 1974, FA Davis.
9. Daniels L, Worthingham C: *Muscle testing: techniques of manual examination,* Philadelphia, 1982, WB Saunders.
10. Fairbanks BL: *Vigor and vitality,* Salt Lake City, 1982, Hawkes Publishing.
11. Fisher AC, Domm MA, Wuest DA: Adherence to sport-injury programs, *Phys Sports Med* 16:47-50, 1988.
12. Francis FS: Scoliosis screening for 3,000 college-aged women: the Utah study—phase II, *Phys Ther* 68:1513-1516, 1988.
13. Garrison L, Read AK: *Fitness for every body,* Palo Alto, Calif, 1980, Mayfield Publishing.
14. Kelsey JL, White AA, Pastides H: The impact of musculoskeletal disorders on the population of the United States, *J Bone Joint Surg* 61(4):959-960, 1979.
15. Langrana NA, Lee CK, Alexander H: Quantitative assessment of back strength using isokinetic testing, *Spine* 10:287-290, 1984.
16. Linton SJ, Kamwendo K: Low back schools: a critical review, *Phys Ther* 678:1375-1383, 1987.
17. Miller DK, Allen TE: *Fitness: a lifetime commitment,* Minneapolis, 1982, Burgess Publishing.
18. Nachemson A: Work for all, *Clin Orthop* 79:77-85, 1983.
19. Pollock ML et al: Effects of resistance training on lumbar extension strength, *Am J Sports Med* 17:624-628, 1989.
20. Ratcliffe KT et al: Effects of approximation on postural sway in healthy subjects, *Phys Ther* 67:502-506, 1987.
21. Sharpe GL, Liemohn WP, Snodgrasss LB: Exercise prescription and low back, *J Health Phys Educ Rec Dance* 59(9):74-78, 1988.
22. Sherrill C: *Adapted physical education and recreation, ed 3,* Dubuque, Iowa, 1986, Wm C Brown Publishing.
23. Sherill C: Posture training as a means of normalization, *Ment Retard* 18:135-138, 1980.
24. Stelmach GE et al: Age related decline in postural control mechanisms, *Aging Human Dev* 9:205-223, 1989.
25. Subotnick SI: Foot orthoses: an update, *Phys Sports Med* 11:103-109, 1983.
26. Tenhula JA, Rose SJ, DSelitto A: Association between direction of lateral lumbar shift, movement tests and side of symptoms in patients with low back pain syndrome, *Phys Ther* 70:480-485, 1990.
27. The National Scoliosis Foundation: *One in every ten persons has scoliosis,* Belmont, Mass, 1985, The Foundation.
28. Tigny RL: Anterior dysfunction of the sacroiliac joint as a major factor in the etiology of idiopathic low back pain syndrome, *Phys Ther* 70:250-262, 1990.
29. Waddell B: A new clinical model for the treatment of low back pain, *Spine* 12:632-644, 1987.
30. Walker ML et al: Relationships between lumbar lordosis, pelvic tilt and abdominal muscle performance, *Phys Ther* 67:512-516, 1987.
31. Woolacott MH, Shumway-Cook A, Nashner LM: Aging and postural control: changes in sensory organization and muscular coordination, *Int Aging Hum Dev* 23:97-114, 1986.

SUGGESTED READINGS

Blackman JA, editor: *Medical aspects of developmental disabilities in children birth to three,* Rockville, Md, 1984, Aspen Systems Corporation.

Cailliet R: *Low back pain syndrome, ed 3,* Philadelphia, 1981, FA Davis.

Daniels L: *Therapeutic exercises for body alignment and function, ed 2,* Philadelphia, 1977, WB Saunders.

15

OBJECTIVES

Cite the causes of poor physical fitness and the purposes of physical fitness programming.

Determine a unique physical fitness need.

Describe the different types of physical fitness tests and their implications for programming.

List the basic principles for conducting a physical fitness program for individuals with disabilities.

State the physical fitness characteristics and problems associated with specific disabilities.

Construct a circuit training program and an interval training program.

Explain the problems associated with overweight, underweight, and obesity.

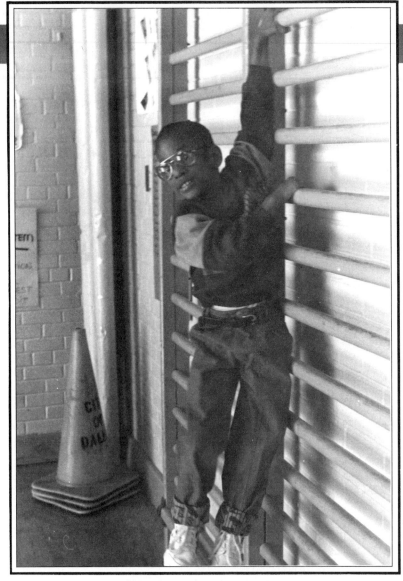

Courtesy Dallas Independent School District

Physical and Motor Development

*O*ne of the objectives of physical educators is to develop in their students the physical characteristics necessary to perform the activities of daily living without undue fatigue. Furthermore, the outcome of the development of these physical characteristics is the ability to perform motor skills competently.

The physical and motor underdevelopment and low vitality of persons with disabilities constitute a major concern of physical education. Chronically ill persons with debilitating conditions are particularly prone to poor physical vitality and development. Persons with cardiorespiratory conditions such as chronic bronchitis and various heart defects also tend toward poor physical fitness. More such medically fragile children are now being educated in the public schools and represent a serious challenge for the physical educator. Children with disabilities and children without disabilities often lack the physical and motor abilities prerequisite to successful participation in sports and the activities of daily living. This chapter includes a discussion of physical and motor fitness and special problems demonstrated by undernourished, obese, visually impaired, and physically impaired persons.

DEFINITION

In general, physical fitness can be defined as being fit enough to meet the demands of everyday life. However, in reality there are as many different definitions of physical fitness as there are different ways to evaluate fitness status. Some tests are designed to measure dynamic and static strength, some to measure muscular power, and some include measures of flexibility. The test used to evaluate fitness usually dictates the type of program designed to improve fitness. When working with populations with disabilities, the long-range goal is to develop the types of fitness that are functionally related to independent living in the community.[7] Therefore it is important to select the type of fitness test that will best meet the needs of individuals with specific disabilities.

It is important for children with disabilities to move as efficiently as possible. To move efficiently a person must possess both physical fitness and motor fitness. Physical fitness is maintaining appropriate levels of muscular strength, joint flexibility, muscular endurance, and cardiovascular endurance to carry out everyday activities. Motor fitness is achieving the agility, balance, and coordination levels necessary to perform tasks and skills such as running, jumping, playing basketball, and playing soccer. Both physical fitness and motor fitness are important prerequisites to participation in movement activities, therefore both must be considered when programs for individuals with disabilities are being developed. An emphasis should be placed on promoting a lifestyle of physical fitness because the enhancement of muscle strength, cardiac output, and supply of blood to the muscles will contribute to motor fitness.[3,14]

THE FITNESS CONTINUUM

There are three purposes of physical fitness: (1) to promote and maintain health, (2) to develop prerequisites for functional motor skills for independent living, and (3) to develop prerequisites for sport and leisure skills.

According to Falls, Baylor, and Dishman,[8] health-related fitness refers to those aspects of physiological and psychological functioning that are believed to offer protection against degenerative conditions such as obesity and coronary heart disease. Also, health-related fitness includes the ability to maintain proper postural alignment.

Physical fitness for the purpose of performing daily living, sport, and leisure skills refers to developing and maintaining levels of strength, flexibility, and muscular and cardiovascular endurance to contribute to the agility, balance, coordination, and stamina needed to participate in those tasks.

Persons with severe disabilities need to develop physical fitness to be able to lift the head, roll over, maintain a sitting position, and achieve range of motion in the joints. For less severely disabled individuals, physical fitness can contribute to the ability to walk, engage in sports, or swim.

Because a person needs basic levels of physical fitness before agility, balance, and coordination can be developed, it can be said that physical fitness is prerequisite to motor fitness. Once minimum levels of physical fitness are achieved, development and use of motor fitness can contribute to additional physical fitness development. That is, once an individual begins to use agility, balance, and coordination in daily living activities, as well as in games and sports, physical fitness levels continue to rise.

PHYSICAL FITNESS IN THE UNITED STATES

Although the United States appears to be involved in a fitness boom, there is evidence that the general population is not as active as one would believe. According to Brooks,[5] slightly more than 20% of the population is active more than 30 days out of the year; however, the study does not indicate the quality of participation of physical activity. The quantitative performance of American youth has been studied by Allen,[1] who found that half of the girls in the United States, ages 6 to 15 years, and 30% of the boys, ages 6 to 12 years, cannot run a mile in less than 12 minutes, which is just over walking speed. Allen also found that 55% of the girls, ages 6 to 15 years, and 25% of the boys, ages 6 to 12 years, cannot do one pull-up; and 40% of children ages 5 to 8 years show at least one potential heart disease factor (e.g., obesity, high cholesterol levels, or high blood pressure). According to Humphrey,[11] there appears to be renewed concern about the status of childhood fitness for the following reasons: (1) the nation's school children have become fatter and less fit during the past decade; (2) if this trend continues, it is predicted that these children will be at greater risk for illness when they become adults; and (3) less than one half (46%) of physical education teachers have as their major goal improvement of physical fitness of students. It is apparent that children in the United States are not as physically fit as experts believe they should be, and it is evident that youth with disabilities are less fit than their peers without disabilities. Out-of-school programs are needed in the community. These programs can be sponsored by community recreation centers, boys' and girls' clubs, and other agencies.[25]

Values of Physical Fitness

Physical fitness is considered a prerequisite to healthful and recreational living, not an end unto itself. Physical fitness can be health related inasmuch as it preserves healthful function of the body over extended periods into adult life. Physical conditioning can keep the cardiovascular and the muscular systems from deterioration and assist in maintaining good mechanical posture. Good alignment of the body is particularly important

to persons with disabilities because it enhances appearance, which aids in social development. Physical fitness programs for individuals with disabilities should contribute in every way possible to independent life patterns.

Physical Fitness Through Lifelong Activity

A central issue of physical fitness is whether the objective of a program should develop lifestyles of physical activity rather than training for specific physical fitness dimensions, such as cardiovascular endurance or strength in a given set of muscles.[6,24] A classic study that supports functional lifestyle fitness is the letter carrier study done at the University of Pittsburgh.[6] The letter carriers walked 25 miles a week at a slow pace and with intermittent stops, making it unlikely that they reached their target heart rate. However, their cholesterol levels were low enough to place them in the low-risk coronary category. In the words of Sheehan,[18] "slow and steady are the watch words for the maintenance of physical fitness."

FACTORS CONTRIBUTING TO POOR FITNESS

There are several factors that contribute to poor physical and motor fitness. Low physical fitness levels are

FIGURE 15-1. Saratoga Cycle. (Courtesy Saratoga Access and Fitness.)

caused by obesity; asthma and other chronic respiratory problems; susceptibility to infectious diseases, including the common cold; poor nutrition; inadequate sleep; and a lifestyle that does not include physical exercise.

There is evidence that individuals with disabilities may be exceptionally self-conscious, and they may lack self-confidence. Their fear of failure may result in avoidance of both instructional and extracurricular physical activity.[17] It is important to determine why a person's fitness is low (i.e., why they are avoiding physical activity) so that the physical fitness program that is developed will focus on cause as well as effect.

Low motor fitness levels can result from abnormal reflex development, delayed vestibular function, poor vision, delayed cross-lateral integration, inadequate spatial awareness, poor body image, and any other factor that limits the ability to move efficiently.

Before a physical educator can decide how best to improve physical and motor ability, present levels of performance must be determined through evaluation.

EVALUATING PHYSICAL AND MOTOR FITNESS

The full evaluation of the physical and motor fitness of a child with a disability requires comprehensive assessment of ability areas identified through research (see Chapter 3). One does not just measure strength as a single entity. Rather, one measures the strength of specific muscle groups such as the knee extensors, elbow flexors, or abdominal muscles. In the same manner, when flexibility is evaluated it is necessary to determine range of motion at specific joints in the body. A severe loss of strength in any muscle group or limited range of motion in any joint could seriously affect the attainment of specific daily living or sport skills. Thus a full evaluation of physical education needs would involve assessing the strength of major muscle groups, range of motion of many joints, and factors that affect cardiovascular efficiency.

The procedures for determining educational needs have been previously described. In review, an educational need is determined by identifying a discrepancy between an individual's performance on a physical or motor fitness task and normative expectations for that task. For example, if the normative expectation of a 6-year-old child's long jump is 60 inches, but the child can only jump 45 inches, then long-jumping ability needs to be developed. Thus full evaluation to determine the unique needs of an individual is based on discrepancy between actual performance and normative performance.

It should be obvious that there is seldom enough time or personnel in a school system to comprehensively assess every child. Therefore the physical educator usually only samples some physical and motor fitness components. Which components are measured is usually determined one of two ways. Either a specific test (e.g., the Health Related Physical Fitness Test) is administered, or test items that measure specific aspects that contribute to a given daily living skill or motor skill are selected and administered.

The ultimate purpose of preevaluation in the areas of physical and motor fitness is to determine which activities will meet the unique needs of the child with disabilities. The procedures to be employed for determining the needs in the areas of physical and motor fitness are as follows:

1. Identify motor skills to be taught in the physical education program that can be expressed as recreational skills and activities of daily living for independence in the community.
2. Select physical and motor fitness areas associated with the skills needed for independent living in the community.
3. Identify levels of physical and motor fitness necessary for independent recreation and activities of daily living in the community.
4. Test for present levels of educational performance in physical and motor fitness domains.
5. Compare the child's performance with normative community standards to determine whether there is sufficient discrepancy to indicate an educational need.
6. If it is determined that there is a need in an identified domain, then ascertain present levels of educational performance on tasks related to the domain and postulate short-term instructional objectives.

TYPES OF PHYSICAL FITNESS TESTS

There are at least three different orientations to physical fitness testing. One type is "health-related fitness," which refers to those components of physiological functioning that are believed to offer protection against such degenerative diseases as obesity and coronary heart disease. A second type are those tests designed to develop physical or motor fitness such as optimal strength, endurance, flexibility, power, agility, and balance to be used in sport activities. A third orientation, which is preferred by Evans and Meyer[7] for individuals with disabilities, is a functional specific type of physical fitness that relates to independent functioning in the

---

TABLE 15-1

Types of fitness tests for individuals with disabilities

Health related	Motor fitness	Functional walking tasks for community living
Cardiovascular fitness 300-yard walk-run[3] 8-minute run[26] 12-minute run[27]	*Explosive leg strength* Standing broad jump[3,26,27] 50-yard dash[3]	*Walking endurance* Improve distance over time
		Ability to maintain balance while walking Widen width of support Shorten stride
Abdominal strength Number of sit-ups in 30 seconds[3] Curlups[26] Bent-knee sit-ups in 60 seconds[27]	*Softball throws*[27] *Static balance* Modified stork stand[27] *Agility* Shuttle run[27]	*Improve heel strike* Modify degree of incline Increase number of heel strikes
Percent body fat Caliper measures[27]	Rise to stand[27] Mat creep[27]	
Flexibility Sit and reach		

---

community. Examples of different types of physical and motor fitness tests are included in Table 15-1.

Health-related tests include measures of cardiovascular endurance, abdominal strength, percentage of body fat, and flexibility. Motor fitness that is prerequisite to specific motor tasks is related to total physical fitness. Some test items included in this type of test are shuttle run, softball throw, stork stand, and standing broad jump. Functional physical fitness tests relate specifically to what an individual needs to meet the daily demands of the environment. Individuals with severe disabilities would require these types of physical fitness tests. Examples of these test items would be walking to develop endurance to walk to and from one's home from designated areas in the neighborhood, developing sufficient balance to remedy a wide shuffling gait, and specific practice to lengthen tight heel cords so that the entire foot will strike the ground when walking. The type of fitness test selected depends on the goals and objectives of the physical education program.

There are two types of normative-referenced tests. One type references a normal population and the other references specific disabilities by age. The purpose of normative-referenced testing is to compare persons of a given classification against the performance of others in that population. Winnick and Short[27] have done considerable work in normative-referenced testing of the abilities of individuals with specific disabilities with their Project UNIQUE. Other tests that have merit for testing disabled individuals are Ulrich's Test of Motor Development,[24] the Peabody Developmental Motor Scales by Folio and Fewell,[10] and The Henderson Revi-

sion of the Stotts Test of Motor Impairment by Stott, Henderson, and Moyes.[22]

These normative-referenced tests for individuals with disabilities are based on the assumption that the tests measure entity-type qualities that are demonstrated by other individuals within the same classification. This assumption has been questioned in other fields such as psychology. Stott, Henderson, and Moyes[22] have studied this approach to motor impairment assessment and have compiled a qualitative diagnostic test of physical fitness to aid practitioners in clarifying what the test measures. Their test assesses the nature of a child's failure of motor control; it also provides behavioral information about poor performance and a checklist to use to analyze motor faults. However, even after the information has been recorded, there is still a problem of how to use the information to make decisions about instruction in specific motor skills that can be used in independent community recreational physical activities.

PROGRAMMING FOR PHYSICAL AND MOTOR FITNESS

Once the unique physical and motor fitness needs of an individual with disabilities have been determined, the teacher has several programming alternatives from which to select. The most popular techniques for developing physical and motor fitness are circuit training and interval training.

Circuit training involves setting up a series of exercise stations to fulfill specific deficiencies. Interval training consists of running, swimming, rope skipping, and bicycle riding for the purpose of improving circulorespiratory endurance. The physical educator should select the training technique that best meets the unique needs of the students in the physical education program.

Circuit Training

Circuit training has the potential to fulfill specific diagnosed areas of deficiencies among students through the selection of carefully arranged exercises. Each numbered exercise in a circuit is called a station. There can be many stations throughout a particular gymnasium, with persons of varying disabilities routed to the exercise stations appropriate to the specific disability. The circuit training system is extremely adaptable to a great variety of situations and has the potential to meet individual differences within a particular class. The advantages of a circuit training system in developing subaverage physical and motor factors are that (1) it can cope with most diagnosed disabilities, (2) it has the potential of applying the progressive overload principle, and (3) it enables a large number of performers to

FIGURE 15-2. Muscle-stim power trainer, offers muscle stimulation for inactive leg muscles. (Courtesy Sinties Scientific, Inc.)

train at the same time and yet meets the individual needs of each performer.

Circuit training usually involves the introduction of a time element into exercise, which often forces the participant to perform at submaximum levels. However, this need not be entirely the case. Each performer can be assigned a specific circuit for a prescribed number of repetitions at each station. If a person wishes to develop both cardiovascular and strength variables, the load may be of a submaximum nature so that the person may continuously engage in exercise while moving from station to station. However, if the strength component is a more desirable outcome, then fewer repetitions with more weight should be achieved before the person moves to the next station. After one circuit lap has been completed, it is at the discretion of the instructor to move the student through a second or third lap, depending on the total dosage desired for a given student. The advantages of the circuit system are as follows:

1. It is adaptable to a number of varying situations.
2. It can be used by 1 or 100 persons and fits almost any time requirements.
3. It assures progression.
4. It allows a person to always work at his or her present capacity and then progress beyond that.
5. It provides a series of progressive goals, which is a powerful motivating force.
6. It may use variables such as load, repetition, and time and consequently it may develop motor and physical characteristics that have been identified as deficient by diagnostic testing.
7. It has the possibility of providing a vigorous bout of exercise in a relatively short period.
8. It can provide any number of stations to meet any identifiable need.
9. The student knows what must be done because of the construction of an individual program.

Regardless of the system of training used in the developmental program, it should always be kept in mind that the primary goal of the system is to meet the individually diagnosed needs of each child in the program through planned progressive exercise. If this principle is applied, chances are that the program will be beneficial to the physical and motor development of the child. Fig. 15-3 shows the implementation of a circuit program. This circuit program consists of 10 different exercises at separate stations, each performed according to a prescribed number of repetitions and load. It must be remembered that there are as many stations possible as there are exercises or areas of subdevelopment. The illustration shows five different levels at

Name of exercise	Developmental levels*				
	I	II	III	IV	V
	Wt.	Wt.	Wt.	Wt.	Wt.
Two arm curl	40	50	55	60	65
Military press	50	60	65	70	75
Deep knee bends	70	80	85	90	95
Dead lift (straight leg)	70	80	85	90	95
French curl (or dip) with dumbbell	10	15	20	25	30
Situps (time)	--	--	--	--	--
Bench step-ups (time)	--	--	--	--	--
Bench press	55	60	65	75	85
Lateral raises (dumbbell)	5	10	15	20	25
Pushups (time)	--	--	--	--	--

*When 10 repetitions are reached, advance to the next developmental level.

FIGURE 15-3. A suggested circuit training program.

each station, permitting four steps of progression. Individuals subjectively select a starting level, and when a criterion of 10 repetitions is reached they move to the next level. Progression depends on the ability to meet a set number of repetitions, which will enable the person to move on to the next progressive level. At each station, it is desirable to place on the wall a card naming the exercise and showing the five levels of performance. The load and number of repetitions should be initially selected to meet the capabilities of the average students in the class; however, from this point weights are adjusted to determine students' present levels of performance so that short-term instructional objectives can be determined. Also, it must be remembered that it is not necessary for all students to participate at each of the stations. Therefore students may be routed to four, five, or six stations according to their needs as compared with normative performance. Any station may be devised that meets a physical or motor need of children, and a progressive program may be established.

Interval Training

Interval training involves short periods of exercise with a rest interval in between. This training technique can be applied to most activities that require muscular strength and endurance. The interval training prescription should be planned for each student individually. A typical interval training prescription for 1 day is repre-

sented in the box below. Target times are used as motivation to encourage all-out performance.

Sherrill lists six components of an interval training program. They are as follows[19]:

1. *Set:* The work interval and the rest interval. An interval training program (ITP) may have any number of sets.
2. *Work interval:* A prescribed number of repetitions of the same activity under identical conditions. Work intervals may involve optimum number of sit-ups or push-ups within a prescribed number of seconds.
3. *Rest interval:* The number of seconds or minutes of rest between work intervals during which the student recovers from fatigue for the next set of repetitions. During the rest period the student

Use of Target Times for the Sit-up*

DAY	PROGRESSION OF REPETITIONS
First 3 days	10
Fourth day	11
Fifth day	12
Sixth day	13
Seventh day	14
Eighth day	15

*Target time: sequence of 10 to 15 repetitions of the sit-up in 20 seconds.

should walk rather than sit, lie, or assume a stationary position.

4. *Repetitions:* The number of times the work interval is repeated under identical conditions.

5. *Target:* The best score that a student can make on the prescribed activity. Target times are usually determined by present levels of performance from data sheets.

6. *Goals:* A statement made by the student of the score the student believes he or she can attain in a particular activity. All-out effort is often motivated after the first few weeks by prescribing a behavioral goal.

Older children may be guided in developing individual exercise sessions comprised of sets that reflect their own levels of aspiration. Presumably, the child will be more motivated to accomplish a goal established by himself or herself than one imposed by an adult.

In keeping with the overload principle, the exercise sessions become increasingly more demanding each week.

The following list of procedures may help the adapted physical education specialist in planning each ITP.

1. Test each student individually to determine the present level of performance.

2. Organize the children for performance based on test data.

3. Develop specific behavioral objectives for each individual.

4. Explain the principle of interval training to the group and establish a card file where the students may pick up their individualized ITPs at the beginning of each physical education period.

5. Review data to determine if behavioral goals are being met, and readjust programs if necessary.

Static Stretching Exercises

Adapted physical education requires that tasks be adapted to the ability level of each learner. When this occurs, each student with a disability can be accommodated. Usually, individuals with disabilities have tight muscles that limit joint range of motion. Stretching is an important activity for increasing movement of desired joints. Ways to evaluate joint flexibility and to stretch muscles include the following:

1. While holding a yardstick between the middle fingers of both hands, bend forward from the

FIGURE 15-4. A child experiences success with a 3-foot high basketball hoop. (Courtesy Dallas Independent School District.)

waist keeping knees straight. Check the yardstick to determine how far the fingers are from the floor. This exercise stretches the lower back.

2. Stand facing a wall with toes and waist touching the wall. Hyperextend the back and bring the chin as far away from the wall as possible. Have a partner measure the distance the chin is from the wall. This exercise stretches the pectoral muscles and promotes appropriate alignment of the shoulders and thoracic spine.

3. Lie on your back on a narrow bench and let your arms, which are straight, hang down toward the floor. Have a partner measure the distance the tips of the fingers are from the floor. This activity stretches the pectoral muscles.

Jumping Rope for Cardiovascular Endurance

When conducting a cardiovascular fitness program for individuals with disabilities, each individualized program should have specific objectives tailored to the present level of ability of the student. A continuum of exercise activities can be used to accommodate individual differences. A procedure for constructing an individualized physical fitness program of rope jumping may be as follows:

1. Make a 4-minute musical tape recording that uses a cadence of 70 jumps per minute.
2. Test the students to determine how long they can jump without a rest interval.
3. Prescribe each individual to continue for 2 seconds longer each day.
4. When an individual can continuously jump for 4 minutes, substitute another tape that uses a cadence of 80 jumps per minute.

Under these conditions there would be two stations of different frequencies, but each person at each of those stations would be performing for specific lengths of time commensurate with their present levels of ability. Increasing cadences could be added to the program as individuals increase in cardiovascular endurance. Another factor that could be introduced into the program to make it more or less difficult is to vary the length of the rest intervals between repeated bouts of exercise.

Walk-Run Program for Cardiovascular Endurance

A walk-run program has at least two variables that can be manipulated to make it more or less difficult: (1) the distance that the individual should run and (2) the length of time permitted to travel the prescribed distance. Suggested distance intervals are 1 mile, 1¼ miles, 1½ miles, 1¾ miles, and 2 miles. Suggested tar-

FIGURE 15-5. A child develops fitness using age-appropriate sport activities. (Courtesy Dallas Independent School District.)

get criterion times for each distance could be 15 minutes for 1 mile, 17 minutes for 1¼ miles, 20 minutes for 1½ miles, 24 minutes for 1¾ miles, and 28 minutes for 2 miles. The learner should be reinforced for improving performance on each subsequent day.

PRINCIPLES OF TRAINING

Fitness programs for most individuals should include resistance training and aerobic activities. Resistance training focuses on developing muscular strength and endurance. The exercise periods (sets) are relatively brief with rest between each exercise bout. Aerobic training is designed to increase cardiorespiratory endurance. The activity is sustained over a prolonged period. Principles of exercise that apply to both resistance and aerobic training are (1) frequency, (2) intensity, and (3) duration.

Frequency of exercise—Frequency of exercise refers to the number of training sessions per week. Rest periods are interspersed between training sessions to permit the body to recover.[9] For aerobic conditioning programs, the American College of Sports Medicine recommends at least three, but not more than five sessions per week.[20] For resistance training, the classical frequency is three times per week.[15] However, some advanced programs of resistance training may be as frequent as six times per week.[23]

Intensity of exercise—Intensity refers to the magnitude (percentage of one's capacity) of exercise during one exercise session. Usually the higher the intensity, the greater the benefit from the activity. In aerobic activity the faster the pace, the greater the intensity. In resistance training, the heavier the weight, the greater the intensity.[13] With individuals with disabilities, low to moderate intensity will provide these advantages: (1) less of a chance of cardiovascular problems, (2) possibly fewer injuries, and (3) a greater probability the students will continue their exercise programs after formal instruction.

Duration of exercise—Duration refers to the length of time a person exercises at a given time. Duration of exercise applies primarily to cardiorespiratory endurance development. Twenty to 60 minutes of sustained activity is recommended.[19] The duration time should include at least a 5-minute warmup period and a 5- to 10-minute cooldown period. The intensity of the aerobic activity will effect the duration of the exercise. In general, the more intense the exercise, the shorter the duration. When working with students who have disabilities it is better to begin with a shorter duration of less intense activity and gradually work toward lengthening the time and intensity of the activity.

The training principles of frequency, intensity, and duration apply to both aerobic and resistance exercise. However, there are some principles that are specific to resistance training. These include volume, repetition continuum, and maximum voluntary contraction.

□ The volume of exercise in resistance training relates to the amount of work performed during the lifting exercise.[9] The amount of work performed depends on the amount of force exerted and the distance the resistance is moved. Volume of training is determined by counting the number of repetitions a given weight is moved during each exercise set. To develop strength it is recommended that 60% of the maximum resistance a person can move be used.

The number of times the weight is moved depends on the repetition continuum selected.

□ The repetition continuum refers to the number of times a given amount of resistance can be moved. The training effect is increased as the number of times an exercise is repeated, up to a point.[4] It is recommended that exercises be repeated three to six times in a row (one set) to increase strength.[9] Once a student can repeat the exercise six times in a row with ease, the number of sets should be increased by one. As the amount of resistance is increased, the number of repetitions is decreased, and then gradually increased.

□ Maximum voluntary contraction is the ability to use (recruit) as many muscle fibers as possible to develop force. As a muscle begins to tire, more muscle

FIGURE 15-6. A high ropes course provides a physical challenge and an opportunity for physical development. (Courtesy Wisconsin Lions Camp, Rosholt, Wisconsin.)

fibers are recruited to move the force. The maximum voluntary contraction is the last repetition of an exercise when maximum force can be generated before the muscle fatigues. Successful training programs include at least one maximum voluntary contraction.[23] For the sedentary person the maximum voluntary contraction will occur after very few repetitions have been completed. Students with disabilities who are just beginning exercise programs should be closely monitored to prevent injuries that may occur because of muscle fatigue.

DEVELOPING TRAINING PROGRAMS

The American Academy of Pediatrics[2] and the National Strength Conditioning Association[16] agree that strength training is permissible for children under the age of puberty only when expert supervision is provided.

Fitness instruction for students with disablities should be conducted in conformance with the individual education program (IEP). This means that there should be measurable, observable objectives and present levels of educational performance for each student when the activity program is conducted. To accommodate the changing demands of the ability level of each learner, the following principles are suggested:

□ *Individual differences:* Every student's IEP should be based on specific assessment data, which indicate the unique needs for alleviating deficits in prerequisites for self-sufficient living.

□ *Overload/shaping principle:* Increases in strength and endurance result from small increments of workload greater than present ability. Overload can be achieved in the following ways:
1. Increase the number of repetitions or sets.
2. Increase the distance covered.
3. Increase the speed with which the exercise is executed.
4. Increase the number of minutes of continuous effort.
5. Decrease the rest interval between active sessions.
6. Any combination of the above.

□ *Maintenance or development of physical fitness:* Training sessions can be used to maintain or develop physical fitness. The data on the frequency of the training will indicate whether the training results maintain or develop physical fitness levels.

□ *Physical fitness for a purpose:* Values gained from exercises should be relevant to development of functional skills of health components. Exercises are highly specific; they need to be done at intensity levels commensurate with the ability of the student.

□ *Active/voluntary movement:* Benefits are greatest when the exercise is active (done by the student) rather than passive (done by the therapist or teacher). When the student performs the activity, it is possible to provide behavioral measurement and apply learning principles from research and demonstration.

□ *Recovery/cool-down:* Students with dyspnea (breathlessness, breathing difficulty) should not lie or sit down immediately after high-intensity exercise. This tends to subvert return of blood to the heart and cause dizziness. Cool-down should entail continued slow walking or mild activity.

□ *Warm-up:* A few minutes of warm-up exercises using movements specific to training should precede high-intensity exercise sessions or competitive games. Warm-up is particularly important for persons with chronic respiratory problems or cardiovascular conditions. Warm-ups should emphasize stretching exercises that facilitate range of motion (flexibility) rather than ballistic (rhythmic bouncing) exercises.

□ *Contraindications:* Physical educators should know what exercises or activities are contraindicated for each individual. This information may be obtained from medical records.

□ *Task analysis of activity:* Physical educators should know how to task analyze exercises to determine which specific muscles should be exercise targets. A principle often used in adapting exercises is *leverage;* the shorter the lever, the easier the exercise. For instance, straight leg lifts from a supine position to develop or assess abdominal strength are difficult since the body (as a lever) is in its longest position. By doing bent-knee leg lifts, the body lever is shortened and the exercise is made easier.

□ *Sequence of activity:* Reduction of lever length usually makes a task less difficult and enables sequencing in activities where the body or its parts move against gravity from a prone position. For instance, bending at the waist or knees makes a push-up less difficult.

MODIFICATION OF THE PHYSICAL FITNESS TRAINING SYSTEM

Circuit and interval training systems can be modified to accommodate persons with disabilities. All students need to participate in activities that are commensurate with their needs with respect to work loads. However, specific types of disabilities require special adaptations to adequately meet unique physical activity needs. General disabilities that need special accommodation

FIGURE 15-7. A student develops age-appropriate sport skills. (Courtesy Adapted Physical Education Department, Jefferson Parish Public School System, Louisiana.)

are those of sensory impairment, physical impairment, and intellectual impairment.

Accommodation of Individual Differences in Interval Training

There are at least four ways that activity can be modified to accommodate the ability level of each student with a disability in interval training. First, the number of repetitions can be modified. The fewer the number of repetitions the less difficult the activity. Second, the nature of the activity can be modified. For instance, if the activity requires that a weight be lifted overhead, the required distance of the upward lift can be reduced. Rather than starting with a lift over the head with arms sraight, a series of intermediate steps can be built into the task (i.e., raise the weight to the level of the chin, nose, forehead, above the head, and finally, straighten the arms above the head.) The greater the upward distance of the lift, the more difficult the activity. Third, the time that it takes to complete a set of repetitions can be lengthened. The shorter the time interval for completing the work the more difficult the

exercise task. Fourth, the number of sets of repetitions can be modified. Greater numbers of sets are associated with more intense and difficult training regimens. The number of sets can be decreased to accommodate the individual's present level of ability. Applying these principles to interval training for persons with disabilities will permit participation in and benefit from these exercise routines.

Accommodating Individual Differences in Circuit Training

Accommodation for individual differences for most students with disabilities in circuit training can be made through reduction of intensity and work load. However, it is necessary to identify the problems of each individual child who will participate in a specific exercise program. To meet the individual physical needs of each child in circuit training, the following modifications can be made.

1. Develop a wide variety of activity levels, the lower of which can accommodate most children with disabilities.

2. Assign students with disabilties to only those stations in the circuit that meet their assessed needs.

3. Modify the nature of the activity at each station so that each student can participate at the appropriate ability level.

4. Provide peer assistance, if available, and special instructions for use of specific apparatus or equipment.

Accommodating for Specific Types of Disabilities

Students with varying types of disabilities may need specific accommodation in circuit training exercises. Visually impaired and deaf students need assistance with comunication systems that provide them with instructional information, whereas students with physical disabilities need accommodation for impaired motor functioning. Students who are mentally retarded or have a specific learning disability, on the other hand, may need assistance in comprehending the task. Suggestions for accommodating visually and physically disabled students are listed below.

Visual Disabilities

Students with visual impairments need confidence to cope with training programs. They may need for the exercise environment to be modified or they may need aid from others to participate in training activities. Some environmental aids and supplemental assistance that may enable the student with a visual disability to benefit from circuit training are listed below.

1. Provide boundaries that define the general exercise area to facilitate mobility of the student within the exercise area.

2. Use boundaries to define the location of each specific exercise station.

3. Use sighted peers, if available, to assist the student with visual disabilities move from station to station and comprehend each task.

4. Provide a complete explanation of the way to use specific apparatus or equipment.

5. Arrange the exercise area the same way every time so that the student with visual disabilities will be able to move through a familiar environment.

6. Arrange for enlarged type or braille descriptions of the activity at each session.

7. Actually move the student through the exercise several times.

8. Plan the circuit so that movement to different areas for exercise is minimized.

FIGURE 15-8. A student performs warm-up activities during the physical fitness component of a daily lesson. (Courtesy Dallas Independent School District.)

9. Provide initial reference points that indicate where the student starts performance in the circuit.

10. Use brightly colored objects as boundaries to assist students with residual vision.

Physical Disabilities

Students with physical disabilities may need accommodations to physically move through the environment and to manipulate exercise equipment. Some accommodations to enable these individuals to participate in circuit training follow.

1. Select activities that involve functional body parts (e.g., if the legs are impaired, prescribe activities for the arms).

2. If an individual has limited function of the wrists and fingers, place pads on the forearms and select activities that will enable the individual to move the weights with the padded forearms.

3. If necessary, attach weights to the body or attach a body part to a piece of equipment with velcro straps (e.g., if the student has difficulty keeping feet in bicycle stirrups, attach feet to pedals with velcro straps).

4. Establish an exercise environment that is accessible for students in wheelchairs.

SELECTED FITNESS PROBLEMS

As mentioned earlier in this chapter, the problems of underdevelopment and low physical vitality are closely associated with a great number of organic, mental, physiological, and emotional problems discussed throughout this book. However, two major problem areas transcend the others—namely, malnutrition and overweight.

Malnutrition

The term *malnutrition* means poor nutrition, whether there is an excess or a lack of nutrients to the body. In either instance the malnourished individual has relatively poor physical fitness and other serious disadvantages.

It is important that the cause of physical underdevelopment be identified. One cause of physical underdevelopment may be a lack of physical activity, which, consequently, does not provide opportunity for the body to develop its potential. However, some children are physically underdeveloped partially because of undernutrition. When a person's body weight is more than 10% below the ideal weight indicated by standard age and weight tables, undernutrition may be a cause. Tension, anxiety, depression, and other emotional factors may restrict a person's appetite, causing insufficient caloric intake and weight loss. The most severe emotional disturbances causing insufficient calorie intake and weight loss are anorexia nervosa and/or bulimia. Impairment in physical development may also ensue. In culturally deprived areas, common in the urban inner city, children may lack proper nutrition as a result of insufficient food resulting from poverty or use of money for other priorities (e.g., drugs), idiosyncrasy, or loss of appetite caused by some organic problem. Proper nutrition and exercise go hand in hand in growing children. One without the other may cause lack of optimum physical development. The role of the physical educator in dealing with the underweight person is to help establish sound living habits with particular emphasis paid to proper diet, rest, and relaxation. The student should be encouraged to keep a 3-day food intake diary, after which, with the help of the teacher, a daily average of calories consumed is computed. After determining the average number of calories taken in, the student is encouraged to increase the daily intake by eating extra meals that are both nutritious and high in calories. The physical educator must be sensitive to the unique problems of the homeless child, the child living in poverty, and the nutritionally abused child. A change in calorie intake is not a simple matter of the child understanding the relationship between calorie intake and health. Often the child is a victim, unable to control the powerful forces around him/her. The physical educator may take the lead in arranging for the child to have a federally or state-subsidized free breakfast or free lunch. This may be the only meal the child eats during the day. In addition, the physical educator may use fresh fruit as a reward, always seeking an opportunity to allow the hungry child to earn the reward.

Overweight

Many persons in the United States are overweight. Obesity, particularly in adults, is considered one of the great current medical problems because of its relation to cardiovascular and other diseases. The frequency of overweight among patients with angina pectoris, coronary insufficiency, hypertension, and coronary occlusions is considerable.

Overweight may be defined as any excess of 10% or more above the ideal weight for a person, and obesity is any excess of 20% or more above the ideal weight. Obesity constitutes pathological overweight that requires correction. Several factors must be considered in determining whether a person is overweight. Among these are gender, weight, height, age, general body build, bone size, muscular development, and accumulations of subcutaneous fat.

In the past there has not been sufficient attention given to the diagnosis of overweight among many children in our society. The incidence of overweight among children in our schools has been estimated at 10% or more—a rate of such significance that attention to prevention and remediation should be provided by public school doctors, nurses, and health and physical educators.

Overweight persons have a greater tendency to contract diseases of the heart, circulatory system, kidneys, and pancreas. They also have a predisposition to structural foot and joint conditions because of their excess weight and lack of motor skill to accommodate the weight.

FIGURE 15-9. An athlete competes in a doubles tennis competition. (Courtesy Texas Special Olympics.)

The basic reason for overweight is that the body's food and calorie consumption is greater than the physical activity or energy expended to utilize them. Consequently, the excess energy food is stored in the body as fat, leading to overweight. In many instances overeating is a matter of habit. Thus the body is continually in the process of acquiring more calories than are needed to maintain a normal weight.

Overweight and obesity have many causes. Among them are (1) caloric imbalance from eating incorrectly in relationship to energy expended in the form of activity; (2) dysfunction of the endocrine glands, particularly the pituitary and the thyroid, which regulate fat distribution in the body; and (3) emotional disturbance.

There is impressive evidence that obesity in adults has its origin in childhood habits. There seems to be a substantial number of overweight adults whose difficulty in controlling their appetite stems from childhood. The social environment may have some influence on obesity. In the preschool years, thinness rather than obesity is the general developmental characteristic of children. However, during the early school years and up to early adolescence, children seem susceptible to excess fat deposition.

A belief prevalent among some authorities is that a great portion of obesity is caused by emotional problems. They theorize that children at the age of 7 years are particularly susceptible to obesity from overeating in order to compensate for being unhappy and lonely. Evidently eating may give comfort to children. This particular period is significant because it is when children are transferring close emotional ties from the family to peer relationships. In the event that children do not successfully establish close friendships with other children, they feel alone. Therefore a compensatory mechanism of adjustment is eating, which gives comfort. Eating also may be used as a comfort when children have trouble at home or at school.

Adverse effects of obesity

Obese children, in many instances, exhibit immature social and emotional characteristics. It is not uncommon for obese children to dislike the games played by their peers, for obesity handicaps them in being adept at the games in which their peers are adequate. These children are often clumsy and slow, objects of many stereotyped jokes, and incapable of holding a secure social position among other children. Consequently, they may become oversensitive and unable to defend themselves and thus may withdraw from healthy play and exercise. This withdrawal from activity decreases the energy expenditure needed to maintain the balance that combats obesity. Therefore in many instances obesity leads to sedentary habits. It is often difficult to encourage these children to participate in forms of exercise that permit great expenditure of energy.

Obesity may be an important factor as children form ideas about themselves as persons and about how they think they appear to others. The ideas that they have about themselves will be influenced by their own discoveries, by what others say about them, and by the attitudes shown toward them. If the children find that their appearance elicits hostility, disrespect, or negative attention from parents and peers, these feelings may affect their self-concept. Traits described by their parents and peers may affect their inner feelings and may be manifested in their behavior, for children often assess their worth in terms of their relationships with peers, parents, and other authority figures.

When children pass from the child-centered atmosphere of the home into the competitive activities of the early school years, social stresses are encountered. They must demonstrate physical abilities, courage, manipulative skill, and social adeptness in direct comparison with other children of their age. The penalties for failure are humiliation, ridicule, and rejection from the group. Obesity places a tremendous social and emotional handicap on children. Therefore educators should give these children all possible assistance and guidance in alleviating or adjusting to obesity.

Measurement of obesity

There are a number of ways to determine whether an individual is obese. The simplest way is to look at a person to see if an overweight condition exists. Another simple method is to compare one's weight with a height and weight table. If this technique is used, allowances must be made for frame differences (e.g., small, medium, or large body frame).[12] More sophisticated ways of measuring weight include anthropometric data, underwater weighing of volume displacement, radiographic analysis, potassium-40 analysis, isotropic dilution, ultrasound techniques, computerized tomography, and nuclear magnetic resins. However, these methods are difficult to adapt to a school setting. One technique that is extensively used by physical educators is measurement of skin fold thickness to determine existing percentages of body fat.[12]

Skin fold measurement provides a simple and accurate method of assessing quantitatively the fat content of the human body. The skin fold caliper is applied to locations on the body where a fold of skin and subcutaneous fat can be lifted between the thumb and the forefinger so that it is held free of the muscular and bony structure. The skin fold caliper has become an evaluation tool for universal comparison of fat fold measurements. The accepted national recommendation is to have a caliper designed so as to exert a pressure of 10 grams per millimeter on the caliper face. The surface area to be measured should be in the neighborhood of 20 to 40 millimeters. The recommended method is to pinch a full fold of skin and subcutaneous tissue between the thumb and forefinger, at about 1 centimeter from the site on which the caliper is to be placed, and then to pull the fold away from the underlying muscle. The calipers are then applied to the fold about 1 centimeter below the fingers so that the pressure on the fold at the point measured is exerted by the faces of the calipers and not by the fingers. The handle of the caliper is then released and a recording is made to the nearest 0.5 millimeter. The recording should be made 2 or 3 seconds after the caliper pressure is applied.

Although the skin fold at the triceps site has been thought by many authorities to adequately represent total body fat, it is advisable, for the greatest accuracy, to take measurements at several body sites. It is common practice to use four sites to study body content of 13- to 34-year-old persons: the biceps, triceps, subscapular, and suprailiac areas (see Table 15-3). A method of taking skin fold measurements is as follows:

1. The subject is seated.
2. Only measurements of the right side are taken.
3. The biceps area is measured over the midpoint of the muscle while the forearm is resting on the subject's thigh.
4. The triceps area is measured at a point half the distance between the olecranon and acromion process while the arm is hanging down.
5. The subscapular region can be measured just below and to the lateral side of the inferior angle of the scapula.
6. The suprailiac region can be measured just above the iliac crest at the midaxillary line.

Formulas can be used to determine ideal body weight, which serves as the basis for determining obesity. Katch and McArdle[12] list the following formula for determining desirable body weight:

$$\frac{\text{lean body weight}}{1 - \text{desired percent body fat}}$$

Once the ideal body weight is established, programming can be monitored based on how close one's weight comes to the ideal weight.

Programming for the obese child

Since overweight children often cannot perform the activities of the physical education program efficiently, it is not uncommon for them to dislike many of these activities. As a result of their inability to participate in the program, they are often the objects of practical jokes and disparaging remarks made by other children. In such an environment obese and overweight boys and girls become unhappy and ashamed and often withdraw from the activity to circumvent emotional involvement with the group. The physical educator should attempt to create an environment that will enable the obese child to have successful experiences in the class, thus minimizing situations that could degrade the child's position as a person of worth. The physical educator is also challenged with regard to developing the attitudes of the nondisabled majority. Consequently, proposing to the class the acceptance of children who are different is an important and worthwhile goal of the physical educator.

Conduction of a weight control program

The conduction of a weight control program should follow the basic procedures according to the instructional process of the Education of the Handicapped Act. First, there must be a goal—a desirable body weight that the individual is to achieve. Next, the present level should portray the weight of the person at the present. Third, short-term instructional objectives that lead from the present weight to the eventual goal must be developed. For instance, if the present body weight is 100 pounds and the desirable body weight is 90 pounds, then the series of short-term objectives could be in 1- or 2-pound increments. The weight loss goal will be reached most quickly if diet control is practiced while the exercise program is conducted. Appropriate goal setting will contribute not only to immediate weight loss, but also to changes in lifelong diet and exercise habits.

The use of behavioral management techniques contribute to success in weight control programs by controlling the positive influences and minimizing the negative variables. Some of the positive aspects of behavior management that will strengthen weight control behaviors are (1) encouragement by the instructor, (2) a safe environment that keeps the student free from injury, (3) a variety of activities to reduce boredom, (4) a regularly scheduled routine, (5) a compatible, supportive social group, (6) feedback about progress toward short-term objectives that have been set, and (7) social reinforcement when weight losses occur. Punishing features that should be minimized are (1) poor program advice, (2) inconvenient time and place, (3) muscle soreness and/or injury, (4) lack of progress, and (5) disapproval of participation in the program by peers and family. Table 15-2 portrays these variables.

There can be no one program for the remediation of children who are overweight. It is necessary that the true cause of the problem be found. When the cause of overweight or obesity is known, there are several avenues available for treatment. Some rules to be applied for successful weight control are

1. Know your desirable weight.
2. Count calories.
3. Try to calculate the energy expenditure through controlled workouts.
4. Do not cut out the food you like, cut down on the amounts you eat.
5. Seek medical treatment in the case of a glandular dysfunction.
6. Seek counseling when emotional causes are at the root of the problem.
7. Seek counseling on the consequences of obesity to the total personality.
8. Disrupt sedentary ways of living.

Obese or overweight students should be guided into activities that can be safely performed and successfully achieved. This will tend to encourage them to participate in more vigorous activities. Some of the activities that can be used to combat obesity are general conditioning exercises, jogging, dancing, rhythmical activities, swimming, and sports and games. Much can be done for these children with personal individual guidance, encouragement, and selection of the proper developmental experiences.

Weekly weigh-ins in which a certain number of pounds is scheduled to be lost in a given week provide program incentives. Sustained reduction may afford opportunities for establishing permanent patterns for ex-

---

TABLE 15-2

Behavior management techniques to control when conducting a weight control program

Program punishers	Program reinforcers
Poor program advice	Adequate program advice
Inappropriate schedule for activity	Convenient and regular routine
Musculoskeletal injury	Care of self and free from injury
Lack of progress in program	Measureable progress
Peer disapproval	Social approval

TABLE 15-3

Measurements required to determine total skin fold thickness at four skin fold sites (biceps, triceps, subscapular, and suprailiac)

Body build	Skin fold measurement (mm)			
	Men	Women	Boys	Girls
Thin				
Mean	24.0	31.2	22.4	33.3
Standard deviation	7.1	6.3	5.3	9.5
Intermediate				
Mean	34.7	39.9	29.7	36.2
Standard deviation	15.7	10.0	7.6	8.8
Plump and obese				
Mean	57.2	66.0	43.2	49.0
Standard deviation	21.4	22.7	13.2	13.6

Modified from Durnin JVGA, Rahaman MM: Br J Nutr 21:681-689, 1967.

ercise and eating. The value of the weigh-in is that it projects a precise goal for the student to achieve each week. Furthermore, the exercise program in which the student engages should be progressive. Exercises based on calculated energy expenditures are initiated with slight progression ensured in the program with each successive day of attendance. Suggested activities are walking, jogging, bicycle riding, rope jumping, swimming, stair and hill climbing, and stepping up on and down from a bench.

Spot reducing

Loss of weight results in a decrease in the amount of stored adipose tissue; however, which stores of adipose tissue will decrease cannot be predicted. Therefore it really is impossible to spot reduce.

Educational versus medical diets

If a physician indicates that there is a pathological condition that is associated with a weight condition, then a medically prescribed diet and exercise program should be provided by the physician. When no medical pathological condition exists and the obesity can be treated by a change in caloric intake and by raising energy expenditure, then an educationally prepared prescription can be conducted. The educational prescription involves changing behaviors that enable the individual to conform to lifestyle patterns that may be maintained over a long period. According to Steiner,[21] of the many persons who make rapid and large weight losses, only 10% of them achieve lifetime weight control. Fad diets should be discouraged because of their potential threat to nutritional balance and their short-lived results.

IMPLICATIONS FOR PHYSICAL EDUCATION

Physical education has emerged with new importance as awareness of the deleterious effect of inactivity on the sedentary adult population has increased. Through the efforts of many disciplines, the public is beginning to realize that proper exercise can be a deterrent to many characteristics of premature physiological aging as well as to their concomitant diseases.

Research and studies have resulted in new concepts about the type of physical fitness activities best suited for adults. Continuity of well-planned activities can serve as a preventive conditioner. Isotonic exercise is preferable to isometric exercise, particularly for persons with a history of cardiovascular disease. Isometric exercise may result in irregular heartbeats, premature ventricular contractions, and abnormally fast heartbeats in heart disease patients.

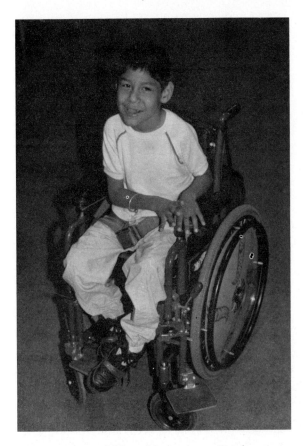

FIGURE 15-10. A child participates in creative dance activities. (Courtesy Dallas Independent School District.)

A multidisciplinary approach has resulted from medicine's concern for premature cardiovascular disease and the positive effects of proper exercise. The physician, physical educator, exercise physiologist, sport nutritionist, and many other professionals are lending their skills to help solve the problem of lack of physical fitness among adults. With the implementation of many medically oriented adult physical education programs, there is an increased need for trained teachers of adapted physical education who understand the problems and needs of the adult population. Establishing individual physical education programs for adults is one of the greatest challenges of our times.

SUMMARY

There are three purposes of physical and motor fitness: (1) to promote and maintain health, (2) to develop prerequisites for maximum performance of daily living

Behavioral Statements for Development of Physical and Motor Fitness

Many physical and motor fitness tasks are measurable. Usually, if measure can be incorporated into a tasks, performance difficulty can be prescribed for the individual learner. Below are statements that involve physical and motor tasks requiring specifications of measurement to be ascribed to the tasks. Many handicapped children will be able to participate in these tasks at their ability level if objectives are sequenced.

1. Walk a specified distance at a heart rate of 120 beats per minute.
2. Jog and walk alternately 50 steps for a specified distance.
3. Run in place lifting the foot a specified distance from the floor a specified number of times for a specified period of time.
4. Run in place 100 steps in a specified amount of time.
5. Run a specified distance in a specified period of time.
6. Perform a modified push-up a specified number of times.
7. Perform a modified chin-up a specified number of times.
8. Climb a rope a specified distance in a specified amount of time.
9. Perform knee dips to a specified amount of flexion in the knee a specified number of repetitions.
10. Perform toe raises with a specified amount of weight a specified number of repetitions.
11. Perform prone lift of a specified weight a specified number of repetitions.
12. Perform a sit-up (modified if necessary) a specified number of repetitions; sit-up difficulty can be modified by performance on an incline where gravity assists with the sit-up.
13. Lift a ball of specified weight with the soles of the feet a specified number of times.
14. Perform a specified number of dips on the parallel bars (lower and raise the body by straightening and bending the arms) with a specified amount of weight attached to a belt. If one dip cannot be done reduce the range of motion of the dip.
15. Perform arm curls with a specified weight and a specified number of repetitions.
16. Perform a prone arch (hands under the hips in prone position) in which the hands and feet are moved a specified distance from one another.
17. Curl the toes and pick up a specified number of pencils or sticks of the same size; move them a specified distance to a target of a specified size over a specified time frame.
18. Perform a wrist roll in which a rope of specified length has a weight of specified pounds attached to it a specified number of repetitions over a specified time frame.
19. Perform toe curls with a towel with the heels flat on the floor; bunch up the towel under the feet and put a weight of a specified number of pounds on the towel a specified distance from the toes.
20. Perform a wrist curl in which the wrist is over the edge of a table or a chair, then bend and straighten the wrist holding a weight of a specified amount a specified number of repetitions.
21. Jump and reach a specified height.
22. Throw a medicine ball of specified weight from a sitting position a specified distance.
23. Perform back extensions from a prone position, so the low back reaches a specified height a specified number of repetitions over a specified amount of time.
24. From a standing position with the knees straight, bend forward at the hips and measure the distance the tips of the fingers are from the floor. If the person can touch the floor, place a book or object on the floor and measure the distance the fingers are below the surface of the object on which the student is standing.
25. Run a specified distance over a specified period of time.
26. Run around a hoop 4 feet in diameter a specified number of times over a specified time frame.
27. Leap over a rope placed at a specified height.
28. Leap over two lines on the floor that are a specified distance apart.
29. Step up and then down on a bench of a specified height a specified number of repetitions over a specified time frame.
30. Run in a figure 8 fashion around a specified number of cones set a specified distance apart a specified number of times during a specified time frame.
31. Perform a shuttle run in which the parallel lines are a specified distance apart a specified number of trips in a specified amount of time.
32. Jump with two feet successively in each of four quadrants formed by two lines crossing at right angles a specified number of repetitions over a specified time frame.

Behavioral Statements for Development of Physical and Motor Fitness—cont'd

33. Perform a specified number of squat thrusts (from a stand, bend the knees and place the hands on the floor, throw the legs back, return the legs to the squat position, stand erect and repeat) during a specified time frame.
34. Run in place so one foot strikes the floor a specified number of times over a specified time frame.
35. Stand on one foot for a specified number of seconds.
36. Stand on sticks of specified width for a specified number of seconds
37. Walk on a balance beam of specified width for a specified number of steps.
38. Walk backward on a balance beam of specified width for a specified number of steps.
39. Balance a bean bag on the head and walk a specified distance.
40. Balance a bean bag on the head and hop a specified number of times over a specified distance.
41. Run, skip, leap, and gallop specified distances over time with a bean bag on the head.
42. Stand on stilts that are a specified distance above the ground a specified period of time.
43. Walk on stilts, which are a specified distance above the ground, a specified distance in a specified period of time.
44. Walk backwards on stilts, which are a specified distance above the ground, a specified distance over a specified time.
45. Stand on one foot and on a stick/beam of specified width, raise the free leg to the rear a specified height and hold for a specified amount of time.
46. From a kneeling position on one knee and with one hand on a beam of known width, lower the head a specified distance from the beam and raise the leg a specified distance from the floor.
47. Walk with an eraser on the top of the head on a beam of specified width a specified distance without letting the eraser fall off the head.
48. Using stilts, walk a specified distance in a specified time frame and stay within a pathway of a specified width.
49. Balance on one foot and bring the toe of the other foot to a point a specified distance from the forehead.
50. On a beam of specified width and length perform the following tasks: (a) Hold the left foot at toes with the right hand behind the right knee, move the left knee a specified distance from the beam and return. Perform the task a specified number of consecutive times. (b) Raise the left leg forward with the knee straight, bend the right knee and lower the seat a specified distance from the beam, and return to a stand.
51. From a standing position on one or two feet move the left knee a specified distance from the floor without losing balance. Grasp the left foot with the right hand behind the right leg. Repeat on opposite side a specified number of times.
52. Run the 50-yard dash in a specified amount of time.

skills, and (3) to develop prerequisites for leisure and sport skills. Each person possesses a unique composition of physical and motor abilities and therefore should be assessed and provided with an individual physical and motor fitness program. Activity programs should be constructed so that the physical and motor fitness tasks can be adapted to the ability level of each learner. Interval training programs are desirable for the development of endurance, while circuit training can be used to develop a wide range of performance levels. Fitness training should include both resistance training and aerobic activities. Principles of exercise that should be controlled include frequency, intensity, duration, volume of exercise, repetition continuum, and maximum voluntary contraction. Physical and motor fitness is important for all persons. Although collec-

tively persons with the same disability may be similar, each student with a disability needs an individualized physical fitness program.

Physical and motor fitness programs are beneficial as deterrents to obesity. Weight control is a product of energy expenditure and balanced caloric intake. Therefore the amount of exercise is an important factor in the control of obesity. Behavior management techniques may assist control of weight.

REVIEW QUESTIONS

1. Describe two types of physical fitness programs.
2. What are the causes of low physical fitness?
3. How would one determine a unique physical fitness need for an individual for functional skill?
4. What are the principles for conducting a physical fitness program for students with disabilities?

5. What are some behavioral management principles that can be applied to conduction of a weight control program?
6. Construct an interval training program.
7. Evaluate and design a program for persons who are overweight.

STUDENT ACTIVITIES

1. Administer a physical fitness test to determine the strengths and weaknesses of a child with a disability, another student, or yourself. Have a test for each of the physical and motor fitness abilities.
2. Select a person with poor physical fitness and determine the activities that might assist in raising the level of fitness.
3. Design an interval training program for yourself or a friend.
4. Write a paper on the causes of and procedures for correcting overweight and underweight.
5. Develop a slide presentation or videotape that promotes the value and need for physical fitness programs for individuals with disabilities.
6. Design and implement a weight reduction program of exercise and diet that incorporates behavior management principles.
7. Discuss the differences between a medical and an educationally prescribed weight reduction program for students with disabilities.

REFERENCES

1. Allen G: *Physical fitness of American youth,* press release to Washington Post, Washington, DC, 1987, President's Council on Physical Fitness.
2. American Academy of Pediatrics: Weight training and weight lifting: information for the pediatrician, *Phys Sportsmed* 11:157-161, 1983.
3. American Association of Health, Physical Education, and Recreation: *Special fitness test manual for the mentally retarded,* Washington, DC, 1968, The Association.
4. Bar-Or O: Trainability of physical fitness measures, *Phys Sportsmed* 17:70-82, 1989.
5. Brooks CM: Adult participation in physical activities requiring moderate tohigh levels of energy expenditure, *Phys Sportsmed* 15:119-132, 1987.
6. Cook TC, Laporte RE, Washburn RA: Chronic low level physical activity as a determinant of high density lipoprotein cholesterol and subfractions, *Sport Exer* 18:653-657, 1990.
7. Evans IM, Meyer L: *An educative approach to behavior problems,* Baltimore, 1985, Paul H Brookes Publishing.
8. Falls H, Baylor A, Dishman R: Essentials of fitness, New York, 1980, WB Saunders.
9. Fleck SJ, Kraemer WJ: Resistance training: basic principles, *Phys Sportsmed* 16:160-171, 1988.
10. Folio MR, Fewell R: *Peabody developmental motor scales and activity cards,* Allen, Tex, 1983, DLM Teaching Resources.
11. Humphrey JH: *An overview of childhood fitness,* Springfield, Ill, 1991, Charles C Thomas Publishers.
12. Katch FI, McArdle WS: *Nutrition, weight control and exercise, ed 2,* Philadelphia, 1983, Lea & Febiger.
13. Kraemer WJ, Fleck SJ: Resistance training: exercise prescription, *Phys Sportsmed* 16:69-81, 1988.
14. Makrides L, Heigenhauser JF, Jones NL: High intensity endurance training in 20 to 30 and 60 to 70 year old healthy men, *Appl Physio* 57:362-370, 1989.
15. McDonagh MJ, Davies CT: Adaptive response of mammalian skeletal muscles to exercise with high loads, *Eur Appl Physio* 52: 139-155, 1984.
16. National Strength and Conditioning Association: Position statement on prepubescent strength training, *Natl Strength Condit* 7:27-31, 1985.
17. Pagenoff SA: The use of aquatics with cerebral palsied adolescents, *Am J Occup Ther* 38:469-473, 1984.
18. Sheehan G: On-the job training, *Phys Sportsmed* 15:73, 1987.
19. Sherrill C: *Adapted physical education and recreation, ed 3,* Dubuque, Iowa, 1986, Wm C Brown Publishers.
20. Sparling PB, Tinklepaugh MP: *A fitness primer: A guide to exercise and diet for enhanced health,* Dubuque, Iowa, 1991, Kendall/Hunt Publishing.
21. Steiner MM: *Clinical approach to endocrine problems in childhood,* St Louis, 1970, Mosby–Year Book.
22. Stott DH, Henderson SE, Moyes FA: The Henderson revision of the Stotts test of motor impairment: a comprehensive approach to assessment, *Am J Ment Defic* 3:204-216, 1986.
23. Tesch PA, Colliander EB, Kaiser P: Metabolism during intensity heavy-resistance exercise, *Eur Appl Physio* 55:362-366, 1986.
24. Ulrich D: *Test of gross motor development,* Austin, Tex, 1985, PRO-ED.
25. Virgiollio SJ, Berenson GS: A comprehensive fitness intervention model for elementary schools, *J Health Phys Educ Rec Dance* 59:19-25, 1988.
26. Wessel JA: *I can primary skills,* Northbrook, Ill, 1976, Hubbard Scientific.
27. Winnick J, Short F: *Physical fitness testing for the disabled: project UNIQUE,* Champaign, Ill, 1985, Human Kinetics Publishers.

SUGGESTED READINGS

Eichstaedt CB, Kalakian LH: *Developmental/adapted physical education,* New York, 1987, Macmillan Publishing.

Humphrey JH: *An overview of childhood fitness,* Springfield, Ill, 1991, Charles C Thomas Publishers.

Katch FI, McArdle WD: *Nutrition, weight control, and exercise, ed 2,* Philadelphia, 1983, Lea & Febiger.

Sparling PB, Tinklpaugh MP: *A fitness primer: a guide to exercise and diet for enhanced health,* Dubuque, Iowa, 1991, Kendall/Hunt Publishing.

Winnick J, Short F: *Physical fitness testing for the disabled: project UNIQUE,* Champaign, Ill, 1985, Human Kinetics Publishers.

16

OBJECTIVES

Explain the nature of AIDS and its impact on children.

Describe the characteristics of a person with anemia.

Describe the role of exercise in asthma.

List the signs and symptoms of physical abuse, sexual abuse, neglect, and psychological abuse.

Describe the role of exercise in the child with cystic fibrosis.

Explain the value of exercise for individuals with diabetes.

List emergency procedures for treating a diabetic attack brought on by hyperglycemia or hypoglycemia.

Explain the effect of diet and activity on dysmenorrhea.

Describe three exercises that can be used to reduce most dysmenorrhea.

Describe the primary characteristic of students with Prader-Willi syndrome.

List the characteristics of Tourette syndrome.

Explain the relationship between the schools and the hospital in the rehabilitation of the child with a traumatic brain injury.

Courtesy Texas Special Olympics

Other Conditions

The federal laws that have been passed in the United States during the last 15 years virtually ensure a free and appropriate public education to every individual who has a real or perceived impairment that limits major life activities. Conditions that may qualify students for adapted physical education that are included in this chapter are acquired immunodeficiency syndrome (AIDS), anemia, asthma, child abuse, childhood cancer, cystic fibrosis, diabetes, menstruation and dysmenorrhea, Prader-Willi syndrome, Tourette syndrome, and traumatic head injury.

It is believed that when children with health impairments improve their motor performance they also benefit socially and psychologically. Physical education programs that increase exercise tolerance and recreational sport skills may also improve self-care and social competence. Improved physical performance capability usually gives the student a great psychological boost. Involving students in skill and physical development activity programs often helps break a cycle of passive debilitating physical and social lifestyles.

AIDS

Acquired immunodeficiency syndrome (AIDS) has swept a deadly path. Although AIDS was not recognized as a disease entity until 1981, it is spreading throughout the world, with the most rapid spread in Africa. As of 1991, there were approximately 200,000 cases of AIDS reported in the United States and 125,000 deaths. It is clearly one of the most serious health problems that is confronting the United States. More than 1 million Americans are believed to be infected with the human immunodeficiency virus (HIV), which causes AIDS. However, most do not realize that they carry this AIDS-causing virus (HIV). It is estimated that in 1991, some 40,000 Americans learned that they were HIV positive, with higher incidences of the disease expected in future years.[46]

AIDS is a secondary immune deficiency caused by a virus[43] (HIV) and characterized by severe immune deficiency resulting in opportunistic infections and neurological lesions in individuals without prior history of immunologic abnormality. When the HIV virus enters the blood stream, it begins to attack certain white blood cells, which results in functional abnormalities of the cells related to the immune system.

Persons who test positive for HIV can be expected to live as long as 10 to 15 years relatively free of symptoms.[47] In the early 1980s it took an average of 7 years after infection with HIV for full-blown AIDS symptoms to develop. Furthermore, in the early years of the epidemic, most people with AIDS died within 6 months to 1 year after diagnosis. In the early 1990s, the average survival after the AIDS diagnosis increased to more than 2 years.

Physical and Psychological Characteristics

The onset of AIDS presents many different physical and psychological characteristics. Some of these characteristics are mild shortness of breath, weight loss, cough-

ing, persistent headache, muscular incoordination, seizures, hallucinations, progressive deterioration of the mental processes, and sensory losses including visual focusing. Thus it can be expected that students with AIDS will eventually manifest adverse physical education performance.

The AIDS-related Complex

Once a person has acquired AIDS there are several possible outcomes. Some persons may not be afflicted by adverse health conditions while others may develop AIDS-related complexes. There are several common illnesses related to AIDS. Some of these are:

1. Pneumocystis carinii pneumonia, a life-threatening form of pneumonia caused by reactivation of chronic latent infections
2. Kaposi's sarcoma, a malignant tumor that may be present in the gastrointestinal tract, lymph nodes, brain, liver, spleen, or heart
3. Mycobacterial infections that cause severe disease localized to the lung or lymph-nodes
4. Other disorders such as cytomegalovirus, herpes simplex, disseminated toxoplasmosis, and cryptococcal meningitis (see The Merck Manual for details)[46]

Transmission of AIDS

AIDS is not transmitted by casual contact or even the close, non-sexual contact that normally occurs in school or in the home. The extremely low risk of transmission by casual contact deserves emphasis. Transmission to another person requires transmission of body substances containing infected cells. HIV has been found in semen, blood, saliva, tears, and vaginal secretions. However, transmission by tears and saliva has not been reported. Most infections occur as a result of repeated and close contact with a carrier of HIV mucous membranes or contact with blood or body fluids of carriers. Sexual contacts are the major source of such infections.

A second source of infection is exchange of blood-to-blood contact between an infected person and someone else. This mode of transmission is usually through sharing of drug needles and syringes. Persons also may become infected through blood transfusions of infected blood. Within recent years techniques for screening blood supplies for the presence of HIV have been developed.

A third source of HIV infection is from mother to child. Under these conditions a child gets the AIDS virus from the mother during pregnancy, childbirth, or breastfeeding.

Physical Activity

Children with AIDS who are in the public school should have an individual education program (IEP) commensurate with their needs. The physical education teacher should consult with the student's physician to determine activity levels. Because of the progressive nature of the disease, students' levels of physical and motor performance should be assessed frequently, and their program modified to accommodate their levels of function. Surburg[58] has suggested that procedures to follow when implementing physical education programs for high school students with AIDS should include providing appropriate rest periods, monitoring pulse rate, generally increasing the intensity level of exercise, and reducing activity in hot and/or humid conditions. However, for children who are rapidly deteriorating physically, it may be realistic to develop a program that will promote maintenance of existing skills and capabilities. Each child with AIDS will be different, because of the many different forms of the illness; however, the ultimate goal should always be to include the student in as many activities as possible.

Precautions

Because of the manner in which the virus is spread, caution should be exercised if the child with AIDS becomes injured and there is blood loss. Although the risk of contracting AIDS through providing first-aid assistance is minimal, it may be decreased by following the guidelines suggested by Dunn and Fait.[20] These suggestions are:

1. Wear disposable plastic or latex gloves.
2. Clean any blood spills with soap and water and use a disinfectant afterward.
3. Put the blood-soaked item in a plastic bag and dispose of it in a place that will minimize exposure to others.
4. Wash your hands with soap and water when finished.

ANEMIA

Anemia is a condition of the blood in which there is a deficiency of hemoglobin, which delivers oxygen to body tissues. This deficiency of hemoglobin may be a result of the quantity contained in the red corpuscles of the blood or a reduction in the number of red corpuscles themselves.

The physical education teacher should be aware of the characteristics that anemic persons display. In many instances, anemic persons appear to be pale because their blood is not as red as that of typical persons. Persons with anemia tire easily because of impaired oxidation in the muscles, and they also may become short of breath. Consequently, in many instances the rate of breathing is increased. As a rule, children with anemia become fatigued more easily than do typical children, are often unable to make gains in physical strength, and are impaired in learning motor skills.

Some of the symptoms that signify anemia are an increased rate of breathing, a bluish tinge of the lips and nails (because the blood is not as red), headache, nausea, faintness, weakness, and fatigue.

Causes

There are many causes of anemia; however, the two general types are congenital and acquired. The congenital form is present at birth. An example of this form is sickle cell anemia, which is perhaps the most publicized form of anemia. The acquired form may occur at any time during one's life and persist or move into remission. Some of the specific causes of anemia are as follows:

1. Chronic post-hemorrhaging when there is prolonged moderate blood loss, such as that caused by a peptic ulcer
2. Iron deficiencies in the diet
3. Inadequate or abnormal utilization of iron in the blood
4. Decreased production of bone marrow
5. Vitamin B_{12} deficiency
6. Deficiency in folic acid, which is destroyed in long-term cooking
7. Mechanical injury or trauma that impacts on blood circulation
8. Disorders of red blood cell metabolism
9. Defective hemoglobin synthesis[46,47]

There are primary diseases that give rise to anemia as a secondary condition. Some of these diseases are malaria, septic infections, and cirrhosis. In addition, poisons such as lead, insecticides, intestinal parasites, and arsenobenzene may contribute to anemia. Diseases associated with endocrine and vitamin deficiencies such as chronic dysentery and intestinal parasites may also cause anemia.

Anemia is symptomatic of a disturbance that in many cases can be remedied. Inasmuch as there are several varieties of anemia, the method of treatment depends on the type of anemia present.

Types

There are several forms of anemia. Chlorosis, or iron deficiency anemia, is characterized by a reduced amount of hemoglobin in the corpuscles and usually occurs in young women at about the time of puberty.

Anemia can be caused by excessive hemorrhage, in which case the specific gravity of the blood is reduced because there is a greater proportion of fluid in comparison with corpuscles in the blood. Occurring less often than chlorosis, pernicious anemia is characterized by a decrease in the number of red corpuscles. It can cause changes in the nervous system, along with loss of sensation in the hands and feet. In aplastic anemia, the red bone marrow that forms blood cells is replaced by fatty marrow. This form of anemia can be caused by radiation, radioactive isotopes, and atomic fallout. Certain antibiotics also may be causative factors. One prevalent type of anemia among African-Americans is sickle cell anemia.

Sickle cell anemia

Sickle cell anemia is one of the most well-known forms of anemia. It is an inherited disorder. The sickle cell trait is carried by about 60 million people in the world, of whom 50 million live in Africa. It is estimated that over 100,000 babies are born each year with sickle cell disease.[46] Specific sites of the body that are most commonly affected by sickle cell anemia are bones (usually the hands and feet in young children), intestines, spleen, gall bladder, brain, and lungs. Chronic ankle ulcers are a recurrent problem. Episodes of severe abdominal pain with vomiting may simulate severe abdominal disorders. Such painful crises usually are associated with back and joint pain.

There is no drug therapy for sickle cell anemia. The symptoms of the disease are treated as they appear. It is suggested by Dunn and Fait[20] that those suffering from sickle cell anemia should avoid high altitudes and other situations in which there is less oxygen available.

Treatment

The various forms of anemia require different treatments. Chlorosis may be remedied by an increase in the amount of iron-bearing foods in the diet or by taking iron supplements. However, pernicious anemia requires the intramuscular injection of liver extracts. Aplastic anemia may be corrected by transplantation of bone marrow from healthy persons and by use of the male hormone testosterone, which is known to stimulate the production of cells by the bone marrow if enough red marrow is present for the hormone to act on. Vitamin B_{12} is stored in the liver and released as required for the formation of red blood cells in the bone marrow.

Another form of anemia is referred to as sports anemia. It apparently afflicts athletes with low values of

red blood cells or hemoglobin. These athletes may range from fit individuals performing daily submaximum exercise to individuals participating in prolonged severe exercise and strenuous endurance training.[7] Persons who have anemia because of a disease process have different medical needs than do athletes with sports anemia who are apparently healthy. Sports anemia in the athlete occurs as a consequence of physical activity and is only marginal.[11]

Programming for the Anemic Student

The final decision regarding the nature of physical education activities for a child with anemia should be made by medical personnel. A well-conceived and supervised physical education program can be of great value to the child who has anemia. Exercise stimulates the production of red blood cells through the increased demand for oxygen. However, to be beneficial, an activity must be planned qualitatively with regard to the specific anemic condition. It is not uncommon for children who have anemia to be retarded in the development of physical strength and endurance. The alert physical educator should be able to assist in the identification of anemia and thus refer the student to medical authorities. Undiagnosed anemia may curtail motor skill and physical development and thus may set the child apart from peers in social experiences.

For the most part, students with anemia can participate in physical activities in the regular program; however, they should be closely monitored. Appropriate activities include modified (if needed) activities and prerequisite activities such as balance, eye-hand coordination, gross body coordination, and agility, as well as physical fitness components such as strength, endurance, and flexibility. Experiences that minimize access to a ready supply of oxygen, such as underwater swimming where students may be required to hold their breath for prolonged periods, should be avoided.[20]

ASTHMA

Asthma is a chronic disorder that causes periodic breathing difficulties. It is a bronchial condition with intermittent symptoms of wheezing, chest tightness, and cough. Attacks vary greatly in severity and duration and usually require some intervention to resume normal and comfortable breathing. The attack often begins with an irritating cough. The student complains of difficulty breathing, especially during inspiration, and may describe tightness in the chest.[46] The symptoms of attack can come on rapidly, transforming the student from apparent normality to a state of severe disability within 30 minutes or less. Miller and Keane[47] have described the stages of severity of an acute attack of asthma, ranging on a four-point scale from diffuse wheezing on the less severe end and respiratory distress, lethargy, and confusion at the higher end of the scale.

Asthma affects approximately 3% of the children and adults in the United States. The incidence of asthma is slightly higher among males than females.

Exercise-induced Asthma

Exercise-induced asthma (EIA) results from excessive and prolonged exercise and affects approximately 12% of the population. Exercise-induced asthma precipitates muscular constriction of the bronchial tubes and may cause wheezing and labored breathing. The Asthma and Allergy Foundation of America[5] estimates that 60% to 90% of all asthmatics are susceptible to EIA.

EIA students should be provided with individualized programming. Their present levels of performance should be assessed to determine exercise tolerance. This can be done through behavioral assessments that measure distance over time, or it can be done through exercise tests administered by physicians.[9] To assess the individual's present level of performance, cardiovascular endurance tests can be done using treadmills, bicycle ergometers, or free running. Heart rate and breathing efficiency are usually monitored at 1-, 5-, 10-, 15-, and 20-minute intervals. In the case of the asthmatic, the physical educator may choose to limit testing time to 5 to 10 minutes and evaluate vital signs every minute.

Environmental factors related to EIA that can be controlled are (1) avoiding cold and dry environments; (2) breathing through the nose; (3) exercising below maximum effort; (4) keeping the duration of the exercise to 5-minute intervals or less, followed by rest; (5) performing a good warmup; and (6) exercising within 1 hour of the warmup.[12] In the event of an asthma attack, a person should slow the intensity of the exercise sufficiently or stop altogether.

Benefit of Exercise

Bundgaard's[9] review of the literature on the benefits of exercise on asthma indicated mixed overall results; however, the consensus is that exercise is beneficial. One study evaluated the effects of an exercise program on asthmatic children. The findings suggest that endurance training in asthmatic children with EIA can increase aerobic capacity.[36] Another study reported that a 4-day-a-week program for 6 weeks, which involved gradually increasing the running distance, resulted in

about one half of the asthmatic population tested developing EIA repeatedly.[5] However, use of an aerosol bronchodilator reversed symptoms readily. As the weeks passed, the involved runners were able to run greater distances in a given period. Thus the asthmatic condition apparently was not a deterrent to improved cardiovascular endurance performance.

Breathing Exercises

There is evidence that progressive programs designed to improve breathing patterns may be beneficial to asthmatic children. If such programs are undertaken, Sherrill[56] recommends that the following interaction take place when teaching breathing exercises: (1) provide each child with an exercise mat, a waste paper container, and a box of tissues; (2) encourage the child to blow the nose and cough up accumulated phlegm; (3) explain to the child that the exercises may initially cause some anxiety; and (4) warn the child to expect coughing and wheezing during the first few seconds of abnormal breathing.

According to Dunn and Fait,[20] children with breathing problems should begin their physical education program with breathing exercises. However, they warned that in the first few seconds of exercise, when the diaphragm is forced to do most of the work of exhaling the air, students with asthma may be expected to cough and wheeze.

Program Management

Students with asthma need to participate in a physical education program that is warm and accepting where activities and instructional environments are modified to meet their needs. Aspects of the physical education program that must be planned carefully include (1) the psychosocial environment, (2) instruction commensurate with abilities and needs, (3) modification of activities and the environment to accommodate physical limitations, and (4) appropriate activities.

Psychosocial Management

Although children with asthma may participate in normal physical education activity with their peers, under certain conditions they may be viewed as different from others during physical education activity. Because the disorder can limit their physical capabilities, children with asthma sometimes have anxieties about doing well in class. Further anxieties may result from fear of having an attack of asthma during class. A severe attack can be socially devastating to the child with asthma because it draws attention to his or her differences. Therefore it is desirable for the teacher to promote mutual respect between the youngster with asthma and the student's classmates. The physical educator who takes an active role in fostering understanding between class peers and the asthmatic child will help alleviate anxieties of the child with asthma.

Modification of Activity and the Environment

Both the nature of the activity and the instructional environment can be modified to accommodate the individual needs of children with asthma. Because children with asthma may have limited capabilities to sustain activities, frequent rest periods should be provided to accommodate the tolerance level of these students. In addition, activities that require low levels of intensity, such as golf, shuffleboard, archery, and bowling, can be included in the students' program. Also, when needed, rules of games may be modified to reduce the intensity and level of activity required of the children. For instance, in the game of softball, the distance between bases can be reduced. In addition to modification of activities, the physical educator should also be sensitive to other ways to assist the child with asthma. These may include checking for air pollution levels, which may aggravate respiratory conditions, and providing tissues for managing excess mucus.

Physical Education Instruction

Children with asthma are to have an individual physical education program that meets their unique needs. These children, because of less-than-normal stamina and ability, may need to be motivated to benefit from and enjoy activity in physical education. One of the most difficult challenges is to provide opportunities for success and yet not exceed tolerance levels of the student. Thus Dunn and Fait[20] have suggested a system of progressive overload where a sequence of activities from lesser to greater degree of difficulty is designed. They proposed a walking program that varies the degree of difficulty and intensity by increasing/decreasing the distance and speed of walking with the eventual addition of stair climbing to increase intensity. Once the sequence of activity intensity has been developed, it is possible to determine where in the sequence the student can perform comfortably and then progress from that point. Procedures used in systems of interval training (i.e., variable rest periods) and other forms of progressive overload can be applied to promote development of physical skills and performance while keeping the activity within the tolerance level of children with asthma. Movement education is an excellent approach to use to teach children because it is self-regulating and permits the inclusion of children with different levels of development and exercise tolerance. Regardless of the instructional approach, it is essential that the physical education program produce a training effect.

Activities

Inasmuch as children with asthma vary in their capabilities to participate in activity that is intense, each child's physical education program should be individualized. Clearly, many persons with asthma are world class athletes. In the 1984 Olympics, approximately 11% of the U.S. Olympians suffered from asthma or related disorders. Forty-one of these athletes won medals. Therefore assumptions should not be made about the physical capabilities of students with asthma. For the most part, children with asthma can participate in physical activity with their peers without modification of activity. However, in general, many children with asthma need special attention. Participation in activity that improves breathing is important. Thus it is suggested that exercises be provided to strengthen the chest muscles that aid the breathing process, as well as activity that develops breathing. Weight training and cardiovascular exercises, which include swimming, jogging, and cycling, may develop the chest muscles to improve breathing. Dunn and Fait[20] have described games that are designed specifically to improve breathing per se. However, these exercises would be of decreased benefit to non-affected students. Therefore, whenever possible, games and activities included in the regular physical eduation program should be modified to accommodate the special needs of children with asthma.

Medication

Many students with asthma are taking medication prescribed by a physician. One group of drugs is corticosteroids, which reduce the number of inflammatory cells in the airways. Another medication is sodium cromoglycate, which was developed for its antiallergic properties. It assists in protection against attacks by allergens and exercise. Other drugs that may be used to treat asthma are ephedrine, isoproterenol, metaproterenol, atropine, theophylline, and beta-2 agonists.[47] It may be helpful for physical educators to be knowledgeable about drug treatment to students so they can monitor asthmatic behavior while the student is participating in physical activity.

CHILD ABUSE AND NEGLECT

The physical educator must be aware of the nature of child abuse and neglect and be alert for the signs and indications. Not only does the teacher have a moral imperative to report suspected child abuse and neglect, but teachers are among a large group of professionals required by law to report suspected child abuse and neglect.

Child abuse and neglect must be considered within the context of the child's total ecosystem. Child abuse is not usually "something" done to a child by an unknown stranger. Child abusers are most often parents, siblings, other relatives, or people entrusted with the care of the child—baby sitters, child care workers, and youth group leaders, for example. Indeed, one of the most tragic issues surrounding child abuse and neglect is that the abuser is almost always someone the child trusts and/or someone upon whom the child is dependent.

Child abuse is difficult to consider within the context of a society that endorses the notion that children are the property of the parent. The courts typically have supported the notion that the best possible place for a child to be raised is with the natural parents. The efforts of professionals involved in child protection are often thwarted by the interpretation of laws that continue to support the notion that a parent "owns" his/her child and, subsequently, has the right to treat the child, the "property," as he/she sees fit. Teachers who report suspected child abuse are often dismayed to learn that an abused child is returned to the home, or place where abuse occurs, after investigation. The issue of child abuse is also difficult to address in a society that endorses corporal punishment and assumes that parents have the right to spank, slap, and in other ways physically punish their children. If a woman hits another person's child on the street, that woman would be prosecuted for assault and battery. If that same woman strikes her own child on the street, passersby are fearful to intervene. Corporal punishment as a technique for child rearing is still endorsed in some states and allowed by some school districts. It is based in folklore that suggests that to "spare the rod" is to "spoil the child."

In essence, child abuse (and any other form of abuse) is a function of lack of empowerment. An individual who feels helpless, hopeless, and unempowered may need to demonstrate control or mastery. That person may choose to abuse another to feel power. A child is often a victim of this need for power—as the child is unable to fight back.

The incidence of child abuse and neglect has escalated in this society as more and more people feel unempowered. This is a result of a number of factors, including alcohol and other drug abuse, poverty, homelessness, unemployment, inadequate parental educa-

tion, teenage pregnancy, unwanted pregnancy, and family history of abuse. Refer to Chapter 6 for a discussion of abuse as it relates to children with disabilities.

Murphy et al.[50] found that, of their sample of 206 cases of serious child abuse/neglect brought before a Boston metropolitan court judge, 50% of parents involved in persistent child abuse/neglect abused alcohol, cocaine, or heroin. The researchers found that these drug-abusing parents were much more likely to be perceived by child protective service personnel as presenting a "high risk" to their children. In addition, these parents were most likely to have a history of reports of child abuse. They did not follow court-ordered mandates regarding the care of their children and were more likely than non-drug-abusing parents to have the children permanently removed from the "home." The researchers suggested that maternal drug abuse was a more significant factor than paternal drug abuse in the abuse of children.[50]

Poverty and homelessness are also significant factors in child abuse and neglect.[35,50] Severe poverty and homelessness contribute particularly to the neglect of children. This neglect includes inadequate nutrition; lack of appropriate clothing; lack of access to appropriate medical care, including immunizations; and inability to provide a secure, safe place to grow. Growing unemployment is significantly related to increasing levels of poverty and homelessness and is a major factor in the increased incidence of abuse.

Inadequate education is a factor in child abuse and neglect, as well.[35,50] This is particularly true of young, teenage mothers who do not have the skills or knowledge to raise a baby or young child.

Child abuse also tends to be part of a vicious family cycle.[33,35] An individual who was abused as a child is more likely to be an abuser as an adult. Indeed, the abusive behavior is the only parental "model" the individual has had and, subsequently, the only parenting behavior the individual ever learned.

Types of Child Abuse and Neglect

The types of child abuse and mistreatment considered in this chapter include physical abuse, sexual abuse, physical neglect, and psychological abuse. In most cases, it is difficult to separate the different types of abuse. It is unusual, for example, for a child to be the victim of physical abuse and not also suffer from neglect and psychological abuse, as well.

Physical abuse

Physical abuse has been defind by the Children's Hospital in Columbus, Ohio as:

An injury to a child caused by a caretaker—for any reason, including injury resulting from a caretaker's reaction to an unwanted behavior. Injury includes tissue damage beyond erythema or redness from a slap to any area other than the hand or buttocks....Tissue damage includes bruises, burns, tears, punctures, fractures, rupture of organs, and disruption of functions. The use of an instrument on any part of the body is abuse. The injury may be caused by impact, penetration, heat, a caustic, a chemical, or a drug.[13]

Indicators of possible physical child abuse include[1,33-35,44,63]:

1. Affective disturbances
   a. Lower self-esteem
   b. Hopelessness
   c. Depression
   d. Non-responsiveness
   e. Flat affect
2. Soft-tissue damage (most common site—buttocks, hips)

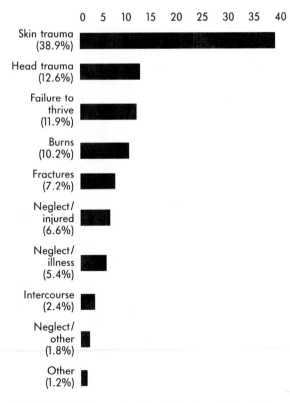

FIGURE 16-1. Reasons for hospitalization of physically abused children by percent.

a. Soft-tissue bruises, particularly multiple bruises
b. Bruises in different stages of healing (Day 1-2: red/blue; Day 3-5: blue/purple; Day 6-7: green; Day 8-10: yellow/brown)
c. Bruises that occur before a child can walk
d. Bruises with shapes of objects used for abuse (hand, knuckles [fist], belt, belt buckle, looped electrical cord, stick/whip, fly swatter, coat hanger, board or spatula, paddles, hair brush, spoon, sauce pan)
3. Burns
   a. Burns in areas child could not reach
   b. Burns shaped in patterns of objects used to inflict burn (hot plate, light bulb, curling iron, cigarette lighter, steam iron, hot knife, immersion burns)
4. Head trauma, from blows or shaking the child
   a. Cephalohematoma
   b. Intercranial soft-tissue damage
   c. Skull fracture
5. Sternum or scapula fracture
6. Transverse or spiral fractures
7. Joint dislocation
8. Abdominal trauma

In 1987, Children's Hospital in Columbus, Ohio had 852 child abuse referrals.[13] Of these children, 313 (36.7%) were physically abused; and of this 313, 80 required hospitalization. The reasons for the hospitalization of the abused children are described in Figure 16-1.

Sexual abuse

Once again, perhaps the most frightening aspect of the sexual abuse of children is the fact that the abuser is usually someone the child knows and trusts. The abuser is generally a parent, sibling, or other relative; this may include the extended family, such as the mother's boyfriend.

The signs of sexual abuse may include[23,33,34]:

1. Pregnancy
2. Sexually transmitted disease
3. Affective disturbances
   a. Deficit in age-appropriate social skills
   b. Fearfulness of adults
   c. Feelings of hopelessness and despair
   d. Preoccupation with issues of sexuality, age-inappropriate
   e. Deficit in age-appropriate play skills
4. Physical indicators
   a. Genital, urethral, or anal injuries
   b. Genital, urethral, or anal lesions

c. Genital, urethral, or anal discharge

d. Soft-tissue injuries on or around the mouth and breasts

e. Rope burns about the wrists and ankles

f. Difficulty sitting

g. Pain and irritation during urination

Physical neglect

The increased incidence of physical neglect appears to be tied to increased unemployment, poverty, and homelessness. Caregivers who may really care about their children are often forced by their circumstances into patterns of neglect.

The indicators of physical neglect include:

1. Failure to thrive
   a. Below-average height for age
   b. Underweight for age
2. Malnutrition
3. Poor physical fitness levels
4. Low energy levels
5. Complaints of hunger
6. Inappropriate clothing for weather (e.g., no socks in winter)

Some of the indicators of physical neglect include failure to provide adequate medical intervention, including regular physical examinations and regular inoculations against childhood disease.

Psychological abuse

The literature is replete with indications that a child may be as damaged by psychological abuse and emotional neglect as by any physical abuse.

Psychological abuse and maltreatment can result from acts of ommission (neglect) or commission (abuse).[25,26,28] These forms of psychological abuse and maltreatment include the acts of rejecting, threatening, terrorizing, teasing, isolating, and exploiting the child. For example, the parent who sells a child's food to buy drugs is exploiting the child. The parent who keeps a child chained in the basement is abusing the child by isolating the child. In addition, psychological abuse may include degrading and corrupting the child. For example, the parent who forces a child into prostitution is guilty of corrupting and degrading the child. In addition, forcing the child to deny his/her emotions may be psychologically abusive, as well.

Claussen and Crittendon[14] have noted that psychological damage is not usually done in one isolated incident, but in repeated ommissions or commissions. Long-term psychological deprivation, the absence of appropriate nurturing, can have long-term affects on the mental, social, and emotional health of the child.

The indicators of psychological abuse include[14,25,26,28,33]:

1. Affective disturbances
   a. Flat affect
   b. Volatility or "acting out" behaviors
   c. Inability to maintain significant relationships/friendships
   d. Inability to participate in age-appropriate play
2. Physical indicators
   a. Failure to thrive
   b. Malnutrition

The physical educator is in a unique position to see the signs and indications of child abuse. Routine physical fitness assessments may give evidence of a child who is failing to develop normally according to height and weight measurements. Observations of children at play will give clear evidence of those who have difficulty demonstrating age-appropriate play and personal-social interaction skills. In addition, the physical educator is more likely than other school personnel to see children/adolescents who are not fully clothed. A child with legs badly bruised from being kicked may be able to hide them in the regular classroom, but may have difficulty hiding the bruises if the required dress is shorts, for example. A child in a swimming suit may find it difficult to hide vaginal or anal discharge.

If a physical educator suspects abuse, it must be reported. Most school districts have policies that outline the steps the teacher should take to report it. Some referrals are made to child protective service agencies through principals, school nurses, and/or school counselors.

CHILDHOOD CANCER

Childhood cancer, a devastating childhood disease, is the major cause of death by disease in children between the years of 1 and 15.[65] Between 6000 and 7000 children under the age of 16 are diagnosed with cancer each year in the United States. The distribution of cancers of childhood are reported in Table 16-1.

Leukemia and lymphomas account for 45% of childhood cancer in children of Anglo heritage and 35% of childhood cancer in children of African heritage.[53] Central nervous system tumors and tumors of the sympathetic nervous system account for 26% of childhood cancer in children of Anglo heritage and 29% of childhood cancer in children of African heritage.[53]

Causes of Cancer

The onset of childhood cancer appears to be related to the relationship between the child's genetic/familial endowment and the child's environment. If the child has

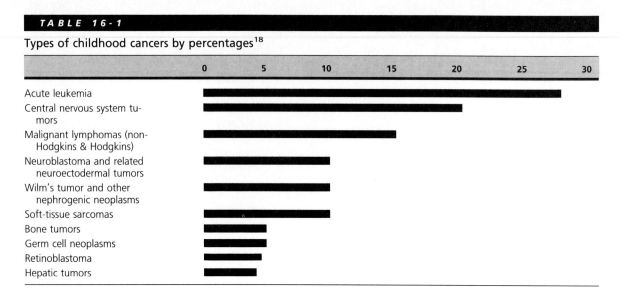

TABLE 16-1

Types of childhood cancers by percentages[18]

	0	5	10	15	20	25	30
Acute leukemia							
Central nervous system tumors							
Malignant lymphomas (non-Hodgkins & Hodgkins)							
Neuroblastoma and related neuroectodermal tumors							
Wilm's tumor and other nephrogenic neoplasms							
Soft-tissue sarcomas							
Bone tumors							
Germ cell neoplasms							
Retinoblastoma							
Hepatic tumors							

a chromosomal aberration, as is seen in Down syndrome, Trisomy G, or Klinefelter's syndrome, for example, the child is more likely than another to develop childhood cancers. In fact, children with Down syndrome are 15 times more likely than other children to develop acute lymphoblastic leukemia.[52] Chromosomal instability is also related to the development of childhood cancers, as are inherited traits for immunodeficiency. The best example of this is the child born with AIDS; that child is highly likely to develop AIDS-related cancers.

Pratt[53] suggested the following environmental factors may be related to the development of childhood cancer: ultraviolet light, ionizing radiation, asbestos, viruses, and chemical agents. Chronic Dilantin use, for example, has been found to be related to lymphoma.[49]

Description of Cancer

Cancer is a cellular malignancy whose unique characteristic is a loss of normal cell control. The body literally loses control of its cells' growth and the distribution of cells by function. Uncontrolled cell growth is common. There is also a lack of differentiation of cells. The cells tend not to assume a particular function in the body. In addition, these unique, apparently random cells have the ability to invade local, healthy tissues and metastasize (spread), destroying the healthy cells.[7]

It has been discovered that there are cellular proto-oncogenes, normal cells that have a latent capability to transform into malignant cells. In addition, there appear to be genes that suppress the tendency for a cell to become malignant. These tumor-suppressor genes are growth-regulating genes with encoding proteins that suppress the tumor formation.[16] The formation of cancerous, malignant cells in the body appears to be a function of the relationship between the two. Many malignant cells appear to be a function of a body with activated proto-oncogenes and inactive or ineffectual tumor suppressor genes.[16]

The transformation of a cell from normalcy to malignancy is thought to occur in one cell through a series of two or more steps. The development of cancer cells or malignancies are initiated by a cell that is affected by an event. This cell then becomes an "initiated" cell. If this cell is further stimulated by an event, the cell may become pre-cancerous. Any subsequent conversion or modification of this cell causes it to become malignant. Then the malignant cell "clones" itself. It appears that most tumors are "clonal" expansions of cells that grow unchecked because of acquired changes or alterations in the genes that regularly control the growth and development of cells.[61]

For example, if an infant is exposed to a large dose of radiation, one of the child's cells may become an "initiated" cell. If that cell is, subsequently, exposed to additional large doses of radiation, precancerous cell growth may be promoted. Any further modification of the cell may cause it to become malignant and then "clone" itself, metastasizing into other healthy tissues.[30]

Characteristics

The general symptoms of childhood cancer include the following[7]:

□ Fatigue
□ Weight loss
□ Cough
□ Changes in blood composition
□ Changes in bowel activity
□ Persistent pain
□ Skeletal pain
□ Fever
□ Sweating

Types of Childhood Cancers
Leukemia

Leukemia is a condition in which malignant neoplasms (tumors) have a significant negative impact on the blood-forming tissues of the body.[46] The factors that predispose a child to the develoment of leukemia are the same as those that predispose a child to the development of other forms of childhood cancer. These include the Epstein-Barr virus, human T-cell lymphotrophic virus, exposure to ionizing radiation, genetic defects (like Down syndrome), and familial disorders (Fanconi's anemia).[7]

Acute leukemia is the most common form of malignancy in childhood.[52]

There are two major forms of childhood leukemia. They are acute lymphoblastic leukemia (ALL) and acute nonlymphoblastic leukemia (ANLL). Acute lymphoblastic anemia accounts for 75% of the 2000 cases of leukemia diagnosed each year.[52] The peak incidence is between the ages of 2 and 6 years. ALL is twice as likely to affect children of Anglo heritage than children of African heritage. Like other forms of childhood cancer, it is more common in boys than girls.[52]

The signs and symptoms of ALL include[52]:

□ Anemia
□ Pallor
□ Extreme fatigue
□ Bleeding
□ Bone and joint pain
□ Enlargement of the spleen
□ Enlargement of the liver
□ Significantly elevated white blood cell count
□ Lymph node pathology

Acute nonlymphoblastic leukemia represents less than 25% of the cases of acute leukemia.[27] The incidence of ANLL is constant from birth through 10 years, and then there is a slight peak in adolescence. Children predisposed to ANLL include those treated with alkylating agents for solid tumors like Hodgkin's disease, and those with genetic or chromosomal disorders like Fanconi's anemia or Bloom's syndrome.[30] The cancerous cells eventually dominate the bone marrow and make it impossible for the production of blood cells to occur.

Central nervous system tumors

The most common primary childhood brain tumors are medulloblastomas, astrocytomas, and brainstem gliomas.[2,16,24] These primary childhood tumors tend to remain confined to tissues within the central nervous system but are devastating in their impact on the total human being.

Most of the general signs and symptoms of brain tumors are significantly related to elevated levels of intracranial pressure caused by the presence of abnormal tissue growth. These include[7,16]:

□ Headaches
□ Nausea and vomiting
□ Swelling and distention of the head
□ Convulsive and focal seizures
□ Visual disturbances
□ Ataxia

Depending on the site of the tumor, the following mental/emotional indicators may be present[7]:

□ Drowsiness
□ Lethargy
□ Obtuseness
□ Personality changes
□ Conduct disorders
□ Impaired mental faculty, including impaired short- and long-term memory
□ Psychotic symptoms

Hodgkin's disease

Hodgkin's disease in childhood is similar to Hodgkin's disease that affects adults. About 15% of those affected by Hodgkin's disease are younger than 16 years of age. It is a chronic condition in which large multinucleated reticulum cells (Reed-Sternberg cells) are present in lymph node tissue or in other non-reticular formation sites. The presence of these cells cause lesions. The primary lesions are located in the lymph nodes, spleen, and bone marrow.

The most common signs and symptoms include:

□ Enlarged lymph nodes
□ Enlarged spleen
□ Changes in the composition of blood
□ Anemia
□ Fever[19]

Late effects of Hodgkin's disease include skeletal and bone growth abnormalities, sterility, and tendency to develop subsequent malignant tumors.[53] In fact, the survivors of childhood cancers are 20 times more likely to experience a second malignant neoplasm than the general population.[53]

Neuroblastoma

A neuroblastoma is a common solid tumor of childhood of the embryonal neural crest of the sympathetic nervous system. One in 7000 children under the age of 5 years is affected. Approximately 75% of the cases are found in children under the age of 5 years.[7,59]

Wilms' tumor

Wilms' tumor is a form of nephroblastoma or renal embryoma. It is a very aggressive, commonly lethal tumor.[18] It is important to note that Wilms' tumor can be accounted for by heredity in 100% of the cases where tumors exist on both sides of the body.[4]

Soft-Tissue Tumors

One of the more common forms of soft-tissue tumors in children is rhabdomyosarcoma, representing approximately 65% of childhood soft-tissue sarcomas.[16] This malignancy affects the muscle tissue. In fact, the malignant cells arise from progenitor cells of the striated muscles.

Bone tumors

The two best known childhood bone malignancies are Ewing's sarcoma and osteosarcoma. Ewing's sarcoma is the second most comon form of malignant primary bone tumor of childhood.[32] It is a round cell bone tumor of childhood, the primary symptoms of which are pain and swelling, fever, and a mass. The primary bone tumor usually appears in the extremities and most commonly metastasizes to the lungs and bone marrow. Osteosarcoma is a form of childhood bone cancer that appears between the ages of 10 and 20 years. Pain and a noticeable mass are the usual symptoms. It is most common in the knee joint. It is highly malignant.

Retinoblastoma

A retinoblastoma is a malignant tumor that arises from the immature retina. The disease may be inherited and has been traced to an autosomal dominant trait.[7] It has a significant negative impact on the child's vision.

THE ROLE OF THE PHYSICAL EDUCATOR

New and innovative treatments of childhood cancer have increased the likelihood that children who are diagnosed early will have a chance of survival. The re-

markable advances in medicine have made it possible for so many to survive that by the turn of the century, 1 in every 1000 young adults will be survivors of childhood cancer. The physical educator must be aware of the fact that many of these survivors return to school and attempt to re-establish relative normalcy to their lives. The teacher must be aware of the side-effects of the cancer and the treatment of cancer and must be sensitive to the psychosocial needs of the student.

The side effects of the childhood cancers and their treatments include[39,45,53]:

☐ Retardation of growth
☐ Impaired fertility
☐ Scoliosis or other skeletal impairments
☐ Impaired renal, pulmonary, hepatic, or cardiac function
☐ Neuropsychological deficits
☐ Psychosocial deficits, including vastly affected peer relationships

The teacher needs to be sensitive to the physical deficits and needs of the child survivor of cancer. The physical educator must work in close cooperation with the child's physician, rehabilitation therapists, and parents in the development of a program that addresses the unique health needs of the student.

In addition, the teacher must be aware of the significant psychosocial affects that a life-threatening illness has on the child, his/her parents and siblings, members of the extended family, and friends. The child who is able to return to school, able to move from the more restricted hospital/homebound education program to the less restricted public school program, will face peers with a history of markedly different experiences. It is often difficult for the child to find and make friends who are not fearful of cancer. It is frequently difficult for the child to make the difficult transition from a life-and-death situation to a life of play and games and sport. However, play, games, and sport often serve as a vital link to normalcy for the child.

CYSTIC FIBROSIS

Cystic fibrosis is an inherited childhood disorder that is generally fatal. It is the most common inherited life-shortening disease and affects 1 in every 2000 Caucasion births, and 1 in every 17,000 African-American births.[46] During the last 20 years the median lifespan of individuals with cystic fibrosis has improved from 4.5 to 20 years, with some living into their 30s.

Characteristics

The disease is characterized by the production of abnormally thick mucus, impaired absorption of fat and protein, a high concentration of sodium and chloride in the sweat, and progressive lung damage. The more rapid the progression of lung damage, the faster the debilitation of the individual.[57]

The symptoms and severity of cystic fibrosis vary from apparently "normal" to markedly impaired health. Although in young school-age children there are often chronic problems with the lungs and with malnutrition, in about 20% of the cases the diagnosis of cystic fibrosis is not made until the student is in the late teens.[46] There is usually continuing destruction of pancreatic tissue. The proportion of children with residual pancreatic function is less than 20%.[47] Older children may also have diabetes. Thus the varied impact of the disorder on the functioning of the individual accounts for considerable variance in the physical capabilities of children with cystic fibrosis.

Increased understanding about cystic fibrosis and the value of aggressive intervention programs have resulted in improved prognosis over the last 40 years. Successful intervention includes a special diet, salt supplements, control of infection, pulmonary therapy, and physical exercise.

Diet

To offset the undernourishment that results from underabsorption of fat and protein, additions to the diet and supplements are utilized. The recommended special diet includes an intake of calories and protein that exceeds Recommended Dietary Allowance (RDA) by 50%, and includes a high fat intake. Double the recommended daily allowance of multivitamins and supplemental vitamin E are used to strengthen the immune system. Salt supplements during periods of exposure to high temperature and sweating reduces the chances of heat-associated illnesses.[17]

Control of infection

A high incidence of pulmonary infections requires intermediate to long-term use of antiobiotics, depending on the individual. Immunizations against whooping cough, measles, and flu are routine.

Pulmonary therapy

Progressive bronchiolar and bronchical obstruction leads to infection of the bronchi and breakdown of lung tissue. Every effort is made to clear the bronchi of thick mucus that continually accumulates. Pulmonary involvement leads to death in over 90% of individuals with cystic fibrosis. Pulmonary therapy to lessen the accumulation of mucus consists of postural drainage, percussion, vibration, and assistance with coughing upon indication of pulmonary involvement. Oral and/or aerosol bronchodilators are also used to reverse

airway ostruction.[7] In severe cases constant use of supplemental oxygen is necessary.

Physical activity

During the last 10 years, research has validated the value of exercise for the vast majority of persons with cystic fibrosis.[10] Ongoing exercise programs have been shown to improve flow of mucus from the lungs, build endurance of the breathing muscles,[17] and improve clinical status, sense of well-being, overall morale, and independence.[10]

Each program should be tailored to the individual's physical capability. After consulting with the person's physician, a cardiovascular endurance test should be administered to determine exercise tolerance and maximum heart rate. The exercise program should begin with low intensity exercise and gradually increase to a target intensity of 70% to 80% of maximum rate for 20 to 30 minutes per session. Three to five times weekly is recommended.[10] Types of exercise programs that have been shown to benefit the individual with cystic fibrosis include running, swimming (no diving), bicycling, and active play.[21]

It may be helpful for physical education teachers to understand behavior and medical treatments of children with cystic fibrosis. Some observations that have been adapted from Harvey[29] are as follows:

1. Children with cystic fibrosis need to cough out the mucus in their lungs. Therefore they should be encouraged to do so. Other children need to be taught that cystic fibrosis is not a communicable disease.
2. The diet of the student may be different from the norm; as such, the child may need to make frequent trips to the restroom.
3. Although children with cystic fibrosis may have less stamina than normal children, it is important that they participate in modified physical activity commensurate with their abilities.
4. Some children with cystic fibrosis may be on medication for both pancreatic and lung involvement and may, subsequently, need to take medication during physical education class.
5. Aerosol administration of bronchiodilator drugs is valuable and may be taken in class.
6. Precautions should be taken to minimize the probability of respiratory infections.

DIABETES

Diabetes is a general term referring to a variety of disorders, of which diabetes mellitus is the most well known. This is a chronic metabolic disorder where there is an inability of the cells to use glucose. In this form of diabetes, the body is unable to burn up its intake of carbohydrates because of the lack of insulin produced by the pancreas. The lack of insulin in the blood prevents storage of glucose in the cells of the liver. Consequently, blood sugar accumulates in the bloodstream in greater than usual amounts. Other forms of diabetes are:

1. Bronze: a primary disorder of iron metabolism with deposits of iron-containing pigments in the body
2. Insipidus: characterized by a urinary output of from 2 to 10 liters per day, and an intake of fluids that does not match the output
3. Gestational: characterized by impaired glucose tolerance during the second and third trimesters of pregnancy.

Leon[40] reports that there are 5,000,000 persons with diabetes in the United States. It has been estimated that approximately 65,000 new cases of diabetes develop each year and that approximately 4,750,000 persons presently residing in the United States, who are now free of diabetic symptoms, will develop diabetes during their lifetimes. About 10% of the recorded cases occur among children.[20] However, there is greater prevalence of diabetes with increasing age. The American Diabetes Association estimates that for every 10,000 persons in the United States there is 1 diabetic under 20 years old, 10 between 20 and 40 years old, 100 between 50 and 60 years old, and 1000 over 60 years old.

The incidence of diabetes appears to double each 15 years.[46] The alarming increase in the incidence of known cases of diabetes may be explained, in part, by improved methods of case finding and reporting.

Teachers should be aware of the symptoms of diabetes to help identify the disease if it should appear in any of their students, since early identification and treatment promise the best hope. Symptoms of diabetes include infections that may be slow to heal, fatigue, excessive hunger, itching, impairment in visual acuity, excessive urination and thirst, and skin afflictions such as boils, carbuncles, ulcers, and gangrenous sores.

The etiological factors of diabetes are, as yet, unknown. This condition may be caused by too much food, infection, resistance to insulin, injury, surgical shock, pregnancy, or emotional stress.[55] There seem to be hereditary predispositions for the acquisition of the disease. Also, 70% to 90% of diagnosed diabetics have a history of obesity as a result of having a high fat and carbohydrate content in their diets. Endocrine imbalances, mental trauma, and sedentary living also appear as precipitating factors in the onset of diabetes.

Although the symptoms mentioned may be important in identifying diabetes, the most reliable method of detecting the disorder is urinalysis.

Characteristics

There are two different designated types of diabetes that relate to the time of onset. When individuals up to 20 years old contract diabetes, it is termed *Type I.* This type is very serious, and the youngster must have daily insulin injections to maintain health. *Type II* diabetes is acquired after the age of 20. In its early stages, type II diabetes can be controlled with diet and exercise. Although some adults do develop type I and some children do develop type II diabetes, these instances are quite rare. Children at high risk for type II diabetes may be obese.[17]

The two types of diabetes reflect differing degrees of insulin deficiency. Type I children are usually slender and cannot produce insulin, whereas type II children gain some ability to produce natural insulin but exhibit excess body fat. Thus the two clinical forms of diabetes (insulin dependent and non–insulin dependent) require differing types of exercise.[12] Full understanding of diabetes and its management, along with the effects of exercise and its implications, are essential when dealing with this prevalent population.

There are many different adverse characteristics that may affect individuals with diabetes. Typical of rapid onset with older persons may be sudden weakness at the hips and knees. In addition, intermittent diarrhea may occur for a few days with increasing frequency as the condition becomes worse. Obesity is often associated with diabetes. In addition, the diabetic may be more subject to viral infections. There may be autoimmunity in which the number of antibodies continue to decrease. There may be higher incidence of renal failure and there may be general fatigue and muscle weakness. Individuals with diabetes are prone to infection, delayed healing, vascular disease, and visual disturbances.

Treatment

It is important that the physical educator understand diabetes treatment procedures so that cooperative efforts with the medical profession can enhance the total development of the child. Effective control of diabetes solely by diet and oral medication has long been sought. Progress toward this objective has been made in recent years through the development of therapeutic drugs that have the properties of insulin. However, another factor is important in the control of diabetes. Participation in exercise functions like insulin in that it burns glucose so less insulin is needed to convert it to glycogen for storage. Many individuals with diabetes take insulin orally; however, some still require insulin injections that are usually self-administered with a hypodermic needle. Also important in the treatment of diabetes is the psychological adjustment patients must make. In addition, patients must undergo regular health checkups and have periodic urinalyses recorded by medical personnel. They must also realize that the condition still is not curable, although it can be controlled. By adjusting to the disciplines placed on them by the physician, diabetic persons can expect to live lives as long and productive as those of nondiabetic persons.

There are two main goals of treatment for diabetes. The first is to prevent day-to-day symptoms secondary to the disorder (e.g., sweating and headache) and the second is to prevent long-term complications from tissue damage.[47] The second is the more difficult to achieve and there is no consensus among medical personnel about how tissue damage should be prevented. It is worthy to note that specific treatments should be matched with specific types of diabetes.

Emergency treatment of hypoglycemia

A hypoglycemic reaction, which results from low blood sugar, is the most common type of diabetic reaction.[41] This condition can arise when the diabetic participates in excessive physical activity without eating extra food. Bodily functioning requires that the chemical processes be kept in balance. Symptoms of hypoglycemia are (1) paleness around the mouth and across the bridge of the nose, (2) perspiration in the palms of the hands, (3) little facial expression, (4) outer trembling, and (5) a general sense of weakness. Physical activity greatly decreases blood sugar levels. The onset of a reaction to hypoglycemia is usually quite rapid and may be marked with jerky movements and incoordination.

When a reaction related to hypoglycemia is detected, there should be an immediate intake of carbohydrates to counteract the hypoglycemic reaction. It is suggested that the following treatment be applied for an individual having such a reaction: (1) give some form of sugar immediately (improvement should be evident within a few minutes), (2) when improvement occurs, give additional food and then have the child resume normal activities, and (3) if the child does not improve after sugar intake, call parents, the physician, and emergency medical assistance. If the student becomes unconscious or is unable to take the sugar, immediately call for medical assistance.

Emergency treatment of hyperglycemia

Hyperglycemic reactions may result in a coma. Such reactions may occur from failure to hold to a prescribed diet or from failure to take insulin. Sugar and free fatty acids build up in the blood. If insulin is not administered, an individual may pass into a coma. Immediate treatment is critical. If a coma occurs, the student should be rushed to a physician or to a hospital for proper administration of controlled insulin. This treatment cannot be done by the physical educator.[22] Sherrill[56] lists some causes of diabetic coma. They are (1) insufficient insulin, (2) neglecting to take injections, (3) onset of infection or mild illness, (4) overeating or excessive consumption of alcohol, and (5) emotional stress.

Exercise and diabetes

Physical activity has long been advocated in the management of diabetes, but without full knowledge of benefit mechanisms or boundaries for caution. Exercise and training may have therapeutic value in diabetic control, but careful planning is necessary when introducing intensive activity. Exercise appears to be a necessary part of the treatment of diabetes.[40] Before the discovery of insulin in the late 1920s, diabetes was controlled primarily through diet and mild exercise. Although scanty, studies conducted before the discovery of insulin show that the number of deaths from diabetes was higher among the group of persons whose occupations were of a sedentary nature than among those with more physically active jobs. From these findings, it might be inferred that exercise is a variable in the longevity of the diabetic. Exercise has been considered so valuable to diabetic persons that it should be looked on as a duty and incorporated into their daily lives. Walking and mild exercise were thought to be of sufficient value.

There is evidence that diabetics can improve their physical fitness. Also, control of the diabetes improves during the period of training. In addition, the motor fitness of an experimental group subjected to exercise increased during the training period, whereas the motor fitness of a nonexercising control group decreased.

Regular exercise programs are of value to children with diabetes, because exercise may help stimulate pancreatic secretion as well as contribute to overall body health and assist in maintaining optimum weight, which is a problem for many diabetics. The child with diabetes can participate, in general, in the activities of the unrestricted class. However, in many cases, diabetic patients are more susceptible to fatigue than their non-diabetic peers. Therefore the physical educator should be understanding in the event the diabetic cannot withstand prolonged bouts of more strenuous exercise.

Leon[40] has indicated that exercise is an essential

component of an effective treatment program for many diabetics. He reports that an exercise program may be helpful in the following ways:

1. It may improve diabetic control by decreasing the insulin requirements for insulin-dependent diabetics.
2. Strengthening of skeletal muscles can make a significant contribution to the control of diabetes.
3. It reduces the risk of coronary heart disease by controlling risk factors such as overweight.
4. It provides increased stamina and physical functioning to improve work capacity.
5. The benefits of exercise provide a sense of well-being and self-confidence.

Programming for the Diabetic Student

School medical records should be examined in an effort to identify children with diabetes as well as other conditions that may impair their education. After the identification of such students, programs of exercise should be established (with medical counsel) according to the needs of each student. The limits to the activity each diabetic child can perform vary. Continuous evaluation must be made to determine the capabilities and limitations of each diabetic child in the performance of physical and motor activity. The physical education program for the diabetic child, as all other physical education programs, should follow specific progressive sequences ranging from light to intense and simple to complex with regard to the development of physical characteristics and motor skills. It is suggested that the initial capabilities of the child be identified precisely so that no exercise will be prescribed that is more intense or difficult than the child's capabilities permit. Such a situation could be physiologically and psychologically damaging and might retard the child's receptivity to subsequent activity. The setting most suitable for the child with diabetes is a regular physical education class. In the event that the condition warrants adaptation of exercise and games, these adaptations should be made. The social values accrued from participation with peers seem to far outweigh the possible slight stigma that may be placed on the child because of the adaptations in the physical education program.

Student Education

Successful management of diabetes requires that the student participate in a regimen of care. Noncompliance with health practices relted to diabetes can have serious short- and long-term effects. In general, a student's education program should include the following

components[42]:

1. Glucose monitoring. Students can learn to use a glucometer.
2. Monitoring the blood sugar status.
3. Managing appropriate insulin administration.
4. Monitoring signs and symptoms of hyperglycemia and insulin reaction.
5. Adherance to personal hygiene practices of daily living such as skin and foot care and treatment of minor injuries to prevent infections.
6. Wearing a medical identification tag or carrying a medical identification card with vital medical information.
7. Avoiding exercise on days when nausea or respiratory infections are present.
8. Exercising with a partner who is aware of a possible hyperglycemic response.

Diet for Diabetes

All students should meet the basic requirements of a diet that provides adequate calories and necessary nutrients to achieve desirable weight and sustain normal growth and development. However, Miller and Keane[47] offer practical advice that may assist with the control of diabetes:

1. Ingest enough calories to support necessary activity and growth and maintain the individual's weight at the proper level.
2. Spread food intake through the day.
3. Meals should consist primarily of complex carbohydrates that are slowly digested.
4. The total carbohydrate content of the diet should provide 50% to 55% of the total calorie intake.
5. Students should be thoroughly instructed in the calorie as well as the carbohydrate content of their food.
6. Eat meals at regular intervals.

Exercise Program

There are few activities that are contraindicated for persons with diabetes. In developing an exercise program, it is desirable to provide activity that meets the student's interests and needs yet utilizes the large muscles of the body. Sport activity and aerobic exercise such as walking, jogging, cycling, swimming, and cross country skiing are particularly desirable.

Some precautions

Children with diabetes should drink plenty of water. As a rule, water should be provided every 15 minutes when the student is doing strenuous activity. Another precaution should be consideration of the muscle site where the diabetic injects insulin. It is best, prior to strenuous physical activity, to inject insulin in a muscle group that is not primarily involved in heavy activity. Thus it may be desirable for the injection to be made in the trunk rather than the arms or legs. Care should be taken that diabetics not be exposed to foot infections through excessive foot friction, sunburn, and other potential sources of infection. Coram and Mangum[15] have suggested the following precautions for individuals with diabetes:

(1) Have up-to-date medical information, (2) wear diabetes mellitus identification, (3) participate in graded exercise testing, (4) have a consistent time for regular sustained exercise, (5) understand the importance of careful timing of medication and food intake and exercise, (6) keep fast-acting sugar handy, and (7) know what exercise conditions are contraindicated for their form of diabetes.

MENSTRUATION AND DYSMENORRHEA

Menstruation is a complex process that involves the endocrine glands, uterus, and ovaries. The average menstrual cycle lasts for 28 days. However, each woman has her own rhythmic cycle of menstrual function. The cycle periods usually range from 21 to 35 days, but they occasionally may be longer or shorter and still fall within the range of normality.

The average total amount of blood lost during the normal menstrual period is 3 ounces; however, a woman may lose from 1½ to 5 ounces. This blood is replaced by the active formation of blood cells in bone marrow and consequently does not cause anemia. On occasion, some women may have excessive menstrual flow, and in this event a physician should be consulted. The average menstrual period lasts 3 to 5 days, but 2 to 7 days may be considered normal. The average age of onset of menstruation is 12.5 years, although the range of onset may be from 9 to 18 years.

Dysmenorrhea, or painful menstruation, is a common occurrence among some girls and women. The ratio may be as low as 1 to 4 among college women, indicating that it is the exception rather than the rule. It has been estimated that only 20% to 30% of cases of dysmenorrhea are a result of organic causes such as ovarian cysts, endocrine imbalance, or infections. Most of the causes are of functional origin such as poor posture, insufficient exercise, fatigue, weak abdominal muscles, or improper diet.

Diet and Its Effects on the Menstrual Period

Many women are unaware of the effects dietary habits can have on their degree of comfort during the onset of their menstrual flow. During this age of fast foods saturated with salt, the modern woman needs to understand how her diet choices can influence her comfort during the menstrual period. With such knowledge many women can reduce the painful discomfort of dysmenorrhea. Reduction of pain is directly associated with the amount of salt stored in the body.

Approximately 1 week prior to the onset of the menstrual period, the body begins storing sodium chloride. When this storing process begins, a woman craves salt. If she yields to the craving for salt at that time in her cycle, a whole series of events occur that result in abdominal bloating, which increases the pain associated with the first 2 days of the menstrual flow.

What occurs is that when salt intake is increased, it tends to move into and be held by the body tissues. The salt stored in the body tissues draws water toward those tissues, thereby upsetting the osmotic balance in the body. Much of the water that is drawn into the tissues is pulled from fecal matter moving through the large intestine. When large amounts of water are removed from the fecal mass, the mass begins to harden and its progress is slowed. Thus the net result of increasing salt intake 1 week prior to the onset of the menstrual period is bloating from stored water and accumulating fecal material. This increased congestion presses against nerves in the abdominal and lower back area and causes pain.

The entire chain of events can be avoided (or markedly reduced) if, 1 week prior to the onset of her menstrual flow, a woman will decrease (or at least not increase) salt intake and, at the same time, increase water and roughage (raw celery, carrots, apples) intake. By following these simple guidelines a woman can preserve the osmotic balance of water in the body, and softness and progress of the fecal mass through the large intestine can be maintained. Regular movement of the fecal mass results in reduction of the amount of bloating associated with the menstrual period. Reduced bloating and faithful adherence to exercises described later in this chapter will relieve most of the pain associated with menstruation.

Physical Activity during the Menstrual Period

There have been questions raised about the desirability of young women participating in physical education and exercise during the menstrual period. There is a perception among some that exercise during a period of discomfort is undesirable and that young women during this period should be excused from physical education classes. Young women have varying experiences as they pass through the menstrual cycle. Thus judgments about physical exercise during menstruation should be made on an individual basis. However, there is evidence that there are benefits from physical exercise as it relates to physical fitness and postural efficiency in lessening the pain associated with menstruation. Furthermore, it appears that menstruation does not impair physical performance.

The consensus among physicians and gynecologists is that restriction from participation in vigorous physical activity, intensive sport competition, and swimming during all phases of the menstrual period are unwarranted for girls who are free of menstrual disturbances. However, with regard to the first half of the menstrual period, some physicians advise moderation with limited participation in intensive sport competition. The reason for moderation during the first half of the menstrual period is that the flow is heavier during the first 2 or 3 days and some women experience cramps during this time.

Exercises for Dysmenorrhea

The question has often been asked as to what effect exercise has on dysmenorrhea. Studies indicate that women previously suffering from moderate or severe cases of dysmenorrhea showed a decrease in severity of cramps after performing prescribed abdominal exercises for 8 weeks. These exercises, prescribed for women who had no organic causes for dysmenorrhea, provided relief of congestion in the abdominal cavity caused by gravity, poor posture, poor circulation, or poor abdominal muscle tone. Physical activity also assists relief of leg and back pains by stretching lumbar and pelvic ligaments in the fascia to minimize pressure on spinal nerves. Undue muscular tension also may have a bearing on painful menstruation; therefore relaxation techniques and positioning of the body, accompanied by heat from a heating pad on the lower back area, may relax tensions and consequently lessen the pain. Other relaxation techniques and exercises also may be used to reduce tension in the body (see Appendix B).

Women who suffer from dysmenorrhea may benefit from a daily exercise program designed to alleviate this condition. The exercises should provide for improvement of posture (especially lordosis), stimulation of circulation, and stretching of tight fascia and ligaments. The exercises discussed here are suggested to alleviate the symptoms of dysmenorrhea.

Fascial stretch

The purpose of fascial exercise is to stretch the shortened fascial ligamentous bands that extend be-

FIGURE 16-2. Fascial stretch.

tween the lower back and the anterior aspect of the pelvis and legs. These shortened bands may result in increased pelvic tilt, which may irritate peripheral nerves passing through or near the fascia. The irritation of these nerves may be the cause of the pain. This exercise produces a stretching effect on the hip flexors and increases mobility of the hip joint (Fig. 16-2). To perform the exercise, the woman should stand erect, with the left side of her body about the distance of the bent elbow from a wall; the feet should be together, with the left forearm and palm against the wall, the elbow at shoulder height, and the heel of the other hand placed against the posterior aspect of the hollow portion of the right hip. From this position, abdominal and gluteal muscles should be contracted strongly to tilt the pelvis backward. The hips should slowly be pushed forward and diagonally toward the wall and pressure applied with the right hand. This position should be held for a few counts, then a slow return should be made to the starting position. The stretch should be performed three times on each side of the body. The exercise should be continued even after relief has been obtained from dysmenorrhea. It has been suggested that the exercise be performed three times daily. To increase motivation women should record the number of days and times they perform the exercise.

Abdominal pumping

The purpose of abdominal pumping is to increase circulation of the blood throughout the pelvic region. The exercise is performed by assuming a hook-lying position placing the hands lightly on the abdomen, slowly and smoothly distending the abdomen on the count of one, then retracting the abdomen on the count of two, and relaxing (Fig. 16-3). The exercise should be repeated 8 to 10 times.

Pelvic tilt with abdominal pumping

The purpose of the pelvic tilt with abdominal pumping is to increase the tone of the abdominal muscles. In a hook-lying position, with the feet and knees together, heels 1 inch apart, and hands on the abdomen, the abdominal and gluteal muscles are contracted. The pelvis is rotated so that the tip of the coccyx comes forward and upward and the hips are slightly raised from the floor. The abdomen is distended and retracted. The hips are lowered slowly, vertebra by vertebra, until the original starting position is attained (Fig. 16-4). The exercise is to be repeated 8 to 10 times.

Knee-chest position

The purpose of the knee-chest exercise is to stretch the extensors of the lumbar spine and strengthen the

FIGURE 16-3. Abdominal pumping.

FIGURE 16-4. Pelvic tilt with abdominal pumping.

FIGURE 16-5. Knee-chest position.

abdominal muscles. The exercise is performed by bending forward at the hips and placing the hands and arms on a mat. The chest is lowered toward the mat, in a knee-chest position, and held as close to the mat as possible for 3 to 5 minutes[14] (Fig. 16-5). This exercise should be performed once or twice per day.

PRADER-WILLI SYNDROME

Waters, Clarke, and Corbett[60] reported that Prader-Willi syndrome was first described in the mid-1950s by Prader, Labhart, and Willi. The incidence of the condition is reported to be 1 in every 10,000 live births.[31]

Characteristics

Prader-Willi syndrome is characterized by neonatal hypotonia and feeding difficulty followed by excessive appetite, pica behavior (eating indiscriminately—dirt, crayons, paste, paper, etc.), and obesity starting in early childhood. Adults are short, have small hands and feet, almond-shaped eyes, a triangular shaped mouth, a prominent nasal bridge, and have underdeveloped gonads. Children with Prader-Willi syndrome share the same characteristics. As a group individuals with Prader-Willi syndrome are very heterogeneous with IQs ranging from less than 20 to 100. Individuals with intelligence in the normal range frequently have learning disabilities, but do demonstrate strong visual-spatial perception.[60]

Physical Activity

Because of the characteristic obesity, precautions must be taken to avoid overtaxing the cardiovascular system. It is crucial that these individuals participate in calorie-burning activities, activities that will elevate the body's metabolism. These individuals should participate in activities commensurate with their abilities, however, heart rate should be routinely monitored.

In addition, it is vital that these individuals learn the skills necessary to participate in leisure and recreation activities. This is a better alternative than sedentary activities, which tend to be the choice of obese individuals. It should be noted that when behavior modification programs are used to motivate students with Prader-Willi syndrome, food should never be used as a reinforcer.

TOURETTE SYNDROME

Tourette syndrome (TS) is an inherited neurological disorder with some associated symptoms that affect behavior. Characteristics of individuals with this syndrome include involuntary motor and vocal tics and symptoms that come and go and change over time.[8] A high percentage of children with TS also have problems with attention, activity, and impulse control; learning disabilities; and visual motor integration problems.[8] Some also demonstrate obsessive-compulsive behaviors. The prevalence rate is estimated to be 1:2000 and is three times more common in males than females.[3]

Characteristics

Diagnostic criteria developed by the American Psychiatric Association[3] are:

□ Both multiple motor and one or more vocal tics have been present for some time.

□ The tics occur many times a day (usually in bouts), nearly every day, or intermittently throughout a period of more than 1 year.

□ The anatomic location, number, frequency, complexity, and severity of the tics change over time.

□ Onset before age 21.

□ Occurrence not exclusively during Psychoactive Substance Intoxication of known central nervous system disease, such as Huntington's chorea or postviral encephalitis.

The teacher of the child with TS may be the first to observe the symptoms. The motor tics that may be seen include sudden twitches of the entire body, shoulders, and/or head; eyeblinks or rolling of the head; repetitive tapping, drumming, or touching behaviors; or grimacing. The vocal tics are involuntary uttering of noises, words, or phrases including sniffing, throat clearing, or repeated coughing, coprolalia (saying socially inappropriate words), laughing involuntarily, uttering a variety of sounds or yells, and echolalia (repeating what others or oneself has just said).[8] Sometimes the symptoms are very frequent and sometimes the child does not demonstrate them at all. Also, they change from one year to the next.

Physical Activity

Other than learning to tolerate the child's involuntary tics, the physical educator's primary concern will probably be the visual-motor integration problems the student experiences. These range from alternating visual suppression (using each eye independently from the other) to mild depth perception difficulties. The performance clues will include poor striking success, inability to catch a thrown ball, avoidance of climbing apparatus, and/or descending stairs one step at a time. Before designing a physical education program, the child should be referred for an orthoptic visual examination and remediation (see Chapter 13).

TRAUMATIC HEAD INJURIES

The number of school-age children with head injuries is significant. One in 500 school-aged children are hospitalized with head injuries each year, and by age 15, 3% of the school population will have sustained a head injury.[48] Causes of head injuries include motor vehicle accidents (most common in adolescence), falls, bicycle accidents, child abuse, assaults, and sports injuries. The effects of head injuries on school behavior depend on the extent of the insult to the brain tissue.

Severity

Although no classification system exists, a commonly used system for grading severity of brain damage is[38]:

Minor	Common bumps to the head with no evidence of concussion; generally, these cases are not seen by a physician.
Mild	Only brief loss of consciousness, if any, with accompanying symptoms of concussion such as vomiting, lethargy, or lack of recall of the injury.
Moderate	Evidence of concussion; loss of consciousness, less than 5 minutes.
Severe	Concussion or skull fracture; loss of consciousness 5 to 30 minutes.
Serious	Loss of consciousness more than 30 minutes; concussion or skull fracture and notable neurological sequelae.

Characteristics

The location and severity of brain damage greatly effects the characteristic behaviors of the child and the speed of recovery.

Generally cognitive, motor, behavior, and language functions are impaired to some extent. These posttrauma reactions frequently lead to a misdiagnosis of learning disabled, mentally retarded, or emotionally disturbed.[51] Although rapid recovery of most functions occurs during the first 2 or 3 years after injury, problems frequently persist for longer periods. Cognitive problems include difficulty with organization of sensory input, concept formation, understanding complex instructions, coherent organiztion of verbal and written reports, and flexible thinking.[54] Motor impairments include speed of execution of refined and complex movements.[6] Difficulty processing and integrating information as well as abnormal brain activity contribute to negative behaviors including low tolerance for frustration, aggression, impulsiveness, and noncompliance.[51] Ongoing language problems include difficulty finding words, organizing sequences of words, and comprehension of complex instructions.[64] Extent and frequency of these problems should be addressed in the student's individual education plan.

Educational Modifications

Educational modifications that may need to be included in the IEP are:[48]

☐ Reduced course load
☐ Scheduling the most demanding courses in the morning when the student is fresh
☐ Resource room with the assistance of an aide
☐ Rest breaks as needed
☐ Adapted physical education or a modified regular physical education program
☐ Peer tutoring
☐ Counseling
☐ Provisions for taping lectures and extra time for completing written work and examinations

Physical education personnel should be particularly attentive to the posttrauma student's ongoing psychomotor, cognitive, and behavior problems. Care must be exercised in sequencing motor tasks, providing instructions, and simplifying motor demands. Any adjustment that will reduce frustration to a minimum will contribute to the possibility of success in physical education.

REFERRAL TO SUPPORT SERVICES

There are specific procedures that should be followed to involve the appropriate personnel when developing individualized physical education programs for health-impaired persons. First of all, a clinical assessment should be made to determine whether an individual has a disability. Then, an appropriate physical education assessment should be done to determine the physical education needs of the student. Once these needs have been determined, an individualized physical education program can be developed commensurate with the present levels of performance of each child. The physical demands made on the individual should not exceed the capabilities of the learner. If the student does not make gains toward the goals and objectives included on the IEP, he/she should be referred to a physician and psychological personnel for additional clinical evaluations. Those additional evaluations should provide instructions about what activities and levels of exercise the student can safely participate in. Thus there are two instructional conditions to be considered when conducting an individual physical education program: (1) follow the initial medical/psychological evaluation recommendations and (2) seek additional information if the students do not benefit from the initial physical education program. When students are referred for a second evaluation, their history of problems in physical education should be made available to the evaluators. Once the contraindicated activities are identified, the IEP should be modified to reflect these instructions.

SUMMARY

Some other conditions in the laws that qualify a student for special programming consideration are anemia, AIDS, asthma, child abuse, childhood cancer, cystic fibrosis, diabetes, Prader-Willi syndrome, Tourette syndrome, and traumatic head injury. Additional conditions that may limit a student's strength, vitality, or alertness are menstruation and dysmenorrhea. The physical educator should understand the nature of each of these conditions, how the condition can affect a student's performance capabilities, and types of program modifications that best meet the needs of each student.

Most of the conditions discussed in this chapter require medical attention. When this is the case, it is advisable to consult with the student's physician to assure that the type of exercises and activities selected for the student will not aggravate the condition. In most situations mild exercise will benefit the student. However, in the case of the diabetic, the type of diabetes must be known before specific exercise programs can be developed.

REVIEW QUESTIONS

1. What causes painful menstruation?
2. What diet changes might decrease pain during the first 2 days of menstruation?
3. What is the effect of activity during menstruation?
4. What are two exercises that can reduce dysmenorrhea?
5. What are four symptoms of diabetes?
6. What is the effect of exercise on glucose levels in the body?
7. How does exercise affect diabetic individuals?
8. Name the ways AIDS may be acquired.
9. What are some of the physical characterisitcs of a child with AIDS?
10. Describe the similarities and differences between each of the types of child abuse and neglect.
11. Explain cautions that must be used in developing an individual exercise program for a child with cystic fibrosis.
12. What are three characteristics of an anemic person?
13. Describe emergency treatment procedures for hypoglycemia.

14. What are emergency treatment procedures for hyperglycemia?
15. What is the primary characteristic of the child with Tourette syndrome? How does this interfere with the child's psychosocial development?
16. What are some precautions the physical educator should take with children who have asthma?
17. What is the major characteristic of a child with Prader-Willi syndrome? What cautions must be taken in the development of an exercise program for children with Prader-Willi syndrome?
18. What are the levels of severity of trauma associated with head injury?

STUDENT ACTIVITIES

1. Working with a partner, demonstrate the three exercises to reduce dysmenorrhea that are described in this chapter. Have your partner check the exercises for accuracy. Exchange roles.
2. Look through six recent issues of the *Journal of the American Medical Association.* List the articles that relate to the conditions described in this chapter. Read through some of the articles to see if exercise is mentioned as a possible way to relieve the condition.
3. Interview a person with diabetes. Find out what type of medication the person takes and how often it must be taken. Ask if the person ever failed to take the medication and how he or she felt because of missing the dosage.
4. Interview a school nurse. Find out what percentage of the students in the nurse's school have the conditions discussed in this chapter.
5. Contact an organization that advocates for other health-impaired children and study their literature. Identify the information that is relevant to conducting a physical education program for individuals with other health impairments.
6. Identify an athlete who is/was afflicted with another health impairment. Write a paper on accommodations that had to be made for the athlete.
7. Conduct a case study of a child who has a health impairment with respect to participation in recreational physical activities.

REFERENCES

1. Allen DM, Tarnowski KJ: Depressive characteristics of physically abused children, *J Abnorm Child Psychol* 17:1-11, 1989.
2. Allen JC: Childhood brain tumors: current status of clinical trials in newly diagnosed and recurrent disease, *Pediatr Clin North Am* 32:633-651, 1985.
3. American Psychiatric Association. *DSM-III-R Diagnostic and statistical manual of mental disorders (revised),* Washington DC, 1987.
4. Arthur DC: Genetics and cytogenetics of pediatric cancers, *Cancer* 58:534, 1986.
5. Asthma and Allergy Foundation of America: *The allergy and asthma advance* 2:9-10, 1984.
6. Bawden H, Knights R, Winogron H: Speeded performance following head injury in children, *J Clin Exp Neuropsychol* 7:30-54, 1985.
7. Berkow R, Fletcher AJ, editors: *The Merck manual of diagnosis and therapy, ed 15,* Rahway, NJ, 1987, Merck & Co.
8. Bronheim S: *An educator's guide to Tourette syndrome.* 42-40 Bell Blvd, Bayside (1990), NY, 11361, Tourette Syndrome Association.
9. Bundgaard A: Exercise and the asthmatics, *Sports Med* 2:254-266, 1985.
10. Canny GJ, Levison H: Exercise response and rehabilitation in cystic fibrosis, *Sports Med* 4:143-152, 1987.
11. Carlson DL, Mawdsley RH: Sports anemia: a review of the literature, *Am J Sports Med* 14:109-122, 1986.
12. Casey JL: Step safely into sports, *Diabetes Forecast* 2:38-41, 1985.
13. Child Abuse Program: Annual Report Children's Hospital, Columbus, Ohio, 1986-87.
14. Claussen AH, Crittenden PM: Physical and psychological maltreatment: relations among types of maltreatment, *Child Abuse Negl* 15:5-18, 1991.
15. Coram SJ, Mangum M: Exercise risks and benefits for diabetic individuals: a review, *Adapt Phys Ed Q* 3:35-57, 1986.
16. Crist WM, Kun LE: Common solid tumors of childhood, *N Engl J Med* 324:461-471, 1991.
17. Cystic Fibrosis Foundation: *Cystic fibrosis and exercise: a beginner's guide,* Rockville, Md, 1984.
18. Dehner LP: A contemporary view of neoplasms in children, *Pediatr Clin North Am* 36:113-136, 1989.
19. Donaldson SS, Link MP: Hodgkin's disease: treatment of the young child, *Pediatr Clin North Am* 38:457-473, 1991.
20. Dunn JM, Fait H: *Special physical education,* Dubuque, Iowa, 1989, Wm C Brown Publishers.
21. Edlund DJ et al: Effects of a swimming program on children with cystic fibrosis, *Am J Dis Child* 140:80-83, 1986.
22. Eichstaedt CB, Kalakian LH: *Developmental/adapted physical education,* New York, 1987, Macmillan Publishing.
23. Elliott DJ, Tarnowski KJ: Depressive characteristics of sexually abused chidlren, *Child Pyschiatry Hum Dev* 21:37-47, 1989.
24. Friedman HS, Horowitz M, Oakes WJ: Tumors of the central nervous system: improvement in outcome through a multimodality approach, *Pediatr Clin North Am* 38:381-391, 1991.
25. Garbarino J, Garbarino AC: *Emotional maltreatment of children,* Chicago, 1986, National Committee for Prevention of Child Abuse.
26. Garbarino J, Guttman E, Seely JW: *The psychologically battered child,* San Francisco, 1986, Jossey-Bass.
27. Grier HE, Weinstein HJ: Acute nonlymphocytic lukemia, *Pediatr Clin North Am* 32:653-668, 1985.

28. Hart SN, Grassard MR: A major threat to children's mental health: psychological maltreatment, *Am Psychol* 42:160-165, 1987.

29. Harvey B: Asthma. In Bleck EE, Nagel DA, editors: *Physically handicapped children: a medical atlas for teachers,* ed 2, New York, 1982, Grune & Stratton.

30. Helman LJ, Thiele CJ: New insights into the causes of cancer, *Pediatr Clin North Am* 38:201-221, 1991.

31. Holm VA: The diagnosis of Prader-Willi syndrome. In Holm VA, Salzbacher S, Pipes PL, editors: *The Prader-Willi syndrome,* Baltimore, 1981, University Park Press.

32. Horowitz ME, Neff JR, Kun LE: Ewing's sarcoma: radiotherapy versus surgery for local control, *Pediatr Clin North Am* 38:365-380, 1991.

33. Huettig C, DiBrezzo R: *Factors in abuse and neglect of handicapped children.* Paper presented at American Alliance of Health, Physical Education, Recreation and Dance National Convention, Las Vegas, April 1987.

34. Jason J: Child abuse or maltreatment. In Conn RB, editor: *Current diagnosis 7,* Philadelphia, 1985, WB Saunders.

35. Johnson CF: Inflicted injury versus accidental injury, *Pediatr Clin North Am* 37:791-814, 1990.

36. Katz R: Prevention with and without the use of medications for exercise induced asthma, *Med Sci Sports Exerc* 18:331-333, 1986.

37. Kelly ED: *Adapted and corrective physical education,* New York, 1965, Ronald Press Co.

38. Klonoff H, Low M, Clark C: Head injuries in children: a prospective five year follow-up, *J Neurol Neurosurg Psychiatry* 40:1211-1219, 1977.

39. Lansky SB: Management of stressful periods in childhood cancer, *Pediatr Clin North Am* 32:625-632, 1985.

40. Leon AS: Diabetes. In Skinner JS, editor: *Exercise testing and exercise prescription for special cases,* Philadelphia, 1987, Lea & Febiger.

41. Lodewick P: How to treat low blood sugar, *Diabetes,* Spring 1984, pp 7-12.

42. Malone JI: Diabetes mellitus in childhood and adolescence. In Rakel RE, editor: *Conn's current therapy,* Philadelphia, 1984, WB Saunders.

43. Mann JM: AIDS: a global challenge, *World Health Organization J* March, 1988, pp 4-8.

44. McClelland CQ, Kingsbury GH: Fractures in the first year of life: a diagnostic dilemma, *Am J Dis Child* 136:26-29, 1982.

45. Meadows AT, Krejimas NL, Belasco JB: The medical cost of cure: sequelae in survivors of childhood cancer. In van Eys J, Sullivan MP, editors: *Status of curability of childhood cancers,* New York, 1980, Raven Press.

46. Merck JB, Sharp GM: *The Merck manual of diagnosis and therapy,* Rahway NJ, 1990, Merck Co.

47. Miller J, Keane RR: *Encyclopedia and dictionary of medicine, nursing, and allied health,* Philadelphia, 1987, WB Saunders.

48. Mira M, Tyler J: Students with traumatic brain injury: making the transition from hospital to school, *Focus Except Child* 23:1-12, 1991.

49. Mulvihill JJ: Ecogenetic origins of cancer in the young: environmental and genetic determinants. In Levine AS, editor: *Cancer in the young,* Paris, 1981, Mosson.

50. Murphy JM et al: Substance abuse and serious child mistreatment: prevalence, risk, and outcome in a court sample, *Child Abuse Negl* 15:197-211, 1991.

51. New Medico Head Injury System. Emotionally charged: why do head injuries make some people seem out of control, *Headlines* 1:2-9, 1990.

52. Poplack DG: Acute lymphoblastic leukemia in childhood, *Pediatr Clin North Am* 32:669-681, 1985.

53. Pratt CB: Some aspects of childhood cancer epidemiology, *Pediatr Clin North Am* 32:541-556, 1985.

54. Routke B, Fisk J, Strong J: *Neuropsychological assessment of children: a treatment-oriented approach,* New York, 1986, The Guilford Press.

55. Schmitt GF: *Diabetes for diabetics: a practical guide,* Miami, 1973, Diabetes Press of America, Inc.

56. Sherrill C: *Adapted physical education and recreation, ed 3,* Dubuque, Iowa, 1986, Wm C Brown Publishers.

57. Shor DP: Cystic fibrosis. In Blackman JA, editor: *Medical aspects of developmental disabilities in children birth to three.* Rockville, Md, 1984, Aspen Publishers.

58. Surburg PR: Are adapted physical educators ready for the students with AIDS? *Adapt Phys Ed Q* 5:25 9-263, 1988.

59. Tuchman et al: Screening for neuroblastoma at 3 weeks of age: methods and preliminary results from the Quebec neuroblastoma screening project, *Pediatrics* 86:76 5-775, 1990.

60. Waters J, Clarke DJ, Corbett JA: Educational and occupational outcome in Prader-Willi syndrome, *Child Care Health Dev* 16:271-282, 1990.

61. Weinberg RA: Oncogenes, antioncogenes and the molecular bases of multistep carcinogenesis, *Cancer Res* 49:3713-3721, 1989.

62. Welfer RE: The neglect of our children, *Pediatr Clin North Am* 37:923-942, 1990.

63. Wilson EF: Estimation of the age of cutaneous contusions in child abuse, *Pediatrics* 60:750-752, 1977.

64. Ylvisaker M: Language and comunication disorders following pediatric head injury, *J Head Trauma Rehab* 1:48-56, 1986.

65. Young et al: Cancer incidence, survival and mortality for children younger than age 15 years, *Cancer* 58: Supplement 2:598-602, 1986.

SUGGESTED READINGS

Dunn JM, Fait H: *Special physical education,* Dubuque, Iowa, 1989, Wm C Brown Publishers.

Surburg PR: Are adapted physical educators ready for the students with AIDS? *Adapt Phys Ed Q* 5:259-263, 1988.

ORGANIZATION AND ADMINISTRATION

THE ROLES OF THE adapted physical education teacher and other

critical professionals who contribute to the individual education

program are discussed in Chapter 17. Options for structuring

physical education classes to best meet a variety of specific

individual needs are presented. Types of equipment needed and

effective ways to administer programs for students with

disabilities are discussed in detail.

17

OBJECTIVES

Define accountability.

Explain the rights of parents/guardians in the IEP process.

List school personnel designated as "direct" service rather than "related" service personnel.

Describe the roles and responsibilities of direct service and related service personnel involved in the IEP process.

List the components of the IEP.

List the individuals who should attend the IEP meeting.

Explain the individual physical education plan.

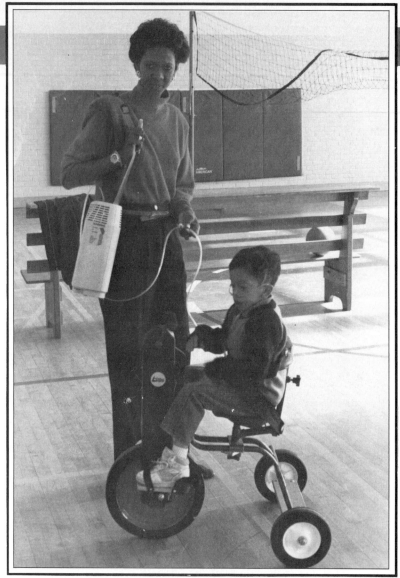

Courtesy Dallas Independent School District

The Individual Education Program Process

*T*he intent of the Individuals with Disabilities Education Act (IDEA) of 1990 was to ensure that children with disabilities be given the same educational opportunity as their nondisabled peers. The findings of the 101st Congress of the United States include:

1. There are more than 8 million children with disabilities in the United States today

2. The special educational needs of such children are not being fully met

3. More than half of the children with disabilities in the United States do not receive appropriate educational services which would enable them to have full equality of opportunity

4. One million of the children with disabilities in the United States are excluded entirely from the public school system and will not go through the educational process with their peers

5. There are many children with disabilities throughout the United States participating in regular school programs whose disabilities prevent them from having a successful educational experience because their disabilities are undetected

6. Because of the lack of adequate services within the public school system, families are often forced to find services outside the public school system, often at great distance from their residence and at their own expense (IDEA, Section 1400 b)

Fifteen years after the passage of the Education of the Handicapped Act (1975), the educational needs of children and young adults with disabilities are still not being met. In an attempt to correct this injustice, IDEA expanded and further explained the intent of the U.S. Congress—to meet the educational needs of children with disabilities in order to assure equal protection under the law; that is, a free public education.

Every child in the United States is entitled to a free, public education. This is true of a child with a disability, as well. However, each child with a disability has unique abilities and unique needs. The very nature of a disability simply enhances the uniqueness and requires that the child be more carefully taught.

To ensure that a child with a disability, a child with unique abilities and needs, receives an appropriate education, the Education of the Handicapped Act mandated that an individual education plan (IEP) be developed for each student with a disability. The IEP requires, by its very nature, that educators and administrators be accountable for the education of the child with a disability. The IEP process, by and through which a child's education is planned and executed, requires a specific education plan to be developed for each child with a disability. The federal mandates regarding the development of the IEP and the content of the IEP necessitate accountability. Educators and administrators must be able to document the child's need, based on a comprehensive assessment and evaluation, and outline specifically the methods, techniques, and procedures that will be used to educate the child, while keeping in mind the child's specific and unique needs.

Once a child is identified as having a specific and unique educational need the IEP process is initiated. There are many ways to identify children's needs for special intervention. The child's parent, the child's educator, a pre-kindergarten screening team, or Child-Find personnel may identify a developmental delay, behavior that interferes with learning, or a performance deficit. Once this is noted, the child is referred for a comprehensive evaluation to determine if, indeed, the child has a unique educational need. The procedure to be followed is clearly defined:

1. The parents of a child with a suspected disability must be made aware of their rights and of the child's rights prior to evaluation. In many school districts, a handbook explaining these rights is disseminated to the parents. In Texas, for example, a manual titled *Special Education: Parent and Student Rights*[27] is disseminated. Although this handbook is available in English and Spanish, it may need to be translated into another language. It is vital that the contents of the parents' rights handbook be explained to the parents in their native language or mode of communication. The parents cannot simply be handed a document to read. This is crucial because of the increasing numbers of illiterate adults, as well as parents with developmental and learning disabilities, raising school-age children who may also have disabilities. A thorough explanation of their rights protected by law, given by a competent and caring professional, can set the tone for a working "partnership" between the school and the parents. It should be noted that when the parent is unable or unwilling to participate in the process of educating the child, the courts may assign a "child advocate" to serve in that capacity.

2. The parents must give informed consent for the child to be tested. (Please refer to Figures 17-1 and 17-2, samples of forms used to obtain parent consent for assessment/evaluation of a child with a suspected disability.)

   (Please refer to Figure 17-3, a sample of a form used to notify parents of the need for intervention by special education personnel, a form which seeks consent for observation of the child and school and in-home interviews.)

3. The child must be evaluated with tests that are valid; the tests must measure that which they claim to measure. The tests must be non-discriminatory. For example, a child of a migrant farm worker should not be evaluated with an instrument that reflects the upper middle-class suburban experience. In addition, the tests must be administered in the

8-29-10
Form SE-74A (Rev.) — 10M — 2292 — 90-E
SC-03-30490

WHITE — Central File
CANARY — Local
PINK — Parent

2.0
Page 1 of 2

Dallas Independent
School District

PARENTAL CONSENT FOR INDIVIDUAL EVALUATION

Student _____ I.D. _____ D.O.B. _____ Grade _____

To the Parent(s):

Members of the staff at _____ School have been considering your child's
need for additional help because of the following school-related problems:

_____

_____

They have considered the following information: attendance records, grades and test scores, observations of your child in the classroom, reports about your child's vision and hearing, information about your child's health, information about your child's language, and information you have given the school about the child.

Alternatives that have been tried to help your child include:

Alternative	Outcome
1. _____	_____
2. _____	_____
3. _____	_____
4. _____	_____

Based on these results, it has been determined that a comprehensive evaluation is needed to adequately plan your child's education program. The evaluation procedures to be used will cover the following major areas:

LANGUAGE/COMMUNICATION: If your child knows more than one language, these tests will help us to find out which is the best language for his/her learning. Also, this will let us know which language to use for all of the other testing. If his/her best language is not English, an interpreter will give all the other tests in the language that your child speaks and understands best. If your child has trouble speaking clearly, a speech teacher may test him/her to find out what the speech problem is. We also want to test how well your child understands what is said to him/her and how well he/she can express his/her thoughts. Some of the tests we may give are: **Goldman-Fristoe Tests of Articulation and Auditory Discrimination** and **Test of Language Development** or similar tests.

PHYSICAL: We need to know if any physical health problems make it difficult for your child to do his/her school work. We may ask the school nurse, nurse practitioner/physician's assistant, and physical or occupational therapist to test in these areas. We may wish to give him/her tests, such as: vision and hearing screening, medical examination, gross and fine motor assessment and **Connor's Rating Scale** for hyperactivity.

EMOTIONAL/BEHAVIORAL: We want to know how well your child gets along with others at school and at home. We will talk with you, your child, and his/her teachers. Also, we may want to see how he/she works in one of his/her classes at school. To find out what your child thinks about himself/herself, a school psychologist or associate school psychologist may use such techniques as drawing pictures, making up stories, or completing sentences.

SOCIOLOGICAL: We will want to talk with you to get information about your child's home life and kinds of experiences he/she has had in your family. School staff members may be calling to talk with you about this.

FIGURE 17-1. Parental consent for individual evaluation form. (Courtesy Dallas Independent School District.)

10-10-28
Form SE-74 (Rev.)—3M—10224—88-E
SC-03-30480

WHITE — Central File
CANARY — Local
PINK — Parent

2.0
Page 2 of 2

PARENTAL CONSENT FOR INDIVIDUAL EVALUATION

Dallas Independent
School District

In the event your child is eligible and will continue to need special education services, a comprehensive evaluation assessing the areas above will be completed within a minimum of every three years. Formal and informal assessments will be ongoing as needed.

You will be notified following the completion of your child's evaluation and invited to a meeting to discuss the results. At this time, any recommended changes in your child's program and/or special education placement will be reviewed.

I have been informed of the referral of my child for individual testing or other evaluation procedures described above. I have received a copy of **Special Education: Parent and Student Rights, 1986**. This handbook documents for me the local school procedures for prior notice (pages 2, 4), consent procedures (pages 2, 4), my rights in the assessment process (pages 5, 6), the confidentially of records (pages 13, 14), the complaint process (pages 15-17) and the least restrictive environment (page 2, 10). I do understand my rights.

_____ YES   _____ NO

_____ I give my consent to conduct the evaluation described. I understand that my consent is voluntary and may be revoked at any time.

_____ I request a conference to discuss the referral of my child.

_____ I request a conference to discuss my rights.

_____ I do not want my child evaluated at this time.

_____   _____
Date   Signature of Parent/Guardian

_____   _____
Signature of Interpreter (if used)   Signature of person obtaining informed consent and phone number

---

FIGURE 17-1, cont'd. Parental consent for individual evaluation form.

child's native language and/or mode of communication. A Spanish-speaking child cannot be asked to take a test in English. A deaf child must be evaluated via an interpreter. A severely multiply disabled child may need to be evaluated using a picture board. The law is also clear that more than one instrument must be used to evaluate the child before decisions can be made regarding the child's education program. The dates of evaluation and the names of the instruments used to gather data must be included on the child's IEP.

4. The child must be educated in the least restrictive environment. The decision regarding placement must be made by a multidisciplinary team in a meeting that includes the child's parent(s) (IEP meeting).

5. The test results and proposed educational procedures must be reviewed by a multidisciplinary team in a meeting that includes the child's parents (IEP meeting).

6. The parents have the right, under the law, to seek an independent evaluation if they do not agree with the results of the multidisciplinary team evaluation.

Each of these provisions ensures that the best possible decisions will be made regarding the child's education. The provisions mandate a series of checks and balances that increase the likelihood that a child will receive an appropriate education.

PERSONNEL

This section describes the variety of personnel who provide both direct and related services and may be involved in the initial evaluation and in the child's subsequent individually designed education program.

IDEA stipulates those services that are to be "direct" and those that are to be "related." Direct services are

08-8960-0005—7-2-246
500—4499—86-E

Dallas Independent School District

TEMA: NOTICIA Y PERMISO PARA COLOCACION INICIAL

PARA: _____ TOCANTE A _____ _____
         Nombre del Padre   Nombre del estudiante   Fecha

DE MIEMBROS DE PERSONAL _____ S.S.# _____
                    Nombre De La Escuela

NOTICIA PARENTAL DE COLOCACION INICIAL

El Comité de Admisión, Repaso, y Retiro (ARD) ha repasado con cuidado toda la información recogida para la Avaluación Comprensiva Individual. Basado en este repaso, el Comité ARD ha determinado que_____ está elegible para los servicios de la Educación Especial. Una noticia escrita por miembros del Comité ARD y un Plan Educacional Individual (PEI) registran la decisión de colocar a su niño en un mejor programa educacional. Se necesita su permiso antes de que pueda empezar esta colocación propuesta.

PERMISO PARENTAL PARA LA COLOCACION INICIAL

Esta forma debe ser completada por el padre, guardián, o padre subrogado de:

_____ _____ _____
Nombre del Estudiante   Edad Cronológica   Fecha de Nacimiento

Favor de marcar ☑ los recuadros de "sí" solamente si está de acuerdo que las declaraciones son correctas. Si las declaraciones no son correctas, marque los recuadros de "no." Cuando termine, favor de firmar su nombre y la fecha y devolver esta forma a la escuela lo más pronto posible.

☐ ☐ He recibido y comprendo el reporte del Comite de Admisión, Repaso,
sí no y Retiro (ARD), de la fecha _____, que se ha preparado para

         _____
         Nombre del Estudiante

☐ ☐ Me han dado el nombre y el numero de teléfono de un miembro de personal de la
sí no escuela a quien puedo llamar si deseo obtener más información o si tengo preguntas.

☐ ☐ Estoy de acuerdo con la decision del Comité ARD y doy mi permiso para la colocación
sí no educacional especial que se ha propuesto para mi niño.

☐ ☐ Entiendo que mi permiso es voluntario y puede ser revocado por escrito a cualquier
sí no tiempo.

☐ ☐ Me han dado una copia del folleto, "Los Derechos de Los Padres y Estudiantes a Una
sí no Educación Especial." Un miembro de personal de la escuela me ha explicado cada
         sección de este folleto, incluyendo las páginas número _____.

Después de repasar el reporte del Comité ARD haga favor de completar la forma de aviso parental y devolverla a:
MIEMBRO DE PERSONAL DE LA ESCUELA: _____
ESCUELA_____ DIRECCION _____

Si desea tener información o si tiene preguntas, favor de llamar a:

MIEMBRO DE PERSONAL DE LA ESCUELA _____ NUMERO DE TELEFONO _____

_____   _____
Firma del Padre, Guardian, Padre Subrogado   Fecha

_____   _____
Firma del Intérprete (si se usa)   Fecha

FIGURE 17-2. Noticia y permiso para colocacion inicial form. (Courtesy Dallas Independent School District.)

WHITE — Central File
CANARY — Local School
PINK — Parent

DISD

Dallas Independent School District

PARENTAL NOTICE AND CONSENT FOR
TECHNICAL ASSISTANCE BY SPECIAL EDUCATION

Student: _____ I.D. # _____

School: _____ Grade: _____ Birth Date: _____

Members of the staff at _____ School have been considering your child's need for additional help at school because of the following school related problems:

_____

_____

We have considered the following information: attendance records, grades and test scores, observations of your child in the classroom, reports about your child's vision and hearing, information about your child's health, information about your child's language, and information you have given the school about your child.

Alternatives that have been tried to help your child include:

Alternative	Length of Time	Outcome
1. _____	_____	_____
2. _____	_____	_____
3. _____	_____	_____
4. _____	_____	_____

After discussing the results of the above alternatives, we are requesting further observation and review of your child's records by special education personnel to help us better understand your child's educational needs.

If you agree with this request, please sign this approval for special education personnel to conduct the following activities at this time:*

Review of school records _____   Parent interview _____
Classroom observation _____   School staff interview _____
Student interview _____

_____ I do give my consent for all the activities checked above.

_____ I do not give my consent for the activities listed above.

_____   _____
Signature of Parent Guardian   Date

If you wish to have more information or if you have any questions, please call:

_____   _____
School Staff Person   Telephone Number

_____   _____
Signature of Interpreter (if used)   Date

*If further assessment is recommended, a Special Education Visiting Teacher will schedule a meeting with you to get your written permission for this assessment.

FIGURE 17-3. Parental notice and consent for technical assistance by special education form. (Courtesy Dallas Independent School District.)

those to be provided as part of the child's special education. These include (1) instruction conducted in the classroom, in the home, in hospitals and institutions, and in other settings, as well as (2) instruction in physical education. The personnel involved in the provision of these services are described below.

Special Educators

Special educators are professional personnel who have received specific training in the techniques and methodology of educating children with disabilities. In the past, special educators were trained primarily to provide instruction to children with one particular disability. For example, special educators received training and subsequent certification in "mental retardation," "emotional disturbance" or "deaf education." Today, most professional preparation programs provide training that leads to a generic (general) special education certification. This general training and certification better prepares educators to serve disabled children in the public schools, who frequently have more than one disability. For example, one child may be diagnosed as learning disabled, emotionally disturbed, and may have a hyperactive attention deficit disorder. Each disabling condition must be considered when designing the learning environment.

The level and type of instruction provided to children with disabilities depends on the child's present level of performance and expectations for future performance. For example, special educators working with profoundly mentally retarded, multi-disabled, medically fragile children provide sensory stimulation experiences and health care. Special educators working with autistic, developmentally delayed children provide a very structured pre-vocational, self-care program. Those teachers working with severely emotionally disturbed, abused children may present a pre-academic or academic curriculum within the framework of a structured behavior management program. The special educator, a classroom teacher, has primary responsibility for the child with disabilities.

Generally, as the child's primary teacher, the child's special educator is responsible for the implementation and monitoring of the IEP. The special educator should work closely with other professionals, including the physical educator and the adapted physical educator, to ensure that the child acquires developmentally appropriate motor skills. The physical educator should regularly communicate with the classroom teacher.

The child's special educator is also a tremendous resource, because that teacher works with the child closely on a daily basis. This professional may provide vital information regarding techniques to manage the child's behavior and to enhance instruction.

Hospital/Homebound Instructors

Hospital/homebound instructors are trained professionals who provide special education instruction to children who are hospitalized or who, because of severe medical disabilities, cannot be educated within the typical school setting. The education is the same, only the setting is different.

Instructors in Institutions and Other Settings

For a variety of reasons, some children, often the profoundly, multiply disabled, receive their education within an institutional setting. Within recent years court mandates have significantly improved the quality of both instruction and care within these facilities.

Adapted Physical Educators

The art, the science, and the profession of adapted physical education is described throughout the entire text. The role of the adapted physical educator, as part of the multidisciplinary team, is summarized below.

Adapted physical educators are physical educators with specialized training; the extent of required training is determined on a state-by-state basis. Specifically, these professionals have training in the assessment and evaluation of motor behavior and physical fitness, the development of the child's individual physical education program (IPEP), the implementation of the child's IPEP, and the processes of teaching and managing the behavior of children with disabilities. Their services are required by law.

The Education of the Handicapped Act mandated that physical education was to be a vital part of each child's special education program. In fact, physical education was the only curricular area designated specifically as a required, direct service. The intent of the law was that specially trained, adapted physical educators would provide quality, direct, "hands-on," daily physical education instruction to children with disabilities. A lack of financial and personnel resources, as well as a lack of commitment to physical education in general, has made this scenario a dream, rather than a reality, in most school districts.

In many school districts with full-time, on-staff, adapted physical educators, the caseloads (the numbers of children served) are often huge. The adapted physical educator is often itinerant; that is, the teacher travels from school to school, carrying assessment tools and equipment in his or her car. Because the adapted physical education teacher may actually only provide direct service to the child one or two times per week, the teacher must rely on the regular physical educator and the child's special educator to provide day-to-day instruction.

Not all adapted physical educators are hired on a full-time basis. Many school districts, meeting only the "letter of the law," hire adapted physical educators on a part-time basis as consultants. The consultant assesses and develops an IPEP for a child. However, once again, the regular physical educator and the child's special educator have to assume responsibility for the implementation of the IPEP. As a result, more and more children with disabilties receive physical education services within the "mainstream." The schedule of the regular physical educator usually makes it impossible for him/her to provide direct service to children with disabilities except as part of regularly scheduled classes. The child's special educator, often overwhelmed by the extent of the required curriculum, finds it the "path of least resistance" to allow the child with a disability to receive physical education services in the "regular" physical education class. Unfortunately, this often occurs even when the "regular" physical education class is not the child's least restrictive environment.

The physical educator, faced with serving large numbers of children with disabilities in the "regular" physical education class should actively seek the support and assistance of the adapted physical educator. The physical educator may get the following types of help from the adapted physical educator: information about how to design a humane, caring, mainstreamed physical education environment; completion and interpretation of a full-scale motor and physical fitness eval-uation; recommendations for programming; instruction about how to modify grading criteria and standards; and suggestions for how to revise the curriculum to meet the special needs of children with disabilities.

Vision Specialists

Historically, a severely visually impaired child received educational services within a segregated environment. Typically, educational services were delivered in a separate residential school facility or within a self-contained room in a given school building. In that setting, the child's primary teacher was a vision teacher specially trained to meet the educational needs of the blind child.

The Regular Education Initiative (REI), the federally supported concept that suggests that children with special needs should be educated within the "regular" education program, has had a significant impact on the education of the visually impaired. Specifically, the visually impaired child, whenever possible, is educated in his/her home school with support from vision specialists and orientation and mobility specialists. Children who are totally blind, legally blind, partially sighted, or multiply handicapped (whose visual loss is only one of their impairments) may be educated with support within the regular education classroom in school districts embracing the concept of the REI.

The vision specialists and the orientation and mobility specialists have the skills necessary to complete a visual evaluation and educational assessment to determine the extent of visual disability and the types and kinds of intervention that will make possible a successful educational experience. The vision therapist/

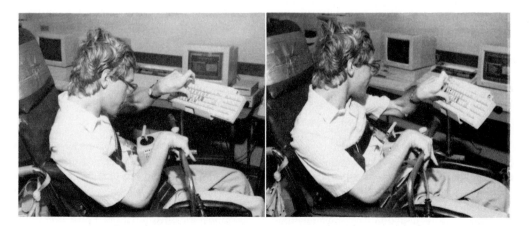

FIGURE 17-4. Assistive technology may be mandated on the student's IEP.
(Courtesy Dallas Independent School District.)

teacher focuses on modification of instruction, which may include specific visual, tactile, and/or auditory learning techniques. Other modifications also may be required for the child to learn in the designated education setting. The therapist may suggest augmentative aids, like a Braille typewriter, an abacus, or a text enlarger to meet the unique needs of the child.

The orientation and mobility specialist will work with the child and his or her regular or special educators to help develop the skills necessary, for example, to use a cane or to successfully ascend/descend school bus stairs.

The vision specialist and orientation and mobility specialist will work closely with the physical educator and adapted physical educator to ensure the child has a successful experience in the regular physical education program, if appropriate. They may suggest modifications, which include a "buddy system" or a "peer tutor system."

RELATED SERVICES

The law also specifies and defines "related services." These are services that must be provided to the child with disabilities so that the child can benefit from instruction. The related services are described below.

Audiologists

The audiologist is trained to complete a comprehensive evaluation of a child's hearing capabilities. This includes an evaluation of the child's response to the qualities of sound—intensity, pitch, frequency, and timbre. Based on the results of the evaluation, the audiologist makes recommendations to school personnel. The audiologist may suggest, for example, simple modifications in the education environment of the mildly hearing impaired child to facilitate learning; specifically, the child may be placed close to the teacher for instructional purposes. The audiologist may recommend that a hearing aid be provided for the more severely hearing impaired child and may work closely with trained special educators who will help the child develop total communication skills, including sign language, speech reading, and oral language.

Counselors

Counseling services are becoming increasingly important in the total education process for all children, particularly children with disabilities. These services may take a variety of forms. The school-based counselor may serve children with disabilities by implementing programs designed to enhance self-esteem, to teach children to identify and avoid sexual abuse, to share

techniques for values identification and clarification, or by teaching techniques and methods for dealing with grief.

Children with disabilities living within dysfunctional families may need a more comprehensive intervention. These children may need individual counseling services in order to benefit from educational services. Because the family unit must be addressed if counseling is to be of value and have long-lasting effects, the most effective programs involve each member of the family in the counseling process.

Medical Diagnostic Service Personnel

IDEA indicates that medical diagnostic services must be provided for a child who needs these services in order to benefit from his or her education. Many school districts have working partnerships with a hospital or rehabilitation facility so that children who require medical diagnostic services can be referred to that hospital or center. It is important to note, however, that the law does not mandate medical services, just medical diagnostics; wisely, it was decided that the provision of medical services for children with disabilities would be financially prohibitive for school districts.

In order to be eligible for special education services a child with an orthopedic impairment or other health impairment must be diagnosed as having a disability; this diagnosis must be made by a licensed physician. In order for a child to be identified as "emotionally disturbed," a licensed psychiatrist must confirm the diagnosis.

In addition, physicians and rehabilitation specialists work closely with members of the occupational therapy, physical therapy, recreation therapy, and adapted physical education staff. These professionals work in cooperation to assure that the child's medical needs are being addressed in the school setting.

Many school districts hire a physician's assistant or nurse as part of the special education staff. These trained professionals serve as liaisons between the special education department and the hospital or rehabilitation facility.

Occupational Therapists

The Education of the Handicapped Act mandated that occupational therapy must be made available to a child with a disability who requires this service in order to allow the child to be successful in the educational environment. Prior to passage of this act, the pediatric occupational therapist functioned primarily within hospitals, community-based agencies, home-health care agencies, and rehabilitation facilities. Now pediatric occupational therapists are a vital part of the total education process and can be an integral part of a motor development team.

The American Occupational Therapy Association has adopted the following occupational therapy performance areas.[4] These are the focus of occupational therapists in all settings.

1. Activities of daily living
   a. Grooming
   b. Oral hygiene
   c. Bathing
   d. Toilet hygiene
   e. Dressing
   f. Feeding and eating
   g. Medication routine
   h. Socialization
   i. Functional communication
   j. Functional mobility
   k. Sexual expression
2. Work activities
   a. Home management
   b. Care of others
   c. Educational activities
   d. Vocational activities
3. Play or leisure activities
   a. Play or leisure exploration
   b. Play or leisure performance

Occupational therapists working within the educational setting have had to define their role and focus in relationship to special education. As a result, the school-based therapist has had to develop a strategy to function within the educational model rather than the medical model. The American Occupational Therapy Association has described the occupational therapist serving in the schools in the following way[5]:

> Registered occupational therapists in education systems are considered to be related service personnel. The occupational therapist is responsible for assessment, planning, and goal development and for providing appropriate intervention services designed to enhance the student's potential for learning, to assist the student in acquiring those functional performance skills needed to participate in and benefit from the educational environment, and to help the student function independently.

According to Orr, Gott, and Kainer,[24] the occupational therapist in the school setting must focus on the student role. Within the schools, these professionals concentrate on activities of daily living that are part and parcel of the process of going to school. In addition, the school-based occupational therapist defines "school" as a child's "work." The occupational therapist

is responsible for assuring that the student with a disability can assume the role of student and benefit from instruction within the school setting. They define behaviors and activities that comprise the role of the student and then develop strategies to allow the child to be successful in the student role.

The school-based occupational therapist might contribute to the child's school success in a number of ways. The therapist may help wheelchair-enabled students move independently within the school by teaching them to carry a lunch tray on their lap, manage a ramp to and from the playground, and move through crowded halls without running into classmates. The therapist may assist a learning disabled student by providing sensorimotor training to ready the child to receive instruction. The therapist may help the autistic child develop basic play skills.

The occupational therapist will often work in cooperation with the physical educator, particularly to ensure student success in managing travel around the gymnasium or playground, in developing strategies to maximize the development of appropriate social skills/play behavior, and to contribute to the physical education individual exercise plan.

Parent Counselors and Trainers

IDEA affirmed the fact that the parent is the child's first and primary teacher. This echoes mandates in PL 99-457 (Education for All Handicapped Children Amendments of 1986) for parental involvement in early intervention.

Parent counseling and training is vital for those facing the reality of raising a child with a disability. This counseling and training addresses the grief process. Parents of a child with a congenital disability (one present at birth) experience a great deal of grief for the child who "would have been" president...a Harvard graduate...a basketball superstar. The parents must grieve the loss of the child who "would have been" before they can rejoice in the child who is.

This counseling and training is even more crucial for a single parent raising a disabled child. The financial struggles, the loneliness, and the fears are overwhelming.

Parent counseling and training focuses, as well, on helping the parent(s) develop appropriate expectations regarding the child's growth and development. The parent must be helped to develop realistic, yet hopeful, goals for the child.

Parent counseling and training also introduces home teaching methodologies and therapy that can be conducted in the home. The adapted physical educator

Occupational Therapy
Defined Student Role Tasks

STUDENT ROLE TASKS

Manage school environment

Physical space
  Access school
  Access classroom(s)
  Access lunchroom
  Access gym
  Place self at desk
  Manage stairs/ramp
  Access class worksites
  Access bus
Schedules
  Keep precise schedule
  Stay within 15 minutes of schedule
  Stay within 30 minutes of schedule
Self-help
  Manage coat
  Manage books
  Manage locker
  Manage school supplies
  Manage toilet needs
  Eat lunch
  Manage lunchline

Participate in instructional activities

Use of education tools
  Manipulate educational objects
  Produce printed shapes, letters, numbers
  Produce printed words, number groups
  Produce printed sentences
  Use work sheets
  Cut
  Construct
  Record information (notes, board copy)
Readiness for instruction
  Maintain learning ready posture
  Prepare supplies for use

Manage school social interactions

Orientation to activity
  Orient body toward instruction
  Direct response to class/teacher
  Work independently
Group member function
  Wait for turn
  Stand in line
  Remain in instruction area
  Share workspace
Relationship formation
  Cooperate in group assignments
  Share materials

---

might be asked, for example, to develop a home fitness program or to provide the parent(s) with information on techniques for modifying a favorite sport or game so that the child with a disability can be included.

Physical Therapists

The physical therapist is trained to provide services that address range of motion, maintenance and development of muscle tonus, gait therapy, and mobility assistance with and without physical aids or equipment. The physical therapist can be a vital and integral part of the motor development team. The therapist brings to the child with disabilities a vast wealth of information regarding human motion.

One of the major problems facing the public schools that are attempting to meet the mandates of the federal law is that it is increasingly difficult to hire a physical therapist to work within the schools. The services of physical therapists are sought by hospitals, rehabilitation facilities, and nursing homes; generally, the public schools cannot compete financially to hire and retain physical therapists.

Psychologists

Psychological services for children with disabilities, and if necessary for their parent(s), have been designated as a related service. Many school districts provide these services by hiring a psychologist or psychiatrist as a consultant or on a per-child basis. Larger school districts may hire school-based psychologists as part of the assessment and intervention team.

These professionals are involved in the assessment of children with disabilities referred because of emotional disturbance, aggressive behavior toward other children or their parent(s), severe depression, suicidal tendencies or attempted suicides, or because of reports of sexual or physical abuse or serious neglect.

Psychological services to children with disabilities

must include assessment within the child's home or residential facility, the development of an in-home or in-residence intervention program, and parent training.

Recreation Therapists

The recreation therapist approaches the child and adolescent with disabilities with the knowledge that these individuals will, throughout the lifespan, have a great deal of leisure time. They frequently have a large amount of leisure time because, unfortunately, while current unemployment rates among the general population average 7% to 8%, depending on geographical location and population distribution by race, the unemployment rate among individuals with disabilities hovers near 65%.[28]

The school-based recreation therapist provides instruction so individuals with disabilities will be able to make wise choices in the use of leisure time. The intent is to provide instruction so that their students will be able to participate in community and culturally-based leisure activities. For example, the wellness program for individuals with disabilities at Vinland Center, in Loretta, Minnesota, introduces paraplegics to pulk ice hockey, quadriplegics to toboganning, and blind athletes to downhill skiing. Equest, a Dallas-based horseback riding program for those with disabilities, introduces children and adults to a "Texas tradition"— horseback riding. A recreation therapist in "Little Italy" in New York city might teach Boccii to his/her students.

The recreation therapist works closely with the adapted physical educator and the physical educator. Individuals with disabilities need to be taught, carefully taught, the skills necessary to enjoy recreation and leisure. In most school systems, the adapted physical educator, in collaboration with the physical educator, focuses on the development of skills that are prerequisites (basic) to the development of leisure and recreation competency. The recreation therapist focuses on the use of motor skills within a community-based recreational setting; for example, a bowling alley, a roller skating rink, a swimming pool, or a YMCA/YWCA.

Because of the commitment of recreation therapists to community-based, lifetime activity development, these professionals plays a vital role in the development of the child's transition plan. The child's IEP in middle school and high school must include specific goals and objectives related to community-based leisure and recreation activities.

Rehabilitation Counselor

Rehabilitation counseling focuses on helping the child with a disability gain the confidence and learn the skills necessary to function as normally as possible. Most rehabilitation counseling and rehabilitation services address the needs of children with adventitious injuries or disabilities; these are injuries or disabilities that occur after the child has already experienced "normal" development.

Rehabilitation counseling addresses grief; specifically, the child with a new injury or disability must grieve the loss of function or ability before he or she can get on with life. It also addresses strategies for the reestablishment of self-esteem. Techniques are taught so that the child can adapt or compensate for the injury or disability and live a full life.

Play, games, and sports have been found to be effective tools in the rehabilitation process. Indeed, most major rehabilitation facilities encourage participation in these activities to facilitate recovery and development.

One of the major roles of the rehabilitation counselor is to provide a link between the school and community agencies, including the school-based social worker.

Assistive Technology Service Personnel

Congress defined assistive technology service as:

> Any service that directly assists an individual with a disability in the selection, acquisition, or use of an assistive technology device. Such term includes—(A) the evaluation of the needs of an individual with a disability, including a functional evaluation of the individual in the individual's customary environment; (B) purchasing, leasing, or otherwise providing for the acquisition of assistive technology devices by individuals with disabilities; (C) selecting, designing, fitting, customizing, adapting, applying, maintaining, repairing or replacing of assistive technology devices; (D) coordinating and using other therapies, interventions, or services with assistive technology devices, such as those associated with existing education and rehabilitation plans and programs; (E) training or technical assistance for an individual with disabilities, or, where appropriate, the family of an individual with disabilities; and (F) training or technical assistance for professionals (including individuals providing education and rehabilitation services), employers, or other individuals who provide services to, employ, or are otherwise substantially involved in the major life functions of individuals with disabilities.[12]

IDEA focused on the fact that an individual living in the twenty-first century must be comfortable with technology in order to thrive, in order to survive. Assistive technology services is a related service that must be provided to a child who needs such services in order to benefit from the educational experience. The technologies that must be made available to a child with disabilities include computers, sophisticated mobility equipment, modified work stations, and communication systems.

Lavine[17] suggested, "Personal computers may offer their greatest benefits to still another group of people—those who, for one reason or another, have limited abilities to influence and interact with the outside world...For them, personal computers can help bridge the barriers imposed by their handicaps." A statement of the Instruction Systems Technology Division of the Dallas Independent School District[1] included, "The population of students who stand to gain the most from microcomputer technology are those who have physical, sensory, emotional and/or cognitive limitations which have caused them to be isolated from their 'regular' peers."

Cain[8] suggested six reasons why computer technology must be included within special education programs. They are:

1. Computer technology is a vital component of "regular" education so it should be a vital component of special education to ensure program equity.
2. These technologies prepare individuals with disabilities for the most productive life possible.
3. Computers can serve as a vital tool for compensatory, expressive and receptive language.
4. Computers provide the opportunity for children with disabilities to experience the real world through simulation activities.
5. Computers serve as a prosthetic communication device for dyslexics, the deaf, the hard of hearing, the visually impaired, and the language-disordered.
6. Computers can provide a recreational alternative for children to enable them to "play" soccer, golf, football, or ping pong via computer.

Adaptations that allow all children to use and learn with the aid of a computer include alternative keyboards, enlarged keyboards, communication board overlays tied to "talking" computer systems, touch windows, single switch input devices, and voice-activated systems.

Assistive technology may also take the form of sophisticated, or simple, mobility aids. Equipment is available that provides muscle stimulation and allows independent exercise for individuals with muscle atrophy. Equipment has been designed that allows a quadriplegic to control his or her motor function using electrodes. Tricycles have been modified with velcro straps to help hold hands to handlebars and feet to pedals.

School Health Service Personnel

School health services must be provided to children with disabilities. In most school districts, these services are provided by a school nurse. These health services include monitoring immunization records and monitoring and/or completing health procedures like catheterization or tracheostomy tube suction. In the Irving Independent School District v. Tatro, 1984, the U.S. Supreme Court decided that health services that are needed to enable a child to reach, enter, exit, or remain in school during the day were required.[13]

School health services for children with disabilities become more complex as more medically fragile children pursue their right to a free, appropriate public education as mandated by IDEA and Section 504 of the Rehabilitation Act.

Social Workers

Social work services, which include group and individual counseling with children and their families (home-centered where possible), are a vital part of related services required by law. The licensed social worker intervenes within the family, seen as part of the total community, and helps the child with disabilities and his or her family deal with issues that directly relate to the disability—discrimination, fear, guilt, substance abuse, child-abuse, medical expenses, and the intrusion of well-meaning professionals into their lives.

The social worker is trained to assist the family to cope with the vast and often complex system designed to provide support for families in trouble. The social worker can, for example, help a parent apply for Aid for Dependent Children or, if necessary, unemployment compensation.

In some large school districts community social service agencies have opened offices within the schools to improve access to needed social services. This strategy has proved valuable in providing assistance to non–English-speaking children and their families.

Speech Pathologists

Speech and language therapy has as its goal the improvement of communication behaviors of students whose speech and/or language deficits affect educational performance. Haynes[11] has identified four separate speech and language components that must be addressed by the therapist: (1) semantics (language content or meaning); (2) syntax (language structure or grammar); (3) pragmatics (language use or function); and (4) phonology, the sound system of language.

Service delivery in speech and language programs was historically based on a medical model in which the speech and language therapist provided therapy to children with speech and language deficits in a clinical, isolated setting. That is, the clinician provided speech and language programming in a setting removed from the child's regular education or special education classroom. That practice is changing.

Current, innovative practice in speech and language programs is based on the notion that speech and language is a basic and integral part of the child's total life experience. As Achilles, Yates, and Freese have suggested,[2] the child uses speech and language throughout the day, in a variety of environments, in response to a variety of stimuli, and in interaction with many different people; and as such, it is an on-going process. Therefore speech and language therapy must be embedded within the total academic and non-academic curriculum.

To allow classroom-based therapy to occur, the speech and language therapist functions collaboratively with the child's regular educator and/or special educator.[21] The therapist is often willing to collaborate with the physical educator or the adapted physical educator because the advantages identified in classroom-based language instruction pertain to the physical education "classroom," or adapted physical education "classroom," as well. In fact, the very nature of physical education makes it an exciting, language-rich opportunity. Children involved in dance, play, or games are functioning within their most natural environment; this environment demands communication in a variety of forms—gesture, sign, expressive facial behaviors, or expressive/receptive speech.

In addition, the therapist collaborates with the physical educator/adapted physical educator because of the obvious relationship between gross and fine motor development and the development of speech and language. Indeed, movement is speech; speech is movement.

Transportation Specialists

In Alamo Heights v. State Board of Education (1986) the court mandated that transportation, like other related services, must be included on the child's IEP.[3] The Office of Civil Rights has decreed that a child with a disability should not have to ride the school bus longer than other children. The Office of Civil Rights also indicates it is a violation of civil rights if a child with a disability has a shorter instructional day than other children because of the school bus schedule. In addition, the child with a disability should have the same access to extracurricular, before-school or after-school, programs as any other child.[23]

If the child needs an aide on the bus during transportation to and from school, recent litigation indicates it should be included on the IEP, as well. In Macomb County Intermediate School District v. Joshua S., 1989, the court mandated that the school district must provide an aide to help a multiply handicapped student who needed positioning in a wheelchair and a tracheostomy tube suctioned during the ride to and from school.[18]

A representative of the transportation department may need to be invited to the meeting at which the child's IEP is formulated.

The law also mandates the provision of transition services. These services are designed to help the child or adolescent with a disability move comfortably into the community.

Transition Service Personnel

Transition services are vital if an individual with a disability is to function in the mainstream of life. Ultimately that is the goal of all special education and rehabilitation programs.

These transition services may take a variety of forms. One of the major transition services offered through special education is vocational education. A quality vocational education program includes a comprehensive assessment of vocational potential and capabilities. The student with a disability is given the opportunity to demonstrate his or her unique skills and talents so that appropriate job training can be provided. As the student enters middle school and high school, the focus of the education provided is vocational. Special education instruction focuses on the skills necessary to function within a workplace. Actual work-related opportunities are provided in "work production" or "work simulation" classes. Some progressive school districts have job placement opportunities for children with disabilities in the last years of their special education career. In fact, some provide "job coaches." The primary responsibility of the job coach is to work "shoulder to shoulder" with a student with a disability at the actual job site to assist the student with the technical aspects of the job as well as the social nuances of the job. For example, if the student is being trained as a maid for a major hotel chain, the job coach accompanies the student to the hotel, both wearing the same uniform as every other employee, and helps the student learn the day-to-day routine and processes involved in being a successful employee.

Other transition services include continuing and adult education, adult and independent living services, and introduction to community services. Transition services that should be addressed on the student's IEP include transition into community-based recreation and sports programs. The adapted physical educator and the recreation therapist work with students with disabilities to help the child develop the skills necessary to play and recreate in the community. For example, it is not enough to teach a student with a disability to bowl. That student must also be able to enter the alley, pay for shoes, put them on, choose a ball, find the right lane and, if possible, keep score.

Each of these professionals brings a special expertise to the child with a disability. Seldom does one child require the services of all these specialized professionals. However, the intent of the law is that, these personnel must be made available if necessary for the child to benefit from the educational process.

Seldom are all these professionals on-staff personnel within a given district. Small school districts may rely on a special education center to provide such services. These centers are called by different names in different states. In Kansas, the term *cooperative special education center* is used. In Michigan, the title *intermediate school district* is given to centers that provide specialized services. In Texas, *regional special education service centers* work in close cooperation with local school districts. When this type of special education center is not available, school districts hire their own specialized personnel on a contractual basis or refer children to private practitioners and/or hospitals or rehabilitation centers for assessment/evaluation services and/or programming.

Regardless of the arrangement used to ensure that students with disabilities receive appropriate assessment/evaluation and intervention, the process of determining which students need services (evaluating the children's performances and determining appropriate placement and services) is similar in most school districts. The first step in the process is to identify the child with special needs.

IDENTIFYING THE CHILD WITH SPECIAL NEEDS

Children who have serious disabilities are usually identified as needing special services before they reach school age. Many school districts now have cooperative agreements with hospitals and social service agencies that improve the likelihood of early identification of at-risk children. In some states, this early identification process begins with the identification of mothers-at-risk during pregnancy. This early identification of mothers-at-risk is particularly crucial if parents are drug abusers, carriers of sexually transmitted diseases,

human immunodeficiency virus (HIV) positive, or have a history of child abuse with other children in the family.

Early identification and early intervention are the only way real strides will be made in preventing and meeting the needs of children with disabilities.

When children with disabilities are identified before they enter the formal school setting, the more fortunate child may have a history of receiving professional help from as early as birth. The less fortunate, the homeless child with a disability, for example, may have received no services while living a transient life in and out of shelters, abandoned buildings, and abandoned cars. Children who have received services early in life usually arrive at school with a large portfolio that includes assessment and intervention information. Generally, they offer no surprises other than that they perform at higher levels than do children who did not have the benefit of early intervention programs. Indeed, these are the lucky ones — the ones who have the best possible opportunity to thrive.

Children with less apparent disabling conditions are often not so fortunate. Even with the active searches that have been conducted by Child Find programs and pre-kindergarten screening programs, sooner or later every school district discovers a child who is entitled to, who needs, and should have been receiving special services. These children are eventually classified as mildly mentally retarded, learning disabled, or emotionally disturbed. It is not until the child enters the formal schooling years that deficits and an inability to keep up with other children are recognized. These children are first identified by school personnel. Most often the classroom or physical education teacher is the first to become aware of these children's learning problems. Figure 17-5 is a sample of a form used by classroom personnel to identify a child's learning problems.

The physical educator may identify a child's disability early in the school year when screening tests are routinely administered to all children in the physical education class. However, whether the teacher administers a test or not, as children participate in activities with their classmates the slow-developing children soon become apparent. It is often in play that the child is seen in the most natural state and can most readily be identified as one with a developmental delay or unique need. While a child can literally "hide" a disability in a classroom setting (particularly if well-behaved), gait abnormalities, postural deformities, and abnormal movement patterns are easily identified in the physical education setting.

7-12-60
Form SE-1 (Rev)—5M—2202—90-E
SC-03-30320

WHITE — Central File
CANARY — Local

PUPIL ASSISTANCE SUPPORT SYSTEM
TECHNICAL ASSISTANCE/SPECIAL EDUCATION

Dallas Independent
School District

Student: _____ I.D. #: _____ School: _____ Date: _____

Parent/Guardian: _____ Address: _____

D.O.B. _____ Grade: _____ Telephone: Home _____ Bus. _____

TEACHER/CLASSROOM OBSERVATIONS

		YES	NO	P	N/A
1. Does student attend to task when information is presented orally?	1.	☐	☐	☐	☐
2. Does student attend to task when information is presented visually?	2.	☐	☐	☐	☐
3. Does student attend to task when information is presented orally and visually?	3.	☐	☐	☐	☐
4. Are student's fine motor skills adequate for completing activities such as handwriting without reversals, copying assignments, or taking dictation?	4.	☐	☐	☐	☐
5. Does student follow the class rules and routine schedule?	5.	☐	☐	☐	☐
6. Does student exhibit significant disruptive, overactive, or fidgety behavior?	6.	☐	☐	☐	☐
7. Does student exhibit significant shyness or withdrawal behavior?	7.	☐	☐	☐	☐
8. Are emotional disturbances suspected? If so, attach Special Education Student Behavior Record sheet.	8.	☐	☐	☐	☐
9. Has student been referred to psychological services?	9.	☐	☐	☐	☐

PREVIOUS OPPORTUNITY TO LEARN

		YES	NO	P	N/A
10. Is attendance good (cumulative absences_____)?	10.	☐	☐	☐	☐
11. Did student attend kindergarten in public school?	11.	☐	☐	☐	☐
12. Have services such as Chapter I, tutoring, and compensatory programs been tried at least 30 school days?	12.	☐	☐	☐	☐
13. Has student been retained in a grade?	13.	☐	☐	☐	☐

GRADES/ACHIEVEMENT

		YES	NO	P	N/A
14. Is student being taught on grade placement Learner Standards?	14.	☐	☐	☐	☐
15. Does student routinely earn grades less than 70 on his progress reports in reading/language arts?	15.	☐	☐	☐	☐
16. Does student routinely earn grades less than 70 on his progress reports in math?	16.	☐	☐	☐	☐
17. Are student's grades significantly lower than his classmates?	17.	☐	☐	☐	☐
18. Are student's achievement scores historically below the 40th percentile?	18.	☐	☐	☐	☐
19. Has the student mastered the TEAMS?	19.	☐	☐	☐	☐

LANGUAGE FACTORS

		YES	NO	P	N/A
20. Is this a LEP student? If so, indicate LAS score: English_____, Spanish_____, Date_____ What language is normally spoken in the home? _____	20.	☐	☐	☐	☐
21. Is student in a sheltered bilingual class?	21.	☐	☐	☐	☐
22. Has this request for technical assistance been reviewed by a LPAC member?	22.	☐	☐	☐	☐
23. Is the student receiving speech and language service or is assessment recommended?	23.	☐	☐	☐	☐
24. Is learning disability the suspected handicap?	24.	☐	☐	☐	☐

MEDICAL FACTORS AND PARENT INFORMATION

		YES	NO	P	N/A
25. Is the student free of medical problems that may adversely affect learning?	25.	☐	☐	☐	☐
26. If not, have corrective devices or medical solutions been attempted?	26.	☐	☐	☐	☐
27. Is ADHD the suspected handicap? If so, attach the report of the results of medical referral.	27.	☐	☐	☐	☐
28. Have significant factors been identified by the parents? If so, attach explanation.	28.	☐	☐	☐	☐

Primary Reason for technical assistance request: _____

_____

Documentation for review by assessment specialist:

_____ Cumulative records   _____ Results of other districtwide interventions, as appropriate

_____ Health records   _____ ADHD medical referal report

_____ Work samples   _____ Other relevant information

_____ Specific documentation of behavior concerns

_____   _____   _____
Administrator   Referrant   Nurse

_____   _____   _____
LPAC Member   Support Staff   Other/Position

P   = Progressing adequately
N/A = Not applicable

FIGURE 17-5. Pupil assistance support system; technical assistance/special education form. (Courtesy Dallas Independent School District.)

In a time when more and more school districts are moving toward site-based management (decision-making and control by parents, teachers, and the school principal), the school principal or the principal's designated representative—case manager or counselor—assumes the major responsibility for ensuring that the child receives appropriate services. The principal or the principal's designate represents the local education agency in all meetings regarding the child's education.

The principal is contacted either by the child's parents, guardian, or professionals who have been providing services to the severely disabled child or by a teacher who first suspects a child is not performing to the standards expected in the classroom or gymnasium. Once the principal has been notified, a preliminary meeting is usually scheduled. This initial meeting includes a minimum of educational professionals. The personnel involved are the principal or the principal's representative, the teacher, an educational psychologist or educational diagnostician, and a representative of the special education department. The child's learning problems and special needs are discussed, and then the parents or guardian are contacted for their approval to complete a comprehensive assessment on the child. Prior to seeking parental approval for the evaluation, the parents must be notified of their rights and their child's rights. If the parents or guardian agree that the child needs to be evaluated, one member of the professional staff is designated as the assessment/evaluation coordinator. The coordinator then makes arrangements with each of the professionals who is to assess the child and ensures that the assessment is comprehensive and appropriate.

ROLE OF THE PHYSICAL EDUCATOR IN THE PRELIMINARY STAFFING

The physical educator may be asked to provide data on the child's physical fitness level, gross motor competency, and play behavior. Most physical educators do not, however, have the training necessary to complete a comprehensive motor assessment. This is particularly true with the more severely disabled child. In that case, an adapted physical educator should complete the comprehensive motor assessment prior to the IEP staff meeting.

It is vital that the assessment be comprehensive enough to determine the child's present level of performance. Only by identifying the child's competencies, deficits, strengths, and needs can a plan be determined by which the child can be educated.

THE PRELIMINARY IEP STAFF MEETING

In some school districts, a meeting of school personnel, both on-staff and consultant personnel involved with the comprehensive assessment, is held prior to meeting with the child's parents or guardians. This is often done so that school district personnel can approach the parents or guardians with a concensus. That is, however, not the intent of the law. Ideally, the parents or guardians should meet with all professionals involved in the assessment of the child and have access to their information, their insight, and their thoughts regarding the child's performance and subsequent education before a decision is made concerning services and placement.

It is important to note that in some instances a pre-staffing meeting may be necessary because of the nature of the child's parents or guardians. This is true when dealing, for example, with the mentally retarded parents of a mentally retarded child or when dealing with the alcoholic mother of a child with fetal alcohol syndrome. This may also be the case when the child in question is a recently traumatic brain injured child and the parent is in a state of denial, one of the stages of grieving. A pre-staffing meeting may be held to discuss the best possible strategy for sharing information with a parent with unique needs.

THE IEP MEETING

Ideally, the IEP meeting should be attended by each individual who tested the child, the coordinator, the principal or the principal's representative, the classroom teacher and the physical educator, and the child's parents or guardian.

As more and more non-English speaking children and their parents are receiving educational services, the interpreter becomes a vital part of the IEP meeting, as well. The intent of the IEP meeting is that every individual with important information about the child should meet with every other individual with important information about the child and share their information so that, in the end, the child receives the best possible education. Unfortunately, this is not always possible. Often, because of time limitations, not all the people who actually tested the child can attend every meeting. The argument is made that it is neither expedient nor necessary for all evaluators and teachers to be present if those who do attend can interpret the test results. Adapted physical education teachers who find themselves in this situation should be certain that the person making the physical education report understands what the evaluation results were and why it is important to follow the physical education recommendations.

Unfortunately, it is not uncommon for parents of a child with a disability to miss the IEP meeting. This may be the result of a number of factors:

1. The parent is overwhelmed by the educational system and chooses to avoid interacting with professionals involved with the child. This is common particularly when the parent has not been treated, at previous IEP meetings, as a valuable member of the team of individuals seeking to educate the child.

2. The parent, despite repeated attempts to notify, is unaware of the meeting. Difficulty notifying parents is typical in non-English speaking families. It is also typical if parents are illiterate. Difficulty with notification is a particular issue with homeless families; as a rule they are so transient it is difficult to maintain contact over the period of time required to complete evaluation/paperwork.

3. The parent is unable to attend the IEP meeting at the time it is scheduled. A constantly changing work schedule may be one reason for this problem. This is particularly true of migrant farm workers and other members of a temporary work force. School professionals also may have been unwilling to accommodate the parent by scheduling a meeting at night; and the parent may be unaware that it is his or her right to demand a rescheduled meeting.

4. The parent cannot find transportation to the meeting site.

5. The parent is unable to find a "babysitter" and is hesitant to bring other, younger children to the meeting.

6. The parent's cultural background is such that he or she feels obligated to accept the decisions of the professionals involved; as such, the parent feels as if he or she has no input of value.

7. The parent simply doesn't care. As difficult as it is to believe, parents often choose not to attend the IEP meeting because of a lack of interest in the education of their child.

8. The parent may have significant developmental disabilities or emotional disturbances, drug-related and non drug-related, which preclude their participation, without careful assistance, in the IEP process.

If the IEP meeting is held without the parent, a representative of the school must contact the parent to explain the results of the meeting and secure a signature indicating agreement or disagreement with the findings of the committee.

THE IEP MEETING PROCESS

The IEP meeting proceeds as follows:

1. The principal or coordinator gives general background on the child, including the reason the child was referred for testing and the professionals included in the overall evaluation.

2. Each evaluator then gives a concise report that includes the name of the tests administered, the results of the testing (including strengths and deficits demonstrated by the child), and the goals and objectives that should be set for the child. Whenever possible, it is important to tie the physical education findings to results found by other evaluators (e.g., poor balance often can be tied to fine motor delays, visual problems can be tied to reading difficulties, poor self-concept can be associated with motivational problems in the classroom).

3. An open discussion among the people present at the meeting usually is the next step. During this discussion all the needs of the child and alternative methods for meeting these needs are explored. At this point the true multidisciplinary nature of the meeting should surface. Each person must be willing to recognize the value of the services that other persons, particularly the parents, have to offer, as well as the value of his or her own expertise. The knowledgeable physical educator will understand and appreciate services that can be provided by the various therapies; however, he or she must also recognize that many activities in physical education can accomplish the physical and motor goals of the child in an interesting, novel fashion unique to the discipline.

4. Agreement must be reached among the professionals in attendance about which of the child's needs are most pressing and which goals and objectives take precedence over others. When contributing to these decisions, the physical educator should focus on the present level of educational performance evidenced by the child in the physical and motor areas. If through testing the child was found to have basic level deficits such as reflex abnormalities, vestibular delays, or range of motion limitations the physical educator does not believe can be included in the physical education program activities, referral to a related therapy may be the best recommendation. Such a recommendation does not mean the

child should not or cannot participate in some type of physical education class. It simply means that the related therapies should focus on the immediate low level deficits while the child continues to participate in a physical education program that is designed to reinforce the intervention programs provided by the other services. None of the related therapies should replace physical education; however, they could be used to help the student take a more active role in the physical education class.

5. Alternative placements are discussed and agreed on. Once again, physical educators should remember that their services are valuable, regardless of the child's demonstrated functioning levels. Under no circumstances should the physical educator agree that the child should automatically be "mainstreamed" into physical education. Unfortunately some school personnel continue to perceive physical education as supervised "free play." Their perception that physical education is a non-academic experience causes them to devalue physical educa-

FIGURE 17-6. The individual physical education plan must include transition strategies to enhance development of community-based leisure/recreation skills form. (Courtesy Texas Special Olympics.)

tion. Careful consideration should be given the decision regarding placement.

CONTENT OF THE IEP

IDEA explains the IEP and describes its required content as follows[12]:

> The term 'individualized education program' means a written statement for each child with a disability developed in any meeting by a representative of the local education agency or an intermediate educational unit who shall be qualified to provide, or supervise the provision of, specially designed instruction to meet the unique needs of children with disabilities, the teacher, the parents or guardian of such child, and, whenever appropriate, such child, which statement shall include—(A) a statement of the present level of educational performance of such child, (B) a statement of annual goals, including short-term instructional objectives, (C) a statement of the specific educational services to be provided to such child, and the extent to which such child will be able to participate in regular educational programs, (D) a statement of the needed transition services for students beginning no later than age 16 and annually thereafter (and, when determined appropriate for the individual, beginning at age 14 or younger), including, when appropriate, a statement of interagency responsibilities or linkages (or both) before a student leaves the school setting, (E) the projected date for initiation and anticipated duration of such services, and (F) appropriate objective criteria and evaluation procedures and schedules for determining, on at least an annual basis, whether instructional objectives are being achieved. (Sect. 1401.20.)

Figure 17-7 is an example of an IEP.

Process of Writing the IEP

Developing the individualized education program is a procedure that is followed to assure that an appropriate educational experience is designed for each student with a disability. The process provides a mechanism for the student with a disability and family members as well as teachers and professionals from related services to reach joint decisions about goals and objectives and their relative importance. These decisions are, of course, based on the findings of the comprehensive assessment used to determine the child's present level of educational performance. Wilcox and Bellamy[34] have recommended the following sequence at the IEP meeting: (1) each participant proposes activity goals and provides a brief rationale for their selections; (2) the proposed goals are written out for all to see; (3) the group discusses the proposals for the purpose of identifying high-priority goals; and (4) the group agrees on a final list of goals that are believed to be

Text continued on p. 414.

I-30-89
Form SE-89 (Rev I—5M—10827—89-E
SC-03-30640

WHITE — Central File
CANARY — Local School
PINK — Parent

**ADMISSION, REVIEW, AND DISMISSAL
(ARD) COMMITTEE MEETING**

5.0

Page 1 of ___

Dallas Independent
School District

3700 Ross Avenue
Dallas, Texas 75204-5491

☐ Admission

☐ Review

☐ Dismissal

DATE OF MEETING: _____

Student: _____ I.D. #: _____ S.S. #: _____

Birth Date: _____ School: _____ Grade: _____

Parent/Guardian: _____ Phone Numbers: Bus. _____ Home _____

Home Address: _____ K-3 School: _____

☐ ☐ An interpreter was used to assist in conducting the meeting. If YES, specify language/modality:_____
YES NO

I.   **REVIEW OF ASSESSMENT DATA** (☑ if applicable)

Comprehensive Individual Assessment Reports

☐ Intellectual assessment or re-evaluation dated: _____

☐ Educational assessment or re-evaluation dated: _____

☐ Developmental and Sociological information dated: _____

☐ Adaptive behavior assessment dated: _____

☐ Emotional/Behavioral assessment dated: _____

☐ Physical exam or health update dated: _____

☐ Speech and language assessment dated: _____

☐ Language dominance assessment dated: _____

☐ Vocational assessment dated: _____

☐ Related services assessment dated: _____

☐ Other assessment: _____

_____

_____

II. **DETERMINATION OF ELIGIBILITY** (☑ if applicable)

Based on the assessment data reviewed, the committee has determined that the student:

☐ does not meet eligibility criteria as a handicapped student.

☐ meets eligibility criteria for _____.
                                          HANDICAPPING CONDITION

A

FIGURE 17-7. **A,** Admission, review, and dismissal (ARD) committee meeting
form. (Courtesy Dallas Independent School District.)

Continued.

B

**ADMISSION, REVIEW, AND DISMISSAL
(ARD) COMMITTEE MEETING**

5.1

Page 2 of ____

Dallas Independent
School District

3700 Ross Avenue
Dallas, Texas 75204-5491

Student: _____ I.D. #: _____ S.S. #: _____

III. DEVELOPMENT OF THE INDIVIDUAL EDUCATIONAL PLAN (IEP)

Present Competencies (☑ if applicable)

A. Academic/Developmental (Grade or age levels not acceptable.)

Content areas in which the student CAN receive instruction in the essential elements in the regular program WITHOUT modifications or special education:

☐ Language Arts/English   ☐ Science/Health

☐ Mathematics   ☐ Non-Academics/Electives

☐ Social Studies/History   ☐ Other:

Content areas in which the student CANNOT receive instruction in the essential elements in the regular program WITHOUT modifications or special education (for each, specify present competencies):

B. Physical, as it affects participation in

instructional settings:

physical education:

☐ ☐ The student is capable of receiving instruction in the essential elements of physical education through
YES NO   the regular program without modifications.

C. Behavioral, as it affects

educational placement and programming:

ability to follow disciplinary rules:

☐ ☐ The student is capable of following regular disciplinary rules without modifications. If NO, specify:
YES NO

D. Prevocational/Vocational (when appropriate)

FIGURE 17-7. cont'd. **B,** ARD committee meeting form.

Continued.

10-24-78
Form SE-89 (Rev.)   5M   10383   .88 E
NE-03-206410

WHITE — Central File
CANARY — Local School
PINK — Parent

DISD

Dallas Independent
School District

**ARD/IEP COMMITTEE REPORT: Individual Education Program
ANNUAL GOALS AND SHORT-TERM INSTRUCTIONAL OBJECTIVES
FOR INDIVIDUAL INSTRUCTIONAL PLAN**

Page _____ of _____

☐ Draft _____
                    Date

☐ Accepted by ARD _____
                                Date

Student: _____ I.D. #: _____ S.S. #: _____

Birth Date: _____ School: _____ Grade: _____

IV. ☐ Instructional Services: ☐ Related Services: Specify: _____

Duration of Services: from _____ to _____ Responsible Implementator (title only): _____
                                M/D/Y   *M/D/Y*

Goal Area: _____   Annual Goal:
Instructional Level: _____

SHORT TERM OBJECTIVES The student will be able to:	Circle Review Code and Evaluation Criteria	Date of Review	EVALUATION CRITERIA (PERFORMANCE STANDARDS MEASURING INSTRUMENT)
_____	A B C D E 1 2 3 4 5	_____	A. Brigance Inventory
_____	A B C D E 1 2 3 4 5	_____	B. Teacher Observation
_____	A B C D E 1 2 3 4 5	_____	C. Teacher made tests
_____	A B C D E 1 2 3 4 5	_____	D. Informal Inventories
_____	A B C D E 1 2 3 4 5	_____	E. Other: _____
	A B C D E 1 2 3 4 5		With _____ % accuracy

Goal Area: _____   Annual Goal:
Instructional Level: _____

SHORT TERM OBJECTIVES The student will be able to:	Circle Review Code and Evaluation Criteria	Date of Review	EVALUATION CRITERIA (PERFORMANCE STANDARDS MEASURING INSTRUMENT)
_____	A B C D E 1 2 3 4 5	_____	A. Brigance Inventory
_____	A B C D E 1 2 3 4 5	_____	B. Teacher Observation
_____	A B C D E 1 2 3 4 5	_____	C. Teacher made tests
_____	A B C D E 1 2 3 4 5	_____	D. Informal Inventories
_____	A B C D E 1 2 3 4 5	_____	E. Other: _____
	A B C D E 1 2 3 4 5		With _____ % accuracy

Review Codes
1. Mastered
2. Continued — progress satisfactory

3. Continued — progress unsatisfactory
4. Continued with modifications as indicated and attached
5. Discontinued — inappropriate

Attach additional goals as needed.

Comments attached: yes _____ no _____

C

FIGURE 17-7. cont'd. **C,** ARD/IEP committee report: individual education
program; Annual goals and short-term instructional objectives for individual instructional plan form.   *Continued.*

10-24-78
Form SE-89/Rev I—5M—10361—88-E
SC-03-30640

WHITE—Central File
CANARY—Local School
PINK—Parent

**ADMISSION, REVIEW, AND DISMISSAL
(ARD) COMMITTEE MEETING**

5.3

Page ___ of ___

Dallas Independent
School District

3700 Ross Avenue
Dallas, Texas 75204-5491

Student: _____ I.D. #: _____ S.S. #: _____

V. DETERMINATION OF PLACEMENT

Placement Alternatives Reviewed and Additional Services Discussed. (Include consideration of occupational training needs for students at or before entry into high school.)

___ Regular education only
___ Regular education with modifications
___ Regular education with support from
    special education

___ _____ vocational program
___ _____ special education
    class program

___ Special transportation
_____ therapy
___ Services for auditorially handicapped (AH)
___ Orientation and Mobility (VH)
___ Vision training/instruction
___ Adaptive equipment
___ Other (specify) _____

The committee recommends placement in _____ at _____
                                     name of program   *name of local school*

☐ ☐ This is the school which the student would attend if not handicapped. If NO, explain:
YES NO

    ☐ instructional option unavailable in home school.

    ☐ other: _____.

☐ For the visually handicapped or auditorially handicapped students, the committee has completed and attached additional IEP Requirements for Visually Handicapped and/or Auditorially Handicapped Students.

VI. SCHEDULE OF SERVICES (List content areas/courses.)

Special Education:	Amount of time per day/week
Related Services:	
Speech	
OT/PT	
Transportation	"D" "C" "P"
Other:	

☑ if applies	Regular Education:	Amount of time per day/week
	Language Arts/English	
	Mathematics	
	Social Studies/History	
	Science/Health	
	Physical Education	
	Fine Arts	
	Non-Academics/Electives	
	Other:	

Cite justification for special transportation:

☐ instructional option unavailable in home school.

☐ other: _____

Specify pick-up and/or delivery address if different from the one listed on page 1 _____

_____

Modifications recommended for regular, remedial and supportive programs (☑ if applicable):

☐ see attached page.

☐ other: _____

TEAMS Required: ☐ Yes ☐ No (If YES, see attached page.)

D

FIGURE 17-7, cont'd. **D,** ARD committee meeting form.

10-24-78—
Form SE-89 (Rev.)—5M.— 10361—86-E
SC-03-30640

WHITE — Central File
CANARY — Local School
PINK — Parent

5.4

**Admission, Review and Dismissal
(ARD) Committee Meeting**

Page ___ of ___

Dallas Independent
School District

Student: _____ I.D. #: _____ S.S. #: _____

VII. Review for consideration for evaluation by; ____Speech Clinician; ____OT/PT;

____Adaptive PE Specialist; ____Other_____

Professional to be notified by_____
                                                 Local School Staff Person/Position

VIII. **ASSURANCES** (☑ if applicable)

The committee assures that special education placement

(A) of national origin minority group students or linguistically different students is not based on criteria which were developed solely on command of the English language.

   Basis of assurance: ☐ adaptations in testing procedures

   ☐ use of interpreter

   ☐ review of parent/student information

   ☐ review of language assessment

(B) is not based on deficiencies identified as directly attributable to a different culture, lifestyle, or lack of educational opportunities.

   Basis of assurance: ☐ review of parent/student information

   ☐ review of sociological assessment

(C) is in the least restrictive environment.

   Basis of assurance: Parents were given an explanation of the procedural safeguard or referred to the Parent and Students Rights Document — page 10.

SIGNATURE	POSITION	COMMITTEE AGREE	DECISIONS DISAGREE (Comments must be attached)
	*Administration		
	*Parent		
	*Instruction		
	*Special Education		
	*Assessment[1]		

*Required for decision

Assessment[1] personnel are required when interpretations of assessment data are being considered.

IX. **FOR INITIAL PLACEMENT**

   ☐ Parent approval obtained (see attachment).

   ☐ Parent/guardian not present. Person designated to obtain parent approval _____ .

E

FIGURE 17-7, cont'd. **E,** ARD committee meeting form.

most important for building and maintaining a desirable lifestyle for the disabled student. Wilcox and Bellamy[34] recommend that supportive program materials be made available to give the parents a clear idea of the process that will be followed to assure that the agreed-upon goals are achieved.

Process of the Individualized Instructional Program

The product of the process of the individualized physical education instructional program is objective data that focus on the learning of motor and physical skills. The three interrelated components of the process of the individualized instructional program are the present levels of educational performance, annual goals, and short-term instructional objectives. The present levels of educational performance define the existing limits of performance at a given point in time on which the short-term objectives are developed. Goals are measurable, observable, broad instructional tasks that are achieved over time. It is essential that they are well defined so that they can be broken down and converted into observable and measurable short-term instructional objectives, which are the intermediate steps to goal acquisition.

Figure 17-8 shows the relationship of goals, objectives, and present levels of educational performance as they interface with sequential learning tasks on an instructional time frame.

It must be pointed out that if no specific goals are formulated, then the rest of the program fails. No short-term objectives can be developed and no sequence of learning that can be measured is on a continuum toward goals. If the small steps (short-term instructional objectives leading to the goal) are too large or are improperly sequenced, then the experiences will be a punishing failure.[20] If the steps can already be demonstrated by the student, there can be no learning. Children do not need to relearn things they already can do. Thus the programmed instruction task analysis of the behaviors to be taught provides the structure and opportunity for application of the individualized instructional process.

DESCRIPTION OF EACH COMPONENT OF THE IEP
Present Level of Educational Performance

Each IEP must include a specific description of the child's present level of educational performance. This may include a description of the child's need for related services in order to function within the educational environment. The statement describing the child's present level of performance must be based on the results of more than one assessment instrument. This is particularly vital as placement decisions are made on the basis of this assessment. The statement of the child's present level of performance in physical education may, for example, include a description of the child's locomotor competencies and physical fitness levels. Refer to the box on pp. 415-416 for a sample of an example of a description of present level of performance.

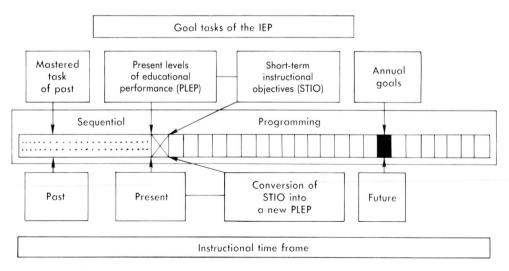

FIGURE 17-8. A description of the instructional components of the IEP.

Present Level of Motor Performance (Example)

SCHOOL DISTRICT
ADAPTED PHYSICAL EDUCATION

Student: J. Guitterez

ID#:

School:

Grade:

Report by:

Date:

At the request of J's mother and sister, I did a complete motor evaluation and physical fitness evaluation on two consecutive days—October 11, 1991 and October 12, 1991. At the time of the test, J was 8 years and 11 months of age. His birthday is November 3. I evaluated J using the complete battery of the Bruininks-Oseretsky Test of Motor Proficiency. It is a norm-referenced instrument that allows evaluation of gross motor and fine motor skill and upper-limb coordination.

J was a delight! He is bright and personable and has an excellent sense of humor. He gave me his very best performance.

Following is a summary of the results of the evaluation. I have included age-equivalencies because of the ease of interpretation. It should be noted, however, that age-equivalencies should be viewed with some caution. An age equivalency suggests the approximate age at which a non-delayed child would be likely to acquire a given skill.

	Point score	Age equivalency
Gross motor subtests		
Running speed and agility	0	<4.2
Balance	7	<4.2
Bilateral coordination	15	8.8
Strength	5	4.1
Upper limb coordination	18	10.5
Fine motor subtests		
Response speed	4	5.8
Visual-motor control	22	15.8
Upper-limb speed and dexterity	34	7.11

His motor profile is one of great variability. His particular strengths are activities associated with visual-motor control. These tasks included: cutting a circle with preferred hand; drawing a line through a crooked, straight, and curved path; and copying a circle, triangle, diamond, and overlapping pencils. In these tasks he performed like a child aged 15.8 years. He also performed exceptionally well on those items that required upper limb coordination; specifically, he scored as a child aged 10.5 years would be likely to score. These tasks included: bouncing and catching a tennis ball with both hands and preferred hand; catching a tossed ball with both hands and preferred hand; throwing a ball at a target; touching a swinging ball, touching nose with index fingers (eyes closed); touching thumb to fingertips (eyes closed); and pivoting thumb and index finger. J performed at or near age level on those items that required bilateral coordination and upper-limb speed and dexterity.

He performed well below his age level on the test of running speed and agility. This is, simply, a shuttle run. He also performed below age level on items that evaluated balance. These included: standing in a stationary position on one foot with eyes open and closed; and walking on a line and a balance beam with eyes opened and closed. He also performed below age level on the strength items; these included sit-ups, push-ups, and a standing broad jump.

I believe the performance on the test of running speed and agility to be a function of lack of practice rather than lack of ability. Until recently, J avoided all running activities because of fear of incontinence.

I was concerned with his performance on the items that evaluated balance. However, his performance was similar in the performance of the same skill with eyes opened and eyes closed. This appears to negate my initial suspicion of a vestibular dysfunction. I believe this performance deficit to be a function of lack of hip stability. I evaluated J's physical fitness using

Continued.

Present Level of Motor Performance (Example)—cont'd

SCHOOL DISTRICT
ADAPTED PHYSICAL EDUCATION

the American Alliance of Health, Physical Education, Recreation and Dance (AAHPERD) Health-Related Fitness Test. The AAHPERD Health-Related Fitness Test is a norm-referenced instrument that examines several components of fitness that relate directly to health. The normative data are based on evaluations of non-delayed children. J was cooperative throughout the evaluation and gave me what I believe to be his "best effort." Below is a summary of the results.

	Performance/results	Percentile
Nine-minute run	920 yards	<5
Sum of skinfolds	22 mm	25
Bent-knee sit-ups	26	15
Sit and reach	23 cm	40

J had significant difficulty in the performance of the 9-minute run, a means for measuring cardiovascular-respiratory endurance. He began walking only 1 minute and 15 seconds into the run and told me he

was "tired." He then alternated walking and running throughout the 9-minute time period. His immediate post-exercise pulse was 180 beats/minute. After a 1-minute walking "cool-down," his pulse was 138 beats/minute. His performance placed him at less than the fifth percentile.

J's body fat percentage was measured using Lange Skinfold Calipers to measure skinfolds at two sites—triceps and subscapular. The result is the sum of the two skinfold measurements.

The bent-knee sit-up was used to evaluate J's abdominal strength. He was able to perform 26 in a 1-minute period. His score was at the 15th percentile. This means that J's performance was equal to or better than 15% of boys his age.

The sit-and-reach test was used to evaluate his lower back and hip flexibility. His performance of 23 centimeters was at the 40th percentile. This means that his performance was equal to or better than 40% of boys his age.

Annual Goals

Goals are statements that describe what a child with a disability should be able to accomplish over a specified time. There should be a direct relationship between the present level of educational performance (written in measurable objective terms), the goals, and the short-term instructional objectives. Annual goals should be reviewed throughout the year.[9] Examples of appropriate and inappropriate goals are listed in Table 17-1.

There are arguments as to how precise goals need be. The more specific the goals, however, the easier it is to judge the effectiveness of the educational program. Martin[20] has made the following comments about the characteristics of quality goals:

1. There must *be* goals. Actions not related to any goal cannot be judged as either worthwhile or pointless.
2. They must be concrete. They must be actual and realizable.
3. They must be visible. There must be no dispute about whether they are being obtained.
4. They must be objectively stated. Administrators, students, and parents all can use the same language and agree on results and subsequent decisions made as to whether the goal was achieved.
5. Each goal can be divided into a sequence of

tasks. Without subtasks there can be no measure of progress. Evaluation would have to wait until the terminal goal was reached, with no feedback provided.
6. There must be a measure for successful completion of the task. No comparisons can be made to measure progress of change.
7. The goal must bear a reasonable relationship as to why the person is in special education. Either the persons are acquiring skills to return to normative levels in regular class, or they are being prepared for self-sufficient living in specific natural environments.
8. Goals should be individualized. Grouping must come after a goal has been postulated, not before.

There are two aspects of learning motor tasks that can be incorporated into an IEP or that can comprise the major components of an IPEP. One is the correct execution of form of the skill, and the other is improved performance of the skill. Task analysis is used to express goals, objectives, and present levels of educational performance in the acquisition of the form of a skill. The box on p. 417 shows a task analysis of running a mile, which was designed for the Special Olympics curriculum.

All prerequisite behavioral components of the form

TABLE 17-1

Acceptable and unacceptable goals and objectives through evaluation of appropriate criteria and conditions

Action	Condition	Criterion
Acceptable objectives		
Run	1 mile	In 5 minutes 30 seconds
Walk	A balance beam 4 inches wide, heel to toe, eyes closed, and hands on hips	For 8 feet
Swim	Using the American crawl in a 25-yard pool for 50 yards	In 35 seconds
Unacceptable objectives		
Run		As fast as you can
Walk	On a balance beam	Without falling off
Swim		The length of the pool

and strategy are marked with an X. These behaviors are within the repertoire of the learner. This constitutes the present level of educational performance. All unmastered components of the task analysis of acquisition of form are short-term instructional objectives. Achievement of all of the unmastered objectives constitutes acquisition of the goal. This is the sum total of

all form components and strategies necessary to run a mile. Improved performance would require that the learner better his or her time for running a mile. This requires measurable ongoing performance of student participation in the mile run. Shaping is used to communicate the instructional process of the IEP. The best performance to date might be 8 minutes and 30 seconds (present level of performance). The goal might be 8 minutes, and the short-term instructional objectives are times between 8 minutes and 8 minutes and 30 seconds. The setup that follows below indicates the relationship of the components of the instructional process of the IEP.

Goals	Present level of performance	Objectives
Run the mile in 8 minutes	8 minutes and 30 seconds	8:25, 8:20, 8:15, 8:10, 8:05

Form versus performance goals

Goals can be written for the development of skills in two areas: (1) the form that the skill is to take and (2) the performance outcome of the skill. For example, in throwing a softball, a form goal would be a description of how the individual would grip the ball, step toward the target, move the arm, and maneuver the body. A performance goal would be how far the child with a disability could throw the ball or how accurately the ball could be thrown. Most task analyses are directed toward achieving a desired form. However,

---

Cognitive Acquisition of Sound Running Strategy While Participating in the 1-Mile Distance Event (Special Olympics Rules)
Task analysis

X   1. Assume a crouched starting position.
X   2. Move on the command to start.
X   3. Demonstrate a steady running pace if more than four paces from the runner ahead.
     4. Stay close to the inside of the track.
X   5. Run to the right of the runner ahead to pass.
     6. Increase arm action to lengthen the stride while passing.
X   7. Listen for approaching runners and take longer strides to increase the distance from them.
     8. Gradually accelerate during the final lap and try to sprint the last 100 meters.

X = Behaviors mastered and present level of performance. All behaviors unmarked are short-term objectives. Acquisition of all of the behaviors represents attainment of a goal.

A modification of the Special Olympics Track and Field Sports Skills Instructional Program provides a data base for measuring acquisition of running strategies while participating in the mile distance event. Data to indicate present levels of performance, goals, and objectives require a record of specific components mastered. When all short-term objectives are satisfied, the goal of sound running strategy will be achieved.

The Joseph P. Kennedy, Jr. Foundation; accredited by Special Olympics, Inc. for the Benefit of Mentally Retarded Citizens.

the "do exactly as I do" approach to teaching form and converting it to goal setting has been criticized because it overlooks the possibility that there may be more than one way to accomplish the same basic end (i.e., throwing a softball for distance or for increased accuracy). For example, a child with quadriplegic spastic cerebral palsy might actually throw the ball further if the ball is thrown backward, over the shoulder. White[33] has suggested that emphasis should be placed on what the individual is to accomplish (e.g., performance) rather than on the specific form.

Critical function of behavior when stating goals

There is evidence that instruction and goal setting should be toward the critical functioning of a skill. The critical function is that aspect of the skill for which there is a functional use. For instance, in throwing a softball, throwing the ball in and of itself is insignificant. The critical function is to be able to throw a ball consistently enough, for example, to play "catch" with a friend. This is very different from focusing on the form that one uses to throw the ball. Clearly, successful functioning in any given play situation in physical activity is identified not only by the form of the skill, but by a careful analysis of the environmental demands and consequences for which the skill will be used. Defining skill goals in terms of their critical functions can be useful in deciding which specific skills should be developed or used to achieve that delicate balance between the individual's personal abilities and the environmental sport and physical activity demands. It is important to remember that the physical prerequisites of a form of a skill are just tools that must be blended and orchestrated to accomplish the critical effect of a functional task in a meaningful, culturally relevant sport or physical event. Thus, in the writing of goals, it is important to identify the specific need of the individual as well as the critical elements of each skill that is to be attained so that meaningful behavior can be developed to permit the individual with a disability to participate in physical activity and sport.

Decisions for goal selection

A child, by public policy, must demonstrate an adverse performance on physical education tasks before that child is deemed to require specially designed physical education. Once adverse performance in physical education is determined, a decision should be made as to whether the purpose of the special physical education is to facilitate development of skills for unrestricted participation and normative functioning, or whether it serves to plan for specific education and

training for independence in specific community environments. All children with disabilities, including the moderately and severely disabled, need to be trained for self-sufficiency. Two proposed approaches for achieving this end are the developmental model and the community-based ecological (task-specific) model described by Brown et al.[7]

Developmental model	Community-based ecological model
1. Goals are selected from developmental sequences or longitudinal sequences.	1. Goals are selected from tasks of adult life and broken down to present level.
2. Each step in the developmental sequence is prerequisite to the next.	2. Teach what is necessary, not what is next.
3. The developmental level of the child determines the next goals (the concept of readiness).	3. The next environment the individual functions in will indicate the goals.
4. Simple behaviors can be elaborated into more complex forms.	4. Design functional alternatives to participation in normal activities.
5. Goals portray the characteristics of those of a young age.[25]	

Value judgments assume critical importance in the selection of possible physical education goals for the IEP or the IPEP. Goals that are achieved should enhance performance and participation for independence in daily living. Curricula designed for universal audiences may serve higher functioning children, but not the severely disabled. With these students, local-referenced goals that are functional in the student's own community should be targets of instruction.

Brown et al.[7] advocate an analysis of each individual's various environments to inventory skills necessary for successful participation. The skills physical educators should focus on are community recreational activity and the motor skills needed for independent living. The environments where these skills can be used are at school, in the home, and in the community. The goals of the IEP should reflect the activities of nondisabled peers. The identification of these goals can be accomplished in a number of ways:

☐ Observe peers and adults without disabilities.

☐ Interview persons knowledgeable about the community.

☐ Determine the important activities of peers who live independently.

□ Analyze needs.
□ Analyze community leisure, recreation, and sport resources for individuals with disabilities.
□ Study the lifestyle of persons with disabilities thriving in the community.

The individualization of goals implies that two broad sets of decisions have been made independently for each pupil. The individualization of the goal affects, in essence, both the content and sequential rate at which instruction is presented. The scheduled instruction is a function of the student progress. Individualization is not synonymous with personal attention, rather it denotes student-by-student selection of goals and flexibility in how they are taught.

Short-Term Instructional Objectives

Short-term instructional objectives are "measurable intermediate steps between present levels of educational performance and the annual goals."[34] The sum of all of the short-term instructional objectives should equal one goal. Because the present levels of performance

FIGURE 17-9. The IEP should include leisure and recreation activities.

are observable and measurable and all components of the IEP instructional process are related, the goals and objectives also should be observable and measurable. They are "the cornerstone of the individual education program."[29]

Objectives occur at different levels of curricular development and must be appropriate for the ability level of a specifically diagnosed individual. They require an assessment of the learner's capabilities. In the event that mastery of a specific behavior is not possible, the question is asked: What prerequisites are needed for this individual to achieve mastery of this task? This question, once answered, is restated until the student's present level of performance is determined and the appropriate instructional objective is determined. A sequence of prerequisite activities thus provides a chain of instructional events that leads the learner from lower to higher levels of mastery within the instructional content. The use of this instructional process requires that detailed records be kept on each learner so that the responsible personnel can determine the student's position in a learning activity sequence. The mastery of one objective is the prerequisite that gives rise to a more complex objective, making development progressive.

In the shaping process that uses programmed instruction to formulate objectives, hierarchies enable measurement of learner progress. A hierarchy is a continuum of ordered activities in which a task of lesser difficulty is prerequisite to acquisition of a task of greater difficulty. Progress from one task to another in a hierarchy serves as a measure of student development and answers three vital, educationally relevant questions: (1) What is the student's present level of educational performance? (2) What short-term instructional objectives should be provided to extend the present level of educational performance for development? and (3) How much development has already occurred? Task analysis is a valuable tool for the development of instructional hierarchies.

The instructional objective must incorporate four concepts: (1) it must possess an action, (2) it must establish conditions under which actions occur, (3) it must establish a criterion for mastery of a specific task, and (4) it must lie outside the child's present level of educational performance.

Specific Educational Services and the Extent to Which the Child Will Participate in Regular Educational Programs

In the broadest sense the specific educational services to be rendered means what professional services (e.g.,

Goals, Short-Term Objectives, and Present Levels of Education Performance of an Individualized Physical Education Program

GOALS, SPORT SKILLS, AND TEAM GAMES	PRESENT LEVELS OF PERFORMANCE	SHORT-TERM OBJECTIVES
Perform the track and field skills of the Special Olympics (SSIP)	Relay exchange, sprinting, and high jump	Throw and distance running*
Perform the soccer skills of the Special Olympics (SSIP)	Soccer kick and trap	Soccer pass and dribble*
Perform the basketball skills of the Special Olympics (SSIP)	Pass and dribble	Shooting and guarding*
Perform the volleyball skills of the Special Olympics (SSIP)	Set and bump	Spike and serve*
Perform the gymnastic skills of the Special Olympics (SSIP Task Analysis)	Forward roll and side roll	Headstand and backward roll*
Physical and motor fitness		
Run a mile in 8 minutes	8 minutes and 45 seconds	8:40, 8:35, 8:30, 8:25, 8:20, 8:15, 8:10, 8:05
Perform a military press with 70 pounds, 10 repetitions	60 pounds, 7 repetitions	60 pounds/10 repetitions, 65 pounds/10 repetitions
Perform 30 bent-knee sit-ups	18 bent-knee sit-ups	20 repetitions, 22 repetitions, 25 repetitions, 27 repetitions, 29 repetitions
Balance on a 3/4-inch stick for 10 seconds	1-inch stick for 5 seconds	10 seconds on a 1-inch stick, 5 seconds on a 3/4-inch stick
With the knees straight, bend forward and touch the tips of the fingers to the floor	5 inches from the floor	4 inches, 3 inches, 2 inches, 1 inch
Perform a vertical jump to 7 inches	A height of 4 inches	5 inches, 6 inches
Fundamental motor pattern		
Skip 30 feet in 15 seconds	20 seconds	19 seconds, 18 seconds, 17 seconds, 16 seconds
Run 60 feet in 5 seconds	50 feet	52 feet, 54 feet, 56 feet, 58 feet
Fundamental motor skills		
Throw a 4-inch ball so it hits a 12 × 12 inch target from a distance of 20 feet	From a distance of 7 feet	8, 9, 10, 11, 12, 13, 14, 15, 16, 17, 18, 19, 20
Bounce an 8-inch ball and travel a distance of 30 feet in 6 seconds	23 feet with an 8-inch ball	24, 25, 26, 27, 28, 29, 30
Kick an 8-inch ball into a 6 × 2 foot target from a distance of 20 feet five times in a row	From 10 feet into a 6 × 2 foot target	11, 12, 13, 14, 15, 16, 17, 18

*Indicates a need for further specification of objectives from Special Olympics (SSIP) curricula.

remedial reading, speech therapy) will be made available to the student. In a stricter sense specific educational services has been interpreted to mean what activities (e.g., aerobic activities, weight lifting) the student will engage in. This latter example relates directly to the instructional plan that will be used to achieve the goals and objectives included on the IEP. Every activity selected should contribute toward reaching specific objectives.

Related services

Related services help the child with disabilities benefit from the educational process. The goals and objectives of related service personnel may be a vital part of the child's IEP and should be consistent with those of direct service personnel. If there are gross or fine motor goals on the IEP that the physical educator cannot fulfill, related services personnel (occupational and physical therapists) may be called on for assistance. These services should focus on offsetting or reducing the problems resulting from the child's disability that interfere with learning and physical education performance in school.[29] For instance, for a child with a recurring hip dislocation that prevents participation in physical education, the physical therapist might treat the condition until a transfer of programming to the physical educator is feasible. Or for a child who lacks some equilibrium reflexes, the physical educator might contact either an occupational or physical therapist for help in selecting appropriate activities to facilitate development of those reflexes. The length of time that is required for the related service to produce the result should be specified. Duration limitations gauge the effectiveness of the service.

Participation in Regular Physical Education

The IEP for each child with a disability must include a statement of "the extent to which the child will be able to participate in regular (physical) education programs."[11] One way of meeting this requirement is to indicate the percent of time the child will be spending in the regular (physical) education program with nondisabled students. Another way is to list the specific regular (physical) education classes the child will be attending.[30]

The regular education initiative

Assistant Secretary of Education Madeline Will wrote the position paper, "Educating Students with Learning Problems—A Shared Responsibility"[35] that is generally considered the foundation for the regular education initiative. Will encouraged, "special programs to form a partnership with regular education. The objective of this partnership for special education and the other special programs is to use their knowledge and expertise to support regular education in educating children with learning problems." The position paper encouraged more inclusive education for all students, particularly those with special needs. This was based on her belief that there are four fundamental problems in current special education practice:

1. Services meant to reach children are lost in a maze of distinct categories; children can fall through the cracks.
2. "Regular" and "Special" education programs function separately. This reduces the accountability of the regular classroom educator. Children are "pulled-out" of the regular classroom for special services and this instruction is not coordinated with that received in the regular classroom.
3. Students in segregated programs are labeled and may be stigmatized; this may result in lowered self-esteem.
4. Eligibility requirements may create conflicts between parents and educators.

Some educators have embraced the notion of inclusion as a method of education that reduces "segregationism" they believe typical of special education. Wang and Walberg[31] wrote, "The extant literature provides no solid scientific or moral basis for the continued segregation of services for students with special needs." The notion that special education is segregationist is enhanced by data that indicate a disproportionate number of African-American and Hispanic children are placed in special education programs. As a result, the national trend is toward the provision of services for all children within regular education.

There are educators who feel strongly that this is a vital mistake. Kauffman[15] stated:

> One of the primary hypotheses on which the REI [Regular Education Initiative] is based is that students with disabilities would be best served by the improvement of education for all students, such that students of every description are fully integrated into regular classes, no student is given a special designation [label], costs are lowered by the elimination of special budget and administrative categories, the focus becomes excellence for all, and federal regulations are withdrawn in favor of local control...Implementation of education policies based on a trickle-down hypothesis will very likely produce parallel results for those students who learn most easily and those who are most difficult to teach—high performers will make remarkable progress, but the benefits for students having the most difficulty in school will never arrive.

FIGURE 17-10. Participation in Special Olympics may be addressed in student's IEP. (Courtesy Wisconsin Special Olympics.)

Indeed, the "trickle-down" economic policy of recent administrations increased the wealth of the most wealthy, while the poor simply became poorer. It is reasonable to expect the same result of a "trickle-down" education policy.

Another of the problems associated with the REI, or the push for normalization, is the message it sends to the disabled child and to their families. Meisbov[22] said:

> Another problem with the normalization principle as a guiding force for programs involving handicapped individuals and their families is that it promotes an undesirable value system from their perspective...Handicapped people are discouraged from spending large amounts of time with other handicapped citizens and are regularly encouraged to move into settings with nonhandicapped peers. The continuous message is that nonhandicapped peers are more desirable than handicapped people like themselves.

Despite its opponents, the REI is being embraced in school districts throughout the nation. One of the major reasons for its embrace is its perceived cost-effectiveness.

Inclusion of children with disabilities into regular physical education

The REI has grave implications for the regular physical educator. Some school districts are encouraging unilateral inclusion of *all* children with disabilities, even those with severe disabilities, into regular physical education programs. As such, the regular physical educator is faced, constantly, with pressure to "mainstream" children with disabilities into the regular physical education program, even if the "mainstream" is not the child's least restrictive environment.

The decision that must be made regarding placement in physical education, a vital part of the IEP process, is one of the most important decisions that must be made. The physical educator and the adapted physical educator must be aware of the complex myriad of issues that must be considered before placement in regular physical education. (Refer to Chapter 18 for a more complete discussion of the placement alternatives in specially designed physical education.)

A Statement of Needed Transition Services

A statement that describes the process by which a child with a disabilty will make the transition into community-based living must be included on the IEP of each child no later than age 16 years. In some cases, it may be determined that the needs of the child justify inclusion of transition services earlier in the child's educational career. The Louisiana Department of Education has developed an "Individualized Transition Plan" which targets the following areas for "holistic" adult

TABLE 17-2

Target areas for holistic adult lifestyle transition planning

1. Postsecondary education (choose one)

___1.1 College
___1.2 Junior college
___1.3 Adult education
___1.4 Vocational technical/training school
___1.5 GED program
___1.6 Other_____

2. Employment (choose one)

___2.1 Competitive employment—no support
___2.2 Competitive employment—transition support
___2.3 Supported employment—at or above minimum wage, individual placement
___2.4 Supported employment—subminimum wage, individual placement
___2.5 Enclave—small group in business setting, on-going support
___2.6 Mobile crew—small group in a variety of businesses, on-going support
___2.7 Sheltered workshop
___2.8 Day activity center
___2.9 Other_____

3. Living arrangements (choose one)

___3.1 Living on own—no support
___3.2 Living on own—with support
___3.3 With family or relative
___3.4 Adult foster care
___3.5 Group Home—specialized training
___3.6 ICF-MR—training, on-going support
___3.7 Adult nursing home
___3.8 Other_____

4. Homemaking activities (choose all that apply)

___4.1 Independent—needs no services
___4.2 Needs personal care assistance
___4.3 Needs housekeeping, laundry assistance
___4.4 Needs meal preparation assistance
___4.5 Needs menu planning, budgeting assistance
___4.6 Other_____

5. Financial/income needs (choose all that apply)

___5.1 Earned Wages
___5.2 SSI
___5.3 SSDI
___5.4 SSI/SSDI and earned wages
___5.5 Unearned income—gifts, family support
___5.6 Trust/Will
___5.7 Food stamps
___5.8 Other_____

6. Community resources (choose all that apply)

___6.1 Independent—needs no services
___6.2 Needs banking assistance
___6.3 Needs shopping assistance
___6.4 Needs assistance with identifying and using some resources (daycare, voting, etc.)
___6.5 Needs assistance to use all or most community activities
___6.6 Other_____

7. Recreation and leisure (choose all that apply)

___7.1 Independent—needs no services
___7.2 Needs assistance—needs support to participate in all or almost all activities
___7.3 Participates in family activities
___7.4 Attends community recreation activities with disabled peers
___7.5 Attends community recreation activities with disabled and non-disabled peers
___7.6 Participates in church groups, clubs
___7.7 Other_____

8. Transportation (choose all that apply)

___8.1 Independent—needs no services
___8.2 Needs assistance—uses public transportation
___8.3 Needs assistance—uses specialized transportation
___8.4 Uses family transportation
___8.5 Uses car pool
___8.6 Uses group home or residential transportation
___8.7 Other_____

9. Medical services (choose all that apply)

___9.1 Covered by group insurance—Blue Cross, Medicaid, etc. and needs no assistance
___9.2 Covered by group insurance but needs assistance—monitoring medical needs, appointments, etc.
___9.3 Needs extensive medical services and support—regular tests and/or daily monitoring of medicine and/or therapy
___9.4 Other_____

10. Relationships (choose all that apply)

___10.1 Independent—needs no services
___10.2 Desires family planning assistance
___10.3 Desires support group
___10.4 Desires counseling assistance
___10.5 Desires family respite or family support services
___10.6 Desires peer or "buddy" friendship network
___10.7 Other_____

11. Advocacy/legal (choose all that apply)

___11.1 Independent—needs no services
___11.2 Desires some assistance—estate planning, will, etc.
___11.3 Desires extensive assistance—guardianship, etc.
___11.4 Other_____

lifestyle transition planning (see to Table 17-2). These include: (1) post-secondary education, (2) employment, (3) living arrangements, (4) homemaking activities, (5) financial/income needs, (6) community resources, (7) recreation and leisure, (8) transportation, (9) medical services, (10) relationships, and (11) advocacy/legal needs.

The individualized transition plan addresses each of these issues and designates the desired adult outcome for each of the areas. (Refer to Figure 17-11.) This plan then defines the process required to ensure the individual meets the goals or desired adult outcomes by stipulating the responsibilities of the school, the family, and adult agencies in meeting these outcomes. Included for each desired adult outcome are "school action steps," "family action steps" and "adult agency action steps."

The major role of the physical educator and adapted physical educator in the development of the transition plan is, obviously, in the area of recreation and leisure.

INDIVIDUALIZED TRANSITION PLAN
LOUISIANA DEPARTMENT OF EDUCATION   Page___ of___

Comprehensive transition planning should consider each of the following areas.
Check each area that was addressed for this student in this year's plan.

1. ___ Postsecondary Education   4. ___ Homemaking Needs   7. ___ Recreation and Leisure   10. ___ Relationships
2. ___ Employment   5. ___ Financial/Income Needs 8. ___ Transportation Needs   11. ___ Advocacy/Legal Needs
3. ___ Living Arrangements   6. ___ Community Resources   9. ___ Medical Services   12. ___ Other _____

We, the undersigned, have participated in this transition plan and support its intent and recommendations.

STUDENT	STATE ID #	SCHOOL SYSTEM	DATE
PARENT/GUARDIAN		RELATED SERVICE PROVIDER(S)	
TEACHER			
ITP COORDINATOR		ADULT AGENCY SERVICE PROVIDER(S)	
ODR			

DATE	DESIRED ADULT OUTCOMES	SCHOOL ACTION STEPS	DATE	FAMILY ACTION STEPS	DATE	ADULT AGENCY ACTION STEPS	DATE

July, 1991

FIGURE 17-11. Individualized transition plan form. (Courtesy Louisiana Department of Education.)

However, the good physical educator and adapted physical educator address the functional needs of the individuals served. As such, the specially designed physical education program may address issues related, for example, to community resources. For example, the program may be designed to help the individual with disabilities to push a shopping cart, walk with a bag of groceries, or carry a box down a series of bus steps. Or, the program may be designed to help an adolescent with behavior difficulties learn to play/interact with others.

Projected Date for Initiation/Duration of Services

The projected date for beginning and terminating educational and related services must be included on the IEP. This is just one more technique intended to assure accountability.

All IEPs must include a date when services should begin and an anticipated date when goals will be reached. Whenever possible, delays in beginning a program should be avoided. The sooner the student with disabilities can begin to receive program services, the greater the progress that can be expected. Well-coordinated programs move students in and out of class assignments with minimal disruptions. Established policies and procedures should facilitate appropriate placement within a short period after needs have been identified and the IEP is written and approved.

Perhaps the most difficult task when writing an IEP is determining when each student will reach his or her specific goals. Every person is unique. Learning pace, motivation level, present performance level, and severity of the disabling condition all affect performance progress. Often it is not until the physical educator has worked with a student that it becomes possible to estimate how much progress to expect. The law does not mandate that goals be reached within the specified time, but that progress toward those goals be demonstrated. The alert physical educator will monitor progress closely and modify the instructional plan when it becomes evident that objectives are not being reached.

Appropriate Objective Criteria and Evaluation Procedures

Each IEP must also include a description of the techniques that were used to determine the child's present level of performance and to determine whether the child accomplishes each of the goals/objectives stipulated on the IEP. These must include specific evaluation/assessment instruments that allow each participant in the IEP staffing process to determine whether the child accomplished the goals/objectives in a clear and non-biased way.

Independent of legal issues, data suggest that IEPs fulfilling the conditions delineated in the regulations are judged to be more useful programmatically than are incomplete IEPs.[19] The Department of Education[30] regulations provide a workable model to increase the effectiveness of improving student learning. The requirements for concrete goals and sequenced tasks to which there can be feedback regarding progress provide the essential framework for an efficient delivery system. The completed IEP becomes the standard for evaluating the effectiveness of educational efforts during the implementation period.

THE ROLE OF THE PHYSICAL EDUCATOR

As mentioned earlier in this chapter, the REI increases the likelihood that the regular physical education teacher will deliver services to children with disabilities. The regular physical education teacher has new responsibilities for the development and implementation of IEPs for students with disabilities:

> Whenever a child with a disability is placed in a regular classroom, the responsibility of the regular educator for that child is the same as for any other child in the classroom. Because all children differ with respect to amount of learning, rate of learning, and learning style, modifications in methodology, curriculum, or environment are often necessary for both nonhandicapped and handicapped children. Special education, which involves significant modifications in methodology, curriculum, or environment may also be delivered to some handicapped children in regular classrooms. Whenever this arrangement is specified in the child's IEP, the development of such specially designed instruction is the responsibility of special educators. Regular educators are responsible for assisting the child in carrying out the program. Overall classroom management also continues to be the responsibility of the regular teacher.[6]

Regular educators have any or all of the following duties with respect to children with disabilities[8]:
1. Identification of possible disabling conditions
2. Referral of children for evaluation and placement
3. Data gathering
4. Assisting children with disabilities with special equipment
5. Participation in developing IEPs
6. Sharing information with parents
7. Integrating children with and without disabilities in the school environment

INDIVIDUAL PHYSICAL EDUCATION PLAN OR INDIVIDUAL MOTOR EDUCATION PLAN

As mentioned previously, children with disabilities are to receive an individual physical education plan (IPEP) or individual motor education plan (IMEP) to meet their unique physical education needs. The program includes annual goals, present levels of educational performance, and short-term instructional objectives. Furthermore, there should be a full preevaluation of the physical education needs of the child. The unique physical education needs of children with disabilities are determined by identifying discrepancies between existing levels of performance and minimum standards on physical education tasks set by local school districts. Therefore the *physical educator* determines what will be on the IPEP by assessing children on tasks from the regular curriculum. Once a task deficiency is noted, present levels of performance are determined, goals are set for remediation of the deficiency, and short-term objectives are postulated. The physical educator is the *only* person who knows the curriculum tasks to carry out this mission and should be the primary author of the short-term objectives of an IPEP. The physical educator knows how each child functions on curriculum tasks implemented in his or her class.

When a child is placed in special physical education, it should be determined why he or she is there. If participation in a special physical education program can remediate the adverse physical education performance and get the child back in a regular unrestricted class, that is the reason for placement. If it is judged that the child will not acquire skills to enable return to the regular physical education class, specific goals that relate directly to independent functioning in natural community environments should be incorporated into the IPEP. Provisions should be made to generalize motor skills attained through instruction to domestic and community recreational settings.

Advantages

A separately written physical education or motor plan has some distinct advantages:
1. The unique contributions that can be made to the child given a quality physical education or adapted physical education program are clear.
2. The physical educator and/or adapted physical educator accepts full responsibility for implementation of the physical education or motor program.
3. The physical educator and/or adapted physical educator, who often carrying huge caseloads, can computer generate the IPEP or IMEP. (Refer to

Chapter 19 for a thorough discussion of techniques to generate an IPEP or IMEP using a computer.)

The box on p. 427 is a sample IPEP.

SOME PROBLEMS WITH IMPLEMENTING IEPS

The IEP has become, in some school districts, a paper chase that is unrelated to the actual process of educating the child with a disability.

Indeed, school personnel are asked, "Are you done with Juan's IEP?" or "Have you written the IPEP for Demetric?" The IEP is seen as an end product rather than an on-going process of evaluation, review, and adaptation of the program to meet the child's unique educational needs.

Smith[26] has criticized the IEP process:

> ...despite overwhelming evidence that IEPs have failed to accomplish their mission, little has been done to rectify the situation...the IEP should be an essential component of instructional design and delivery that enhances and accounts for students' learning and teachers' teaching. Yet, data support the contention that IEPs are not functioning as designed, including being inept at structuring 'specially designed instruction.'

Indeed, Gerardi et al.[10] suggested that the IEP may well be the "single most critical detriment to appropriate programming" for children in need of special education services. The researchers suggested that the IEP process has created a huge ineffective bureaucracy.

While the potential for maximizing educational benefits for children with disabilities through the IEP process is great, there have been problems with IEP implementation. Specific problems and suggested solutions follow.
1. The regular physical educators fail to test students to identify those persons whose performance is adversely affected (criteria for determining the disabling condition).[32]

   Local school districts should set minimum standards for physical education curriculum tasks.

   If this is not done, then there is no basis for determining adverse educational performance. School districts or states need to design curricula with standards so that adverse educational performance can be determined. Furthermore, measurement for the most part is not an integral part of the physical education instructional delivery system. Measurement needs to be incorporated into the curriculum, data collected by teachers,

Individual Physical Education Plan

Student_____   ID#_____   Date_____
School_____   DOB_____   Grade_____
Nature of disability_____
Responsible implementor(s)_____

Present level of performance (summary)   **Evaluation Instruments**

_____   ___   Bruininks-Oseretsky
_____   ___   OSU Sigma
_____   ___   Project Mobilitee
_____   ___   Health-Related Fit
_____   ___   Brigance Inventory
_____   ___   Other:_____

Detailed evaluation report attached   ___yes ___no

Duration of services: from_____to_____
Date of annual review_____

PHYSICAL EDUCATION PLACEMENT:

___ Regular physical education
___ Regular physical education with assistance. Specify:_____
_____

ANNUAL GOAL: _____
Student objective: _____
Student objective: _____

ANNUAL GOAL: _____
Student objective: _____
Student objective: _____

ANNUAL TRANSITION GOAL: _____
Student transition objective: _____
Student transition objective: _____

Community Based Agency	**/Facilitator/Community**
Contact ___ Special Olympics Unified Sports Program	_____
___ Disabled Sports Association. Specify:	_____
_____	_____
___ YMCA/YWCA	_____
___ Recreation agency. Specify:	_____
_____	_____

and judgments made from the data to determine which children are having problems.

2. School districts fail to include short-term instructional objectives before the child is placed in special physical education.[29]

Short-term instructional objectives are behaviors taught by the teacher that relate to goals (physical education). Therefore teachers need to be involved in developing the goals. If they are not involved, they may not know how to structure the short-term instructional objectives that will support the goals.

3. School districts are writing IEPs with goals and objectives that bear little relation to the teacher's instructional plans.[29]

Schools often do not write goals that can be

broken down into behaviors that can be incorporated into instructional plans. Also, some teachers cannot make an instructional plan and implement it so that it relates to the goals of the IEP. The problem can be partially solved by training personnel to write clearer goals and develop the instructional plans that support the goals.

4. Educators fear they will be held accountable if the child fails to achieve the goals of the IEP. The IEP is not a performance contract.[29]

It appears that the IEP process can be used to hide ineffectual and inappropriate education for children with disabilities. The IEP process can, however, be used to carefully monitor the education of children with special needs.

Good goals on an IPEP are not sufficient to change one's lifestyle so that persons may engage in physical and sport activity patterns that are meaningful in leisure. A process of lifestyle planning is needed to coordinate the formal instruction of the public schools and the informal services in the community so that the skills gained in physical education instruction may generalize into adult lifestyles of physically active leisure. Thus a part of the planning process might well be directed toward the generalization of motor skills acquired in the physical education program to community-based sport activities or intramural programs that accommodate the needs of individuals with disabilities within the school setting. IDEA addresses this need, specifically, in the mandate that a "transition plan" must be included as part of the IEP.

This problem requires education of teachers by supervisory personnel. A sound data base will indicate progress of children in physical education. Goals are calculated guesses of the degree to which learning takes place. They give instruction direction. Indeed, administrators and parents must help teachers believe that it is vital that they be held accountable for their actions. The good teacher embraces the notion that he or she can and must be able to carefully document the child's progress and, more important, can and must be able to design an instructional environment so the child can accomplish the specific goals and objectives.

Thus the physical educator assesses children with disabilities in the physical education curriculum. The physical educator develops an IPEP from the needs assessment, implements the IEP, and records data on the progress of objectives achieved and goals met. If a child does not progress in the physical education component of the IEP, related services may be secured to help the child benefit from the IPEP. The physical educator must be an active participant in the development of the IPEP.

HELPING THOSE WHO ARE NOT CLASSIFIED AS DISABLED

There are many children in the public schools whose performance is adversely affected but who do not qualify for special education servies. These individuals may still need special help. Keogh and Sugden[16] indicate that 3 in 40 individuals are awkward. Will[35] states that 20% of the school-age population who are considered normal need special academic assistance. Will believes systems need to be developed to provide individualized instruction for all children so that those who have special needs, whether classified as disabled or not, can have their needs met.

SUMMARY

The process of designing individual education programs (IEPs) in physical education for the student with a disability is a basic component of effective programming. The nature of the program will depend on the intended outcomes for specific children. The goal for children with mild disabilities may be alleviating deficits so they may participate in a regular class. The purpose of the IEP for young children with severe disabilities may be to promote developmental functioning; however, self-sufficiency in their community is the desired outcome for older individuals. Those goals that are directed specifically toward self-sufficiency should focus on performance of functional behavior that can be put to immediate use.

Appropriate IEPs necessitate ongoing assessment of the attainment of short-term objectives of the IEP, which takes place in both the IEP and the instructional daily plan of the teacher. Related service personnel are crucial in the development and implementation of the IEP. IEPs for persons with severe disabilities should focus on use of functional facilitations or adaptations so the children may participate in age-appropriate activities. IEPs for the severely disabled should also emphasize goals and objectives that represent discrepancies between existing motor skills and those needed for self-sufficiency in the community. The IEP is a link between the student and the demands of his or her environment. The child with a mild disability should be prepared for environments where they have options similar to those without disabilities. The IEP for the student with more severe disabilities is a link between instruction and the demands of the community; it is an important element in the transition from school to adult independent life in specified environments.

REVIEW QUESTIONS

1. Can you explain the contents of the IEP?
2. Who attends the IEP meeting?
3. Explain current legislative mandates to include transition planning in the IEP.
4. Explain the difference between direct service and related service personnel. Give an example of each and explain their role in service delivery to children with disabilities.

STUDENT ACTIVITIES

1. Ask your instructor to help arrange an opportunity for you to attend an IEP meeting in a local school district.
2. Interview a parent of a child with a disability. Ask what the parent expects of professionals who work with his/her child.
3. Observe a special education class. Ask the instructor to explain how his/her lesson plan relates to the annual goals on the students' IEPs.
4. Arrange to observe an adapted physical education teacher assess a child. Determine the contents of the IPEP based on the data.
5. Arrange to observe one of the professionals designated as a related sevice provider. Talk with the individual about the nature of his/her professional relationship with adapted physical educators and "regular" physical educators.
6. Read a current article from a journal representing a related service field. These include, for example, *Corrective Therapy Journal, Language, Speech and Hearing in the Schools, Journal of Communicative Disorders,* and *American Journal of Physical Therapy.*
7. Interview a physical educator whose classes include children with disabilities. Ask the teacher about the nature of the these children's problems, challenges, and joys.

REFERENCES

1. *A four-year plan to systematically integrate microcomputers, videodiscs, and other state-of-the-art technology into special education administration, management and classroom instruction.* Dallas Independent School District, January, 1987, Instruction Systems Technology Division, Department of Special Education.
2. Achilles J, Yates R, Freese J: Perspectives from the field: collaborative consultation in the speech and language program of the Dallas Independent School District, *Lang, Speech, Hearing in the Schools* 22:154-155, 1991.
3. *Alamo Heights v. State Board of Education,* 790 F.2d 1153 (5th Cir. 1986).
4. American Occupational Therapy Association: *Uniform terminology for occupational therapy, ed 2,* Rockville, Md, 1989, The Association.
5. American Occupational Therapy Association: *Guidelines for occupational therapy services in school systems,* Rockville, Md, 1989, The Association.
6. Barresi J, Mack J: Responsibilities of regular classroom teachers for handicapped students. In: *ERIC fact sheet,* Reston, Va, 1989, ERIC Clearinghouse on Handicapped and Gifted Children.
7. Brown L et al: A strategy for developing chronological age appropriate and functional curricular content for severely handicapped adolescents and young adults, *J Spec Educ* 13:81-90, 1979.
8. Cain EJ: The role of the computer in special education: some philosophical considerations, *The Pointer* 28:6-11, 1984.
9. Fiscus ED, Nandell C: *Developing individual education programs,* St Paul, Minn, 1983, West Publishing.
10. Gerardi RJ et al: IEP—more paperwork and wasted time, *Contemp Ed* 56:39-42, 1984.
11. Haynes C: Language development in the school years—what can go wrong? In Mogford K, Sadler J, editors: *Child language disability,* Clevedon, England, 1989, Multilingual Matters.
12. *Individuals with Disabilities Education Act.* US Congress: Public Law 101-476, October 30, 1990.
13. *Irving Independent School District v. Tatro,* 1984, 468 US 883.
14. Jenkins JR, Pious CG, Jewell M: Special education and the regular education initiative: basic assumptions, *Except Child* 56:479-491, 1990.
15. Kauffman J: The regular education initiative as Reagan-Bush education policy: a trickle-down theory of education of the hard-to-teach, *J Spec Educ* 23:256-278, 1989.
16. Keogh J, Sugden D: *Movement skill development,* New York, 1985, Macmillan Publishing.
17. Lavine RA: *Personal computers serving people: a guide to human service applications,* Washington, DC, 1980, Hawkins & Associates.
18. *Macomb County Intermediate School District v. Joshua S.,* 715 F Suppl 824 (ED Mich 1989).
19. Maher C: Training special service teams to develop IEPs, *Except Child* 47:206-211, 1980.
20. Martin R: *Legal challenges to behavioral modification trends in schools, corrections and mental health,* Champaign, Ill, 1979, Research Press.
21. Marvin CA: Consultation services: changing roles for SLP's, *J Child Comm Dis* 11:1-16, 1987.
22. Meisbov G: Normalization and its relevance today, *J Autism Dev Disord* 20:379-390, 1990.
23. Office of Civil Rights, 1989, EHLR 326.
24. Orr C, Gott C, Kainer M: *Model of student role adaptation: merging the values of occupational therapy and special education,* Dallas Independent School District, 1990.
25. Seaman JA, DePauw KP: *The new adapted physical education: a developmental approach,* Palo Alto, Calif, 1989, Mayfield Publishing.
26. Smith SW: Individualized education programs (IEPs) in special education—from intent to acquiescence, *Except Child,* September:6-13, 1990.
27. Special education: parent and student rights, *Texas Education Agency,* September, 1986.

28. Tiritelli W, Director, Dallas Independent School District Special Education Vocational Instruction Program, *personal conversation,* October, 1991.

29. US Department of Education: Assistance to states for education of handicapped children: interpretation of the individual education program, *Fed Reg,* Jan 19, 1981.

30. *US General Accounting Office: Report to Congress,* Feb 5, 1981.

31. Wang MC, Walberg HJ: Four fallacies of segregationism, *Except Child* 55:128-137, 1988.

32. Wessell J, editor: *Planning individualized educational programs in special education with examples from I CAN,* Northbrook, Ill, 1977, Hubbard Publishing.

33. White OR: Adaptive performance objectives: form versus function. In Sailor W, Wilcox B, Brown L: *Methods of instruction of severely handicapped students,* Baltimore, 1985, Paul H Brookes Publishing.

34. Wilcox B, Bellamy G: *Design of high school programs for severely handicapped students,* Baltimore, 1982, Paul H Brookes Publishing.

35. Will M: *Educating students with learning problems—a shared responsibility. A report to the secretary,* Washington, DC, 1986, US Department of Education.

SUGGESTED READINGS

Meisbov G: Normalization and its relevance today, *J Autism Dev Disord* 20:379-390, 1990.

Smith SW: Individualized education programs (IEPs) in special education—from intent to acquiescense, *Except Child,* September:6-13, 1990.

Wang MC, Walberg HJ: Four fallacies of segregationism, *Except Child* 55:128-137, 1988.

OBJECTIVES

Describe the least restrictive environment concept as it applies to students with disabilities in physical education.

Explain the preservice and inservice requirements of paraprofessionals, peer buddies, and student assistants.

Effectively group students.

Explain computer-aided instructional management in physical education for children with disabilities.

Monitor pupil performance and progress.

Manage instructional time.

Write a lesson plan that corresponds to a child's IPEP.

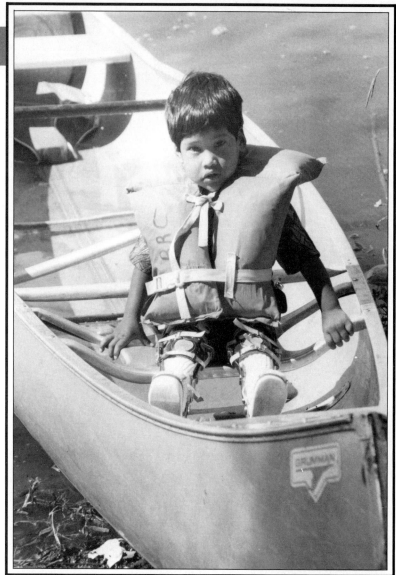

Courtesy Dallas Independent School District

Class Organization

S trategies for organizing the learning experience to meet the needs of children with disabilities are discussed in this chapter. These organizational strategies include application of the concept of least restrictive environment in physical education and strategies for creating and managing an effective learning environment.

Physical education for children with disabilities can be organized for instruction in several different ways. Many factors have an impact on the organization of physical education for children with disabilities. These factors include:

□ The number of days per week physical education is required by the state's Department of Public Instruction or Education Agency

□ The school district's interpretation of "physical education; some school districts wrongly include any time spent in supervised play (recess) as part of the child's physical education program

□ The number of minutes allocated in the total physical education program for physical activity

□ Administrative commitment or lack of commitment to physical education

□ Administrative commitment or lack of commitment to physical education for children with disabilities

□ The availability of physical educators trained to teach children with disabilities in the regular physical education program

□ The availability of specially trained physical educators, adapted physical educators

□ The relationship between regular physical education and adapted physical education

□ The availability of an accessible facility

□ The availability of equipment, specialized if necessary

The most important consideration, however, is the fact that children with disabilities have an ethical and legal right to be educated in their least restrictive environment.

PHYSICAL EDUCATION IN THE LEAST RESTRICTIVE ENVIRONMENT

The Education of the Handicapped Act mandates that a child with a disability should be educated in the least restrictive environment. This is true of the child's specially designed physical education, as well. The regular education initiative, the national trend toward returning children with disabilities into the "regular" education program, has caused some misunderstanding, however, of the intent of the law. Specifically, the regular education initiative has caused renewed interest in education within the "mainstream." However, it must be noted that the term *mainstreaming* is not to be found anywhere in the Education of the Handicapped Act. The law mandates that a child should be educated within the least restrictive environment.

Aufsesser[2] has described changes in programming within special education that can have an impact on the concept of the least restrictive environment in physical education. They are as follows:

□ Focus on transition from school, to work, to home

□ Utilize community based instruction with all students, regardless of the nature or severity of the disability

□ Use technological advances like computers and communication boards to improve the educational environment

□ Focus on improved fitness required for independent living and vocational success

□ Focus on the development of functional skills

□ Foster participation of children with and without disabilities in unified sport and recreation programs.

The trend toward education of all children within the "regular" education program has caused increased problems for the regular physical educator. Historically, children unable to be "mainstreamed" into any other classroom have been mainstreamed into art, music, and physical education. Lavay and DePaepe[13] have cautioned that a student with a disability must be "integrated" into the physical education program rather than just "included."

Grosse[7] has addressed the issue that the "mainstream" may not be the appropriate placement for some children with disabilities. Grosse has outlined her concerns as follows[7]:

STUDENT

The mainstream is not always a better place to be when...

□ A full physical evaluation, including movement patterns, skills knowledge, and fitness, is not performed prior to placement decisions

□ A student is placed based on a decision about an entire special education class rather than on an individual basis

□ A student is placed there even though the student cannot follow directions, attend, or demonstrate on-task behaviors necessary to participate in a group

□ A student is placed without appropriate support personnel

□ A student does not have the experience or skills necessary to participate actively in the education process

□ A student is teased or ridiculed by classmates

□ A student is unable to make friends within the class

□ A student is unable to benefit from the class.

TEACHER

The mainstream is not always a better place to be when the teacher...

□ Is not receptive to having a child with a disability in the regular class

□ Is not trained in adapting equipment, curriculum, and teaching techniques to meet individual needs, nor is able to receive support/assistance from an adapted physical education specialist

ENVIRONMENT

The mainstream is not always a better place to be when...
☐ Facilities and equipment are inappropriate
☐ The class is overcrowded
☐ Participation in mainstream physical education hinders the student's development in other subjects/classes

To prevent misuse of the mainstream physical education placement, the physical educator must be prepared to function as a vital part of the multidisciplinary team that decides on the child's placement in physical education. This section addresses a cascade of service delivery environments in physical education. However, they are not presented in a hierarchy. Specifically, there is no one best physical education environment for all children. There is, however, a "best," least restrictive physical education environment for each child with a disability.

Regular Physical Education

In order for a child with a disability, even a mild disability, to be educated in the regular physical education class, careful preparation must be made. There are four variables tht must be considered before making a decision to place a child into the regular physical education program: (1) the professional preparation of the physical educator to teach a child with disabilities, (2)

FIGURE 18-1. Staff members of Disabled Sports Association of North Texas give wheelchair sports demonstration for a class of fifth graders. (Courtesy Disabled Sports Association of North Texas.)

the attitude of the physical educator toward the disabled child, (3) the support of the primary campus adminstrator of the concept of inclusion, and (4) the readiness of the non-disabled children in the school to accept and interact with the child. These four factors all must be considered.

The first variable to be considered in the decision to include children with disabilities in regular physical education programs is the preparation of the physical education teacher. In order to serve children with disabilities in the regular physical education class, the teacher must have knowlede of the following:

1. Physical, mental, and emotional characteristics of children with disabilities
2. Learning styles of children with disabilities
3. Teaching techniques and methodologies appropriate for children with and without disabilities
4. Behavior management strategies appropriate for children with and without disabilities
5. Techniques for modifying play, games, and sport activities to include children with disabilities
6. Methods for modifying curricular objectives to meet the needs of children with disabilities
7. Methods for modifying evaluation and grading for children with disabilities.

If the physical educator did not acquire this knowledge during undergraduate or graduate professional preparation, the physical educator must be provided access to this information through inservice preparation *before* a child with disabilities is included in the regular program.

The second variable that must be considered before placing a child with a disability into the regular physical education classroom is the teacher's attitude toward teaching those with disabilities. If the teacher has a negative attitude about including a child with a disability in the class, the child will know it instantly and be devastated by it; the child with a disability simply cannot be placed in a classroom/gymnasium in which he or she is not wanted.

Teachers may have negative attitudes toward a disabled child for a variety of reasons, but attitudes are learned behaviors which, when necessary, can be changed. Clark, French, and Henderson[5] noted:

> It is important to find ways to teach physical educators the knowledge and skills necessary to work effectively with students with disabilities in the regular classroom *and* increase positive attitudes toward them. These are not mutually exclusive. Teachers may have negative attitudes toward students with disabilities because they do not know how to teach them.

Clark, French, and Henderson[5] recommended preservice or inservice training that would include empathy experiences, values clarification, volunteerism, experiences with children with disabilities, group discussions, and lectures as vehicles for attitude change. Below are suggested techniques for preservice or inservice presentations intended to alter the attitudes of physical educators toward the disabled.

Empathy experiences

The physical educator would be provided experiences that simulate the experience of being disabled. For example, the individual could be asked to spend a day teaching in a wheelchair or to spend a night at home with his or her family while blindfolded.

"Humbling" experiences

The physical educator would be exposed to information about the physical performance of elite disabled athletes. The educator would be asked, for example, to compare his or her running performance to the national marathon record of male and female wheelchair racers. Better still, the physical educator would be given the opportunity to compete against an elite disabled athlete. The teacher would have the opportunity to bowl, for example, against a member of the American Wheelchair Bowling Association or to play golf against a low handicap player of the National Amputee Golf Assocation.

Observation experiences

The physical educator would be invited to attend a local or regional sports competition for individuals with disabilities. These would include events sponsored by, for example, the Special Olympics, the National Wheelchair Athletic Association, or the National Association of Sports for Cerebral Palsy. If this is not possible, the teacher would be given the opportunity to view tapes, for example, of the 1991 International Special Olympics Competition in Minneapolis, Minnesota or of the wheelchair division of the 1992 Boston Marathon.

Volunteer experiences

The physical educator would be given the opportunity to volunteer, particularly at sporting events for the disabled individual. The thread throughout the development of attitude change is the common experience of movement and sport.

Values clarification

The physical educator would be led by a trained psychologist or school counselor through the process of identifying and clarifying prejudices, attitudes, and notions about individuals with disabilities. These values might best be clarified in and through conversations with disabled adults or with parents of children with disabilities. This type of conversation should be led by a psychologist or counselor, at first, to ensure the individuals have a quality human interaction. Clark, French, and Henderson[5] suggested that a "trigger story" may also help physical educators sort out feelings and attitudes toward teaching the disabled. For example, the physical educator would be asked to react to the following types of scenarios, by identifying the emotions of the child, his or her classmates, and the fears or concerns the physical educator may have about the inclusion process:

> Atlantis is a moderately mentally retarded, emotionally disturbed child who cries for an hour before being made to join the fifth grade physical education class. No one in the class has befriended her; indeed, her classmates taunt and jeer at her throughout.
> *or*
> Guadalupe is a 5-year-old child with mild spina bifida. He is ambulatory and loves to play. He is not being allowed to come to the gym with his classmates and is depressed because of the decision.

This type of values clarification can also be encouraged by asking the physical educator to read books like *Breaking Through*, the Harry Cordellos story (Cordellos H: *Breaking through,* Mountain View, Calif, 1981, Anderson World) or to watch movies, readily available on videotape, like "My Left Foot" or "Children of a Lesser God." In addition, the physical educator could be asked to view contemporary television programs that feature disabled actors (e.g., "Life Goes On" or "Reasonable Doubts").

Jansma and Schultz[12] demonstrated that even a short, 2-day inservice workshop could promote the development of positive attitude change in physical educators toward students with disabilities. Most teachers have chosen their field because of a love of children; these indiviudals usually can be touched, in a positive way, so that they develop a positive attitude toward teaching children with disabilities.

There are other variables that also must be considered before a decision is made to include children with disabilities in the regular physical education program.

The third variable that must be considered is administrative support for the inclusion of children with disabilities into the regular physical education classroom. If the local campus administrator, principal, or dean of instruction supports the notion that children with disabilities should be integrated into the regular physical education program, then that administrator must be in a position to support the physical educator in a number of ways. The local campus administrator cannot expect that a physical educator can create a nurturing, supportive environment for a child with a disability—for any child, for that matter—if saddled with huge class sizes. It is not uncommon, for example, for a physical educator in the Dallas Independent School District to have a class size in excess of 80 students. It is impossible to address the needs of each child in the class in this situation and it is ridiculous to assume that even the best teacher could accommodate even one more child, particularly a child with a disability. The administrator committed to inclusion in physical education will do one of three things to ensure that a quality physical education is received by all:

1. Decrease class size by hiring additional professional personnel or arranging alternate scheduling patterns
2. Decrease teacher-student ratio by assigning trained paraprofessionals to assist the teacher
3. Decrease teacher-student ratio by assigning school volunteers to assist the physical educator in the gymnasium.

In addition to limiting the teacher-student ratio in physical education, the campus administrator must also provide support for the physical educator by addressing other concerns:

1. The physical educator must be encouraged to attend classes and in-service presentations that address the education of children with disabilities in the regular physical education program
2. The physical educator must be given release time to participate actively as part of the motor development team or the multidisciplinary team in the assessment/evaluation of the child's gross motor skills and the creation/implementation of the child's individual motor education plan (IMEP) or individual physical education plan (IPEP).

The fourth consideration that must be addressed before including a child with disabilities into the regular physical education program is the readiness of the other children to accept and interact with the child. Indeed, the same type of experiences must be given the other children in the school as were suggested for improving the attitude of the physical educator—empathy experiences, "humbling" experiences, group discussions, observations, and volunteerism.

If the physical educator has been trained to accommodate the child with a disability into the regular class, *if* the physical educator has a positive attitude about including the child into the regular program, *if* the

campus administrator is supportive of the inclusion model, **and** *if* the children in the school have been prepared to accept the child, it is possible to include a child with a disability into the regular physical education program. The most successful of these programs have been those that used cooperative learning activities to involve the children with and without disabilities in activity together.[6] Specific suggestions for methods and techniques for modifying the physical education program for a child with a disability are included in Chapters 7 to 16.

Regular Physical Education with Instructional Support

It is often necessary to provide support in the regular physical education environment to allow a child with a disability to learn and thrive in that setting. A number of variations are available to accommodate the child.

Regular physical education with peer buddy

Often the only accommodation that must be made to allow the child to learn within the regular physical education class is to ask a given child in the same class, a child the same age, to be a special "buddy."[9] The child is asked to include the disabled child in play, games, or activities; often this is the only "ice breaker" necessary to allow the child to thrive in the regular program.

Regular physical education with older buddy

A child unable to function within the regular physical education class with a same-age buddy may thrive if given the opportunity to work with an older buddy or "teacher's assistant." This assistant should be carefully trained to help meet the special needs of the child without interfering with instruction and without setting the child apart from the others. This older, more mature student should receive training in the nature of the child's disability, in techniques for communicating effectively with the child, in methods, for example, of assisting the child move his or her wheelchair or, if blind, orient himself or herself in the gymnasium.

Regular physical education with adult volunteer support

Like the older buddy, the adult volunteer must be carefully trained to meet the needs of the child with a disability in the regular physical education classroom. This may be a more effective learning environment (the least restrictive one) for a child with behavior disorders that are difficult for another child to manage, but that can be handled by an adult.

Regular physical education with paraprofessional support

The child's least restrictive physical education environment may be the regular physical education class with the support/assistance of a physical education or special education paraprofessional. This paraprofessional literally serves as a second physical education teacher, who focuses interest and efforts on the children with special needs. In some instances the regular physical education teacher must insist that if a child with a disability or children with disabilities are to be included in the physical education class a paraprofessional must be available.

Regular Physical Education by Unit/Activity

On occasion, rather than making a decision solely on the basis of instructional support, a decision about the least restrictive environment must be made on a per unit/activity basis. For example, an autistic child may be able to participate in the structured warm-up/fitness phase of the physical education class but would be unable to handle the less restrictive play, game, and sport phase of the class. A blind child may be able to participate in individual sport activities like bowling or archery (with beeper supplements, for example), but would be unable to participate in team sports. A least restrictive environment decision based on unit/activity is one option for consideration when seeking inclusion.

Regular Physical Education with Younger Children

Occasionally it may be appropriate to integrate children with disabilities into physical education classes with younger children. This may be appropriate with children with delayed social and play skills. Under no circumstances, however, should a child with a disability be integrated into a physical education class serving children more than 2 years younger. To place a mildly emotionally disturbed first grader into a physical education class with kindergartners may prove a humane and creative way of allowing the child to develop social and play skills that the child lacks. It would, however, be inhumane to place that same child into a kindergarten class when the child has reached fourth-grade age. The child is not "included" in that environment; the child is set apart for ridicule by the very nature of size differences.

Reverse "Mainstreaming"

When it is deemed that education within the regular physical education program, even with instructional support or modifications, is inappropriate for the child—that is, it is not the least restrictive educational environment—there are other strategies that can be used to allow the disabled child to participate and learn with other children. If the child is receiving physical education instruction in a separate class setting, children without disabilities can be invited to participate in the class, as well.

This is the type of program that is the basis for the Special Olympics Unified Sports Concept. The intent of that instructional, recreational, and sport program is to allow individuals with mental retardation to be taught with, to recreate with, and to compete with individuals without disabilities.

Separate, but Equal, Physical Education Instruction

Some children receiving their education within the public schools, because of the nature and the severity of their disabilities, need to be educated in self-contained classes. For example, severely emotionally disturbed children may need to be educated in a self-contained class. That is, the children stay in their class throughout the day and receive physical education instruction as a group. This, because of the nature and the severity of the disability is the least restrictive

FIGURE 18-2. Adapted physical education teacher provides one-to-one assistance in class activity. (Courtesy Dallas Independent School District.)

learning environment for these children. It must be noted, however, that this physical education must be provided by a trained physical educator. This may be the school's regular physical educator working in the gymnasium or it may be the district's adapted physical educator providing service in the gymnasium or classroom.

Physical Education within Institutions, Hospitals, or Home-Bound Programs

Occasionally, the nature or the severity of a child's disability requires segregated educational placement within institutions, hospitals, or home-bound programs. The Education of the Handicapped Act mandates that a child receiving educational services within one of these environments must receive physical education services if physical education is required of his or her peers. For example, an emotionally disturbed, suicidal adolescent may receive physical education services in the psychiatric ward of a rehabilitation facility while receiving crisis intervention. A child struggling with the last phases of Acquired Immunodeficiency Syndrome (AIDS) may require physical education services in the hospital or at home.

It is vital in the consideration of the least restrictive physical education environment, however, that it is understood that the placement must vary depending on the student's needs at the time. For example, the suicidal adolescent mentioned earlier may, upon completion of the crisis intervention program at the rehabilitation center, return to school and receive physical education with instructional support in the regular physical education program. The child with AIDS should, during the initial phases of the illness, receive physical education within the the regular physical education program with support from the medical community.

In each of these situations the physical education teacher must adapt instruction, manage behavior, and promote social acceptance of children with disabilities. Furthermore, the teacher is responsible for arranging and managing the total instructional environment in physical education.

PRE-SERVICE TRAINING AND MANAGEMENT OF SUPPORT PERSONNEL

The physical educator who serves children with disabilities in any of the above settings may be responsible for managing support personnel. In many instances, the availability of support personnel is one of the major factors in decisions regarding the least restrictive environment for children with disabilities. The teacher may need a responsible paraprofessional, a student buddy, a

student teacher's assistant, or an adult volunteer to integrate children with disabilities into the regular physical education program. Consideration is given in this chapter to the role of the teacher in the management of personnel within the physical education environment.

Paraprofessional

In many school districts paraprofessionals or teacher's aides are assigned to assist a teacher in a given program without regard to their training or background. As such, it is possible that the physical education teacher will need to ensure that the paraprofessional attend preservice and in-service programs regarding physical education and, if children with disabilities are to be served, regarding physical education for children with disabilities.

At the very least, the paraprofessional must have the opportunity to share the same type of experiences recommended for teachers. Clark, French, and Henderson[5] have recommended preservice or in-service training for physical education teachers that would include empathy experiences, values clarification, volunteerism, experiences with children with disabilities, group discussions, and lectures as vehicles for attitude change. This same type of preservice or in-service training must be included in the training regimen of the paraprofessional.

One of the most significant aspects of the supervision of a paraprofessional is the description of the paraprofessional's role and responsibilities. Most school districts have a job description for the paraprofessional. This description is, however, often vague and leaves questions regarding the specific role and responsibilities of the paraprofessional. In addition, the job description for the paraprofessional is usually prepared for the individual who will assist a classroom teacher. The duties and responsibilities of the paraprofessional working in the gymnasium are different from the duties and responsibilities of the paraprofessional in the classroom. As such, the physical education teacher or adapted physical education teacher must work closely with the building principal to design a specific job description, particularly if the paraprofessional is to help teach children with disabilities. An example of a description for one class period follows:

Specific responsibilities for _____,
P.E. paraprofessional

Class #1, 8:00 - 8:45

7:55   Go to Room 103 to accompany Kaneisha to the gym. Insist she push her own chair.

FIGURE 18-3. Paraprofessional leads class in rhythm activity to develop body part identification skills. (Courtesy Dallas Independent School District.)

8:00-8:15 Roam throughout the gymnasium while children are doing warm-up exercises encouraging all the children to do well. If necessary, remind Kaneisha to do her modified warm-ups which are posted on the wall.

8:15-8:40 Monitor Kaneisha's interactions with others in the class. Record and describe any inappropriate interactions on her behavior chart in teacher's office. Refer to the description of appropriate/inappropriate behaviors on her chart.

8:40-8:45 Accompany Kaneisha to her room.

A specific job description significantly alleviates potential problems. If respective roles and responsibilities are clear to both the physical education teacher and the paraprofessional, they can work together as a professional team, serving children in the best possible way. In addition, the wise physical educator should take every opportunity to reinforce the efforts of the paraprofessional. For example, the physical educator should write a letter to the principal praising the efforts of the paraprofessional. A copy should be shared with the paraprofessional. Or, the physical educator should routinely orchestrate a class "thank-you" for the paraprofessional with cards, cake, and punch.

Peer Buddies and Teacher's Assistants

One's peers are powerful facilitators of learning. Once instruction becomes specific, it is not difficult for students to learn what it is they are to do and then com-municate information to their peers. The peer instruction or modeling can be done by children with and without disabilities.[22] Buddies must know what is to be done and have the ability to communicate with the child with a disability. Such instructional activity is what Mosston[15] calls *reciprocal teaching.* The PEOPEL Project (Physical Education Opportunity Program for Exceptional Learners) is nationally recognized. This organization has effectively used peer teachers.

The buddies and teacher's assistants should receive the same type of preservice and in-service training as does the paraprofessional. Armstrong, Rosenbaum, and King[1] found that a controlled, direct-contact experience between children with and children without disabilities can significantly improve the attitudes of the non-disabled child toward the disabled child. Empathy experiences are particularly valuable in the training of peer buddies and teacher's assistants. And, just like paraprofessionals, the buddy or teacher's assistant should have a specific job description. Working in close cooperation with the student's classroom teacher, this experience can be valuable for the peer buddy, the teacher's assistant, and the child with a disability, as well.

Older students may also serve as excellent models and teacher's assistants in physical education. Peer teachers can be indispensable in individualized learning environments. They can assume several responsibilities that contribute to class management and record progress in physical education, such as setting up and storing equipment before and after class, collecting data on self and others, and assisting with the instruction of peers. These students are often honor students who are released from school or are scheduled with younger and slower-learning children. They serve for a short time and usually feed back information about errors in task performance and student collection of data. These students need to be thoroughly familiar with the programming if their assistance is to be valuable. Research indicates that third-grade children are capable of correcting one another's movement errors. However, in a structured behavioral program that uses stick figures to represent objectives, kindergarten students and trainable mentally retarded children can learn to self-instruct; by first grade some can feed back information to peers.[20,27]

The process of organizing a successful peer buddy or student assistant program is complex. The steps are outlined below:

1. Discuss the peer buddy/teacher's assistant plan with the local campus administrator. Secure support and approval.
2. Discuss the peer buddy/teacher's assistant plan with the classroom teachers whose schedules will be affected. Secure support/approval.
3. Schedule a preservice orientation meeting for all teachers and students. The preservice orientation should include:
   A. Description of the peer buddy/teacher's assistant program.
   B. Role/responsibilities of the peer buddies and teacher's assistants.
   C. Characteristics of the children with disabilities who will be served. (Care must be taken to protect, at all costs, the privacy rights of the children who will be served. Information may be shared, for example, about the nature of mental retardation, but specific information about "Bobby" must not be shared with these children.)
4. Develop a schedule for each teacher/child involved in the program. Share copies with the principal.
5. Have on-going in-service education with peer buddies and teacher's assistants during each lesson. Spend a few moments before each class reminding the students of their roles and responsibilities.
6. Evaluate the performance of the peer buddies and teacher's assistants during each lesson. Provide feedback (positive, whenever possible) with students after each lesson.

7. Arrange to honor the peer buddies and teacher's assistants at the end of the unit, semester, or year. Ask to be involved in the school's honor assembly and award certificates of participation or certificates of thanks during the award ceremony.
8. If possible, present a slide presentation that highlights the peer buddies/teacher's assistant program at a Parent Teacher Association (PTA) meeting.

Adult Volunteers

In some school districts adult volunteers are active in the total education process. Refer to Chapter 19 for a discussion of techniques for recruitment and retention of volunteers.

CLASS ORGANIZATION STRATEGIES

The very nature of the physical education experience demands that the physical education class is well-organized. Belka[3] has suggested that poor class organization has a negative impact on how and what children learn and may contribute to poor behavior in sport skills teaching lessons. The physical education teacher must organize the class to maximize the experience of children, all very anxious to move and play. The physical education teacher, particularly one serving children with disabilities in the regular physical education program, must provide a structured learning environment. Ratliffe, Ratliffe, and Bie[17] wrote, "Effective learning environments allow teachers to provide learning tasks, refine students' performance, and focus on students' skill and knowledge rather than on their behavior. Until such a learning environment has been established, most of the teacher's time is spent attending to students' behavior and trying to keep students on task."

The physical education teacher must have significant management skills to coordinate the learning environment. Stephens[24] has outlined six classroom elements that teachers should consider:

1. *Demographics:* The group's composition
2. *Physical environment:* The use of the play area and its surroundings
3. *Time:* The amount of time available each week for the program
4. *Student motivation:* Ways in which students are reinforced for performance
5. *Provision for interacting:* Mixing students among peers and the teacher
6. *Differentiating instruction:* The extent to which and how the instruction is individualized

Ratliffe, Ratliffe, and Bie[17] outlined creative strategies for organizing instruction in the regular elementary physical education class. The techniques and strategies are appropriate for any physical education setting. The teacher approaches classroom organization proactively and creates a situation that enhances learning and prevents inappropriate behavior. Their suggestions include[17]:

☐ Reinforce appropriate behavior.

☐ Reward appropriate behavior (e.g., smiley faces, stars, "happy-grams," stickers, hugs, smiles, or free time).

☐ Before starting a lesson, remove distractions from the area.

☐ Provide equipment of the same type and color for all children, to help prevent fights.

☐ Strategically place students who are likely to exhibit inappropriate behavior in designated spots within the gymnasium (e.g., close to the teacher or near children who will be good models.)

☐ Have students practice "stopping" an activity, by placing equipment on the floor in front of their feet. Have students practice returning equipment to the original storage place.

☐ Develop a strategy for transition from the classroom to the gymnasium that allows maximum control. For example, have the students practice walking in a line with hands behind the back.

☐ Consider an immediate individual activity when students sit on their designated spot, waiting for further instruction. For example, have the children join in singing a song while waiting for the entire class to be seated.

☐ Reward students who listen and cooperate by letting them choose equipment first and take turns first.

☐ Stand near a disruptive student. Make your immediate presence known by placing your hand firmly on the student's shoulder.

☐ Provide a designated time-out area separate from the group, but easily monitored.

There are three basic techniques for organizing instruction in the physical education program. First, the class can be organized so that each student has an individual exercise and/or activity program. Through the use of self-instructional and evaluative standard teaching sequences, students can participate in individual exercise programs. The major advantage of this method is that students have programs specifically planned to meet their needs and interests. The exercises, the number of repetitions, the amount of resistance used, the rest periods, and the special equipment needed are all assigned to enable students to meet predetermined objectives. Students can be strongly motivated to work toward correction or improvement of

their disabilities in this type of class. Some teachers may find that controlling a group of 20 to 25 students who are all working on individual programs is more difficult than class control of students who are all doing the same program simultaneously. However, the advantages of having each student engage in an individual program of activities outweigh such problems. Preparation of individual programs is time consuming, but certain shortcuts can be used to enable the teacher to prepare these individual programs in a minimum amount of time. It must be noted that some physical education classes are prohibitively large and make this type of individualization impossible. A good physical education teacher may be able to design individual programs for 20 to 25 students, but would be unable to do so with 80 to 100 students.

Second, a class also may be organized formally for exercises and other selected activities. In this class, all the students perform the same activity at the same time, usually under the direction of the teacher, paraprofessional, or teacher's assistant. However, each student performs to his or her present level of educational performance on the specific instructional task. This type of program lends itself well to the instruction of younger children in elementary school or to the instruction of students who cannot assume the responsibility of an individual program. The advantages of this type of organization are that it gives teachers good control of the class and allows them to observe the performance of all the students more adequately than if they were watching 20 students, each doing something different. A disadvantage of this system is the lack of opportunity to give individually assigned activities to students with special needs.

A third method of class organization involves grouping students for instruction and practice. When skills and abilities are the focus of instruction, homogeneous grouping can ensure accommodation of individual differences. When populations of students with and without disabilities are diverse, techniques are needed to coordinate groups of students so that activity in games can be mutually beneficial. Heterogeneous groupings also can be used for instruction. Smith, Neisworth, and Greer[23] point out that in this type of group, lower functioning students are provided with models if higher functioning children are also in the class.

Some of the questions that need to be answered when selecting groups for specific activities are:

1. Does the learner have the prerequisite skills to play the game?

2. If there are deficient skills, what modifications can be made for participation?

3. Does the learner know the rules?
4. Does the learner have the social discipline to play the game without impairing the benefits of other participants?
5. What is the maximum size of the group?
6. What is the minimum number of persons who should participate in the group?

No hard rules can be given for the selection of participants for a group. In the final analysis professional judgments are needed by the physical education teacher to decide the composition of a group formulated to achieve a specific educational purpose.

Most teachers prefer to use a combination of each of the three preceding types of class organization to meet the individual needs of the students, to provide for some small group activities and some individual exercise and activity sessions during which the teacher more directly controls the amount of work done.

This combination plan might be organized as follows:

FIGURE 18-4. A child is assigned to a station to develop climbing skills. (Courtesy Dallas Independent School District.)

5 minutes: Formal warm-up consists of all students doing the same exercises under the leadership and direction of the teacher or a student leader.

5 minutes: Students are divided into homogeneous groups according to their needs and perform three activities or exercises with the members of their group under direction of a student leader.

10 minutes: Each student performs five exercises or activities specifically assigned to him or her, doing the number of repetitions assigned and recording progress on the exercise card. (Activities using special equipment can be assigned here, since students are able to take turns in the use of special pieces of apparatus.)

5-10 minutes: Play, games, and sport activities are organized and led by the teacher, finishing with formal dismissal of the class, if desired.

ALLOCATION OF TIME FOR INSTRUCTION

In general, there are two ways of organizing the academic year to accomplish curricular goals and objectives. In many regular physical education programs, the academic year is broken into instructional units. For example, a semester might include 6 weeks of swimming, 6 weeks of archery, and 6 weeks of tumbling. Thus student and instructor attention and interest can be focused on one activity at a time. These units are determined based on the following: (1) age of students, (2) number of students in the class, (3) available facilities and equipment, and (4) seasons of the year. The specially designed physical education program may reflect the unit organization of the regular physical education program; this may be particularly important if the intent is to prepare students with disabilities to make a transition into the regular physical education program.

The second basic strategy for organizing instruction to accomplish curricular goals and objectives is to use particular classes/portions of classes for specific instruction throughout the year. For example, a middle school physical education program may emphasize the development of physical fitness by devoting 3 class periods per week to the development of physical fitness. The other 2 days may be devoted to the development of leisure, recreation, and sport competencies.

The third basic strategy for organizing instruction to accomplish curricular goals and objectives is to organize each class period using the same structure. The first 20 minutes may be devoted to the development of physical fitness and may include warm-up exercises, activities designed to develop cardiovascular respiratory fitness, and exercises designed to develop strength.

The next 15 minutes may be devoted to perceptual-motor skill acquisition. The last 15 minutes may be devoted to play, games, and/or leisure, recreation, and sport activity. Some teachers have found that this method, in which up to 15 minutes of each class period are devoted to games and sports (usually after the exercise portion of the class is finished), serves as a good motivation device, keeping interest at a high level in the play, games, and/or leisure, recreation, and sport activity.

MANAGEMENT OF INDIVIDUALIZED PROGRAMS

Physical education teachers must be able to cope with individual differences of their students. It is no longer desirable for physical education teachers to stand in front of a class and instruct all pupils on the same task and expect that they will all be successful and learn at the same rate. The need for individualized instruction requires that the teacher be a facilitator and manager of learning. This is particularly true if children with disabilities are integrated into the regular physical education program.

Some of the strategies for accommodating children with disabilities in the regular physical education program have already been discussed. Training of paraprofessionals, teacher's assistants, and peer buddies may make it possible for the child with a disability to be included in the regular physical education class. However, the unique needs of **all** the children, particularly the children with disabilities, must be adressed.

To ensure that the goals of the individual physical education programs are met, it is necessary to structure the programs. This can be accomplished with paraprofessionals, student teacher's assistants, and peer buddies. There are many related component parts to individualized physical education programs. A well-managed program includes identification of (1) the name of the instructor who will provide the physical education activities, (2) the names of pupils who will participate in the activities during specific sessions, (3) the activities for each of the students, (4) the functions that those who are involved in the instruction must carry out, (5) the facility where the activities will be carried out, and (6) when the activity will take place.

Activities: Physical activities that are the goals of instruction should be functional. When possible, they should include the natural routines that occur in the daily lives of most persons. The schedule of activities should consider the learners' present and future environments for participation in leisure, recreation, and sport activities.

Functions: Instructors perform several functions. Some of the functions are (1) assessment of learners, (2) formulation of objectives, (3) management of equipment that is associated with programs, (4) training of paraprofessionals, student teacher's assistants, peer buddies, and adult volunteers who assist with the instructional program, and (5) readjustment of the program each day based on the results of what has been learned previously.

Location: Locations of activity are areas of the environment in which the activities occur. The location should, if possible, be natural and functional.

The instructor: In a given class there may be more than one instructor. Aides, student teachers, and peer buddies should be involved in the instructional program whenever possible. Each of these individuals should be carefully matched to the students with disabilities and be assigned specific duties within the program.

Time of the activity: The time during a given instructional period should be indicated as should the duration of each of the activities. When this is done, the learner, instructors, physical activities, and location of the activities are brought together in a specific time frame.

Students: Students with disabilities have differing needs. Therefore those persons who have similar needs can be grouped together to be served during certain time frames by instructors who have the appropriate capabilities to enable all learners to profit from physical education instruction. The pupils' activities should require that all students be active most of the time. All pupils should participate in the planning of activities whenever possible.[8] This is particularly true of older, more mature students.

The component parts of an activity program can be scheduled so that each instructor knows what he or she is to do, with whom, what is to be done, where it is to be done, and for how long it is to be continued.

Learning Stations

An effective method of class organization to maximize individual learning opportunities consists of learning stations. Each station should be supervised by a paraprofessional, student teacher's assistant, or peer buddy. Children move to appropriate stations and learn skills appropriate to their needs. This requires that much of the planning for programming and reviewing student progress, teacher plans, and development of material be done before class. Under these conditions effective learning is contingent on excellent classroom organization, planning, and management.

Learning stations are areas in the facility where activity is conducted to achieve specific objectives. Often stations are used to improve skills through behavioral programming. Learning stations vary in number, nature of the learning task, or permanency of the assignment. Playing a game may be considered a learning station.

Once learning stations have been established, it is necessary to manage each student at the stations during the entire class period so the unique learning needs of each child can be met. Several systems can be used to assign students to stations that meet their learning needs:

☐ *Rotation:* Every student participates at every learning station.
☐ *Free movement:* Students have individualized programs and move to the learning stations at their own discretion or with direction from paraprofessional, student teacher's assistant, or peer buddy.
☐ *Structured movement:* Students are assigned to stations that meet their learning needs and spend a specified amount of time at each station. There is a period when all students move to stations to start other activities.

Each of these systems requires a particular degree of skill management by the physical education teacher. The rotation system requires initial assignment of students to groups with accommodation for specific learners. The groups are rotated after a specified time frame. Free movement rotation may be necessary when IPEPs are provided for each student. This management system enables students to participate in activities that meet their unique needs. Therefore it is unlikely that any two students will be assigned to the same learning stations. Each student manages his or her own time, perhaps with support from the paraprofessional. Structured movement requires that the teacher make individual schedules of participation for each child. Under these conditions rotation is structured so each child participates in necessary activities in a structured manner. The younger the child and the more severe the disability, the greater the need for structured movement.

Characteristics of learning stations

Most learning stations have a set of general characteristics. Minimum requirements for most learning stations are that they be a designated area for participation, they include specific learning activities designed to meet an educational need, and the equipment is related to the physical activity.

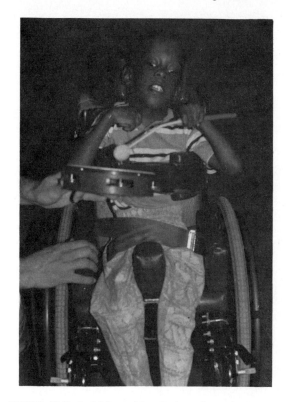

FIGURE 18-5. A child provides the beat for a class rhythm activity. (Courtesy Dallas Independent School District.)

Learning systems involving behavioral programming and structured movement require more elaborate designs. Additional items might be (1) lines and targets to specify the conditions of the objectives, (2) measuring instruments, such as time clocks and tapes, (3) program cards (chart) with all of the behavioral objectives, (4) labels to indicate the number of the station, and (5) a data sheet on which progress can be recorded. Each learning station should be designed to maximize the independence of each learner.

Advantages of learning stations

Some advantages of using learning stations to conduct individualized programming include the following:

☐ The number of students at any learning station at a specific time can vary.
☐ Learning stations can accommodate persons with differing skill levels.
☐ The length of time one spends at a learning station can vary.

□ The nature of the activity is specified so other persons can assist with instruction.

Learning stations need not be used all the time. Many of the activities, such as games, require the entire group; in this case the use of learning stations is undesirable. However, to accommodate the unique physical education needs of children with diverse skill and ability levels, group instruction alone will not suffice.

MONITORING STUDENT PERFORMANCE

There are two general phases of instruction—presenting new material and practicing what has been learned from the presentation to improve performance. During practice, methods should be incorporated into instruction to monitor student performance. Self-instructional behavioral programs, in which the learner performs alone, enable students to receive feedback from performance and practice independently without the assistance of the teacher. This frees the teacher from direct instruction. When objectives are specific, students know when the task has been performed correctly. This works well with students who have a history of failure, since a behavioral shaping program ensures more success than failure.[14] In behavioral programming learners progress at their own rate through small, incremental steps that build on previous learning.[10]

MONITORING PROGRESS

It is necessary to monitor the progress of children with disabilities in the acquisition of objectives listed on the IPEP according to the nature of the activity and the type of instructional approach. If standardized normative-referenced tests are used, testers must be trained to measure continuous instructional progress and learning outcomes before the post-test is given. Then it can be decided whether the programming is effective. If behavioral hierarchical programming is used, progress can be monitored daily. However, in the event that the students participate in self-instructional and evaluative activity, these student skills also must be monitored to verify the validity of progress. If student data collection proves invalid (unsuccessful), the physical education teacher, the paraprofessional, or a student teacher's assistant must monitor student progress.

The acquisition of cognitive objectives such as rules of the game and strategies can be reported from written/oral tests or checklists designed to evaluate participation. Clearly, the progress of each child should be monitored to determine whether programming is effective. If it is not effective, it should be changed.

MANAGING INSTRUCTIONAL TIME EFFICIENTLY

Physical education teachers often have limited time with their students with disabilities. To maximize benefits, class time should be managed efficiently by establishing a daily schedule for each class. Schedules tell what activities will occur and when they will occur; also, schedules divide the class periods into time blocks and ascribe specific amounts of time to the activities. Highest priority should be given to instructional activity. Noninstructional activities should be kept to a minimum. Mercer and Mercer[14] suggest the following:
□ Move from definite to flexible schedules.
□ Alternate highly preferred with less preferred activities.
□ Plan for leeway time.
□ Provide a daily schedule for each student.
□ Provide a variety of activities.
It is usually best to keep the activity periods short. The more mature the learner, the longer the activity period. The schedule should be shared with students and assistive personnel, and the format should be consistent from day to day.

Time on Task

Efficient class organization requires that students be managed so they are on task a considerable portion of the class period. Long lines where children wait for their turn to participate is an unacceptable situation. A system should be developed to control the frequency of an individual's positive response.

Dead time is that portion of the class when students are not working to achieve objectives of the instructional program. Children may be active, but the instructional tasks may be irrelevant or detrimental to learning. For instance, participation in an activity that is well within the capability of the learner has little benefit. Activity reinforcers, where children participate in tasks of interest that do not contribute to objectives, are also dead time. The two dimensions of time on task are (1) percentage of time spent learning a task and (2) the qualitative aspects of the learning experience.

DAILY LESSON PLANS

The daily lesson plan can be written and generated using a word processor, particularly in conjunction with an integrated data base. The daily lesson plan is taken from the unit plan so that appropriate elements of implementation are followed and all essential topics and plans are included in the time scheduled for a given unit. Unit plans need not be rigidly followed. As student or class needs are discovered, the curriculum should be modified to meet these special circumstances.

In a similar way, a daily lesson plan should help teachers and students plan ahead for desired learning experiences. A typical lesson plan should include the following information:

1. Name (title of unit)
2. Subunit
3. Activities of the day
4. School level or grade
5. Date
6. Major objective(s) for the teacher
7. Procedures
8. Facilities and equipment necessary
9. Evaluation after completion of lesson

ORGANIZING THE INSTRUCTIONAL ENVIRONMENT

The instructional environment of a physical education class facility comprises the procedures, materials, and equipment used by the teacher to improve pupil achievement. The teacher selects the curriculum, manages the individual learning of students, and sets up the delivery systems for instruction and improved performance of the skills. The management structure directly affects social conduct as well as student achievement in motor skills. Students actively involved in appropriate instruction are less likely to exhibit behavioral problems.

Functional Arrangement of Space

The physical environment is made up of space and equipment. The nature of the physical environment and how it is arranged can affect behavior[23] and exerts great influence on performance of students. Weinstein[26] concludes that classroom characteristics affect attitudes and social behavior.

The arrangement of students in relation to one another can affect social behavior and thus acquisition of motor skills. Peers influence one another in both positive and negative directions. If students have an adverse effect on one another (act out or disrupt class), they should be separated. The physical environment of the class facility can be arranged in many ways to promote successful pupil achievement.

The initial class organization must be structured. This is particularly true if there are large numbers of children and if some of the children have attention deficit disorders or behavior disorders. The gymnasium or playground area must be marked with designated spaces for the children to sit and wait for instruction. The most effective class organization system is to have each child seated separately from the others in the class. A diagram of this type of system is shown below.

The students' designated spots can be painted on the gymnasium floor or can be marked by plastic dots or carpet squares. A designated spot can be marked on the playground by a chalk mark, by plastic dots, or by cones.

Gymnasium space should be divided into performance areas or zones to accommodate routine activities and tasks.[14] Stowitschek, Gable, and Hendrickson[25] suggest that when planning the arrangement, teachers should consider typical storage needs for materials and equipment and should develop procedures for distribution and collection of equipment and student work.

In some gymnasiums, small group instructional areas are set up for specific subjects or activities. For example, in classrooms that use learning stations, there may be separate areas for physical fitness, perceptual-motor skills, and health. These areas can be used by the teacher for direct instruction or by students for independent performance in programmed activity.

In addition to instructional areas, each student should have an individual work space. A separate stor-

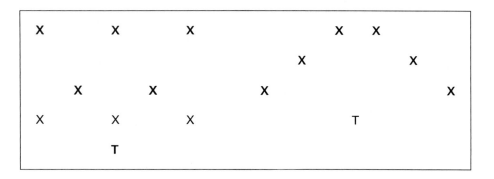

age area may be needed if there is a considerable amount of equipment. Some teachers set up a specific area where students pick up their work for the day and return their score sheets. Free times or recreational areas are common for leisure activities such as games, records, and tapes. Time in this area may be used as a reinforcement for appropriate behavior, completed work, or accurate performance. It is also possible to designate a time-out area to which students can be removed for inappropriate or disruptive behavior.

The relationship between different areas within the gymnasium should be carefully planned by considering the following important factors:

□ *Convenience:* Store equipment, supplies, and materials near where they are used.
□ *Movement efficiency:* Make traffic patterns direct; discourage routes that lead to disruptions (e.g., students distracting others when turning in assignments or moving to activities).
□ *Density:* Arrange students so that personal space is preserved; avoid crowding.

Safe and Accessible Environment

A primary concern with any environment is the safety of the students. Students with physical and sensory disabilities require special precautions. For example, objects and other clutter on the playing surfaces are haz-ards for students with balance problems or poor eyesight. Students with mobility problems may need accommodation to participate in active games, and deaf and other hearing impaired students may need visual cues to react in emergency situations.

Another major consideration is *access* to the gymnasium. Many of the newer school buildings are designed to be barrier free; that is, *architectural barriers* are removed to allow disabled individuals entry to and use of the facility. Elevators and ramps are available, stairs have handrails for persons with crutches or canes, doorways are wide enough to allow entry of wheelchairs, and bathroom facilities are specially designed. Drinking fountains, lockers, vending machines, trash cans, towel dispensers, and telephones are accessible to persons in a wheelchair. However, it may be necessary to make more modifications for students with disabilities. The environment of the gymnasium also should be barrier free. The room should be arranged to allow easy travel to and from restrooms and showers.

GENERALIZATION OF INSTRUCTIONAL SKILLS TO THE COMMUNITY AND SPORTS ORGANIZATIONS

The activities and skills learned in the physical education class should generalize and be applicable to community activity. Therefore the general nature of physi-

FIGURE 18-6. Partners pedal for fitness and enjoyment of a beautiful lake.
(Courtesy Wisconsin Lions Camp, Rosholt, Wisconsin.)

cal activity should represent, to the greatest extent possible, the sports and skills being taught in a regular class or sports currently being played in the community.

Special Olympics and other sports organizations for individuals with disabling conditions comprise many sports. Each sport is conducted during a particular time of the year. Interscholastic events of sports organizations provide an opportunity for widespread participation. Therefore the selection of the physical education content should take into consideration linkage with culminating sports events in the community that relate directly to the instructional skills.

INDIVIDUALIZED CURRICULUM SEQUENCES

Individualized curriculum sequences or clusters of skills should be selected to enable students to participate in physical and sport activities in the community. Guess and Helmstetter[8] suggested that rather than teach a multitude of skills, it may be better to teach a relatively small number of skills needed to interact effectively in one's environment. Such a procedure would require that the behaviors demonstrated in the community be systematically observed and the content of skill sequences taught to individuals with disabilities be modified accordingly.[4] The thrust of the individualized curriculum sequences is to make the learner an active rather than a passive agent in the environment and to engage the learner in initiating meaningful community-based recreational motor behavior.[8]

The Need to Prioritize the Goals

For maintenance and generalization to community-based leisure, recreation, and sports programs to occur, it is essential that the skills that are acquired by individuals with disabilities in physical education class are functional. Therefore there are several considerations that should be observed in the selection and prioritization of goals. Some of these priorities suggested by Sailor and Guess[21] include the following:

1. *Immediate usefulness of the skill:* Develop the skill if it can be used immediately. This will enable maintenance and generalization to occur.
2. *Time available:* If many years remain in the curricula, develop the most generalizable skills that contribute to a broad range of physical activities. However, as time nears adulthood, there is more need to develop the critical functional skills for independent recreational and domestic living in the community.
3. *Demand:* Maintenance and generalization of specific skills attained in physical education depend

on the consistency of the demand for the use of that skill. If environments do not demand the utilization of the specific skills, then there is a chance that they will not be maintained.
4. *Availability of devices and persons for external dependency:* The program should be designed to reduce dependencies. This can occur by using the principle of partial participation and by gradually fading the assistance needed to participate successfully in a community-based activity.

Instructional Materials

Preplanned learning materials are essential for conduction of the IPEP. These take the form of task-analyzed materials, recording instruments, assessment instruments, and audiovisual packages. Examples of these preplanned materials are included in Chapters 2 to 5. These learning materials must be managed so that the individual needs of the learner are served.

Guidelines for Selection

Several different types of instructional aids can be introduced into the physical education classroom to instruct all children, including children with disabilities. These include (1) audio tapes; (2) books, models of skill sequences; (3) filmstrips; (4) slides; (5) overhead transparencies; (6) motion pictures; (7) videotapes; and (8) interactive computer programs. Each of these media has different attributes, which should be considered in the selection of the materials. Some of these attributes are motion, pacing, random access, sign type, and sensory mode. Appropriate selection of instructional aids should consider the instructional objective to be achieved in relation to the specific attributes of the media.

Instructional Attributes of Media

The question to be answered by those who select instructional materials is "Which aid is best suited to help children, including those with disabilities, attain physical education objectives?" A description of the specific attributes of media follow:

Motion: Film and videotape possess the attribute of showing motion. When motion is an attribute of the media, there is a presentation of a total picture of the task or the instructional event.

Pacing: Pacing permits the teacher or the student to spend as much time on each piece of information as is desired. Written material such as books and models of skill sequences that are printed belong to this category. Once films, videotapes, and audiotapes are set in motion they are uncontrolled.

Random access: Random access refers to the degree to which the student can go directly to any specific part of the instructional materials, such as printed matter.

Sensory mode: Most media used by teachers are transmitted through the ears or eyes. Educators of the blind find the tactile mode very useful and may make extensive use of three-dimensional models. Media for the blind should be auditory, and media for the deaf should be visual.

The utility of instructional materials and aids is a consideration in the selection process, as is the feasibility of acquisition and continued use. The following considerations apply:

☐ *Cost:* How expensive are the materials to purchase initially?

☐ *Accessibility:* Are the materials and equipment accessible to the children and teachers?

☐ *Training required to use the materials:* Are extensive training and skill required to use the materials?

☐ *Durability:* Are the instructional materials and related equipment easily damaged or are they durable?

☐ *Technical quality:* Is the technical quality of the materials and related equipment acceptable?

CLASS ORGANIZATION THROUGH COMPUTER TECHNOLOGY

The single most significant advance in the science and art of teaching is the computer. Computer technology has made it possible for educators to open the world to children. In addition, computer technology has made possible computer assisted instructional management and computer assisted instruction.

Computer assisted instructional management is particularly important in the fields of physical education and adapted physical education where teachers commonly have large caseloads. This is particularly true of the adapted physical educator who must be accountable for the learning process. It is possible to generate the IEP or IPEP on the computer.[18] A.W.A.R.E. (Apple-Works Assisted Resource for Educators), a system for generating goals and objectives for IEPs in adapted physical education, utilizes the AppleWorks integration of database and word processor files. With A.W.A.R.E., adapted physical education goals and objectives are selected from a database file. Then, using programming macros, goals and objectives are transferred to a word processor to create a professional-looking IEP. Contained in the system is an IEP word processor template, a database of goals and objectives, and AutoWorks.[16] The same type of computer-generated IEP program is currently being developed for use with the Macintosh line of personal computers.[19]

Word processors can be used to write and generate assessment reports, write weekly/daily lesson plans, maintain behavior records, maintain a record of skill acquisition, and generate communications with parents and other school personnel.[11] The process of describing the results of assessments and evaluations, critical in effective adapted physical education programming, can be simplified by the use of templates developed for use on word-processing software. The template provides evaluators with a fast and effective format for recording and then reporting information.[19] The process of writing the evaluation report is made even simpler when phrases used often are saved for re-use in macro files. For example, the evaluator might save the phrase, "The Ohio State University SIGMA is a criterion-referenced instrument, validated by the wealth of research/literature on the process of normal and abnormal motor development." The evaluator can use a simple key-

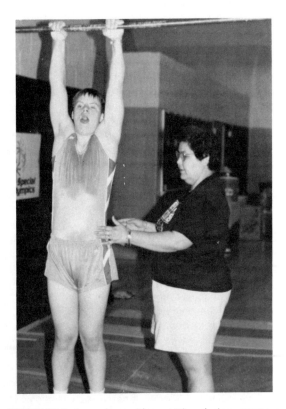

FIGURE 18-7. A coach provides spotting during warm-up for competition. (Courtesy Texas Special Olympics.)

TABLE 18-1				

Sample "window" of data base of music for young children

Song	Album	Author	Area	Level
All part of you	Activities and	Stallman	Body Ident	1
Walk don't run	Activities and	Stallman	Locomotor	1
Your body	Activities and	Stallman	Body Ident	1
Jello	Aerobic dances	Glass	Imitation	2
Kangaroo	Aerobic dances	Glass	Body awareness	2
Bouncing back	Aerobics for	Stewart	General	1

stroke combination to write this statement instead of having to type it over and over and over again.

Database programs can be used to maintain student records, including demographic data and height/weight records, as well as to maintain a list of the child's medications. In addition, database programs can be used to organize information about equipment, music, or games (Table 18-1).[11] These can be valuable as the physical educator makes decisions, for example, about the type of games that would be appropriate for a particular child, with a particular objective.

Information stored in the database can be retrieved for easy use by the physical educator. For example, the database can retrieve and list all of the Level 1 songs that address body awareness. Or it can list all the songs written by Hap Palmer.

Spreadsheet programs can be used to monitor grades. In addition, they can be used to monitor instructional time. For example, a spreadsheet can be used effectively to give the instructor an accurate report of curricular areas addressed, activities selected for remediation, the number of minutes spent on a given area (e.g., equilibrium or body image), and the total percentage of time devoted to the areas emphasized. In addition, spreadsheets can be used for developing and maintaining equipment inventories and budgets.

Computers can also be used to manage the instructional process. For example, curricular materials can and should be written and updated via computer programs. This provides the opportunity for constant and on-going revision of curriculum, which prevents the curriculum from becoming stagnant.

GRADING (MARKING) IN ADAPTED PHYSICAL EDUCATION

A grade in any subject should promote educational goals and should reflect educational aims and objectives. For programs to be most effective, established objectives must indicate the desired goals of instruction so that they become the criteria on which grades are based. If they are valid criteria, successful measurement will result in valid evaluation. The grade, if one desires to translate behavioral performance, could reflect how well these criteria have been met.

The complexity of grading physical education classes is magnified when an attempt is made to evaluate the performance of students with disabilities. The one common denominator among all students is the mastery of individual performance objectives. If students are graded on the basis of how well they meet their objectives, a student with poor posture, a student with a cardiac disorder, an obese student, and a student who has just had surgery all can be properly evaluated for their grades in the class.

The following criteria might be applied to students to determine how well they have met objectives in the adapted physical education class:

1. *Performance:* Standard of performance in reference to individual limitations, such as vigorous work on specific activities and posture exercise for obese students, control of the amount and intensity of work for cardiac and postoperative students
2. *Persistence:* Accomplishment of individual performance objectives determined in the IPEP

Suggestions for recording and computing the grade are as follows:

1. Since the grade may involve some subjective judgments on the part of the instructor, the student should be observed and graded many times throughout the semester (daily or weekly).
2. Numerical ratings (recorded on the exercise card and in the roll book or in a class spreadsheet) can be given to the student; in this way, the student and the instructor are always aware

of the student's progress toward stated behavioral objectives.

3. These numerical grades can be averaged and then should be considered, along with other factors that may influence the final grade (knowledge examinations and health factors, if they are considered), to determine the final mark for the semester.

4. Objective measurements should be used to test skill and knowledge.

SUMMARY

The nature and needs of children with disabilities differ greatly. The size of the classes as well as the nature of the physical education content also differ. Therefore a number of considerations need to be taken into account in the formulation of the organization of physical education classes to accommodate the individual needs of students. Some of these considerations are: effective grouping of students for certain types of tasks; effective management of time; the physical environment; use of paraprofessionals, student teacher's assistants, and peer buddies; the development of learning stations; and effective organization of the instructional environment. Flexible daily lesson plans should be developed to facilitate meeting the needs of all learners. Students should be graded on both performance and persistence as objectively as possible. As a student gets older it may be better to teach a relatively small number of skills needed to interact effectively in one's environment.

REVIEW QUESTIONS

1. What are some of the different types of class organization needed for physical education that serve all children in a range of physical activities?
2. What are the characteristics of a learning station that is capable of accommodating individual differences?
3. What type of training is necessary before a physical education teacher, a paraprofessional, or a student assistant can work effectively with children with disabilities?
4. What are some considerations for effectively grouping students for instruction?
5. What are the components needed to conduct an efficient individualized instructional management system?
6. Explain the role of the personal computer in the management of physical education/adapted physical education instruction.

STUDENT ACTIVITIES

1. Talk to a teacher who has used student teacher's assistants and buddies. Determine how they were selected, the nature of their training program, methods of communication between the teacher and the tutors, and the advantages and disadvantages of such an instructional system.

2. The development of technology provides many opportunities for upgrading practice in physical education. Indicate some of the technology that can be used and how it might be employed in the integrated physical education class.

3. Visit a class and describe the organization. What would you do differently to more efficiently arrange the physical environment, manage instructional time, and effectively group students?

4. Set up a learning station.

5. Interview a paraprofessional. Ask questions regarding his/her motivations, objectives, and concerns. Ask specific questions regarding his/her expectations of the physical education teacher.

6. Design a hypothetical individualized management system that involves paraprofessionals and buddies.

REFERENCES

1. Armstrong RW, Rosenbaum PL, King SM: A randomized controlled trial of a 'buddy' programme to improve children's attitudes toward the disabled, *Dev Med Child Neurol* 29:327-336, 1987.
2. Aufsesser PM: Mainstreaming and least restrictive environment: how do they differ? *Palaestra* 7:31-34, 1991.
3. Belka DE: Let's manage to have some order, *J Phys Educ Rec Dance* 62:21-23, 1991.
4. Bricker D, Schiefelbusch RL: Infants at risk. In McCormick L, Schiefelbusch RL, editors: *Language intervention,* Columbus, Ohio, 1984, Charles E Merrill Publishing.
5. Clark G, French R, Henderson H: Attitude development of physical educators working with the disabled, *Palaestra,* 1:26-28, 1986.
6. Grineski S: Promotion success in physical education: cooperatively structured learning, *Palaestra* 7:26-29, 1991.
7. Grosse S: Is the mainstream always a better place to be? *Palaestra* 7:40-49, 1991.
8. Guess D, Helmstetter E: Skill cluster instruction and the individualized curriculum sequencing model. In Horner RH, Meyer LH, Fredericks HD, editors: *Education of learners with severe handicaps: exemplary service strategies,* Baltimore, 1985, Paul H Brookes Publishing.
9. Guralnick MJ: Integrated preschools as educational and therapeutic environments: concepts, designs, and analysis. In Guralnick MJ, editor: *Early intervention and the integration of handicapped and non-handicapped children,* Baltimore, 1978, University Park Press.
10. Heron TE, Harris KC: *The educational consultant: helping professionals, parents, and mainstreamed students,* Boston, 1982, Allyn & Bacon.
11. Huettig C, Reinhardt A: A joint university and public school commitment to adapted physical education, *Palaestra* 2:23-26, 1986.
12. Jansma P, Schultz G: Validation and use of a mainstreaming attitude inventory with physical educators, *Am Corr Ther J* 36:150-158, 1982.

13. Lavay B, DePaepe J: The harbering helper: why main-streaming in physical education doesn't always work, *J Phys Educ Rec Dance* 58:98-103, 1987.

14. Mercer CD, Mercer AR: *Teaching students with learning problems,* Columbus, Ohio, 1983, Charles E Merrill Publishing.

15. Mosston M: *Teaching physical education,* Columbus, Ohio, 1966, Charles E Merrill Publishing.

16. Rademaker B, Shirer W, Stocco D: *Project communicate: computer aided instruction for handicapped students,* Mosinee, Wis, 1990, Mosinee School District.

17. Rattliffe T, Ratliffe L, Bie B: Creating a learning environment: class management strategies for elementary physical education teachers, *J Phys Educ Rec Dance* 62:24-27, 1991.

18. Reinhardt A: *Computer assisted instruction and management in adapted physical education,* a working draft of the Wisconsin Department of Public Instruction Adapted Physical Education Curriculum, 1992.

19. Reinhardt A, Adapted Physical Education Specialist, Stevens Point (Wis) Area Public Schools, 1992, *(personal communication).*

20. Runac M: *Acquisition of motor awareness related tasks between kindergarten and primary mentally retarded children through individually prescribed instruction,* Slippery Rock State College, 1971 (unpublished master's thesis).

21. Sailor W, Guess D: *Severely handicapped students: an instructional design,* Boston, 1983, Houghton Mifflin Co.

22. Sherrill C: *Adapted physical education and recreation, ed 3,* Dubuque, Iowa, 1985, Wm C Brown Publishers.

23. Smith RM, Neisworth JT, Greer JG: *Evaluating educational environments,* Columbus, Ohio, 1978, Charles E Merrill Publishing.

24. Stephens TM: Teachers as managers, *Directive Teacher* 2:4, 1980.

25. Stowitschek JJ, Gable RA, Hendrickson JM: *Instructional materials for exceptional children,* Germantown, Md, 1980, Aspen Systems Corp.

26. Weinstein CS: The physical environment of the school: a review of the research, *Rev Educ Res* 49:577-610, 1979.

27. While C: *Acquisition of lateral balance between trainable mentally retarded children and kindergarten children in an individually prescribed instructional program,* Slippery Rock State College, 1972 (unpublished master's thesis).

SUGGESTED READINGS

Grineski S: Promotion success in physical education: cooperatively structured learning, *Palaestra* 7:26-29, 1991.

Grosse S: Is the mainstream always a better place to be? *Palaestra* 7:40-49, 1991.

Rademaker B, Shirer W, Stocco D: *Project communicate: computer aided instruction for handicapped students,* Mosinee School District, Mosinee, Wis, 1990.

Rattliffe T, Ratliffe L, Rie B: Creating a learning environment: class management srategies for elementary physical education teachers, *J Phys Educ Rec Dance* 62:24-27, 1991.

OBJECTIVES

Draw administrative hierarchies typical in adapted physical education.

Describe techniques for communicating effectively with the program supervisor or Director of Special Education.

Explain the motor development team.

Describe the relationship between the adapted physical educator and the regular physical educator.

List techniques that are effective in promoting communication with parents.

Describe the nature of parent involvement in quality home intervention programs.

List several techniques for developing good public relations.

Describe the volunteer recruitment and retention process in adapted physical education.

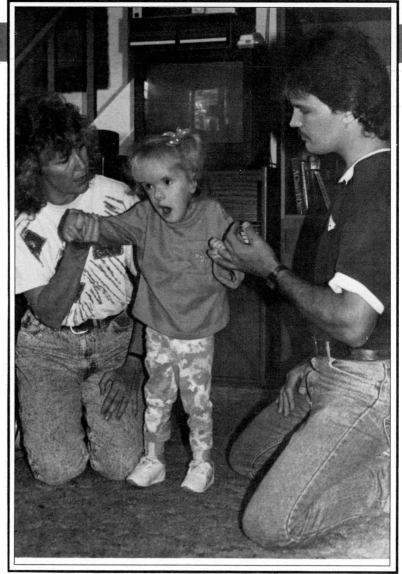

Parents are the child's most important teachers.

Program Organization and Administration

*T*he essence of effective organization and administration in adapted physical education or in any other program, for that matter, is communication. In order to serve students with disabilities, the adapted physical education program must be designed to allow a flow of communication between those with responsibilities for the education of the student. In this chapter, organization and administration strategies to enhance communication between personnel are discussed. Communication strategies for interaction with administrators, other special education personnel, physical education teachers, parents, and students are considered.

Excellent organization and administration are essential if children with disabilities are to be included in increasing numbers in our schools. This is particularly important when educational costs are rising and when pressures exist to examine carefully the total curricular offerings at all school levels.

The definition of physical education in the Education of the Handicapped Act signifies an implicit relationship between instruction in the schools and utilization and participation in the community. Physical education curricula should include individual sport skills, team sports and skills, aquatics, dance, and physical and motor fitness activities. These fundamental motor patterns and skills are prerequisites to community-based recreational sport and physical activity. Thus physical education should assure that children with disabilities have the opportunity to develop functional sport and physical activity that can be used in recreational activity in the community.

GUIDING PRINCIPLES OF ADAPTED PHYSICAL EDUCATION*

It is the responsibility of the school to contribute to the fullest possible development of the potentialities of each individual entrusted to its care. This is a basic tenet of our democratic structure.

1. There is need for common understanding regarding the nature of adapted physical education.
2. There is need for adapted physical education in schools and colleges.
3. Adapted physical education has much to offer the individual who faces the combined problem of seeking an education and living most effectively with a disability.

    Through adapted physical education the individual can: a) be observed and referred when the need for medical or other services is suspected; b) be guided in avoidance of situations which would aggravate the condition or subject him/her to unnecessary risks or injury; c) improve neuromuscular skills, general strength and endurance following convalescence from acute illness or injury; d) be provided with opportunities for improved psychological adjustment and social development.
4. The direct and related services essential for the proper conduct of adapted physical education should be available to our schools.

*Presented by permission of the Committee on Adapted Physical Education, American Alliance for Health, Physical Education, Recreation, and Dance.

These services should include: a) adequate and periodic health examination; b) classification for physical education based on the health examination and other pertinent tests and observations; c) guidance of individuals needing special consideration with respect to physical activity, general health practices, recreational pursuits, vocational planning, psychological adjustment, and social development; d) arrangement of appropriate adapted physical education programs; e) evaluation and recording of progress through observations, appropriate measurements and consultations; f) integrated relationships with other school personnel, medical and its auxiliary services, and family to assure continuous guidance and supervisory services; g) cumulative records for each individual, which should be transferred from school to school.

5. It is essential that adequate medical guidance be available for teachers of adapted physical education.

    The possibility of serious pathology requires that programs of adapted physical education should not be attempted without the diagnosis, written recommendation, and supervision of a physician. The planned program of activities must be predicated upon medical findings and accomplished by competent teachers working with medical supervision and guidance. There should be an effective supervision and guidance, and referral service between physicians, physical educators, and parents aimed at proper safeguards and maximum student benefits. School administrators, alert to the special needs of children with disabilities, should make every effort to provide adequate staff and facilities necessary for a program of adapted physical education.
6. Teachers of adapted physical education have a great responsibility as well as an unusual opportunity.

    Physical educators engaged in teaching adapted physical education should: a) have adequate professional education to implement the recommendations provided by medical personnel; b) be motivated by the highest ideals with respect to the importance of total student development and satisfactory human relationships; c) develop the ability to establish rapport with students who may exhibit social maladjustment as a result of a disability; d) be aware of a student's attitude toward his disability; e) be objective in relationships with students; f) be prepared to give the time and effort necessary to help a student overcome a difficulty; g) consider as strictly confidential information related to personal problems of the student; h) stress similarities rather than deviations, and abilities instead of disabilities.
7. Adapted physical education is necessary at all school levels.

    The student with a disability faces the dual problem of overcoming a disabiliy and acquiring an education that will enable that person to take a place in society as a respected citizen. Failure to assist a student with problems may retard the growth and development process.

Offering adapted physical education in the elementary grades, and continuing through the secondary school and college, will assist the individuals to improve function and make adequate psychological and social adjustments. It will be a factor in attaining maximum growth and development within the limits of the disability. It will minimize attitudes of defeat and fears of insecurity. It will help the student face the future with confidence.

ADMINISTRATIVE RESPONSIBILITY AND ADAPTED PHYSICAL EDUCATION

In the public schools, adapted physical education is usually aligned administratively with the special education rather than the physical education department. This is expedient because of the unique requirements of the law regarding specially designed physical education programs for children with disabilities. This is also administratively effective because of federal and state funding that provides dollars for salaries for those individuals who serve students with disabilities within local school districts or special service cooperatives. In fact, the allocation of personnel dollars is usually directly tied to the numbers of students with disabilities identified within the district or cooperative who will require the services of special education.

In a small school district or small special education cooperative, the adapted physical educator or adapted physical education consultant may be directly responsible to the Director of Special Education. The adapted physical educator is accountable to the Director of Special Education for the provision of quality adapted physical education services, which include:

□ Assessment and prescription within the psychomotor domain
□ Development of the individual physical education plan (IPEP)
□ Implementation of the IPEP
□ Representing adapted physical education at individual education program (IEP) or multidisciplinary team meetings
□ Provision of direct service to children with disabilities, when appropriate
□ Consultation with regular special education and regular physical education personnel
□ Consultation with community-based leisure, recreation, and sport facilities' managers regarding program and facility accessibility
□ Curriculum development and/or revision
□ Communication with parents
□ Management of budget
□ Purchase and maintenance of equipment

In a large school district or large special service cooperative, one member of the adapted physical education staff may be designated as the "Lead Teacher" or the "Department Chair." This person is directly accountable for the activities of the staff and must report to the Director of Special Education. The responsibilities of the staff members are the same as those of educators in smaller districts. The layers of bureaucracy may simply be more complex.

For example, the adapted physical education teacher may be responsible within the following administrative hierarchy:

Director of Special Education
Supervisor of Support Personnel
Lead Teacher—Adapted Physical Education
Adapted physical education teacher

This administrative hierarchy may be more complex in large school districts that also have site-based management. Site-based management is an attempt to bring the control of schools to those most involved in the school—the principal, teachers, and parents. In the city of Chicago a radical shift was made to site-based management of the schools. Each local school is managed by a committee of school administrators, teachers, and parents. The committee is empowered to make **all** decisions regarding the operation and management of the school. This includes the right and the responsibility of hiring and firing teachers and the principal. In a school district with site-based management, the adapted physical education teacher may be ultimately accountable to the Director of Special Education and to the principal of the schools that are served. As illustrated in the diagram below, the adapted physical education teacher may, at once, be responsible to a building principal and to the Director of Special Education.

Director of Special Education	Principal
Supervisor of Support Personnel	Assistant Principal
Department Chair	Dean of Instruction

Adapted Physical Education Teacher

The adapted physical educator must be accountable for the delivery of appropriate services. In some school districts, the teacher is responsible for daily service logs, which must be turned in to the direct supervisor. In some states, federal and state funding of the local special education program are based on the numbers of documented contact hours between the professional and the student. A sample of such a log is provided in Table 19-1.

TABLE 19-1

Daily service log

Date	Service	Student(s) served/school	Time
2/10	Direct service—teaching*	EC Class/Adams	8:00-9:00
	Direct service—teaching*	S/Ph Class/Adams	9:00-10:00
	Travel to Cabell		10:00-10:15
	Motor/fitness assessment	J. Flores/Cabell	10:15-12:00
	Lunch/travel to White		12:00-12:45
	Consultation—PE teacher	K. Black/White	12:45-1:30
	Travel to office		1:30-1:45
	Written report*	J. Flores/Cabell	1:45-3:15
	Prepare for IEP meeting		3:15-3:45
2/11	Direct service—teaching*	EC Class/Foster	8:00-8:45
	Direct service—teaching*	HI Class/Foster	9:00-9:45
	Travel to Cabell		9:50-10:00
	IEP meeting	J. Flores/Cabell	10:30-12:00
	Travel/lunch		12:00-12:45
	Direct service—teaching	S/Ph Class/Grant	1:00-1:45
	Travel to community pool		1:45-2:00
	Direct service	MD students/district	2:15-3:30
	Swimming instruction*		

*See attached lesson plans.

In addition to a daily log, accounting for time and student contact, the adapted physical educator may be responsible, like other teachers in the district, for lesson plans. Adapted physical education teachers with large case loads (more than 50 students) will find it impossible to manage the paperwork, including daily lesson plans, without the use of computer technology. The teacher can generate daily lesson plans using a basic word processing system and a prepared template. This simplifies the process of writing plans when the same basic plan may be used for several classes. For example, if the teacher serves three early childhood classes, the teacher may use the same basic plan for each of the three classes, keeping in mind, of course, the IEP goals for each student. In addition, generating the plans on the computer allows the teacher to trace the progress of each student within each class. A sam-

ple lesson plan, which corresponds to one class listed on daily log above, is included below:

Daily Lesson Plan

Teacher:	Buddy Nelson
Class:	Early childhood/Foster
Date:	2/11/92
Warm-up:	If you're happy and you know it
Rhythms:	What a miracle; Swing, shake, twist, stretch; Flick a fly
Equilibrium activities:	Magic carpet ride; Crazy sidewalk; Freeze

One of the major responsibilities of the adapted physical educator is to communicate regularly and effectively with his or her direct supervisor. It may be important for the adapted physical education teacher to "lobby" with the Director of Special Education or with a building principal regarding the specific requirements of the law as it applies to adapted physical education. The teacher should share legal updates, current articles describing state-of-the-art practices in adapted physical education, and student and parent testimony regarding effectiveness of the program.

Unfortunately, many administrators simply do not understand the nature or scope of the field of adapted physical education. As a student, the administrator may have had a bad experience in "PE" and, as such, does not understand the desperate need for quality instruction. Timely information that describes the "before and after" status of students served in adapted physical education may help the administrator understand the potential of the program. If possible, the administrator should be invited to attend a class or activity that highlights the skills of the students served and demonstrates the necessity for quality programming to meet student need.

It is vital that the adapted physical educator secure the support of the administrator if the program is to receive its share of district and school resources. The administrator can help by:

□ Giving enthusiastic support to the total program
□ Providing an adequate budget
□ Requiring adequately trained teachers
□ Supporting necessary student schedule changes
□ Providing auxiliary services such as medical aid, nursing, transportation, and maintenance.

INTERACTION WITH OTHER SPECIAL EDUCATION PERSONNEL

The adapted physical education teacher works in close cooperation with other direct service providers and with related service personnel, as well. The most crucial interactions are with the special education teacher(s) and related service personnel serving a given child.

The relationship between the adapted physical educator and the physical therapist, occupational therapist, and recreation therapist is particularly crucial given the direct concern of each professional regarding the child's motor efficiency and the role of each as part of the multidisciplinary team. Related service personnel play an important role in physical education programs for children with disabilities. In addition to providing services that will help the children benefit from the program, they may also enhance the program by:

☐ Interpreting the program to medical personnel in the district, to parents, and to the total school population

☐ Handling or making referrals of students with special problems

☐ Recommending exercises and activities

The multidisciplinary team involved in the IEP process was described in Chapter 17. The intent of the Education of the Handicapped Act was for the myriad of professionals involved in the education of the child with a disability to share their knowledge, expertise, and technical skill not only with the child but with each other, as well. In some school districts and special service cooperatives, professionals responsible for the development and implementation of the IEP have agreed to expand the communication between the members of the multidisciplinary team. This is typical especially when the team members have a common interest in a particular phase of the child's development.

A number of professionals involved in the education of a child with a disability have an interest in and a commitment to the child's motor development and motor proficiency. In order to best meet the needs of the child, creative and competent professionals have explored the possibility of interdisciplinary approaches to the education of students. In some school districts and special education service cooperatives, professionals who address the motor needs of children with disabilities have developed interdisciplinary motor development "teams." The members of the interdisciplinary motor development team often include the adapted physical educator, the physical therapist, the occupational therapist, and the recreational therapist. The regular physical educator and the speech therapist may also function as part of the motor development team. Sugars[21] identified several common functions of members of a motor development team comprised of adapted physical educators, physical therapists, occu-

pational therapists, and recreation therapists. They are:

1. To screen and evaluate students with functional and/or educational problems to determine needs for special services.

The first common function of motor development team members mentioned by Sugars was to screen and evaluate students to determine needs for special services.[21] The District 19 (Oregon) Motor Team has developed a Motor Team Screening Form for use by district personnel. A modification of this screening form is presented in Table 19-2.

This screening instrument allows classroom educators, special educators, and physical educators to refer children to the motor developent team if problems are observed in the classroom or in the gymnasium. Given this information, members of the motor development team decide which specialist should serve as the lead member of the motor development team. That lead person then initiates and organizes a subsequent full-scale gross motor evaluation. One of the benefits of the cooperative nature of the motor development team is that professionals do not need to duplicate efforts in evaluation and assessment. For example, both the occupational therapist and the adapted physical educator routinely use the Bruininks-Oseretsky Test of Motor Impairment. If functioning as a member of a motor development team, the adapted physical educator may share the results (data) of the assessment with the occupational therapist.

2. To develop an IEP, as part of the total multidisciplinary team, to address the child's motor needs.

The members of the motor development team develop an IEP that addresses the motor development needs of the child. In some school districts and special service cooperatives the members of the motor development team actually create an Individual Motor Education Plan (IMEP) or Individual Physical Education Plan (IPEP).

3. To implement an intervention program that facilitates learning.

Once the IMEP or IPEP is approved by the total multidisciplinary team and by the child's parents/guardians, the members of the motor development team implement the intervention program. Like the evaluation/assessment, the intervention program is cooperative in nature. Each member of the team addresses the child's motor needs. Instead of limiting focus to one specific component of motor development, each team professional shares responsibility for implementing a program that has been designed by the team.

4. To manage/supervise motor programs.

Each member of the motor development team as-

TABLE 19-2

District 19 motor team screening form

Name:_____DOB_____
Date of referral:_____Grade:_____Teacher:_____
School:_____
Specialist:_____Physician_____
Was student retained?:___Yes ___No
PE Time:_____Recess time:_____
Current disabling conditions:_____
_____

Does the student use adaptive equipment (braces, crutches, etc.)?_____
_____

Please check those items that have been observed.

Gross motor

___ Lacks age-appropriate strength and endurance
___ Difficulty with run, jump, hop, or skip compared with others his/her age
___ Stiff and awkward in his/her movements
___ Clumsy, seems not to know how to move body, bumps into things, falls out of chair
___ Demonstrates mixed dominance
___ Reluctant to participate in playground activities
___ Play pattern is inappropriate for age group (does not play, plays by self, plays beside but not with, stereotypical) (Circle one)
___ Has postural deviations
___ Complains of pain during physical activities
___ Demonstrates unusual wear patterns on shoes and/or clothing

Fine motor

___ Poor desk posture (slumps, leans on arm, head too close to work) (Circle)
___ Difficulty drawing, coloring, copying, cutting
___ Poor pencil grasp and/or drops pencil frequently
___ Lines drawn are light, wobbly, too faint or too dark
___ Breaks pencil often
___ Lack of well-established dominance after 6 years of age
___ Student has difficulty using both hands together (stabilization of paper during cutting and paper activities)

Self-care skills

___ Difficulty with fasteners (buttons, zippers, snaps, shoe tying, lacing) (Circle)
___ Wears clothes backwards or inside out; appears messy
___ Has difficulty putting clothes on or taking them off
___ Difficulty with the eating process (opening packages, feeding self, spilling, using utensils) (Circle)
___ Oral-motor problems (drools, difficulty chewing, swallowing, difficulty drinking from straws) (Circle)
___ Needs assistance with toileting (wiping, flushing, replacing underwear/clothes) (Circle)

Academic (check those areas presenting problems)

___ Distractibility	___ Slow work	___ Restlessness
___ Following directions		___ Organizing work
___ Hyperactivity		___ Finishing tasks
___ Memory deficit		___ Attention deficit
___Difficulty naming body parts		

Tactile sensation

___ Seems to withdraw from touch
___ Craves touch
___ Tends to wear coat when not needed; will not allow shirtsleeves pulled up
___ Has trouble keeping hands to self, will poke or push other children
___ Apt to touch everything he/she sees ("learns through fingers")
___ Dislikes being hugged or cuddled
___ Avoids certain textures of foods
___ Dislikes arts and crafts activities involving different textures (clay, finger paints)
___ Complains of numbness, tingling, and other abnormal sensations

Continued.

TABLE 19-2, cont'd

District 19 motor team screening form

Auditory perception

___ Appears overly sensitive to sounds
___ Talks excessively
___ Likes to make loud noises
___ Has difficulty making self understood
___ Appears to have difficulty understanding teacher/paraprofessionals/peers
___ Tends to repeat directions to self

Visual perception

___ Difficulty discriminating colors and shapes doing puzzles
___ Letter and/or number reversals after first grade
___ Difficulty with eye-tracking (following objects with eyes, eyes and head move together)
___ Difficulty copying designs, numbers, or letters
___ Has and wears/doesn't wear glasses
___ Difficulty transcribing from blackboard or book to paper
___ Difficulty with eye-hand or eye-foot coordination (catching, striking, kicking)

Emotional

___ Does not accept changes in routine easily
___ Becomes easily frustrated
___ Acts out behaviorally; difficulty getting along with others
___ Tends to be impulsive, heedless, accident prone
___ Easier to handle in large group, small group, or individually (Circle)
___ Marked mood variations, outbursts or tantrums
___ Marked out-of-seat behavior
___ Noncompliant
___ Unstable home situation
___ Notable self-stimulatory behaviors

Additional concerns:

Assigned to:_____
Date received:_____ Evaluation date:_____

---

sumes a specific responsibility for the management and supervision of the total motor program. One professional may be designated as the child's motor development case manager. Every member of the motor development team will communicate directly with the motor development case manager regarding the child's progress or difficulties in implementation of the motor program.

5. To document service delivery.

Careful documentation of services delivered is a vital part of the service delivery process. Each member of the team must be accountable not only to the child served but to each other, as well. The motor development team, if it is to function effectively, demands professional accountability. This is often done by using a service provider log. Table 19-3 is a sample of a motor development team log that may reflect service delivery to a child lacking abdominal strength, whose IMEP or IPEP included this annual goal: The child will be able to perform 10 bent-knee sit-ups independently.

TABLE 19-3

Ernesto Gamboa (child's name)—motor development team service provider log

Date	Service provider	IMEP goal	Child's performance
10/1	C. Jones, OTR	10 sit-ups	3 reverse sit-ups
10/2	J. Hernandez, LPT	10 sit-ups	4 reverse sit-ups
10/4	J. Smith, APE Spec	10 sit-ups	3 minutes supine scooter play; 5 minutes supine cageball kick
10/5	G. Meza, RTR	10 sit-ups	25 minutes horseback riding
10/8	C. Jones, OTR	10 sit-ups	5 reverse sit-ups

This type of log is vital for communication between professional members of the motor development team and may serve as crucial documentation of services provided during the annual review of the child's progress.

6. To cooperatively provide or create resources that help other professionals meet the motor needs of students

In some school districts or special service cooperatives, the members of the motor development team have created motor development handbooks for use by teachers in early childhood classrooms or physical education programs. In others, the members of the motor development team have developed curricula for use by special educators in pre-vocational preparation programs.

7. To conduct cooperative in-service motor-development training for other school personnel, parents, and volunteers.

In the Dallas Independent School District, for example, the physical therapist, occupational therapist, speech and language therapist, and adapted physical education specialist provide joint orientation programs for all special education personnel. The staff of the

Achievement Center for the Handicapped, in Stevens Point, Wisconsin, an early-intervention program, provide comprehensive parent training in the home. The staff members represent the professions of physical therapy, occupational therapy, and special education.

□ □ □

Professionals in this motor development team model share common functions yet retain professional integrity and responsibility for the motor development and motor proficiency of the child served.

The traditional emphasis by each professional who may function as a member of a motor development team is illustrated in Figure 19-1. It is important, however, to note that this model is not restrictive. The intent of the motor development team is to share professional competency, judgment, and expertise. For example, the adapted physical educator trained in techniques to enhance sensory integration may work in close cooperation with the occupational therapist in the development of a sensory integration program. Members of the adapted physical education staff of the Jefferson Parish, Louisiana, Project Creole, are actively involved in in-service and pre-service education of

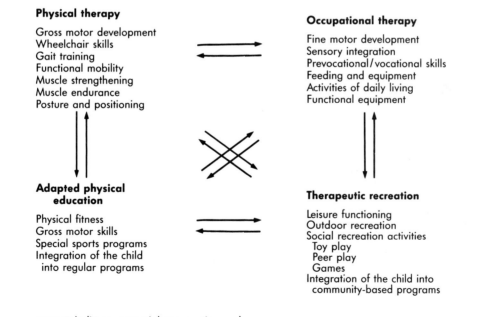

Physical therapy

Gross motor development
Wheelchair skills
Gait training
Functional mobility
Muscle strengthening
Muscle endurance
Posture and positioning

Occupational therapy

Fine motor development
Sensory integration
Prevocational/vocational skills
Feeding and equipment
Activities of daily living
Functional equipment

Adapted physical education

Physical fitness
Gross motor skills
Special sports programs
Integration of the child
  into regular programs

Therapeutic recreation

Leisure functioning
Outdoor recreation
Social recreation activities
  Toy play
  Peer play
  Games
Integration of the child into
  community-based programs

⟶ Indicates potential cooperation and crossover

FIGURE 19-1. Motor development team. (From Sugars A: The adapted physical educator as a member of the motor development team, TAHPERD State Convention, Lubbock, Texas, 1990. Reprinted with permission.)

physical and occupational therapists to train those professionals to teach orthopedically disabled children to use their wheelchairs in sport, leisure, recreation, and functional mobility skills.

This type of model for the delivery of service to children with motor deficits is particularly important in school districts and cooperatives unable to locate sufficient certified, trained professional staff. For example, if a school district is unable to hire and retain a licensed physical therapist as a part of the staff, it may be necessary for other professionals to implement the program designed by the therapist. In school districts with limited adapted physical education specialists it is vital that the regular physical educator be included as part of the motor development team. The regular physical educator may provide the majority of direct service to the child with a disability and must, by necessity, be an informed part of the professional team.

INTERACTION WITH REGULAR PHYSICAL EDUCATION PERSONNEL

The Regular Education Initiative has created an educational environment in which there is widespread demand from educators and parents to educate children with disabilities in the regular education program. As mentioned earlier in the text, this has had a significant impact on the regular physical education teacher and the regular physical education class.

The adapted physical educator must work in close cooperation with regular physical education personnel who are providing services to children with disabilities in the regular physical education class. The physical educator may assume several roles in the capacity of delivering services to children with disabilities. Whatever the role, it is clear that an organizational system needs to be developed that coordinates the efforts of aides, volunteers, and special and elementary classroom teachers who deliver services, as well as itinerant and resource room teachers if they are involved in the program.

The first and primary role of the adapted physical educator is to complete a comprehensive assessment to determine if the child's needs can be met in the regular physical education class without significantly disrupting the education of other students.

The adapted physical educator must provide avenues of communication for the regular physical educator so the two professionals can work to provide the best learning environment for all the children placed in the class. Art Reinhardt, Adapted Physical Education Specialist in the Stevens Point (Wisconsin) Area Public Schools has developed a spreadsheet[18] with which the

physical educator can monitor the performance of children with disabilities within the mainstream. An adaptation is shown in Table 19-4.

This evaluation form, developed on a spreadsheet, allows the regular physical educator and the adapted physical educator to make significant decisions regarding intervention with a child functioning, at least temporarily, within the mainstream. The process of quanti-

---

TABLE 19-4

Mainstream physical education

Student: JC
Class: K
Regular PE teacher: Mr. Shirly
Observer: Art Reinhardt
Date: 2/14/93

Observation	1st	2nd	3rd	4th	5th	Avg
Psychomotor skills	2	2	2	2	2	2.0
Fitness	2	1	2	1	2	1.6
Knowledge/understanding	3	3	3	3	4	3.2
Attitude/behavior	1	2	2	1	1	1.4
Participation in groups	1	1	1	1	1	1.0
Participation with partner	1	1	1	2	1	1.2
Individual activities	3	3	3	2	3	2.8
Total average:	1.8	1.8	2.0	1.7	1.8	

Activities and comments

JC participated well in warm-up activities. Disrupted group parachute activity.
Rating scale: Give the point rating below for the student's performance on that given day.

1 Point

If the student needs to be pulled from class and would require 1-1 assistance
If the regular PE program must be totally modified to meet the student's needs
If the student is unable to participate

2 Points

If 1-1 assistance is required greater than 50% of the time
If significant modifications must be made for more than 50% of the activities
If the student requires full assistance to participate

3 Points

If partial assistance is required for 25% or less of the activities
If slight modifications to regular PE are necessary
If the student requires partial assistance to participate

4 Points

No asistance is required
No modifications are necessary

Reprinted with permission from Mainstream Physical Education Evaluation.

fying behaviors required for successful participation in the mainstream is vital if thoughtful decisions are to be made regarding a child's ultimate placement; and the beauty of the spreadsheet is that repeated observations can be made and calculations performed instantly for review. In addition, quantifying behaviors allows the adapted physical educator to work closely with the regular physical educator to modify the program, if necessary, to allow the child to participate successfully in the program.

For example, the student described in the above mainstream observation appears to have the skills and knowledges necessary to participate in the program, but lacks the social skills necessary to function with partners or with groups, as indicated by 1.0 and 1.2 average scores on "participation within group" or "participation with partner."

The professionals serving this child have several apparent choices based on these data. The first is to remove the child from the mainstream physical education class until the child acquires the social skills necessary to function with a partner or within a small group.

The second is to develop a behavior management system, implemented by a paraprofessional, to shape the child's social behavior while the child remains in the regular physical education class. The third, and least practical, is to modify the regular physical education class so that the emphasis is on indiviudal, self-testing activities that do not require partner or group interaction.

COMMUNICATION WITH PARENTS

Perhaps the most difficult aspect of the role of the adapted physical educator is effective communication with the parents. This vital communication, which can and should lead to an effective partnership between the teacher and the parent and between the school and the home, is often challenging because of cultural, ethnic, and socioeconomic differences. Olson suggested,[17] "As the two major forces entrusted with educating and socializing children in society, parents and teachers should be natural allies. But far too often, they find themselves on opposite sides of an exceedingly high fence."

The 1986 Amendments of the Education of the Handicapped Act, PL 99-457, which went into effect in 1991, mandated comprehensive intervention for infants and toddlers with disabilities. One of the major components of this legislation was the recognition of the home as the child's primary school and the parents as the child's primary teachers. The adapted physical educator, like other professionals who have an interest in the development of infants and toddlers, must be a positive force in the alliance of parents and teachers so that the needs of children with and without disabilities may be met.

To provide an effective home and family intervention program, the adapted physical education specialist must be aware of the comprehensive effects of a child's disability on the total ecology of the family. There are three major theories regarding the impact of a child's disability on the child's parents, siblings, and extended family: chronic sorrow syndrome, stage theory, and nonsequential stage theory. Chronic sorrow syndrome describes the reactions of parents or siblings when faced with the constant reminder of "loss" associated with disability. The parent or sibling with chronic sorrow syndrome may cope relatively well with the day to day requirements of providing support for the child with a disability, but the individual's underlying emotions include sadness, fear, anger, and guilt.[16]

The dominant stage theory suggests that the parent or sibling of a child with a disability experiences emotions and reactions that are identical to those that are experienced by an individual facing the death of a loved one or facing a terminal illness. These stages of grief—denial, bargaining, anger, depression, and acceptance were first described in the teachings of Dr. Elizabeth Kübler-Ross.[11] It is important to note that these emotional stages also parallel those experienced by a child or adult with an adventitious disability (a condition acquired after a history of "normal" development).

The non-sequential stage theory suggests that the parents, siblings, or extended family members may experience some or all of the stages of grief described by Kübler-Ross, but not necessarily in predictable stages. The non-sequential stage theory suggests that a response to the child's disability may be the result of facing particular milestones.[2] The initial diagnosis of disability may cause denial, anger, and depression. These emotions may resurface when the parents are faced with the fact that their child needs to receive special education services; again as the child reaches adolescence and the parents must deal with the realities of sexuality; and/or as the parents deal with their aging and the inevitability of providing alternate care for their offspring.

Understanding the response to a child with a disability is further complicated by the fact that there appear to be socio-cultural differences in parent reactions. Mary[13] studied the reactions of black, Hispanic, and white mothers toward their child with a disability. Mary found that Hispanic mothers reported an attitude of self-sacrifice more often than the other mothers. In addition, Hispanic mothers noted greater spousal denial of the disability than other mothers.

The adapted physical educator hoping to work successfully in the home must recognize not only the emotional responses of family members to a child with a disability, but must also be sensitive to the forces that affect the family. The family is often overwhelmed by the need to interact with the huge, often impersonal, medical bureaucracy. The sense of despair is often heightened by the sense of feeling helpless and unempowered when facing the barrage of medical personnel, hostile medical insurance representatives, and incomprehensible medical bills. The family may experience a sense of isolation as friends and others in the community respond in fear. The family may be frustrated by huge time constraints involved in the care of a child with a disability. Brantlinger[2] writes, "Parenting is always demanding, but having a child with a handicapping condition usually adds to the complexity of the task." Sexton[19] reported that parents of children with disabilities are more likely than others to experience significant stress, and Blacher[1] reported that these parents are more likely to develop emotional and personality disorders. Dyson[4] found that such stress is persistent even in the absence of other socioeconomic disadvantages.

Weiss reported that parents of children with pervasive developmental disorders experience six major stressors[24]:

1. Dealing with professional and other support services
2. Family strains
3. Stigmatization
4. The child's aberrent behavior
5. Concerns regarding their own future mental/emotional health
6. Fears regarding the child's future

These stressors are not uncommon to the parents of any child with a disability. The nature and severity of the disability have a direct bearing on the extent and type of stress.

The Nature of the Effective Home Program

Brantlinger[2] noted that the most significant need of parents with disabilities is to have accurate and honest information about the child's disability and programs/resources that may help the parents deal with the child. Kroth[10] suggested that programs that best serve the families of children with disabilities are responsive to the diverse needs of the families. Turnbull[23] sug-

gested that only those programs that are voluntary in nature can be truly successful.

The school-supported home program can and must meet many needs. First, the parents must be given accurate and honest information about the child's disability. The adapted physical education specialist may provide a vital service by describing both "normal" developmental motor milestones and those that should be expected from the particular child. Second, the parents must be made aware of all resources that may help them meet the needs of the child with a disability. These resources include assessment and diagnostic personnel, early intervention programs, school and community-based programs that serve children with disabilities, modified or adapted equipment for home use, and respite therapy programs.

Third, the program should provide opportunities for parents, particularly young parents, to learn appropriate parenting skills. Most parents imitate the behaviors of their own parents. The parents of children with disabilities need access to successful models; they need to have the opportunity to learn parenting skills from those who have successfully raised a child with a disability. Fourth, the school-supported home program should provide the opportunity for parents and siblings of a child with a disability to meet and interact with others. A "support" group may serve many needs.

A vital consideration in the development of family support programs is the diverse need of families that represent different socioeconomic strata, different cultures, and different values. Educators must recognize and embrace the diversity of the American experience if they are to be able to truly welcome parents into the education system.

Parents as Teachers

Ehlers and Ruffin[5] described the Missouri "Parents as Teachers" project, which evolved in 1984 when Missouri became the first state in the nation to mandate parent education and family support services, beginning at the child's birth, in every school district. According to Ehlers and Ruffin, the Parents as Teachers project is based on the following premises[5]:

☐ Parents are the first and most important teachers of their children.
☐ The home is the child's first schoolhouse.
☐ Children will learn more during the early years than at any other time in life.
☐ All parents want to be good parents and care about their child's development.

The Parents as Teachers (PAT) project provided the following information for parents, beginning in the third trimester of pregnancy and continuing until the child reached age 3 years[5]:

☐ Counseling and information to prepare the parents for their new role.

☐ Timely information about the child's language, cognitive, social and motor skill development.

☐ Techniques to foster and develop the acquisition of language, cognition, and social and motor skills.

☐ Periodic screening to detect possible educational, hearing, visual, or motor deficits.

☐ If deficits were present, PAT provided referrals to appropriate medical personnel or social service agencies.

☐ Monthly visits to the home by trained parent educators who developed and monitored the child's individualized home program.

☐ Monthly parent support group meetings for information and experience exchange.

This highly successful Missouri project demonstrated that such early intervention produced remarkable results. Diamond[3] wrote of the PAT program, "The approach is simple: If parents have the information and support they need to do the best job possible as their children's first teachers, those children will have a jump start on life." Children whose parents participated in the project demonstrated language, problem solving, coping behaviors, and skills required to interact with adults, which were significantly more advanced than those of children whose parents did not participate. Perhaps most remarkable is the fact that those children who were believed to be at risk because of young parents, parents with low traditional educational achievement, low income families, or single-parent families, demonstrated the same results as other children whose parents were involved.[5]

Lazar and Darlington[12] completed a 15-year longitudinal study of children who participated in home preschool programs. They concluded that the direct participation of children in home preschool programs improved children's functioning capability later in life. They also found that providing services for the whole family resulted in even more significant gains for the child.

McConachie found that parents of young children with learning problems are willing and able to conscientiously follow a program of play when provided a simple recording system.[14] She noted, however, that parents differ greatly in the amount of professional advice and direction they require to be successful teachers.

Home-School Partnerships

Benson, after studying the achievement of 700 sixth graders in Oakland, California found that those students whose parents were involved in their education achieved more in school than those whose parents were not involved. He found that this occurred regardless of family income, but that parent intervention in the school process could not, in and of itself, completely close the educational achievement gap between poor and non-poor children.[17]

McNair and Rusch[15] found that parents expressed an interest in being actively involved in the process of aiding in the transition of their young adult children with disabilities from the school into the community.

Teachers and other school administrators can begin the process of fostering parent involvement in the schools in a number of ways. These include improving communication between the teacher and the parent. Communication can be enhanced by frequent telephone conversations, frequent notes from teacher to parent(s), and frequent notes from parent(s) to teacher. Informal gatherings of parents and teachers can foster increased communication more effectively than more formal, structured meetings (e.g., parent-teacher conferences). Informal gatherings may include spaghetti suppers, pancake breakfasts, or school picnics. It should be noted that improvement of the vital parent-teacher link is often more difficult with poor, non-formally educated parents. Though they may care deeply about their child, they may be intimidated by the educational process and the school itself. This communication is made even more difficult given the vast numbers of non-English speaking parents.

Epstein and Dauber[6] identified five types of parent involvement in the education process:

1. *Basic obligations of parents:* These include the responsibility to provide for the health and safety of the child, to prepare the child for school, to teach family-life schools, and to create home conditions that support school learning and behavior.

2. *Basic obligations of schools:* The school has the responsibility to communicate with parents about the schools' programs and the progress of the individual student.

3. *Parent involvement at school:* Parents may serve as volunteers to assist teachers and administrators and/or to tutor individual children. The parent may attend student performances, sports events, and school plays, or participate in workshops or other programs for their own education and/or training.

4. *Parent involvement in learning activities at home:* The parent may monitor or assist the child at home with learning activities associated with the child's school assignments. The parent may initiate other learning activities in the home.

5. *Parent involvement in governance and advocacy:* The parent may serve in decision-making roles in parent groups, advisory councils, or other committees/groups at the school, district, or state level. The parent may serve as an advocate for groups that monitor the schools and fight for school improvement.

Ten Truths of Parent Involvement

□ All parents have hopes and goals for their children. They differ in how they support their children's efforts to achieve those goals.

□ The home is one of several spheres that simultaneously influence a child. The school must work with other spheres for the child's benefit, not push them apart.

□ The parent is the central contributor to a child's education. Schools can either co-opt that role or recognize the potential of the parent.

□ Parent involvement must be a legitimate element of education. It deserves equal elements such as program improvement and evaluation.

□ Parent involvement is a process, not a program of activities. It requires ongoing energy and effort.

□ Parent involvement requires a vision, policy, and framework. A concensus of understanding is important.

□ Parents' interaction with their own children is the cornerstone of parent involvement. A program must recognize the value, diversity, and difficulty of this role.

□ Most barriers to parent involvement are found within school practices. They are not found within parents.

□ Any parent can be "hard to reach." Parents must be identified and approached individually; they are not defined by gender, ethnicity, family situation, education, or income.

□ Successful parent involvement nurtures relationships and partnerships. It strengthens bonds between home and school, parent and educator, parent and child, school and community.

Reprinted with permission from *Ten Truths of Parent Involvement,* Dallas Independent School District Bilingual and English as a Second Language Program, April, 1990.

The bilingual and English as a Second Language (ESL) programs of the Dallas Independent School District distributed the box below to teachers in the bilingual and ESL programs.[22]

Parent Involvement in Adapted Physical Education Programs

The adapted physical educator should be actively involved in the motor development of the child from birth through adult transition into community-based living and work arrangements. Throughout the lifespan, the adapted physical educator can and must provide vital information and programming assistance to the parents of individuals with disabilities.

The types of information and programming assistance that the adapted physical educator can provide are outlined in Table 19-5.

The Parent-Teacher Association

One of the major avenues for communication with parents is the Parent-Teacher Association. The adapted physical educator should ask to be part of the program on a regular basis. Successful presentations may include activity demonstrations in which the teacher may give children with disabilities the opportunity to demonstrate their skills and abilities. These programs may also highlight the successes of children participat-

TABLE 19-5

Adapted physical education information and programming assistance for parents

Age	Information	Programming assistance
0-3	Reflexes	Sensory stimulation activities
	Equilibrium responses	Equilibrium development
	Locomotor patterns	Locomotor Development
3-5	Locomotor patterns	Locomotor development
	Receipt and propulsion	Receipt and propulsion skills
	Play behavior	Activities to foster play
		Activities to develop body image
		Activities to develop rhythmicity
		Sensory-motor integration
5-12	Locomotor patterns	Locomotor development
	Receipt and Propulsion	Receipt and propulsion skills
	Play behavior	Low organization games
12-15	Fitness	Activities to promote fitness
	Leisure skills	Leisure activities
	Recreation skills	Recreation activities
15-	Fitness	Activities to promote fitness
	Leisure skills	Leisure activities
	Recreation skills	Recreation activities
		Transition skills

ing in rhythms, low organization games, Special Olympics, wheelchair sports organizations, and/or community-based leisure/recreation programs.

It is vital that the parents of *all* children within the district have the opportunity to receive information about effective adapted physical education programming. It is particularly important that the parents of children without disabilities are familiar with the intervention strategies that will be used in providing an appropriate least restrictive learning environment for all children. This type of information may help parents learn to welcome children with disabilities into the "regular" education setting.

Parent Advisory Committee

Recognizing the vital role that parents can and should play in the education of children, many school districts have created parent advisory committees. It is hoped that these committees will open lines of communication with parents that can not only enhance interaction but can, perhaps, forestall adversary relationships between parents and the school district. The parent advisory committee may be district-wide or may be set up to advise at one particular school. This advisory committee helps establish and interpret policy, fosters good public relations, and procures funds.

An advisory committee at the school level has responsibilities similar to those of the district committee. It should advise and support the teachers, including the adapted physical education teacher. It is concerned with interpretation of the program and with public relations at the school level.

The supervisor and the teachers of adapted physical education will find that the parent advisory committee can give them invaluable aid in planning for and interpreting this special type of program. Therefore the members of these committees must be selected with great care.

After the advisory committee has been selected, the members can be helpful with establishing a quality adapted physical education program. Tasks they can assist with include surveying the involved schools, assisting with attainment of objectives, interpreting the program, securing support for the program, and agreeing on general principles that will be followed. A discussion of each of these tasks follows.

Surveying the schools

A survey of a school or district must be conducted to determine what will be required to implement or improve an adapted physical education program and should include information about the following factors:

1. Availability of teachers and their education and experience
2. Time allotment necessary for the program
3. Cost of the program
4. Existing facilities and equipment and amount of additional space and supplies needed
5. Special problems concerning related services
6. Special problems involved in counseling these students and scheduling them for classes at special hours during the day

The caliber of the adapted physical education teacher is the single most important factor of those listed. Money, equipment, support from related service care providers, and other teachers all are important, but an enthusiastic, well-qualified teacher is a necessity. The teacher of children with disabilities must not only be a good instructor, but also must have the understanding and the ability to establish rapport with students who are seeking an education despite their disabilities.

Because the adapted physical education program involves special classes for only a portion of the total student enrollment of a school and because class size often should be limited to allow for considerable individual instruction, schedule problems sometimes result. School administrators and counselors must be convinced that students who have special needs should be scheduled for physical education class early in the selection of their class schedule. The IEP requires that each child with a disability receive instruction that meets his or her specific needs. Furthermore, the placement of the child (where the instruction is to take place) is cooperatively decided by the parents and the school.

An adapted physical education program does cost a school or school district additional money. Small classes, special equipment, a special room, and additional related services increase costs over what is spent on regular physical education classes. These costs need not be exorbitant, however. An excellent program can be provided with a minimum of special equipment and even without a special room if one is not available. Refer to Chapter 20 for a discussion of inexpensive equipment that may be used in the quality adapted physical education program.

Interpreting the Program

Promoting an adapted physical education program in a school or school district requires excellence in program planning and teaching, demonstrating that positive results can be obtained through the conduct of a quality program. Effective communication with administrators, special education personnel, related service personnel, physical education personnel, parents, and the public can be enhanced through the use of computer technology. For example, it is now relatively simple to create an adapted physical education newsletter or newspaper, which can be distributed to share information regarding the adapted physical education program. The adapted physical educator can share information monthly with parents and other teachers using computer-assisted graphs to demonstrate program effectiveness.

Determining the Program's Cost Effectiveness

School administrators often think of their programs in terms of costs, rather than the effectiveness of total human services over a person's lifetime or the humane benefits that can be achieved through well-constructed programs. There is impressive evidence that lifestyles that involve physical activity result in considerable reduction of health care costs over a lifetime.[20] Particularly important for individuals with disabilities is the acquisition of sport skills and physical activity regimens that can be generalized into community environments where active lifestyles, which include leisure, recreation, and sports, can be maintained. The physical education program in the public schools is the most logical and cost-effective way to launch lifestyles of physical activity.

It is now accepted in many countries throughout the world that there is more to life than a roof over one's head and a job. Clearly, the quality of life is contingent upon how well one uses leisure time. Inasmuch as there is a preponderance of evidence that links the physically active lifestyle with health, physical education programs in the public schools should be a high priority not only for students without disabilities, but even more importantly for students with disabilities, who are more apt to adopt sedentary lifestyles.[7]

PUBLIC RELATIONS

The wise adapted physical educator is a public relations specialist. Unfortunately, our field is poorly understood and often ill-respected. The adapted physical educator should take every opportunity to communicate information about the program in the local newspapers, in local radio and television programs, and through presentations to local service groups and corporate groups.

Adapted physical education is often best publicized through special events, which include local, area, and state Special Olympics competitions, competitions of other sports organizations, and/or school play days or sports days.

The adapted physical education program can be highlighted by a school-sponsored leisure, recreation, or sporting event that includes individuals with disabilities. For example, the school or school district could sponsor a fund-raising 10 K road race that highlights the participation of wheelchair road racers. Or, the school or school district could have a fund-raising wheelchair basketball tournament in which talented local wheelchair athletes play basketball against a "celebrity" team (mayor, council members, local radio and television personnel, etc.) in wheelchairs. Or, the school could sponsor a doubles tennis competition in which a local sports celebrity is paired with a mentally retarded athlete. This type of event not only provides vital public awareness opportunities, but also may raise desperately needed money to support the adapted physical education program.

OTHER PROGRAM ORGANIZATION/ ADMINISTRATION CONSIDERATIONS
Schedules

Because the adapted physical education program requires a teacher with special training, certain problems may develop in scheduling the classes of that teacher. The primary consideration in the development of a teaching and/or assessment schedule should be the child. The student's schedule should be developed given the following considerations:
- Child's chronological age
- Child's developmental age
- Nature and severity of the child's disability
- Child's medication and medication schedule
- Child's therapy or treatment schedule, if appropriate
- Child's ability to benefit from instruction as part of a group or need for one-to-one or small group instruction

A primary consideration also should be the state mandates for physical education instruction for children without disabilities. If the state Department of Public Instruction or Education Agency mandates daily physical education for children in elementary school, children with disabilities in the elementary school must also be guaranteed daily physical education instruction.

School-Based Physical Education Teacher

Only rarely does a school district or education agency have the resources to place a full-time adapted physical education teacher within one school. This may occur if a school district has a large school designed primarily for children with special needs. This may also be the case in large facilities designed to serve children with a particular type of disability (e.g., the Wisconsin School For the Blind, in Janesville, Wisconsin).

In the event that a school/facility has a full-time adapted physical educator, that teacher's class schedule should parallel those of other teachers within the school/facility. Classes should be regularly scheduled throughout the day, with a 5 minute break between classes, if possible. The teacher should have a lunch period and planning period as part of the day. If possible, the teacher should have at least one period during the week designed specifically for assessment/evaluation for new referrals and transfers, and/or as part of the 3-year comprehensive review process.

Itinerant Adapted Physical Education Teacher

The schedule of the itinerant adapted physical education teacher may be more difficult to arrange. The schedule should be designed to maximize contact time with students, to minimize time needed for transition/travel, and to allow some flexibility for assessment/evaluation. If an itinerant teacher travels to a school where more than one class is offered, it is advantageous to have the classes scheduled consecutively. This will streamline preparation of the facility and arrangement of equipment for instruction. A hypothetical schedule of the itinerant adapted physical education teacher who serves three elementary schools is outlined below.

Time	M	T	W	Th	F
8:00-12:00	Foster	Grant	Foster	Grant	Foster
1:00-4:00	Adams	assess	Adams	assess	Adams

This teacher's schedule on Monday may resemble the following:

Foster

8:00-8:50	Young's early childhood class
9:00-9:50	Supervision of Jason, James, Talitha, Josue, and Shamika in kindergarten regular physical education
10:00-10:50	Wilson's daily living skills class
11:00-11:50	Stone's pre-vocational skills class

Adams

12:30-1:15	Jones's severe/profound class
1:20-2:00	Pedford's severe hearing impaired class
2:10-3:00	Hammer's reverse mainstream visually impaired class
3:10-3:40	Planning period

There are additional matters that also should be considered in the determination of class schedule. If the special exercise room, the pool, or the special game areas used by the adapted physical education classes are available only during certain periods of the day, the schedule should be arranged so that the adapted classes can be held in as many of these areas as possible during the course of the year. Often adapted physical education classes are held in the gymnasium, the dance studio, or the gymnastics, weight-training, or wrestling room. When this is done, it should be a part of the master schedule of this particular facility. These rooms may be used in lieu of a special adapted room, or they may be used as a facility for one of the activities offered in the adapted sports and activity program.

The adapted sports and activity program usually can be quite flexible and can be organized to permit facilities to be used when they are not needed by the other physical education classes that meet during the same period. However, it is important that a block of time be provided for the adapted class for each activity area, including the pool, so that students in this program have a rich and varied experience in a wide range of physical education activities.

Transfer of Students

One of the important features of a quality program of adapted physical education is to provide for the easy transfer of students to a less restrictive physical education class. The provision of a system of easy transfer of students to and from the adapted physical education class does much to erase the stigma sometimes attached to a separate class for students who have disabilities. This may be necessary in the least restrictive environment continuum if a child is having behavior problems associated with a particular type of activity or has a disability that contraindicates participation in a particular activity.

Budget

The adapted physical educator or the direct supervisor may be responsible for the purchase and maintenance of equipment. The management of this equipment budget is facilitated by the use of a spreadsheet so that the type of equipment, the number of pieces of each type of equipment, and the cost of each unit can be maintained. The spreadsheet calculation capabilities allow the teacher to "play" with the figures to determine what to purchase and in what quantity. If for example, the Director of Special Education indicates that the adapted physical education teacher has a new equipment purchase budget of $1000 for the 1993-1994

TABLE 19-6

Sample budget

Item	No.	Unit	Cost/unit (dollars)	Total cost (dollars)
Fleece balls				
3"	2	8/set	21.89	43.78
4"	2	8/set	29.13	58.26
Parachutes				
6' deluxe	1	1	39.55	39.55
30' deluxe	1	1	197.42	197.42
Scooters				
16"	12	1	17.75	213.00
Cageballs				
36"	1	1	53.47	53.47
5'	1	1	150.98	150.98
Playground balls				
6"	12		2.55	30.60
8"	12		3.35	42.60
Spot markers				
Yellow	1set	12	19.95	19.95
Mesh ball bags				
24" × 36"	5	1	5.95	29.75
Portable cones				
12"	12	1	3.95	47.40
Hoola hoops				
36"	1set	dozen	31.40	31.40
			Total	**939.36**

school year, the teacher can use the automatic calculation capabilities to consider purchases. A sample is provided in Table 19-6.

The teacher, using the spreadsheet, can adjust the figures to determine if, for example, ordering no mesh ball bags would allow the purchase of one dozen more hoola hoops.

This type of spreadsheet can be used to manage and maintain a record of equipment that will facilitate the budget process during subsequent years. This also can be expanded to include a check-out process.

Recruitment and retention of volunteers

As funds become increasingly scarce, administrators and teachers have become increasingly dependent on the use of volunteer resources to continue or to improve programs. The effective recruitment and retention of volunteers is enhanced by all the means of communication discussed earlier in this chapter. However, it is important for the adapted physical education teacher or the physical education teacher to understand the nature of the volunteer to effectively use the volunteer to meet program goals.

Huettig[8] found that Special Olympics volunteers were motivated by the fact that they found the experience to be personally rewarding and fulfilling and were, in addition, anxious to bring joy and happiness into the lives of the Special Olympians. This is consistent with the findings of other volunteer researchers. Individuals who are willing to volunteer usually do so because of a sense of classic altruism, wishing to do "good works" for other people, but continue to be volunteers because they find the experience is meaningful and rewarding.

Schools and school districts have begun the process of actively recruiting volunteers to work with children within the schools. Schools may be "adopted" by a corporation or a civic organization. Corporate employees or members of a civic group may each serve the school in a unique way, as a part of the "adopt a school" program. The physical education teacher or adapted physical education teacher can increase the likelihood that a volunteer will choose to work in the gymnasium in the following ways:

□ Develop a poster recruiting campaign that features the fact that it is "fun" and a great "change of pace" to work with children with disabilities in a play, leisure, recreation, or sport setting.

□ Actively recruit volunteers on the basis of their athletic skills; it is easier to recruit someone who perceives the self to be needed because of particular skills.

□ Indicate the potential for learning new skills, particularly those that might be marketable. This is particularly valuable in recruiting individuals who are unemployed or seeking alternate employment opportunities.

□ Share program goals and objectives with the volunteer. Share specific goals and objectives for specific children the volunteer serves.

□ Write a specific job description for the volunteer. This is the key to successful volunteer recruitment and retention. The volunteer needs to understand his or her role within the program.

□ Ensure that the volunteer is recognized for his or her efforts. Help the children in the program express their thanks—this is perhaps the most valuable form of recognition for most volunteers.

□ Develop a systematic strategy for recognizing the volunteer. This includes "volunteer highlights" in the adapted physical education newsletter, thank-you notes, plaques, and/or recognition dinners.

The use of volunteers in the schools can greatly enhance the opportunities that can be given to children with disabilities. The adapted physical educator can provide a chance for children to thrive and grow, while encouraged by the presence of program volunteers.

SUMMARY

The adapted physical educator functions within an environment in which communication with administrators, special educators, physical educators, related service personnel, parents, and volunteers is crucial to program success. The key to the development of effective interaction within the school district or school is to honestly and openly and, in a timely fashion, share vital information about the nature of the adapted physical education program with key personnel.

REVIEW QUESTIONS

1. What strategies can be used to ensure administrative support for the adapted physical education program?
2. What is the function of the motor development team? Describe the role of each of the members of the team.
3. What types of public relation strategies are effective in promoting the adapted physical education program?
4. What is site-based management?
5. What types of responsibilities may be appropriate for a parent advisory council?
6. Describe some of the primary considerations in the development of effective comunication with parents.
7. Describe techniques for recruitment and retention of volunteers for adapted physical education programs.

STUDENT ACTIVITIES

1. Interview the Director of Special Education in a nearby community. Ask the administrator to describe the adapted physical education program.
2. Develop an information sheet or brochure describing the adapted physical education program that would be suitable to send to parents.
3. Survey five parents of children with disabilities. Inquire about what they believe an adapted physical education program is and what benefits they believe their children will realize from such a program. Ask the parents what types of information about their child's motor development would be helpful to them.
4. Interview a physical therapist, occupational therapist, or recreation therapist. Ask the individual to share their views regarding the concept of a motor development team.
5. Attend a Parent-Teacher Association meeting.
6. Talk with a volunteer coordinator of a large social service agency. Discuss strategies for recruitment and retention of volunteers.
7. Talk with a member of a public relations firm and discuss a strategy for the development of a community-wide campaign regarding physical education, leisure, recreation, and sports for individuals with disabilities.

REFERENCES

1. Blacher J: Sequential stages of parental adjustment to the birth of a child with handicaps: fact or artifact? *Ment Retard* 22:55-68, 1984.
2. Bratlinger E: Home-school partnerships that benefit children with special needs, *El School J* 91:249-259, 1991.
3. Diamond DB: Program helps parents think of themselves as teachers, *Chicago Tribune,* August 11, 1991.
4. Dyson LL: Families of young children with handicaps: parental stress and functioning, *Am J Ment Retard* 95:623-629, 1991.
5. Ehlers VL, Ruffin M: The Missouri project—parents as teachers, *Focus Except Child* 23:1-14, 1990.
6. Epstein JL, Dauber SL: *Teachers' attitudes and practices of parent involvement in inner-city elementary and middle schools,* Baltimore, 1989, The Johns Hopkins University Center for Research on Elementary and Middle Schools.
7. Heikkinen W, Pohjolainen P: Physical activity and cardiovascular disease among the elderly, *Finnish Sports Exer Med* 2:54-61, 1983.
8. Huettig C: Motive and meaning—the Special Olympics volunteer. In Auxter D, editor: *Completed research at the International Special Olympics Games,* Washington, DC, 1988, International Special Olympics.
9. Jowett S: Working with parents—a study of policy and practice, *Early Child Dev Care* 58:45-50, 1990.
10. Kroth R: School-based parent involvement problems. In Fine MJ, editor: *Second handbook on parent education: contemporary perspectives,* San Diego, 1989, Academic Press.
11. Kübler-Ross E: *On death and dying,* New York, 1969, Macmillan Publishing.
12. Lazar I, Darlington R: Lasting effects of early education: a report from the consortium for longitudinal studies, *Monogr Soc Res Child Dev* 195:47, 1982.
13. Mary NL: Reactions of black, Hispanic and white mothers to having a child with handicaps, *Ment Retard* 28:1-5, 1990.
14. McConachie HR: Home-based teaching: what are we asking of parents? *Child Care Health Dev* 17:123-126, 1991.
15. McNair J, Rusch FR: Parent involvement in transition programs, *Ment Retard* 29:93-101, 1991.
16. Olshansky S: Chronic sorrow: a response to having a mentally retarded child, *Soc Casework* 43:190-193, 1962.
17. Olson L: Parents as partners: redefining the social contract between families and schools, *Educ Week* April:17-24, 1990.
18. Reinhardt A, Adapted Physical Education Specialist, Stevens Point (Wis) Area Public Schools, 1992 [personal communication].
19. Sexton D: *Working with parents of handicapped children.* Presentation at the Institute for the Study of Developmental Disabilities, Bloomington, Ind, 1989.
20. Shephard RJ: The impact of exercise upon medical costs, *Sports Med* 2:133-143, 1985.

21. Sugars A: *The adapted physical educator as a member of the motor development team,* TAHPERD State Convention, 1990, Lubbock, Tex.

22. *Ten Truths of Parent Involvement,* Dallas Independent School District Bilingual and English as a Second Language Program, April, 1990.

23. Turnbull AP: The challenge of providing comprehensive support to families whose children have learning and behavior problems, *Beh Disord* 14:40-47, 1988.

24. Weiss SJ: Stressors experienced by family caregivers of children with pervasive developmental disorders, *Child Psychiatry Hum Dev* 21:203-215, 1991.

SUGGESTED READINGS

Falvey MA: *Community-based curriculum: instructional strategies for students with severe handicaps,* Baltimore, 1986, Paul H Brookes Publishing.

OBJECTIVES

Describe the types of equipment needed for elementary level adapted physical education programs and for secondary and college level adapted physical education programs.

List inexpensive equipment that can be used in the physical education program for children with and without disabilities

Identify ways in which special equipment can be used in the adapted physical education program.

Describe equipment that is now available to maximize the participation of individuals with disabilities in leisure, recreation, and sport activities.

Courtesy Stand-N-Go, Inc.

Facilities and Equipment

*P*roper facilities and equipment are as important for classes that serve children with disabilities as they are for the regular physical education program. They are as vital to quality instruction in physical education as are books and paper/pencils in the regular classroom.

In these days of endless budget cuts and fiscal crises, it is often difficult for the physical educator or adapted physical educator to secure the facilities and equipment desired. A dedicated physical education teacher or adapted physical education teacher must learn to provide a quality program with minimum facilities and equipment by using some imagination and improvisation. However, good facilities and equipment make the teacher's job easier, make the program more meaningful, and provide motivation for the student.

The facilities and equipment needed for children with disabilities may vary somewhat according to the type of students served. Children with disabilities receiving physical education instruction in the regular physical education program generally share the facility and equipment used by other class members. If the students receive physical education instruction in a segregated class, consideration must be given the following factors when making decisions regarding the type of facility and equipment needed. These factors include:

☐ The number of children in the class
☐ The age of the students
☐ The nature and severity of their disabilities

This chapter includes information about the kinds of facilities and equipment that should be provided in physical education classes that serve children, youth, and adults with disabilities at the elementary, junior and senior high school, and college levels.

FACILITIES FOR ELEMENTARY SCHOOLS
Facilities for Use in Regular Physical Education Programs

Facilities for physical education at the elementary school level vary extensively from district to district and from state to state. Most elementary schools have a small indoor gymnasium/play area and an outdoor playground area that is available for class use. Students with disabilities who receive physical education instruction within the regular physical education program share these facilities with children in their class. It is, of course, necessary to evaluate the facilities with regard to the safety of all the children. In addition, it is vital that the physical educator critically appraise the facility with the unique needs of children with disabilities in mind. The physical educator must ask the following questions regarding the learning environment:

☐ Is the indoor gymnasium/play area accessible for a child who is wheelchair-enabled, crutch-enabled, or walker-enabled?
☐ Can the child with a physical or neurological disability make an easy transition from the indoor gymnasium/play area to the outdoor play area?

☐ If the gymnasium/play area is not easily accessible, what accommodations can be made to ensure that a child is not limited by a disability?
☐ If the child is unable to make an easy transition from the gymnasium to the outdoor play area, because of stair steps, for example, what accommodations can be made to ensure that the child is not limited by the disability?
☐ Can the gymnasium/playground be modified to provide a safe and secure nurturing learning environment for all children?
☐ Is there an accessible washroom close to the gymnasium or playground area?
☐ Can all children, including children with disabilities, be safely evacuated from the gymnasium/play area in the event of a fire?

It is important for the teacher to understand that Section 504 of the Rehabilitation Act of 1973 and subsequent legislation, specifically the Americans with Disabilities Act of 1990, mandate that all new public facilities must be built to ensure access for individuals with disabilities. In the event, however, that the teacher is serving in an old building, the law mandates that a "reasonable accommodation" must be made to ensure the child has access to programs offered to other children. For example, if the primary pathway from the gymnasium to the playground is down a set of stairs, a child in a wheelchair may be unable to get to the playground using that route. A reasonable accommodation is for the physical education teacher to have the entire class use an accessible route, one with a ramp, for example, so that the child using the wheelchair feels part of the group.

The gymnasium and playground areas can be modified to make them more user-friendly for children with disabilities. For example,

☐ A constant sound source could be placed in the gymnasium or on the playground to allow the visually impaired child to orient self in both settings.
☐ A "safety strip," made of a material different from that of the major play area, could surround the gymnasium or playground area to warn the visually impaired/blind child of walls or fences.
☐ The playground area must be completely surrounded by fences if a severely emotionally disturbed child, an autistic child, or a behaviorally disordered "wanderer" is to be allowed to play outside.
☐ The gymnasium should be well-lighted to ensure best use by a child with a visual disability.
☐ The gymnasium should have good acoustics to ensure a child with a hearing impairment can hear the teacher's instructions.

□ The teacher should have access to a microphone to speak at levels that can be heard by a child with a hearing impairment.

□ Major equipment should be stored within the gymnasium always in the same place, to provide consistency for the visually impaired and autistic child.

Special Physical Education in a Less-Integrated Facility

Those children with disabilities who need to be physically educated in a less integrated program may need to receive services in a separate facility.

It is unusual, however, for children with disabilities who require physical education instruction in a more controlled environment to have access to their own separate special physical education room. Indeed, these children may receive their physical education instruction in the regular classroom, the auditorium, the cafeteria, or outside play areas. Adapted physical education teachers have been known to use any available free space to provide instruction, including hallways, foyers, and storage rooms.

Occasionally, school districts have attempted to meet the physical education needs of children with disabilities at the elementary school level by providing special centers, located strategically in the district, where the students can be taken for this important part of their educational experience. Students from a number of schools in the district are transported to the center where a specialist in adapted physical education, with a properly equipped facility, is able to offer them expert instruction with the assistance of specialists from the school district and other qualified personnel. This type of arrangement also may be used in school districts seeking to provide community-based leisure/recreation experiences for their students as part of the special physical education program. Children may be transported to a swimming pool, bowling alley, or miniature golf course where they receive instruction from trained personnel.

Another possible arrangement that can be used to provide better facilities and equipment for elementary school children who require special physical education in a segregated setting is to schedule children for a class at a nearby junior or senior high school where the adapted physical education room and equipment are available. Using this arrangement, classroom teachers of several elementary schools can bring their children to the nearby secondary school for an exercise and/or activity program conducted by a district specialist. Some modified equipment may be necessary for such a program, but the room and much of the equipment can be adapted for this type of class.

FIGURE 20-1. Physical educators must appraise play facilities with the needs of disabled students in mind. (Courtesy Collier Center for Communicative Disorders.)

EQUIPMENT FOR ELEMENTARY SCHOOL PHYSICAL EDUCATION FOR CHILDREN WITH DISABILITIES

As mentioned earlier, if children with disabilities are able to receive physical education instruction in the regular physical education program, they generally share equipment with the other children. The physical education teacher who serves children with disabilities in the regular elementary physical education program may wish to supplement basic equipment needed for quality elementary physical education instruction with additional equipment. The basic equipment needed for such a program is listed below. This list also represents the basic requirements for an adapted physical education program in a more restricted environment:

1. Locomotor skills
   A. Wide balance beams or balance boards (6", 8", 10", and 12" wide)
   B. Plastic "feet" for demonstrating foot placement on floor
   C. Large, oversized scooter boards
   D. Colorful, plastic tape for marking floors
   E. Plastic hoops
   F. Jump ropes
2. Manipulative skills
   A. Balloons
   B. Punch balls
   C. Assorted nerf-type balls for catching and kicking
   D. Assorted, including large size, playground balls
   E. Velcro paddles and Velcro balls for catching
   F. Wands with ribbons attached
   G. Small balls with ribbons attached
3. Low organized group games
   A. Huge group parachutes
   B. Cage balls
   C. Tug-of-war rope
4. Lead-up games for individual and team sports
   A. Oversize tennis and badminton racquets
   B. Oversize bats
   C. Nerf-type soccer balls, footballs, and volleyballs
   D. Junior size basketballs
   E. Adjustable basketball hoop that can be lowered
5. Tumbling and developmental gymnastics
   A. Floor mats
   B. Incline mats
   C. Carpeted barrels
   D. Inner tubes (covered for jumping)

6. Rhythms and dance
   A. Portable boom box
   B. Assorted tapes and records
   C. Music-making equipment (bells, drums, maracas, etc.)

Refer to "Sources of Adapted Physical Education Equipment" at the end of the chapter.

With some ingenuity, the teacher can provide an excellent adapted physical education program for students at the elementary school with minimum equipment. Play equipment can be made inexpensively. Following are suggested inexpensive equipment for use in the physical education program:

☐ Rope for skipping, making shapes, jumping over, or climbing under
☐ Cardboard boxes to climb in and through, to catch with, or to use as targets (particularly empty refrigerator, television, or washer/dryer boxes)
☐ Tape to make shapes on the floor for moving on, around, and in
☐ Chalk for making "own body" shapes/puzzles
☐ Half-gallon or gallon plastic jugs (this is also great for the recycling effort!) for catching, throwing, knocking over, etc.
☐ Scrap lumber for balance beams
☐ Yarn for yarn balls
☐ Carpet squares to skate on, slide on, sit on, or use as targets
☐ Cardboard barrels to roll in or throw objects into
☐ Old garden hoses to make hula hoops[15]
☐ Old ladder to walk on, through
☐ Traffic cones for obstacle courses
☐ Balloons
☐ Wire clothes hangers and old nylons (nylons suspended around the clothes hangers make inexpensive racquets)
☐ Bean bags
☐ Butcher paper
☐ Paper bags filled with sand for "barbells"
☐ Tin cans filled with cement, held together with pipe for "barbells"
☐ Dowel rods, cut into sections, for lumni sticks
☐ Rags, tied into knots to make balls

Play equipment for adapted physical education students at the elementary school level usually may be borrowed from the regular physical education teacher. Also, a wide variety of excellent specialized equipment for use by persons of all ages and most types of disabilities has been developed by numerous manufacturers. Any adaptations to modify the activities in terms of equipment or facilities can be worked out by the phys-

FIGURE 20-2. Equalizer 5000 home and office gym. (Courtesy Equalizer Exercise Machines.)

ical education teacher with the help of an adapted physical education specialist.

FACILITIES FOR SECONDARY SCHOOLS AND COLLEGES

Facilities and equipment for adapted physical education in secondary schools and colleges are usually far more extensive than those found in the typical elementary school. Once again, the Regular Education Initiative has integrated many adolescents and adults into the regular physical education program. These students share pre-existing facilities and equipment with other students.

Special Exercise Room

Occasionally, one room is designated for adapted physical education at the junior high school, senior high school, and college levels for those students who are unable to receive physical education services within the regular program. This specially designated room has become increasingly unlikely, however, given current budget constraints.

The size of the adapted physical education room, if it exists, and related facilities adjacent to it depend on the philosophy of adapted physical education program in each school and in each school district. The adapted physical education room is usually designed to handle a limited number of students. Since students in this program have individualized programs, fewer students can be handled satisfactorily than in the regular physical education class. However, it must be remembered that this room must accommodate special equipment that occupies a considerable amount of floor, wall, and ceiling space. A clear area also must be provided for exercises and activities that do not involve the use of special equipment. The room therefore must be of sufficient size to comfortably meet these special needs. The minimum size of an adapted physical education room for a junior or senior high school would be 40 by 60 feet if the room is limited to use by adapted physical education classes.[16] If the room is used as a multipurpose facility accommodating regular physical education classes for special kinds of activities such as gymnastics or wrestling, additional space is necessary.

This multipurpose arrangement has limitations, however, since much of the adapted equipment should be permanently installed on the floor, ceiling, and walls. An often-recommended 15-foot ceiling height is not sufficient if this room is also used for gymnastics or ball games, in which case the minimum height should be 20 to 25 feet.

A regular spring construction hardwood floor is preferred for this room, although parquet flooring has been used successfully in some facilities. The walls, at least to door height, should be of material that will withstand hard use (resistant to scarring and marking) and should provide for the mountings of special equipment. The ceiling may be of acoustical tile if ball games are not played in the room. High windows are suggested for two sides of the room to allow for ample light and fresh air and to provide space for equipment on all four walls. Proper lighting and ventilation are important for a special exercise room. Doorways leading to this room from the locker area, hallways, and fields should be extra wide, with ramps leading to them. This arrangement allows for the easy movement of equipment and for the passing of students with wheelchairs or crutches. Bulletin boards and blackboards should be mounted on the walls.

Considerable planning is required before the equipment is located in the adapted physical education room. Efficient use should be made of the available space so that students who are using special apparatus and equipment are able to use it effectively and so that hazards are not created while they use equipment such as barbells, the horizontal ladder, pulleys, and jump ropes (Figs. 20-3 and 20-4).

Recreation/Sports Area

A recreation/sports area may be located immediately adjacent to the gymnasium or adapted physical education room. This area should consist of blacktop and grass for multipurpose use and space for special games. Activities that can be conducted on the blacktop include volleyball, paddle tennis, badminton, and deck tennis. A smooth concrete area provides space for shuffleboard, quoits, table tennis, and other adapted activities. A grass or dirt area provides space for horseshoes and croquet. The horseshoe-pitching area must be carefully laid out to ensure safety.

Other adapted sport activities often can be conducted between or adjacent to the regular physical education classes that are using a facility. They also can be conducted when an area such as that for archery, tennis, or swimming is not scheduled for other classes.

Students in the modified program should have many opportunities to participate in activities that are similar to those engaged in by students in the regular physical

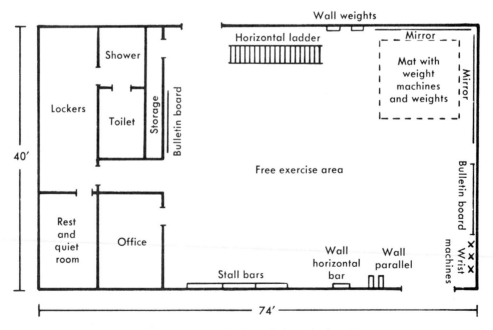

FIGURE 20-3. Self-contained adapted physical education room.

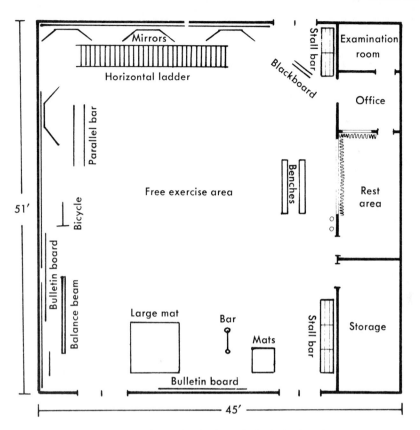

FIGURE 20-4. Secondary school adapted physical education room.

education program so that they can be mainstreamed into regular classes at the earliest possible time. Instructors of regular physical education classes can accomplish this by making minor adaptations in the games, sports, and activities that are being conducted in the regular physical education curriculum.

There is a recent trend toward the use of community and private facilities by students in adapted physical education. Nearby recreation centers, private pools, bowling alleys, special exercise facilities, and badminton, racquetball, golf, miniature golf, and archery facilities are often made available; and, in some instances, expert instruction is provided for persons with disabilities by the personnel at the facility. In the event that the personnel at the community-based and private facilities lack training, the adapted physical education specialist could offer a vital service by providing in-service instruction for the personnel.

Since swimming is such an important activity for persons with disabilities, every effort must be made to provide pool experiences for as many of the students as possible. A small, warm, therapeutic pool is an ideal facility for students with disabilities, but in most schools both hydrotherapy activities and swimming or scuba instruction for students with disabilities can be conducted in the regular pool. Some school districts have successfully used a portable pool (Fig. 20-5), which is put on a blacktop or grass area and then moved from school to school every 2 or 3 weeks so that all students with disabilities in the district can participate in a swimming unit. This works especially well at the elementary school level, where a pool is seldom included in the physical education facilities. Another practice for either a school or therapy unit for any age level is to use a portable pool built on a trailer. This type of pool can be drained and easily transported to different facilities for use without the expense of building a pool or the problems of labor and time required to move and set up a portable pool at each new locality.

FIGURE 20-5. A portable pool.

STUDENT ORIENTATION TO FACILITIES AND EQUIPMENT

Orientation for students with and without disabilities during the first week of school should include information on the rules that relate to the use of the physical education facility and its equipment. These rules include the following:

1. Students may participate in activity only with proper supervision.
2. It is necessary to be instructed in the use of any specialized equipment before using it.
3. Exercises and activities should be performed only when they have been assigned or approved for use by the instructor; careful instruction in the execution of each exercise must precede its use.
4. It is necessary to be instructed in the proper use and care of barbells, dumbbells, and other resistance equipment before beginning a progressive resistance program.
5. All equipment must be returned to its proper place immediately after use.
6. Information about any faulty equipment must be reported immediately to an instructor.
7. Hazardous types of equipment (weights, horizontal ladders, Stegel, trampoline, ropes, cargo ladder, etc.) must be tested by the instructor before being used by students, and spotters should always be present to prevent accidents and injuries.
8. Students must stop their exercise or activity programs and report to an instructor immediately if they experience undue pain, dyspnea, or general discomfort.
9. Students must be aware of the consequences for not following any of the above rules.

It should be noted that such orientation should be carefully done to ensure that all students understand the rules and know the consequences for breaking the rules. Rules and consequences should be posted in conspicuous places in the native languages of the majority of the students (usually English and Spanish). In addition, rules must be explained in a concrete manner to students with learning disabilities and mental retardation. The hearing-impaired student should be given the opportunity to read the rules and see a signed interpretation of the rules and consequences.

EQUIPMENT

The equipment needs of each of the special facilities just described are somewhat unique, depending on factors such as the number of students using each facility; whether the area is used for boys or girls or is coeducational; whether it is for elementary school, junior or senior high school, college, or community use; and whether minimum or ideal equipment is to be furnished.

Minimum Equipment

The minimum equipment needed in any special physical education room in a secondary school or college-level facility includes the following: sufficient individual 1-inch thick plastic-covered body mats to accommodate the peak class load plus five or six more, 2-inch thick mats of sufficient size to cover the floor under hazardous types of equipment such as the horizontal ladder or the horizontal bar, a platform or firm rubber mats to cover the floor where weight-training activities will take place, towels for use in the exercise program, a plumb line or posture screen for posture examinations, and miscellaneous inexpensive pieces of testing equipment such as measuring tapes and skin pencils. School benches usually can be obtained from the maintenance department of the school. Since resistance exercises are desired in most programs, homemade weights can be constructed by the instructor or by the students. Thus, with a minimum of expenditure, sufficient equipment can be obtained to start a good adapted physical education program. Special equipment for perceptual-motor training can be purchased or borrowed from regular classes or it can be improvised until funds are available. Equipment for most adapted sports can be borrowed from the regular physical education program.

Additional Equipment

Standard equipment for a special physical education room includes the minimum equipment already described and, if possible, the following items:

1. A posture screen and plumb line
2. Manufactured adjustable barbells and dumbbells and racks for their storage or resistive equipment constructed at the school
3. Stahl bars
4. A horizontal ladder
5. An incline board
6. A balance beam
7. Mirrors
8. Wide, padded benches
9. A multistation heavy resistance machine on which students can exercise a number of different areas of the body (this provides six to eight stations); if possible, a Universal Gym, Nautilus equipment, or other isokinetic machines should be used.
10. A stationary bicycle

FIGURE 20-6. A child examines her equipment. (Courtesy Dallas Independent School District.)

11. A stationary rowing maching
12. A stationary cross-country skiing simulator
13. Dynamometers and tensiometers
14. Treadmill

Equipment for leisure, recreation, and sports should include the following:

1. Archery
   A. Lightweight bows
   B. Large, fluorescent target faces
   C. Beepers to attach to target
2. Badminton
   A. Oversize racquets
   B. Oversize shuttlecocks
3. Basketball
   A. Adjustable height basketball standards
   B. Basketball standards with return nets
   C. Junior basketballs
4. Bowling
   A. Bowling ball with retractable handle
   B. Portable bowling ramp
   C. Wooden shuffleboard sticks for pushing the ball down the floor
   D. Lightweight balls with appropriate holes (4-6" balls)
   E. Beepers for target at end of lane
5. Goal ball
   A. Goal ball with beeper
   B. Goal ball nets
6. Golf
   A. Clubs with enlarged head size
   B. Fluorescent golf balls
   C. Fluorescent golf-size wiffle balls
7. Rhythms and dance
   A. Boom box with excellent bass adjustment
   B. Lumni sticks
   C. Tambourines
   D. Percussion instruments
8. Snow skiing
   A. Sit-skis
   B. Pulk skis
9. Softball
   A. Adjustable T-ball stands
   B. Beeper softballs
   C. Large, *soft*, softballs
   D. Oversize bats
   E. Fluorescent bases
10. Tennis
    A. Oversize racquets
    B. Fluorescent balls
11. Track and field
    A. Beep cones
    B. Guideropes with moveable plastic holder

12. Volleyball
    A. Beach balls, brightly colored
13. Waterskiing
    A. Sit-skis

Outdoor play equipment such as slides, swings, tee-ter-totters, rings, sandboxes, tires, and jungle gyms provide opportunity for a variety of perceptual-motor activities in the fresh air and sunshine. The equipment should be placed on grass or on a surface of shaved wood. Manufacturers have created playground environments that are accessible to children with disabilities. These include:

Barrier-free playground equipment	Mainstreamers Quality Industries, Inc. 2151 Mechanic Street PO Box 278 Hillsdale, MI 49242
Playground equipment for children with/without disabilities	Landscape Structures/Mexico Forge 601 7th Street S Delano, MN 55328

FIGURE 20-7. A tricycle provides an opportunity for development of motor competency. (Courtesy Dallas Independent School District.)

Evaluation Equipment

Evaluation equipment includes marked mats (or floor), stopwatches, yardsticks and metric tapes or sticks, targets, traffic cones, mats, ropes, hoops, beads, tapping board test equipment, and blocks. Some standard tests and test kits that might be used include the following:

1. Purdue Perceptual Motor Survey[11]
2. Stott Motor Impairment Test[13]
3. Individual Motor Behavior Survey and Diagnostic Motor Ability Test[2]
4. Frostig Movement Skills Test[9]
5. Draw-a-Man Test[8]
6. Visual Perception Test[7]
7. Fiorentino Reflex Tests[6]
8. The Ayres Space Test, Figure-Ground Visual Perception Test, kinesthesia and tactual perception tests, and motor accuracy tests[3]
9. Physical fitness tests by the American Alliance for Health, Physical Education, Recreation and Dance[9,12,14]
10. Bruininks-Oseretsky Test of Motor Proficiency[4]

LEISURE, RECREATION, AND SPORT FACILITIES AND EQUIPMENT

The Americans with Disabilities Act of 1990, P.L. 101-336, has expanded the federally mandated accessibility requirements of Section 504 of the Rehabilitation Act of 1973. The findings of the Congress included the following[1]:

1. Some 43,000,000 Americans have one or more physical or mental disabilities, and this number is increasing as the population as a whole is growing older
2. Historically, society has tended to isolate and segregate individuals with disabilities, and, despite some improvements, such forms of discrimination against individuals with disabilities continue to be a serious and pervasive social problem
3. Discrimination against individuals with disabilities persists in such critical areas as employment, housing, public accommodations, education, transportation, communication, **recreation**, institutionalization, health services, voting, and access to public services
4. Individuals with disabilities continually encounter various forms of discrimination, including outright intentional exclusion, the discriminatory effects of architectural, transportation and communication barriers, overprotective rules and policies, failures to make modifications to existing facilities and practices, exclusionary qualifica-

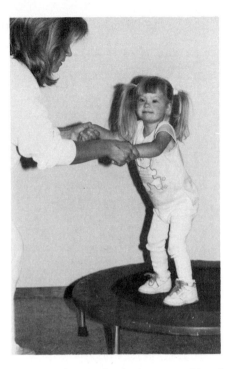

FIGURE 20-8. Equipment for the home provides play opportunity for child and parent.

tion standards and criteria, segregation and relegation to lesser servies, programs, activities, benefits, jobs, or other opportunities

In essence, the Americans with Disabilities Act of 1990 expands the mandates of Section 504 of the Rehabilitation Act of 1973. That law indicated that no individual can, solely on the basis of a disability, be denied access to publicly supported facilities and programs. The Americans with Disabilities Act of 1990 expands that to include privately owned public facilities. The law states that:

> No individual shall be discriminated against on the basis of disability in the full and equal enjoyment of the goods, services, facilities, privileges, advantages or accommodations of any place of public accommodation by any person who owns, leases (or leases to), or operates a place of public accommodation.[1]

In addition, the law mandates that individuals with disabilities should be able to participate in the programs and activities of the public facility in the most integrated setting appropriate to the needs of the individual. A reasonable accommodation must be made to ensure access. A reasonable accommodation may include modifications of rules and policies, providing access to assistive devices, or provision of support personnel.

Text continued on p. 486.

FIGURE 20-9. A safe and secure instructional aquatic environment. (Courtesy Wisconsin Lions Camp, Rosholt, Wisconsin.)

TABLE 20-1

Equipment for the disabled

Equipment/modification	Brand name	Corporation
Sport wheelchairs	Quickie's	Sunrise Medical 2842 Business Park Ave Fresno, CA 93727
Sport wheelchairs	Fortress Edge	Fortress PO Box 489 Clovis, CA 93613
Sport wheelchairs	Action's	Action Technology 34655 Mills Road North Ridgeville, OH 44039
Sport wheelchairs		SOPUR WEST, Inc. 601 East Sola St Santa Barbara, CA 93103
Sport wheelchairs	Max	Kuschall of America 753 Calle Plano Camarillo, CA 93012
Sport wheelchairs	Heat The Predator (hand-crank)	Top End 6551 44th St N, #5002 Pinellas Park, FL 33565
Sport wheelchairs	Avatar	Wheel Ring, Inc. 199 Forest St Manchester, CT 06040
Sport wheelchairs	Screaming Eagle	Eagle Sportschairs 2351 Parkwood Road Snellville, GA 30278
Sport wheelchairs for children	Hall's Wheels	Bob Hall PO Box 784 Cambridge, MA 02238
Sport wheelchairs Electric wheelchair Three-wheel scooter	Action Pro-T The Arrow	Invacare Corporation 34655 Mills Road North Ridgeville, OH 44039
Suspension wheelchair	The Iron Horse	Iron Horse Productions, Inc. 2624 Conner St Port Huron, MI 48060
Off-road wheelchair	Cobra	Up and Over Engineering 1509 Liberty St El Cerrito, CA 94530
Sport wheelchairs Easy-Stand	ALTimate	ALT, Inc. 913 South Washington Redwood Falls, MN 56283
Wheelchair/walker	Stand-N-Go	Stand-N-Go Rt 5 Box 22A Fergus Falls, MN 56537
All-terrain vehicles Hand-controlled (motor)		Recreative Industries 60 Depot St. Buffalo, NY 14206
All-terrain hand cycle	Quantum Leap	Quantum Leap 974 Pinson Blvd Rockledge, FL 32955
Electric scooter .Wheelchair van lift	Tri-Wheeler	Braun Corporation 1014 S Monticello Winamac, IN 46996
Wheelchair/standing box	Lifestand	IDC Medical Equipment 20 Independence Ct Folcroft, PA 19032
Transfer machine	EasyPivot	Rand-Scot Inc. 401 Linden Center Dr Fort Collins, CO 30524

Continued.

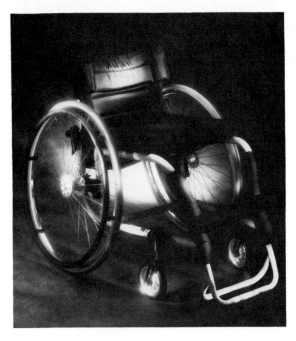

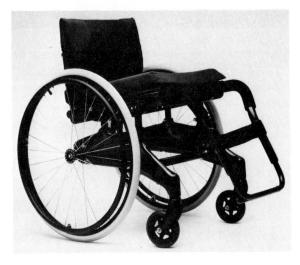

Action Pro-T—Aircraft aluminum high-performance rigid frame wheelchair. (Courtesy Action Technology.)

Action AC—Advanced carbon fiber composite wheelchair for everyday use. (Courtesy Invacare Corporation.)

The Arrow—A powered wheelchair controlled by a micro-computer control gives users with limited mobility a greater level of independence. (Courtesy Invacare Corporation.)

Stand-N-Go. (Courtesy Stand-N-Go, Inc.)

TABLE 20-1—cont'd

Equipment for the disabled

Equipment/modification	Brand name	Corporation
Wheelchair treadmill	The Bug Roller	Mclain Cycle Products 1718 106th Ave Otsego, MI 49078
Stationary aerobic hand cycle with: 　Limited-grasp handgrips 　Adjustable-loop handgrips 　Gripp Cuffs	Saratoga cycle	Saratoga Access & Fitness PO Box 2346 Clifton, Park NY 12065
Weight training machine	Versatrainer	Pro-Max Bowflex of America Inc. 2200 NE 65th Ave Suite C Vancouver, WA 98661
Weight training machine	Equalizer Home Gym	Helm Distributing, Inc. 911 Kings Point Road Polson, MT 59860
Weight training machine	Freedom Machine	2323 W Encanto Blvd Phoenix, AZ 85009
Weight training machine	FreeForm ProLink	James Design Co., Inc. 412 S Wade Blvd Millville, NJ 08332
Weight training machine		Moto's Custom Iron Works 3787 Shasta Dam Blvd Central Valley, CA 96019
Weight training machine	The Activator	Magic Industries 11906 Northeast Halsey Portland, OR 97220
Muscle stimulator/Exerciser	Power Trainer	Sinties Scientific, Inc. 1216 N Lansing Ave Suite B Tulsa, OK 74106
Prosthetic foot development	Seattle Lightfoot	Model & Instrument 861 Poplar Place S Seattle, WA 98144
Prosthetic foot	Quantum Foot	Hosmer Dorrance Corp. 561 Division St Campbell, CA 95008
Prosthetic foot	Natural Toes	Kingsley Mfg. Co. Costa Mesa, CA
Knee/ankle prosthesis	Endolite	1-800-LITE-LEG
Lower leg prosthesis	Flex-Foot and Flex-Walk II	Flex-Foot Inc. 27071 Cabot, Suite 106 Laguna Hills, CA 92653
Lower leg prosthesis	Swing-N-Stance	Mauch Laboratories 3035 Dryden Road Dayton, OH 45439
Para golf/golf Cart for wheelchair users		Para Golf PO Box 24303 Houston, TX 77229
Three-wheel racer	Shadow Racer	Magic in Motion, Inc. 20604 84th Avenue S Kent, WA 98032
Mono-ski (snow)	Shadow Mono-ski	
Mono-ski boot (snow)		
Hand-cycle attachment for wheelchair	Shadow Cycl-one	
Mono-ski (snow)	Yetti	Radventure, Inc. 20755 SW 238th Place Sherwood, OR 97140

Continued.

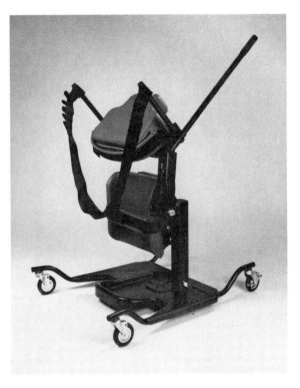

Easy Pivot EP-250, patient transfer machine. (Courtesy Rand-Scot, Inc.)

Tri-Wheeler. (Courtesy the Braun Corporation.)

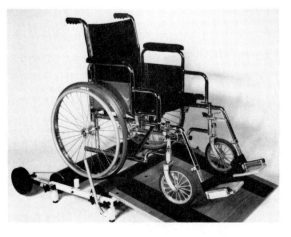

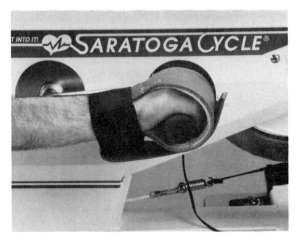

The Bug Roller for muscular and cardiovascular conditioning. (Courtesy McClain Cycle Products Corporation.)

Saratoga Gripp Cuffs for the Saratoga cycle. (Courtesy Saratoga Access & Fitness, Inc.)

TABLE 20-1—cont'd

Equipment for the disabled

Equipment/modification	Brand name	Corporation
Sit-ski (water)	Kan Ski	Kan Ski 2704 Hwy 99E Biggs, CA 95917
Ski pick (snow)		Innovator of Disability Equipment & Adaptations 1393 Meadowcreek Dr Suite 2 Pewaukee, WI 53072
Fishing rod holder	Strong-Arm	Strong Arm Fishing Products 2046A Pharmacy Ave Scarborough, Ontario Canada M1T 1H8
Rowing single shell	Pocock	U.S. Rowing Association
Double rowing shell	Pocock Double Wherry	
Rowing pontoon	Rowcat	
Adjustable basketball hoop	Rim Ball	Snitz Manufacturing 2096 S Church St East Troy, WI 53120
Automatic return basketball hoop		Jayfro Corporation PO Box 400 Waterford, CT 06385
Bowling ramp		Flaghouse, Inc. 150 N MacQuesten Pkwy Mt Vernon, NY 10550
Automatic grip release bowling ball		Flaghouse, Inc. 150 N MacQuesten Pkwy Mt Vernon, NY 10550
Custom-seat kayak		Gopher Sports Equipment 220 24th Ave NW Owatonna, MN 55060
Sports gloves for wheelchair athletes		Mega Bike 916 N. Western Ave #226 San Pedro, CA 90732
Racing rims for sport wheelchairs	Mistral M19A II	Sun Metal Products, Inc. PO Box 1508 Warsaw, IN 46581
Snow chains for wheelchairs	Sno-Traks	Handi-Trak, Inc. 1521 S 85th St Milwaukee, WI 53214
Wheelchair accessible motor home	Freedom Edition	Rehabilitation Equipment and Supply 311 N Western Ave Peoria, IL 61604

One of the most dramatic results of the emphasis on inclusion of individuals with disabilities in all public programs and facilities can be seen in the efforts of the National Park Service and the United States Forest Service. According to Ellis,[5] the National Park Service and the United States Forest Service have made a concerted effort to provide opportunities for individuals with disabilities to use and enjoy the programs and opportunities offered in the national parks. Ellis[5] has included some of the following national parks in a list of those accessible for individuals with disabilities:

- ☐ Denali National Park and Preserve
- ☐ Grand Canyon National Park
- ☐ Death Valley National Monument
- ☐ Sequoia National Park
- ☐ Mesa Verde National Park
- ☐ Rocky Mountain National Park
- ☐ Everglades National Park
- ☐ Gulf Islands National Seashore
- ☐ Mammoth Cave National Park
- ☐ Blue Ridge Parkway
- ☐ Prince William Forest Park

Modular III Flex Foot and Flex-Walk II prostheses. (Courtesy Flex-Foot, Inc.)

Swing-N-Stance, for lower extremity amputees. (Courtesy Mauch Laboratories, Inc.)

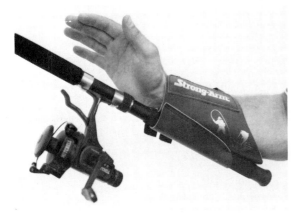

The Strong-Arm. (Courtesy Strong-Arm Fishing Products.)

The Tri-Rolls is a three-wheeled scooter designed for both rugged outdoor use and precise control indoors. (Courtesy Invacare Corporation.)

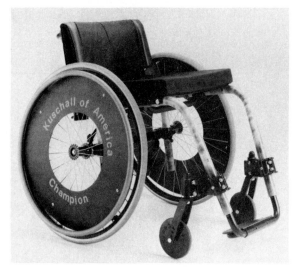

Champion 3000 ST. (Courtesy Kuschall of America.)

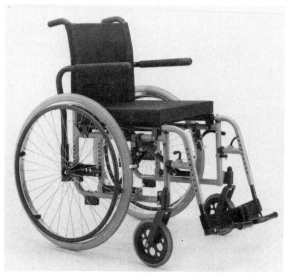

Champion 1000, folding cross-brace wheelchair swing-away footrest model. (Courtesy Kuschall of America.)

Racing chair. (Courtesy Top End.)

In addition to the impact on public leisure and recreation programs supported by the federal government, there has been a significant growth of leisure, recreation, and sport programs specifically designed to meet the needs of individuals with disabilities. For example, the "Classifieds" section of *Sports n' Spokes* routinely includes advertisements for vacation packages for individuals with disabilities, for sports training camps and programs for individuals with disabilities, and for integrated recreation and sport programs like Wilderness Inquiry.

Modification of equipment frequently enables individuals with disabilities to participate in leisure, recreation, and sport activities from which they would otherwise be excluded. Entrepreneurs have come to understand that individuals with disabilities are as serious about quality leisure, recreation, and sport activities as the non-disabled population. Within the past few years, there has been a remarkable growth in equipment that enhances athletic performance for individuals with and without disabilities. There are hundreds of types of shoes that can be selected specifically to improve performance in a given activity. There are also a wide variety of sport wheelchairs and modified equipment designed to improve performance in a given activity. There are now, for example, specific wheelchairs designed for sprint racing, distance road racing, basketball, tennis, rugby, football, and wilderness trekking. Some innovations in equipment and modifications of equipment for individuals with disabilities are listed in Table 20-1: (Please note: the inclusion of equipment on this list does not in any way indicate the authors' specific endorsement of the product; the list is included to provide a clear example of the extent of equipment modifications making possible the participation of individuals with disabilities in leisure, recreation, and sport activities.)

For more information about regular and sport wheelchairs, please refer to Sunderlin A: 8th annual survey of the lightweights, *Sports n' Spokes* 15:24-51, 1990.

SUMMARY

The student participating in the regular physical education program shares the facilities and equipment used by other students. In the event that the student requires special accommodation, specific equipment may be used to enhance performance. This equipment may be inexpensive. Always, the program must be innovative.

There have been major advances in the types of facilities and equipment now available to enhance the participation of individuals with disabilities in public leisure, recreation, and sports programs.

REVIEW QUESTIONS

1. What are six inexpensive (or homemade) pieces of equipment that might be used in elementary physical education?
2. What types of equipment would an elementary physical educator wish to include in an inventory if children with disabilities are included in the regular physical education program?
3. Describe a special physical education room at a middle school, high school, or college.
4. What types of sports equipment are available for individuals with disabilities to enhance their performance.

STUDENT ACTIVITIES

1. Collect five inexpensive items (e.g., milk cartons, boards, coat hangers, boxes, and hose) and construct equipment that could be used in an adapted physical education program and donate the equipment to a local elementary school.
2. Describe how three pieces of equipment used in a regular physical education program could be modified for use in an adapted physical education program.
3. Design an adapted physical education room using only the equipment available in a regular physical education program. Tell how you would use each piece of equipment.
4. Make up a list of equipment you would buy for an elementary adapted physical education room if you had $100 to spend.
5. Read current issues of *Sports n' Spokes* and *Palaestra: The Forum of Sport, Physical Education and Recreation for the Disabled* and notice advertisements for equipment/programs.
6. Attend a recreation/sport event that includes individuals with disabilities. Talk with an athlete about his or her equipment.
7. Secure a wheelchair. Go to a sport/recreation facility and determine its accessibility, via experience. Try to enter the building. Try to enter and use a restroom. Try to get a drink of water. Ask to sign up for a sports league.

REFERENCES

1. *Americans with Disabilities Act of 1990, PL 101-336,* National Mental Health Association, Alexandria, Va, 1991, pp 1-44.
2. Arnheim DD, Sinclair WA: *The clumsy child: a program of motor therapy, ed 2,* St Louis, 1979, Mosby—Year Book.
3. Ayres AJ: *Southern California sensory integration tests,* Los Angeles, 1972, Western Psychological Services.
4. *Bruininks-Oseretsky Test of Motor Proficiency,* Circle Pines, Minn, 1978, American Guidance Service.
5. Ellis WK: Accessible camping in the national parks, *Sports n' Spokes* 17:47-51, 1992.
6. Fiorentino MR: *Reflex testing methods for evaluating*

CNS development, ed 2, Springfield, Ill, 1973, Charles C Thomas, Publisher.

7. Frostig M: *Marianne Frostig Developmental Test of Visual Perception,* Palo Alto, Calif, 1964, Consulting Psychologists Press.

8. Goodenough RL, Harris DB: *Goodenough-Harris Drawing Test,* New York, 1963, Harcourt Brace Jovanovich.

9. *Health Related Physical Fitness Test,* Reston, Va, 1980, American Alliance for Health, Physical Education, Recreation, and Dance.

10. Orpet RE: *Frostig movement skills tests battery,* Los Angeles, 1972, Marianne Frostig Center of Educational Therapy.

11. Roach EG, Kephart NC: *The Purdue Perceptual Motor Survey,* Columbus, Ohio, 1966, Charles E Merrill Publishing.

12. *Special fitness test manual for mildly mentally retarded persons,* Reston, Va, 1976, American Alliance for Health, Physical Education, Recreation, and Dance.

13. Stott DH: A general test of motor impairment for children, *Dev Med Child Neurol* 8:523-531, 1966.

14. Sunderlin A: 8th annual survey of the lightweights, *Sports n' Spokes* 15:24-51, 1990.

15. Werner P, Rini L: *Perceptual motor equipment: inexpensive ideas and activities,* New York, 1975, John Wiley & Sons Inc.

16. *Youth fitness test manual, rev,* Washington, DC, 1961, The American Association for Health, Physical Education, and Recreation.

SOURCES OF ADAPTED PHYSICAL EDUCATION EQUIPMENT

BSN Sports PO Box 7726 Dallas, TX 75209 1-800-527-7510

Early Learning Materials ABC School Sypply, Inc. 3312 N Berkeley Lake Road PO Box 100019 Duluth, GA 30136 1-800-669-4ABC

Sporttime Select Service and Supply Co, Inc. One Sportime Way Atlanta, GA 30340 1-800-283-5700

Thingz From Bell 230 Mechanic Street PO Box 206 Princeton, WI 54968 1-800-543-1458

SUGGESTED READINGS

Schurr E: *Movement experiences for children: a humanistic aproach to elementary school physical education,* Englewood Cliffs, NJ, 1980, Prentice-Hall.

Sunderlin A: 8th annual survey of the lightweights, *Sports n' Spokes* 15:24-51, 1990.

Appendixes

Selected Assessment Tests

A norm- and criterion-referenced developmental scale.

Adaptation of the Denver Developmental Scale

STO: lifts head	Chin off table	1 month
STO: lifts head	Face 45° to surface	1½ months
STO: lifts head	Face 90° to surface	2 months
STO: arm support	Chest up, on forearms	3 months
Sit: head steady	Head upright for 10 seconds	3½ months
Rolls over	Completely two times or more	4 months
Pulls to sit	Head does not hang at any time	5 months
Weight on legs	Brief support of weight on legs	5½ months
Sits without support	5 seconds or more	5 months
Pulls self to stand	On a solid object	8 months
Gets to sitting	Without assistance	8½ months
Walks holding furniture	5 steps	10 months
Stands momentarily	2 or more seconds	11 months
Stoops and recovers	Pick and return without touching floor	12 months
Walks	Does not tip from side to side	13 months
Walks backward	Two or more steps	17 months
Walks up steps	Upright (assisted by rail)	18 months
Kicks ball	Without support	19 months
Throws ball overhand	3 feet	22 months
Balances on one foot	1 second two out of three times	26 months
Jumps in place	Both feet off floor at the same time	28 months
Broad jump	8½ inches, feet together	32 months
Balances on one foot	5 seconds	41 months
Balances on one foot	10 seconds	52 months
Hops on one foot	Two or more times	48 months
Heel-toe walk	Four or more steps, two out of three times	51 months
Catches bounced ball	3 feet, uses hands, two out of three times	52 months
Backward heel-toe walk	Four steps without falling off	60 months

Profile Chart for North Carolina Fitness Test

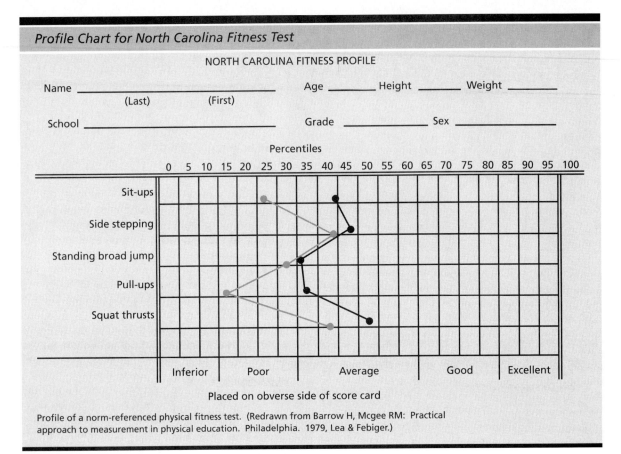

NORTH CAROLINA FITNESS PROFILE

Name _____ Age _____ Height _____ Weight _____
      (Last)   (First)

School _____ Grade _____ Sex _____

Percentiles

0   5   10 15 20 25 30 35 40 45 50 55 60 65 70 75 80 85 90 95 100

Sit-ups
Side stepping
Standing broad jump
Pull-ups
Squat thrusts

Inferior   Poor   Average   Good   Excellent

Placed on obverse side of score card

Profile of a norm-referenced physical fitness test. (Redrawn from Barrow H, Mcgee RM: Practical approach to measurement in physical education. Philadelphia. 1979, Lea & Febiger.)

Red Cross Progressive Swimming Courses

BEGINNER SKILLS

1. Water adjustment skills
2. Hold breath—10 sec.
3. Rhythmic breathing—10 times
4. Prone float and recovery
5. Prone glide
6. Back glide and recovery
7. Survival float
8. Prone glide with kick
9. Back glide with kick
10. Beginner stroke or crawl stroke—15 yds.
11. Combined stroke on back—15 yds.
12. Leveling off and swimming
13. Jump (shallow water), swim
14. Jump (deep water), level, swim
15. Jump (deep water), level, turn over, swim on back
16. Changing directions
17. Turning over
18. Release of cramp
19. Assist nonswimmer to feet
20. Reaching and extension rescues
21. Use of personal flotation device (PFD)
22. Demonstration of artificial respiration
23. Safety information
24. Combined skills no. 1
25. Combined skills no. 2

ADVANCED BEGINNER SKILLS

1. Bobbing—deep water
2. Rhythmic breathing to side
3. Survival float—2 min.
4. Crawl stroke
5. Elementary backstroke
6. Survival stroke
7. Treading water—30 to 45 sec.
8. Changing positions and treading water—30 sec.
9. Standing front dive
10. Underwater swim—3 to 4 body lengths
11. PFD—swimming
12. PFD—jumping into water
13. Artificial respiration
14. Basic rescue skills
15. Personal safety skills
16. Safety information
17. Combined skills no. 1
18. Combined skills no. 2
19. Combined skills no. 3

INTERMEDIATE SKILLS

1. Sidestroke—arms
2. Sidestroke—scissors kick
3. Sidestroke—coordination
4. Breaststroke—arms
5. Breaststroke—kick
6. Breaststroke—coordination
7. Crawl stroke—improve
8. Elementary backstroke—improve
9. Survival float—3 min.
10. Survival stroke—3 min.
11. Back float—1 min.
12. Sculling on back—10 yds.
13. Open turns—front and side
14. Open turn—back
15. Tread water—1 min.
16. Swim underwater—15 to 20 ft.
17. Standing front dive
18. Use of backboard—demonstration only
19. Donning PFD—deep water
20. Basic rescues
21. Artificial respiration
22. Safety information
23. Combined skills no. 1
24. Combined skills no. 2
25. Combined skills no. 3
26. Combined skills no. 4
27. Combined skills no. 5

SWIMMER SKILLS

1. Sidestroke—review/improve
2. Back crawl
3. Breaststroke—review/improve
4. Crawl stroke—review/improve
5. Surface dives—pike, tuck
6. Feet-first surface dive
7. Long shallow dive
8. 1 meter board—jumping entry
9. 1 meter board—standing dive
10. Stride jump
11. Inverted scissors kick
12. Sculling—snail and canoe
13. Open turn—front
14. Open turn—back
15. Open turn—side
16. Survival float—review
17. Survival stroke—5 min.
18. Underwater swim—20 to 25 ft.
19. Basic rescues
20. Artificial respiration
21. Safety information
22. Combined skills no. 1
23. Combined skills no. 2
24. Combined skills no. 3
25. Combined skills no. 4
26. Combined skills no. 5
27. Combined skills no. 6

Continued.

Red Cross Progressive Swimming Courses—cont'd

ADVANCED SWIMMER SKILLS
(must meet prerequisites)

1. Elementary backstroke—review
2. Back crawl—review/improve
3. Breaststroke—review/improve
4. Sidestroke—both sides, both kicks
5. Crawl stroke—review/improve
6. Overarm sidestroke
7. Inverted breaststroke
8. Trudgen stroke
9. Open turns—review/improve
10. Surface dives—review/improve
11. Survival float/survival stroke—fully clothed
12. Standing dives—review/improve
13. Jumping—1 meter board—review
14. Running front dive—1 meter board
15. Combined skills no. 1
16. Combined skills no. 2
17. Combined skills no. 3
18. Combined skills no. 4
19. Combined skills no. 5
20. Combined skills no. 6
21. Combined skills no. 7
22. Combined skills no. 8

Checklist of Gymnastic Vaulting Tasks

Test item 15 difficulty	Vault no. 1 skills
1.0	a. Knee mount
2.0	b. Squat mount
2.5	c. Straddle mount
3.0	d. Squat vault
3.5	e. Flank vault
4.0	f. Straddle vault
4.0	g. Wolf vault
4.5	h. Rear vault
5.0	i. Front vault
6.0	j. Thief vault
6.5	k. Headspring vault
7.0	l. Straddle half twist
9.0	m. Horizontal squat
9.5	n. Horizontal straddle
10.0	o. Horizontal stoop
11.0	p. Layout squat
11.5	q. Layout straddle
12.0	r. Layout stoop
13.0	s. Handspring vault
13.0	t. Giant cartwheel
14.0	u. Hecht vault
15.0	v. Yamashita
15.0	w. Handspring with half twist (on or off)

From Ellenbrand DA: Gymnastics skills test for college women. In Baumgartner TA, Jackson AS: Measurement and evaluation in physical education, Dubuque, Iowa. Copyright 1980 by WC Brown Publishers.

Checklist of Social Traits

Name_____ Date_____

Directions: Read each statement and think how it will describe your behavior. Put a check in the column that tells most nearly what statement is correct for you.

Always   Often   Seldom   Never   **Self-Direction**

_____ 1. I work diligently even though I am not supervised.
_____ 2. I practice to improve the skills I use with least success.
_____ 3. I follow carefully directions that have been given me.
_____ 4. I willingly accept constructive criticism and try to correct faults.
_____ 5. I play games as cheerfully as I can.
_____ 6. I appraise my progress in each of my endeavors to learn.

                                                                      Social adjustment

_____ 1. I am considerate of the rights of others.
_____ 2. I am courteous.
_____ 3. I am cooperative in group activities.
_____ 4. I accept gladly responsibility assigned me by a squad leader.
_____ 5. I accept disappointment without being unnecessarily disturbed.
_____ 6. I expect from the members of my group only the consideration to which I am entitled.

Always   Often   Seldom   Never   **Participation**

_____ 1. I am prompt in reporting for each class.
_____ 2. I dislike being absent from class.
_____ 3. I ask to be excused from an activity only when it is necessary.
_____ 4. I do the best I can regardless of the activity in which I am participating.
_____ 5. I give full attention to all instructions that are given in class.
_____ 6. I encourage others with whom I am participating in an activity.

Reprinted from Teachers' Guide to Physical Education for Girls in High School, compiled by Genevie Dexter, California State Department of Education. Sacramento, 1957, p. 318. Used by permission of the Department.

A checklist from a content analysis. There is no criterion for correctness. The list indicates what is incorrect, not what is correct.

Checklist for Rating Softball Batting Skills

Student's Name_____ Date_____

Rated by_____ Score_____

Directions: First check student's performance as good, fair, or poor on each item and then check deviations noted. Determine the student's score by assigning 1 point for poor, 2 for fair, and 3 for good, and totaling points.

	Rating	**Deviations from standard performance**
1. Grip	_____Good	_____Hands too far apart
	_____Fair	_____Wrong hand on top
	_____Poor	_____Hands too far from end of bat
2. Preliminary stance	_____Good	_____Stands too near the plate
	_____Fair	_____Stands too far from plate
	_____Poor	_____Stands too far forward toward pitcher
		_____Stands too far backward toward catcher
		_____Feet not parallel to line from pitcher to catcher
		_____Rests bat on shoulder
		_____Shoulders not horizontal
3. Stride or footwork	_____Good	_____Fails to step forward
	_____Fair	_____Fails to transfer weight
	_____Poor	_____Lifts back foot from ground before swing
4. Pivot or body twist	_____Good	_____Fails to "wind up"
	_____Fair	_____Fails to follow through with body
	_____Poor	_____Has less than 90° pivot
5. Arm movement or swing	_____Good	_____Arms held too close to body
	_____Fair	_____Rear elbow held too high
	_____Poor	_____Bat not held approximately, parallel to ground
		_____Not enough wrist motion used
		_____Wrists not uncocked forcefully enough
6. General (eyes on ball, judgment of pitches, and the like)	_____Good	_____Body movements jerky
	_____Fair	_____Tries too hard; "presses"
	_____Poor	_____Fails to look at center of ball
		_____Poor judgment of pitches
		_____Appears to lack confidence
		_____Bat used not suitable

Reprinted from Teachers' Guide to Physical Education for Girls in High School, compiled by Genevie Dexter, California State Department of Education. Sacramento, 1957, p. 315. Used by permission of the Department.

A content analysis of the breaststroke, with a subjective weighting of value of each component. Deficiencies are determined through study of the skill.

Breaststroke Whip Kick Weighted Checklist

Name_____ Evaluator_____

Date: pretest_____ posttest_____

	Weighted value	Check fault pretest	Check fault posttest
PHASE I. GLIDE PHASE			
1. Legs not fully extended	1	_____	_____
2. Ankles too far apart	1	_____	_____
3. Feet and ankles not in same plane as the body	2	_____	_____
4. Feet not plantar-flexed	2	_____	_____
PHASE II. RECOVERY PHASE			
1. Knees flexed too much or not enough	2	_____	_____
2. Hips flexed too much or not enough	2	_____	_____
3. Heels not brought close enough to the buttocks	2	_____	_____
4. Feet not pronated	2	_____	_____
5. Thighs not medially rotated at the hip joint	3	_____	_____
6. Feet not dorsiflexed	3	_____	_____
PHASE III. PROPULSIVE PHASE			
1. Legs are extended straight back instead of in a rounded or circular path	3	_____	_____
2. Feet travel laterally to an abducted leg position instead of in a rounded or circular path	3	_____	_____
3. Legs do not travel in the same or similar horizontal plane(s)	3	_____	_____
4. Legs travel in such a manner that the body is propelled toward or away from the surface of the water, instead of parallel to it	3	_____	_____
5. Vigorous action of the kick not sufficient to create an adequate propelling force	3	_____	_____
6. Legs actively squeezed together instead of coming together naturally	2	_____	_____
7. Feet not inverted as they come together	2	_____	_____
8. No inertial glide before the next kick is begun	2	_____	_____
Score		_____	_____

From Mansfield JR: The effect of using videotape and loop films as aids in teaching the breaststroke whip kick. Master's thesis, Pennsylvania State University, 1972. Used by permission of the author.

Golf Swing Classification

7. Excellent   Full swing, coordination and timing consistently produce full speed at contact, flight of ball straight, trajectory appropriate to club.

6. Very good   Does not achieve full swing, timing and coordination consistent.

5. Good   Some inconsistency in swing, contact good most of the time, does not achieve full power.

4. Average   Inconsistent in swing and contact, no major faults.

3. Fair   Inconsistent in swing, some faults in form, does not maintain body relationship to ball, contact erratic.

2. Poor   Several faults in swing, makes contact most of the time, but contact seldom produces proper flight.

1. Very poor   Many faults in swing, frequently misses ball, contact usually poor.

Relaxation Techniques

STRESS

Selye[19] suggested the existence of a general adaptation syndrome that occurs in animals and humans when they are subjected to continual emotional stress. This syndrome is composed of three consecutive stages: (1) the alarm reaction, which represents normal body changes caused by emotion; (2) the resistance to stress, or one's adjustment to the alarm reaction, which requires considerable energy resources; and (3) the exhaustion stage, in which the store of energy is used up. The exhaustion stage may lead to the death of single cells, organs, organ systems, or the entire organism. Some authorities have suggested stress as a possible cause of hypertension, rheumatism, arthritis, ulcers, allergies, cancer, and other conditions. An individual with uncontrolled stress has a high level of cerebral and emotional activity, coupled with nervous muscular tension, which may eventually lead to the exhaustion stage and perhaps to psychosomatic disorders. It is commonly accepted in medicine that long-term stress may lead to one or more disease states.[19]

THE RELAXATION RESPONSE
Exercise

Electromyographic studies show that neuromuscular tension levels decrease significantly with vigorous exercise, particularly in persons with high tension levels; however, effects are usually transitory.[8]

Some forms of exercise that result in a relaxed state are rhythmical motion, muscle stretching, and the physical exercise system of hatha-yoga, known as *asana*. Music and rhythm are used extensively to initiate coordinated movement and relaxation. Synchronization of specific movement patterns, as expressed through kinesthesia, is the basis for skilled activity. According to Rathbone,[17] rhythmical exercise relieves the feeling of fatigue and residual tension. Activities that are based on a continuous or even sequence of movement (e.g., walking, dancing, swimming, and bicycle riding) result in reduced tension. Muscle stretching, which increases joint flexibility, also tends to re-

duce tension within the musculotendinous unit. Therefore it is logical to presume that an articulation that is unencumbered by tight restricting tissue will also be one that is capable of relaxation. Stretching the body helps one overcome stiffness and allows the various body segments to relax. Research indicates that a steady progressive stretch tends to decrease the myotatic reflex and reduce muscle tension, whereas the ballistic or jerky stretch increases tension. Many of the asanas of hatha-yoga tend to improve joint range of motion. Each yoga posture is executed slowly and deliberately. Devotees consider that relaxation occurs as the mind and body become harmonious.

CONSCIOUS CONTROL OF MUSCULAR TENSION

The most easily learned beneficial means of reducing nervous tension is that of conscious control.[9] Physiological benefits from willed relaxation include reductions in oxygen consumption, respiratory rate, heart rate, and muscle tension.

There are several specific techniques that may be employed in relaxation training. Some of those that have been reported to work well include helping students (1) discriminate between tense and relaxed states of different muscle groups on the body, (2) give themselves a silent cue to relax while taking deep breaths and then slowly exhaling,[15] and (3) use audiotapes that include suggestions of heaviness, warmth, and calmness while concentrating on each part of the body from the feet to the head. Before beginning relaxation techniques it is helpful to practice some exercises to loosen muscles in the neck and shoulder areas (head rolls and neck and shoulder stretches). Cue-controlled relaxation can be practiced by pairing a silent cue word to the sensation of relaxation. Relaxation can be practiced in several positions—standing, reclining, straight sitting, and walking. Relaxation skills also may be used to reduce tension before or during anxiety-producing situations (e.g., an important test, a big athletic game, confronting an angry person).

Three excellent techniques for consciously reducing tension are progressive relaxation, autogenic training, and differential relaxation.

Progressive Relaxation

Edmund Jacobson, a physiologist-physician, is known as the father of progressive relaxation.[11] His technique emphasizes relaxation of voluntary skeletal muscles. During progressive relaxation training an individual becomes aware of muscular tension and learns to consciously release tension in specific muscle groups. Jacobson's system starts with muscles of the left upper extremity and moves to the right upper extremity, followed by the left lower extremity, right lower extremity, abdominal muscles, respiratory muscles, back pectoral region, shoulder muscles, and facial muscles. Persons are encouraged to gradually stiffen each body part and then to slowly release that tension.[16]

Progressive muscular relaxation is a standardized method that can be learned within a short period and can be practiced in the home.[6] Furthermore, according to Larson and Melin,[15] relaxation training can have positive effects on tension-type headaches of school children in a school setting. Moreover, recent reports show that a home-based relaxation approach may be as effective as a clinically delivered treatment.[12,21] The effectiveness of using audiotaped suggestions of heaviness, warmth, calmness, and regular breathing by Sorbi[20] further indicate the importance of extending relaxation training into the home.

Autogenic Training

Autogenic training in relaxation was devloped by H.H. Schulz, a German neurologist.[18] This technique is designed to reduce exteroceptive and proprioceptive stimulation through mental activity described as passive concentration. Using this method an individual brings to mind images that promote a relaxed state.

Autogenic training begins with phrases that suggest heaviness of the whole body and the individual parts, followed by phrases that suggest warmth or regularity to the body, heart, respiratory system, and abdominal area. A third set of phrases promotes images of colors and relaxing in warm, soft, pleasant surroundings.[18]

Differential Relaxation

Decreasing and increasing muscular tension levels at will require varying degrees of coordination. All skilled movement requires differential relaxation. A technique that has been found beneficial for training individuals to selectively control specific muscles is known as the muscle tension recognition and release method.[3,4] This technique starts with the subject tensing and relaxing the entire body and then learning bilateral body control (control of both upper limbs and then of both lower limbs). Following demonstration of bilateral limb control the subject advances to unilateral body control,whereby muscular tension is increased on one side of the body and completely released on the other—for example, with tensing of the right arm and leg and relaxing of the left arm and leg. From unilateral control the subject progresses to cross-lateral body control, which involves tensing of the opposite arm and leg. The last stage of differential relaxation training involves the isolation and relaxation of specific body parts at will. In general, differential relaxation training is a useful tool for developing total body control, increasing body awareness, and reducing anxiety. However, this technique should be limited to the particular developmental level of the individual. These techniques, used individually and in combination, reduce nervous tension and tactile defensive responses in children.[2]

Stress-Coping Training

Stress-coping training requires an individual to differentiate between desirable and undesirable states of tension (e.g., having no headache versus having a headache). The learner is taught to identify relationships between situations that create tension in the body, bodily sensations of distress, emotional states, and thoughts that lead to tension. To help a person discriminate between anxiety-producing situations and nonthreatening situations, the person should keep a log of circumstances surrounding the times when he or she feels tense and when he or she feels relaxed. Once he or she learns to identify tension-producing situations, he or she can begin practicing relaxation before or when confronted with these situations. In most medical settings, relaxation techniques are used in combination with some form of drug therapy. As a person improves his or her ability to relax through self-suggestion, drug use is decreased and, hopefully, eventually terminated.[7]

Benefits

Learning to relax is a motor skill and must be considered an important part of the total education program or physical education program. As a skill, relaxation must be taught and practiced for competency. Too often teachers of physical education are concerned with gross movement activities alone. To lie down when tired or to practice relaxation when tense or overanxious is considered a waste of time by many teachers.

This narrow point of view ignores an important aspect of the field of physical education—that relaxation is of special importance to many atypical as well as typical students.

A number of positive benefits can be accrued by disabled children who have conscious control of their tension levels. Energy can be conserved and better control of emotions can result (fears and anxieties become less intense). Sleep comes easier, the acquisition and performance of motor skills are enhanced, pain and physical discomfort become less intense, and the ability to learn may be improved. Relaxation therefore becomes a vital tool in the total machinery of the educational process.

To the physiologist, relaxation indicates a complete absence of neuromuscular activity (zero state).[16] The relaxed body part does not resist stretch but rather reflects the lengthening of muscle fibers. An overt sign of relaxation is a limp and completely motionless body part. Through relaxation of overly tense muscles, a number of positive effects may occur in respiration, circulation, and neuromuscular coordination.

Respiration

The reduction of tension in the thorax and muscles of respiration allows for a greater capacity of inspiration and expiration. With this increased capacity, there is a more efficient exchange of oxygen and carbon dioxide within the body. For persons with breathing disorders, relaxation of the thoracic mechanism allows for a greater respiratory potential.

Circulation

Relaxation of tense skeletal muscles allows the blood to circulate unimpeded by constricted blood vessels to all the body tissues. A person with cardiovascular disease is greatly aided when the ability to reduce muscular tension at will is achieved. Blood pressure may be reduced by diminishing outside resistance, which subsequently decreases the strain on heart and blood vessels.

Neuromuscular coordination

In order for the body to move uninhibited, there must be a smooth synchronization of muscles. Differential relaxation or controlled tension attributable to the reciprocal action of agonist and antagonist muscles provides for coordinated movement without undue fatigue. Persons who exhibit poor coordination as a result of neuromuscular or cerebral problems must learn to relax tense muscles differentially in order for their purposeful movement to be smooth, accurate, and enduring.

Experiments are being done to determine whether relaxation techniques can affect physiological functioning. One such group of studies has attempted to alleviate headaches through relaxation techniques. Larson and Melin[15] report that relaxation therapy alone led to significant reductions in headaches of school-aged children. They reported that children seemed to react in an "all or none" fashion (either the headache totally disappeared, or it continued with no relief whatsoever).

Much attention in clinical experimentation has been devoted to muscle contraction as an underlying cause of headaches.[5] Attempts have been made to control headaches with relaxation training of the frontalis (forehead) muscle through electromyography (EMG).[13] Cottier, Shapiro, and Julius[6] have indicated that relaxation does affect physiological measures. They found that responders to progressive muscle relaxation were characterized by faster heart rates and higher plasma norepinephrine levels. They also found that with progressive relaxation the treated group had a significant decrease of oxygen consumption compared to the control group. Furthermore, Agras[1] noted that relaxation training has a direct effect on catecholamines and results in the blocking of noradrenergic receptors. While there is evidence of physiological changes as a result of relaxation training, as yet it is difficult to apply these findings to daily living behavior. LaCroix et al.[14] concluded that the link between frontalis EMG results and "muscle contraction" headaches is a questionable one. Thus, according to these researchers, the changes brought about in headaches through biofeedback or relaxation training are most likely attributable to a generalization of feelings of mastery over the environment or an increase in self-esteem resulting from the subjects' apparent success at the task.

TEACHING A SYSTEM OF RELAXATION

Relaxation therapy is a treatment that involves teaching a person to achieve a state of both muscular and mental tension reduction by the systematic use of environmental cues.[10] Relaxation training focuses primarily on promoting a balance between the sympathetic and parasympathetic subsystems. For the most part it can be learned in a short period and produces an overall feeling of well-being and relaxation.[1]

The instructor of adapted physical education can teach a variety of relaxation techniques depending on the time and conditions available. As has been described earlier in this discussion, imagery and recognition of tension provide a convenient means of learning to relax. These methods may be combined and used with success in the typical 30-minute physical education period.

Identification of abnormal tension areas in the body requires the performance of a series of muscle contractions and relaxations. In this modified system of progressive relaxation, muscle contractions should be performed gradually and slowly for 30 seconds and then the muscles should be relaxed for 30 seconds in an attempt to obtain a "negative" state. The student is reminded to tense only the muscles the instructor indicates and to keep all other body areas relaxed while tensing a single part. Special consideration is given to the areas of the body that are difficult to relax—for example, the lower back and the abdominal, shoulder, neck, and eye regions. After the guided session, the student makes a record of the areas that were difficult to relax. Eventually, with diligent practice, the student will have to tense and relax only those areas that are difficult to relax. In doing so the student can achieve at will a general decrease of muscular tonus throughout the body.

Preliminary Requirements

In order for the student to develop a keen perception of tension and to learn to relax, the instructor should consider a number of environmental and learning factors that may strongly affect the ability to reduce body tension.

Room

The room in which relaxation exercises are conducted should have a comfortable temperature (between 72° and 76° F); it should be well ventilated with nochilling drafts. The light may be dimmed or turned off and signs posted outside to prevent interruption of the relaxation lesson.

Dress

The student should wear comfortable, warm, loose-fitting apparel and no shoes.

Equipment

In actuality, very little equipment is needed to teach relaxation. Ideally, five small pillows or rolled-up towels and a firm mat are useful; however, relaxation can be accomplished on any comfortable surface without the use of props. All students should have a pencil and paper nearby so that they can record personal reactions after the session.

Positioning

Although a person can learn to relax while standing or sitting, the ideal position for tension recognition is that of lying on a firm mat with each body curve comfortably supported by a pillow or towel (Fig. B-1). Contour support is afforded the curves of the cervical and lumbar vertebrae; each forearm is supported, resulting in a slight bend to each elbow; and the knees, like the elbows, are maintained in a slightly flexed position with the thighs externally rotated. With minimum support given to the body curves and limbs, free muscle contraction can take place while the individual is in a comfortable, relaxed position. However, if equipment for joint support is not available, a flat mat surface will suffice.

Sound

A number of techniques utilizing sound may be used by the teacher to aid thestudent in acquiring the right frame of mind for relaxation. Soft music playing in the background may be beneficial. If music is not available, the monotonous pattern of a metronome clicking at 48 or fewer beats per minute may be helpful. However, the most important sound is the voice of the instructor, which should be quiet, slow, rhythmical, and distant.

Breathing

During the relaxation session the student is instructed to take slow, deep inhalations through the nose and make long, slow exhalations through the

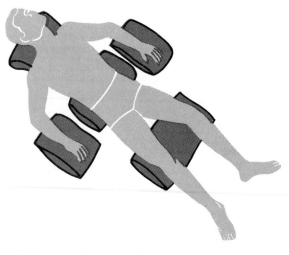

FIGURE B-1. Basic position for tension reduction exercises (see also Figures B-2 to B-18).

mouth. Gradually, through breathing control, the student consciously tries to let go of all the body tension. As relaxation occurs, breathing becomes slower and more shallow.

Imagery

The tension recognition technique involves two distinct phases: a contraction phase, whereby the subject contracts a particular muscle or group of muscles to sense tension; and a "let go" phase, whereby the subject seeks a complete lack of tension, or negativeness. To aid the pupil in the second phase the teacher encourages the use of imagery. The student is told to imagine very relaxing things. Image-inducing statements such as "your body is heavy against the floor," "your heart is beating regularly and calmly, like a clock ticking," and "listen to the sound of your breathing" may help the student relax. Children at the elementary school level have keen imaginations and respond readily to suggestions such as imagining their bodies as snowmen on a hot day or as butter in a hot pan.

Sleep

The pupil should be instructed that the main purpose of the exercise session is to develop awareness of tense body areas and the ability to relax consciously without falling asleep. However, if sleep does occur during the session, it should be considered a positive reaction.

Principles of Teaching Relaxation

There are a number of ways the instructor can proceed with relaxation guidance. The teacher can begin by having the pupils contract their facial muscles and then move downward to finish in the lower limbs or, conversely, by having them contract muscles from foot to head. If less time is available, contraction of large muscle groups with progression to the smaller muscles of the body is another alternative. Whatever the technique used, the goals are the same and the teacher will soon develop a style that seems to work best.

Because of the limited amount of time available in the physical education period, many sessions may be required before desired results are attained. A home program should be encouraged for persons who find it difficult to let go of tension.

Directions to the Student

For expediency in the physical education setting, each muscular contraction phase and each relaxation phase is conducted for approximately 30 seconds, providing a total of 1 minute for each step. During the in-

troductory session the muscle contraction should be intense enough to cause a degree of fatigue. The tension is reduced gradually with each subsequent session, requiring a greater perceptual sensitivity. The following is a sample of a relaxation session given to a group of students in a typical school setting.

Step 1: Lie still for a minute and stare at an object on the ceiling. Do the eyes feel as though they are getting heavy? As this occurs, gradually let them close. Take five deep breaths, inhaling and exhaling slowly. Think of all the joints of the body as being very relaxed.

Step 2: Curl the toes downward and point both feet downward toward the end of the mat (Fig. B-2). Feel the tension in the bottoms of the feet and behind the legs. Keep the mouth relaxed and continue to breathe deeply and slowly. While tensing one area of the body, all other parts should be relaxed. Now release the muscle contractions slowly, letting go to a complete relaxed state. Feel the body getting extremely heavy and sinking into the mat.

Step 3: Curl the toes and both feet upward toward the head (Fig. B-3). Sense the tenseness on the tops of the feet and legs. Remember not to reinforce the movement by tensing other parts of the body. Breathe easily and relax. Let go of the muscle contraction, allowing the feet and ankles to go limp slowly.

Step 4: Leaving the legs in their original position, with the knees slightly bent, press the legs down (Fig. B-4). Feel the tension in the back of the thighs and buttocks. Remember, while holding this contraction, all other parts of the body should be at ease. Relax, slowly feeling the discomfort of tension completely leave the body.

Step 5: Remain in the position as for step 4 and straighten the legs to full extension (Fig. B-5). Feel the tightness in the tops of the thighs. Now let go. Breathing should be easy and relaxed, and a profound sense of heaviness should be present throughout the body.

Step 6: With the legs and thighs in the original resting position, draw the thighs upward to a bent-knee position, with the heels raised from the mat about 3 inches (Fig. B-6). The tension should be felt primarily in the bend of the hip. Try to keep all other muscle groups relaxed. Return slowly to the starting position and then let go to a negative state again.

Step 7: Forcibly rotate the thighs outward (Fig. B-7). Feel the muscle tension in the outer hip region. Do not let tension creep into other parts of the body. Now slowly relax the hip rotators. Go limp.

Step 8: Rotate the thighs inward (Fig. B-8). Feel the muscle tension deep in the inner thighs. Relax slowly, let go of all tension, and let the thighs again rotate outward. Sense the body sinking deeper into the mat.

Step 9: Squeeze the buttocks (gluteal muscles) together tightly and tilt the hips backward (Fig. B-9). Muscular tension should only be felt in the buttocks and lower back region. Again, be aware of other tensions that may

FIGURE B-2. Step 2.

FIGURE B-3. Step 3.

FIGURE B-4. Step 4.

FIGURE B-5. Step 5.

FIGURE B-6. Step 6.

FIGURE B-7. Step 7.

FIGURE B-8. Step 8.

FIGURE B-9. Step 9.

FIGURE B-10. Step 10.

FIGURE B-11. Step 11.

FIGURE B-12. Step 12.

FIGURE B-13. Step 14.

FIGURE B-14. Step 15.

FIGURE B-15. Step 17.

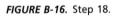

FIGURE B-16. Step 18.

FIGURE B-17. Step 19.

FIGURE B-18. Step 21.

be occurring in the body. Now let go of the contraction and try to sense the joints becoming extremely loose.

Step 10: Tighten the abdominal muscles by pressing downward on the rib cage while rolling the hips backward; at the same time, flatten the lower back (Fig. B-10). The tension is felt both in the abdominal muscles and in the lower back region. Inhale slowly and let the back settle into the mat.

Step 11: Inhale and exhale slowly and as deeply as possible three times (Fig. B-11). A general tension should be felt throughout the rib cage. After the last forced inspiration and expiration, return to normal quiet breathing and sense the difference in tension levels.

Step 12: Accentuating the curve of the neck (cervical spine), press the head back and lift the upper back off the mat (Fig. B-12). The tension should be felt in the back of the neck and upper back. Settle slowly back to the mat.

Step 13: Pinch the shoulders back, squeezing the two shoulder blades together. Tension is felt in the back of the shoulders. Release the contraction slowly and fall easily back to the mat. Be aware of any residual tension that might remain after returning to the mat.

Step 14: Leaving the arms in the resting position, lift and roll shoulders inward so that tension is felt in the front of the chest (Fig. B-13). Do not allow the shoulders to drop back to the mat in the resting position. Feel the tension leave the chest.

Step 15: Spread and grip the fingers of both hands. Do this three times (Fig. B-14). The tension is felt in the hands and forearms. As the fingers are gripped and spread, be sure not to lift the elbows from the mat. After the third series, let the hands and forearms fall limply back to their supports.

Step 16: Make a tight fist with both hands and slowly curl the wrists backward, forward, and to both sides. Tension should primarily be felt at the fist, wrist, and forearm. After these movements, allow fingers and thumbs to open gradually.

Step 17: Make a tight fist with both hands and slowly bend (flex) the arms at the elbows until the forearms rest against the upper arms, at the same time lifting the shoulders (Fig. B-15). Tension is felt in the front part of the forearms, in the bicep regions, and in the front part of the shoulders. After the arms are slowly uncurled and returned to the resting position, relax each segment separately until they become limp, motionless, and negative.

Step 18: Make a tight fist with both hands, stiffen the arms, and press hard against the mat (Fig. B-16). Tension should be felt in the forearms and the back of the upper arms and shoulders. Hold the pressure against the mat for 30 seconds and then release slowly.

Step 19: Shrug the right shoulder, then bend the head sideways (laterally flex neck), touching the ear to the elevated shoulder (Fig. B-17).

Step 20: As in step 19, shrug the left shoulder; then laterally flex the neck, touching the ear to the elevated shoulder. Tension should only be felt in the upper left shoulder and the lateral muscles of the neck. Release the contraction, slowly returning the neck and shoulder to the resting position.

Step 21: Bend the head forward, touching the chin to the chest (Fig. B-18). Tension is felt in the front of the neck. Relax and slowly return the head to the resting position. Continue to concentrate on the body as being extremely heavy and at a zero state.

Step 22: Lift the eyebrows upward and wrinkle the forehead. Feel the tension in the forehead. Let the face go blank.

Step 23: Close the eyelids tightly and wrinkle the nose. Tension is felt in the nose and eyes. Let the face relax slowly. Concentrate on the tension leaving the face.

Step 24: Open the mouth widely as if to yawn. Feel the tension in the jaw. Now let the mouth close slowly and lightly.

Step 25: Bite down hard and then show the teeth in a forced smile. Tension should be felt in the jaw and lips. Slowly allow the face to return to a blank expression. Be sure not to tense other parts of the body when contracting the facial muscles.

Step 26: Pucker the lips hard as if to whistle. Sense tension at the edge of the mouth. Let the tension melt away.

Step 27: Push the tongue hard against the roof of the mouth. Let go. Push the tongue against the roof of the mouth again as hard as possible. Relax. Push the tongue against the upper teeth. Relax. Sense the contraction of the tongue muscles. Try not to use any other body parts. Relax.

Step 28: Lie very still for a short while and try to be conscious of the body areas that were difficult to relax. Move slowly and take any position desired. Relax and rest.

Step 29: Try to hold the color of black or white in the mind's eye. Once you see one color, do not let any other color or picture slip into your mind.

Step 30: Roll to one side and sit up slowly.

Evaluation

Although the most accurate indication of abnormal tension is provided by electromyographic tests, subjective evaluation still has its place for the physical education instructor. Tension is easily observable through mannerisms such as extraneous movements or muscle twitches (eye twitches, finger movements, stiffness, changes of position, and playing with hands) and vocal sounds. The instructor should test muscle resistance by lifting the student's arms and legs after the relaxation session. Limbs that have residual tension do not feel limp or lifeless; they tend to feel stiff and unyielding. The instructor tells the student that he or she will be tested for relaxation at the end of the session. The following four factors may be made apparent by the tests: (1) whether the student assists the movement, (2) whether the student resists the movement, (3) whether the student engages in positioning body parts, or (4) whether the student ideally displays a complete lack of tension.

After the exercise session, the students are asked to answer questions about their personal reactions, writing their answers on a sheet of paper by their side. Some suggested questions include the following:

1. What was your general reaction to the session—good, bad, or indifferent?
2. Were you comfortable for the entire session? If not, what disturbed you?
3. Did you sense the tensions and relaxations at all times? If not, why not?
4. Were there areas of the body that you just could not continually relax? What were they?

Questions such as these help the student identify reactions to the relaxation session. The student may require a number of sessions before being able to identify tense body regions accurately. While learning to relax individual parts, the student will gradually be able to relax larger segments and eventually the whole body at will.

REFERENCES

1. Agras WS: Medical uses of relaxation training, *Paper presented at Grand Rounds,* University of Wisconsin, Department of Psychiatry, 1983.
2. Anneberg L: A study of the effect of different relaxation techniques on tactile deficient and tactile defensive children, *Unpublished master's thesis,* University of Kansas, 1977.
3. Arnheim DD, Pestolisi RA: *Developing motor behavior in children: a balanced approach to elementary physical education,* St Louis, 1973, Mosby—Year Book.
4. Arnheim DD, Sinclair WW: *The clumsy child: a program of motor therapy, ed 2,* St Louis, 1979, Mosby—Year Book.
5. Blanchard EB et al: Biofeedback and relaxation training with three kinds of headache: treatment effects and their prediction, *J Consult Clin Psychol* 50:562-575, 1982.
6. Cottier C, Shaprio K, Julius S: Treatment of mild hypertension with progressive muscle relaxation, *Arch Intern Med* 144:1954-1958, 1984.
7. Curb JD, Borhani NO, Blaszkowski TP: Long-term surveillance for adverse effects of antihypertensive drugs, *JAMA* 253:3263-3268, 1985.
8. DeVries HA: *Physiology of exercise, ed 3,* Dubuque, Iowa, 1980, Wm C Brown Publishers.
9. Frederick AB: Tension control, *J Health Phys Educ Rec Dance* 38:42-44, 72-80, 1967.
10. Jacob RS et al: Relaxation therapy for hypertension: comparison of effects with concomitant Piacaho, Diuretic, and B-blocker, *Arch Intern Med* 146:2335-2391, 1986.
11. Jacobson EO: *Modern treatment of tense patients,* Springfield, Ill, 1970, Charles C Thomas, Publishers.
12. Jurish SE et al: Home- versus clinic-based treatment of vascular headache, *J Consult Clin Psychol* 51:749-751, 1983.
13. LaCroix JM: Mechanisms of biofeedback control on the importance of verbal (conscious) processing. In Davidson RJ, Schwartz GE, Shaprio, editors: *Consciousness and self-regulation: advances in research, vol 4,* New York, 1986, Plenum.
14. LaCroix et al: Physiological changes after biofeedback and relaxation training for multiple-pain tension-headache patients, *Percept Mot Skills* 63:139-153, 1986.
15. Larson B, Melin C: Chronic headaches in adolescents: treatment in a school setting with relaxation training as compared with information-contact and self-regulation, *Pain* 25:325-336, 1986.
16. Moback R: The promise of biofeedback: don't hold the party yet, *Psychology Today* 9:18-22, 80-81, 1975.
17. Rathbone JL: *Relaxation,* Philadelphia, 1969, Lea & Febiger.
18. Schulz HH, Luthe W: *Autogenic training,* New York, 1959, George A Straton, Inc.
19. Selye H: *The stress of life,* New York, 1976, McGraw-Hill Book Co.
20. Sorbi M, Tellegen B: Differential effects of training in relaxation and stress coping in patients with migraine, *Pain* 29:473-481, 1986.
21. Teders SJ et al: Relaxation training for tension headache: comparative efficacy and cost effectiveness of a minimal therapist contact versus a therapist-delivered procedure, *Behav Ther* 15:59-70, 1984.

SUGGESTED READINGS

Davidson RJ, Schwartz GE, Shapiro D: Consciousness and self-regulation: advances in research, New York, 1986, Plenum.
Larson B: Chronic headaches in adolescents: treatment in a school setting with relaxation training as compared with information-contact and self-regulation, *Pain* 25:325-336, 1986.

Glossary

A

ABC analysis Functional analysis of a behavior in a systematic way to determine the antecedent, behavior, and consequence of an act.

Abdominal pumping An exercise to increase circulation of the blood through the pelvic region.

accountability To the physical educator this means being responsible for ensuring that the physical education programs provided to students with disabilities ultimately lead to independent functioning in the community.

Acquired Immunodeficiency Syndrome (AIDS) A disease that gradually destroys the body's immune system and eventually results in death.

acute Condition having a quick onset and a short duration.

ADA Americans with Disabilities Act of 1990, P.L. 191-336, expanded the federally mandated accessibility and participation requirements of Section 504 of the Rehabilitation Act of 1973.

Adam's position Position to determine the extent to which a scoliosis is structural. The subject bends over from the waist with arms relaxed in a hanging position.

adapted physical education The art and science of assessment and prescription within the psychomotor domain to ensure that an individual with a disability has access to programs designed to develop physical and motor fitness, fundamental motor skills and patterns, and skills in aquatics, dance, and individual and group games and sports so that the individual can, ultimately, participate in community-based leisure, recreation, and sport activities and, as such, enjoy an enhanced quality of life.

adapted physical educator A professional with specialized training in evaluating, designing, and implementing specialized physical education programs.

adaptive behavior The effectiveness of adapting to the natural and social demands of one's environment.

adaptive skill areas Communication, home living, community use, health and safety, leisure, self-care, social skills, self-direction, functional academics, and work.

adult-initiated activity Social activity that is initiated by another person.

adventitious blindness Acquired conditions causing loss of sight.

adverse physical performance A condition that exists when a child's performance level is below the performance standard of the majority of students in the regular physical education class.

aerobics A progressive conditioning program that stimulates circulorespiratory activity for a time sufficient to produce beneficial changes in the body.

aggression Offensive action or procedure.

agonist Muscle that is directly engaged in action.

allergy Hypersensitive reaction to certain foreign substances that are harmless in similar amounts to nonsensitive individuals.

Amendments to the Education of the Handicapped Act Federal legislation that required states to collect data to determine the anticipated service needs for children with disabilities.

Amendments to the Elementary and Secondary Act Federal legislation creating the Bureau of Education for the Handicapped.

anatomic task analysis Evaluation of the functional level of ability of specific muscles that contribute to a pattern of a skill.

anemia Condition of the blood in which there is a deficiency of hemoglobin.

ankle and foot pronation Abnormal turning of the ankle downward and medially (eversion and abduction)

ankle and foot supination Position of the foot when it is turned inward (inversion and adduction)

ankylosis Abnormal immobility of a joint (fusion)

antagonist Muscle that opposes the action of another muscle.

antigravity muscles Muscles that keep the body in an upright posture.

aphasia Impairment in use of words as symbols of ideas.

arthritis Inflammation of a joint.

asocial Not knowing or exhibiting the expected normative behavior of the group.

Asperger's syndrome A condition known as "high level autism" that shares many of the same symptoms as classic autism, but that also includes motor clumsiness and a family history of Asperger traits.

assistive technology personnel Specially trained professionals who provide assistive technology services.

assistive technology service Any service that directly assists an individual with a disability in the selection, acquisition, or use of an assistive technology device.

asthma Labored breathing associated with a sense of constriction in the chest.

astigmatism Refractive error caused by an irregularity in the curvature of the cornea of the lens; vision may become blurred.

asymmetric tonic neck reflex A reflex that causes extension of the arm on the face side and flexion of the arm on the posterior skull side when the head is turned.

ataxia Clinical type of cerebral palsy that is characterized by a disturbance of equilibrium.

athetoid Clinical type of cerebral palsy that is characterized by uncoordinated movements of the voluntary muscles, often accompanied by impaired muscle control of the hands and impaired speech and swallowing.

atonia Clinical type of cerebral palsy that is characterized by a lack of muscle tone.

at-risk infants, children, and adolescents Individuals whose development is jeopardized by factors that include poverty, homelessness, prenatal and postnatal maternal neglect, environmental deprivation, child abuse, violence, drug abuse, and racism.

atrophy Wasting away of muscular tissue.

attention-deficit disorder—residual (AD-R) The adolescent or young adult who has not outgrown the attention-deficit disorder.

attention-deficit disorder without hyperactivity (ADD) Loss of thought patterns, shifts from initial impressions, delays in delivery responses, and delays in recalling names and descriptions.

attention-deficit hyperactivity deficit (ADHD) A condition characterized by short attention span, easy distractibility, impulsivity, restlessness, poor listening skills, and inappropriate excessive motor activity.

audible ball A ball that emits a beeping sound for easy location. It is used in activity for the blind.

audible goal locators Motor-driven noisemakers that enable the visually impaired to position objects in space.

audiologist A specially trained professional who can provide comprehensive evaluations of individuals' hearing capabilities.

aura Warning (sound, feeling, sight) preceding a seizure

autism *See* classic autism

B

backward chaining The last of a series of steps is taught first.

barrel chest Abnormally rounded chest.

behavior modification Changing of behavioral characteristics through application of learning principles.

behavioral objectives Objectives that contain an action, conditions, and criteria and that have not been mastered by the learner.

bilateral Pertaining to two sides.

blind Lacking the sense of sight.

BMR Basal metabolism rate; expenditure of energy of the body in a resting state.

body image System of ideas and feelings that a person has about his or her structure.

body righting Reflex that enables segmental rotation of the trunk and hips when the head is turned.

bronchial asthma Condition that affects the respiratory system and usually results from allergic states in which there is an obstruction of the bronchial tubes, the lungs, or a combination of both.

C

cancer A cellular malignancy resulting in loss of normal cell function and uncontrolled cell growth.

cataract A condition in which the normally transparent lens of the eye becomes opaque.

central deafness Condition in which the receiving mechanism of hearing functions properly, but an abnormality in the central nervous system prevents one from hearing.

cephalocaudal control Gross motor control that starts with the head and progresses down the axial skeleton to the feet.

cerebral palsy Conditions in which damage inflicted to the brain resulted in a motor function disorder.

chaining Leading a person through a series of teachable components of a motor task.

chromosomal anomalies Chromosomal patterns that differ from normal.

chronic Condition having a gradual onset and a long duration.

chronologic-age–appropriate skills Culturally appropriate skills performed by normal persons.

circumduction Moving a part in a manner that describes a cone.

classic autism A disorder originally known as Kanner's syndrome. Characteristics include global language disorder, abnormal (bizarre) behavior patterns, social isolation, and usually, but not always, mental retardation.

community-based assessment Assessment that focuses on skills needed to live independently in the community.

community-based physical education programs Physical education curricula that focus on behaviors and skills that an adult will be able to use in the community environment.

community-based programming Activities that enable acquisition of skills through habilitation/education and lead to independent living in the community.

competencies Predetermined standards of behavior.

competition Intense participation between performers using skills to their best advantage.

component building Pairing of a positive and a neutral event, then fading the positive in such a manner that there is transfer from the positive to the neutral to make the neutral positive.

component model of functional routines Breaking down a person's daily sport and other physical activities into a series of routines that are composed of several skills.

condition shifting program Program in which several conditions of behavioral objectives are altered to produce activities that are sequenced from lesser to greater difficulty.

conditions A description of *how* the learner is to perform an objective.

conductive hearing loss   Condition in which the intensity of sound is reduced before reaching the inner ear, where the auditory nerve begins.

congenital   Present at birth.

content analysis   Breaking a task down into teachable components.

content-referenced assessment   The process of determining which activities or components of a task have and have not been mastered.

content-referenced social assessment   The acquisition of information about what an individual can and cannot do within the context of social sport and play activities of the specific physical education curriculum of a given school district.

contingency   An agreement between the student and the teacher that indicates what the student must do to earn a specific reward.

contingency observation   A technique in which an error is corrected by taking the person out of the activity to observe a peer doing the behavior correctly.

contracture (muscle)   Abnormal contraction of a muscle.

cooperation   The ability to work with others to achieve a common group goal.

cooperative learning   Working together to carry out responsibilities and reach common goals.

corrective physical education   Activity designed to habilitate or rehabilitate deficiencies in posture or mechanical alignment of the body.

corrective therapy   System of therapy using physical activities for the rehabilitation of a disability.

coxa plana   Also known as Legg-Calvé-Perthes disease; avascular, necrotic flattening of the head of the femur.

coxa valga   Increase in the angle of the neck of the head of the femur to more than 120 degrees.

coxa vara   Decrease in the angle of the neck of the head of the femur to less than 120 degrees.

criterion   The standard for mastery of an objective.

criterion-referenced tests   A test that is constructed to give scores that tell what types of behaviors individuals can demonstrate.

critical function   Objectives and goals that enable immediate and meaningful improvement of function in school and the community setting.

cross-lateral integration   The ability to coordinate use of both sides of the body.

curriculum-based assessment and programming   A system in which students are evaluated and classified in relation to their ability to learn a specific curriculum content.

cycle constancy   The continual recurrence of a specific motor task within similar time periods.

D

data-based curriculum   Curricula composed of goals and objectives of functional motor skills.

deaf   Nonfunctional hearing for the ordinary purposes of life.

delay of gratification   Ability to control emotional responses so one's social status in a group is not jeopardized.

development   Proceeding from lower to higher; progression; process of growing to maturity.

developmental checklist   A task list of chronologically sequenced behaviors in prerequisite order selected from developmental scales.

developmental delay   Retarded or arrested stages of performance that hinder a child's ability to be successful at a task.

developmental disabilities   A term to describe all disabilities collectively.

Developmental Disabilities Assistance and Bill of Rights Act   Federal legislation that affirmed the rights of the mentally retarded and other developmentally disabled individuals.

developmental teaching approach (bottom, up)   Intervening in a child's life as early as possible to eliminate deficits in input systems, abilities, and skills.

deviant   When some characteristic is judged different by others who consider the characteristic of importance and who view this difference negatively.

diabetes   A chronic metabolic disorder in which the cells cannot use glucose.

diagnostic-prescriptive integrity   A direct relationship between the assessment and the programming to remediate the assessed disabilities.

differential reinforcement of high rates   Provision of reinforcement when high rates of desirable behavior are demonstrated.

differential reinforcement of low rates   Reinforcing inappropriate behaviors as they are gradually decreased. For instance, a child who acts out in class is reinforced as the behavior is reduced.

differential reinforcement of other behaviors   A reinforcer is delivered after any response except the undesirable target response.

differentiation to integration   Isolated movements of body parts become differentiated, and partial patterns emerge to permit purposive movement.

direct service   Such services as physical education that provide instruction in the curricula designed by the schools.

directionality   Perception of direction in space.

disability   An obstacle.

disabled   An individual with physical, social, or psychologic variations that significantly interfere with normal growth and development.

discrimination   The cognitive ability to detect variations between sensory stimuli.

dislocation   Abnormal displacement of a bone in relation to its position in a joint.

disorder   General mental, physical, or psychologic malfunction of the processes.

displacement   Disguising of a particular goal by substituting another in its place.

distal   A point away from an origin, as opposed to proximal.

domain-referenced assessment   Tests a specific behavior to measure a general ability from which inference's are made about a student's general capability.

domain-referenced test A test that measures a general ability.

dorsal Refers to back, back of hand, back of thoracic region, or top of foot.

dorsiflexion The act of bending the foot upward (flexion).

drug therapy The use of drugs to relieve symptoms and to control unusual aggressive behaviors or other types of behaviors that interfere with learning and social interaction.

duration recording The length of time a behavior occurs.

dynamic balance The ability to maintain equilibrium while moving.

dysmenorrhea Painful menstruation.

E

ecologic inventory A checklist of behaviors the learner should master to become self-sufficient in the natural environment.

Education of the Handicapped Act Preferred title for the Education for All Handicapped Children Act of 1975 (PL 94-142).

Education for All Handicapped Children Act of 1975 Federal legislation that created a free appropriate public education for all handicapped children between the ages of 3 and 21 years.

Education of the Handicapped Amendments of 1986 Federal legislation mandating states to develop comprehensive interdisciplinary services for handicapped infants, birth through age 2 years, and to expand services for preschool children ages 3 through 5 years.

education accountability A particular educational program, method, or intervention can be demonstrated to cause a significant positive change in one or more behaviors.

educational integrity Evidence that the educational process is of value to the individual.

educational validity An educational program that contributes to meaningful independent participation in activities.

electromyogram Recording of the action potential of skeletal muscles.

Elementary and Secondary Education Act Federal legislation that enabled the states and local school districts to develop programs for economically disadvantaged children.

empirical validity Evidence that a particular accomplishment contributes to a person's ability to participate in current and future environments and activities.

epilepsy Disturbance in electrochemical activity of the brain that causes seizures and convulsions.

epiphysis Ossification center at the end of each developing long bone.

equal educational opportunity Compensatory education provided to children with disabilities that enables attainment of equal benefits or educational goals as compared with children without disabilities.

equally effective education Education that is not identical but that provides opportunity to achieve equal benefit or

goals through the individual education program (IEP) in the least restrictive environment.

equilibrium reactions A reflex that helps a person maintain an upright position when the center of gravity is suddenly moved beyond the base of support.

esophoria A tendency for an eye to deviate medially toward the nose.

esoptropia A condition in which the eyes turn inward, such as cross-eyes.

etiology Study of the origin of disease (term often misused for "cause").

event recording Noting the number of times a specifically defined behavior occurs within a time interval.

eversion Lifting the outer border of the foot upward.

exercise intensity Amount of work load in relation to the functional capacity of the individual.

exercise-induced asthma Muscular constriction of the bronchial tubes resulting from excessive and prolonged exercise.

exophoria A tendency for an eye to deviate laterally away from the nose.

exotropia A condition wherein an eye deviates laterally away from the nose.

extension Movement of a part that increases a joint angle.

external evaluation Refers to a situation in which a person independent of the project evaluates the extent to which predetermined behaviors are acquired by pupils and also the processes employed for achieving objectives.

extinction Removal of reinforcers that previously followed the behavior.

extrinsic Originating outside a part.

F

fading Gradually withdrawing help from a task.

fascial stretch An exercise designed to stretch the shortened fascial ligamentous bands that extend between the low back and anterior aspect of the pelvis and legs.

form objective Defining how a skill is to be executed.

formative assessment Determination of whether a student's form or techniques replicate a defined model of performance.

forward chaining The first step of a series of tasks is taught first.

functional adaptation Modification by using assistive devices or by changing the demands of a task to permit participation.

functional physical fitness tests Assessment instruments that relate specifically to what an individual needs to meet the daily demands of the environment.

fundamental motor skills Motor skills that are generic to several specific sport skills, such as catching, striking, kicking, and throwing.

G

gait Walking pattern.

gallop A gain in which a leap is followed by a small step on the trailing foot, followed by another leap.

general abilities Prerequisites, such as strength, flexibility, and endurance, to performance of specific motor skills.

general intellectual functioning Assessment of performance on an IQ test.

generalization The transfer of abilities and skills from the training to nontraining environments.

generalization variables Factors that affect the ability of an individual to generalize.

general-to-specific The progression of motor development from mass undifferentiated movements to specific voluntary motor control.

genu recurvatum Hyperextension at the knee joint.

genu valgum Knock-knee.

genu varum Bowleg.

glaucoma A condition in which the pressure of the fluid inside the eye is too high, causing loss of vision.

goal A measurable, observable behavior achieved through attainment of several short-term instructional objectives.

goal ball A game for the blind in which gross motor movement is a response to auditory stimuli in a ball.

grand mal seizure Seizure that involves severe convulsions accompanied by stiffening, twisting, alternating contractions and relaxations, and unconsciousness.

gross motor to fine motor control The individual gains control over large muscles before small muscles.

growth Development of or increased size of a living organism.

H

habilitation An educational term that indicates the person with a disability is to be taught basic skills needed for independence.

hallux valgus (pl. halluces) Displacement of the great toe toward the other toes, as occurs with a bunion.

Handicapped Children's Protection Act Federal legislation permitting reimbursement of attorney's fees to parents forced to go to court to secure appropriate education for their child with a disability.

hard-or-hearing Conditions of hearing impairment or persons who have hearing impairments but who can function with or without a hearing aid.

health-related tests Assessment instruments that include measures of cardiovascular endurance, muscular strength, percent body fat, and flexibility.

hemoplegia Neurologic affliction of one half of the body or the limbs on one side of the body.

hernia Protrusion of an organ through an abnormal opening.

heteroptropias Malalignments of the eyes in which one or both eyes consistently deviate from the central axis.

hierarchy A continuum of ordered activities in which a task of lower order and lesser difficulty is prerequisite to acquisition of a related task of greater difficulty.

Hodgkin's disease A chronic condition in which large multinucleated reticulum cells are present in lymph node tissue or in other nonreticular formation sites.

hopping Taking off from one foot into a flight phase and landing on the same foot.

hospital/homebound instructors Trained professionals who provide special education instruction to children who are hospitalized or homebound, and, as such, cannot be educated within the typical school setting.

hyperactivity Excessive activity of an individual.

hyperglycemia A type of diabetes that results in too much blood sugar.

hyperopia A condition in which the light rays focus behind the retina, causing an unclear image of objects closer than 20 feet from the eye.

hyperphoria A tendency for an eye to deviate in an upward direction.

hyperresponsiveness Overreaction to sensory stimuli.

hypertropia A condition in which one or both eyes swing upward.

hypoglycemia A type of diabetes that results in too little blood sugar.

hypophoria A tendency for an eye to deviate in a downward direction.

hyporesponsiveness Underreaction to sensory stimuli.

hypotropia A condition in which one or both eyes turn downward.

I

IDEA Individuals with Disabilities Education Act of 1990 (P.L. 101-476). Federal legislation that mandates educational services to school-aged persons with disabilities.

idiopathic Refers to disease of unknown cause.

Individual education program (IEP) process The procedure followed to develop an appropriate educational experience.

incidental learning Learning that in unplanned.

Individual Education Program (IEP) Specially designed instruction to meet the unique needs of a person for self-sufficient living.

individualized curriculum sequences Specific clusters of skills selected to enable students to participate in physical and sport activities in the community.

inflammation Reaction of the tissue to trauma, heat and cold, chemicals, electricity, or microorganisms.

inhibition of primitive reflexes Overriding of primitive reflexes by higher control of the central nervous system to permit voluntary movement.

instruction Organized principles with established technical procedure involving action and practice.

interval measure A common unit of measure with no true zero point.

interval recording The occurrence or nonoccurrence of a behavior within a specific time interval.

intrinsic Originating within a part.

inventory assessment Checklists of tasks to be accomplished with little functional relationship that usually are not in sequential order.

inversion Turning upward of the medial border of the foot.

isometric muscle contraction Muscle contraction without any appreciable change in its length.

isotonic muscle contraction Muscle contraction whereby origin and insertion move toward one another.

itinerant adapted physical educators Adapted physical educators who provide services to students in many schools.

K

kinesthesis Awareness of the position of the limbs.

kypholordosis Exaggerated thoracic and lumbar spinal curves (round swayback).

kyphosis Exaggerated thoracic spinal curve (humpback).

L

laterality An awareness of the difference between both sides of the body.

leadership Provision of motivation for a group to achieve its goals.

leaping Taking off from one foot into a flight phase and then landing on the opposite foot.

learning by correction Advancement made from feedback provided about errors made after performing a skill.

learning stations Areas in a facility where activity is conducted to achieve specific objectives.

least restrictive alternative The alternatives available for placement in least restrictive environments.

least restrictive environment The setting that enables an individual with disabilities to function to the fullest of his or her capability.

leukemia A type of cancer which negatively affects the body's flood-forming tissues.

lordosis Exaggerated lumbar vertebral curve (swayback).

M

main task Of less difficulty than a skill and prerequisite to skills.

mainstreaming Placement of children with disabilities in regular class, based on an IEP.

maintenance The perpetuation of a trained behavior after all formal intervention has ceased.

manual communication systems Techniques for communicating, including Pidgin Sign Language, American Sign Language, Manually Coded English, and finger spelling.

maturation The rate of sequential development of self-help skills of infancy, development of locomotor skills, and interaction with peers, all of which would occur irrespective of instructional intervention.

medical diagnostic service personnel Medical personnel who provide diagnostic services to children with disabilities and verify the disability status of individuals.

memory The length of time that information can be retained.

menarche Onset on menstruation.

meningitis Acute contagious disease characterized by inflammation of the meninges of the spinal cord.

menstruation The monthly loss of blood in mature females in response to hormonal cues.

mental retardation Significantly subaverage general intellectual functioning existing concurrently with deficits in adaptive behavior, manifesting before age 18 years.

metatarsalgia Also known as Morton's toe; severe pain or cramp in metatarsus in the region of the fourth toe.

mildly mentally retarded The person's functioning level is either self-sufficient, or needed supports can be provided on his or her own, or intermittent help or support is needed in areas such as case management, transportation, home living, physical health, leisure, employment, and/or self-advocacy.

mobility training An adaptive technique that is applied to the blind and enhances the ability to travel.

modeling Demonstration of a task by the teacher or reinforcement by another student who performs a desirable behavior in the presence of the targeted student.

mononucleosis Disease of low virulence that affects the lymphocytes.

monoplegia Neurologic affliction of one extremity of the body.

morbidity Number of disease cases in a calendar year per 100,000 population.

Moro reflex Startle reflex elicited by jarring or removing the supporting surface.

mortality Death rate.

most appropriate placement Children with disabilities should be placed in educational settings that best met their physical education needs.

motor fitness Characteristics of movement that are essential to the efficient coordination of the body.

motor fitness tests Assessment instruments that include measures of explosive strength, coordination, agility, and balance.

motor planning The ability to organize information in sequential segments and then carry out the plan in a smooth and integrated fashion.

motor skill Reasonable complex motor performance.

muscle setting Statically tensing a muscle without moving a part.

muscular dystrophy Chronic, progressive, degenerative, noncontagious disease of the muscular system, characterized by weakness and atrophy of muscles.

myopia A refractive condition in which the rays of the light focus in front of the retina when a person views an object 20 feet away or more.

N

narcotics Derivatives of opium used for sedative and analgesic actions.

natural environment generalization Spontaneous generalization by individuals with disabilities to stimulus and response variations that occur outside of the training setting.

naturalistic observations A social assessment technique that involves observing an individual interacting with others in a variety of natural social settings.

negative reinforcer An event or stimuli that, when terminated, increases the frequency of the preceding response.

negative support A reflex in which there is flexion of the knees when pressure is removed from the feet.

neuromotor disorders Medical conditions in which damage inflicted to the brain is accompanied by motor involvement.

nominal measure A statement that represents a dichotomous value.

normalization Making available to disabled individuals patterns and conditions of everyday life that are as close as possible to the norms and patterns of the mainstreaming of society.

normative-referenced assessment Tests administered under similar conditions in which the results can be classified according to percentiles.

norm-referenced social assessments Tests used to identify specific behavioral characteristics that generalize across persons, environments, and activities.

nystagmus Rapid movement of the eyes from side to side, up and down, in a rotary motion, or in a combination of these movements.

O

obesity Pathologically overweight in which a person is 20% or more above the normal weight (compare with overweight)

objective Acceptance of events without distortion or prejudice; action toward which effort is directed for a purpose; to achieve goals that can be evaluated without prejudice.

occupational therapist Professionals who improve functional living and employment skills.

ocular control The ability to fixate on and to visually track moving objects.

Office of Civil Rights A forum to address grievances resulting from exclusion or denial of accessibility, education, employment, or services to persons with disabilities.

ontogeny Historical development of an individual organism

ophthalmologist Licensed physician who specializes in the treatment of eye disease and optical defects.

optical righting reaction A reflex that causes the head to move to an upright position when the body is suddenly tipped.

optician Technician who grinds lenses and makes up glasses.

optometrist Person who provides examination of the eye for defects and faults of refraction and the prescription of correctional lenses and exercises.

oral communication method Hearing-impaired persons are provided amplification of sound and are taught through speech reading (lipreading).

organic brain injury Condition in which damage to the central nervous system exists.

orientation Obtaining the response and reinforcing the response.

orientation and mobility specialist A specially trained professional who works with visually impaired individuals to improve movement skills needed to function in the environment.

orthopedics Branch of medicine primarily concerned with treatment of disorders of the musculoskeletal system.

orthoptic vision The ability to use the extraocular muscles of the eyes in unison.

orthoptist Person who provides eye exercises and orthoptic training as prescribed by medical personnel.

orthotics Construction of self-help devices to aid the patient in rehabilitation (e.g., braces).

Osgood-Schlatter disease Epiphysitis of the tibial tubercle.

osteoarthritis Chronic and degenerative disease of joints.

osteochondritis Inflammation of cartilage and bone.

osteoporosis Increased porosity of bone by the absorption of calcareous material.

otitis media Infection of the middle ear.

overweight Any deviation of 10% or more above the ideal weight for a person (compare with obesity).

P

parallel activity Play at the ability level of the individual in observable proximity of other play participants.

paralysis Permanent or temporary suspension of a motor function because of the loss of integrity of a motor nerve.

paraplegia Neurologic affliction of both legs.

parent counselors and trainers Specially trained professionals who provide education and support services to parents of children with disabilities.

paresis Local paralysis.

pathology Study of disease (term often misused for "diseased" or "pathologic" conditions).

pattern analysis Study of sequential arrangement of movement behaviors to achieve a purpose.

peer isolation Removing an individual from a group setting.

peer tutoring Situation in which classmates learn material and assist peers who do not understand the material.

peer-mediated reinforcement Use of similarly aged students to reinforce specific behaviors.

pelvic tilt Increase or decrease of pelvic inclination.

perceptive deafness Inability to hear caused by a defect of the inner ear or of the auditory nerve in transmitting the impulse to the brain.

perceptual-motor programming Use of activities believed to promote the development of balance, body image, spatial awareness, laterality, and directionality.

performance objective Defining what is to be achieved to ensure successful participation.

personality disorder Chronic maladaptive behavioral patterns that are culturally and socially unacceptable.

pes Refers to the foot.

pes cavus Exaggerated height of the longitudinal arch of the foot (hollow arch).

pes planus Extreme flatness of the longitudinal arch of the foot.

petit mal seizure Nonconvulsive seizure in which consciousness is lost for a few seconds.

phagocytosis Process of ingestion in injurious cells or particles by a phagocyte (white blood cell).

phenylketonuria (PKU) Physiologic disturbance caused by an imbalance in the animo acids and resulting in mental limitations.

phobias Abnormal fears of specific objects, people, or situations.

phylogeny Development of a race or group of animals.

physiatrist Physician in physical medicine.

physical education Development of physical and motor fitness and fundamental motor patterns and skills.

physical fitness Refers to physical properties of muscular activity such as strength, flexibility, endurance, and cardiovascular endurance.

physical medicine Phase of medicine that uses various therapies to bring about a healing response.

physical priming Physically holding and moving the body parts of the learner through the activity.

physical therapist A professional who evaluates and treats physical impairments through the use of various physical modalities.

pigeon chest Abnormal priminence of the sternum.

plantar flexion Moving the foot toward its plantar surface at the ankle joint (extension)

play therapy A type of intervention used with emotionally disturbed children that involves using play to provide insight into emotional problems.

pneumonia An infection of the air spaces of the lungs.

positive support A reflex that causes the legs to extend and the feet to plantas flex when one is standing.

posture Mechanical efficiency or inefficiency of body parts.

Prader-Willi syndrome A condition characterized by neonatal phyptonia and feeding difficulty followed by excessive appetite, pica behavior, and obesity starting in early childhood.

prerequisite analysis The analysis of a complex task to determine the ability prerequisites.

prescription Specification of action based on diagnosis before program implementation.

present level of educational performance The existing limits of measured capability.

probe generalization Responding to a similar stimulus-and-response situation that was originally structured by the teacher.

process Steps that lead to objectives in a particular manner; a progressive series of operations to be followed in a definite order that directs action toward achievement of objectives.

process-oriented analysis assessment Systematically measuring performance outcomes of intervention strategies.

prognosis Prediction of the course of a disease.

program Sequential order of behavioral objectives that go from lesser to greater difficulty.

programmed instruction A set of hierarchical objectives that lead to a specific learning outcome. The outcome of each objective is used to make an instructional decision.

progressive muscular dystrophy Progressive wasting and atrophy of muscles.

projection Disguising a conflict by excluding one's motives; blaming someone else.

prompting Physically holding and moving the body parts of the learner through an activity.

prone position Lying in a face-down position.

prosthesis Artificial limb or appliance.

protective extensor thrust A reflex that causes immediate extension of the arms when the head and upper body are tipped suddenly forward.

protraction Forward movement of a part; for example, shoulder girdle.

proximal Refers to a point nearest to the origin of an organ or body part, as opposed to distal.

proximal-distal Referring to body parts closest to the midline of the body, which develop first, followed by development of the shoulder, elbows, wrist, and then fingers.

psychogenic deafness Condition in which receptive organs are not impaired, but for emotional reasons the person does not respond to sound.

psychometrist A professional who administers and interprets cognitive achievement and behavioral tests.

psychomotor seizure Seizure in which one may lose contact with reality and manifest bizarre psychogenic behavior.

ptosis Weakness and prolapse of an organ; for example, prominent abdomen.

punishment An aversive event that follows an undesirable behavior.

Q

quadriplegia Neurologic affliction of all four extremities

R

ratio measure A common unit of measure between each score and a true zero point.

recreation therapy System of therapy using recreation as a means to rehabilitation.

recreational therapy A related service that provides leisure time evaluation, instruction, and activities to a variety of populations with special needs.

reflexes Innate responses that all normal children develop.

refractive vision The process by which light rays are bent as they enter the eyes.

regular class Public school class in which typical children are educated.

regular education initiative A federally endorsed effort to return children with disabilities to regular education programs to receive the majority of services regardless of the child's unique needs.

rehabilitation Restoration of a disabled person to greater efficiency and health.

Rehabilitation Act of 1973 Civil rights legislation for individuals with disabilities that states that there is to be no exclusion or denial of benefits to those with disabilities.

rehabilitation counselor Specially trained person who helps individuals with disabilities gain the confidence and learn the skills necessary to function as normally as possible.

reinforcement schedule The frequency with which reinforcers are given.

reinforcer Any consequence that follows an action and strengthens that act.

related services Services that help a person benefit from direct services.

relaxation Lessening of anxiety and muscle tension.

reliability The consistency with which one carries out an assigned responsibility.

remedial physical education Activity designed to habilitate or rehabilitate functional motor movements and develop physical and motor prerequisites for functional skills.

repetitions The number of times the work interval is repeated under identical conditions.

response cost The withdrawal of earned reinforcers or privileges following an inappropriate behavior.

responsibility Carrying out a role that has been assigned by an authority figure of a social group.

rest interval The time between work intervals in progressive resistive exercise.

retraction Backward movement of a part; for example, shoulder girdle.

Rett syndrome A neurologic disorder characterized by normal development during the first 6 months of life followed by loss of acquired fine motor skills and development of impaired language skills, gait apraxia, and stereotypical hand movements.

reverse mainstreaming The infusion of individuals without disabilities into educational and recreation settings to interact with persons with disabilities.

rigidity Clinical classification of cerebral palsy characterized by rigid functional uncoordination of reciprocal muscle groups.

risk Used to describe persons who have a majority of factors pointing toward the potential development of disease or disability.

round shoulders Postural condition whereby the scapulae are abducted and the shoulders are forward.

S

schizophrenia Abnormal behavior patterns and personality disorganization accompanied by less-than-adequate contact with reality.

scoliosis Lateral and rotational deviation of the vertebral column.

sedatives Drugs that induce sleep and have a calming effect.

self-evaluation Accurate interpretation of the consequences of instructional performance without the aid of outside information.

self-initiated activity Voluntary participation in activity that is initiated by the individual.

self-instruction Engaging in procedures to achieve one's objectives without personal and direct input from the instructor.

self-mutilating behavior Acts that injure oneself.

sensory inputs Information received through the senses, such as vision, hearing, kinesthesis, and vestibular and tactile responses.

sensory integration Administration of activities believed to promote processing of sensory stimuli.

set The time between the work and the rest interval in progressive resistive exercise.

severely mentally retarded The person's functioning level requires regular on-going support and includes instruction and/or supervision within a designated adaptive skill area or needs constant care on a 24-hour basis.

shaping Reinforcement of small progressive steps that lead toward the desired behavior.

short-term instructional objectives A specific observable and measurable behavior that functions as an intermediate step to extend present levels of educational performance toward the goals of the IEP.

skill Utilization of abilities to perform complex tasks competently as a result of reinforced practice.

slide A sideways gallop.

social adjustment Degree to which the individual is able to function independently in the community, achieve gainful employment, and conform to other personal and social responsibilities and standards set by the community.

social goals Accepted social behavior standards.

social interaction Interaction among persons who are engaged in common activities.

social validity Evidence that instruction received by individuals with disabilities is beneficial to meaningful everyday life.

social worker A professional who is the link between the home and the school through work with intraprofessional specialties.

sociometric measures A social assessment technique that involves the use of peer ratings.

somatotype Certain body type (endomorphy, mesomorphy, or ectomorphy).

spasm Involuntary muscle contraction.

spastic Clinical type of cerebral palsy characterized by muscle contractures and jerky, uncertain moments of the muscles.

spatial relations The position of objects in space, particularly as the objects relate to the position of the body.

special class Class designed to give special educational help to children with disabilities.

Special Education Act Federal legislation designed to train professionals to prepare teachers of deaf children.

special educator A professional involved directly or indirectly with the instruction of children with disabilities.

specific learning disability A disorder in one or more of the basic psychologic processes involved in understanding or in using language, spoken or written, which may manifest itself in the imperfect ability to listen, speak, read, write, spell, or do mathematical calculations.

speech therapist A professional who evaluates children with speech and language deficits and provides intervention programs.

spina bifida   Congenital separation or lack of union of the vertebral arches.

splinter skill   Particular perceptual or motor acts that are performed in isolation and do not generalize to other areas of performance.

standard teaching sequence   A scquence of hierarchic potential short-term instructional objectives that enable the determination of a pupil's present level of educational performance, of short-term instructional objectives, and of learning gains made over a certain period.

static balance   The ability to maintain equilibrium during held positions.

stereotyped behavior   Specific acts that are repeated over and over.

strabismus   Crossed eyes resulting from inability of the eye muscles to coordinate.

stress   Condition that causes the inability of an organism to maintain a constant internal environment.

sublimation   Substitution of one activity for another, more accessible, activity.

submaximal intensity   Below the functional level of maximum performance.

subtask   Subdivision of a task; several subtasks compose the main task.

supination   Rotation of the palm of the hand upward, or abduction and inversion of the foot.

supine position   Lying on the back and facing upward.

survey   Assessment that provides broad guidelines for selection of instructional content.

symmetric tonic neck reflex   A reflex in which the upper limbs tend to flex and the lower limbs extend when ventroflexing the head. If the head is dorsiflexed, the upper limbs extend and the lower limbs flex.

system   Interdependent items that relate to a whole operation and function as a unit.

T

tactile sense   Knowledge of where the body ends and space begins and the ability to discriminate between pressure, texture, and size.

talipes equinus   Walking on the toes or the anterior portion of the foot.

talipes valgus   Walking on the inside of the foot (pronated)

talipes varus   Walking on the outside of the foot (supinated).

target level   Desired performance level of an individual while participating in activity.

task analysis   Identification of prerequisite behaviors of tasks to be targets of instruction.

task-specific approach (top, down)   Teaching a skill directly and generalizing it to a variety of environments. If it cannot be learned, teach the prerequisites.

teacher ratings   A social assessment technique that involves the use of teacher rating scales to gather social data.

tenotomy   Surgical operation on the tendons.

terminal objective   Synthesis of all subobjectives that enable mastery of the main or general objective.

tetralogy of Fallot   Abnormality of the opening of the septum between ventricles or positioning of the aorta to the right in such a manner that it lies over the defect of the septum of the left ventricle.

therapeutic modality   Device designed to bring about a therapeutic response; for example, heat, cold, light, electro stimulation.

therapy   Treatment of a disease or disability.

throwing   Projection of an object through space with the arm.

tibial torsion   Medial twisting of the lower leg on its long axis.

time out from reinforcement   Withdrawal of reinforcement for a certain period of time.

token economy   A form of contingency management in which tokens are earned for desirable behavior.

tonic labyrinthine reflexes   Reflexes that are present when one maintains trunk extension when supine and trunk flexion when prone.

torticollis   Also known as wryneck; contraction of neck muscles resulting in drawing the head to one side.

total communication method   The hearing-impaired person elects to communicate through speech, signs, gesture, or writing.

Tourette syndrome   An inherited neurologic disorder characterized by spasmodic, involuntary motor and vocal tics.

tranquilizers   Drugs that reduce tension or anxiety. They affect the sympathetic nervous system by suppressing synaptic stimuli.

transition service personnel   Specially trained professionals who provide the expertise to ensure that individuals with disabilities have the skills needed to work and function in the community.

transition services   Services that assist in the process by which a child with a disability moves smoothly from the school setting into community-based living. By law, these services must be included on a child's IEP at no later than 16 years of age.

transportation specialists   Individuals who assist in ensuring disabled students are provided appropriate and timely transportation services.

trauma   Injury or wound.

traumatic head injuries   Blows to the head that result in insult to brain tissue.

travel vision   Residual vision in the blind that enables travel.

treatment-referenced assessment   Tests to determine which teaching strategy would be most successful with a given student.

tremor   Clinical type of cerebral palsy evidenced by a rhythmic movement caused by alternating contractions between flexor and extensor muscles.

Trendelenburg sign   Dropping of the pelvis on the unsupported side because of weakness or paralysis of hip abductor muscles.

U

unified process of development The conception of intellectual, physical, social, and emotional development as a unified process.

uniformity of sequence The sequence of development is the same in all normal children.

unique need A behavior that is a target of instruction in the form of goals of the IEP; deficiencies are determined by a comparison of behaviors required for self-sufficiency in the community with present levels of performance.

V

valgus (valgum) Angling of a part in the direction away from the midline of the body (bent outward).

varus (varum) Angling of a part in the direction of the midline of the body (bent inward).

vestibular sense Response for balance; located in the nonauditory section of the inner ear.

vision specialist A specially trained professional who evaluated the extent of visual disabilities and designs intervention programs that make possible a successful educational experience.

visual motor control Ability to fixate on and visually track moving objects as well as the ability to match visual input with appropriate motor responses.

vocational counselors Professionals who guide disabled persons in seeking employment.

W

whiplash injury Deep-tissue neck injury resulting from the head being forcefully snapped forward and backward.

winged scapula Vertebral border of the scapula project outward because of weakness of the serratus anterior or the middle and lower trapezius muscles.

Wolff's law of bone growth Bone alters its internal structure and external form according to the manner in which it is used.

work interval A prescribed number of repetitions of the same activity under identical conditions.

Index